Dream, Death, and the Self

Dream, Death, and the Self

J. J. Valberg

PRINCETON UNIVERSITY PRESS

PRINCETON AND OXFORD

Copyright © 2007 by Princeton University Press
Published by Princeton University Press, 41 William Street,
Princeton, New Jersey 08540
In the United Kingdom: Princeton University Press, 3 Market Place,
Woodstock, Oxfordshire OX20 1SY

Library of Congress Cataloging-in-Publication Data

Valberg, J. J.
Dream, death, and the self / J. J. Valberg.
p.   cm.
Includes bibliographical references and index.
ISBN-13: 978-0-691-12858-0 (cl : alk. paper)
ISBN-10: 0-691-12858-8 (cl : alk. paper)
ISBN-13: 978-0-691-12859-7 (pbk. : alk. paper)
ISBN-10: 0-691-12859-6 (pbk. : alk. paper)
1. Experience. 2. Self-knowledge, Theory of. 3. Solipsism. 4. Death. I. Title.
B105.E9V34 2007
128—dc22   2006053165

British Library Cataloging-in-Publication Data is available

This book has been composed in Sabon

Printed on acid-free paper. ∞

press.princeton.edu

Printed in the United States of America

10   9   8   7   6   5   4   3   2   1

To Anna, Flo, and Leo

Contents

Part Two: *Death*

PART THREE: *The Self*

Preface

THIS BOOK was written at different intervals, often separated by long gaps, over a period of more than twenty years. Much has changed over the time of writing. The café briefly described at the outset (the Dorice) has long since been displaced as one of my regular working venues; in fact, it has long since ceased to exist: a building society now stands in its place. Gone too are most of the habitués of the café. They belonged to a community of middle Europeans, mainly German-speaking Jews, who emigrated to London in the 1930s and 1940s and whose presence in the Swiss Cottage area (after the war, a German war reparations office was established there) accounted for the many local continental-style cafés, patisseries, confectioners, delis, and restaurants that were still flourishing in the mid-1970s when I moved to the neighborhood. That community, in fact, the whole little world of Finchley *Strasse*, has now all but disappeared. Yet in various rewritings of the book, in countless other cafés elsewhere in the city, I have—partly for sentimental reasons, partly out of laziness—retained the original description of myself philosophizing in that no longer existent environment. Pen and paper have long since given way to a laptop, and my daughter, who figures in the Dream discussions as a "little girl," has long since arrived at adulthood.

In writing the early parts, not all of the organizing themes of the book were yet clear. Insofar as these have been superimposed on the beginnings (primarily in the introduction, but also in the form of a few hints and foreshadowings in the chapters that follow), one might gain the impression of a greater unity of purpose over time than was actually the case. However, a sense of the central subject matter of the book was always present, and in this respect there was right from page 1 a sense of where the book was going—if it went anywhere at all.

There have been lengthy delays and the inevitable need for revisions. The original manuscript was radically shortened in response to comments from readers for Princeton University Press. As well as to these and later readers for the Press, I am grateful to James Tartaglia for laboring through the original version, and for his many insightful queries and criticisms (of course an author cannot escape total responsibility for what comes out at the end); and to Hong Yu Wong, both for his probing commentary and for preparing the index.

Dream, Death, and the Self

Philosophical Discovery and Philosophical Puzzles

Int.1 Discovering What We Already Know

Anyone who has acquired the hang of philosophical dialogue and reflection, who has (so to speak) learned to play this "game," will recognize that it is possible in philosophical reflection to make discoveries; but he[1] will also recognize that such discoveries differ from what counts as discovery in other areas of intellectual endeavor (science, mathematics, history, economics, etc.) as well as everyday life. The main difference is this: what we discover and thus come to know outside philosophy is something new, something we do not already know (how else, one wants to ask, could we *discover* it?), while it seems that in philosophy we discover only what we already know.

On the surface this is puzzling; yet it is an old and familiar idea. You can find it in Plato, Kant, Hegel, Wittgenstein, Heidegger, and many other philosophers. It is part of philosophy's image of itself. And it deserves to be. However we explain it, there is such a thing as discovering what we already know. As anyone who has philosophized knows.

The possibility is not confined to philosophical reflection. If someone draws my attention to the fact that I feel pressure on my back from the chair on which I am sitting, or that I am kidding myself about so-and-so's intentions, I may discover something. But what I discover, what comes to light, does not come as a surprise. In the first case, I discover a fact about how things are within my experience; in the second case, a fact about how things are within my life. But in both cases what I discover is something I already know. The same possibility—that which exists in the phenomenological and self-knowledge cases—exists in the philosophical case. In fact, as will be clear, the three cases are connected.

Philosophical reflection differs in that it is impersonal. In realizing that I feel pressure on my back, or that I am kidding myself, my interest is restricted to my experience, my life. Of course, experience and the self (my life) are themselves legitimate topics of philosophical reflection; but insofar as they become topics of philosophical reflection, I regard myself—my experience, my life—only as a representative of the general case.

---

[1] Apart from cases where it refers to specific individuals, "he," etc., is always meant in a gender-neutral way.

I am, you could say, impersonally interested in myself: impersonally interested in what is "mine," in what is first personal. Insofar as self- reflection and phenomenological reflection are impersonal, they are philosophical.

To repeat: in philosophy we discover what we already know. Indeed, this is (or may be) itself something we discover philosophically. If we have acquired the hang of philosophical reflection but have yet to reflect on the nature of such reflection, the fact that in philosophical reflection we discover what we already know will, when it comes to us, come to us as something we already know. We will make a philosophical discovery about philosophical discovery.

Int.2 The Socratic Conception of Philosophical Discovery

If philosophical discovery is possible, it seems there must be a way of knowing, a kind of knowledge, that makes such discovery possible: a way of knowing, etc., that allows for the possibility of discovering what we already know. Let us distinguish three cases here. We may be in the position (1) of having already made a philosophical discovery, that is, of having reflected and explicitly spelled out what we know, or (2) of being ready to begin reflecting but without yet having carried through our reflections. Finally, in contrast to both of these cases, (3) it may be that we not in a position, that we do not have the wherewithal, to begin reflecting. Corresponding to (2) and (3), there are different senses of "not knowing": a sense that (3) entails not being in a position to begin reflecting, and a sense that (2) entails being in a position to begin but without yet having carried through our reflections. It is in the latter sense that we do not know at the outset of philosophical reflection.

Thus, at the outset of philosophical reflection there is, as philosophers have long observed, a sense in which we "know" and a sense in which we do "not know." The sense in which we do not know is that we have not yet spelled out or made explicit to ourselves what we know. But in what sense, or way, do we know? What kind of knowledge is it that puts us in a position to make a philosophical discovery?

This is the question that Socrates attempts to answer in Plato's *Meno*. For Socrates, the aim of philosophical reflection is to spell out, to make explicit, the content of a Form or concept. With this aim, we put to ourselves a question of the schema "What is Φ?" ("What is virtue?" "What is justice?" "What is knowledge?" and so on.) Socrates' idea is that at the outset of philosophical reflection we know the answer to such questions in the way that someone can be said to "know" what he has learned but finds himself unable to recollect. Philosophical reflection is the process (for Socrates, a dialectical process) of provoking ourselves to recollect what we once learned but are now (when the question is raised) unable to recollect. Obviously, this raises the further question of how and when we originally learned the things that we are unable to recollect. It is not likely that we shall accept Plato's view that we have had, in a disembodied state, a prior confrontation with the Forms.

But there is a more immediate problem. In whatever way we gain the relevant knowledge, recollection does not seem like the correct model for the philosophical discovery of what we thereby know. For example, it can happen that at the very moment when we cannot recollect something we are nonetheless confident that we know it. "Wait, it will come to me." Such a reaction seems totally out of place in philosophical reflection. Again, whereas the content of a thought that prompts a recollection may—via the psychological mechanism of association—be more or less anything, the content of a thought that opens the mind to a philosophical discovery must be related in a very particular way to the content of the discovery (say, by illustrating the possibility or impossibility discovered). Recollection is one thing; philosophical discovery is something else.

Int.3 Wittgenstein: Insidership and Philosophical Discovery

We need a different model, a different conception of philosophical discovery. In fact, we have (I think) in passing indicated the conception we need. Consider our example of philosophical discovery about philosophical discovery: that in philosophy we discover what we already know. Not everyone is in a position to discover this. If you tell someone who has never engaged in philosophical reflection that in philosophy we discover what we already know, that person may be puzzled, or accept it without understanding it, or reject it as nonsense. But he will not recognize it as true: he will not make the relevant philosophical discovery. To do that, he must have (as we put it) acquired the hang of philosophical reflection: he must be an "insider" of this type of activity or game. We who are insiders—let me assume that I am addressing insiders—were drawn into the game, the activity of philosophizing, by others who were already insiders. As insiders, we know what it is to philosophize. We know it in a way that only insiders can know it, and whether or not we have ever reflected on what we know.

This idea—which comes from Wittgenstein—the idea of being an insider of a game, an activity governed by rules in which we are mutually engaged with others, is philosophically fundamental. We can get a handle on the idea by reflecting on ordinary games, on what it is to be drawn into and gradually master the rules of ordinary games (chess, ball games, card games, etc.). We all know what it is gradually to get drawn into such a game, to pick up the rules, to catch on, to get the hang of things. We all know then what it is to become, and to be, an insider. It is by becoming an insider of a system of games, the system of what Wittgenstein calls "language-games" (the games whose rules govern the use of expressions in our language), that we master concepts, that we become thinkers. And we all find ourselves now in the position of insiders. We find ourselves with others on the inside of our system of language-games. We find ourselves thinkers.

Language-games are evidently not ordinary games: they exist at a more basic level. Our becoming insiders of ordinary games presupposes, at least for sophisticated games (say blackjack or chess),[2] that we are already insiders of a system of language-games; insidership in the latter presupposes only that we have the natural capacities (memory, perception, the ability to imitate, etc.) essential to the process by which others, those who are already insiders, draw us into the game. At the ground level, this happens without our being given explanations. (It has to, since we are not yet in a position to understand explanations.) We imitate the insiders and are corrected and encouraged by them. Gradually we ourselves become insiders—"with" the others who are already on the inside. Gradually we master concepts. Gradually the world acquires meaning: we become thinkers. The world acquires meaning by our becoming insiders. Apart from this, the world might be there, but it would have no meaning.

Consider, for example, a child's coming to grasp the concept of color or number. The child must be able to react to the different appearances of objects, to distinguish objects as separate, to remember and repeat the numerals, and so on. If we knew enough about the brain, we might correlate different stages of the child's conceptual development with different stages in the development of its brain, or identify certain stages of brain development as necessary or sufficient for certain stages of conceptual development. In this sense, we might "explain" the child's acquisition of the relevant concepts. But there is at the ground level no way of gaining insight into the child's conceptual development—in the way that we gain insight into the mind of a fellow subject; for that presupposes that we can already impute a grasp of concepts to the child, that the child is already with us on the inside, etc. It presupposes the very insidership that the development we are describing is meant to realize.[3]

---

[2] The games we play with infants (like peek-a-boo) are themselves part of the process by which infants become insiders of the system of language-games.

[3] This is what is wrong with the notion that we learn concepts by abstraction from particular cases: we imagine that the infant figures something out, or solves a problem ("If this is Φ and that is Φ, then being Φ must be . . . "). There is, certainly, such a thing as abstracting a concept from particular cases, but the capacity to do this presupposes a relatively sophisticated level of conceptual development.

First the world has no meaning, then it has meaning: first we are outside the system of language-games, then we are inside. And once we are inside, our situation is in a sense inescapable. In the case of an ordinary game, we can choose to withdraw from it, to put ourselves back outside the game—from where entered it—or to play a different game. But we cannot, just like that, choose to be inside a different system of language-games, nor, except by a radical act that would deprive the world of meaning altogether, put ourselves outside the system. We did not consciously put ourselves inside the system but were drawn inside and now *simply find* ourselves here; and given that we are here, there is nowhere else to be.

The thought, then—to return to the Socratic question—is that what we discover or bring to light in philosophical reflection is our insider's knowledge, that is, the knowledge we have picked up in becoming insiders of our system of language-games. The sense in which at the outset of philosophical reflection we "know" the answer to the question we have posed is that in which insiders of a system of language-games know what they have picked up (the rules of the games) in being drawn into the system: we have insider's knowledge. The sense in which we "do not know" is that we are not yet *open* to what we know—in the way that a self-deceived subject is not open to what he knows, or that a subject may not be open to how things are within his experience. In becoming open to our insider's knowledge, in making this explicit to ourselves, we make a philosophical discovery.

It is thus our insider's knowledge that puts us in a position to philosophize. This holds, note, for the special case of philosophical discovery about philosophical discovery. If we tell someone who is not yet a philosophical insider (who has not studied philosophy, or hung around with philosophers) that in philosophical reflection we discover what we already know, he may understand our words, but he will not recognize the truth of what we tell him. He will not will not recognize this—he will not philosophically discover its truth—until he too becomes a philosophical insider, that is, until he is drawn into the game and is thus with us on the inside.

Notice, in picking up the system of language-games, we do not thereby pick up the meta-game of philosophical reflection. This constitutes a further step, which is not essential to being an insider of the system, and which we might never make. (The philosophical game, the activity of philosophizing, might strike us as eccentric, ridiculous, or just a waste of time. Or it might just never come our way.) Being insiders of the system puts us in a position to philosophize; but being in a position to philosophize does not automatically make philosophers of us.[4]

---

[4] The ubiquitous "we" of philosophical discourse is ambiguous: sometimes it has in view a wider, sometimes a narrower, audience. Thus sometimes it is intended (narrowly) to include only those who are with us as insiders of philosophy, but other times (widely) to

Int.4 Philosophical Discovery and Resistance

The Socratic question is: In what way do we know what we know at the outset of philosophical reflection? That is: In what way do we know what we then discover? Our answer is that we know in a way that insiders know. But one might wonder why, if we already know what we discover philosophically, such discovery should be difficult—why it should require work or effort. (Think of how philosophers rack their brains devising thought experiments concerning personal identity, freedom of the will, causation, and so on.) Why does not that which is discovered present itself effortlessly to the philosophizing mind? Why should there be resistance to our being open to what we already know?

Consider self-deception (to which we have, in passing, already referred).[5] In this case, what is discovered is personal: I discover, i.e., become open to, a fact about myself, about something internal to my life. But not only that, a particular motivation is involved: the fact to which I become open is a fact that I want not to be true (that is why I hide it). In the philosophical case we have no motive for not being open to what we already know. The resistance in this case comes from a different quarter.

The world, we said, emerges as meaningful for us only insofar as we become insiders of our system of language-games. This process depends not just on the guidance and example of those already on the inside but on our having, right from the start, a primitive involvement with the world. Thus as we are drawn into the system, as the world acquires meaning, it is the world itself, with its meaning, not the system of language-games from within which the world has its meaning, that occupies or engrosses us. The world is the locus of meaning. We look to the world—and in doing so look right past that from within which it has meaning. To convert the system of language-games into an explicit topic of reflection, to place it rather than the engrossing world at the focal point of our attention and thereby let ourselves become open to what we (in virtue of being insiders of the system) already know, requires an attitude or effort of mind that not only is not essential to the immediate business of everyday affairs, which is out in the world, but runs counter to it. This—i.e., our engrossment in the world—is the source (or at least one source) of resistance. It is what makes philosophical reflection and discovery difficult.

---

include all those who are with us on the inside of our system of language-games—the community (one might say) of thinkers.

[5] Cf. the discussion in 2.4–6 of my *The Puzzle of Experience* (Oxford University Press, 1992).

Int.5 The Presumptuousness of a Claim to Philosophical Discovery

The present conception of philosophical reflection and discovery (let us call it the "insider conception,") seems to fit what philosophers often refer to as conceptual analysis. The aim of conceptual analysis is to bring to light the possibilities, necessities, and impossibilities implicit in our concepts. What does this mean?

Generally, from within a game certain things are possible (necessary, impossible). The game sets the limits on what is possible, etc., from within it. We, insofar as we are insiders of the game, cannot but grasp these possibilities. Moreover, by reflecting in the right way we can become open to what we thus grasp. It is, on the insider conception, the same with conceptual possibilities (necessities, impossibilities). Conceptual possibilities are possibilities, etc., that are internal to, and thus set by, our system of language-games. If we reflect in the right way, we can become open to these possibilities—to the possibilities that, as insiders, we cannot but already grasp. In this way, we discover what is conceptually possible (impossible, necessary).

If this appears to trivialize conceptual analysis, it is because we have failed to take on board the earlier point that our language-games—the games that set the limits on conceptual possibility; the games inside of which we simply find ourselves and outside of which there is nowhere for us to be—exist at a different level from ordinary games. (We have failed, you might say, to radicalize our model.) The rules of an ordinary game can, in principle, be altered at will. Of course we do this not from within the game, as a "move" in the game, but only from a position outside the game. We thereby alter what is possible within the game, or, perhaps, if you say that it will no longer be the same game, we create new possibilities by creating a new game. In the case of our language-games, however, we have no external vantage point from which to contemplate alternatives; no vantage point, then, from which we might decide to alter or create new possibilities. (They may evolve; but evolution is not decision.) Hence the possibilities that hold from within our language-games, conceptual possibilities, figure not as holding "from within" but as holding absolutely; that is, as simply holding: as holding *period*. We discover these possibilities by letting ourselves become open to how things are from with the games in which the possibilities hold; but the possibilities we thereby discover figure with us as holding absolutely.

Something else. The resources of a language-game have a richness, a depth, absent in the case of ordinary games. There is always more to them than we ever bring to light. (Thus analytical truths and lexical definitions do not scratch the surface of the knowledge possessed by insiders of a language-game.) Moreover, any putative discovery of a conceptual possibility, etc., is, in principle, open to being overthrown by further reflection. (A clever person may always come up with a counterexample, which brings to light a previously unremarked possibility, etc.[6]) In contrast to the possibilities internal to an ordinary game, reflection on conceptual possibilities is open-ended. Of course at some point we stop reflecting; but there is no point that reveals itself as the final stopping point. Herein lies the true meaning of Socratic modesty.

But modesty in this case involves a kind of double-mindedness. If we take ourselves to have philosophically discovered something, to have brought it into the open, then "there it is"—in the open. How can we be modest? On the contrary, there is a certain presumptuousness inherent in laying claim to a philosophical discovery. We are referring now not to the familiar point that it is rare to come up with anything new in philosophy (everything is a "footnote to Plato and Aristotle"), but to the fact that in making such a claim we put ourselves in the position of speaking on behalf of those to whom we address the claim. In effect, we are saying to someone: "Here is what we have discovered—and you already know it." Suppose the response is: "We do not see what you claim to have discovered." Then, of course, neither will these people accept that they already know it.

What can we say, or do? We can only say something else. There is no substitute for talking, and thereby trying to get those we address to see what we think they already know.

In fact it may turn out, if we keep talking, that it is we who are wrong. This may be our philosophical discovery, that we were wrong. So we were wrong about what those we were addressing knew. And, it seems, *we* already knew this: that we were wrong: that we were wrong about what they, and perforce we, knew. How do we know when we know? Again, there is no secret formula. We do the best we can. We keep talking.

---

[6] Consider the following example. Since Hume, most philosophers have accepted as a conceptual necessity that a singular causal fact entails the existence of a covering law (or generalization); but this apparently settled and "evident" conceptual truth has been shaken by Elisabeth Anscombe's inviting us to reflect that in the case of the behavior of subatomic phenomena, we seem prepared to judge that, say, a collision of particles caused one to move in a particular way, at the same time that we acknowledge the absence of a covering law. "Causality and Determination," in *The Collected Papers of G.E.M. Anscombe* (Blackwell, 1981). Even if we think that this does not settle the issue, even if we remain a partisan of Hume's original intuition, Anscombe's thought experiment illustrates the possibility of drawing upon the resources of our concepts, our language-games (in this case, of causation), to overturn a previously accepted conceptual truth: the possibility, we might say, of one philosophical discovery overturning another.

Int.6 Conceptual Analysis and the Communal Horizon

The insider conception answers, I believe, the Socratic question of how philosophical discovery is possible. Or rather, it answers this question insofar as philosophical discovery is a matter of conceptual analysis. Is all philosophical discovery a matter of conceptual analysis?

One thing seems clear. Whatever we say about discovery, conceptual analysis does not exhaust philosophical thinking or reflection. Thus we must at least acknowledge as belonging to philosophical reflection the construction of arguments and reasoning: the drawing out of consequences, implications, entailments. Thus, once we bring to light the philosophical possibility of discovering things we already know, we may draw the general conclusion that not all discovery involves surprise. In contrast to the discovery itself, this may seem surprising. The reason is that when we draw the conclusion—that is to say, when, in light of the discovery, we see that we are rationally forced to accept the possibility of discovery in the absence of surprise—we go beyond what we already know, what we have philosophically discovered, viz., that in philosophy we discover what we already know.

In philosophical reflection there is a constant interplay between reasoning (argument, inference) and discovery. It can happen also that what has the form of an argument opens us up to something and thus serves as the instrument of discovery. (We shall give an example later in the book.) Yet in principle, the two are different: seeing that such-and-such follows from what we already know, that we are thereby rationally forced or required to accept it—this is different from the kind of opening up that constitutes philosophical discovery. In the first case we move, because we are forced to move, to new ground. In the case of philosophical discovery, we mark time. We end up where we begin, with what we already know—except that now we are open to it. Nor are we forced. We may be in various ways prodded, jogged, urged, reminded, directed, and so on, but in the end we must *let ourselves* be open to what we already know. The contrast between philosophical reasoning (argument) and philosophical discovery is like the contrast between external constraint and our own will.[7]

---

[7] Wittgenstein's advice not to "think" but to "look" means that we should think, reflect, in the way of letting ourselves be open to what we already know. See Wittgenstein, *Philosophical Investigations*, trans. G.E.M. Anscombe (Basil Blackwell & Mott, 1958), 66. Becoming open to a conceptual possibility is (in terms of the "looking" metaphor) opening our eyes to what goes on in this or that language-game, i.e., looking rather than forming a hypothesis or making an inference. Yet it should be clear that argument or reasoning also belongs to philosophical reflection. It is not everything, but it is something.

Our question, however, is not whether conceptual analysis exhausts philosophical thinking (reflection), but whether conceptual analysis exhausts philosophical discovery. Here it may occur to us that our present reflections on the insider conception, by means of which we have attempted to gain insight into the nature of conceptual analysis, themselves bring to light a fact that transcends anything that might be discovered by conceptual analysis, viz., the fact that there *is* such a subject matter as our system of language-games. This fact expresses not another possibility (necessity, impossibility) internal to the system, another conceptual possibility, but the existence of *that from within which* any such possibility holds: the "horizon" (as we shall say) of conceptual possibility. That there is such a subject matter, when it dawns on us, is a discovery not of a conceptual possibility but a fact, a fact of existence—of the existence of the very subject matter to which conceptual possibilities are internal.[8]

If there is such a subject matter, a horizon to which conceptual possibilities, etc., are internal, there must be truths about it to which, like the possibilities that hold from within it, we can become open; that is to say, truths which, like the conceptual truths (the possibilities, etc.) that hold from within it, can be discovered philosophically. Thus the system of our language-games, the horizon, is revealed, or uncovered, as the system into which we are drawn gradually, and not piecemeal but (to use the jargon) holistically; as the subject matter of which we simply find ourselves, inescapably, on the inside with others, i.e., the horizon that is "ours" (the communal horizon); as the subject matter, the horizon, that sets the limits on possibility and from within which the world means what it means. These are truths about the communal horizon, about our system of language-games, truths of which we already know and to which we can, if we reflect in a certain way, become open.

Generally, if there exists such a thing as X, X must have its own essence or way of being. So there must be truths that hold of (about) X. In the case where the existence of X is discovered philosophically, the truths

---

[8] Our use here of the term "horizon" to refer to this subject matter is suggested by the dictionary definition of a horizon as "the boundary line of one's vision on the surface of the earth ... hence the limit of one's experience, knowledge or observation" (see *Webster's New Twentieth Century Dictionary*, unabridged). Husserl uses "horizon" in a related way to refer to the space of possibilities implicit in our grasp of a material object. See, e.g., *Cartesian Meditations* (Kluwer, 1995), sections 9, 18; *Ideas* (George Allen & Unwin, 1958), section 44. Again, in Heidegger, the term "horizon" also refers to an implicitly grasped structure of possibilities—though for Heidegger these possibilities are not perceptual but "ontological," i.e., possibilities essential to what he calls our "Being." See *Being and Time* (Basil Blackwell, 1973), 116, 365. In the next section we shall introduce a further use of the term "horizon." This further use of the term—which we shall employ throughout the book, and for which I hope the reader will gradually acquire a feel—retains the underlying notion of a limit but redirects our attention from a communal to a personal subject matter.

that express the essence of X and thus hold of X—the truths that, so to speak, come with X's existence (being)—must be such that they too can be discovered philosophically. However, these truths are not conceptual truths. They are not, once again, truths expressing possibilities (impossibilities, necessities) internal to the communal horizon, our system of language-games. In fact, in the present case, they are truths that hold of (about) the communal horizon itself, the horizon of conceptual truth. They are not conceptual truths, yet, like conceptual truths, they are discoverable philosophically.

Int.7 The Personal Horizon

Thus far, our reflections on philosophical discovery have revolved around the subject matter that is "ours," the communal horizon. It is now time to point out that our main interest in the book, though it will, inevitably, keep referring us back to the communal horizon, concerns not what is "ours" but what is "mine"; not the communal but, as we shall initially call it, the "personal" horizon. This, the personal horizon, is the subject matter that in the course of our reflections will emerge as the subject matter of the dream hypothesis, and of death: the subject matter, the horizon, that is (in a certain sense) the self.

The personal and communal horizons stand at the same level. In fact they have a way of competing with one another. There is also a way in which they depend on one another. On the one hand, it is only from within the communal horizon, the horizon that is "ours," that anything has meaning. If nothing had meaning, nothing would be "mine": there would be no personal horizon. On the other hand, the fact that the communal horizon is "ours," that it is communal, entails a multiplicity of subjects (those who are together on the inside of it). At the same time—anticipating an idea that we shall discuss at great length later in the book—it is only by being "at the center" of the personal horizon, of the horizon that is "mine," that something (a human being) is a "subject." Without the horizon that is "mine," then, there can be no horizon that is "ours."

But drawing attention to its interdependence with the communal horizon does not yet bring the personal horizon into the open. If there is a personal horizon, a horizon that is "mine" and that stands in interdependence with the communal horizon, it needs itself to be philosophically discovered. And here, I think, we encounter more difficulty, more resistance, than in the case of the communal horizon.

In part, the resistance has the same source as in the communal case: our engrossment in the world. Given that we are engrossed in the world, we tend to pass over that from within which the world is present and appears—just as we pass over that from within which the world has meaning. The world appears from within my horizon (my consciousness, my experience, my life), while that from within which it appears, the horizon that is "mine," passes us by.

There is something else that contributes to resistance in the case of the personal horizon. The communal horizon is our system of language-games. It actually consists in the activity, the communal life, of the system. In contrast, there seems to be nothing in which the personal horizon consists. The horizon that is "mine"—my consciousness, my experience, my life—is in a sense *nothing*: it is nothing *in itself* (something else we shall have to explain). Hence the extra resistance in the case of the personal horizon. Not only do we habitually look to the world, the subject matter from which we look away, and thus tend to pass by, i.e., the personal horizon, is, being nothing in itself, by its very nature such that we tend to pass it by. By its very nature, the personal horizon tends to remain a hidden subject matter.

In part 1 of the book, we shall pursue a line of reflection about the dream hypothesis whose main purpose is to bring the hidden subject matter, the horizon that is "mine," into view. In a way, this will be our purpose throughout the book. As we go along, we shall be discussing many familiar philosophical problems. In each case, we shall try to show that the correct analysis of the problem requires reference to the personal horizon. But while in each case our focus will be on this or that problem, there will always be the background agenda of enhancing our grasp of the hidden subject matter, the horizon that is "mine." It, the personal horizon, might be described as the subject matter of the book.

Perhaps we can now indicate in outline how the book is organized and hint at the main topics that will be discussed.

We said that in part 1, for the purpose of bringing into view the personal horizon, we shall consider the dream hypothesis (the hypothesis that this might be a dream). But once the hypothesis is raised, the challenge of dream skepticism is unavoidable. In part 1, then, in addition to inquiring into the meaning and subject matter of the dream hypothesis, we shall be required to confront dream skepticism and to formulate a response to it.

Part 2 deals not with a hypothesis but with a fact, the fact (faced by each of us) that: I will die. What is the meaning of this fact, the meaning of my death? Death holds up the prospect of a ceasing to be, i.e., of the ceasing to be of something that is "mine." The ceasing to be of what? And in what sense is it "mine"? The answer to the first of these questions points back to the subject matter that comes to light in our reflections on the dream hypothesis, the personal horizon. The answer to the second question points to solipsism: the thought that my horizon is (in a certain sense) *the* horizon. Solipsism, as it appears in the context of death, is not a quirky philosophical "view" to be refuted or dismissed out of hand, but something that we all know to be true and thus believe, and to whose truth we can—by reflecting on the meaning of death—become philosophically open.

Part 3 builds on the first two parts. Here we shall attempt to come to grips with a wide range of philosophical questions: about the first person and first-person reference; about imagination and possibility; about the self and the self in time (the problem of personal identity). This is the longest and most complicated part of the book. However there is an underlying unity. Everything turns around the same hidden subject matter, the horizon that is "mine" in the way that nothing else is: the subject matter of the dream hypothesis and death. The more we use and develop our conception of this subject matter, the more the conception should take hold. But remember, however much we go on about it, nothing can rationally force us to accept that there is such a subject matter. Nothing can guarantee that it comes into view—except our being open to it.

Becoming open to the existence of the personal horizon, to the fact that there is such a subject matter—this is a philosophical discovery in the same sense that becoming open to the existence of the communal horizon, to the system of language-games, is a philosophical discovery: it is the discovery of something we that already know. In the communal case, we distinguished two categories of philosophically discoverable truths: first, conceptual truths, truths expressing possibilities (impossibilities, necessities) that presuppose (in that they hold only from within) the communal horizon; second, truths that hold of or about the horizon. A similar distinction can be drawn with respect to the personal horizon, except that the truths of the first category, precisely because they are internal not to the communal horizon (the system of language-games) but to the personal horizon, are not conceptual truths. Here again, we need a distinction, viz., between phenomenological truths (these will be important later in book) and ontological truths (we shall briefly comment on these in following section).

Int.8 Philosophical Anticipations of the Personal Horizon

The personal horizon is, of course, not unanticipated in philosophy. How could it be? The personal horizon figures (as we shall attempt to spell out; see part 3) in our conception of ourselves. In that case, how could it fail to play a role in philosophical reflection? Yet, as the hidden subject matter, it plays for the most part a hidden role.

Kant's Transcendental Idealism is good example of what I have in mind. The starting point of Transcendental Idealism is the idea of something, an X, appearing and thus figuring within our experience or consciousness. All we can possibly know of the X is based on this, on the way the X appears from within our consciousness. It follows, for Kant, that we can know nothing of what the X is "in itself," i.e., apart from the way it appears. Thus what we conceive as the world in space and time is not the X as it is in itself but only the X as it appears. This contrast between the X as it appears versus is in itself is the core of Kant's Transcendental Idealism. All the transcendental arguments in the "Analytic" as well as the resolutions of the puzzles raised in the "Dialectic" depend on the contrast. But the contrast itself depends on a conception of consciousness or experience that Kant never makes explicit, on the conception of consciousness as the "that within which" the X appears/figures as the world in space in time; on what we shall call the "horizonal" conception of consciousness.

There will, as we proceed, be occasion to discuss in detail the hidden role played by the horizonal conception of consciousness both in Kant's views and in the views of other philosophers. But, leaving Kant aside, let us mention a few examples where the conception is pretty much out in the open.

The horizon that is "mine," we said, tends to remain out of view not just because of our preoccupation with the world but because of its own nature, its peculiar nothingness: the fact that it is nothing in itself. Such a characterization is reminiscent of Sartre's characterization of consciousness, the "for-itself," in *Being and Nothingness*. The nothingness of the for-itself is a central theme of Sartre's book. Consider, for example, the following statement from the conclusion: "The for-itself is not nothingness in general but a particular privation; it constitutes itself as the privation of *this* being . . . it is in no way an autonomous substance."[9] This, it will be clear, pretty well fits our conception of consciousness as the personal horizon. The reason the for-itself, consciousness, cannot be described as "nothingness in general" is quite simply that there *is* such a thing as consciousness. Yet there is such a thing only insofar as something is present/appears from within it and thus figures from within it as demonstratively given: as *this* being. Apart from the presence, the demonstrative givenness, of something within it, there is no "it"—no such thing as consciousness. Consciousness, in short, is nothing in itself.

However, the above quote contains an element that jars with our conception of consciousness as the personal horizon. Sartre says that the for-itself "constitutes itself" as the privation, etc. This suggests that the for-itself is itself active (it must, in fact, keep constituting itself anew—another theme in Sartre's book). Now, we may accept that without the personal

[9] *Being and Nothingness*, trans. H. Barnes (Methuen, 1969), p. 618.

horizon there would be no such thing as reason-grounded activity, as will, in that there is such a thing only from within the horizon (see part 3); however that which is active (that which wills, which constitutes itself) is not the horizon, which is nothing in itself, but the one at the center of the horizon, the subject. And the subject is the human being. If anything is rationally active it is the human being, who is part of the world and therefore not nothing in itself.

The second philosopher we shall mention in this regard is Heidegger. In Heidegger's work there are two closely related conceptions with which, for different reasons, we might be tempted to identify that of the personal horizon, the horizon that is "mine." The first is the conception, articulated at great length in *Being and Time* (this is really what the book is all about), of what Heidegger calls "Dasein's Being"—the kind or way of being that we, we human beings, have: the way in which we "be." [10] What suggests the identification with the personal horizon is that Heidegger repeatedly characterizes Dasein's Being as the way of being that "is in each case mine." [11] But as he gets further into the working out of this way of being (that to be in this way is to be "in the world," "with others," "ahead of oneself," and so on), the richness of the subject matter, the potentially endless detail, makes it evident that, in contrast to the personal horizon, it cannot be described as something that is nothing in itself. [12] (Perhaps this should have been evident just from the fact that it is "a way of being.")

In this respect, Heidegger's subject matter in *Being and Time*) resembles not the personal but the communal horizon, our system of language-games. Like our system of language-games, the way of being that is Dasein's way of being (that is Dasein's Being) constitutes an inexhaustible subject matter for philosophical discovery. In one case what comes to light are the possibilities and necessities internal to the communal horizon (our system of language-games), in the other case, the structures essential to Dasein's way of being. We might then regard Dasein's way of being, the way of being that is in each case "mine," as the first-person singular counterpart of the life or activity of the communal horizon. Or to put it the other way around, we might regard our life as insiders of the communal horizon, of our system of language-games, as the communal counterpart of Dasein's Being. [13] But in that case, as we said, Dasein's

---

[10] Here "be" must be taken as an activity verb, for which we might substitute (not as an exact synonym, but to give the flavor of Heidegger's idea) a verb like "live" or "carry on."

[11] See, e.g., H 41, 42, 43, 53.

[12] Thus the question of what Dasein's Being consists in, so far from being the most general, is said to be "the most basic and concrete." Ibid., H 9.

[13] Notice, though, it is part of Dasein's being to be "with others," just as from within our system of language-games each of us acquires the conception of "myself."

Being cannot be identified with the subject matter that is nothing in itself, the personal horizon.

There is, however, another conception in Heidegger—of which we get an occasional glimpse in *Being and Time* but which becomes more prominent in his later writings—that seems cut out to be the conception of a subject matter that is nothing in itself, viz., his conception of "the clearing (*die Lichtung*)." Thus in "The End of Philosophy and the Task of Thinking," he suggests that even in thinking of those philosophers (he is here discussing Husserl and Hegel) whose aim is to uncover, to bring things into the open, there remains something that "conceals itself precisely where philosophy has brought its matter to absolute evidence [Hegel] and to ultimate evidence [Husserl]," viz., a "free region" an "openness that grants a possible letting appear." This subject matter, this free region from within which alone things appear, Heidegger calls "the clearing."[14] It is, he says, "the open region for everything that becomes present and absent." In itself the clearing, as a free region, is nothing—i.e., it is nothing apart from things figuring from within it as present or absent. The clearing, in other words, is nothing in itself.

It is worth noting that, whereas Dasein's Being "is in each case mine," there is no mention here of the "mineness" of the clearing. Yet if it is not "mine," what distinguishes the clearing from *space*, i.e., the space that spreads out endlessly around me and that might in its own way be described "the open region for everything that becomes present and absent"? Space, the space around me and in which I move about, is not "mine" or anyone else's. In contrast to the impersonal nature of space, the clearing is personal: it is the personal horizon, the horizon that is "mine."

We must ask, then, about the relation between the clearing and Dasein's Being. The clearing is the horizon of Dasein's Being. That is to say, there is such a way of being, the way of being whose structure is uncovered for us in *Being and Time*, only from within the clearing; only from within the subject matter that is nothing in itself, the personal horizon. This is the source of the "mineness" of Dasein's Being. Dasein's Being "is in each case mine" by virtue of being internal to the horizon that "is in each case mine." Of course we do not yet know in what *this* "mineness" consists. Heidegger never tells us.

Thus the truths that elaborate the structure of Dasein's Being are truths that hold only from within the personal horizon, the clearing. They are truths about Dasein's Being that hold only from within the personal horizon. Such truths, which Heidegger calls "ontological" truths, are therefore to be distinguished from truths that are internal to the personal hori-

---

[14] *Basic Writings, Martin Heidegger*, ed. D. F. Krell (Routledge, 1994), p. 440ff.

zon but do not concern Dasein's Being, that is, from "phenomenological" truths. (See the final paragraph of Int.7 above.)

Wittgenstein—that is, Wittgenstein of the *Tractatus*—is the last philosopher we shall mention in this regard. Wittgenstein's conception of the "metaphysical subject," the subject that is not part of the world but its "limit,"[15] is, I believe, the conception of the personal horizon, the subject matter with which we shall be occupied in this book. The details of Wittgenstein's view will be considered in part 2, when we come to grapple with questions about solipsism and the meaning of death. But perhaps we might in advance enter a general observation about Wittgenstein's philosophy.

The often remarked upon shift between the earlier and later Wittgenstein may be viewed in light of the contrast between the personal and communal horizon.[16] In the Tractatus, the deepest truths, like the "truth" in solipsism,[17] are truths that have reference to the personal horizon, to the "limit" of the world (the metaphysical subject). In the *Investigations*, as we have pointed out, the focus is on our system of language-games, on the communal horizon.[18] The conception of the personal horizon, of the metaphysical subject, etc., seems no longer to play any role—as if it embodied a philosophical mistake. What happens then to the truth in solipsism? Is this to be reevaluated as a mistake? In that case, what death means to us is a mistake. No, we may philosophically turn away from it, but the personal horizon, the metaphysical subject, will still be there for us.

The following remark from On Certainty is of interest in this connection: "You must bear in mind that the language-game is so to say something unpredictable. I mean: it is not based on grounds. It is not reasonable (or unreasonable). It is there—like our life." What is "there like our life" is the system of language-games. But what is it to which the system is being compared when Wittgenstein says that the language-game (i.e., the system of language-games) is there like our life? What is "our life"? It is what for each of us is "my life." It is the subject matter that is "mine" in the way that nothing else is (life in the horizonal sense). It seems to me

[15] *Tractatus*, 5.632–33.

[16] Cf. Bernard Williams, "Wittgenstein and Idealism," in G. Vesey, ed. *Understanding Wittgenstein*, Royal Institute of Philosophy Lectures, vol. 7 (Macmillan, 1974).

[17] *Tractatus*, 5.62.

[18] This is indirectly evident in countless remarks and by Wittgenstein's procedure throughout the book; but the thought is also directly expressed, e.g., in the advice to "Look at the language-game as the primary thing" (656; see also 654–55), and again, to "accept the everyday language-game, and to note *false* accounts of the matter as false." He continues: "The primitive language-game which children are taught needs no justification; attempts at justification need to be rejected" (p. 200).

that Wittgenstein, in reaching for an analogy with the communal horizon, takes hold of the subject matter that he thinks he has left behind, the personal horizon: the metaphysical subject, the "limit" of the world.

Int.9 Two Types of Philosophical Puzzle

There is an idea that reoccurs throughout the book, a theme (you might say) that is interwoven with the other material, to which we have yet to draw attention. It relates to a certain general type of philosophical puzzle. The puzzles of this type have various structures; but they have in common that, though they are all philosophical, they are also, in a way, "extraphilosophical," and as such contrast with "intraphilosophical" or "purely philosophical" puzzles.[19] All philosophical puzzles (i.e., both extra- and intraphilosophical puzzles) depend on philosophy for their articulation and analysis. Intraphilosophical puzzles, however, are philosophical in the further sense that without philosophical reflection there would be no relevant puzzlement. In the case of the extraphilosophical puzzles, on the other hand, we may be puzzled in the absence of philosophical reflection. These are puzzles that may come over us, as it were, in the course of everyday life, without any philosophical preparation: without arguments, analyses, thought experiments, and so on.

The clearest examples of purely or intraphilosophical puzzles are Zeno's paradoxes about motion. Apart from something like Zeno's arguments, I do not think anyone would be puzzled about motion. (Would it ever occur to us, just like that, that it is impossible that anything should move?) A few other examples: Russell's paradox about classes, Goodman's "grue" paradox, the various paradoxes of confirmation (e.g., the ravens paradox), the surprise examination paradox, the sorites paradox, the preface paradox, Kant's antinomies of space, time, and matter. Obviously, this list is not exhaustive or systematic. There is, however, a unifying element. In all these cases it is essential to our actually being puzzled that we actually follow a certain argument or thought experiment, etc.; otherwise we will not be puzzled, at least not in the right way.

In leading us into puzzlement, philosophy exploits unclarities present in our concepts or language-games; unclarities that enable us to construct arguments that lead to conclusions that are self-contradictory, or patently false. Naturally, we assume that the arguments contain mistakes, fallacies. It falls to philosophy, through further analysis, to expose the mistakes and thereby to lead us out of the puzzlement into which it has led us.

[19] See *The Puzzle of Experience*, 9.3.

In the case of the intraphilosophical puzzles, everything—the generation, analysis, and solution of the puzzles—is philosophical business.[20]

In the case of the extraphilosophical (philosophical) puzzles, however, the puzzles that we bring to light philosophically have a way of making themselves known outside philosophy—that is to say, without any philosophical argument or analysis, without, as we put it, any philosophical preparation; a way of breaking into and disturbing everyday consciousness from a level where they exist whether or not we are disturbed by them.

Thus, for example, the fact that I (each of us for himself) will die, when it hits home, may strike us as incomprehensible. The incomprehensibility of death is the incomprehensibility of something intrinsically puzzling, of something that is impossible yet a fact: an impossible fact. If we are ever to get to the bottom of the impossibility (that death is a fact is all too evident), we need philosophy; but the elements of the impossibility, and thus of the puzzle itself—in other words, the very things we must attempt philosophically to uncover and analyze—these things are already there for us, independently of philosophy. Thus, whereas philosophy is required to expose the elements, to bring them to light and make clear how they give rise to the puzzle, our prior unarticulated grasp of puzzle may make itself known to us outside philosophical reflection, i.e., without any argument or analysis whatever. And once everything is out in the open, there is nothing more (philosophically) that we can do. The puzzle has no solution.

Not all the philosophical puzzles (problems, difficulties, etc.) discussed in the book have the extraphilosophical dimension that puts them beyond the reach of a philosophical solution, and in a number of cases we shall in fact propose "solutions" (e.g., in the case of certain familiar puzzles about first-person reference and personal identity; part 3). Now there is no doubting the fascination that such (intra- or purely philosophical) puzzles can exercise on the philosophical mind; they are, in fact, a mainstay of philosophical reflection. However, it is the extraphilosophical puzzles that can really get to us (though, admittedly, not all to the same degree[21]).

---

[20] The fact that philosophical reflection generates the intraphilosophical puzzles does not mean that philosophical reflection will find it easy to expose the mistake and thereby solve the puzzles, as the huge literature on Zeno's paradoxes will testify. Or consider Russell's paradox about classes, or the liar's paradox, or the paradoxes of confirmation, or the surprise examination paradox, or the preface paradox, etc. Are the solutions to these puzzles obvious? A particularly interesting case is the sorites paradox. Here, I think, we have a puzzle that not only makes itself manifest in everyday life, but does so in manner that almost mimics the philosophical formulation of the puzzle. The philosophical puzzle in this case appears extraphilosophically. But the sorites not only appears extraphilosophically, when it thus appears we know how to deal with it. You could say that it both appears and is solved extraphilosophically (although we overlook this when we deal with the puzzle philosophically). Of course these assertions require backing up and explanation.

[21] Puzzlement about death is, no doubt, the most immediate and easy to relate to—which, of course, is why I have chosen it to illustrate the conception of an extraphilosophical puzzle.

Thus these are the puzzles that offer philosophy the opportunity of pursuing its ancient task. For although in bringing into the open the source of our puzzlement we do not solve anything, we may come to understand something—something about ourselves. Has this not always been conceived as a philosophical task, to understand ourselves?

Insofar as they depend on unclarities in our language-games (concepts), the purely philosophical puzzles might be described as "puzzles of the communal horizon." The extraphilosophical puzzles, on the other hand, are all "puzzles of the personal horizon." They depend not on unclarities but on difficult truths, i.e., on difficult truths whose expression in one way or another requires reference to the personal horizon. Let us conclude our introductory remarks by offering a brief characterization of the extraphilosophical puzzles, and indicating how the personal horizon figures in each case.

Int.10 The Extraphilosophical Puzzles

Note, to begin with, when we speak in this context of extraphilosophical puzzles we refer not to the surface puzzlement but to the underlying puzzle that philosophical reflection aims to articulate. The surface puzzlement, if it occurs (it need not occur; we need never be thus puzzled), takes the form of incomprehension, a sense of something uncanny or impossible. "How can this be?" The underlying puzzle takes the form of an antinomy or contradiction. The idea is that the surface puzzlement manifests an unarticulated grasp of the underlying puzzle. If we are able to bring the puzzle to light (with everything on which it depends), then we will have discovered something, viz., why we are puzzled. We will have made a philosophical discovery. (Of course, this cannot be expected on the basis of the preliminary characterizations we shall now offer—which merely hint at the puzzles.)

The puzzles of death.[22]   There are two puzzles that find their way to the surface in our sense that death—"my" death—cannot be comprehended. The first is the "solipsistic puzzle of death": the prospect of my death looms as the end of everything and in that sense as *the* death; yet I know it is like that for everyone. How could a multitude of deaths each be "the" death? The second puzzle may be called the "temporal puzzle of death." The subject matter of death is the personal horizon: the personal horizon is what ceases to be in death. The personal horizon, however,

[22] See chapter 11.

emerges (in our reflections on the dream hypothesis) as a subject matter that is outside time and therefore cannot cease to be.

The puzzle of the causation of consciousness.[23]   In this case, the extraphilosophical manifestation of the puzzle requires knowledge that consciousness depends on the activity of our brains: that there is such a thing as my consciousness because of what is going on in my brain. This is a fact—but how could it be? If we are puzzled in this way it is, I think, because we have a sense of the personal horizon. The personal horizon, i.e., consciousness in the horizonal sense, cannot itself be included in time. Causation, however, presupposes temporality: only what is in time can be caused to be. Consciousness (in the horizonal sense), since it is not in time, is not a possible term of the causal relation—and yet, right now, because of what is happening in my brain, there is such a thing as my consciousness.

The puzzle of experience, and the puzzle of memory.[24]   These puzzles, like the puzzle of the causation of consciousness, depend on our knowledge of the causal role of the brain, except that what concerns us now is the causing to be of what is available from within the personal horizon rather than the causing to be of the horizon itself. Thus the puzzle of experience concerns the experiential presence of objects from within the horizon (experience in the horizonal sense), and the puzzle of memory, the availability of past events from within the horizon. At the surface, it can seem baffling that something happening "up here" in my brain should cause the presence in my experience of something "out there" in the world, or that something happening "now" in my brain should cause the availability (givenness) of something that no longer is, something that happened "back then." The underlying puzzle (roughly) is this: the presence/availability of what is caused cannot be the object "out there" or the event "back then," since that would mean that events happening in my brain bring the world/the past into being. What is caused by the brain must rather be some kind of internal object (a sense-datum, a memory image); yet (we know) it is precisely the world and the past that are present/available from within consciousness.[25]

[23] See chapter 11. To avoid confusion, we should stress that the puzzle we are concerned with here has nothing to do with what philosophers call the "qualitative character of experience" or with what has recently come to be known as "the problem of the explanatory gap."

[24] See chapter 21.

[25] Since I have discussed it at length elsewhere, our discussion of the puzzle of experience will be perfunctory (see *The Puzzle of Experience*). Its main purpose in the present book is to serve as an object of comparison for the puzzle of memory.

The puzzles of experience and memory, like the puzzle of the causation of consciousness (and the puzzle of division, which we will come to in a moment) depend on what we might call our causal entrapment in the world, on the fact that both the existence of the personal horizon and the way things are from within it are the causal upshot of what is happening right now in that bit of the world that is my brain. In contrast, the puzzles of death depend solely on the status of the personal horizon: on its claim to uniqueness, on its nontemporality. On the other hand, since causal entrapment depends on temporality, the temporal puzzle of death seems close to puzzles of causal entrapment in contrast to the solipsistic puzzle of death, which stands apart.

That we are causally entrapped in the world is something we all know. We know too, about the same world that causally entraps us, that this world and its past are given from within the personal horizon. We know these things—but we are not yet open to them: we have not yet philosophically discovered what we already know. Now, as we pointed out in Int.4, philosophical discovery presupposes resistance. The peculiar thing about the puzzles of experience and memory is that in these cases the resistance comes from philosophy itself, viz., from philosophical arguments whose conclusions (that objects in the world and past events cannot be what is given from within the horizon) conflict with what we know. Thus in expounding the arguments that (by creating resistance) put us in a position philosophically to discover the givenness of the world and past, we at the same time philosophically discover the puzzles. But the puzzles we thereby discover are already there for us, implicit in the fact of our causal entrapment and the facts of availability.

In contrast, however, to the purely philosophical puzzles, philosophy does not enter in these cases as a necessary preliminary to our puzzlement. It enters rather as part of the reflections by means of which we explicate a puzzle that may make itself known to us without any need for philosophical reflection.

The puzzle of division.[26] The puzzle of division, which is related to the puzzle of the causation of consciousness, is an imperfect example of an extraphilosophical puzzle (a puzzle of causal entrapment): it does not have its own extraphilosophical manifestation. The puzzle the causation of consciousness concerns a fact about the personal horizon, that it is causally maintained by the activity of my brain. The puzzle of division, however, concerns not a fact but a possibility about this subject matter:

---

[26] See chapter 23.

the possibility of its dividing, of my horizon (my consciousness, experience, life) becoming two horizons.

The puzzle is that whereas from the standpoint of experiential possibility division seems impossible, given the brain's role in maintaining the horizon, and given further the metaphysical possibility of splitting the brain in such a way that each half (appropriately enhanced) could maintain my horizon, from the standpoint of causal and metaphysical possibility, there seems to be nothing that excludes the possibility of division (of my horizon doubling); nothing, in other words, that excludes something that I cannot make sense of as a possible experience; nothing that excludes a possibility that conflicts with what Kant called "the necessary unity of consciousness."

Of course, what we have just described (helping ourselves to philosophical jargon) is, if our description is correct, the underlying puzzle rather than a kind of puzzlement that is not apt to break in upon everyday consciousness without special philosophical prompting. The existence of my horizon (consciousness, experience, life); that it will cease to be (death); that it is causally maintained in existence by my brain; that the world and the past are given from within my horizon—these are all facts. They are, you might say, facts that we live with. Thus the puzzles that attach to these facts have the ever-present potential of breaking through the surface of everyday consciousness. The puzzle of division, in contrast, concerns (as we remarked) not a *fact* but a *possibility*—a possibility that we evoke with the aid of arguments and thought experiments (about brain-splitting, etc.). Hence there is no extraphilosophical symptom of the puzzle.

Yet once we are prompted by the puzzle of the causation of consciousness to look beneath the surface, the essence of the puzzle of division is very close at hand. The puzzle of the causation of consciousness concerns the singular and remarkable (and ultimately problematic) fact that my consciousness, the subject matter that is the horizon of the spatio-temporality totality I call the world, is itself maintained in existence by one tiny bit of that totality, one tiny bit of matter. My brain. ("How can this be?") To get the essentials of the puzzle of division—i.e., the metaphysical possibility of an experiential impossibility—we need only add to the puzzle of the causation of consciousness the fact that the brain, as a bit of matter, is divisible. The conflict in this case is merely potential and thus does not manifest itself extraphilosophically (apart from thought experiments, etc.). But it is there for us, implicit in our causally entrapped situation, waiting to be philosophically discovered.

It will not go unremarked that the puzzles of causal entrapment (of experience, memory, consciousness, and division) to one degree or another resemble well-known (and much discussed) puzzles in the philosophical literature. It is, however, important to appreciate that we are regarding these puzzles in a particular way. Our aim is not that of solving the puzzles (we are saying they have no solution), but of getting to the bottom of them, of exposing their elements. This is, as we put it, the philosophical aim of understanding our situation, of understanding ourselves.

PART ONE

Dream

1. The Dream Hypothesis and the Argument from Internality

1.1 Our Purpose in Raising the Dream Hypothesis

The dream hypothesis (DH) is the hypothesis that this is a dream. The DH makes sense only from the first-person singular perspective (if this were a dream, it would be my dream, not yours or ours, etc.). The question philosophers always raise is: How do I know this is not a dream? How do I know this is reality? The DH is thus viewed as posing an epistemological challenge. Assuming that we are certain the hypothesis is false, that this is not a dream, we are in effect asked to justify our conviction and thereby provide grounds for rejecting the DH. Skepticism in this regard (dream skepticism) says that we cannot provide adequate grounds, that we are not justified in rejecting the DH. The skeptic also says that unless we have (adequate) grounds for rejecting the dream hypothesis, none of our everyday beliefs about the world (including that there is a world) are justified. What then are we justified in believing?

It is notoriously difficult to say what justifies us in rejecting the DH. In fact, the difficulty is such that one may come to suspect there is something wrong with the project of looking for a justification. Perhaps the response to the DH should be along different lines altogether. In this vein, it may be said that there is something wrong with the hypothesis, that it is (in some sense) meaningless or empty or nonsensical. If that were so, we would be entitled to dismiss the hypothesis even though we were not able to provide grounds that refute it (show it to be false). We would be entitled to dismiss the hypothesis for the very reason that it is not open to a refutation of this sort.

Our main purpose in raising the DH, however, is not the usual one, since it is independent of the familiar epistemological challenge. Of course, once the hypothesis is raised, the challenge is there, and we shall eventually have to face up to this. But what we must first come to see is that there is a problem about what the DH *means*. If we are not clear what the hypothesis means, we are not clear about the distinction between dream and reality. This would seem to be a fundamental gap in our grasp of things—one worth remedying for its own sake, apart from the epistemological issue concerning the DH. Anyway, how could we hope to deal with the question of what justifies us in rejecting the DH if we are not clear what the hypothesis means?

This is our first aim in the book: to clarify the meaning of the DH. Notice, in undertaking to clarify the meaning of the dream hypothesis we do not prejudice the idea that the hypothesis may turn out to be in some sense meaningless. If the hypothesis proves to be "meaningless," it will not be in the sense that it is gibberish. In some sense the DH has meaning—a meaning that can be clarified. (Gibberish cannot be clarified.) Indeed, it could only be by clarifying its meaning in this sense that we might be able to show that, in another sense, it is meaningless and hence that we are entitled to dismiss it.

1.2 That the Dream/Reality Contrast Is Extrinsic to the Subject Matter of the Dream Hypothesis

I shall describe my present situation. I am sitting in a local café, writing (these very words). The place is full: other customers (most of whom, like the little group of elderly middle-European Jews in the corner who spend half the day here, are well known to me), the manager, the woman who operates the espresso machine, and two waitresses who are constantly bickering. I am at my usual table with a cup of coffee, a notebook and pen, and today's paper. There is a background din of morning table conversation and loud talk coming from the kitchen. If I look up I see shoppers passing by, and traffic on the busy road outside.

You get the picture. I am in a situation in which everything is familiar: a familiar place in a familiar neighborhood in a big city where I have lived for many years. In this familiar setting (where I myself am a familiar, if somewhat marginal, figure), I feel safe and at ease—in the middle of everyday life, so to say. So when I now consider the hypothesis that this is a dream, it is not because something terrifying or strange has happened. What prompts me, then, to raise the hypothesis?

Of course, I have a philosophical motive. But is that essential? Might not the hypothesis simply have occurred to me? The fact is, the hypothesis *can be raised.* Yet when I raise the hypothesis, it is not clear what it means.

If the meaning of the DH is not immediately clear, the logical form of the hypothesis seems, at least on the surface, straightforward enough. When, expressing the dream hypothesis, I use the sentence "this is a dream," I refer to something by "this" and say of it that it is a dream.

We shall speak of what is referred to as the "subject matter" of the DH. If the hypothesis were true, if this were a dream, that to which I refer here by "this," the subject matter of the hypothesis, would be a dream. This, at any rate, is how things seem at the surface.

The DH, thus understood, seems to represent a possible state of affairs. It seems possible that the subject matter to which I refer in expressing the hypothesis, the subject matter of the hypothesis, might be dream.[1] Let us elaborate on this.

First, we need to distinguish between two contrasts: the essential/accidental contrast and the intrinsic/extrinsic contrast. An essential property of X is one that to suppose it lacking is equivalent to supposing there is no such thing as X, that X does not exist; an accidental property of X is thus a property that, to suppose it lacking, is compatible with supposing that X exists. An intrinsic property of X, on the other hand, is a property that, to suppose it lacking is to suppose that X is itself in some way different; whereas an extrinsic property of X is one that, to suppose it lacking, leaves X, the thing itself, in no way different—though, trivially, different propositions would be true of X.

Imagine a convention whereby we describe a cup by reference to the city in which it is located. The cup in front of me is thus a London cup. Being a London cup—versus, say, a New York cup—makes no difference to the cup. Different propositions would be true of the cup; but the object itself, the cup, would be just as it is. Being a London cup is an extrinsic property of the cup. Being chipped, on the other hand, would be an intrinsic property of the cup. It would also be accidental (this very cup, which is chipped, might not be chipped). In contrast, being composed of a certain parcel or bit of porcelain seems essential to the cup. Any object that was not made of this very stuff could not be this very object, this cup.[2] Notice, while being chipped is accidental (versus essential) to the cup, it is nevertheless intrinsic (were the cup not chipped, it would not be in itself exactly as it is). Being a London cup is also accidental to the cup; but it is not intrinsic to the cup (although different propositions would be true of it, were the cup not a London cup, it might itself be exactly as it is). From this it should be evident that if a given property is extrinsic to X, it is thereby accidental to X; but that a property can be accidental to X without being extrinsic to X.

Now I do not wish to claim that these distinctions are crystal clear or that they reflect the ultimate metaphysical truth. Many philosophers regard them with a certain professional skepticism. (I myself am not so

---

[1] Note our double usage of the term "subject matter": on the one hand, in phrases of the form "the subject matter of. . ." (e.g., "the subject matter of the DH"); on the other hand, in phrases of the form "the subject matter that is . . ." (e.g., "the subject matter that is nothing in itself," "the subject matter from within which the world appears," and so on). Thus, using the expression in both ways, we might ask, "What is subject matter that is the subject matter of the DH?"

[2] It will be obvious here that I am borrowing some ideas from Saul Kripke. See his *Naming and Necessity*, (Basil Blackwell, 1980).

skeptical.) But even these philosophers, I submit, see the point of the distinctions; they see what people are trying to get at by means of them. This is really all we need in the present context.

We are mainly interested here in the intrinsic/ extrinsic distinction. Suppose X is F. Being F is extrinsic to X just in case, first, X, one and the same thing, might not be F (being F is accidental, versus essential, to F), and second, the realization of this possibility is compatible with X itself being in itself exactly as it is. If being F is extrinsic to X, then, so (where this is the case) is being not-F.

We said that the DH represents a possible state of affairs; that the subject matter of the hypothesis—what in expressing the hypothesis that this is a dream I refer to by "this"—might be a dream. We can fill this in a bit now by remarking that the possibility in question is formally analogous to the possibility of the cup in our example being a New York cup. This cup is a London cup. But it (being in itself exactly as it is) might be a New York cup. Similarly, this is (let us assume) reality. But it could be a dream: this, being exactly as it is, could be a dream. The idea is that, formally speaking, being a dream has the same relation to the subject matter of the dream hypothesis that being a New York cup has to the cup. Being a dream is (formally) a property that, if it held of the subject matter that is reality, would be extrinsic to it. So, on the assumption that this is reality, being reality is also extrinsic to this. There is a sense, then, in which whether it is a dream or reality *makes no difference* to the subject matter of the dream hypothesis.

It should be plain that we are talking here about what are called metaphysical versus epistemic possibilities. Thus, for the purpose of stating the possibility about the cup, we may take it as given that I know the cup is a London cup. Similarly, for the purpose of stating the possibility about the subject matter of the dream hypothesis, we may take it as given that I know this is reality. (And do I not know it?) I.e., although that to which in expressing the dream hypothesis I refer by "this" could—being exactly as it is—be a dream, we may take it as given that I know it is reality. Of course the skeptic will say that, once we see the metaphysical possibility, we must conclude that in fact I do not know this is reality. He will, in other words, appeal to the metaphysical possibility by way of trying to make us accept the corresponding epistemic possibility (that for all I know, this could be a dream). And perhaps he is right. But for the time being what interests us is just the metaphysical possibility: the possibility that, being exactly as it is, this could be a dream.

We said that this possibility is formally analogous to that of the cup's being a New York cup. Why only "formally" analogous? Consider the modal assertions that we would be prepared to make in each case. On the assumption that this is a London cup, we would assert not just that it might be a New York cup, i.e., that being a New York cup is compatible with its being as it is, but that it *might have been* a New York cup; or again that it might *become* a New York cup. I do not think we would be prepared to make either of these modal assertions about the subject matter of the dream hypothesis. Assuming this is reality, I do not think we would be willing to assert that it, the same subject matter, might have been a dream; or that it might become a dream. Nor, on the assumption that this is a dream, would we be prepared to assert that it might become reality, or that it might have been reality.

Again, where we are not prepared to assert of X, which we know to be F, that X might have been not-F (or might become not-F), this is because we take being F as essential to X. But the dream/reality case is different. On the assumption that it is reality, this could (might) be a dream. That is to say, being a dream is compatible with this (which is reality) being as it is. So, being reality is not essential to this. Indeed, it is *extrinsic* to this. And similarly, for being a dream. Yet, as we said, on the assumption that this is a dream, we would not wish to assert that it might have been reality (or might become reality); or, given that this is reality, that it might have been (or might become) a dream.

But if that to which I refer by "this" in expressing the hypothesis that this is a dream is such that it, being just as it is, might be reality, what is it to which I refer? Here we come to the reason why the meaning of the DH is unclear. The meaning of the hypothesis is unclear because it is unclear what the hypothesis is about. "This (I tell myself) might be a dream." I look around the café. *What* might be a dream? What do I mean (refer to) here by "this"? We may know the form of DH. But what is its subject matter?

I hope that you will react to the question in the way that I do. (I will pretend that it is occurring to me for the first time.) The question throws me, as if—after giving who knows how many tutorials on Descartes—I had never really thought about the DH before. Could it be that there is something wrong with the question, that in setting up the question we have already made a mistake? Well, we can consider that later. Let us first see what happens when, taking it at face value, we try to answer the question.

1.3 The Argument from Internality

Once again: What is the subject matter of the DH? In expressing the hypothesis that this is a dream, to what do I refer by "this"?

One thing should be evident. I am not using the word "this" in the way that it is typically used, viz., to refer demonstratively to something present in my experience (to something directly available for me to pick out or focus on). After all, the DH is not the hypothesis that *this* table, or *this* coffee cup, is a dream.[3]

There is an argument here. No doubt, that the subject matter of the dream hypothesis is not the cup or the table does not need an argument. But the argument in question is one we shall use again and again. So it is worth stating the argument right away, as it applies in the simplest and most obvious type of case.

Consider the table. The table is not the subject matter of the dream hypothesis. Here is the argument. On the DH—on the hypothesis that this is a dream—the table would be an object *in* the dream. Thus it could not *be* the dream. But if it could not be the dream, it could not be that to which I refer to by "this" when I express the hypothesis that this is a dream; for whatever it is to which I refer by "this" in expressing the hypothesis, it is precisely that which would be the dream if this were a dream. We shall call this "the argument from internality."

What holds of the table, holds of the cup. It holds, obviously, of any object now present in my experience. Whatever the object is, if it is now present to me, then, if this were a dream, the object would be in the dream and thus could not be the dream; so, by the argument from internality, it could not be what I refer to here by "this." Then to what do I refer? What is the subject matter of the dream hypothesis?

Perhaps it is not just one or another of the things now present in my experience but the totality of such things. This is not a well-defined totality. But that is not the problem. The reason I cannot regard the totality of objects present to me as the subject matter of the DH hypothesis is basically the same reason that I cannot regard the individual cup or table as the subject matter of the DH. Whatever exactly it includes, the totality is by hypothesis a totality of things now present to me. If this were a dream, the totality in question would be a totality of things now present in the dream. In that case, it (the totality) could not be the dream. So it could not be that to which I refer by "this" when I express the hypothesis that this is a dream.

Once the nature of the reasoning is clear, you start to get an inkling of the difficulty concerning the subject matter, and thus the meaning, of the DH. And things get worse. The pattern of reasoning can be extended. So far, we have considered only objects present now in my experience. On the DH, any such object would be in (part of) the dream. Let us ask: If

[3] Throughout the book we shall employ the convention of emphasizing the word "this" to express the pretence that the object of reference is something present in experience; i.e., something directly available to be picked out and demonstrated. We shall also, to express presence, employ the convention of emphasizing the word "there." Thus we might say, an object can be referred to demonstratively "only on the condition that it is *there*." So there would be a patent redundancy in saying (writing) "*this* object is *there*."

this were a dream, would something have to be in my experience to be in the dream?

Absent-mindedly I finger the under edge of the table at which I am sitting. What is this? An old piece of chewing gum stuck to the table. Suppose, contrary to fact, my fingers had just missed the piece of gum, or had never strayed under the table. Then the piece of gum would not have been, as it is, present now in my experience. We may assume that it would never have been present in my experience, that I never would have known about it at all. Of course, this would take nothing away from the piece of gum. Whether I came across it or not, it would have been there just as it is. It would have continued modestly along the course of its own history, fated perhaps to remain forever undiscovered by human hands.

These thoughts about the piece of gum lead to more general thoughts of the same nature. Just within the confines of this café there are countless objects that are not now, and never will be, present in my experience; things that will never figure in my life in any way. Obviously, I cannot *say* *which* things these things are—but they are there all the same, completely indifferent to whether I happen to come across them or not. And that is only within the little world of the café. If I consider the world at large, the point gets magnified indefinitely. Most people are at one time or another struck by the following, that only a tiny fragment of the world ever shows up within my experience, that which things these are depends ultimately on matters of brute contingency, and that the whole of the remainder, the vast part of the world that falls outside my ken, goes on its own way, following out its own destiny.

What happens if I repeat such reflections—but this time under the DH? I reflect that this piece of gum might have remained undiscovered by me, that there are all sorts of things in the café that not only are but will always remain outside my experience. What is the point of these reflections? The point is just that they seem unaffected by the hypothesis that this is a dream. They do not seem to be in any way undermined or disturbed by the hypothesis.

That is, whatever exactly the hypothesis means, it does not seem to affect the fact that the piece of gum I just discovered might have remained undiscovered. If this were a dream, the piece of gum would have remained undiscovered *in the dream*. Or consider the possibility that there is a piece of gum under the next table. Why should the DH interfere with this possibility? And there is no end to such possibilities. Thus I am led to reflect that, just as is the case in reality, were this a dream it would be true that there are in and about the premises of the café (behind the counter, in the kitchen, and so on) all sorts of things I never have laid eyes on, and never will—things that will never play the smallest role in my life. So the totality that consists of everything in the café (of objects both within and without my experience), this totality would, on the DH, be in or part of the dream. It would be "in" or "part of" the dream in the very way or sense that, given this is reality, it is "in" or "part of" reality. On the DH, the totality of objects in the café includes objects that are *outside my experience in the dream*, in the same way that, given that this is reality, it includes objects that are *outside my experience in reality*.

Once again, then, the argument from internality applies. Since the totality of objects in the café would be in the dream, it could not be the dream. It could not, therefore, be the subject matter of the DH.

1.4 Dream and the Law of Excluded Middle

By this time we may begin to suspect that there is no stopping the argument, that we can keep reapplying it to ever more inclusive totalities. But there is an objection that would cut off the reasoning where it moves from what is inside my experience (actually present within my experience) to what is outside (not present within) my experience.

Consider the point in our reflections where I light upon some previously unnoticed object (like the piece of gum) and assert that, if this were a dream, the object would have been there in the dream even had it never come to my attention. What may seem hard to swallow is the idea that something that never reveals itself, something of whose existence I know nothing at all, should nonetheless (on the DH) be in my dream. Our uneasiness here is based, I think, on a correct perception about the logic of dreams; but there is an element of confusion as well.

The correct perception is closely related to a point that philosophers often make about fiction and the law of excluded middle (LEM), the logical principle that every proposition is either true or false, that there is no third possibility (having another truth-value, or no truth-value). It is often maintained that LEM breaks down in the case of fictive entities. To take the usual sort of example, it might be said that it is neither true nor false that Hamlet had a mole behind his ear. So, LEM breaks down here. The explanation is not that "Hamlet" is an empty singular term (like "the present king of France"), but that what is true of Hamlet depends on what is said of him in the story in which he exists (plus what can be inferred from this)—and there is a limit to what can be said in a story. In the case a fictive entity, then, we run out of truths. Thus it can happen that a question is raised about such an entity to which there is no answer, no truth that covers the question. In contrast, with a real entity, although we may not know what it is, there always is a truth that covers the question.

The world in a fiction is in this sense logically incomplete, which is why it is possible to formulate propositions about such a world that are neither true nor false. LEM breaks down. The world outside fiction, i.e., the world, is not logically incomplete. Here LEM does not break down.[4] Now the idea is that dreams are a kind of fiction. The author is in this case the dreamer. The facts about the world of the dream depend on what the dreamer dreams, and, since a dreamer can dream only so much, these facts or truths are limited. Hence the world of a dream is logically incomplete— which means there are bound to be propositions about that world for which LEM does not hold.

Consider my dream of the other night. I am seated on a train next to my daughter. I get up for a drink of water. When I return to my seat my daughter is gone. I search the train but cannot find her. These being (let us assume) the main facts of the dream, consider the question of whether there was a piece of gum under my seat on the train. There is no answer: the facts of the dream simply do not cover this case. The world of my dream is incomplete, and thus LEM breaks down. It breaks down in a way that it never breaks down for the world of reality.[5]

It is not hard to see how these ideas relate to the objection expressed above. The objection is that extending the argument from internality to the totality of objects in the café assumes that LEM holds on the DH, that on the DH the world around me is, as it is in reality, logically complete. It assumes, e.g., that even had I not discovered it, the piece of gum would have been there under the table in the dream, just as it is under the table in reality. This assumption is a mistake. Suppose I wonder whether there is spoon behind the espresso machine, or a wallet in the pocket of the man at the next table? When we extend the argument from internality to include objects of whose existence I know nothing, we mistakenly assume that, on the DH, such questions have answers. We mistakenly assume that if this were a dream, the world around me would be, as it is in reality, logically complete.

The trouble with this objection is that it overlooks a complication about standpoint. If this were a dream, then, from the standpoint outside

---

[4] We are ignoring the case of vague predicates, as well as empty singular terms—both of which are irrelevant.

[5] Thus one might say that logic breaks down with respect to dreams. Notice, however, that usually when people say things like this, something rather different is intended. E.g., you go home, it's your street, your house—and yet it isn't. Is it or isn't it? Somehow everything is different. Or again, you seem to be your present age, and yet you are back in childhood. This sort of dream logic is not easy to describe, but we can at least say that it involves strangeness. The house that is and is not mine is, for that reason, strange. In contrast, the seat in my dream, about which there is no answer to the question of whether it has a piece of gum under it, is not for that reason strange. The strangeness of a dream world has nothing to do with the fact that the dream world is logically incomplete. We are all struck by the strangeness of our dreams, but only a philosopher will be interested in the fact of their logical incompleteness.

this, outside the dream, the world around me, JV, would be incomplete. But from *my* standpoint, the standpoint from which we are considering the DH—i.e., from within the subject matter about which we are asking whether it is a dream—that world is complete. It is complete whether or not this is a dream.

In the case of fiction, there is the standpoint we occupy, the standpoint outside the fiction (the external standpoint), and that internal to the fiction (the internal standpoint). A given proposition about a fictive object can be true from one standpoint but not the other. Consider the proposition that Hamlet is one of Shakespeare's most famous characters. This proposition is true from the external standpoint, but not from the standpoint internal to the play. After all, in the play, Hamlet is just a man, a prince. He does not—not in the play—have the property of being a character created by Shakespeare. The proposition that Hamlet has this property is an external not an internal truth about Hamlet. On the other hand, the proposition that Hamlet is a prince is an internal truth. We can, of course, assert this from the outside; but that is because we can, from the outside, assume the internal standpoint. (How else could we understand a fictive world?)

Notice the asymmetry here. We who occupy the external standpoint are like people watching others through a one-way glass. We have access to both standpoints, i.e., to the standpoint we occupy, outside the fiction, and to that internal to the fiction. We *occupy* one standpoint and, from that standpoint, *assume* the other. Those whose standpoint we assume cannot assume our standpoint, the external standpoint, but are confined to the standpoint they occupy. Thus, from outside a fiction, we are in a position to assert both external and internal truths about characters internal to the fiction. Could Hamlet have asserted, "I have been created by Shakespeare"? True, there are plays where characters say things like this. Shakespeare could have (what could stop him?) written the words into Hamlet's mouth. But the effect of this type of (tiresome modernist) device depends precisely on the impossibility to which we are calling attention. (It is only because the device flies in the face of the asymmetry that we meant to chuckle, shake our heads, etc.)

Similar points apply in the case of dreams. Here too we need a distinction between internal and external truths. And there is the same kind of asymmetry. After we have emerged from a dream and occupy the standpoint outside it, we have access to both standpoints. This puts us in a position to assert both external and internal truths about objects in the dream. When we are inside a dream, however, we have access only to the standpoint we occupy. We are in a position only to assert internal truths about objects in the dream, truths that hold from the standpoint we occupy.

There is, however, an important difference between the dream case and that of fiction: there is no such thing as emerging from a fiction to occupy the standpoint outside the fiction—as there in the case of a dream. Hence, from within a dream, I, the subject, may have the thought that I will (or might) emerge from this, in effect, the thought that this is a dream. Perhaps I can even know that this is a dream. But in having such a thought, or such knowledge, I do not have access to, and hence cannot assume, the standpoint of the world outside, the world into which I will emerge. I may know there is such a world, but the objects of that world do not figure with me in such a way that I can think about them.[6] From within a dream, I am not (we might say) in touch with the world outside. If I were in touch with the world outside, I would thereby occupy its standpoint. So it would not be the world "outside" but simply the world. I would already have emerged from the dream.

From the standpoint of reality, i.e., from the standpoint I occupy outside a dream, I can assume the standpoint of the dream. If, however, I can assume the standpoint of reality, I already occupy that standpoint. There is no distinction between assuming and occupying the standpoint of reality, the standpoint outside a dream. But notice, it does not follow that if I do occupy the standpoint of reality, I know that that is the standpoint I occupy (that I know that this is reality).

There are, to be sure, all sorts of peculiar in-between possibilities. For example, under general anaesthesia one might be cognizant of one's situation. This once happened to me as a child (an experience I would not wish to repeat). I was able to hear the conversation of the medics in attendance while lacking all other sensory contact with the world. However, this is not a case of assuming the standpoint of reality from within a dream. My standpoint was not that of a dream but of the world: the same world that included the medics and the operating theater, and from which I was partly cut off. (This would have been true even had I, in the same state, not actually heard anyone around me but just thought about my situation on the operating table, etc.) Similarly, one can emerge from a dream and thus reoccupy the standpoint of the world outside the dream, prior to

[6] This assertion may seem obviously false. In the dream, I am looking for my daughter. Do I not think about my daughter in the dream? Or, say, a bell rings in the world outside and I hear it in the dream. But is the ringing in the dream the identical ringing of the bell in the world outside the dream? Is the girl in my dream identical with the girl in the world outside the dream? There is a difficult question here about identity that we shall address further on in our reflections.

being fully in touch with that world. (One thinks, as he is coming to, "It was a dream.")

OK. When it comes to dreams and being awake or conscious, all sorts of things are possible.[7] But one thing is not possible: both being within a dream, occupying its standpoint, and being back in touch with the world outside. Once I reestablish contact with the world outside—once objects from that world figure with me in such a way that I can think about them—I occupy the standpoint of the world outside, of the world in reality. Whatever peculiar state of consciousness I am in, I have emerged from the dream. It cannot both be true that I am in the dream and that I have emerged from it.

On the other hand, it surely *is* possible that from within a dream the thought that this is a dream should *not* occur to me. The thought is not in any way essential to a dream. Again, it is possible that if from within a dream the thought does occur to me, I dismiss it—in the same way I now (in reality, let us assume) dismiss the thought that this is a dream, or that from within a dream I wish that this were a dream (which depends on my taking it that this is not a dream).[8]

Consider again, to pick up the thread of our argument, my dream of the other night. I am now outside the dream. From this standpoint, certain things are true that are not true from the internal standpoint. Just as Shakespeare created Hamlet, by dreaming I created the train in the dream, I, JV, am the "dream author." This is clearly an external versus internal truth about the train in my dream. From within the dream, it is not true that the train is created by my dreaming. From within the dream, the train I am on is just that: the train I am on, a train. In contrast, that I am on a train is an internal truth. It is true from the standpoint internal to the dream but not from the standpoint I now occupy outside the dream. (I was not, in reality, on a train.) When, having emerged from the dream, I assert that in the dream I was on a train, I represent, from my standpoint outside the dream, how things were from within the dream (a truth internal to the dream): from the external standpoint, I assume the internal standpoint.

The familiar philosophical idea that LEM breaks down for objects in a fictive world has in mind the external standpoint on such objects. From

---

[7] This makes it difficult to remain focused on essentials when discussing these issues: everyone has (first- or second-hand) weird and wonderful sleep/dream experiences to report—vivid dreams, waking dreams, etc.

[8] Dante offers a further twist on this possibility: "*Qual e colui che suo dannagio sogna, che sognando desidera sognare, si che quel che'e, come non fosse, agogna*" (Like one who dreams of something hurtful and, in dreaming, wishes it were a dream, so that he wishes for what is actually the case)." *Inferno*, (Princeton University Press), 1977) Canto 30, 136–38. I am indebted to my friend Elena Marcarini for guiding me through Dante.

the standpoint internal to a fiction, LEM remains in force. From the standpoint internal to the play, e.g., Hamlet is not a logically incomplete human being (he is just a human being): there either is or is not a mole behind his ear. Is it not the same with dreams? If truth is relativized to the standpoint inside or outside a dream, this will apply to truths about LEM and logical incompleteness. In other words, that LEM, etc., breaks down for the world of a dream is true from our standpoint outside a dream, but not from within the dream.

Was there or was there not a piece of gum under my seat on the train? From where I am, outside the dream, the answer is that there is no answer. LEM breaks down here: the train seat is a logically incomplete object. But this is not true from within the dream. In the dream, I am not sitting on a logically incomplete object. I am just sitting on a seat, in a train, and there either is or is not a piece of gum under the seat on which I am sitting. From the standpoint internal to the dream, the world of the dream is as complete as the world around me in reality.

Given that I have emerged from the dream, I have, in a sense, access not just to the standpoint I actually occupy but also to the standpoint internal to the dream: I can assume that standpoint. I am in a position, then, to assert both internal truths about objects and events in the dream (what happened in the dream) and the external truth that, for example, there is no answer to the question of whether there was a piece of gum under the seat on which I was sitting (that the train seat is a logically incomplete object). However, when I occupy the standpoint internal to the dream, I have access only to that standpoint. I have no access to the standpoint of the world outside. (If I did, I would already occupy that standpoint; I would already have emerged from the dream.) I have no access, then, to the standpoint from which the propositions about logical incompleteness, etc., are true, and thus I am not in a position to assert these propositions.

But the DH is the hypothesis that exactly this is the case, that the standpoint I occupy is internal to a dream. By hypothesis, then, the world around me is internal to the dream. It follows that, on the DH, I cannot assert about objects in the world around me, like the table, that these objects are logically incomplete, that LEM breaks down for these objects. To be in a position to assert about the table, about *this* table, that it is logically incomplete, I would have to occupy a standpoint that by hypothesis I do not occupy: the standpoint outside the dream; the very standpoint that the dream hypothesis says I do not occupy.

In the case of a past dream, like that of a fiction, the external standpoint coincides with the standpoint I actually occupy. Thus I have access both to that standpoint and to the standpoint internal to the fiction or dream. But the whole idea (as it were) of the dream hypothesis is to place me inside a dream and thereby deprive me of access to the external stand-point: the standpoint to which I must have access if I am to assert something about, say, the table here that is logically incomplete. Of course, if this were a dream and I emerged from it, *then*, from the new standpoint, the standpoint outside the dream, I would be in a position to assert that LEM fails of the table; just as now, from my standpoint outside the dream of the other night, I can make such assertions about the seat on the train. But, to repeat, this is (by the DH) not my standpoint. If this is a dream, I am not outside but inside a dream.

It is this business about standpoint that is apt to confuse us here. We correctly appreciate that the world of a dream contains logical gaps, but we fail to appreciate that these gaps exist, and can be asserted to exist, only from the standpoint that, on the DH, we do not occupy. Or perhaps we appreciate this, but we somehow fail to keep straight where, on the DH, we are. We reason about the DH as if the dream that concerned us was a past dream, a dream of which we are now outside, whereas the hypothesis itself places us inside a dream. The latter is an example of what we shall call a "confusion of standpoint." We shall, in our further reflections on the DH, encounter further examples of this kind of confusion.

1.5 The Dream Hypothesis and Space

Let us take it then that we are entitled to extend the argument from internality beyond the totality of objects present in my experience; that we are entitled to reason that, if this were a dream, the totality of objects in my immediate environment (in the café)—all these things close around me, including the objects that are not actually present in my experience, including objects that will never be present in my experience and of which I have no knowledge whatever—this totality would be internal to the dream. Hence, the totality of objects close around me is not what we are looking for. It is not what I refer to by "this" when I consider the hypothesis that this is a dream. It is not the subject matter of the DH.

And now we may as well openly assert what we earlier (1.3) expressed as a suspicion, viz., that there is going to be no way of stopping the reasoning on which we have embarked, that the argument from internality can be extended to more and more inclusive totalities. Consider, say, the totality of objects that includes not just everything in the café but everything in the building of which the café is a part; or that which includes not just the building and everything in it but all the surrounding buildings and streets in the neighborhood, along with all the objects and people they contain; or the totality that includes the whole great city of which this neighborhood is a small part; and so on. Where should it end? At Oxford Street? At the river? At the city limits? Why should it end *anywhere*, with any natural or conventional boundary? Why, in other words, should it end before we include everything that is there to be included? All of this is out there right now. So, on the DH, it would be out there right now in the dream.

Think of the totality comprised by the whole of the Earth and every-thing on (and in) it. Would this constitute an ultimate stopping point? Why just there, and no further? We can go further. Once we realize that we are free to take the crucial step beyond the totality of objects present in my experience, we can go on to reason in the same way about, say, the totality that includes, along with the Earth, our solar system and galaxy—and beyond. Why not? The vast totality of things to which I refer (and which, according to the certain cosmologies, is itself expanding) is out there right now. If this were a dream, the whole mind-boggling totality would be out there right now in the dream. It does not matter that only the merest fragment of a fragment of this vast totality is actually present within my experience; or that only the merest fragment ever will be pres-ent in my experience. If this were a dream, it would all be out there, outside my experience, forever outside my experience, in the dream. Just as it is in reality. Thus it, this vast totality, cannot be what in expressing the dream hypothesis I refer to by "this." So it cannot be what we are trying to get hold of: the subject matter of the dream hypothesis.

On the DH, whatever is out there is out there in the dream. Notice, as we are at present using these words, "out there" does not entail being outside my experience. If I point and say, "Look at the moon," the moon, we may assume, is present within my experience; at the same time, it is "out there." "Out there" contrasts with "here." The contrast is spatial. When I locate something as "here," I mean it is close to me; when I locate something as "out there," I mean it is far from me. (Of course, this is just a schematic statement of the meaning: what counts as "close" or "far" varies from context to context.) Two further points are worth noting about the "here/out there" contrast. First, it is egocentric: close to versus far from me. Second, given the spatial meaning of the contrast, the im-plicit first-person reference must be to something that itself has a spatial position—like the human being I am, or my body.

Just as what is "out there" may be present within my experience, what is "here" may be outside my experience (not present, demonstratively available). The pennies in my pocket as well as the moon may be outside my experience, or both may be inside (within) my experience. It should be clear, then, that the contrast between "inside" versus "outside" my experience does not have the kind of spatial significance that belongs to the "here/out there" contrast.

What happens when we mix the DH with these contrasts? If this were a dream, there would be a world of objects outside this (outside the dream): a world that stands to the world around me in the way the world around me stands to the world in my dream the other night. The thing to note is that although objects in the world outside the dream would be outside my experience, such objects could not be said to be (in our sense) "out there"—i.e., "out there" as opposed to "here." An object that is "out there" (as opposed to "here") is far from me, from the human being I am, from my body. An object that is far from me is at some distance from me. Thus, for any object that is "out there," no matter how great the distance, it is in principle possible that that object and myself, the human being that I am, should be connected by a physical continuant of some sort, like a piece of string.

Would this be possible, on the DH, in the case of an object internal to (inside) the dream? Yes. Suppose I am holding one end of a piece of string. The piece of string in my hand might run all the way to the moon. This would remain true on the dream hypothesis. For if this is a dream, what I call "the moon" is internal to the dream. It would remain true quite generally—for all spatial objects. Or rather, it would remain true for all spatial objects so long as we are talking about spatial objects internal to the dream.

If this were a dream, any object "out there" (like the moon, say) would be "out there" in the dream. And, as we just remarked, any such object could be physically connected with myself, the human being I am: a string could run from that object to me. What about objects in the world outside this, that is, outside the dream? Could a string run from such an object to me? Could a string run from *outside to inside* the dream—as it might run from outside to inside the café? Or think of it the other way around. Suppose the string is tied to a leg of the table at which I am sitting, and this is a dream. The string runs out the door of the café and just keeps going. Might the other end be attached to an object outside the dream? Could the string run from *inside to outside* the dream? Imagine I decide to follow the string. I walk alongside it, letting it slip through my fingers. Might I, by following the string, end up outside the dream? (How far would I have to go before I got there?)

The idea behind all these rhetorical questions is the same. If this were a dream, objects in the world outside the dream would have no spatial relation to me. There would be no spatial route between them and me. The space of the world outside the dream and the space that spreads out around me would not be the same space. They would be, as we might put it, discrete spaces.

The same holds with respect to my dream of the other night. That train that I was on was traveling somewhere. Within the dream, it could have kept going and going. But could it have gone so far as to arrive *here*, where I now am? The space of the dream has nothing to do with where I now am.

String often figures in thought experiments about space. This is because it is a handy example of something that is both physically continuous and indefinitely extendible. Physical continuity embodies the continuity, and hence the unity or oneness of space. It is when, and only when, objects can in principle be connected by something physically continuous that the spaces containing these objects are parts of a unified space: that they are spaces that might be added to one another so as to yield a more extensive space. Were this a dream, objects in the world outside this would not be physically connectable with me, the human being I am. There would be no possibility of, say, a string being stretched from those objects to me. The space in which I would be located, that which spreads out around me, and the space of the objects outside the dream would be, as we put it, discrete spaces. You could not "get from" one space to the other. They could not be added together to form a larger space.

Indeed, we may conceive of each of these discrete spaces (the spaces inside and outside the dream) as endless or infinite, in the sense that from any position in either there is no furthest position with that same space; so, for each space, nothing could be larger than it, or added to it.[9] On the other hand, for any two positions within each space, there is a distance between the positions, a path from one to the other.

1.6 The Dream Hypothesis and Time

The application of the argument from internality to time parallels, as we shall see, that of space. This is not to deny that time and space differ in various ways. (1) The temporal counterpart of "here" versus "out there" is "now" (temporal presence) versus past and future; but past and future have no genuine spatial counterparts. (2) An event can be temporally present without being present in my experience, just as an object can be "here" (spatially present) without being present in my experience. However, whereas an object's being present in experience does not entail that the place where it exists is spatially present, an event's being present in experience seems to entail that the time at which the event occurs is "now." (Could *this* event be in the past, or future?) (3) In the case of future versus past/present events, we seem to lack an object of reference. If, for example, we say next year's Christmas party will be a success, there seems to

---

[9] Generally, in what follows we shall assume that space is infinite; whether this accords with the latest views in cosmology will not affect the argument.

be no individual event that is the next year's party to which we refer and about which we say that it will be a success. (We mean, rather, that there will be an event-individual of the relevant kind that will be a success.) There is no comparable asymmetry in the case of "here" versus "out there"; the possibilities of reference in space are uniform. (4) The question of what I mean by "here" has a relatively straightforward answer, viz.: near me, the human being I am. In contrast, when we try to explain the meaning of "now," of temporal presence, we get embroiled in one perplexity after another.

Time (let me just assert this) is philosophically more problematic than space. Of course the seeming differences on which this thought rests raise further issues, some of which will come up later in the book. We mention these things now mainly to forestall the impression, which you might easily get from what we are going to say about time and the DH, that space and time stand in a simple, predictable correspondence—as if there were a formula by which any point we make about one can be automatically transposed into a point about the other. Nevertheless, if we confine ourselves to the question of time and the DH, the parallel with space is relatively straightforward.

The space that spreads out around me, i.e., the space that spreads out from here, is infinite. On the DH, it would still be infinite. Similarly, the time before and after now is infinite—whether or not this is dream. There was no moment before now that was the first moment; there will be no moment after now that will be the last moment. Would it be any different if this were a dream? Would not the time before and after now still be endless, just as endless as it is in reality? Let us think about this in a little more detail.

I take a sip of coffee. If this were a dream, I would be taking the sip of coffee in the dream. So, if this were a dream, I would be taking that sip right now in the dream. We have at least to grant, then, that if this were a dream the time *now* would be in the dream.

I entered the café and sat down here, let us say, about an hour ago; before that I got out of bed, had my breakfast, and so on. What happens to these statements on the dream hypothesis? Nothing. If this were a dream, these statements about my recent past would be as true as we may assume they are in reality. Thus, on the dream hypothesis, the times to which the statements refer would be times internal to the dream. Consider the moment of my entering the café. The time in question is now in the past. That is to say, it is earlier than now. But we have already granted that on the DH the time now would be in the dream. It would be part, let us say, of dreamtime. If the time now would be part of dreamtime, the same must be true of the time at which I entered the café, since that time was *earlier than (before) now*. This parallels "here" and "out there": if the place "here" is internal to a dream, then any place "out there" must also be internal to the dream, since any place "out there" is at a *distance from here*.

You can see straight away that this point (if it is correct) is perfectly general. It holds for any time earlier than now: for any time in the past. Any time in the past would, on the DH, be internal to the dream. If this were a dream, the time now would be internal to the dream; but if the time now is internal to the dream, then so is any time in the past, since any time in the past is a time earlier than (before) now. But the past is endless, infinite: there is no time that was the earliest time before now. On the DH, then, this, the subject matter of the hypothesis, would contain an endless past.

What we say in this respect about time, we must say about events. If any time before now is, on the DH part of the dream-past, any event occurring at that time is an event in the dream-past. My actions yesterday and the day before that, and the things I did last year, and the year before that, and so on, all belong (on the dream hypothesis) to the dream-past.

Notice, so far we have just mentioned things that I do, things that belong (as we might express it) not just to *the* past but to *my* past. But of course most of what belongs to the past does not belong to my past. For an event to belong to the past, all that is necessary is that it have occurred before now. If an event occurred before now, and this a dream, the event belongs to the past in the dream—however long before now it occurred, hence whether or not it is part of my past in the dream. The stock market crash of 1929, the French Revolution, the death of Socrates, these all belong to the past. But not to my past. The development of civilization, the Stone Age, the Great Flood, these also belong to the past. So does the formation of our solar system and galaxy, and the original "bang." All these things occurred at a time earlier than now, i.e., in the (not my) past. So they all get swept along by the DH. If this were a dream, all these things would belong to the past internal to this, the past internal to the dream.

The argument about the past, and past events, carries over in an obvious way to the future, and future events. If this were a dream, the time now would be internal to the dream. Must not the same be true, then, of any of the time that is later than (after) now? But (as with the past) there is no limit to the future, to how much time there is later than (or after) now. However "far ahead" you consider, there is more time than that. The future, like the past, is endless. Were this a dream, then, the endless time "up ahead" would be "up ahead" in the dream. The dream would contain an infinite future—which would outstrip my personal future—in the same way that it contains an infinite past. And along with the infinity of times that would belong to the dream-future, there would be an infinity of events. This would all be, on the DH, internal to the dream.

The inference from what holds of "now" to what holds of any time before or after "now" resembles mathematical induction. We might state the principle like this. If t is now, and now is internal to a dream, then for any n, t plus or minus n hours, etc., is a time internal to the dream. Why, you might ask, should we accept this principle?

Consider the corresponding inference in the case of space. The space right around me, here, would on the dream hypothesis be internal to the dream (the base step for the induction); thus the same would be true of any space at any distance from here, no matter how great the distance. (The principle of "spatial induction": If s is here, and here is internal to a dream, then for any n, n meters from s is a space internal to the dream.) To convince ourselves of the correctness of spatial induction, we appealed to the possibility of something physically connecting the space "here" with that "out there." A physically continuous entity, like a piece of string, embodies (as we put it) the continuity of space. Any two physically connectable positions must belong to the same space. Suppose this is a dream. A piece of string beginning here could not run from inside to outside the dream. However long the string, the position at the other end would be internal to the dream. In order to convince ourselves of the correctness of the relevant temporal inference, i.e., of temporal induction, what we need is something that embodies the continuity of time in the way that a piece of string, or some other indefinitely extendible physically continuous entity, embodies the continuity of space.

A continuous, ongoing activity or event embodies the continuity of time. Thus something like a hum, which is indefinitely extendible, might serve our purposes here. But a better example, since it allows us to exploit the points we have made about spatial continuity and the dream hypothesis, is that of linear physical motion. As an extended piece of string embodies the continuity of the space *through* which it runs, the continuous movement of (say) a ball along that string will embody the continuity of the time *during* which the ball moves. Let us consider, then, the movement of a ball along a string that stretches out from here, where I am.

The ball, we may suppose, is set in motion now and moves away from me along the string at a constant speed. However long the string is, the ball will keep moving along the string at that speed. Thus the farther the ball gets from me, the more the time that will have elapsed, and the later it will be after now. Consider all this under the DH. The string, no matter how long it is, could not, we said, run from inside to outside the dream. Thus, no matter how far along the string the ball moves, the ball would not move from inside to outside the dream. The movement of the ball, however, not only occurs through space along the string, it takes time. The farther the ball moves, the more time it takes. To each of the ever farther (from me) positions that the ball reaches on the string, there corresponds an ever later (than now) moment of time.

Assume the ball starts moving now. On the DH, now is a moment in dreamtime. This is our inductive base. If the movement begins in dreamtime, might it leave dreamtime? The movement occurs along the string. If the string, whatever length it is, cannot leave the space internal to the dream, how could a movement along the string leave the time internal to the dream? Since there is no limit to the length the string might be, hence no limit to the distance the ball might move along the string, there is no limit to of time the movement might take—hence no limit to the time after now internal to the dream. (For any would-be limit, we need only consider a longer piece of string.)

To apply this reasoning to the past, we may think of the ball not as starting out now along the string, but as arriving now along the string. Once we make the reorientation, the argument that on the DH the dream would contain an endless past will mirror the argument about the future. Clearly *now*, the moment when the ball arrives, would on the DH be part of dreamtime (the base step). Could the movement that issues in the arrival of the ball have begun outside dreamtime? Could it have *entered* the time internal to the dream? How did the ball get here? How did it reach me? By moving along the string. Since the string could not have entered dream-space, a movement along the string could not have entered dreamtime. And there is no limit to the possible length of the string, no limit to the distance the ball might have traveled to get here. Thus there is no limit to how long the ball might have been traveling; hence no limit to how long before now the ball might have started traveling.[10] Temporal induction holds for the past as well as the future. On the DH, there would be, as in reality, no moment of time before now that was the earliest moment before now. If this were a dream, the past internal to the dream would be endless, infinite, as endless as it is in reality.

We are entitled then to apply the argument from internality to the infinity of time. On the DH, not just the present time but the infinite past and future would be internal to this, to the subject matter of the hypothesis. So, like the infinity of space, the temporal infinity could not be the subject matter of the DH.

---

[10] Notice, the point is not that to get here the ball might have traveled "across a limitless space" or "for a limitless time," which is impossible (or nonsensical), but that, for any particular distance d from here, and any particular moment of time t before now, the ball could have traveled to here from a distance further away than d, and thus might have started out at a moment earlier than t.

1.7 The Dream Hypothesis and the World

When philosophers speak of "the world," they do not mean what we normally mean, e.g., what we mean in speaking of the ways of the world, or in saying that the world is getting smaller, or that little Hans left home and went out into the world, and so on. They mean, rather, a certain all-inclusive totality, viz., the totality of objects and phenomena in space and time.[11] If the infinity of space and time is internal to the subject matter of the DH, the world (in this sense) is internal to the subject matter of the DH. Thus, on the argument from internality, the world cannot be the subject matter of the DH. What is left? Once we exclude the world, is there anything that might be the subject matter of the DH?

But defining the world as the totality of objects and phenomena in space and time is not sufficiently precise. For one thing, it excludes objects and phenomena that are conceived as being not in space but only in time—like Cartesian souls and phenomena occurring in souls. Although of course we may wish to exclude such things, it would not be right to achieve this by definition. Let us therefore understand being "in space and time" to mean being "in space and/or time."

Another complication concerns objects (phenomena) like afterimages and hallucinatory objects (internal objects). Such objects have their own kind of spatiality but are not literally in space. They are, however, literally in time—yet we would not include them in the world. Notice, if we think the world does not contain Cartesian souls, this is because we think there simply are no such things, whereas it would (or so it seems to me) be a mistake to say that there simply are no such things as afterimages, etc. The reason we do not want to include afterimages in the world is that, although they exist in time, they lack the right kind of independence: they exist only insofar as they are present within experience; their existence is exhausted by their presence within experience. Is this true of souls? We can say that if there are souls, they are part of the world. But we cannot say that if there are afterimages, they are part of the world. Whereas there *are* afterimages, they are *not* part of the world.

Objects whose existence is exhausted by their presence within experience may be called "internal objects." Internal objects contrast with "external objects," i.e., objects whose existence is not exhausted by their pres-

---

[11] We are assuming what may be regarded as the standard or traditional philosophical conception of the world and are ignoring other philosophical conceptions of the world, e.g., Wittgenstein's conception (in the *Tractatus*) of the world as the totality of facts versus objects, and Heidegger's conception (in *Being and Time*) of the world as a structure that cannot be extricated from our way of being (our way of being is, among other things, being-in-the-world).

ence within experience. The world, then, may be defined as the totality of independently existing objects in space and time, that is to say, as the totality of external objects in space in and time. Strictly, then, it is redundant to speak (as philosophers commonly do) of the "external world," since by definition the world includes only what is external. It includes *this* (I fix on the cup), but not *this* (I fix, let us pretend, on an afterimage).

Note, we have defined independence, hence the world, impersonally, i.e., not in terms of "my experience" but simply "experience." In reflecting on the DH, however, we have to adopt the first-person perspective, that of my experience. Here we have another complication. It would not be correct for me to say that something is part of the world just in case it exists independently of my experience; for in that case the world would include objects that exist only insofar as they are present from within your experience (your images, etc.). I include in the world objects present from within your experience only if they are, or have the potential to be, present within my experience. In other words, I include what is outside my experience only if it could be inside my experience. Any currently existing part of the world is potentially present from within anyone's experience, yours and mine. Thus you and I, as part of the world, are potentially present within each other's experience.

Consider the following situation. I point and you point. You and your pointing arm are present in my experience. My pointing arm and I are present within your experience. The indicated lines of our pointing intersect at the same object, which object too is present both in your experience and mine. Not only is this the case, we know that it is the case, and each knows that the other knows, and knows that the other knows that he knows, and so on. That is to say, we *mutually* know, or grasp, our situation. In mutually grasping our situation, we share the world. We share the world, but we do not share everything. And we know that we do not share everything. Thus I know that things can be present within your experience that exist only so far as they are thus present, and hence cannot be present within my experience. And similarly for you. This fact, too, that we do not share everything, is mutually grasped. The mutual grasp of our separateness is part of our togetherness.

Let us say that something that is outside but potentially inside my experience is "empirically" outside my experience, and that something whose existence is confined to the experience of another subject (like an image or sensation) is "transempirically" outside my experience. What belongs to the world, then, has the potential to be empirically, but not transempirically, outside my experience. What is transempirically outside my experience is, for that reason, not part of the world. Notice, although the object in such a case is transempirically outside my experience, the subject within whose experience the object occurs shares the world with me and thus is himself, as part of the world we share, potentially present within my experience.

The DH hypothesis introduces new complications. If this is a dream, what I call "the world" is not the only world. There is a world outside the dream: a world that stands to what I call "the world" in the same way that the latter stands to the world internal to my dream the other night. The objects in the world outside the dream are in some sense "outside" my experience, but, it should be clear, not in either the empirical or the transempirical sense. They are not empirically outside, etc., in that (we shall develop this in a moment) they are not potentially inside my experience. They are not transempirically outside my experience in that they are not internal to the experience of a subject who shares the world with me. Let us say that they are "transcendently" outside my experience.

Perhaps it will help us appreciate what this means if we consider the point that, on the DH, the objects in the world outside the dream would not be empirically outside my experience, i.e., outside but potentially inside my experience. If an object is potentially inside my experience, there must be a possible transition the object can make from outside to inside my experience. The transition may be effected either by some change on my part—by something that happens to me, or by something I do—or by a change on the part of the object. But, one way or another, this presupposes that the object and myself inhabit the same space, which, as we have seen, is not the case, on the DH, for objects outside the dream.

Thus there is no path an object in the world outside might follow to present itself within my experience. What might I do to effect an empirical confrontation? How do I make present to me an object that is not present to me? Not by wishing. I take certain concrete steps. I change my orientation; or I reach out and feel around; or I remove obstacles; or I move myself; or if the object is very small, I interpose a magnifying device between the object and myself. And so on. A few examples. At the moment, the piece of gum under the table is outside my experience. By feeling under the table, or by bending over and craning my neck, I can bring the piece of gum within my experience. The espresso machine (in the café) is right now outside my experience. If I turn my head, it will be present within my experience. The bill the waitress gave me is under my writing tablet; so if I just move the tablet. . . . Or think of objects further afield, like the newsagent a few doors from the café. In this case, I would have to get up, leave the café, turn left, walk a few paces, etc. To get a view of the Thames, I would have to walk much farther, or take a bus. Things at a greater distance would require greater effort and ingenuity, other forms of conveyance. And things that are truly remote (like objects on other planets) might require forms of conveyance and equipment that have not yet been developed on Earth. But the point is the same. In all these cases it is a matter of reorientation, or magnification, or removing (or circumventing) obstacles, or getting closer to the objects in question, and so on. Now suppose this is a dream. Could I, by carrying out operations of the sort just indicated, bring within my experience an object that belongs to the world outside the dream?

Would it help (say) to turn my head, to orient myself differently? As if what lies in *this* direction is in the dream while what lies in *that* direction is outside the dream! By removing the tablet, I reveal the bill. What should I remove to reveal something outside the dream? If I place a powerful magnifying glass between my eyes and the table top, I will see tiny things that otherwise would have been invisible to me. But of course magnification would not render visible to me objects that are outside the dream. Or suppose I get up and leave the café. This would not make any difference. In leaving the café I would not leave the dream.

I act in space—i.e., in the same space that I inhabit, the space that spreads out around me. No action or maneuver on my part could bring an object within my experience unless the object is to be found somewhere in that same space. On the DH, the space I inhabit is internal to the dream. The space I inhabit, though infinite, is discrete from the space of the world outside the dream. An object in that world is neither "here" nor "out there," neither close to me nor at a great distance. How could I bring such an object within my experience by *re*orienting myself to it? I have no orientation to it. How could I bring an object within my experience by getting closer to it, or by removing an obstacle—or interposing a magnifying instrument—between the object and myself, when there is in the first place no such thing as "getting closer" to the object, when there is no such position as a position "between" the object and myself?

Everything but a minute part of the world is empirically outside my experience. This proposition is unaffected by the DH. Right now, for example, the objects on my desk at home are empirically outside my experience. They are outside my experience, but there are steps I could take to bring them within my experience. If this were a dream, exactly the same would be true: the objects on my desk at home would be empirically outside my experience. They would be empirically outside my experience in the dream, but there would be steps I could take that would (in the dream) bring them within my experience. However, since all such steps presuppose that the objects and myself inhabit the same space, it would be absurdly futile to undertake them in the case of objects outside the dream. There is, in principle, nothing I might do that could bring objects outside the dream inside my experience. Such objects would be, as we put it, transcendently outside my experience.

Consider objects that are transempirically outside my experience, e.g., an image within your experience. If this were a dream, such an object would *not* be outside the dream. It would not be transcendently outside my experience. Yet, like an object that is transcendently outside my experience, it would not be potentially present in my experience. The reason, however, is not that the object exists in a discrete space, but that it exists only within your experience: within the experience of the subject who shares the world with me and thus inhabits the same space. Only on the DH are there objects transcendently outside my experience. Given, then, that this is reality, nothing transcends my experience.

Suppose there is an afterimage present in your experience. It may, from within your experience, appear to be at place a few feet from your body. But nothing (relevant) actually occupies that place. What should I do to bring the object within my experience? Should I attempt to look at it from a different vantage point? There are no vantage points in this case—not because the internal object (the image) lies in a discrete space, but because it lies in no space (it only appears to lie in space). Should I get closer to it? I can get closer to *you*, but not to *it*. In the case of an object transcendently outside my experience, there is no way of moving from its position in space to mine; in the case of an object that is transempirically outside my experience, the object has no position from which to move.

Notice, an object that is now transempirically outside my experience would, on the DH, be internal to the dream. If this were a dream, not just my images, etc., but your images would be internal to the dream. Within the dream, you would be (say) having an afterimage: an internal object would be present within your experience.

To summarize, the world is the totality of independently existing objects and phenomena in space and time (i.e., in space/and or time). Independence here, if we conceive it first personally, entails the potential of an object, etc., present within my experience to exist outside my experience, and the potential of an object outside my experience to be present within my experience. The world, thus defined, includes neither objects that are transempirically nor transcendently outside my experience. But it does include everything that is empirically outside my experience. All but a tiny fragment of the world is empirically outside my experience. If this were a dream, not just the totality of objects now present within my experience, or these plus the objects close around me, or the latter plus the neighborhood or city, etc., but *whatever is out there now*, the totality that comprises the world with its endless space and endless past and future, would be internal to the dream. By the argument from internality, then, the whole of the world with its infinite space and time would be internal to the subject matter of the DH, internal to what in Int.7 we called "the personal horizon," and thus could not be identified with that subject matter. We are in this way brought back sharply to our earlier question of whether there is anything left—anything, i.e., with which to identify the subject matter of the DH.

2. The Dream Hypothesis: Identity and the First Person

2.1 A Puzzle about Identity

What do mean by "this" when we contemplate the hypothesis that this is a dream? Insofar as we cannot identify the subject matter of the DH, we do not know what the DH means. We do not know what the hypothesis *is* that we are contemplating. It may occur to us that there is no meaningful hypothesis to contemplate (that hence there is nothing for skepticism to worry about), or that if there is, we have misformulated the hypothesis, or again, that our problem in identifying the subject matter of the DH derives from a mistake in the argument from internality. We shall consider these and other possibilities in due course. But in order to evaluate such possibilities, there are several matters that need to be clarified in advance.

The first of these is a puzzle about identity. The puzzle has been implicit in our reflections all along, but we have allowed it to remain unexpressed. It would seem obvious that one and the same object cannot be part of both the world internal to and the world outside a dream: that if x belongs to the world internal to a dream, and y to the world outside the dream, x is not y. Suppose this is a dream and that x is part of the world internal to this. Then either x would be present to me, present within my experience, or there would be in principle steps I could take that would bring x within my experience. But neither of these things would be true of y, since we are supposing y is outside the dream. Being outside the dream, y would be transcendently outside my experience; thus it could be neither actually nor potentially present within my experience.

For example, if this were a dream, the girl who is my daughter would be part of the world internal to the dream. So although she is outside my experience now, there are ways I could get to her, paths I might follow from where I am to where she is—in school about two miles from here—by following which I could bring her within my experience. (She is only empirically outside my experience.) There is, in contrast, no way of my getting to, of bringing within my experience, anything that belongs to the world outside the dream. No individual, then, that belongs to that world could be the individual who is my daughter. She is part not of a transcendent world but of the world whose space spreads out around me: the world.

Similarly, the world in my dream the other night (the dream about the train that I related earlier) is discrete from the world around me now, the totality I call "the world." No object in this totality, then, can be identical with an object in the world of the dream. Any object in the totality I call "the world" has a spatial relation to *here*, where I am. Objects in the world of my dream have no such spatial relation to where I am. There would have been no way of setting out from a position in the space internal to the dream and arriving here, in the café.

But this clashes with the fact that now, speaking from the standpoint outside my dream of the other night, there seems to be no special problem identifying an individual in the world outside the dream with an individual belonging to the world of the dream. Thus, in telling you my dream, I will say (I did say) without any hesitation or fuss that in the dream such-and-such happened to "my daughter." When in this connection I use the expression "my daughter," it seems I straightforwardly refer to my daughter, the very individual to whom I would refer if I told you now, say, that this morning "my daughter" was off to school before I got up. Or suppose that I now leave the café in order to track down my daughter in school. I could walk right up to her and say, "You were in my dream the other night." To whom should I refer by "you" if not the person I am addressing, my daughter? And what do I tell this person, my daughter, if not that *she* was in my dream the other night?

So now it looks as if my daughter, the girl who is sitting in school two miles from here, was also part of the world internal to the dream; in other words, as if the girl who is part of the totality I call "the world" is identical with the girl in the world of my dream the other night. Yet we have agreed that these are discrete worlds. How can objects belonging to discrete worlds be identical? Suppose I make the two-mile trip and locate my daughter. Then, it seems, I could truly say that *this* girl, my daughter, is the girl in my dream. But again, how could that be? From the standpoint internal to dream, it was no more possible to follow a path to *this* girl than, on the DH, I could now follow a path to an entity in the world outside the dream.

2.2 Representation and Identity

Such is the puzzle. Notice how extreme the conflict is. On the one hand, it can seem "out of the question" that the girl in the dream the other night actually *is* my daughter (the very human being who left home before I got up and who is right now sitting in school two miles from here). On the other hand, we might say "of course" it is my daughter in the dream. This disparity of reactions suggests that some sort of ambiguity is at work here. Consider another case. I catch a glimpse of a teenage girl passing by the café and exclaim with surprise, "That is my daughter." Here, by "is" I clearly mean identity: I mean that the girl outside the café is none other than my daughter. So, one might say, the term "is" in these different statements is ambiguous. When I say that the girl in the dream "is my daughter" I do not mean by "is" what I mean when I say that the girl passing the café "is my daughter." In the latter case I use the word "is" literally: I mean identity. Then what do I mean in the former case, when I say of the girl in the dream that she "is (or was) my daughter"?[1]

I point to a photograph and say, "This is my daughter." By the words "my daughter," I refer, certainly, to my daughter. What am I saying of her? Do I mean to identify her with the printed image to which I point? Of course not. Perhaps I mean that the image to which I point *represents* my daughter. Why not suppose that I mean something like this in the dream case as well?

But it is not yet clear what I would mean. Is it that *the girl in the dream* represents my daughter? In that case, we have drawn the analogy incorrectly. What we should be looking to is not the printed image but *the girl in the picture*. But the girl in the picture just *is* my daughter, the girl in the world. So if we accept the analogy we must say the same thing about the girl in the dream and my daughter—that the girl in the dream just *is* my daughter. But the point of the analogy was to provide a way to avoid saying this.

The photograph analogy can be employed differently. There is, we might say, a dream counterpart of the printed image in the photograph case—a dream-image. When (it may be suggested) I say of my daughter, the girl in the world, that she "was in the dream," what I mean (roughly) is that in the dream there was an image that represented my daughter. Now introducing dream-images here seems to me utterly wrongheaded, but let us go along with it. The problem is that we have yet to be told what to say about the girl in the dream. *She* can no more be identified with a dream-image (whatever that is) than the girl in the picture can be identified with a printed image. The difficulty is that the dream case involves one more element than the photograph case, and it is precisely this

---

[1] It might seem more natural to say that the girl in the dream "was," rather than "is," my daughter? This is because the dreaming of the dream is now in the past, not because the identity in question held in the past but not in the present. We shall sometimes use the present, sometimes the past, tense form of the verb "to be" in this context. It will not affect the issue of identity.

extra element that is at the heart of the puzzle. That is to say, while the girl in the photograph can be straightforwardly identified with the girl outside the photograph, the corresponding identification in the dream case (between the girl in the dream and an individual outside the dream) seems impossible. If we are not talking about images, what is "in a photograph" is simply part of the world; a dream, by contrast, has a world of its own.

In this respect, a fictive work might be a better analogy—a novel, for example, or better still a play—since here we can think about a particular performance. The actors in the play (the performance of the play) might be said, in some cases anyway, to represent people in the world outside the play. The latter, however, would have to be distinguished from the people in the world of the play, the *dramatis personae*. We may accept this, but it is not clear that it will help us sort out the puzzle about dreams and identity. In fact, we may find ourselves faced by an analogous puzzle in the case of plays.

We distinguish the world internal to a play from the world outside the play. Yet it also seems we can refer to someone outside the play as having been "in the play," where we have in mind not that he *acted in* the play but . . . but what? That he is *identical* with someone in the world of the play? Do we not view this world (the world internal to the play) as discrete from the world outside the play? If you say, we mean that a certain actor in the play represents such-and-such person in the world outside the play, i.e., in the world, then we still need an account of the relation between the latter and the relevant *dramatis persona*, the person in the world internal to the play. If they are not identical, how are they related? And this is just like the question we want to answer in the case of dreams. If my daughter and the girl in the dream are not identical, how are they related?

It might be suggested that, in the case of a play, we can distinguish two relations of representation: an actor in the play can be said to represent a particular person in the world; but also, a person in the world of the play can be said to represent a person in the world. The latter relation would be the one appropriate to the dream case. The girl in the world of my dream the other night would represent the girl in the world, my daughter, in the same way or sense that someone in the world of a play would represent such-and-such person in the world.

In certain cases, this may be the correct way to describe the matter; but it is not in general correct. Consider, for example, a play set in the twentieth century in which the main character attracts a following through his inner strength and moral purity. The powers that be come to regard him as a threat; they have him tried and put to death on trumped up charges. A critic might venture that the character (the man in the world of the play) represents Jesus. Compare this with the Passion Play performed at

Oberammergau—there is the Last Supper, the betrayal by Judas, the confrontation with Pilate, and so on. In other words, these things are all acted out in the (performance of the) play. In contrast to the first case, I think we will want to say about the main character in this play not that he represents Jesus, but that he *is* Jesus. A similar contrast can be made out in the case of dreams. I tell you a dream in which, say, a particular flower seems to be very significant (such-and-such happens to the flower, I feel such-and-such emotions, etc.). You suggest that the flower represents my daughter. And this may strike me as right: I may accept that the flower in the dream represents my daughter. In contrast, however, I will say that the girl in my dream of the other night *is* my daughter.

It is only where the mind must first discern a connection (in terms of causation or association or similarity or symbols) between objects respectively inside and outside a dream, or inside and outside a play, that it is correct to describe the first of these objects as "representing" the second. Nothing like that is involved when I think of the girl in my dream of the other night. I simply take that girl to *be* my daughter.

2.3 A Way out of the Puzzle

Is there a way out of the puzzle that does not involve conceiving of the relation between, say, the girl in the dream and my daughter as something other than identity? I believe we can (and in fact do) accept both that objects in the world of a dream can be identical with objects in the world outside and that the worlds inside and outside a dream are discrete. (Similarly for the case of plays; but we shall discuss the matter with reference to dreams.)

Note, first, that when we are dealing with distinct objects both of which are part of the world, we would never (assuming we are not confused or under a misapprehension or trying to mislead someone) be inclined to say, just like that, that one "is (was)" the other—no matter how *alike* the objects in question are. However, when we are dealing with objects inside and outside a dream (play), we may be inclined to insist that one "is (was)" the other even where we recognize dissimilarities between the relevant objects. Consider, for example, Hilary Putnam's well-known Twin Earth idea. Somewhere out there (hence as part of the world) there is a duplicate of our Earth: it has a duplicate geography, duplicate inhabitants, and so on. On Twin Earth, then, there is a duplicate of my daughter. Is there any inclination to say of that girl (assuming no misapprehensions, etc.) that she "is (was)" my daughter? Yet without further ado I will say this about the girl in my dream. I will say this, in fact, while acknowledging that the girl in the dream was in such-and-such ways *different* from my daughter. "My daughter is fair, the girl in the dream dark; but it *was* my daughter in the dream." It is as if, when we identify objects of discrete worlds, the principle of the Indiscernibility of Identicals goes out the window.

Or is that the wrong way to look at it? Perhaps what the foregoing shows is that when we identify objects of discrete worlds, we do not mean "is" or "was" in a literal way. We mean something other than identity. But what? Not representation. The difficulty here is not just that we find it hard to think of a plausible alternative to identity. It is also that identity *seems right*. If you ask what I mean in saying of the girl in the dream that she "was" my daughter, I will say I mean just that: the girl in the dream *was* my daughter. That, just as it stands, seems to be the right answer.

At some stage we must shift from viewing this as the description of a puzzle to viewing it as a description of how things are. How could things be that way? It may appear that what we are offering is not so much a solution to the puzzle about dreams and identity as a paradox. But we mean to be offering a solution, and once you see what it is, the solution will not seem paradoxical. More likely, it will seem trivial. And it is trivial. Which is to say: the puzzle itself is trivial.

Here is the "solution" of the puzzle. Sometimes—in fact usually, or standardly—when we use the expressions "is" and "was" to say of objects *x* and *y* that "*x* is (was) *y*," it is presupposed that *x* and *y* belong to the same world; but sometimes the presupposition is just the opposite, viz., that *x* and *y* belong to discrete worlds. In both cases (the standard and nonstandard) we mean the same thing by "is (was)." That is, we "mean the same thing" in the sense that if we are asked to *say what* we mean by "is" or "was" in these cases, we will give the same answer (which is the only answer we have to give). That is, we will complete the schema "'is (was)' means . . . " in the same way, using the same words. Let us say that in each case "is (was)" has *the same formulatable content*. But there is also a sense in which we do not "mean the same thing" in both cases. We are, as is shown by the different presuppositions, using different concepts of identity (the standard and the nonstandard concept). The concepts are different but very closely related or similar.

In effect, the "solution" of the puzzle is simply to point out (to become open to the fact) that this sort of thing is possible with respect to concepts: concepts can be different and yet so closely related, so similar, that they not provide for a difference in formulatable content. In both cases, not only do we naturally and unthinkingly use the same expression or expressions; if we are asked to say what we mean in each case, the answer we give is the same. There is only one answer to give.

Thus if we ask whether, in "The girl who went past the café was (is) my daughter," I mean the same thing by "was" as I mean in "The girl in the dream was (is) my daughter," the answer must be "Yes" and "No." I "mean the same thing" in the sense that if I try to say what I mean, I will in each case use the same words. There is no difference in formulatable content. This reflects the similarity of the relevant concepts of identity. Yet the concepts are different, they rest on different presuppositions, and in that sense I do not mean the same thing by "was (is)" in each case. Thus in the nonstandard case we may (as remarked above) insist that one object "is" or "was" the other in the face of acknowledged differences between them. The Indiscernibility of Identicals holds, we might say, for standard but not nonstandard identity.[2]

Wittgenstein's idea of an expression being embedded in a language-game is perfectly suited to capture our thought here about identity. Language-games—that is, the rules and practices by which they are constituted—can be (as Wittgenstein often emphasizes) more or less similar. Suppose an expression E figures in two very similar language-games. It has, in this sense, two very similar "uses." The uses are similar, but (we are supposing) on reflection we can point out differences. Now given the differences, there is a sense in which, in one language-game, E does not "have the same meaning" that it has in the other (meaning as use). Yet it does not follow that there will be any difference in formulatable content, that if we are asked to *say what* E means in these two cases we can formulate different meanings. In this sense, E "means the same thing" in both cases.

Wittgenstein gives the following example concerning negation:

> We can easily imagine human beings with a "more primitive" logic in which something corresponding to our negation is applied only to certain sorts of sentence; perhaps to such as do not themselves contain any negation. It would be possible to negate the proposition "He is going into the house," but a negation of the negative proposition would be meaningless, or would count only as a repetition of the negation. (*Investigations*, 554)

Suppose the expression for negation in the primitive language-game is "not." We may assume that if one of the primitives utters "p," and another utters "not-p," they act in ways we would regard as disagreement. (Of course, this in turn assumes all sorts of further similarities, similarities between their whole system of language-games and ours.) But they do not

---

[2] Here is another difference between the two concepts. The girl who passed by the café a little while ago—was she really my daughter? I may be unsure, but there must be an answer. If, however, I am uncertain about the girl in the dream and my daughter, it is not just that I may not know the answer; there may not be an answer. The concept of identity that we use across discrete worlds, the nonstandard concept, seems (unlike the standard concept) to allow for indeterminacy.

have anything like the idea of one negation canceling the effect of another. Consider now what we would say if we were asked to say (to put into words) what people in the primitive language-game mean by "not." Can we say anything except that by "not" they mean *not*? (Can we do anything except just use the word "not," once again?) From that you could take it that they mean what we mean by "not," that we both mean the same thing. But—if we know all the facts about their language-game, including the absence of double negation—I do not think we would want to leave the matter there. I think we would want to say that there is also a sense in which the primitives do not mean the same thing that we mean by "not." The language-games are different. They are different and yet the difference does not issue in a difference in formulatable content.

Do we or don't we mean the same thing by "not" as those other people? We do and we don't. Once we see the difference between the two language-games and the fact that, despite such a difference, there is no difference in formulatable content—more generally, once we see that this sort of thing is possible, that it is no big deal—there is nothing more to see.

The case with dreams and identity is, I submit, parallel. The expression "is (was)" occurs in two closely related but different language-games, two language-games of identity. In one (the standard language-game) it is presupposed that the objects with which we are concerned belong to the same world; in the other, that the objects belong to discrete worlds. (Of course, unlike Wittgenstein's negation example, the language-games we are comparing are both ours.) Do we mean the same thing by "is (was)" in both cases? As in the example with primitive negation, we do and we don't. If we are asked to say what we mean in each case, we shall in each case give the same answer (which reflects the similarity of the language-games). In that sense we mean the same thing. In another sense (meaning as use), we do not mean the same thing: though similar, the language-games are different. Once we see these points we see everything there is to see.[3] We see, in particular, that there is nothing impossible (nothing to fuss about) in the idea of an identity between an object in the world of a dream and an object in the world. How could it be impossible when we

---

[3] Thus it would add nothing if we introduce some way—such as the attachment of a subscript—of making it explicit that we are using the expression "is (was)" in one language-game rather than another. Suppose, referring to the girl in the dream, I say (write) that she "was$_d$" my daughter. The subscript "d" is meant to indicate that I use "was" in the language-game of identity that presupposes we are dealing with objects from discrete worlds. There is no harm in this, but once again, it adds nothing. In particular, it would be an illusion to think that we now had a difference in formulatable content between the two uses of "was." Where should it come from? From the letter "d"? A difference in content either is already there, to be extracted by reflection on the relevant language-games, or is not. We cannot create content by inserting a subscript.

have a language-game (concept) of identity whose sole purpose, as it were, is to provide for the possibility?

This is not to say that there may not be a real and maybe interesting question whether Y (a person in my dream) was X (a person in the world). But the question will be settled by reference to the traits of X and Y and not to the single, radical fact that X is part of my dream whereas Y is part of the world, in other words, the fact that X and Y belong to discrete worlds. *That* fact—hence the (standard) nonidentity of X and Y—is presupposed when we raise the question of their (nonstandard) identity.

2.4 *The Dream Hypothesis and the First-Person Singular*

We turn now to the other topic announced in the title of this chapter: the first person. The first person (singular) is, in fact, one of the central topics of the book. It will crop up, in passing, many times, and we shall discuss it at length in part 3. Here, we shall make a start by considering the first person in light of the dream hypothesis. However, it is impossible to say anything about the first person without introducing ideas that have a general significance for the topic—ideas that, as the book is organized, will not be explained properly until later on. In the meantime there are bound to be loose ends and unanswered questions.

In my dream my daughter was seated next to me. So my daughter was in my dream. And by "my daughter" I mean (who else?) my daughter, the girl in school about two miles from this café. Let us assume that we know what is going on here, that we are not going to get excited about the fact that, although my daughter and the girl in the dream belong to discrete worlds, I am prepared to say that the girl in the dream was (is) my daughter. Of course, the point applies not just to people but to entities of all kinds. Let us suppose I have had a dream in which I am sitting in this café. Would this café, where I am sitting now, have been part of the world internal to the dream? The world internal to the dream is discrete from the world, and this café is part of the world. So how could the café in the dream *be* this one? Could I have traveled from a position in the space of the dream—e.g., from where I was sitting in the café—to *here*, inside this café? Yet in the dream this is where I was, in the café where I am now. So traveling was not necessary. I was already here. *Here?*

Both things are true. The world of the dream is discrete from the world, and the café in which I am sitting (not the Cosmo or Casa Fabrizi but this place, the Dorice) was in the dream. In talking about the DH, we will constantly be making statements with apparent inconsistencies of this sort. I hope we can just go on our untroubled way without always explaining how the apparent inconsistency of such statements is to be resolved.

Consider the human being (or soul; but we shall ignore for now the possibility that I am a soul) that I am. In the dream, my daughter was sitting next to me. Then I went to get a drink of water. To whom do I refer in this connection by "me" and "I"? Well, to whom do I ever refer by "I"? Why should this case be special? I refer to the human being that I am, *this* one (I touch my chest). So it would seem that we can now just transfer what we have said about dreams and identity to the first-person case. If we can handle the superficial puzzlement about my daughter, or this café, being in a dream of mine, there should be no special problem about me— the human being that I am, the one who dreamed those past dreams— being in such a dream. The human being I am was part of the world internal to my dream of the other night, and that world is discrete from the world to which *this* human being (I touch him again) belongs. Still, it is correct to say that I, that very human being (the one I touched), was in my dream the other night—just as it is correct to say that my daughter was in that dream. We have a concept of identity that allows for this.

Again, even though the girl in the dream is dark whereas my daughter is blond, I can insist that the girl in the dream was my daughter. This holds in the first-person case as well. The man in the dream was bald and I am not. Nonetheless, that man was me. In the dream was bald.

So far we have found nothing to distinguish the first-person case. But there are complications here. Suppose I have a dream in which there are two individuals (human beings), X and JV. Yet in the dream I am not JV but X (X is me). This seems possible, but what does it mean? Not that, in the dream, *JV* was X. In the dream, JV and X are distinct individuals. JV is in the dream, but in the dream JV is not me. In the dream I am a human being other than the human being that I am. We can make sense of this sort of thing.

Suppose that my daughter, FV, is also in the dream. On the new count there are, in the dream, three separate individuals: X, FV, and JV. Now, as just remarked, we understand the idea that in the dream I am X; but, if the dream contains the three individuals just mentioned, there seems to be no possibility that my daughter, FV, is X. In the dream she and X are distinct individuals. Yet the fact that JV and X are distinct does not, it seems, exclude the possibility that, in the dream, *I* am X (X is *me*). You see the difference. In the first-person case, given that JV and X are distinct individuals in the dream, there still exists the possibility that in the dream *I* am X. But, in the other-person case, given that in the dream FV is not X, there is no possibility that, in the dream, *she* is X.

Here is something else to think about. If this were a dream, I might emerge from this. What is it to emerge from a dream? It is not like emerging from a house, or a bath. My emerging from my house is something that transpires within the world. Our understanding of what transpires in such a case involves the standard concept of identity. A single human being, the one I am, is first inside and then outside the house. You could track him from inside to outside. There is no comparable tracking possibility in the case of emerging from a dream. I have, let us assume, just emerged from a dream. The human being who I am in the dream belongs to a different world from that of the human being who now contemplates the dream, the human I am. I can correctly say that in the dream I did such-and-such, but this must be understood in terms of the nonstandard concept of identity. However, emerging, it seems, can be understood only in terms of the standard concept of identity. If I emerge from a dream, there must, it seems, be a single human being who is first on the inside of the dream and then, via a trackable transition, finds himself outside the dream, back in reality. But there is no such human being.

Perhaps to say I emerged from a dream is to say that the human I am, JV, was *me* in the dream. But this suggestion is undermined by the possibility that the human being who is me in dream is other than the human being I am. In such a case, someone is me in the dream, but it is not JV, the human being I am. JV need not have been in the dream at all. Yet it would still be true that I have emerged from the dream. And anyway, what is it to be "me" in the dream?

My daughter, FV, was in my dream the other night; but she did not emerge from that dream. It was *I* who emerged from the dream. Again, on the DH, I might emerge from this, from the subject matter we are hypothesizing to be a dream. Is the same true of my daughter? On the DH, my daughter belongs to the world internal to the dream. But could she emerge from this, from the dream? The idea of "emerging" seems to apply only from the first-person perspective.

It might be suggested that to emerge from a dream is nothing more or less than to *wake up* from the dream. But if we think about DH, we will see that this cannot be right. The suggestion would be, if this were a dream, that for me to emerge from this would be for me to wake up. But who is it, exactly, that would wake up? Would it be me, JV, *this* human being (once again, I touch my chest)? The one who would wake up is the one who would be asleep. It would be (let us suppose) a human being. That human being would be asleep, and he would be dreaming. The suggestion, then, is that I am that human being. Thus if we say that, on the DH, for me to emerge from the dream would be for me to wake up, this means that I, the human being that I am, am asleep. But that is obviously not the case. The human being I am, *this* one, is *not* asleep. He is sitting in a café, writing, about to take a sip of coffee. On the DH, whatever human being is asleep, it is not *this* human being. It is not the human being *I am*, the one who just now sipped some coffee. (Did I do that while I was asleep? How did I manage not to spill anything?)

Let us dwell on this point. Assume this is a dream. The dream is being dreamed by (we are supposing) a human being, and that human being is asleep. Consider the brain of the human being who is asleep and dreaming. That brain is in a certain state. There is a certain kind of activity going on in that brain, the kind that goes on in the brain of a dreamer. It is because of this activity that the dream is being dreamed. Now if this were a dream and *I* (JV) were the dreamer, the activity on which the dream depends would be occurring right now in *my* brain, i.e., in the brain up here in *this* head (I reach up and touch it). But the brain up here, my brain, would be part of the world internal to the dream. It would, of course, be empirically outside my experience right now; but it would be outside my experience *in the dream*. Thus if I could arrange for my head to be opened up while I remained conscious, my brain, the brain up here, might (by means of a mirror, or whatever) become present within my experience. To repeat, on the DH, my brain belongs to the world internal to the dream. But the brain on which the (dreaming of the) dream would depend would not belong to the world internal to the dream. Imagine my head is opened up, etc. I can see my own brain. If this were a dream, it would not be on the activity of *this* brain (the one I now point out in the mirror) that the dream depends. The dream, i.e., the dreaming of the dream, could not depend on the activity of a brain that itself belongs to the world internal to the dream.

Clearly, if this were a dream, the brain on whose activity the dream would depend, the brain of the sleeper (dreamer), would be the brain of a human being in the world outside the dream. It would be, you might say, a transcendent brain, the brain of a transcendent human being. Accordingly, it would be the transcendent human being, not *this* human being (the one I am, JV), who would wake up from the dream. So, to return to the suggestion, when we say that on the dream hypothesis I might emerge from the dream, we cannot be understood to mean that I (the human being that I am, JV) might wake up from the dream. With respect to waking up, the human being that I am would not be the right human being. It would not be his brain (my brain) on whose activity the dream depends. It would not be he (me, JV) who is asleep and dreaming and would therefore wake up.

2.5 The Subject versus the Dreamer of a Dream; The Positional Conception of the Self

In light of the foregoing, let us distinguish between the human being who is the *dreamer* of a dream and the human being who is the *subject* of a dream. The dreamer is the one (the human being) who dreams the dream, the one who is asleep and who will wake up. He is the one on whose brain the dreaming of the dream depends. The dreamer is part of the world outside the dream, the transcendent world. The subject, on the other hand, belongs to the world internal to the dream. He is the human being in that world who, one might say, occupies a certain position in the dream. We shall not attempt yet to define or explicate the subject position (this is one of the loose ends to which we alluded earlier), but perhaps it will be suggestive to say that the subject of the dream is the human being at the "center" of the dream. If this were a dream, the subject would be the human being at the center of this: at the center of what, on the DH, would be the dream. The human being in question would be part of the world internal to the dream. Which human being would that be? It would be JV, *this* human being. On the DH, JV would be the subject of the dream—not the dreamer of the dream, but the one at its center.

Notice, the same human being, JV, would be the one at the center of this even if this were not a dream. This, the subject matter that would be a dream if this were a dream is not a dream. It is reality. Who is the human being at the center? JV, *this* human being, the same human being who, if this were a dream, would be the subject of the dream.

From this we get, in outline, the answer to a question that everyone can ask himself. Let me ask it in my own case. I look around in the café. I am not alone: other people, other human beings, are here with me. What do I mean by "other" people, etc.? The idea is not just that there are in the café human beings in addition to *this* one, JV, but that there are human beings in addition to *me*, the human being that I am. This shifts the question from "other" people to "me." Consider the set of human beings in the café. One of them—*this* one, JV—is the one I call "me." On what basis do I select him? What makes *him*, JV, *me*? Once again, when I use the first person I mean (to refer to) one human being rather than any other. Which one? JV. Why JV? What is it about *him*, rather than any other human being, that makes *him*, JV, the human being that I *am*?

This is not a question about identity. We are not asking about JV and a certain human being X what makes JV *identical with* X. If the question were about JV's identity X, it would not matter how we refer to X. Suppose I am also known as "MV." I could ask, What makes JV identical with MV? This would do for the question about identity. But it would not capture the question we are asking. It is essential to the question we are asking that I use the first person. What makes JV *me*? Our question, we might say, seeks an explication not of the concept of identity but of a certain conception of the self.

Again, if *a* is identical with *b*, what makes *a* identical with *b* must be what makes *a* identical with *a*. Hence, if the question "What makes JV me?" concerned identity, it would be the same question as, "What makes JV identical with JV?" Yet it seems obvious that these are different questions.

It may indeed strike us that the question about identity has no answer. What makes *a* identical with *b*? Suppose, by way of an answer, we cite the Identity of Indiscernibles: if whatever is true of *a* is true of *b*, *a* = *b*. In itself this principle seems correct. It is a true principle about identity. But does it tell us in what the identity of *a* and *b* consists? Rather, it is *because* of the identity that the coincidence of properties exists. But then the identity cannot consist in the coincidence of properties. Either *a* is identical with *b* or *a* is not identical with *b*. There is one object or two. And that's it. There are laws or principles about identity. But they do not tell us of what identity "consists." Identity, one is tempted to say, does not consist of anything.

We shall not pursue the point about identity. We need only remark that if we have doubts whether the question about identity has an answer, this should strengthen our sense of a difference between that question and the question about the self. For surely the question about the self has an answer. Surely there is something in virtue of which one human being, JV, rather than any other, is *me*. There may be no way to explicate the concept of identity, but, it seems, there must be some way to explicate the relevant conception of the self, some way to answer to the question of what makes JV me, the human being that I am.

We said that, in outline, the answer is that JV occupies a certain position/role within the subject matter that, if this were a dream, would be the dream. JV is the one at the center of the subject matter of the DH, of that which contains the whole of the world plus the infinity of space and time. Thus if JV, that very human being, did not occupy the position at the center, if it were another human being that occupied the subject position, then that other human being would be *me*. He would of course not be JV, but he, not JV, would be the human being that *I am*.

"*This* human being is *me*." I touch his chest, my chest. What makes his chest *my* chest? His head (brain) *my* head (brain)? It is the chest (head, etc.) of the human being that *I am*. That is to say: it is the chest (head, etc.) of the human being at the center of this, the subject matter of the DH. The "my-ness" of my body derives from its position in this subject matter.

We shall call this conception of a certain position within the subject matter of the DH, viz., the position of being at the center of the subject matter, the "positional" conception of the self. The positional conception of the self is thus the conception of a position. Of course, describing the position as that of "being at the center" is (as we said) only suggestive. We have yet to spell out what it is to be "at the center." However, appreciating that we have such a conception of the self is a step forward, and it enables us to understand the possibility about dreams and the first person that we were puzzling over above.

I have a dream in which X and JV figure as distinct individuals. Yet in the dream JV is not me (I am not JV). It is X who, in the dream, is me; in the dream I am X. How shall we understand this? We know the idea is not that in the dream X is *JV*, since in the dream JV and X are distinct individuals. We may understand the possibility as follows. In the dream it is X, not JV, who occupies the subject position—the position occupied by JV in reality. That is, it is X, not JV, who is at the center of the dream. In reality, JV is the one at the center: JV is me. In the dream X occupies the position at the center: in the dream X is me.

Implicit in the foregoing is an important distinction in the use of the first person. Suppose that from my standpoint outside the dream, I assert, "In the dream, X is me (is the one I am)." It is possible that my intention is to assert an identity between X and JV. (It might be, say, that in the dream X turns out to be JV in disguise.) In that case, "me (the one that I am)" functions as a singular term. It is used to refer to an individual in the world of the dream of whom I assert that that individual and X are one and the same. The use of the first person here is referential, just as it would be if I report that "In the dream I sat next to my daughter (my daughter sat next to me)"; or again, if I tell you that "I arrived in the café an hour ago," or that "I want another coffee," and so on. However, as we have observed, by "In the dream, X is me (is the one I am)" I may mean to assert not an identity but that X occupies the subject position in the dream: X is the one at the center. In that case, my use of "me (I)" is not referential but, as we may call it, "positional." It is used not to refer to X, to an individual in the world of the dream, but to convey a special position occupied by that individual. Or suppose I think (perhaps philosophically), "This human being, JV, is me (the one that I am)." Here too, although we might concoct a story in which I assert an identity, i.e., in which my use of the first person is referential, there is another way to understand my thought, viz., as the thought that JV occupies the subject position within this: he is the one at the center.

There are, then, these two uses of the first person: the referential and the positional. Notice, though, the conception of the self expressed by the positional use of the first person, the positional conception of the self, informs first-person reference. It enters, you might say, into our referential intention, into what we mean when we refer in the first person. When I use "I" referentially, to whom do I (mean to) refer? To a certain human being. Which one? The one that I am (who is me). Here, in this last sentence, I express my referential intention. But in thus expressing my referential intention—i.e., in saying the human being to whom I mean to refer is the one "who is me (that I am)"—my use of the first person is not *again* referential; it is positional. When I use "I" referentially I mean to refer to a certain human being, and the human being to whom I mean to refer is: the one at the center of this. In this way, the positional conception of the self informs first-person reference: it enters into the intention with which I refer.

But if my intention in using "I" is to refer to the human being at the center of this, to what do I refer here by "this"? What is it by being at the center of which a certain human being is me, the one that I am? It is the same subject matter as the subject matter of the DH—and we do not yet know what that subject matter is. Or rather, I would say, we know but we are not yet open to what we know. We are in the process of trying to bring what we know into the open.

2.6 Emerging from a Dream and the First Person

Perhaps we can deal now with the question we raised about emerging from a dream. Emerging from a dream, we remarked, is bound up with the first-person perspective. If this were a dream, it would be *I*, and not (say) the man who just walked into the café, who would emerge from the dream. I would (or might) emerge from this in the same way that I emerged into this from my dream of the other night. What do such statements mean? Not (as we pointed out) that I, JV, the human being that I am, might cross over from the world around me into a transcendent world, the world outside the dream. The world outside the dream would be discrete from the world internal to the dream. Nor is it that I, the human being that I am, might wake up. The human being I am, JV, is already awake. The human being (let us assume it is a human being) who would wake up, the dreamer of the dream, would be part of the world outside the dream.

Just as I, JV, am at the center of this (the subject matter that on the DH is a dream), the human being that would (if this were a dream) wake up would occupy the subject position of a wider, a transcendent, subject matter. The wider subject matter would have its own world and space and time, and there would be in that world an individual, a human being, who would occupy the position at the center. Now, that human being, the transcendent subject, may or may not identify the human being he is with JV, in the same way that I may or may not identify JV with the human being at the center of a dream I have dreamed. But, either way, the transcendent subject would judge that "In the dream JV is me." For it would be JV, the one at the center of this, who is at the center of subject matter that the transcendent subject looks back on as a dream, just as I, JV, judge of the human being X at the center of my dream the other night that (even if I do not identify the human I am with that individual) in the dream X is me. For I, JV, am at the center of the subject matter that, if this were a dream, the transcendent subject would look back on as a dream. In other words, JV, the human being at the center of this, the human being that I am, is, from the standpoint of the transcendent subject, "the one who in the dream is me."

This provides the sense in which, on the DH, it "would be I who emerges" from the dream: it would be I who emerges in the sense that the transcendent subject, the one at center of the wider subject matter, would regard *me*, JV, the one at the center of this (the one who is me), as the one that he (the transcendent subject) is in the dream. He would regard me this way, even if he does not identify the human being that he is (the one at the center of the wider subject matter) with JV.

Note that two types of identification are involved here. Consider my dream about my daughter. From my standpoint outside the dream, (1) I, JV, identify an individual in the world of the dream as "JV," just as I identify someone in that world as "my daughter," but also (2) I identify the first (versus the second) individual as occupying the subject position in the dream (as being the one at the center), i.e., as being "me" in the dream. In (1) I employ the nonstandard concept of identity. In (2), I employ the positional conception of the self.

There is something ungraspable about emerging from a dream. First I am in the world of the dream, then I am in the world of reality (the world). Yet the two worlds are discrete, with discrete spaces and times. Thus the times at which I am "first" in one and "then" in the other are not related as earlier to later; nor is the "I" at these times a single individual who crosses from one world to the other.

In each case, there is a subject matter, a personal horizon (Intro.7), with a position at the center, with its own world and space and time, a subject matter, a horizon, about which the DH can be raised. What interests us right now is the radical break or jump that constitutes my emerging from a dream. Let us say that, in emerging from a dream, one horizon *displaces* another: the horizon that is the dream is displaced by a wider horizon, by the horizon that is reality (or so we may assume). I emerged from my dream of the other night into this, the horizon of which I, JV, am at the center; that is to say, this, the horizon of which I am at the center, displaced the horizon of my dream of the other night. Similarly, if this is a dream and I emerge from it, the wider horizon (with its own subject, its own world and infinity of space and time) will displace this, the horizon of which I, JV, am at the center and which I take to be reality.

One horizon displaces another. It is this business of displacement that is ungraspable. Think of what gets displaced. Everything. The whole of the world with its infinity of space and time. Thus although the displacement of one horizon by another is something that happens, there is no time at which it happens. Consider my dream of the other night. It was displaced by this, the horizon of which I am the center. *Was* displaced? That means the displacement was at a time earlier than now. However, if the displacement occurred earlier than now, it would have occurred in the time internal to this, the displacing horizon. But at any such time, the dream horizon would *have already been* displaced. Perhaps the displacement occurred not before *now*, but in the time internal to the dream. No. At any such time the displacement would *not yet* have occurred. Are we to suppose that it was in the dream that I emerged from the dream?

Again, if this were a dream, I might emerge from this. The horizon of which I, JV, am the center might be displaced by a wider horizon. When would that happen? At some point in the future, i.e., after *now*? But any such time would be a time internal to the horizon we are hypothesizing to be a dream. Could the dream be displaced at a time within the dream? Could it be within the dream that I emerge from the dream? On the other hand, it could not be at a time internal to the wider, displacing horizon. At any such time, the horizon I am hypothesizing to be a dream would already have been displaced. I would already have emerged from this into the wider horizon.

It is hard to avoid the use of tensed expressions in talking about displacement (emerging). Yet there seems to be no time to which displacement can be assigned, no time at which it happens. Surely something happens in this regard to which we can assign a time. I wake up. I cease to dream. Here we have no problem assigning a time. The waking up, the ceasing to dream, happens in the time of the wider horizon, that which displaces the dream. It is the human being at the center of the wider horizon who was asleep, ceased to dream, and awoke. Similarly, if this were a dream and I emerged from it, there would be a waking up, a ceasing to dream, that would happen in the time of the wider horizon. The subject of the wider horizon could say of himself that he ceased to dream at such-and-such time (in the wider horizon), just as I might now make such a statement about my dream of the other night. In contrast, however, the displacement of the dream horizon by the horizon I call reality cannot be assigned to a time in the horizon I call reality. Nor to a time *in* the dream. And there is no other relevant time. One horizon displaces another, but not (it seems) at any time.

3. The Confusion of Standpoint

3.1 Dreams and the Infinity of Time

Our general conclusion about space/time and the dream hypothesis (DH) in chapter 1 was that the DH makes no difference to the space that spreads out from *here*, from where I am, or to the time before and after *now*. The DH, we might say, makes no difference to egocentric space and time. Whether this is a dream or reality, either way egocentric space and time are infinite. Yet if in light of the DH we contemplate the possibility of waking up, the point about infinity may seem less convincing in the case of time than in that of space. For the possibility of waking up seems to place a temporal rather than a spatial limit on the dream. If this, the horizon of which I am at the center, is a dream and I wake up, then, after I wake up, there will be no such thing as this. So there will then be no such time as the time internal to this. How then could the time internal to this, internal to the dream, be infinite? How could a time that in a few minutes will no longer exist be an infinite time? Or think of it as follows. If this is a dream and the time internal to this is infinite, whatever happens after now, i.e., in the future, will happen in the dream-future; so it will happen in the dream. But suppose I wake up. Would not the things I do and that happen after I wake up be done and happen in the future? Yet, by hypothesis, they would not happen in the dream.

However, we must remind ourselves that if this is a dream, I, the human being that I am, would not be the one who wakes up. The one who wakes up would belong to the transcendent world, the world of the wider horizon. If we say that, on the DH, I might emerge from the dream into the wider horizon, this means (as we explained in 2.6) that the subject of the wider horizon, the horizon that would displace this, would identify with me in the way I identify with the subject of my dream of the other night (he would judge that, in the dream, "I am JV").

An individual creature, a human being say, is first asleep and then awake. These are different states a human being can be in. When we talk about "waking up" we are talking about a human being (animal) undergoing a change, going from one state to another. The idea of emerging from a dream cannot be understood in terms of change. Instead of a human being who is in different states, first in one and then the other, we need the utterly different conception of one horizon displacing another. One horizon displaces another, and the subject (the one at the center) of the displacing context identifies himself (in a certain sense) with the subject of the displaced context.

Another point to be clear about is that the horizon we hypothesize to be a dream cannot properly be conceived as temporal. It does not itself "happen" or "occur"; nor does it "last" or "go on" or "endure" for such-and-such period of time. So it does not "begin" or "end" at a certain time. Suppose this is a dream. If this, the subject matter of the supposition, were temporal, it would occur either in the time internal to the dream, dreamtime, or in the time of the wider context, the wider time. Obviously, the dream could not occur in dreamtime, since in that case it would occur in the dream—in itself. So it would have to occur in the wider time. But what occurs in the wider time is not the dream "itself," the horizon that contains an infinity of time, but the *dreaming* of the dream. Let us dwell on this briefly.

A dream is dreamed, but not from within it. How shall we conceive of the dreaming of a dream? The dreaming of a dream is a process or activity or series of states on the part of the dreamer. On the part of the dreamer, note, not the subject of the dream (the one at the center of the dream). Thus it, the dreaming, occurs in the world outside the dream. If this were a dream, the dreaming of this would occur in the world of the wider horizon, the transcendent world, hence not in dreamtime, the time before and after *now*, but in the time of the wider horizon, which has no temporal relation to *now*. And the dream "itself"? It would occur neither in the time internal to the dream, i.e., to itself, nor in the wider time. It would not occur in any time.

The time before and after now is infinite. So if this were a dream, the time internal to the dream would be infinite. But the dream "itself," the horizon to which the temporal infinity would be internal, would not be "itself" in time. It would be outside time.

I have dreamed and awoken from many dreams. The dreamings of these dreams are now as much a part of my history, the history of the human being that I am, as are the many times I have gotten into bed, fallen asleep, slept, and then awoken in the same bed. All such events or happenings are, in turn, part of the history of the world, since my history, the history of the human being I am, is part of the history of the world. But the dreams that I dreamed, i.e., the horizons within which the dream events unfolded, these are not part of my history, or that of the world. Nor can they be included in the histories internal to themselves. They cannot be included in any history.

Of course, we commonly speak of dreams "lasting" for a certain length of time, and we speak of the time "when a dream occurred," and so on. I think that such ways of speaking either embody a confusion or must be viewed as elliptical. What we (really) mean when we give the date or duration of a dream is that the dreaming of the dream had such-and-such date or duration.

There is something else to observe. We said that, if this were a dream, the dreaming (the relevant activity or process or series of states, etc.) would belong to the wider time. How long would that dreaming activity or whatever last in wider time? A few minutes? A few days? The question seems to have no particular answer; this, despite the fact that the time internal to the horizon that would be a dream is, as we said, endless. To contain an endless time, a dream does not have to be endlessly dreamed. Compare the case of a fiction. If we tell a story about ordinary life, the characters in the story see before and behind them an endless time. How long does it take to tell the story? It may be a few minutes or an hour. No particular length of time is required for the telling of the story in order that the story should, in the relevant sense, contain an endless time.

In my dream of the other night (the dream I, JV, dreamed the other night), I got up from my seat on the train for a drink of water. How long ago, i.e., how long before now, did I get up? There is no answer to this question. I can say that the dream in which these things occurred was dreamed three nights ago, but I cannot (correctly, unconfusedly) say of events in the dream that they occurred three nights ago; i.e., three nights prior to now. In the dream, I was first seated next to my daughter; then I got up, etc. Here we are talking about the time internal to the dream. When I was seated, that was dream-present, and my getting up was dream-future. When I got up, that was dream-present, and my being seated was dream-past. But now, in the time of the horizon I call reality, I cannot regard my being seated (in the dream) as past, i.e., before now. My being seated (in the dream) has no temporal relation to *now*. I can say how long ago it was that I dreamed that I got up for a drink of water, but not how long ago I got up. I can no more relate the time of that event to *now* than I can relate the position of the seat from which I got up to the position I now occupy, to *here*.

Similarly, if this were a dream, the horizon into which I would emerge were I to emerge from the dream would have its own past, present, and future. But nothing that occurs in the wider time would have a temporal relation to what is happening *now*. I am now writing. If this were a dream and I emerged from it, the transcendent subject could view as past the dreaming of my present activity of writing, but not the activity of writing. He would view it, rather, as I now view my getting up in my dream of the other night. Again, I, now, cannot properly view as future such actions as the subject of the wider context (the subject who would identify himself with me in the way I identify myself with the subject of the dream the other night) might perform. His actions, his history, would belong to the transcendent time. They would have no temporal relation to *now*.

3.2 Time and the Confusion of Standpoint

As we remarked in 1.4, it is important in reflecting on the DH to keep track of standpoint, i.e., of whether we are considering things from the standpoint internal to the dream or from the standpoint outside the dream, the standpoint (as we may now express it) of the wider horizon. So much should be evident; yet when time enters the equation there is a tendency to get confused in this regard—of which our earlier discussion of emerging from a dream (2.6) already provides a glimpse.

The thoughts to which we gave expression at the beginning of the previous section—viz., that if this were a dream I might awake from it, and that that would place a limit on the time (versus space) internal to the dream; that therefore we are not entitled to assert that on the DH there would be an infinity of time up ahead, and so on—such thoughts exemplify the type of confusion we are attempting to analyze, the confusion of standpoint. We confusedly regard my waking up from the standpoint of the horizon that is the dream, as if my waking might be internal to that horizon and thus in the future. If, however, my waking from the dream were in the future, it would belong to dreamtime, whereas, like the dreaming of the dream, it belongs not to dreamtime but to the time of the transcendent horizon. It would be an event not in the world of the horizon of which I, JV, am the subject, but in the transcendent world, the world of the transcendent horizon, and therefore could not place a limit on the time after *now*, the future.

The confusion is remarkably stubborn. No matter how often I rehearse the foregoing analysis, I find myself tempted to think that, for example, "If this were a dream, in a few minutes time I might wake up"—as though the waking up would occur in the future, i.e., a few minutes from *now*, rather than in a time that has no relation to the present. When I have the thought, "If this were a dream, in a few minutes I might wake up," I confusedly amalgamate two standpoints: that of the horizon I hypothesize to be a dream, and that of the wider horizon, the horizon that would displace the horizon I hypothesize to be a dream.

Some such confusion of standpoint undermines, I think, the way in which philosophers commonly formulate and discuss dream skepticism. Consider the following line of reflection:

Right now I am sitting in a café, writing. Nothing unusual is going on. But many times in the past I have dreamed I was engaged in some perfectly ordinary activity, in perfectly ordinary circumstances. And then I awoke, I ceased to dream, and found myself once again in my familiar bed, in my familiar room. I emerged from the dream back into reality. So how can I be sure now (what justifies me in believing now) that I will not once again awake to find myself in my familiar bed, etc.? How can I be sure that I will not emerge from this back into reality? How can I be sure that this is reality and not just another dream?

This is a typical expression of dream skepticism. But it is incoherent.

When I refer to all the times in the past that I have awoken from dreams and found myself back in reality, by "reality" I mean the horizon of which I am now at the center. For the past to which I refer is the time before *now*, not, surely, the past belonging to the time of any of the dreams in question. I mean times not internal to any of these dreams but the times when I dreamed them, and those times are all times that are *now* in the past, and this is the past of the horizon of which I am now at the center, the horizon into which I emerged from those past dreams when (as we put it) I emerged back into reality. Yet it is about this same horizon that I am expressing uncertainty whether it is a dream or reality. "How can I be sure that I will not emerge from this back into reality?" It would appear that I view as reality both the horizon into which I emerged from all those past dreams, i.e., the horizon I am now in, *and* the horizon into which I would emerge if I emerged from the horizon I am now in. Could this be right? Might I emerge *from* the horizon I am now in *back into* that same horizon? The thought is incoherent. I cannot emerge into the horizon into which I emerged from my past dreams. I am already there.

Consider the references to "my familiar bed," etc. In the first instance, when I have in mind all those times in the past that I have awoken to find myself in "my familiar bed," I refer to something that belongs to the world of the horizon of which I, JV, am now at the center. Is not the bed to which I refer situated right now in a flat about ten minutes walk from here? Could I not take you there right now and show you that bed? But when I in a skeptical vein go on to ask how I can be sure that I will not "once again awake to find myself in my familiar bed," it seems that the bed to which I refer must belong to the world of the wider horizon, the horizon into which I would emerge if I emerged from the dream. So, no matter what I do, I could not show it to you. Then how could it be "my familiar bed"? This bed of mine won't stay still. It jumps from one horizon to another: from the horizon of which I am now at the center to a wider horizon, that which (if this were a dream) would displace the horizon of which I am now at the center.

3.3 Descartes and the Dream Hypothesis

We are going on about the confusion of standpoint because (apart from the fact that the logic of the confusion is intrinsically interesting; or so it seems to me) it is one that is, as we said, very easy to fall into. And philosophers actually do fall into it. The confusion actually occurs in philosophical discussions of the DH. It occurs, I think, in the most famous of all such discussions—the discussion of the dream hypothesis in Descartes' *First Meditation*.

Here is the relevant passage:

> At the same time I must remember that I am a man, and that consequently I am in the habit of sleeping, and in my dreams represent to myself the same things or sometimes even less probable things, than do those who are insane in their waking moments. How often it has happened to me that in the night I dreamt that I found myself seated near the fire, whilst in reality I was lying undressed in bed! At this moment it does indeed seem to me that it is with eyes awake that I am looking at this paper; that this head which I move is not asleep, that it is deliberately and of set purpose that I extend my hand and perceive it; what happens in sleep [i.e., in dreams] does not appear so clear nor so distinct as does all this. But in thinking over this I remind myself that on many occasions I have in sleep [in dreams] been deceived by similar illusions, and in dwelling carefully on this reflection I see so manifestly that there are no certain indications by which we may clearly distinguish wakefulness from sleep [i.e., what happens in reality from what happens in a dream] that I am lost in astonishment. And my astonishment is such that it is almost capable of persuading me that I now dream.[1]

Let us begin by noting that Descartes does not at this stage in the *Meditations* seem to have any qualms about the idea that he is a man (they come later). He says about himself that as a man, a human being, he is "in the habit of sleeping." And while sleeping he sometimes dreams. Often, in the night, he has dreamed he was dressed and seated by the fire, when in fact he was undressed and lying in his bed. Could this (he asks himself) be just another such dream? Certainly it seems to him that he is looking with "eyes awake," that "this head" that he moves "is not asleep," that he deliberately moves his hand, and so on. What happens in a dream, he says, "does not appear so clear nor so distinct as does all this." For a moment it looks as if Descartes thinks he has a way of refuting the DH,

---

[1] *Philosophical Works of Descartes*, trans. Elizabeth Haldane and G.R.T. Ross (Dover, 1955), vol. 1, pp. 145–46.

of answering dream skepticism, but, it seems, the would-be refutation is undermined by a simple thought: it has been just like this in his past dreams, things have been just as "clear" and "distinct" as they are now. So, after all, he cannot be sure that this is not merely another dream. He has no "certain indications" on the basis of which he can rule out the DH.

When Descartes tells us that he has often dreamed he was sitting by the fire, and so forth, the dreaming to which he refers is obviously in the past, i.e., some time before *now*. (Here, obviously, we adopt the standpoint of Descartes' temporal present.) He tells us that he dreamed those dreams at times when, in fact, he lay asleep in his bed. So those times, since they are past with respect to *now*, belong to the time of the horizon of which Descartes occupies the subject position, not to the past of any of his past dreams. And his bed. It must belong to the world of the same horizon as all that sleeping and dreaming he did, since it was in that bed that he did the sleeping and dreaming, and in that bed that he awoke from his sleep, emerged from the dreams. Thus Descartes' thought that—given there are no "certain indications" by which he can distinguish reality from dream—for all he can tell this might be another such dream, hence that for all he can tell he might once again awake to find himself undressed and lying in his bed (is that not what he means?), means in effect that for all he can tell he might emerge from the horizon of which he is now at the center back into the horizon of which he is now at the center. For the horizon of which he is now at the center *is* the horizon into which he has emerged from all those past dreams; it *is* the horizon in whose past he, the man Descartes, has slept and dreamed undressed in his bed.

The confusion of standpoint should be clear. Descartes is implicitly viewing the horizon of which he is at the center both as wider than the dreams he has dreamed (for it is *into* the horizon of which, etc., that he emerged from those dreams) and as being, as far as he can tell, on a par with those dreams (since otherwise he would not suppose that if this were a dream, and he emerged from it, he would find himself back in his old bed, where he has so often slept and dreamed). He is viewing the horizon of which he is at the center as if, impossibly, it were a horizon into which he might emerge.

Again, in trying to rule out the possibility this is a dream, Descartes remarks that "it does indeed seem to me that it is with eyes awake that I am looking at this paper; that this head which I move is not asleep, that it is deliberately and of set purpose that I extend my hand." But then he suggests that the appearance of wakefulness and purpose and so on is undermined by the fact that it has seemed to him like that in dreams. He has had "similar illusions" before. Let us take the point about "this head." Descartes' thought seems to be that since this might (for all he can tell) be a dream, the head to which he refers might be asleep. But think about it. If this were a dream, would this head—*this* one (I touch my head)—be asleep? You need only ask the question to see that something has gone seriously wrong. (We shall come back to this in our discussion of dream skepticism.) If this were a dream, the sleeping head would not be *this* head, the head I call "mine." It would belong not to the dream subject (the human being at the center of the dream, the human being that I am) but to the dreamer of the dream. It would be part of a world that transcends my experience, a world outside the horizon of which I occupy the subject position. So it is equally a mistake to suppose that (as Descartes implies) if this head, i.e., my head, were awake, that would mean that this is *not* a dream. My head, the one up here (the one I now touch), is not the head that matters. If this were a dream, my head would be, along with everything else, *in* the dream. Let it (my head) be ever so wakeful, nothing would change: this would still be a dream.

3.4 Dream Skepticism versus Memory Skepticism

It may be objected that our antiskeptical criticism of Descartes takes a lot for granted. I speak matter-of-factly, as if it were philosophically unproblematic, about my head and my bed, about all the times I have gone to sleep in my bed and dreamed, and then awoken in the same bed. In the same matter-of-fact way, I describe myself as sitting in a café, writing, with lots of familiar objects and other people around. And what was I doing before that? Well, I got out of bed (the same old bed) this morning, got dressed, went about my usual daily business, and then came over here, to the café, where I am now having a coffee and writing. So, what is it that we are supposed to be taking for granted in criticizing Descartes' conception of the dream hypothesis? First and foremost, we are taking for granted that my memory is intact, i.e., that I have a grip on the past. But more generally, we are taking for granted that I know who and what I am, and what I am doing, and what is going on around me.

Now, it may be said, these things that we are taking for granted are things for which a philosopher might demand a justification. There is room for skepticism here. Let us focus on the point about memory. How do I know that I *did* wake up this morning, get out of bed, and all the rest? How do I know that I *have* slept and dreamed on many occasions and then emerged from those dreams? How do I know, then, that I emerged from those dreams into (as we are saying) a wider horizon, that of which I am now at the center and about which I am considering the hypothesis that it is a dream? If my grip on the past is called into question, the whole structure of "emerging" and "horizons" in terms of which we are trying to explicate the DH collapses.

It is true, we are assuming that I know what I have been doing and what has been going on in my life, that the past is basically as it seems. And it is only because we assume this that we can employ the structure of "emerging," etc., in terms of which we have formulated the DH as well as our criticism of Descartes' conception of the DH. But I do not think that in making such assumptions about memory and the past we are being unfair to Descartes. In discussing the DH, Descartes, like *all* philosophers when they discuss this hypothesis, makes the same assumption. Recall: "how often it has happened to me that in the night I dreamt that I found myself seated near the fire, whilst in reality. . . ." In being skeptical about dream and reality, Descartes is not being skeptical about his *memory*, about whether the past is as it seems. And why should he be? Just as we can have skeptical doubts about the past without worrying about how to refute the DH, we may worry about the DH without having any skeptical doubts about the past. These are different kinds of skepticism.

The situation with memory and dream skepticism is in some ways like the situation with memory skepticism and skepticism about inductive reasoning. According to the inductive skeptic, we reason like this: "All the A's we have examined have been B's. So (most likely) the next A will be a B." Based on the fact that the past has been thus-and-so, we infer something about the future. The inductive skeptic challenges us to justify this inference from past to future. He wonders whether anything can justify such an inference. Notice, though, in raising this kind of doubt the skeptic is perfectly happy to take for granted that all the A's we have examined have been B's. He does not challenge us to justify our confidence that the past is as it seems. Is he not entirely within his rights to proceed in this way? After all, he is concerned not with knowledge of the past but with how we get from knowledge of the past to knowledge of the future. Nor is the dream skeptic—qua dream skeptic—concerned with knowledge of the past. He may take it for granted that the past is as it seems. The dream skeptic, if he has not fallen into the confusion of standpoint, is concerned with the status of that to which the past is internal, the horizon of which I am at the center. Given that its past is as it seems, how do I know that this horizon is not a dream? What justifies me in rejecting the hypothesis that there is a wider horizon than this, the context in which I have so often dreamed and into which I have emerged from all those dreams?

On Descartes' conception, which is more or less the usual conception in philosophy, the DH turns out (or so we are arguing) to be incoherent. This seems to provide us with a response to the challenge of dream skepticism, whereby we are asked to justify our rejection of the DH. If the hypothesis is incoherent, there is in a real sense nothing to reject; hence nothing whose rejection requires justification. Does this not give us a way of dealing with dream skepticism once and for all?

Not quite. We have been discussing only one conception of the DH. We cannot claim to have shown that the DH is as such incoherent. Thus although it is incoherent to suppose that in emerging from this, the horizon of which I am at the center, I should at the same time be emerging into this, it does not seem incoherent that I might emerge from this into a wider horizon: that there might be a horizon that stands to this in the way that this stands to my dream of the other night. There may, certainly, be something *wrong* with this hypothesis, a reason for dismissing it or not taking it seriously; but it seems to be a coherent hypothesis. In that case, exposing the incoherence of Descartes' conception of the DH (the usual conception), leaves dream skepticism intact. We shall require a different way of responding to dream skepticism.

3.5 Real-Life Uncertainty about the Dream Hypothesis

If our analysis is correct, Descartes' conception of the DH involves a confusion—a confusion of standpoint—that I believe is common in philosophical discussion of dream skepticism. But the confusion occurs not just in philosophy. Outside philosophy, in the course of everyday life, we sometimes get confused in basically the same way—without any philosophical assistance. The difference between the two cases is that when the confusion occurs in the course of philosophical reflection on dream skepticism, typically the truth-value of the DH is not a real issue for us. We are not seriously wondering whether this is a dream. Thus, despite our confusion, the hypothesis manages to stay alive in philosophical reflection. We keep trying to justify our rejection of an incoherent hypothesis. In contrast, when we fall into the confusion outside philosophy, we seriously (though incoherently, hence confusedly) have the thought that this might be a dream. What happens? Given its incoherence, the hypothesis pretty quickly loses its grip. I do not mean (of course) that, outside philosophy, the analysis of the incoherence is clear to us and for that reason we reject it, but that, because we seriously wonder about the truth-value of the hypothesis, the fact of its incoherence gets through; and this makes it impossible to persist in taking the hypothesis seriously. Let me elaborate on this.

Most people have had the experience of momentarily wondering—not as part of philosophical reflection, but in the course of everyday (real) life—whether this is a dream. What happens in such a case? The thought, the question, is usually provoked by the occurrence of something awful or strange (something "dreamlike," i.e., like what has happened in dreams we have dreamed in the past), or something we overwhelmingly do not want to be true.[2] It is accompanied by a kind panic. Then what? Do we refute the hypothesis? Do we assemble evidence or arguments that this is not a dream?

Think about what actually happens. We do not refute the hypothesis. The question simply goes away, the panic subsides.

The question comes, and then it goes. It passes like a chill. The interesting thing is that although the question goes, we do not feel we are left with an *unanswered* question. This is very different from what happens, typically, when we reflect on the DH in philosophy. Of course, at some point we stop reflecting on the hypothesis. We forget about it and consider some other philosophical problem, or put philosophy aside for a while. But the question remains. It is for us, philosophically, an unanswered question, and we suppose that we will come back to it some other time.

Descartes tells us in the second Meditation that, as a result of reflecting on the dream hypothesis, he is "lost in astonishment," and that his "astonishment is such that it is almost capable of persuading me that I now dream." I find it hard to believe that Descartes is reporting the panicky, real-life experience of wondering whether this is a dream. We said that when in real-life the question goes, it does not seem to remain unanswered. Descartes, however, apparently takes the question he raises in the second Meditation to remain unanswered. Thus he returns to the question at the end of the sixth Meditation.

Maybe I am wrong about what Descartes reports. Maybe—can we rule this out a priori?—it is possible, by philosophical reflection, to induce genuine uncertainty about whether this is a dream, uncertainty of the same kind that occasionally overcomes us in real life. Imagine that this is what happens to Descartes in the second Meditation. But it is obvious that the uncertainty, the panic, does not persist with Descartes. That would be a form of madness, insanity. Descartes, however, goes on pretty calmly and rationally with his philosophical reflections. If we accept that in the second Meditation Descartes really does manage to induce serious uncertainty about whether this is a dream, we must suppose that he proceeds, as it were, on two levels. Philosophically, he puts the question aside. It remains unanswered, for him, until the sixth Meditation. In the real-life way, however, the question has disappeared. Were that not the case, he would not be able to continue his philosophizing.

---

[2] Like the confused and desperate subject, a Russian war veteran who has suffered crippling brain damage, described in A. R. Luria's *The Man with a Shattered World* (Penguin Books, 1975), p. 26: "It's hard to believe this is really life, but if it is a dream (and is it?) I can't just wait until I wake up."

Of course it is possible in real life for a question to engage us, and then for us to put it aside without an answer. I see someone in the distance getting on bus. Was that X? I ponder this for a while and then forget about it. I may never find out whether it was X who got on the bus. The question may remain unanswered. But again, this is not what happens when, in real life, I ask myself whether this is a dream. In the dream case, the question goes, but I do not just forget about it, or put it aside. There is no unanswered question. The question *simply goes*.

What distinguishes philosophical from real-life engagement with the DH is that, as we said, whereas in the real-life case we take seriously the possible truth of hypothesis, in the philosophical case we are just trying to meet an epistemological challenge. What distinguishes real-life engagement with the DH, on the other hand, from real-life engagement with, say, the hypothesis that that was X getting on the bus, is that, while in both cases we seriously think the hypothesis might be true, in the dream case we are engaged with an incoherent hypothesis.

It is because our real-life versus philosophical uncertainty about the DH is serious that it disappears. There is in both cases the same incoherence, the same confusion of standpoint on our part. But when we are serious, the confusion cannot survive. At a stroke, the question of whether this might be a dream evaporates. It is no longer there. Thus, there is nothing to put aside, or forget about. The question comes and then it goes.

The impact on the reflecting mind of dream skepticism pales in comparison with that of real-life uncertainty whether this is a dream. Yet (if we are right) what underlies, or may underlie, our philosophical uncertainty is equally the source of our momentary disorientation outside philosophy. The confusion that comes over us in everyday life, which momentarily takes possession of us and then departs, is the same confusion that (I believe) is present in the usual line of philosophical reflection on the DH: the confusion of standpoint. But note: it is also philosophical reflection on the DH that uncovers the elements—the horizonal subject matter of which I am at the center and to which the infinity of egocentric space and time is internal; the possibility of wider such horizons, of emerging from one horizon to another; and so on—that we are employing in our analysis of the philosophical confusion. Philosophical reflection, it seems, exposes the elements that figure in a confusion about the DH both inside and outside philosophy.

You may recall that in the introduction we pointed ahead to the possibility of philosophically uncovering puzzles that are already there for us extraphilosophically, and in fact may break through into everyday consciousness without the benefit of philosophical reflection. We should point out here that the dream/reality case does not fit this model (examples of which will come later in the book). In the dream/reality case what exists extraphilosophically is not a puzzle but a confusion: a confusion of standpoint. Thus the extraphilosophical manifestation takes the form not of puzzlement but, as we said, of disorientation. Moreover, under the pressure of serious, real-life uncertainty about the DH, the relevant confusion tends very quickly to dissolve, whereas, in contrast, the extraphilosophical puzzles remain. What the two cases have in common is that, in both, the disturbance (the puzzlement, the disorientation) has an extraphilosophical source and does not depend on our working through a philosophical argument or piece of reasoning. Thus whereas in both cases exposing and articulating the source of the disturbance requires philosophical reflection, the existence of what is thereby exposed owes nothing to philosophy.

4. The Subject Matter of the Dream Hypothesis

4.1 Is the Argument from Internality Valid?

The starting point of our reflections on the DH was the question: What is the subject matter of the DH? That is: To what do I refer by "this" when I contemplate the hypothesis that this is a dream? In our attempt to answer the question, we repeatedly employed an argument of the following form (the argument from internality): Consider X; if this were a dream, X would be internal to the dream; therefore X cannot be what I mean, what I refer to, by "this." It seems that whatever we propose as an answer to our question turns out, by the argument from internality, to be internal to the subject matter of the DH and hence cannot be the subject matter of the DH. By this argument the whole of the world with its infinity of space and time turns out to be internal to the subject matter of the DH—which seems to leave us with nothing for that subject matter to be. We are now bound to wonder whether this argument, the argument from internality, involves some kind of fallacy or mistake.

Let us grant that if this were a dream, X (say the objects present to me right now, or the totality of objects here in the café, or the whole of what I call "the world") would be internal to the dream. If this were a dream, then, X would be internal to that to which I refer by "this." So far, everything seems in order. But to get the conclusion that X is not that to which I refer by "this," we must suppose that X is internal to that to which I refer by "this." Here is where we may be going wrong. From the fact that if this were a dream X *would be* internal to (that to which I refer by) "this," does it follow that X *is* internal to "this"? The inference, it may be said, is invalid. It is a simple-minded modal fallacy.

Certainly, the argument from internality is not formally valid. From the fact that if such-and-such were the case, X would be F, it is not a formally valid step to the conclusion that X is F. Think of what we could prove in this manner. I point to the cup. "If this were a ham sandwich, it would be edible (that to which I refer by 'this' would be edible)." Can I infer, "this (that to which I refer) is edible"? But that is exactly the form of reasoning in the argument from internality. From "If this were a dream it would contain the whole of the world," we are inferring "this (that to which I refer by "this") contains the whole of the world."

The argument from internality is not formally valid. Nonetheless it is valid. That is, from the fact that if this were a dream that to which I refer by "this" would contain the whole of the world, it follows that that to which I refer, etc., contains the whole of the world. It follows—but not as a matter of logical form.

It is a philosophical commonplace that there can be valid inferences that are not formally valid. From "this is red," it follows that "this is colored." The inference is valid, despite the fact that "X is F, therefore, X is G," is not a valid inference form.

Let us consider a modal example. If it is true that X might not have been a body, X is not a body. Clearly, this is not a formally valid inference. If it were, we would be entitled to infer from the fact that this cup might not have been a chipped cup, that it is not a chipped cup. Yet many people (I include myself here) would accept the first inference as valid. The reason they would accept the inference as valid is that they regard being a body (as opposed, say, to being chipped) as essential to whatever is a body. So, if something might not have been a body, it is not a body.

In our case, the relevant point concerns not the essential/accidental, but the intrinsic/extrinsic, contrast. Being a dream, or being reality, is, we said (1.2), extrinsic to the subject matter of the DH, i.e., to that to which in expressing the hypothesis I refer by "this." If this were a dream, that to which I refer by "this" would be just as it is. It would, then, contain just what it does contain. So, if on the DH this would contain the whole of the world, it (that to which I refer, etc.) does contain the whole of the world. To repeat, the reasoning is not formally valid, but it is valid.

You could think of the reasoning as having two parts or stages. The first part brings us, step by step, to the conclusion that if this were a dream, the whole of the world with its infinity of space and time would be internal to this. In the second part, we draw the conclusion that the whole of the world, and so on, is internal to this subject matter. What entitles us to take the further step? That is, from our conclusion that if this were a dream the whole of the world *would be* internal to it, what entitles us to infer that the whole of the world *is* internal to this subject matter? It is that being a dream, or being reality, whichever it is, is extrinsic to this subject matter, to the subject matter of the DH.

Suppose we are challenged about whether the status of this as dream or reality is determined by something extrinsic to it (to this), extrinsic, that is, to the subject matter of the DH. Clearly, we cannot appeal to the argument from internality. Then why should we accept the conclusion of the argument?

But this is the wrong way to view the argument—as if from self-evident premises we were logically forced to accept that the world is internal to the subject matter of the DH. I think it works (if it works) differently. We begin by asking to what we refer by "this" in expressing the hypothesis that this is a dream. (Most likely the question has not previously occurred to us.) We then introduce the argument from internality and keep re-applying the argument to ever more inclusive totalities, eventually to the whole of the world with its infinity of space and time. Then what? Do we on the basis of the fact that its status as dream or reality is extrinsic to the subject matter of the DH *draw the conclusion* that the world, etc., is internal to this subject matter? No. Rather, the all-inclusive subject matter has, if it has (there is no guarantee), in the course of our reflections simply come into view. We use the argument not to prove but to open us up to something: to a subject matter to which the world is internal: to a subject matter about which we already know (and of whose existence we there-fore do not need a proof). The argument from internality serves not as an instrument of philosophical proof but as an instrument of philosophical discovery (see Int.6).

4.2 The Subject Matter of the Dream Hypothesis and Grammatical Illusion

At this point a deeper misgiving may arise. Consider my use of "this" in expressing the DH, the hypothesis that this is a dream. The argument from internality—the argument whose repeated use is meant to open us up to a subject matter that contains the world, etc., and thus to serve as an instrument of philosophical discovery—proceeds on the assumption that in expressing the DH I use "this" as a singular term. Thus each time I repeat the argument, I reason that X (the objects around me in the café, the events before and after now, and so on) would be internal to the sub-ject matter that in the present context I refer to by "this"; that therefore X cannot be what I refer to by "this"; that it cannot be the subject matter of the DH. Are we entitled to this assumption? Are we, that is, entitled to assume that in expressing the DH I use "this" as a singular term, to refer to something?

Perhaps the appearance of reference is an illusion. Insofar as it seems that I am referring to something by "this," it seems that there is some-thing, some subject matter, to which I refer. But if it is an illusion that I am referring to something, it is an illusion that there is something to which I refer. It is an illusion, then, that, by repeated use of the argument from internality, something comes into view. We might say: if something comes into view, it is an illusory "something," the product of an illusion of reference. Our philosophical discovery is the discovery of an illusory subject matter.

What kind of illusion is an illusion of reference? Obviously, it is not a perceptual illusion. It is, I take it, an example of what philosophers call a "grammatical illusion." The suggestion would be that, generally, when we use a sentence of form "This is F," we use the expression "this" to refer (as a singular term). So we assume that when (in philosophical reflection) we use the sentence "This is a dream" to express the DH, we refer to something by "this." Given the assumption, we are entitled to ask what the "something" is. Such is the starting point of the argument from internality. Thus we reason that, whatever it is that I refer to by "this" in expressing the DH, it could not be something internal to the dream, since that would mean it is internal to that to which I refer (internal to itself); on this basis, step by step, we go on to exclude as the "something," the object of reference, the whole of the world and the infinity of space and time. If, however, the seeming use of "this" as a singular term is illusory, the argument from internality starts with an illusion. In using the argument we progress from illusion to illusion. We start with an illusion of reference and end with the illusion of an all-inclusive horizon.

Someone who assimilates the "it" in "It is raining" to, say, that in "It is leaking" (said of a faucet) would be under a grammatical illusion of the kind that we are being asked to accept operates when we express the dream hypothesis as the hypothesis that "This is a dream." Just as it is a mistake to project, on the basis of the surface grammatical similarity between "It is raining" and "It [the faucet] is leaking," a semantic similarity (that in both cases "it" is a singular term), it would be a mistake on the basis of their grammatical similarity to project a semantic similarity between "This is a dream" and, say, "This is a cup," i.e., to suppose that in both cases "this" is referential. Someone under the illusion of reference in the rain case will acquire the notion of a strange "something" that emits rain; similarly, someone under the illusion of reference in the dream case will, by repeated use of the argument from internality, acquire the notion of a strange "something" that contains the whole of the world and space and time. In both cases, the "something" is illusory. It is the product of a grammatical illusion.

This idea is tempting: it provides a response to dream skepticism. The dream skeptic is, in effect, asking us to refute a hypothesis about an illusory subject matter. Why—we might ask—should we take such a hypothesis seriously? A hypothesis about an illusory subject matter is not a hypothesis that requires refutation.

The idea may tempt us—yet, on reflection, it is implausible. Whereas the nonreferential use of "it" is a familiar, well-entrenched part of English (would any competent speaker of English ever be taken in by the grammatical similarity between "It is raining" and "It is leaking"?), there is no familiar, etc., nonreferential use of "this." We always use "this" as a singular term.[1] If, however, there is no familiar nonreferential use of "this," there is no use that we might mistake for a referential use. There is, in other words, no basis on which to explain how the supposed illusion of reference in expressing the DH might arise. Like all illusions, a grammatical illusion must be based on something. (There must be something on the basis of which we are led astray.) Illusions do not come from nothing.

4.3 Alternative Formulations of the Dream Hypothesis

This naturally leads to another question. Given that if we express the DH as the hypothesis that "this is a dream" we use "this" referentially, why should we express the DH in that way—as the hypothesis that "this is a dream"? It is not as if there were no alternatives. Instead of "this is a dream," we can express the hypothesis as the hypothesis that "I am dreaming." In fact, this is how the DH is commonly expressed. If the DH is expressed in this way, the line of reflection that is supposed to reveal an all-inclusive horizon as the subject matter of the hypothesis cannot get started.

However, the "I am dreaming" formulation of the DH has a problem of its own (the point will be familiar from our discussion of the first person in 2.4). It would seem that I use "I" here as I normally use it, referentially. To what do I normally refer by "I"? To a particular human being, JV, *this* human being (I point to him). So the DH is the hypothesis that that human being is sleeping. But he is not sleeping. He is sitting here in the café writing about the DH. He (the one whose hand is now holding a pen and in a moment will reach over to pick up the coffee cup) is not the human being that, on the DH, would be sleeping and dreaming but, rather, the human being that would be the subject of the dream (the one at the center). The human being that would be dreaming would not be, as *this* human being would be, part of the world internal to the dream but part of a transcendent world.

There is a mismatch here. When I express the DH as the hypothesis that "I am dreaming," the individual to which I refer by "I" is part of the world internal to the dream. But the individual that would, on the hypothesis, be dreaming would belong to a world outside the dream, a transcendent world. In other words, the individual that would fit the predicative content of the DH would belong to a world other than that of the

---

[1] Which is not to say that we always use "this" to refer to something present in experience; or even that we always use "this" to refer to a material object.

individual to which, in expressing the hypothesis, I refer. I would not be expressing a coherent hypothesis.

It is easy to feel there is something wrong with the DH. But is it incoherent? Someone who answers "No" to this question and yet expresses the DH by the words "I am dreaming" does not grasp the implications of his own words.

Then how should we express the DH? It would seem that if we want the hypothesis to be coherent, we should express it as hypothesis that "this is a dream." In thus expressing the hypothesis, I use "this" to refer to the horizon that contains the world with its infinity of space and time: horizon of which I, JV, am at the center. The horizon is the subject matter of the DH, and the hypothesis is that there is a wider horizon, one with its own world and subject and spatio-temporal infinity. Thus understood, the dream hypothesis is coherent.

There is however another possibility. On both the "I am dreaming" and "this is a dream" formulations, the grammatical subject is referential. What we need, it may be suggested, is a form of words, a way of expressing the DH, that avoids reference altogether.

Some such suggestion is often made with respect to Descartes' famous *Cogito* inference—the inference from "I am thinking" to "I exist." Descartes, it is said, is not entitled to use "I" in his premise. The reason is that, since "I" (like "this") is entrenched in everyday language as a singular term, the use of "I" in the premise presupposes what is meant to be the conclusion of the inference. Descartes needs an alternative way of formulating his premise. Now, as noted earlier, there is in English (and other languages) a familiar nonreferential use of "it," e.g., in "It is raining." Descartes' critics capitalize on this by suggesting (the idea is often associated with the philosopher Lichtenberg, whom I have not read) that Descartes should express his premise not as "I am thinking" but as "It is thinking," where the "it" is understood in the same nonreferential way as in "It is raining" (or *es* in the German *Es regnet)*.

In our case, the suggestion would be that instead of "I am dreaming" we should use the form of words "It is dreaming" or (better) "It is being dreamed" to express the DH. Not only, then, would there be no question of reference to something that turns out, problematically, to contain the whole of the world, etc., there would be no question of first-person reference, hence no question of a reference that renders the hypothesis incoherent. There would be no question of reference at all.

There would, however, be a question: If (as we shall put it) *it is being dreamed*, on whose part would the dreaming occur (who would the dreamer be)? I look at a person asleep, dreaming. I take him to be the dreamer, the one on whose part "It is being dreamed." It is his brain that is responsible for the dreaming. If, retreating to my own case, I contemplate the hypothesis that "It is being dreamed," I know that, if the hypothesis were true, there would be a dreamer. Who would it be? Whose brain would be the brain on which the dreaming depends?

Not, we know, *my* brain (I touch my head), the brain "up here." If my head were opened, I might observe (in a mirror) my brain. But on the hypothesis that "It is being dreamed," that brain would be *in* the dream being dreamed and thus could not be the brain on which the dreaming (hence the dream) depends. Nor would it be some brain "out there." The brain on which the dream depends would not be anywhere in the totality I call "the world." Where then would it be? It would be part of a world outside this, part of a transcendent world. You see what this means. We may, if we wish, express the DH as the hypothesis that "It is being dreamed," but implicit in our grasp of the hypothesis is the contrast between the world that would be internal to the dream, the world that includes my brain, and a transcendent world, the world outside the dream, the world that would include the object on which the dreaming being dreamed depends. This means that we are, in effect, conceiving of the dream, that which contains the world (including my brain) and of which I am the subject, as a horizon, a horizon that can be contrasted with the horizon that contains the world that includes the dreaming brain. We are then recognizing the problematic all-inclusive subject matter, the horizon of which I am at the center, the personal horizon, as the true subject matter of the DH.

In sum, the personal horizon is implicit in our grasp of the DH—however we choose to express the hypothesis. We may employ a form of words that allows the horizon to remain hidden; but it will remain hidden only so long as we fail to reflect properly on what the hypothesis means (to ask the right questions). And even while it remains hidden, we will know it is there. If this is correct, the most perspicuous formulation of the DH is the one in which we refer to the personal horizon; that is, the formulation of the DH as the hypothesis that "this is a dream."

But now we must point out a way in which this form of words is itself misleading—not grammatically but, as we might put it, semantically misleading. The paradigmatic use of "this" is to refer to what is demonstrably available, to what is directly given or present within experience. By "this" in "this is a dream," however, I refer not to something directly given or present but to the all-containing horizon, to *that from within which* whatever is present is present, demonstrably available. I refer, in other words, to a subject matter that by its nature is not, and cannot be, there for me to fix on demonstratively; that is, to a subject matter that is *un*available in the way that the paradigmatic use of "this" presupposes I have something available, something present within the horizon.

Yet the very fact that it is semantically misleading gives the use of "this" in expressing the DH a certain heuristic potential. For when, having raised the possibility that "this is a dream," we put to ourselves the question of what we mean here by "this," we feel—given that its paradigmatic use is to refer to what is demonstratively available—at a loss. Thus in attempting to answer the question of what we mean, it would be natural to gesture about vaguely, indicating at once everything and nothing. Our feeling at a loss, I would say, is the first glimmering of a subject matter that we already know is there: the all-inclusive personal horizon. The use of "this" in expressing the DH may thus, precisely because of its semantically misleading character, act as a kind of prompting or incitement to proceed with the reflections that eventually enable the subject matter of the hypothesis to come openly into view.

Henceforth, to highlight its semantically misleading character—to keep reminding ourselves (as it were) of the fact that, although we are using to it refer, we could not be further from its paradigmatic use—we shall capitalize the word "this" when we use it to refer to the subject matter of the dream hypothesis. Thus we shall express the DH as the hypothesis that "THIS is a dream." And we shall say (write), for example, that the whole of the world with its infinity of space and time is internal to THIS; that I, JV, am at the center of THIS (the one who occupies the subject position); and so on.

4.4 Reality

The hypothesis that THIS is a dream is the hypothesis that I might emerge from THIS into a wider horizon, that there is a horizon that might displace THIS in the way THIS displaced my dream of the other night, and from whose perspective the one at the center might regard THIS, the horizon of which I (JV) am at the center, in the way that I (JV) now regard my dream of the other night. The wider horizon, that into which I would emerge, would have its own world and infinity of space and time, a world, etc., internal to it in the way that what I call "the world" and its infinity of space and time is internal to THIS. Such is the meaning of the DH.

On the hypothesis that THIS is reality (not a dream), there is no wider horizon; no horizon into which I might emerge in the way I emerged into THIS from my dream the other night; no horizon, then, that might displace THIS in the radical way THIS displaced the dream. If THIS is reality, it is the horizon a wider-than-which does not exist: It is the widest horizon of all. Its world (we could say) is the widest world, its infinity of space and time the widest infinity, etc.

Note, if THIS is reality, that which is reality is precisely what would be a dream if THIS were a dream. I ask myself: "Is THIS a dream or reality?" It is a single subject matter whose status is at issue. It is a dream if there is a wider horizon; otherwise it is reality.

It follows that the status of this subject matter as reality versus dream has nothing to do with the nature or character or behavior of what is internal to it. What matters is whether what is internal to it is all there is. If what I call "the world" is indeed *the* world (if there is no wider world), THIS is reality; and if THIS is reality, what I call "the world" is the world. Again, if THIS is reality, whereas only the tiniest fragment of the objects that comprise this totality are actually present in my experience, there is nothing that transcends my experience. Conversely, if nothing transcends my experience, THIS is reality.

The concept of reality that we are using here, that which we use when we contrast dream and reality, is not our only concept of reality. We contrast the real not just with dream but, for example, with the artificial and the illusory. Let us briefly reflect on these other contrasts.

One thing that sets the reality/dream contrast apart from the others is that it does not permit us to differentiate within experience. We can single out particular objects within experience and judge that one is real versus artificial, or again, illusory; that the other is artificial (illusory) versus real. "*This* is a real tree, *that* a fake tree"; "*This* is a tree, *that* is an illusion." Such thoughts have no counterparts in the case of reality/dream contrast. This is because the contrast does not directly apply to objects present within experience, within the horizon that is the subject matter of the DH, but rather to that very subject matter, to the horizon from within which objects are present.

If, indirectly or derivatively, we apply the dream/reality contrast to objects within experience, we must apply it globally. For we could not judge, "*This* is a real object but *that* a dream object." Whichever status is assigned to one object within experience must be assigned to every such object. And not just to what actually is present, but to what is potentially present: to the whole of the world. If THIS is a dream, the whole the world is a dream world; if THIS is reality, the world—the whole of it—is the real world.

It is for a very different reason that objects in the world cannot be distinguished as real and illusory. If I judge, "*This* object is real, *that* illusory," I do not thereby differentiate between objects in the world but rather affirm of one object, and deny of the other, that it is part of the world. I differentiate between objects present within experience, but not between objects in the world thus present.

The real/artificial contrast, on the other hand, is drawn between objects in the world. Objects of a given natural kind K share the same inner nature. Artificial instances of K (artificial trees, say) not only do not share that nature, they may differ from each other in their respective inner natures (they may be made of metal, plastic, or whatever). Thus if a question should arise whether a particular tree is real versus artificial, it can be settled by breaking open a leaf, or stripping off some bark, etc., or by chemical analysis. Compare this with how we settle the question of whether, in a visual case, *this* object is illusory. What do we do? We reach out to determine whether there is anything in place that the object appears to occupy. Roughly: if something is there, the object is real; if nothing is there, it is illusory (it exists only from within our experience). Thus if it is illusory, there is nothing to break open. There is no "inside"—hence no "outside." This is not, notice, because the inner nature of an illusory object is highly rarefied or immaterial, but because an illusory object is not part of the world: it *has* no inner nature.

Dream objects, as we indicated, are not illusory. The contrast between real and illusory applies differentially within experience, whereas, insofar as it applies within experience, the real/dream contrast applies globally. The status of an object as real versus illusory is indifferent to its status as real or dream. Thus within a dream, *this* object may prove to be illusory (I reach out and nothing is there). Or, within the dream, the object may prove to be real (I reach out, in the dream, and take hold of it). An object's status as dream versus real does not register within experience but depends on a fact that transcends experience: on whether there is a wider horizon. Hence, determining the object's inner nature can do nothing to settle the question of whether it is real versus dream. Were I to wonder whether THIS is a dream, would it help resolve my uncertainty if I split open this table top or have it chemically analyzed?

Let us summarize. Consider an object, an F, now present within my experience. What makes it a real versus artificial F is that it has a particular inner nature.[2] What makes it a real versus illusory F is simply that it has an inner nature (any nature); or, what comes to the same thing, that it exists independently of its presence within experience, that it is part of the world. What makes the object a real versus dream object, on the other hand, has nothing to do with its inner nature or independence. It has nothing to do with the object at all. What makes the object a real versus dream object is that THIS is the widest horizon. The object is real because THIS is reality.

---

[2] We are overlooking, to keep things simple, the question of the object's origin.

4.5 What Is the Subject Matter of the Dream Hypothesis?

But what is THIS—the subject matter that is reality and about which I may consider the possibility that it is a dream? What is the subject matter of the DH?

The point, and difficulty, of the question becomes clear when we consider what has been excluded as a possible answer. The whole of the world with its infinity of space and time is internal to THIS, internal to the horizon about which we raise the DH, and thus cannot be the subject matter of the hypothesis (the argument from internality). Suppose, instead of endlessly widening the domain of our reflections, we contract them to the point at the center. We still do not find what we want. When we exclude the whole of the world, etc., we thereby exclude whatever it is that occupies the position at the center of the horizon, the little bit of the world that is *me*—as well as anything occurring in that little bit of the world (in me). It does not matter what kind of thing we take the relevant bit to be: a human being, or a brain, or a soul. Whatever it is, as part of the world it would, if THIS were a dream, be internal to the dream.

Internal objects (sensations, afterimages, illusory objects, and so on), as we explained (1.7), are not part of the world. Might THIS be an internal object? But if THIS is a dream, *this* afterimage, say, is an afterimage in the dream. It is, so to speak, doubly internal: an internal object internal to the dream. The argument is always the same. What is internal to the subject matter of the DH cannot be the subject matter of the DH.

Whether we expand our view of things or contract it to the center, whether we look outward or inward, we do not find what we are looking for. If the subject matter of the DH is the all-containing horizon, that to which the world (including myself), etc., is internal, there is nothing for this subject matter to be; that is, nothing for it to be except just that: the all-containing horizon, that to which everything is internal. This answer, however, may not satisfy us. Indeed, it may serve only to reinforce point of the original question. If the subject matter of the DH is that to which the world is internal, it is not part of the world. In that case, what *is* it? What *is* the subject matter of the DH?

Recall what we said, in the introduction, about our reflections on the DH. The main purpose of these reflections, we said, is to bring into view a subject matter that tends to remain out of view, hidden, but of which we already know; a subject matter that stands in contrast with the communal horizon, the horizon that is "ours" (our system of language-games): a subject matter that is (for each of us) peculiarly "mine"—my experience, my consciousness, my life—the personal horizon. Thus we may identify the subject matter that has emerged in our reflections on the DH as the personal horizon: my experience, my consciousness, my life.

Does this answer our question? So far from answering our question, it merely provides us with new ways of asking the question: What is the subject matter that is "mine" (the personal horizon)? That is, what is my experience, my consciousness, etc.? The subject matter that has emerged in our reflections on the DH is a horizon that contains the world with its infinity of space and time and therefore cannot be included in the world. But if it cannot be included in the world, what *is* it?

Let us try a different tack. As we have indicated, the personal horizon has several guises: it is conceived as my experience, my consciousness, my life. We may speak, then, of a horizonal conception of experience, of consciousness, of life. However, while these are equally conceptions of the same horizon, the subject matter of the DH, when we conceive of this subject matter as "my experience," we restrict our attention to much less of what it contains. For whereas the horizon contains the world with its infinity of space and time, when we conceive of it as my experience, we restrict our attention to what is present and hence appears from within the horizon: we conceive of the horizon, you might say, as the horizon of presence and appearing.[3] Thus we defined (in part) the world as the totality of objects and phenomena whose existence is independent of presence within my experience (1.7). Thus too, though correct, it would be misleading to say that the whole of the world is internal to my experience: it would suggest that there is nothing more to the world than the objects and phenomena now present, etc.

But note, even such a restricted conception of the world would not entail that the world exists only from within my experience. Even if the world were exhausted by the objects present within my experience, it would not follow that these objects exist only from within my experience (that their existence was exhausted by their presence). We must not, in other words, confuse being internal to my horizon with being an internal object (like an afterimage). Internal objects are internal to my horizon. But so are external objects, the objects that comprise the world. In what sense is the world "internal" to my horizon? In the sense that, if THIS were a dream, the world (what I call "the world") would be internal to it, internal to THIS. Go back over our reflections on the DH, over the repeated application of the argument from internality. If you follow these reflections you see the sense in which the world is internal to my horizon.

Implicit in our definition of the world is the distinction between the presence/appearing of the world and the fact of the world's existence.

---

[3] Note that this is meant to include not just visual but tactual and audial, etc., presence and appearing.

Consider the cup in front of me on the table. The cup exists (there is such a thing), and it is present—there for me to fix on demonstratively. These are obviously different facts: the cup could not have been present unless it existed; but it might have existed, just as it is, without being present. The thought we have to be struck by here is that the fact of the cup's presence, hence the fact that it appears thus-and-so, these facts *need* something; they need something in a way that the fact of the cup's existence does not need anything but is, rather, self-standing or autonomous. What does the fact of presence (appearing) need? It needs something from within which to hold. It needs a horizon. *Only from within* experience can there be such a fact. The fact that the cup exists, on the other hand, does not need anything from within which to hold. The fact of the cup's existence holds on its own.[4]

If there were no such thing as experience, nothing would be present. There would be a total absence of presence. Let us think what that involves.

A total absence of presence is not like being immersed in a sensory deprivation tank. We can imagine our experience filled with darkness and silence, having no tactual or bodily feeling whatever. But we have not thereby imagined the complete absence of presence. There would still be *this* darkness, *this* silence—a sensory emptiness that would itself be present. Now suppose that this sensory emptiness were removed as well (and nothing takes its place). What would that be like? It would not be like darkness or silence. It would not be like anything. We cannot imagine it—not because it is somehow too difficult to imagine, but because there is nothing to imagine. Sensory emptiness is a limiting case of presence, an imaginable nothingness. The nothingness that is the total absence of presence is an absolute blank, an unimaginable nothingness.

Perhaps we can gesture at this absolute blank with the capitalized NOTHING. In the absence of presence, there would be NOTHING. The world might exist, just as it is, but there would be NOTHING.

However, if there is NOTHING, an unimaginable absence of presence, there is no such thing as experience: no such thing as THIS. For the horizon to *be*, there must be something present from within it. Not only, then, is it the case that facts of presence hold only from within the horizon; without such facts there would be no horizon, nothing from within which facts of presence might hold. The being of the horizon, the being of THIS, thus stands in reciprocal dependence with presence: there is such a thing as presence only from within experience, only from within the horizon;

---

[4] In the present and following section, I shall repeat a number of points that I make in chapter 6 of *The Puzzle of Experience*. But we shall skirt around the puzzle with which that book deals.

yet without presence, there is NOTHING, and if there is NOTHING there is no horizon, no such thing as THIS.

It follows that the horizon, the subject matter of the DH, is in its own way "nothing": it is nothing apart from there being something present within it. If nothing is present within it, there is no "it" for anything to be present within. There is no horizon.

Suppose I describe something as "that in which I keep my shoes." We may ask, "Yes, but what *is* it?" In asking this question we want to know what the object is *apart from* being that in which I keep my shoes: what it is *in itself*. There may of course be more than one correct answer, but any correct answer must satisfy two conditions. It must specify a kind K such that the object referred to (i) belongs to K and (ii) would have belonged to K even had there been nothing within it. When the "that within which . . . " is, as in our example, an object in the world, so that the relevant containment is spatial, these conditions are always satisfied. Nothing could be that within which I keep my shoes, say, unless it were something in itself—a cardboard box, a cupboard, a wooden crate, etc. The thing is, when we ask about the subject matter of the DH, about that from within which the world is present, we are not dealing with an object in the world. If in this case we say "Yes, but what *is* it?" the question has no answer. The reason is, whatever K we choose, had nothing been present within the horizon, there would have been NOTHING, which means there would have been no horizon, hence nothing that might have belonged to K.

"Yes, but what *is* it?" It makes sense to keep insisting, to keep seeking the relevant K, only where the subject matter is something in itself. This is just what the subject matter of the DH is not. If we think that without an answer to the question the horizonal subject matter will remain mysterious, this is a symptom of our failure to grasp what the horizonal subject matter is. What is it? In a real sense it is *nothing*—i.e., nothing in itself (see Int.7). It is precisely a subject matter about which it is a mistake to keep pressing the question of what it is.

4.6 The Horizonal versus Phenomenal Conception of Mind

In addition, then, to basic existential nothingness (the kind of nothingness expressed by the quantifier, e.g., "there are no . . . ," "there is no such thing as . . . "), we must recognize two further kinds of nothingness: there is the nothingness that is the total absence of presence, NOTHINGNESS, and there is the nothingness of the horizon, i.e., the nothingness of a subject matter that is nothing in itself. Without the subject matter that is nothing in itself, there would be NOTHING. You could say, what stands between us and NOTHINGNESS is a kind of nothingness.

Of the subject matter that is nothing in itself (the personal horizon, that which is "mine"), we have observed that it has different guises. Thus we variously conceive of it as my experience, my consciousness, my life. These are different forms of what might be called the "horizonal" conception of mind: conceptions of the same hidden subject matter that has emerged in our reflections on the DH. It should be evident that this is not the conception of mind with which we typically operate in the philosophy of mind, the conception in terms of which the familiar issues and debates are formulated. The usual conception is the conception not of a horizon from within which the world is present/appears, but rather of a phenomenon, i.e., of something that occurs or goes on in us (and perhaps other animal creatures) and thus is part of the world. We shall call this the "phenomenal" conception of mind (of experience, consciousness, life). It is the phenomenal, not the horizonal, conception of mind that is the dominant philosophical conception of mind.

Consider, for example, the much discussed question of intentionality, the feature that is often supposed to distinguish the mental from the physical. The question is conceived as a question about states (events, processes, activities) on our part. Mental states, it is said, are "directed at" or "of (about)" objects. Right now, say, my perceptual (visual) experience is of this cup. There is, then, an experiential state on my part, a phenomenon, that is of, or directed at, the cup. How are we to understand the relation between state and the cup in virtue of which the experiential state is "of" the cup? Or I am thinking about the cup. There is a state (activity, process) of consciousness that constitutes my thinking and is related to the cup in such a way that it is "about" or "directed at," the cup. Philosophers want an analysis of this relation, i.e., of the relation between the mental state and the object in virtue of which one is "directed at," etc., the other. The familiar problem is that the candidates for an analysis seem always to be either circular or open to counterexamples.

Apart from the relation between mental states and their objects, a question arises about the intrinsic nature of the states. What is an "experiential" state, a state of "consciousness"? Is it a state of the brain, or a state of some nonphysical entity (a soul)? If we say it is a state of the brain (that that is all that is going on here), it may seem that we are missing something essential to mind. If we say it is a state of the soul, a nonphysical entity, we are committed to a dualistic view of the world that seems at odds with the view accepted in science.

So long as the phenomenal conception of mind dominates our philosophizing about mind, so long then as our grasp of the horizonal conception remains obscure, in the background, such questions will continue to vex us. The point is not (of course) to deny that there are states, events, processes, etc., that occur or go on "in us" (in our brains and nervous systems) when we think, perceive, feel, will, and so on. It is not, in other words, to deny the validity of the phenomenal conception of mind but to open us up to a different conception of mind, a conception of which we already have an implicit grasp: a conception of mind not as something occurring in us (in our brains, or souls) or anywhere else in the world, but as that from within which the world is present/appears and to which the world is internal, as something that adds nothing to the content of the world (that could be subtracted while leaving the world as it is). This is the horizonal conception of mind. It is the conception of a subject matter that, since it is nothing itself, tends to remain hidden, the subject matter that emerges in our reflections on the DH.

Nor is the point that, once the horizonal conception of mind becomes explicit (once the subject matter of which it is the conception comes into view), the answers to the familiar philosophical questions about mind will be straightforward. Rather, our perspective on the questions will alter: either they will not arise or they will give way to different questions—which may or may not have answers.

In any case, we are not going to discuss these questions. What has immediate bearing on the theme of this book, however, and therefore should not pass without comment, is the idea (which we have more than once put forward) that even before the horizonal subject matter comes into view—even if it never comes into view (there is no law that says that it must)—it figures within us in a hidden or implicit way; that even while the phenomenal conception of mind dominates our thinking, we have implicit grasp of the horizonal conception of mind.

There is more than one way to approach this point, but let us focus on what is implicit in the phenomenal conception of mind itself. Mind, on this conception, is part of the world. So it is either (let us assume these categories are exhaustive) a physical or nonphysical (spiritual) part of the world. Mind, in other words, is part of the totality of independently existing objects and phenomena. Suppose we now ask: Of *what* is the existence of worldly objects, etc., independent? Well, it is independent of mind.[5] It follows, if mind is part of the world, that the independence of the world consists of one part existing independent of another part: the part that is other than mind exists independently of the part that is mind. Then, obviously, we have not accounted for the independence of the part of the world that is mind. For we cannot suppose that mind exists independently of mind, independently of itself.

---

[5] See, e.g., G. E. Moore's discussion of externality in his "Proof of the External World," in *Philosophical Papers* (Collier Books, 1962), pp. 142–3.

Perhaps things will work out better if we take the relevant independence to be causal independence. The world, let us suppose, is the totality, etc., that is causally independent of mind. That is, the part of the world that is mind is causally dependent on the part of the world that is not mind, but not the other way around. Thus the world (= the part other than mind) could exist in the absence of mind, whereas mind (= the part of the world that is mind) could not exist in the absence of the world (the part of the world other than mind).

The difficulty is that, given that we are conceiving of mind phenomenally, there obviously are cases in which the existence of objects and phenomena in the world are causally dependent on mind. Suppose (with the intention of causing this effect) I keep a light on by keeping my finger pressed down on a button. Then the existence of the light phenomenon depends causally on whatever state it is on my part (a state of my brain, let us assume) that is my mental state, my intending to press the button. Yet it remains true that, in the relevant sense, the light phenomenon exists *independently* of mind. What is the relevant sense? The light phenomenon exists independently in that its existence does not depend on its being present/appearing within experience (mind). But here, clearly, we have abandoned the phenomenal in favor of the horizonal conception of mind: mind as that from within which the world is present/appears: mind as the personal horizon. And mind, on this conception, is a kind of nothingness. It is nothing in itself, a subject matter that adds nothing to the world and therefore cannot be included in the world. Yet it—this subject matter—is implicit in our conception of the world (in our conception of the totality in which it cannot be included). Insofar, then, as we conceive of mind phenomenally, as part of the world, we implicitly rely on a different conception of mind, on the conception of mind as the horizon of the world.

5. The Dream Hypothesis and the Skeptical Challenge

5.1 The Skeptical Argument

Skepticism is basically a challenge, i.e., a challenge that rests on an argument. The skeptic (to characterize him in a general way) first draws our attention to something he says that we unthinkingly believe or accept, and then he argues that, on reflection, we are not justified in believing or accepting this. In light of his argument, he challenges us to produce a justification. So, the dream skeptic says that I unthinkingly accept (believe) that THIS is not a dream, that THIS is reality: I unthinkingly reject the DH. But, he says, if I reflect on what the DH means, it will be clear—here is where he gives his argument—that I am not justified in rejecting it. By our account, this means that I am not justified in accepting that there is no horizon wider than THIS; no horizon, that is, that stands to THIS in the way THIS stands to the dreams I have dreamed in the past; no wider horizon whose subject (the one at the center) would identify with me (the subject of THIS), in the way I identify with the subject of (say) my dream of the other night.[1] What is the skeptical argument?

There are two kinds of justification I might have for believing that THIS is reality (not a dream): a direct justification or an indirect justification. Generally, a justification for the belief that X is F is direct if it rests on facts about X itself; it is indirect if it rests on facts about things other than X. Clearly, an indirect justification of a belief that X is F, in addition to the facts about things other than X, must appeal to a *connection* between these facts and that of X's being F.

As an everyday example, consider what might justify the belief that my cat is hungry. A justification that appeals to the way the cat looks or how the cat is behaving, that is, to facts about the cat itself, would be a direct justification. An indirect justification would appeal to facts about things

---

[1] One might complain here that to say I "believe" or "accept" these things—that THIS is reality, that THIS is not a dream, and so on—misrepresents my actual attitude, that to speak of "belief," etc., does not capture the depth of my commitment. I agree with the complaint, but it does not affect the issue with the dream skeptic. The skeptic's concern is not with the nature of my attitude toward the DH, but with its justification.

other than the cat but which in some way connect with the cat's being hungry. Suppose, for example, I realize that I forgot to put out cat food this morning, and that the food from yesterday is all gone. Given the connection between the nonavailability of food and hunger, I would (we may assume) be indirectly justified in believing that my cat is hungry.

What kind of justification might I have for my belief that THIS is reality? It should be obvious that it could not be a direct justification. A direct justification would appeal to the character and behavior of things present in my experience and, more generally, to the character, etc., of things that are part of what I call "the world," things internal to THIS. But whether THIS is reality versus a dream is determined not by facts about things internal to THIS but by whether there is anything outside THIS—a wider horizon with its own world and space and time. Thus I could not possibly have a direct justification for a belief that THIS is reality, or that THIS is not reality (that THIS is a dream).

Notice how the argument moves from metaphysics to epistemology. Everything within my experience, everything in the world with its infinite past and future, could be just as it is even if THIS were a dream. Here we assert a metaphysical possibility. It derives from the fact that the status of THIS as dream or reality depends not on what holds inside THIS but on what holds outside THIS, on a transcendent fact. Therefore nothing I might know or find out about what holds inside THIS, about what the world and its past and future, could, of itself, justify a belief that THIS is a dream or that THIS is reality. So, given everything I know about the world and its past and future, THIS could be a dream. Here we assert an epistemological possibility.

Think of the sort of remark that teachers of philosophy commonly make in trying to convey to students the seemingly irrefutable character of dream skepticism. "It does not matter how clear and distinct and stable things are within my experience, how orderly and predictable and lawlike, and so on; this could still be a dream." What is the point of such remarks? It is not that, despite their clarity and stability and orderliness and so on, the objects and events in question might, for all I know, be dream counterfeits of real objects (events)—so that if I scrutinized things more thoroughly, or for a longer stretch of time, they might betray their counterfeit nature. The idea is (or should be) that it is possible, metaphysically, that *these very* objects, etc., with their very natures and pasts and futures, are internal to a dream. This is possible because whether these objects are dream versus real objects does not in any way depend on *them*, i.e., on anything intrinsic to the totality I call "the world" and its past and future, but, as we said, on whether there is anything outside this totality: on whether there is a transcendent world and space and time. Thus knowledge of facts about the nature and behavior of the objects in question, about their pasts and futures, could not by itself justify a belief that they, these same objects, are real versus dream objects. The metaphysics of the situation puts me in an epistemological bind.

If it is possible to justify my belief that THIS is not a dream (that THIS is reality), the justification will have to be indirect. It will have to appeal not just to facts about the objects (events) that are part of the world, but to some connection between such facts and the existence or nonexistence of a world outside THIS, a transcendent world with its transcendent space and time. Let us think about this.

Think, first, how we justify beliefs about the existence or nonexistence of things not present in experience on the basis of facts about what is present in experience. This is familiar and unproblematic. For example, I hear the shutter knocking in the next room. We may suppose, in the circumstances, this justifies my belief that there is a wind blowing outside. Or again, the shutter is not knocking. This might justify my belief that there is no wind (whenever it is windy the shutter knocks). In such a case, the justification of my existential or negative existential belief depends in an obvious way on knowledge of some natural law or theory or general causal connection or pattern under which I subsume the objects and events present to me and on which basis I infer the existence (or nonexistence) of something distinct from these objects and events. When we justify beliefs in the existence and nonexistence of things not present to us on the basis of things that are present to us, this is how proceed: by appealing to a law or theory or pattern, and so on. Is there any other way we might justify such beliefs? Do we have any other means of bridging the gulf between what is inside and outside our experience?[2]

It is sometimes said that the testimony of others—both oral and written—is independent of the kind of knowledge of theories and laws and regularities that we have been considering, and that the testimony of others may justify beliefs about the existence and nonexistence of what is not present in our experience. Now as a general point about justification and knowledge, I have sympathy with this view. But in the context of dream skepticism, it is of no use whatever. I cannot appeal to the testimony of others to refute dream skepticism. What should I do? Ask the man at the next table? Consult my newspaper? If THIS were a dream, the man and

---

[2] The point comes from Hume, who writes that when we reason to the existence (or nonexistence) of something that is present in experience, "this conclusion . . . can be founded only on the connexion of *cause* and *effect*." *A Treatise of Human Nature* (Oxford University Press, 1960), book 1, part 3, section 2. Again, he says in *An Inquiry Concerning Human Understanding* (Library of Liberal Arts Press, 1955), section 4, part 1, "If we anatomize all the other reasonings of this nature [reasonings wherein we move from what is present in experience to the existence of something not present in experience], we shall find that they are founded on the relation of cause and effect."

my newspaper would be internal to the dream. Thus the objects and events to which the man and the newspaper refer would be, like the objects and events to which I refer, internal to THIS. But what I need is a way of getting outside THIS, a way of bridging the gulf between what is inside and outside.

Let us return to the kind of indirect justification that appeals to a theory or law or regularity, etc. Certainly, whatever you say about testimony, one way we bridge the gulf between what is inside and outside experience is by appeal to such principles of connection. The problem is that in the case of the DH the gulf that I must bridge is not just between what is inside and outside my experience, but between what is inside and outside THIS—where THIS contains not just what is inside my experience but whatever has been, or might be, inside my experience: the whole of what I call "the world" with its past and future. In order to bridge the gulf from inside to outside THIS, the theory or law, etc., to which I appeal would have to connect things on both sides of this gulf, things inside and outside THIS, and there *are* no such theories or laws. A theory or law connects only things that are in the first place related in space and time, which is just what things inside and outside THIS would not be: related in space and time. If THIS were a dream, things outside THIS would have no spatial relation to *here* or temporal relation to *now*. Such things, then, could not be connected by any law or theory or pattern, etc., to things that happen inside THIS, to anything in what I call "the world," or to anything that has happened in the past or will happen in the future.

Imagine that the cup in front of me suddenly disintegrates, *here* and *now*. There could be laws or theories that, in conjunction with this fact concerning the disintegration of the cup, justify a belief about the existence or nonexistence of objects millions of miles from *here*, or millions of years before or after *now*. Far-fetched—but there could be such laws. There could not, however, be laws or theories that justify a belief about the existence or nonexistence of objects that have no spatial relation to *here*, or temporal relation to *now*. There could not be laws or theories, then, that justify me in believing that THIS is reality, or that THIS is a dream.

In sum, if we leave testimony (which, we observed, is of no help in refuting dream skepticism) aside, the indirect justification of a belief in the existence or nonexistence of something depends on a connecting law or pattern, etc., which in turn presupposes that the things thus connected belong to the same space and time. This presupposition is precisely what fails in the case of things inside and outside THIS. Thus there is no way that I might have an indirect justification for a belief that there is or is not anything outside THIS, that THIS is or is not a dream. And, as we saw, there is no way I might be directly justified in believing THIS is or not a dream. There is, it seems, no way at all I might be justified in such a belief.

5.2 The Usual Argument for Dream Skepticism; Immanent versus Transcendent Dream Skepticism

Once we are clear about the meaning of the dream hypothesis, the argument we have just given for dream skepticism should hold no surprises. It is implicit in the meaning of the hypothesis.

But this is not the argument to which philosophers usually appeal when they make out a case for dream skepticism. Recall, for example, Descartes' remark in *Meditation I* that there are no "certain indications by which we may clearly distinguish wakefulness from sleep" (3.3). By "sleep" we may take it that Descartes means dream. This suggests the following argument, which I think illustrates both how philosophers understand Descartes and how they themselves understand the argument for dream skepticism: any feature belonging to a state of wakeful experience might belong to a state of dreaming; thus, no matter how carefully I examine my current experiential state, nothing I discern in this state will guarantee that it is a state of wakefulness rather than dreaming; so I am not justified in believing that my present state is one of wakefulness, that I am now awake and not asleep (dreaming).[3]

I believe that this argument (the usual argument) involves a confusion about the first person, a confusion between the dreamer and the subject of the dream (see 2.4–5). The state that the argument asks me to examine is supposed to be a current state of mine, i.e., of the human being (or soul) that I am. The argument is that I have no way of telling whether this state of mine, my current experiential state, is a state of wakefulness or sleep (dreaming). So I do not know whether I am now awake. Now, taken in a strict and literal way, either this is just false or the argument is not about what it seems to be about: it is not about my current experiential state. In a sense, it is not about *me* at all.

---

[3] For example, Harry Frankfurt writes that Descartes is interested "in bringing out the impossibility of distinguishing, on the basis of sensory data alone, between dream experience and experience of the real world," in *Demons, Dreamers, and Madmen* (Bobbs-Merrill, 1970), p. 51. Or again, Barry Stroud, in his discussion of Descartes in chapter 1 of his book *The Significance of Philosophical Skepticism* (Oxford University Press, 1984), pp. 20–21, characterizes Descartes' situation as follows: "He realizes that his seeing his hand and seeing and feeling a piece of paper before him and feeling the warmth of the fire—in fact his getting all the sensory experiences or all the sensory information he is then getting—is something that could be happening even if he were dreaming."

Assume the argument is strictly and literally about me, the human being I am. Then, I would say, the conclusion of the argument is false. It is not true that I do not know whether I am now awake. There is no question but that I am now awake. (What I am going to say here will involve a kind of reflection that the reader should by now find familiar.)

I look at my hand. (Do this for yourself.) I bring my hand up and touch my head. I rub it a bit (to rub in, as it were, the fact that the head I am touching is *my* head). Can I doubt that the eyes in this head (*my* eyes) are open now, and that (I move the hand back before my eyes) I now see the hand (*my* hand) with which I just touched my head? If I—the human being whose head I just touched—were actually asleep now, the eyes in that head (my eyes) would not now be open (as they are open). They would be closed. They would not now be seeing (as they are seeing) the hand that just touched the head in which they are located. In other words, I would not be seeing (as I am seeing) my hand.

Let us focus for a moment on the claim that I cannot doubt that my eyes are open and that I am seeing my hand. Will not the skeptic challenge this claim? It must be stressed that the claim is not that I cannot in *any* way doubt that my eyes are now open, or that I now see my hand. But insofar as we allow that such doubts might arise, they do not lead to skepticism about whether I (the human being that I am) am awake. Suppose, for example, the skeptic asserts that, for all I can tell, I might be hallucinating. In that case, *this* object would not be my hand. I would not be seeing my hand. For argument's sake, we may grant that I cannot rule out this possibility. It will not follow that I do not know I am awake. I could be hallucinating while awake. In fact, how could I, the human being that I am (I touch my head again—just to make sure I am clear about who it is that would be hallucinating), be hallucinating unless I were awake? Of course, hallucination is as possible in a dream as in reality. A man who is asleep may dream, and the subject of his dream (the one at the center of the dream) may hallucinate in the dream. But the one who dreams the dream, the sleeping man, cannot hallucinate. For his eyes are closed, and his brain is in the state not of one who hallucinates but of one who dreams.

Yet if from the fact that I was hallucinating and hence was not seeing my hand it would not follow that I am not awake, neither does it follow from the fact that I am seeing my hand, and hence that I am awake, that the DH is false. Thus a philosopher who puts forward the above argument for dream skepticism (the argument that nothing in my present state distinguishes it as a state of wakefulness, etc.) will feel that we have somehow missed the point, that this business about my eyes being open and seeing my hand does nothing to undermine dream skepticism. And he is right. He is right, however, not because *his* argument for dream skepticism entitles him to dismiss as irrelevant to dream skepticism the fact that my eyes are open, etc., but because in an obscure way he appreciates *another* argument for dream skepticism, an argument that does render irrelevant this fact about my eyes. He lacks a clear grasp of the real argument for dream skepticism. The real argument is not an argument about *me*, the human being that I am, or about any state of this human being. More specifically, it is not an argument to the effect that the current experiential state of this human being, *my* current state, might be a state not of wakefulness but of dreaming.

The skeptical argument, correctly understood, may—or rather, should—start by admitting what I know: that my current state is one of wakefulness, that I am awake. I am awake, but, for all that, the DH might be true. Of course, if the DH were true, there would be a dreamer; so there would be a sleeper. There would, then, be someone whose state is not one of wakefulness but of sleep. But this "someone," the sleeper (dreamer), would belong to a transcendent world. He would not be *me*; his state would not be *my* state. I am awake. I am awake, but THIS might be a dream.

Dream skepticism, correctly understood, might be called *a transcendent* skepticism. It asserts that I cannot justify my belief that nothing transcends THIS, the subject matter of the DH; that I cannot justify my belief that there is no wider horizon, no wider world and space and time. In contrast, the usual argument for skepticism, if you take it strictly, leads to an *immanent* skepticism. It asserts that I cannot justify a belief I hold about a certain object—the human being that I am, that is part of the world internal to THIS; internal, therefore, to the horizon that forms the subject matter of transcendent dream skepticism—viz., the belief that that human being is awake.

My view is that, if we are clear about first-person reference in this context, we will see that immanent dream skepticism is easily refuted. I can justify in countless ways my belief that I, the human being that I am, am awake. (Look, the woman over there is complaining about her scrambled eggs. Could *I* have seen *that* were I now asleep? Could *I* have seen *anything* were I now asleep?) On the other hand, transcendent dream skepticism seems impossible to refute. I have no possible basis on which to justify my belief that THIS (which contains the complaining woman, along with everything else) is not a dream, that there is no wider horizon. I think that philosophers confuse, or conflate, these two versions of dream skepticism. When you contemplate the arguments they actually give for dream skepticism, it looks like they have in mind the immanent version. And so they do. But, at the same time, what at bottom fires their interest in dream skepticism and keeps it alive in the face of the patent falsehood of the claim that I do not know I am awake is an obscure appreciation of the transcendent version of dream skepticism.[4] (Henceforth, unless we explicitly indicate otherwise, by "dream skepticism" we shall mean transcendent dream skepticism.)

The idea that I am dreaming seems absurd (does it not?); yet something about dream skepticism will not go away. What seems absurd is immanent dream skepticism; what will not go away is transcendent dream skepticism.

5.3 The Uniqueness of Transcendent Dream Skepticism

Dream skepticism, in its transcendent form, stands apart from all the other familiar kinds of philosophical skepticism. The other kinds of skepticism challenge my right to believe some proposition or other about a subject matter internal to the subject matter of the DH. They are all, then, in contrast to dream skepticism, immanent skepticisms.

Consider, for example, skepticism about the past. Actually, there are different ways of being skeptical about the past. Perhaps it will suffice if we mention what seems the most radical way. In *The Analysis of Mind*, Russell raises the following question: How do I know that the whole world did not come into existence five minutes ago, complete with all the "records" and "traces"—including my "memories"—of the "past"?[5] I am being challenged to provide a justification for rejecting this proposition. Can I do so? This is not our present concern. We need merely observe that the skepticism implicit in Russell's question is an immanent skepticism. That is to say, it does not raise the question of how I know there is no time transcending that which includes the infinity of time before *now*, the infinite past. Rather, it challenges my beliefs about the past, my beliefs about the infinity of time before *now*.

Dream skepticism is independent of skepticism about the past. This is why, as we observed in 3.4, we are entitled in raising dream skepticism to rely on our beliefs about the past; just as we are entitled to rely on these beliefs when we consider inductive skepticism. In fact, since its purpose is to challenge the inferences we make from past to future, inductive skepti-

---

[4] Thus I agree with those philosophers who argue that we cannot doubt that we are awake, e.g., J. L. Austin, *Sense and Sensibilia* (Oxford University Press, 1962), p. 42; Norman Malcolm, *Dreaming* (Routledge and Kegan Paul, 1959), pp. 112–13; and, Bernard Williams, *Descartes* (Penguin Books, 1978), appendix 3. In effect, for one reason or another (the reasons are in each case different), these writers reject immanent dream skepticism. But, since they are not clear about the immanent/transcendent contrast, they do not see it that way: they do not see that the skepticism they reject is immanent (versus transcendent). Thus they do not see that in its transcendent form dream skepticism remains.

[5] Russell, *The Analysis of Mind* (George Allen and Unwin, 1921), chap. 9.

cism presupposes that we rely on our beliefs about the past. Inductive skepticism, like skepticism about the past, is an immanent skepticism. It arises within the subject matter whose status is the concern of dream skepticism and is thus, like skepticism about the past, independent of dream skepticism.

This should make it obvious that there is no hope of refuting dream skepticism by means of an inductive argument. Yet philosophers sometimes appeal to inductive reasoning in the attempt to refute dream skepticism. To give an example, A. J. Ayer, on the last page of his book *The Foundations of Empirical Knowledge*, writes as follows:

> So long as the general structure of my sense-data conforms to the expectations that I derive from the memory of my past experience, I remain convinced that I am not living in a dream; and the longer the series of successful predictions is extended, the smaller becomes the probability that I am mistaken.[6]

Should I then feel more convinced by lunchtime than at breakfast that THIS is not a dream? And by dinner more convinced still? Or is that the wrong time scale? Perhaps I should review the situation every year or so. This will strike us as equally absurd. Why is that?

Whatever beliefs of mine might be confirmed by the fact that "the general structure of my sense-data" continue to conform to my memory-based expectations (if there are any such beliefs), they could include only beliefs about objects in the totality I call "the world," or about the course that events will take in the future, the time after *now*. They could not include any belief whose content has implications, positive or negative, that transcend the horizon of this totality and time. Hence they could not include the belief that it, THIS, is the widest horizon; that THIS is reality, not a dream. Inductive reasoning is immanent reasoning. It may provide grounds for beliefs about what lies in the future—however far into the future we wish to consider. But it cannot provide grounds for a belief about what transcends the future, including the belief that nothing transcends the future.

Another basic and familiar kind of philosophical skepticism concerns "other minds." Let me reflect on the objects and people around me in the café. Or rather, let me reflect on the fact that I take some of the objects around me to be people, objects (let us say) with minds. The skeptic challenges me to justify drawing such a distinction. How do I rule out the hypothesis that the objects I unthinkingly regard as people are in fact sophisticated automata, mindless objects?

---

[6] *The Foundations of Empirical Knowledge* (Macmillan, 1964), p. 274.

Here again, we have a kind of immanent versus transcendent skepticism; a kind of skepticism that falls within the subject matter of the DH and is, therefore, independent of dream skepticism. Suppose THIS is reality. The question of whether any of the objects around me are people, whether they have minds or are mere objects, is not thereby settled. It remains open. Suppose THIS is dream. Would that mean that I am alone in a world of robots? No, the question still remains open. How could the fact of a transcendent world, the fact that there are transcendent objects and transcendent minds, bear on whether any of *these* objects, the objects in the world around me, have minds?

5.4 Dream Skepticism and the External World

Skepticism about other minds will come up again, but right now there is a further kind of immanent skepticism that we ought to consider: skepticism about the existence of an external world. According to the skeptic, I unthinkingly believe that the objects present in my experience are external (versus internal) objects, that they are part of what I call "the world"; so I unthinkingly believe that there are such objects. But, the skeptic argues, the objects present in my experience are universally internal. This means that if my unthinking belief in an external world is to be justified, the justification must be indirect; it must take the form of an inference based on the presence in my experience of internal objects. Of course, the skeptic maintains that any such inference is problematic, and thus that I am not justified in my unthinking belief in the existence of external things.

Given the complexity of the skeptical position here, there is more than one way of attacking it. Some philosophers (this is, no doubt, the most common reaction) question the arguments that the skeptic says establish that external objects are not what is present to me; other philosophers (e.g., Kant and, in a very different way, G. E. Moore) argue, positively, that such objects are what is present to me; other philosophers argue for this same conclusion by offering an analysis of the presence and existence of external objects in terms of the actual and possible presence of internal objects (phenomenalism); other philosophers still (e.g., Descartes, Locke, and Russell), proceeding without the benefit of any such analysis, accept that external objects are not what is present but argue that the inference to such objects can be, nonetheless, indirectly justified.

These responses to skepticism about the external world do not exhaust the possibilities. But the point for us is that the whole tangled area of debate is independent of dream skepticism. Whether THIS is a dream does not bear, one way or the other, on whether *this* is a cup (say), an external object. Similarly, if there are philosophical arguments that show that *this* is not a cup, not an external object, but an internal object (sense-datum), such arguments do nothing to settle the question of whether or not THIS is a dream, i.e., whether there is or is not a wider horizon. In short, dream skepticism is transcendent; skepticism about the external world is immanent. Dream skepticism raises the question of whether THIS, the horizon of the totality I call "the world," is the widest horizon. It leaves my knowledge of this totality, whatever it is, untouched. It leaves untouched, then, precisely the knowledge that skepticism about the external world calls into question.

Thus you could be (philosophically) a convinced dream skeptic and, at the same time, a Naive Realist. There is no inconsistency in such a position. Yet one regularly encounters in the literature on skepticism the notion that dream skepticism entails skepticism about the external world. The reasoning may be represented as follows. If THIS were a dream, the objects present in my experience would all be illusory objects. Illusory objects are not part of what I call "the world." They are internal objects, objects that exist only within my experience. Insofar, then, as I am not justified in rejecting the dream hypothesis, I am not justified in believing that there is an external world (a totality answering to what I call "the world").

Consider, for example, Descartes' move in *Meditation I* from skepticism about his senses to dream skepticism. Descartes begins his skeptical reflections by raising the possibility that, since his senses have sometimes deceived him, they might always deceive him. But he straightaway dismisses the possibility. Maybe his senses could deceive him about "things which are hardly perceptible, or very far away," but not, he says, about the "fact that I am here, seated by the fire, attired in a dressing gown, having this paper in my hands and other similar matters."[7] It would be "mad" to doubt these things; it would be "mad" to suppose that *everything* present in his experience is an illusory object. Maybe *that* thing that seems to be way off there in the distance is illusory, but not *this* thing (the piece of paper, say, in his hand).

So, as Descartes sees it, the possibility of sense deception can deliver skepticism only about this or that isolated element within his experience. The possibility of sense deception, then, does not constitute a basis for questioning the status of everything present within his experience. But of course that is what Descartes is interested in—not piecemeal or isolated doubt, but global doubt. He wants to question the status of everything that is, or might be, present within his experience. This is what lies behind his introduction of dream skepticism. Dream skepticism is global (see 4.4). At a stroke, it calls the status of everything into question.

[7] Ibid., p. 145.

Imagine that Descartes looks at the piece of paper. Could *this* object be illusory? He has just said it would be "mad" to entertain such a doubt. However, he reminds himself that "on many occasions I have in sleep been deceived by similar illusions." Descartes seems to be saying that in a dream everything within one's experience is illusory, and (putting it in our way now) he cannot exclude the possibility that THIS is a dream. Given the global implications of the DH, then, he is led to the conclusion that everything in his experience might be an illusory object, and therefore that he has no way of justifying his belief in an external world.

Now it is true, dream skepticism has global implications—but not in the way that Descartes assumes. If THIS were a dream, all the objects present in my experience would be dream versus real objects. But that is just to say that they would be objects internal to a dream versus reality. From this you cannot, as Descartes tries to do, extract the conclusion that all these objects, i.e., the objects present in my experience, would be *illusory* versus real objects. Descartes, in effect, is conflating two contrasts: the real/dream object contrast and the real/illusory object contrast (see 4.4). If THIS were a dream, everything within my experience would be a dream object. Everything in what I call "the world" would be a dream object. But the division between real and illusory objects would be just as it is. *This* object, for example, would be (just as it is) a cup, a real object.

Dream skepticism calls everything into question. But in a way it leaves everything as it is: it does not touch my knowledge of the external world. This is what philosophers often miss. They ask (in effect), "Can I be sure THIS is not a dream?" and if the answer is "No" they take *that* as a reason for being unsure about the existence of an external world.

Here is another example. It comes from G. E. Moore's paper "Proof of an External World." Before giving his "proof," Moore explains what he means by "external thing" or "external object." His explanation is basically the same as the one we have been using: an external object is an object whose existence is independent of its presence in experience. He says that there are "all kinds of" ordinary things that fit this explanation, so that to prove external things exist, all he has to do is to prove that one such ordinary thing exists. The method of proof Moore advocates is simple. You just point to or hold up an instance of a kind of ordinary thing. So Moore holds up his hand and says, "Here is one hand." He then goes on to say, however, that whether the proof works depends on whether he *knows* that he has actually exhibited a hand. He admits, though, that he cannot *prove* that he has actually exhibited a hand. To prove that, he says,

I should need to prove, for one thing, as Descartes pointed out, that I am not now dreaming. But how can I prove that I am not? I have, no doubt, conclusive reasons for asserting that I am not now dreaming; I have conclusive evidence that I am awake; but that is a very different thing from being able to prove it. I could not tell you what all my evidence is; and I should have to do this at least, in order to give you proof.[8]

Yet Moore asserts that, despite being unable to prove it, he does know that (to put it our way) THIS is not a dream. (He observes that you do not have to be able to prove everything you know.) So, he concludes, his "proof" of an external world is safe against the dream objection.

The interesting thing for us is that he regards it as an objection. Moore seems to be thinking like this: "If being unable to prove that THIS is not a dream entailed not knowing that THIS is not a dream, it would also entail not knowing that here is a hand; so I would have failed to prove the existence of an external thing. But I *do* know, even though I cannot prove it, that THIS is not a dream. So, even though I cannot prove that THIS is not a dream, my knowledge that here is a hand is not threatened; and if my knowledge that here is a hand is not threatened, then, since a hand is an external object, neither is my proof that there exists an external object."

Why does Moore think that not knowing that THIS is not a dream, that THIS is reality, would mean not knowing that here is a hand? Like Descartes, he is (I think) assuming that if THIS were a dream, the objects in his experience would all be illusory. If THIS were a dream, *this* would not be a hand (it would be an illusory object). As we said, Moore seems to be making the same mistake as Descartes. He is conflating the status of being a dream object (an object internal to a dream) with that of being an illusory object. I examine my hand. If THIS were a dream, would the object I am examining, *this* object, be any less of a hand? Would it be of the order of an image, an internal object of some kind? No, it would be just what it is. It would be just as real, that is, just as independent of its presence in my experience, as it is in reality. Whatever else you think of Moore's proof, he might have saved himself this worry about dreaming. If the proof works in reality, it would work in a dream.

5.5 Nozick on the Tank Hypothesis

To summarize, I can (easily) justify rejecting the immanent hypothesis that I (the human being that I am) am dreaming, but not, it seems, the transcendent hypothesis that THIS is a dream. On the other hand, the fact that I cannot justify rejecting the transcendent hypothesis does not threaten my knowledge of an external world. We might say that, in this respect, dream skepticism is both vindicated and disarmed.

---

[8] "Proof of an External World," in *Philosophical Papers* (Collier Books, 1962), p. 148.

The reader will perhaps notice a similarity between the position we have reached and the view developed by Robert Nozick in chapter 3 of his book *Philosophical Explanations*. For the most part, what Nozick actually talks about is not the DH but the "tank hypothesis" (as we might call it). This is, as Nozick formulates it (adjusting the details), the hypothesis that I am floating in a tank on Alpha Centauri with my brain being stimulated in such a way as to make me believe all the things I actually believe, e.g., that I am sitting in a café in London. However, at several points Nozick mentions the DH, and it is pretty clear that, from the standpoint of skepticism, he regards it as equivalent to the tank hypothesis (TH). This view of the two hypotheses seems correct. Imagine watching someone whose brain is hooked up in the manner envisioned by the TH. It would be like watching someone we know to be dreaming. In the latter case, the person would be having a natural dream; in the former, a directly induced and controlled dream—a "tank dream." In both cases you can think of things from the standpoint of the subject of the dream, the one at the center. And if in the tank case you do that, you can have the thought, "Perhaps that is my situation. Perhaps I am the subject of a tank dream." This should bring out the equivalence of the two hypotheses from the standpoint of skepticism. Nozick argues, first, that I cannot refute the TH, but second, that I do know that I am sitting in a café in London. More generally, I cannot refute the TH, but my knowledge of the external world is (for all we need say) what I take it to be. Is this not more or less what we have argued in the case of the (transcendent) DH?

But the similarity is only at the surface. Nozick's view rests on an analysis of knowledge. Our view rests on an analysis of the DH.

Nozick's analysis of knowledge, roughly, is that I know that p just in case I believe that p, it is true that p, and my belief "tracks" the truth (had it been false that p, I would not have believed that p; had it been true that p, I would have believed that p).[9] Nozick claims to draw a rather surprising consequence from this analysis. He argues—the argument depends ultimately on certain delicate judgments in the possible-world semantics underlying the counterfactuals he uses to explicate the idea of "tracking"— that it is a consequence of the analysis that, if I know that p and that p entails q, it does not follow that I know that q. Knowledge, as Nozick puts it, is "not closed under known logical implication." Hence, if I do not know that q, yet do know that p entails q, it will not follow that I do not know that p. So it is compatible with my knowing that p that I both know that p entails q and do not know whether it is the case that q.[10]

[9] *Philosophical Explanations* (Oxford University Press, 1981), pp. 172–78.
[10] Ibid., pp. 204–11.

This is the key point in Nozick's position regarding tank skepticism and skepticism about the external world. If you reflect on it, the point is (as critics have observed) difficult in its own right. But the criticism I wish to make of Nozick's position is independent of his analysis of knowledge. So let us give him the point about nonclosure.

The skeptic, Nozick maintains, is right in asserting that I do not know that I am not floating in a tank on Alpha Centauri with my brain being stimulated to make me believe I am sitting in a café in London. For all I know, the tank hypothesis may be true. For, if it were true, I would not believe that I was floating in a tank, etc. I would believe just what I actually believe: that I am sitting in a café in London, and all the rest. This is part of the hypothesis. The skeptic is also right, Nozick says, in supposing that I know that if I were floating in a tank, etc., I would not be sitting in a café in London. His mistake is to think it follows from this (that is, from the fact that I do not know whether TH is false, and the fact that I do know that if the TH were true, I would not know what I believe to be true about the external world) that I do not know that I am sitting in a café in London. Once we see that knowledge is not closed under known logical implication, we see that this does not follow.[11]

On Nozick's view, then, someone who thinks that tank skepticism entails skepticism about the external world is mistaken about what knowledge involves. Since he mistakenly thinks that knowledge is closed under known logical implication, he mistakenly concludes that my inability to refute the TH entails that I do not know any of the things I take myself to know about the external world, including myself. Now, the assumption here is that *if* the TH were *true*, I would *not* be sitting in a café in London. It is in the face of the seemingly obvious incompatibility between the TH and such everyday beliefs about the external world that Nozick's point regarding nonclosure is meant to save us from skepticism about the external world. The truth, however, is that there is no incompatibility between the TH and our beliefs about the external world. Once this emerges, the point about nonclosure, whether or not we find it plausible, becomes gratuitous. Nozick's conclusion is correct: it is a mistake to think that tank skepticism entails skepticism about the external world. But the mistake lies not in a faulty conception of knowledge, i.e., in the failure to grasp the point regarding nonclosure, but in the failure to grasp the true meaning of the TH.

More specifically, the TH, like the DH (they are essentially the same hypothesis) is a transcendent hypothesis. It contemplates a possibility not about *me*, the human being that I am, but about THIS, the horizon of

[11] Ibid., p. 207.

which I am at the center—viz., the possibility that there is a horizon wider than THIS, a horizon with its own world and space and time.

If you take Nozick's formulation of the TH in a strict and literal way, it seems to be an immanent hypothesis. Who is it that would be in the tank? Does not the hypothesis make it perfectly clear? *I* would be in the tank. Who am I? I am *this* human being. So, if we accept the argument for tank skepticism, it follows that, for all I can tell, I, the human being in question, might now be in a tank on Alpha Centauri. It is hard to know what to make of this. Here I am, surrounded by familiar objects and people, in a café where I have probably been a hundred times before, in a city where I have lived for many years, and the suggestion is that for all I know I may be floating in liquid, in a tank, on a body light years away from Earth.

Perhaps the response will be as follows: "Of course, you *believe* you are surrounded by familiar objects, and so on. But what does that prove? So much follows from the TH itself. It is part of the hypothesis that, although you are in a tank on Alpha Centauri, your brain is being stimulated to make you believe you are leading a normal sort of life in London."

Whose brain would it be that is being stimulated? My brain. *My* brain? The brain *up here* inside *this* head (I touch it), *my* head? In that case, there is no difficulty refuting the TH. It is an immanent hypothesis and, as such, it can be refuted as easily as the hypothesis that I am dreaming. In the latter case, I need only remind myself that my eyes are open, that I see the objects around me. In the case of the TH, all that is required is that I reach up and feel about my head for wires and electrodes, etc. There are none. Could it be that the stimulation of my brain is by means of radio waves? Then I might set about looking for the transmitter. Would Nozick allow that my failure to find evidence of a transmitter goes any way at all toward refuting the TH? Surely he would insist that it is irrelevant whether or not I find wires or a transmitter. You could put it like this. If I did find wires, etc., they would not be the relevant wires; they would not be the wires that according to the hypothesis, are instrumental in causing my belief that I am sitting in a café in London. The instrumental wires would attach not to *this* head but to a transcendent head—a head that is part of a world outside THIS, outside the horizon of what I call "the world."

It is hard to believe that at some level Nozick is not aware of all this. Thus, as we just remarked, it seems clear he would say that my not being able to find any wires attached to *this* head (my head) would have no tendency whatever to refute the TH. But then there is a confusion here (the same kind of confusion that we have been encountering all along). For it also seems clear that, as he actually expresses it, Nozick conceives of the TH as a hypothesis about me, and my head; i.e., as an immanent hypothesis. If he did not conceive of it in this way, as an immanent hypothesis, why would he suppose that the TH is incompatible with my belief that I am sitting in a café in London? Conceived transcendently, the TH is not incompatible with this belief, or with any of the other beliefs I have about the external world (including myself).

Like Descartes and Moore—indeed, like just about every philosopher who discusses the TH/DH—Nozick is, I believe, confusedly viewing the TH in two ways at once, as both an immanent and a transcendent hypothesis. To the extent that he treats the hypothesis as incompatible with our everyday beliefs about the external world, he is thinking of it as an immanent hypothesis. But the fact that he would not (as I take it he would not) allow that the hypothesis can be refuted by the kind of simple-minded procedures indicated above betrays a submerged recognition of its transcendent character.

Let us, in conclusion, focus briefly on the supposed incompatibility between the TH and our beliefs about the external world. Nozick heightens our sense of an incompatibility here by the extra touch of building into the hypothesis the idea that the tank I am in is on Alpha Centauri. Why so far away? Well, my belief is that I am in a café in London. Could I, one and the same human being, be in London and on Alpha Centauri? (Nozick's own example is that he believes he is in a library in Jerusalem—equally far, I guess, from Alpha Centauri.) But once we are clear about the true meaning of the TH, it should be clear that Alpha Centauri is not far away enough. However far away it is, it is at a distance from *here*. So, in principle, I could get to it (see chapter 2). And what, on the tank hypothesis, should I expect to find if I got there? *Myself*? Hooked up to wires and floating in a tank?

To repeat: insofar as Nozick would not accept that the TH can be refuted by (say) my groping about my head for wires, he seems to appreciate the transcendent character of the hypothesis; however, insofar as he regards the TH as standing in conflict with my ordinary beliefs about myself and other objects in what I call "the world," he treats it as an immanent hypothesis. The latter point is, really, the nub of the issue. Most philosophers, when reflecting on the TH/DH, proceed as if it were perfectly obvious that the hypothesis stands in conflict with our ordinary beliefs about ourselves and the world. They take it as obvious because they do not clearly grasp the meaning of the hypothesis. On the TH, THIS, the horizon of what I call "the world," would have the status of a dream (a tank dream, as we put it): a dream the dreaming of which is the result of stimuli being fed into the brain of someone floating in a tank. But *I* (JV, the human being that I am) would not be the one floating in the tank, and the tank would not be located on Alpha Centauri. The tank dreamer, along with his tank, would belong to a transcendent world, whereas the world around *me*, the totality I call "the world," would be internal to the tank dream. And the world around me would include Alpha Centauri. That is, Alpha Centauri would be "out there," light years away, within the tank-dream. Just as it is in reality. Where would I be? Just where I am in reality. In a café in London, contemplating the tank hypothesis.[12]

---

[12] Similar considerations make clear what is wrong with Hilary Putnam's provocative argument that if I were a brain in a vat, then, since what my words (as I think them) mean depends on the kinds of objects that are in general available to me, if I think "I am a brain in a vat," I would think something false. Putnam argues that, on the vat hypothesis, the objects available would not be ordinary external objects but image-objects. So what I would mean by "brain" and "vat" would not be *brains* or *vats* but (let us say) image-brains and image-vats. However, it would, given the vat hypothesis, be false that I am an *image-brain* in an *image-vat*. *Reason, Truth and History* (Cambridge University Press, 1981), pp. 12–17. There are a number of things we might query here, but let me simply point out that, if we understand the vat hypothesis in the right way, it is not touched by Putnam's argument. The main thing to appreciate is that, properly understood, the vat hypothesis is not the hypothesis that *I* am a brain in a vat, or again, that *my* brain is a brain in a vat. On the vat hypothesis, I remain exactly who I am, JV, the one at the center of THIS, the horizon. And the world available to me remains exactly what it is. So, given Putnam's idea about meaning, by "I am a brain in a vat" I would mean what I would in any case mean. Of course, what I would mean is false. (My brain, JV's brain, is not in a vat.) In a way, then, Putnam's conclusion is correct. However, the falsehood of what I would mean is not, as he suggests, due to the fact that I would mean something about an image-brain and an image-vat. On the contrary, it is due to the fact that I would mean something about a brain, JV's brain (the one "up here"), and about an ordinary vat. On the other hand, if it is properly understood, the vat hypothesis is not thereby shown to be false. For the vat hypothesis (properly understood) is not the hypothesis that my brain, JV's brain, is in a vat, but, rather, the hypothesis, first, that there is transcendent world, a world outside THIS; second, that there is in the transcendent world a brain maintained and stimulated in vat; and third, that the transcendent brain-in-a-vat setup is responsible for there being such a thing as THIS, with the world (including JV and his brain) internal to it. In short, properly understood, the vat hypothesis is not an immanent but a transcendent hypothesis.

I am, let us imagine, looking at a brain in a vat. I know that, given how the brain is being stimulated, there is a horizon of which someone is at the center, the subject. The world spreading out around *me* (the one at the center of THIS)—the world that includes the brain in the vat—is, for the vat subject (the one at the center of the vat dream), a transcendent world. In raising the vat hypothesis I raise, in effect, the hypothesis that my situation is analogous to that of the vat subject, the subject whose horizon, along with the world internal to it (including the vat subject) exists because of this brain at which I am looking; the hypothesis that there is a world that transcends the totality I call "the world" in the same way that *that* totality transcends the horizon of the vat subject.

6. Responding to Dream Skepticism

6.1 Is the Dream Hypothesis a Pseudo Hypothesis?

Dream skepticism challenges us to justify rejecting the DH in the face of an argument whose conclusion is that we have no justification. Notice, the dream skeptic can acknowledge that we find the DH "impossible to believe." He may acknowledge that he himself finds it impossible to believe. But finding the DH impossible to believe does not amount to having a justification for rejecting (disbelieving) the hypothesis (a justification for believing that THIS is not a dream but reality). The DH may never occur to us. And if it does occur to us, we may dismiss it as impossible to believe. But, the skeptic says, whether the hypothesis occurs to us not, and whether if it occurs to us we find it impossible to believe, it seems (in light of the argument) that we have no justification for rejecting the DH. How—if we are not content simply to repeat that we find the hypothesis impossible to believe—should we respond to this?

One thing we might wonder about is why, or in what sense, we find it "impossible to believe" the DH. If I say that I find it impossible to believe that X could have stolen your wallet, this might be based on my personal knowledge of X. There are facts about X's character and past behavior, etc., in light of which I find it impossible to believe that X is a thief. In such a case, I find it "impossible to believe" that p because of overwhelming evidence against its being the case that p. But this is a justification for rejecting the hypothesis that p, which is just what we do not have in the case of the DH. I do not have overwhelming evidence for rejecting the DH. I do not have any evidence at all for rejecting the DH.

Nor could I have. The possibility of E—where E is something present/appearing within my experience—counting as evidence for the hypothesis H depends on there being some kind of real (causal, lawlike etc.) connection, direct or indirect, between E and the truth of H. But in this case, since H is a transcendent hypothesis (viz., the hypothesis of a transcendent world with its own infinity of space and time), there is no possibility of any such connection (5.1). For the same reason, there is no way that the truth of the DH might contribute to an explanation of E; no way, in fact, that the truth of the DH could make any difference at all within my experience. One may in light of this be tempted to suggest that the DH is an empirically empty (meaningless) hypothesis.

Of course, the same might be said of analytically/logically/mathematically necessary truths and falsehoods. But the DH does not fall into this category. If it is true, the DH is contingently true. It is a contingent but empirically empty hypothesis. This might seem to place it in the category of what some philosophers regard as pseudo hypotheses—like, for example, the hypothesis that while we were asleep everything doubled in size, or simultaneously shifted eight inches to the right.[1] The point is not that I should suspend belief about the DH (I might suspend belief in the case of an empirically meaningful hypothesis), but that it is, in the first place, a mistake to raise the question of whether the DH should be believed or not. The idea would be that this is why we find the DH impossible to believe.

Notice, if the DH is a pseudo hypothesis, it is correct to say that I am "not justified" in rejecting (disbelieving) it. But the reason would be very different from the case where I am "not justified" in rejecting an empirically meaningful hypothesis (the case, say, where the evidence is too uncertain to justify a rejection). Suppose I am a citizen of Country C and have been put in prison or have no fixed address. Then I may be legally deprived of the right to vote. But if I am not a citizen of C, although I "do not have the right" to vote in C, there is no right of which I am being legally deprived. Similarly, if the DH is a pseudo hypothesis, whereas it follows that I have no justification for rejecting it, there is nothing, i.e., no justification, of which I am epistemically deprived.[2] Not being able to justify rejecting a pseudo hypothesis does not constitute an epistemic deprivation.

This provides a possible response to dream skepticism. Dream skepticism is correct when it says that I lack a justification for rejecting the DH. But, since it fails to appreciate that the DH is a pseudo hypothesis (that it is not an appropriate object of belief), it mistakenly regards this lack as an epistemic deprivation.

What renders a contingent hypothesis empirically empty and thus a pseudo hypothesis is, as anyone who is familiar with the history of the

---

[1] Let us take these familiar examples as suggestive and not worry about whether, as they stand, they are in fact empirically empty. Thus, e.g., once we recognize that taking measurements of objects would not provide evidence against the doubling hypothesis (our yardsticks would have doubled in size), to preserve the empirical emptiness of the doubling hypothesis we would have to qualify the hypothesis (say by assuming changes in the gravitational constant) in a manner that would compensate for the fact that if bodies double in size, their mass, and hence the forces they exert, would much more than double, which would in turn have obvious experiential implications.

[2] In the voting case I might acquire citizenship in C, which possibility has no analogue in the epistemic case. Nonetheless, the point of the analogy should be clear.

verificationist theory of meaning will know, a topic with many twists and turns—which we shall not attempt to follow. The real question is not whether, if it is empirically empty, the DH is a pseudo hypothesis, but whether the DH is empirically empty. Does it not, after all, have a kind of empirical meaning?

If you look at it one way, the DH seems empirically empty. So much follows from its transcendent character, from the fact that it envisions the possibility of a horizon outside THIS, a wider horizon with its own world and space and time—a possibility whose obtaining or nonobtaining could make no difference from within THIS. Yet implicit in this same possibility is the possibility that I might emerge from THIS, from the horizon hypothesized to be a dream. If THIS is a dream, I might emerge from the dream. I might emerge from the dream, that is, into a wider horizon. Of course (as we explained) it would not be me, i.e., *this* human being, JV, who would awake. The one who would awake would be the one who sleeps and dreams the dream, whereas I, JV, the one at the center of THIS, am not asleep. The sleeper, the one who would awake if THIS were a dream, would belong to a transcendent world, the world of the wider horizon. My dream of other night was displaced by THIS. I look back now on that dream and "identify" with the one at the center, the subject of the dream. When I think that if THIS were a dream I might emerge, etc., I contemplate an analogous possibility: that there is a wider horizon, a horizon that might displace THIS in the way THIS displaced my dream of the other might; that the subject of the wider horizon might look back on THIS in the way I look back on that dream; that the subject of the wider horizon might "identify" with me, the one at the center of THIS, in the way now I "identify" with the subject (the one at the center) of that dream.

Thus while there is no way the truth or falsehood of the DH could register within THIS, within my experience, the hypothesis nonetheless envisions an experiential possibility, the possibility of a wider experiential horizon. This distinguishes it from the empty hypotheses that we mentioned above, e.g., the hypothesis that everything has doubled in size. Such hypotheses, notice, concern possibilities about the world, about the totality internal to THIS. The experiential possibilities relevant to their meaning, then, are possibilities that exist from within THIS, from within my experience. Since the hypotheses are contrived to exclude such possibilities, there is no quarter from which they might draw experiential meaning. The DH, in contrast, draws its experiential meaning from a transcendent possibility. Insofar as the possibility that it envisions transcends my experience, the DH is empty; insofar as the envisioned possibility is experiential, however, the hypothesis has experiential meaning. And insofar as it has experiential meaning, it cannot be regarded as a pseudo hypothesis.

6.2 Whether It Would Matter if THIS Were a Dream

Closely related to the idea that the DH lacks experiential content and is thus a pseudo hypothesis is another response we may have to dream skepticism, viz., that—granting the skeptical argument that I cannot justify rejecting the hypothesis—whether the DH is true or false does not matter to me. It does not matter because it would not matter if the DH were true. For all I know, THIS is a dream. The response is a metaphysical shrug of the shoulders: What would it matter? With this thought we turn away from the possibilities of experience (of appearing and presence); it is the possibilities of *value* that now concern us. The DH, we may agree, has a kind of experiential meaning. Yet, in another sense, whether it is true or false does not mean anything. It has, we may say, a kind of experiential meaning but no valuational meaning.

Such is the thought behind the present response to dream skepticism. The skeptic's argument is allowed to stand. (So the response is not antiskeptical.) But, we say, the skeptic's conclusion means nothing to us: it is devoid of valuational meaning. The antiskeptic (as we presented him) is interested in experiential emptiness. If the DH is experientially (empirically) empty, it is not a proper object of belief. In contrast, that the DH is valuationally empty does not entail that it is not a proper object of belief. Then on what basis do we dismiss dream skepticism?

Well, if it does not matter whether THIS is dream, then it does not matter. Hence the skeptical conclusion—that we are not justified in rejecting the DH—does not matter. And if does not matter, it does not matter. The fact of its valuational emptiness speaks for itself. Is this not a basis for dismissing dream skepticism?

But apart from the nagging thought that the skeptical conclusion remains, is it really true that it would not matter if THIS were a dream? There may be a parallel here with what we said about the antiskeptical position. Just as the transcendent implications of the DH give it a kind of experiential content or meaning, despite its valuational emptiness the DH has a transcendent valuational meaning. Thus if we imagine believing the DH, it may first strike us that it would not matter if THIS is a dream. But then it may strike us that nothing could matter more! Why is that?

Why am I inclined in the first place to say that it would not matter if THIS were a dream? It is because everything that matters to me is internal to THIS. Let me try to give an indication of what matters to me. (You will find nothing eccentric here.) The fate of my family matters to me. And the fate of others I know well and care about. And that of others I do not know well, or do not know at all, but care about in an abstract fellow-human way. So I am concerned about all the things that may bear, one way or another on these fates. Then too, of course, I have a special concern regarding my own personal fate (the fate of JV), and the things on which it depends. Moreover, with respect to others, my concern is not spread evenly: the fates of some people matter to me much more than those of other people. Basically, though, what matters to me are the fates of human beings and what affects these fates.

What about the fates of animals other than human beings? And the planet we live on? Say I am bothered by what I read about the apparently irreversible destruction of the environment. Does this rest on concern for the fate of animal life, ultimately on concern for the fate of human beings? Perhaps it all rests on concern about my own fate and that of the few human beings with whom I am personally involved. No, it does not seem like that—though it is not easy to say how it does seem.

However, the precise boundary and structure of my concern is not important. The important thing in the present context is that whatever the boundary and structure of my concern, the fates of the things (the creatures and objects, etc.) that concern me are fates of things that belong to what I call "the world." So the fates that concern me (including my personal fate, the fate of JV) are fates of things internal to THIS. The fates that concern me are all internal to the subject matter of the DH: to that which, if THIS were a dream, would be the dream. However wide the boundary of my concern is drawn, it will be drawn within THIS.

Consider my aims, and the things that I would like to see happen. As *aims*, etc., these relate to the future. But the future, the time after *now*, is internal to THIS, to the horizon that forms the subject matter of the dream hypothesis. Everything that matters is internal to this horizon. All value is internal to THIS.

The sense in which it would not matter if THIS were a dream should now be clear. On the DH, there is a wider horizon, with its own world and space and time: a transcendent world and space and time. Could it matter to me whether there is such a world, etc.? Everything that matters to me is internal to THIS. If everything that matters to me is internal to THIS, how could it matter whether there is anything that transcends THIS? If everything that matters is internal to THIS, then whether anything transcends THIS does not matter.

The horizon to which the world, etc., is internal is the horizon of whatever has importance and value. When I am struck by this fact, I am inclined to say, "It would not matter if THIS is a dream." Clearly, this metaphysical shrug of the shoulders is very different from dismissing a possibility as unimportant in everyday life. In the latter case the point is not that the possibility we are dealing with stands outside the horizon of what has importance, but that, though internal to this horizon, it does not bear on or affect anything of importance. Thus, in the everyday case, what is unimportant now might, given the right circumstances, become important in the future. Or, though it no longer is, it might have been important in the past. In the transcendent case, there is no such possibility, since the past and future are themselves internal to the horizon by reference to which the transcendent case is transcendent.

Yet, assuming we can conjure up a sense of what it would be like actually to believe the DH, I think we can conjure up a sense in which this would matter. In fact, the reason it would matter (in the way it would matter) involves the same fact that we take account of in explaining why it would not matter (in the way it would not matter).

Consider a past dream. Dreams have a way of haunting and puzzling us. Thus we ask what our dreams signify. Dreams are a source of clues for understanding ourselves. In this sense, the events in a past dream may be important to me: they may tell me something about myself. But whatever importance to me the events in a past dream may have, this is set against the background of the fact that they are events in a dream and thus *do not matter at all*. Why do they not matter? Why, for example, do the events in my dream the other night not matter? (Why do I say, "It was only a dream"?) In a way, the question answers itself. The events in my dream the other night do not matter for no other reason than that they are events *in a dream*. That is to say, they do not matter because they are events within a displaced horizon: a horizon that has been displaced by THIS, the horizon of everything that matters. If everything that matters is internal to THIS, what is internal to the horizon that has been displaced by THIS does not matter.

Suppose now, shifting the perspective, I have brought myself to take seriously the possibility that THIS is a dream. Then I must take seriously the possibility of my emerging from THIS: the possibility, that is, of a horizon that would displace THIS and whose subject would "identify" with *me* in the way I now "identify" with the subject of my dream of the other night: the possibility, then, of a horizon from the standpoint of which the events within THIS, the events of my life, would fall outside the horizon of importance and thus would not matter at all in the same total and absolute way that, from the standpoint of THIS, the events in my dream of the other night do not matter at all. But THIS, as we have said, contains everything that matters. What I contemplate, then, if I take seriously the possibility that THIS is a dream, is the possibility *that everything that matters might not matter*, that it might be of no importance at all. Viewed in this light, all value, the mattering of everything that matters, becomes precarious. Would this not, in its own way, matter? It may seem, as we put it, that nothing could matter more.

Perhaps it will be clear now what we meant in saying that the reason it would matter if THIS were a dream involves the same fact to which we have reference in explaining why it would not matter. The reason it would not matter is that everything that matters is internal to THIS. So, in the nature of the case, it would matter whether anything transcends THIS, whether THIS is a dream. But then, if THIS is a dream, I face the possibility of a total displacement of value: everything that matters might not matter. And that seems (in its own way) to matter.

With respect to both meaning and value, then, the DH may evoke ambivalence. Thus we may at first wish to say that the DH is devoid of experiential content, that whether it is true does not matter; but then it may strike us that the hypothesis does have a kind of experiential content or meaning, that in a way it would matter if it were true. In the case of experiential content, we contrasted the DH with the doubling hypothesis. The latter, we said, has no kind of experiential meaning. Here there is no ambivalence. It might be of interest to consider briefly whether there are valuational analogues of this case: hypotheses as devoid of valuational meaning as the doubling hypothesis is devoid of experiential meaning.

I toy with the hypothesis, say, that a thousand years ago a fly landed on this spot. Would it matter? But this is not a genuine analogue of the doubling hypothesis. We can imagine (I leave this to the reader) far-fetched circumstances in which it would matter about the fly.

A better example of what we are looking for is the following. Suppose that friends and family systematically lie to me about things that greatly affect my self-esteem. If I knew the truth, it would make me terribly unhappy, but it is part of the hypothesis that in fact I will never find out the truth. Would this matter to me? The answer may seem obvious. If by hypothesis I never find out, how could it matter? This makes the lie hypothesis seem like a value analogue of the doubling hypothesis. Note too that, like the doubling hypothesis, the lie hypothesis is not transcendent. The lie that I am told concerns objects and phenomena that are internal to THIS, objects, etc., that are part of what I call "the world." The truth behind the lie is a truth that holds in the world—a truth that, though kept hidden from me, is internal to the horizon that, for me, contains everything that matters.

The analogy is not complete, however. In fact, the lie hypothesis seems to generate an ambivalence resembling that which occurs in the case of the DH. Thus we may feel that there is a way or sense in which it would "matter to me" that I am lied to, and further that the very fact that it would not matter to me in the way it would not matter, so far from draining the lie of importance, is part of what gives it the peculiar kind of importance it has; for that I never find out means, we might say, that my whole life rests on a lie. Is there not a sense in which this matters, i.e., a sense in which it matters *to me*? It is precisely because it does not matter in the other sense that in this sense it matters so much. For it is precisely because it in no way matters in the other sense that my life rests on a lie. What could matter more?

In sum, whereas the parallel between experiential content and value holds at the transcendent level, at the immanent level it breaks down: there does not seem to be a value analogue of the empty doubling hypothesis. At least this is true: the example that at first seems like an analogue gives rise, on reflection, to the same sort of ambivalence that we find at the transcendent level. We shall not speculate on the source of this disanalogy.

6.3 The General Form of My Response to the Dream Hypothesis

I find it impossible (do we not all find it impossible?) to believe the DH. Why this is so would be clear if I had overwhelming evidence (or some powerful argument) against the hypothesis; but, as the skeptical argument makes clear, I have no evidence (or argument) at all. Again, if despite being contingent the hypothesis were devoid of experiential content, if it were a pseudo hypothesis, this too would—in a different way—explain the impossibility of believing it. But the DH has a kind of experiential meaning: it is a genuine hypothesis. Similarly, it has a kind of valuation meaning. Thus I cannot dismiss the DH by saying that, although it is a genuine hypothesis, it would not matter if the THIS were a dream. It would (in its own way) matter.

If the DH is a genuine hypothesis, it is an appropriate object of belief. It is an appropriate object of belief and yet it seems impossible to believe. Is the DH self-evidently false? But then its falsehood would be necessary— which it is not. If it is false, it is contingently false. Then why (once again), or in what sense, is it impossible to believe?

The answer to this question, or the general form of the answer, is, I think, as follows. Although I have no evidence on which to reject the DH, there is something else that I believe, another proposition to which I am committed, which excludes the truth of the DH. The other proposition, although incompatible with the DH, is not an evidential proposition. It does not express evidence either against the DH or for the "hypothesis" that THIS is reality (the RH). It is, rather, a proposition on the same level as the DH/RH. Insofar as I am committed to this other proposition and appreciate that it excludes the truth of the DH, I cannot—I find it *rationally impossible to*—believe that the DH might be true.

Let us call the proposition whose truth excludes the truth of the DH "(O)." In advance of actually stating (O) and spelling out its content, let us develop further the form of the overall epistemic situation. (This will be abstract, and it may not mean too much at first.) If proposition (O) is true, the DH is false; i.e., the RH is true. However, the truth of the RH does not entail the truth of (O). In other words, (O) entails that THIS is reality (it excludes the truth of the DH hypothesis), but that THIS is reality does not entail (O). Thus whereas, given my commitment to (O) and my perception that (O) excludes the truth of the DH (we will not always mention the second point), it is rationally impossible for me to believe that the DH might be true, it would, were I not independently committed to (O), be rationally possible for me both to believe (as I do) that the DH is false and yet to be unsure (which I am not) about the truth value of (O).

Then why, you might wonder, do I not simply cite (O) by way of justifying my belief that THIS is reality? It has to do, as we shall see, with the peculiar content of (O). Obviously the content of (O) must differ from that of the RH; otherwise there would not be the one-way entailment. Yet (O) and the RH are (like (O) and the DH) propositions at the same level. (O) is, in its own way, a transcendent proposition. Hence, as in the case of the RH, calling (O) into question leaves everything as it is; everything, that is, within THIS, the subject matter of the RH. Hence too, (O) is, in its own way, as vulnerable to skepticism as the RH. So although my commitment to (O) makes it rationally impossible to believe the DH, it cannot be thought to justify this attitude. Were I to offer (O) in justification of my commitment to the RH (my rejection of the DH), the skeptic would demand the justification for my commitment to (O)—which I could not give him. I live with a commitment to (O), but I cannot justify it. Thus when I appeal to (O) by way of responding to dream skepticism, I am, from a skeptical point of view, merely transferring the burden from one commitment to another. I do not justify my rejection of the DH, but, as we might say, "rationally explain" it.[3]

Yet that such a transfer, and such an explanation, is possible (if it is) is a matter of real interest, since the fact that there is at the level of the DH/RH a proposition *other* than the RH that I believe, and believing which makes it rationally impossible to believe the DH, this is by no means philosophically obvious. Have we not, in the argument for dream skepticism, already taken account of everything—i.e., everything relevant—that I believe?

Note, finally, the asymmetry between my commitment to (O) and to the RH—the fact that believing (O) rationally explains my commitment

---

[3] We ought to remark on a possible ambiguity in what is meant here by being a "skeptic." In one sense, I am a dream skeptic: I accept that I cannot justify my rejection of the DH. I think I can rationally explain it, but I cannot justify it. If, however, a dream skeptic is someone who not only cannot justify rejecting the DH but for that reason takes seriously the possibility that the DH is true, then I am not a dream skeptic. I find it impossible, rationally impossible, to allow (seriously) that THIS might be a dream. I think everyone finds it impossible. So I think that there are no dream skeptics in the second sense.

to the RH, my rejection of the DH, but not the other way around—this asymmetry does not entail that my commitment to (O) is somehow greater or deeper than my commitment to the RH. No commitment could be greater than my commitment to (O); but then no commitment could be greater than my commitment to the proposition that THIS is not a dream but reality. The commitment is equally great, equally deep, in both cases. In light of the asymmetry, this means that my commitment to (O) is transferred in its entirety to the RH. But what is (O)? What is the content of this proposition that, we are saying, both is at the same level as and excludes the DH?

6.4 I Am with Others: Metaphysical Equality and the Claim to Preeminence

(O) may be expressed, in synoptic form, as:

(O) I am with Others (Others are with me).

To understand (O), there are four points of which we must take account. First, by "Others" I refer to other human beings. Perhaps there are nonhuman creatures that, were I familiar with them, I would regard as Others. But I do not know of any such creatures—at least not creatures that I straightforwardly (without qualification) regard in this way, as Others. But in what way is that?

This brings us to the second point. I regard other human beings as other *subjects* (2.5). That is to say, I regard them as being, like myself, at the center of a horizon—a horizon that contains the same totality that I call "the world" and the same endless space and time.

Third, I regard the horizons of which other human beings are the respective subjects, the ones at the center, as coordinate with mine. Metaphysically, you might say, we are equals. This third point, which presupposes the second, is what the capital "O" in "Others" is meant to indicate. I regard other human beings as Others. That is, I regard other human beings as each at the center of a horizon that is coordinate with my horizon. I regard other human beings, all of us, as metaphysical equals.

Finally, in saying that I am "with" Others (that they are "with" me, or that we are "together"), I mean that the fact of our metaphysical equality is mutually recognized: just as I recognize that the Other's horizon is coordinate with my horizon, the Other recognizes that mine is coordinate with his; and each recognizes that the Other recognizes this; again, each recognizes that the Other recognizes that he (the first) recognizes this; and so on.

It is not hard to feel that there is something ungraspable, something we cannot get to the bottom of, about the fact of intersubjectivity, the fact of our being "with" one another, or "together." And there is. Implicit in the mutual recognition that constitutes our "togetherness," the mutual recognition of our coordinate status, exists a potentially infinite complexity. This potential infinity, this ungraspable mutuality that constitutes our togetherness, is presupposed in all our dealings with one another. When I buy a newspaper, produce my ticket for the train conductor, chat with a neighbor, ask a stranger for directions, and so on, I do such things, we all do such things, with our ungraspable mutuality already given.

In light of this mutual recognition of our coordinate status, you could say that we form a community of metaphysical equals. Here again we get the potentially infinite complexity. To belong to a community of metaphysical equals, you must see yourself and your fellows as belonging; hence you must see your fellows as seeing themselves and you as belonging; hence you must see your fellows as seeing you as seeing them as belonging; and so on. We, who form the community, mutually grasp that the fact of our community is ungraspable. I see myself as part of such a community, a community of metaphysical equals. We might take this mutual grasp of our ungraspable togetherness as another way of expressing (O): I am part of a community of metaphysical equals.

How is it that I am, that we are, part of such a community? We were drawn into it in being drawn into our system of language-games, the communal horizon (see Int.6). Those to whom we looked in being drawn in, those who are together with us on the inside, are with us as subjects of coordinate horizons. How do I (we) know this, that I am with Others, metaphysical equals? How, that is, do I know that I am an insider of the communal horizon? There is no argument. It is just where I find myself: on the inside of our system of language-games. Insofar as I find myself an insider of the system, I find myself with Others, part of a community of metaphysical equals. This is why the commitment to (O) is so deep and pervasive: it is rooted in our insidership in the communal horizon, in our finding ourselves together, with Others (metaphysical equals), together on the inside of our system of language-games.

There is, however, something about our (metaphysical) equality, the coordinate status of our respective horizons, that requires further discussion; for it seems that at the same time that I recognize the coordinate status of your horizon, my horizon claims a certain preeminence. But then so does yours. Every horizon claims preeminence for itself. So, in the end, these claims are not incompatible with the mutual recognition of our equality. In fact, they are an aspect of our equality. Let me elaborate on this.

What is the preeminence that each horizon claims for itself? We may first point out something it is not. My horizon includes, or contains, the totality I call "the world"; or, as we have often put it, the totality I call "the world" is internal to THIS, to my horizon. Your horizon includes the totality you call "the world." But there is no clash. Neither side claims that the totality internal to its horizon (the totality he calls "the world"), as opposed to the totality internal to the other horizon (that which the other calls "the world"), is *the* world. For we suppose that these totalities are one and the same: the totality internal to your horizon *is* the totality internal to mine. We do not share the same horizon, but we share the same world. Similar remarks could be repeated for space and time.

The preeminence claimed by my horizon is not that it is the (only) horizon that contains the totality I call "the world," but that it is the horizon that contains or, as we shall henceforth say, *includes* all other horizons. The totality I call "the world" is contained by both your horizon and mine. There is just one totality (and space and time), and my horizon does not claim it for itself; nor does yours. Neither claims preeminence in this respect. The claim to preeminence asserts itself not with respect to the world but with respect to other horizons. The claim is this: your horizon, which contains the world, is included by my horizon. Your horizon is included by my horizon even though yours, like mine, contains the world—and thus me, the human being that I am.

Notice, that my horizon claims to include yours does not mean that I regard your horizon as part of the totality I call "the world." If I were to regard your horizon as part of this totality, I could not regard the totality as internal to it. (I could not regard it as containing the totality.) I could not, in other words, regard it as a *horizon*. I regard *you* (like myself) as part of the totality I call "the world," but not your horizon. I can no more regard your horizon than I can regard my horizon as part of the world. Containment (internality), then, is a relation between a horizon and the world; inclusion (as we are now using this term) is a relation between horizons. More than one horizon can contain the same world: the same world can be internal to more than one horizon. In the case of inclusion, what we must remember is this: if one horizon includes another, it cannot be included by that horizon.

It follows that a claim by one horizon to include another is by its nature a claim to preeminence. My horizon claims to include yours. That is how it represents itself. Given the asymmetry, what my horizon claims (or represents itself as being) entails that your horizon cannot include it. My horizon claims preeminence over yours. Of course, the same holds from the standpoint of your horizon. Your horizon represents itself as including mine, and hence as preeminent over mine. It is like that with every horizon. Every horizon represents itself as including all other horizons. Every horizon represents itself as, in this sense, the all-inclusive horizon.

I (JV, *this* human being) am internal both to my horizon and to your horizon. And you (the human being that, let us say, I address) are internal both to your horizon and to mine. We are both part of the same totality, and this totality (the world) is internal to, or contained by, both horizons. Here there is no clash. The clash relates not to what our horizons contain, but to what they claim to include. Your horizon claims to include mine. Mine claims to include yours. Mine claims to be the all-inclusive horizon, the horizon that includes all others. And so does your horizon. It is like that with all horizons.

I am stating the idea about preeminence in an abstract and jargonistic way, but I think it is something to which we can all relate. To alter the jargon slightly, each of us feels that his life—what for each of us is "my life"—is the all-inclusive life. Not the *only* life, but that within which all others have their place. "All other lives, whatever they include, are included within my life." Does this thought not strike a chord?

It is, we might say, part of what is to be at the center of a horizon that the one at the center, the one for whom it is "mine," views the horizon as the all-inclusive horizon. So this must hold for every subject, for anyone at the center. Am I the only one who grasps this? We all grasp it. We all know that it is "the same for others as for me." And we all know that we all know this, and so on. We all know, mutually, that from within each horizon, that horizon represents itself as all-inclusive, as the horizon that includes all the others. Knowing this, we cannot, it seems, treat the claim to preeminence of our own horizon as valid in an absolute way but as valid only from the perspective of our own horizon; in other words, as valid in a relative way—in the way the claim of every horizon is valid.

My horizon represents itself as the all-inclusive horizon, as preeminent and therefore unique. But I know it is like that from within all horizons. I know, then, that my horizon is just one among many, coordinate with all other horizons. The thing to see is that the claim my horizon makes to preeminence enters into its metaphysical status as one among many. For the claim belongs equally to all horizons, and this is something we all know, and know that we know, etc. We mutually grasp the fact of our metaphysical equality. We are committed to (O).

6.5 The Commitment to (O)

Our commitment to (O) is not just another commitment, another belief. It pervades everything. It is implicit, for example, in what I am doing now. It has been implicit all along, throughout these reflections on the DH—

throughout the very reflections that have led me to the conclusion that I cannot justify my commitment to the RH, i.e., that I cannot justify my rejection of the DH. In being led to the conclusion that I cannot justify my commitment to the RH, I have, implicitly, committed myself to (O). I have, then, in being led to the conclusion that I cannot justify my commitment to the RH, committed myself in a way that makes it rationally impossible not to have this commitment.

Perhaps, most obviously, the commitment to (O) has been displayed in the constant use I have made of the first-person plural. Time and time again I have made claims to the effect that "we" think this way, react that way, and so on. Now in some cases, the use of the first-person plural is stylistic and could be replaced by "I" or an impersonal mode of expression. In some cases, though, the use of the first-person plural has a real point: I have been speaking not just about myself but about Others. It is not just *I* who thinks such-and-such, or reacts thus-and-so; it is *we* who have such thoughts or reactions.

In fact a commitment to (O) is there whether I speak about Others or about myself. For even when I do not speak *about* Others, I speak *to* them: I address them. I have been doing this all along, throughout the whole of the book. I have all along been addressing Others. Not a particular, well-defined group of Others, but a vague group—a vague audience, you might say, of philosophical Others. It would not matter if I determinedly restricted myself to the first-person singular, or expressed myself always in an impersonal way: I would still be addressing Others. Is this an eccentricity? Is it not what you (my philosophical readers) do when you write philosophy?

It is worth dwelling for a bit on this business of writing philosophy. I am not always writing philosophy, or thinking about it. Writing and thinking about philosophy is just one part of my life. It is one way I spend time, one thing that is important to me. I discuss and argue a lot with students and colleagues, but very often (usually, in fact) I philosophize by myself. Indeed, most people would say (this is the popular conception) that, if anything is an isolated and inward-looking occupation, it is philosophizing. Yet in philosophizing we look outward. We have the Other in view. Thus right now, in writing down these sentences, I have the Other in view. I mutter to myself, but I address Others.

There is something else about philosophy. This relates to a point that came up in connection with the idea of philosophical discovery. When we address Others in philosophy and tell them what we have "discovered," we speak not just to them, and perhaps about them, but on their behalf (Int.5). We take our "discovery" to be something about which they already know—whether they are ready to accept this or not. The Other may claim not to know what we are talking about; yet we speak for him.

This is the presumptuous philosophical role: to speak for Others, for the whole community of metaphysical equals. You cannot, then, accuse the philosopher of flagging in his commitment to (O).

So, I have the Other in view now, while writing philosophy. But will it be any different when I cease writing—when, e.g., I ask the waitress for my bill? Forget about the waitress and just think of the bill, and the fact that I have an obligation to pay it. It requires no great leap of thought to appreciate how Others are implicated in such matters. And my life is made up of such matters. This is how I live. It is how we all live: with Others, with a commitment to (O). I live, we live, with our ungraspable mutuality already given.

And clearly, the life-with-Others is there while I philosophize. I philosophize, as it were, in the middle of it. That is, the background commitment to (O), the commitment that comes with the surrounding life (my being in a café, having ordered and now drinking coffee, etc.), is there in addition to the special commitment that comes with philosophizing. So it will, of course, be there when I cease philosophizing. In about half an hour I will leave the café (the surrounding life will change). I will mostly cease philosophizing (for awhile, anyway). I will cease this presumptuous business of speaking, or thinking, on behalf of Others. But I will not extricate myself from the life-with-Others that surrounds me even while I philosophize. My commitment to (O) is not there just when I philosophize. It is always there. It is a constant, all-pervasive commitment.

It is, in fact, implicit in the very fact that I am now thinking (whatever I think). From where do I get the resources to think? From our system of language-games, the communal horizon, that on the inside of which I find myself—that is to say, on the inside of which I find myself *with Others* (6.4). You could say, in the spirit of Descartes: I simply find myself thinking. (Is there an argument for this?) In the same way, I simply find myself an insider of our system of language-games. Finding myself an insider is implicit in the fact that I find myself thinking. And finding myself an insider is already finding myself with Others, committed to (O). There is no more getting between myself and Others than between myself and my own thinking.

We shall come back to this idea. In the discussion that follows, however, we shall leave aside the general, all-pervasive way in which the Other figures in my life, in the very fact of my thinking, and focus (for dramatic effect, as it were) on the special way the Other figures in philosophizing. In philosophizing, I address Others. Imagine that I am addressing you. I am telling you my ideas about dream and reality, and dream skepticism, and so on. That is, imagine that I am doing this in person. You are present within my horizon, and I am present within yours, and I am telling you my ideas about dream skepticism. I tell you the argument that I have no justification for believing that THIS is reality. In telling you this—in telling you anything; in telling anyone anything—I display my commitment to (O). And this commitment, we are saying, is rationally incompatible with my not believing what we just said that I am not justified in believing. It is rationally incompatible with dream skepticism.

But remember, although we are focusing on what I am doing right now (addressing you on the subject of the DH), if a commitment to (O) is rationally incompatible with dream skepticism, the incompatibility will be present not just in my act of addressing you; it will pervade every-thing—the whole of my life. It is not, really, as if I have a *particular reason* for rejecting the DH. Everything in my life makes it impossible to believe the hypothesis (including the very fact that I can think the hypothesis). For everything involves my commitment to (O). Focusing on the context of philosophizing is a device for making the commitment, and its rational incompatibility with dream skepticism, vivid. However, the commitment, the incompatibility, is always there.

6.6 Raising the Dream Hypothesis in Conversation: Forcing a Withdrawal to the First Person

In talking to you, in addressing you, I display a commitment that makes it rationally impossible to take seriously the idea that THIS is a dream. Of course we have not shown this yet. But I suspect that anyone who has ever been a party to a philosophical conversation about the DH (or, in the case of academic philosophers, anyone who has ever "lectured" on this "topic") will have a sense of what I am getting at. He will know the feeling that there is something funny going on when we, when you and I, contemplate together the possibility that THIS is a dream. Let us try to locate where the problem arises.

You and I, say, are discussing the DH. I tell you the argument for dream skepticism. I explain why I cannot refute the hypothesis that THIS is a dream. Now suppose that, while I am telling you these things, I ask my-self: "If THIS is a dream, whose dream would it be?" Would it be *our* dream? No. *Your* dream? No. If THIS is a dream, I want to say, it would be *my* dream. Here we have come to something important, the way the DH has of forcing us to withdraw to the first-person singular.

The subject matter of the DH, THIS, is not part of world. Or the whole of the world. Or the whole of the world plus the infinity of space and time. It is a horizon—that which contains the whole of the world and the infinity of space and time. But whose horizon?

If THIS is a dream and the dream were ours, THIS would be ours. It would be a shared horizon. There is no such horizon. Each of us has our own horizon. I have mine and you have yours.

So if THIS is a dream, it would be either my dream or your dream. My horizon or yours. Let me ask the question again: "If THIS is a dream, whose dream would it be?" Well, who is asking the question? Me. But the only horizon about which I might ask such a question is the horizon of which I am at the center, and of course that horizon is mine. THIS is my horizon.

THIS, the personal horizon, is not "ours" but "mine." (it is the communal horizon that is "ours"); you have yours and I have mine. And, to repeat, THIS is mine. So if THIS is a dream, the dream would be mine. Thus although I am talking to *you*, although *we* are having a conversation about the dream hypothesis, if I ask myself whose dream it would be, I must answer that it would be mine. So much is obvious.

Then what about you? How should I regard you? It seems I must regard you, the one to whom I am talking, as (on the DH) in my dream. Suppose I tell you what I have just thought to myself: that if THIS is a dream, the dream would be mine; that you would be in my dream. Then that is part of our conversation. So, I must think that if THIS is a dream what I have just told you would be part of a conversation in the dream. In whose dream? Once again, there is the inevitable withdrawal to the first-person singular. The dream would be mine. Whatever I tell you in our conversation about the DH, if I ask myself whose dream it would be, the answer I must give is that the dream would be mine. I must bracket my telling you what I tell you inside a withdrawal to the first-person singular. It may be *our* conversation, but it is *my* dream. I have no option, then, but to regard you as someone in my dream.

This is where the problem arises. If I am telling you these things, *addressing* you, I *cannot* at the same time regard you as someone in my dream. Insofar as I address you, I regard you as my metaphysical equal: your horizon is coordinate with mine. Insofar as I regard you as someone in my dream, I cannot regard your horizon as coordinate with my horizon. I cannot regard you as my metaphysical equal. But then I cannot allow that THIS might be a dream. For I *am* addressing you.

This, as we said, is where the problem arises—but the problem may as yet not be clear. Moreover, in indicating where the problem arises, a new and unexplained element has come to the fore. The reader will (I hope) see that there is something to the point about the DH forcing a withdrawal to the first-person singular. But in light of our earlier discussions of the first-person singular, he may wonder how we are to understand the use of the first person in expressing this withdrawal. We said that if while talking to you about the dream hypothesis I ask myself "Whose dream would THIS be?" I must answer that it would be "my" dream; that the dream would be "mine." How am I using "my" and "mine" here? Before trying to explain the problem about my regarding you as being in my dream, we must consider this question about the first person.

6.7 Withdrawing to the First Person and the Horizonal Use of the First Person

If THIS is a dream, you are in the dream. Of course so am I. We, you and I, are having a conversation that, if THIS were a dream, would be taking place in the dream. But the dream (I remind myself) would be mine. So, it seems, if THIS were a dream, you and I would be in my dream.

Consider my use of the three personal pronouns in,

(F) If THIS were a dream, you and I would be in my dream.

By "you" I refer to you, the human being I see before me and to whom I am speaking. By "I" I refer to the human being I am, the one at the center of THIS; hence the one who, if THIS is a dream, would be the subject of the dream. So my use of "you" and "I" is referential in both cases. In both, I refer to an object that, if THIS were a dream, would be part of the world internal to the dream. Then how shall we understand the use in (F) of "my"? What do I mean when I say that if THIS is dream, the dream—the dream that you and I would be in—would be *my* dream?

When I speak of a past dream, e.g., "my dream of the other night," I mean a dream dreamed by the human being that I am. The "my" here is referential: it refers to JV, the human being I am. But I cannot—at least, not without real confusion—mean that if THIS were a dream, I, JV, the human being that I am (the human being talking to you), would be the dreamer, the one dreaming the dream. The human being that I am (the one talking to you) would not, as we have more than once remarked, be the dreamer; the dreamer would belong to a transcendent world.

The "my" in (F), then, is not referential. And yet, it seems, we need the first person here. For there is (I trust you agree) a sense in which I cannot but suppose that if THIS is a dream, and I am talking to you, you and I would be in *my* dream—not yours. So, in addition to the use of the first-person singular to refer to the human being (or soul) that I am, we must recognize another use. Note, the point of this other use here is to draw a contrast between the relevant horizons: the horizon that would be a dream is "my" horizon, not "your" horizon.

In 2.5 we distinguished two uses of the first person: the referential and the positional. If the "my" in (F) is (unlike the "I") not referential, perhaps it is positional.

When I use the first person positionally, it stands in for the specification of a certain position within THIS, within the subject matter of the dream hypothesis; or, if I speak of a past dream, it stands in for a position within that dream. Thus if in "In the dream X was me" I use "me" positionally, I mean that in the dream X occupied the position at the center of the dream (the subject position), the position occupied by JV in reality. Or consider my use of the first person when I speak of JV as "the human being that I am." Here I mean that JV is the human being who occupies the position at the center of THIS, at the center of the subject matter that is the subject matter of the dream hypothesis.

It should be plain, then, that the "my" in (F) is not positional. For, as we remarked, the point of the use of "my" in (F) is to draw a contrast between horizons. I look at you and think, "If THIS were a dream, the dream would be mine (not yours)." But drawing such a contrast is not the point of the positional use of the first person. If I say about JV that he "is the human being that I am," I mean that JV is the human being at the center of THIS. Here, clearly, I do not contrast horizons but specify a position within a horizon; in the present case, a position within THIS, the horizon that is the subject matter of the DH. That is to say, within my horizon. Within "my" horizon? Once again, we are availing ourselves of the previously unremarked use of the first person.

It seems, then, that we have a come upon a third use of the first person. We shall call it the "horizonal" use. When I use the first person horizonally, I use it neither to refer to an object in the totality I call "the world," nor as a stand-in for the specification of a position within the horizon of this totality, i.e., within THIS, but to qualify the horizon: it is "mine" (not "yours"). Of course we have not explained what the qualification amounts to, what it means to say of THIS that it is *my* horizon. We shall come to this later in the book. For the present it will be sufficient simply to register the fact that there is this further, as yet unexplained, use of the first person.

Let us sum up our discussion of the first person so far. We have distinguished three uses of the first person: the referential, the positional, and the horizonal. The referential use is illustrated by "I" in "I am now writing"; the positional use, by "me (I)" in "JV, *this* human being, is the human being who is me (the one I am)"; and the horizonal use, by "my" in (F): "If THIS is a dream, you and I would be in my dream."

The DH, we said, forces a withdrawal to the first-person singular. If, having raised the hypothesis, I ask whose dream it would be, I must answer that the dream would be "mine." We asked how I am using the first person here, when I say the dream would be "mine." What we have in this case is neither the referential nor the positional use, but a third use of the first person: the horizonal use of the first person. The "my" in "my dream," i.e., in "my horizon (experience, consciousness, life)," is the horizonal "my."

6.8 Why It Is Rationally Impossible to Believe the Dream Hypothesis

I am addressing you. I am telling you my ideas about the DH, the hypothesis that THIS is a dream. Given the hypothesis, I must suppose that both you and I would be in the dream. Whose dream? THIS is my horizon. So if THIS were a dream, the dream would be mine. If THIS were a dream, then, I must suppose that you would be in my dream. But in addressing you, I regard you as a metaphysical equal: as being at the center of a horizon coordinate with THIS, with my horizon. Here, we said, is where the problem lies. Insofar as I regard your horizon as coordinate with mine, I cannot regard you as being in my dream. But we also said that the problem may not be obvious.

In fact, it may seem obvious that there is no problem. The DH, we have argued, leaves everything—everything internal to THIS, the subject matter of the hypothesis—as it is. Now the whole of what I call "the world" is internal to THIS. Would that not include you, the person to whom I am talking? Are you not part of what I call "the world"? By our argument, if THIS is a dream and I am talking to you, I would be talking to you in the dream. Where is the problem?

But then you are not just *any* part of what I call "the world." You are a human being, a part of the world with a mind. This suggests that the problem about talking to you in my dream has to do with "other minds," with the fact, say, that I am, in addressing another human being, addressing another mind. Why should that create a problem? If THIS were a dream, you, the human being that I address, hence the other mind that I address, would be part of the dream.

I address another "mind." What does that mean? Let us for the moment hold on to the fact that, in addressing you, I address another subject, a metaphysical equal (an Other). I am committed to (O). I regard you, the human being that I am addressing, as a metaphysical equal: as being at the center of a horizon coordinate with mine. This is what creates the difficulty. Insofar as I regard you as a metaphysical equal, I cannot (it is rationally impossible to) regard you as being in my dream. If THIS were a dream, your horizon would not be coordinate with mine. Thus if I were to take THIS to be a dream, I could not regard you as a metaphysical equal. So I could not regard you as someone I am addressing. I could not regard myself, then, as I actually do: as addressing you. To regard myself in this way is to regard you as a metaphysical equal, as being at the center of a horizon that is coordinate with mine.

We may express this in terms of what we said about how it is for the one at the center of a horizon (6.4). Each horizon represents itself as preeminent, as the all-inclusive horizon. My horizon claims to include yours. Your horizon claims to include mine. Each claim holds from its own perspective. So, metaphysically, things level out: our horizons are coordinate. But if THIS were a dream, my horizon would include yours. Period. The preeminence that my horizon claims would hold not just relatively, from its own perspective, but absolutely. Your horizon then would not be coordinate with mine. You would not be my metaphysical equal.

Assume THIS is a dream. Then there is a horizon wider than THIS, a horizon that can displace THIS; that is, a horizon for whose subject THIS has the kind of status that my dream of the other night has for me (the subject of THIS) now. But THIS, the horizon we are assuming to be a dream, is *my* horizon. Thus, if THIS is a dream, there is a sense in which the being of your horizon (of what for you is "my life") *depends on* the being of my horizon: it depends on whether my horizon (not yours) is displaced by the wider horizon. For if THIS were a dream, it would be THIS that is subject to displacement, and THIS, once again, is *my* horizon (not yours). Our horizons will, after all, not be coordinate: the being of your horizon will depend on mine in a way that mine does not depend on yours. There will be an asymmetry: not only will my horizon claim to include yours, it will include yours. You will not be my metaphysical equal.

Consider, by way of contrast, how things stand if THIS is reality. It will of course remain true that from its perspective my horizon, THIS, includes your horizon. But since on the RH THIS is not subject to displacement, the being of your horizon would not, in the sense just explained, depend on mine. There would be nothing, then, to undermine their coordinate position. Both horizons would claim preeminence. That is to say: each would represent itself as the all-inclusive horizon; so each would, from its own perspective, include the other. These claims to preeminence, since they hold only relatively, would hold side by side. Neither would hold absolutely. In sum, the RH does not conflict with my viewing you as a metaphysical equal. But the DH does. If I were to believe that THIS is a dream, that would make it rationally impossible to view you as a metaphysical equal.

Maybe the point will be more vivid if we consider the situation from your perspective. Imagine I look at you and assert, "THIS is a dream." Now ask yourself what it would be for my assertion to be true. If what I assert were true, you would be in my dream—where (let us be clear) this means, not that you are in a dream being dreamed by the human being who made the assertion (*he*, i.e., JV, would not be the dreamer), but that the horizon of which that human being, JV, is at the center, the subject, is a dream. From your standpoint, this would imply a strange imbalance. Whereas I, JV, could truly say "THIS is a dream," you could not say this. You could not say it because, as we observed, if what I express is true, it would be *my* horizon, not yours, that would be subject to displacement. Does this imbalance not strike you as outrageous—as (so to speak) metaphysically outrageous?

The reason it strikes you this way should now be obvious. You regard your horizon as coordinate with mine. And I do too: I regard your horizon as coordinate with mine. If you were in my dream, your horizon would (as the point about displacement makes clear) depend for its being on my horizon, which means your horizon would not be coordinate with mine. We would not be metaphysical equals. It turns out, then, that your reason for dismissing what I would express by "THIS is a dream" is the same as my reason for dismissing it, viz., that we regard each other as metaphysical equals, that we are committed to (O).

Notice, the thought "He is in my dream" seems less outrageous than "I am in his dream (I am in a dream of which he is the subject)." It seems less outrageous despite the fact that I have the same reason for dismissing both thoughts: the commitment to (O). This is not hard to explain. Both thoughts imply a preeminence of one horizon over another. This conflicts with our commitment to metaphysical equality. But in addition, the thought that "I am in his dream," since it implies the preeminence of the Other's horizon over mine, flies in the face of what it is like to be at the center of a horizon. The claim of my horizon to preeminence allows for the thought, "He is in my dream." Of course I dismiss the thought. I dismiss it because I recognize that the Other's horizon makes the same claim and thus do not assign absolute validity to my claim. I regard the Other as my equal. I am committed to (O). In dismissing the thought, "I am in his dream," however, I am moved not just by the recognition of equality (after all, equality works both ways) but by something else—by my own (metaphysically discounted) claim to preeminence.

I address a group of first-year philosophy students on the subject of Descartes' dream argument. I point out that each person must think through the argument for himself, in the first-person singular. Do I not, even if I achieve my aim of conveying Descartes' argument, sense that something is wrong here? The context in which I tell the students to think through the argument in the first-person singular is a context in which we mutually grasp the conspicuous fact that I am, that we are, "with" other subjects (Others), metaphysical equals (after all, I am addressing them, I am *telling them* something)—a context that makes it rationally impossible to believe the first-person conclusion of the argument (that, for all I know,

THIS is a dream, i.e., that there may be a horizon wider than my horizon). This is not an unusual type of context. It is how we live: with others: committed to (O).

6.9 The Space of Horizons

Someone might be both convinced and puzzled by the foregoing reflections. That is to say, he might acknowledge that he is committed to (O) and that the commitment to (O) rationally blocks dream skepticism, and yet be puzzled as to how it could do this. He might be puzzled because whereas the "Others" to which (O) refers are other human beings, other objects in the world, the DH, as we explained, leaves everything in the world as it is. It is a transcendent hypothesis.

The DH asserts there is a horizon wider than THIS with its own world and space and time. I address you. So I regard you as a metaphysical equal. And you are part of what I call "the world," i.e., the world internal to THIS. Indeed, the assumption is that we are talking face to face. You are present within my experience—present within THIS. How (one might ask) could anything in my attitude toward *you*, who are present *within* THIS, have implications that conflict with a hypothesis that asserts the existence of a transcendent world, that is, a world *outside* THIS?

We anticipated this question when we remarked that, in its own way, (O) is a transcendent proposition (6.3). It refers to objects (human beings) that, like you, are part of the totality I call "the world," the totality that is untouched by the truth or falsehood of the DH—yet it is transcendent. In what way, or sense, is (O) transcendent?

Let us state the question in terms of my attitude toward you. I am talking to you. I regard you both as part of what I call "the world," and as a metaphysical equal. Now the DH is transcendent: it posits a world outside THIS. It posits a world outside the horizon that contains the totality I call "the world," the totality internal to THIS, the totality of which you are a part. If my attitude toward you makes it rationally impossible to take seriously the idea that the DH is true, it too must be in some way transcendent. It must have (so to speak) a transcendent dimension. My attitude toward you—who are part of what I call "the world" and thus internal to THIS; who we are supposing to be in fact present to me, present within THIS—must in some way point outside THIS. It is this transcendent dimension, the pointing outside THIS, that we must try to explain.

I regard you as being (like me) at the center of a horizon. Perhaps right here we have what we are looking for, the transcendent dimension in my attitude toward you. For, as we remarked (6.4), I cannot regard your horizon as part of the totality I call "the world." I regard your horizon (like mine) as containing this totality. Could it contain a totality of which it is part?

This thought is on the right track, but it does not take us all the way. True, I cannot regard your horizon as part of what I call "the world." Thus my horizon claims, as we put it, not to "contain" but to "include" your horizon. It claims preeminence, that is, to include all horizons. But this would seem to undermine the suggestion that my regarding you as a subject, as being at the center of a horizon, constitutes a transcendent dimension in my attitude toward you. The transcendent is what lies outside my horizon. Insofar as my horizon claims to include the horizon of which you are at the center, then its claim seems directly at odds with my assigning a transcendent status to your horizon.

However, there is (as we know) a further twist. My horizon claims to include yours, but I do not take the claim to hold absolutely. I know that your horizon makes the same claim. I grasp that from its perspective, your horizon includes mine. I am not a solipsist: I do not take the claim to preeminence of my horizon as a truth, an absolute preeminence; nor, of course, would I accept the absolute preeminence of your horizon. On the one hand, then, there is what my horizon *represents itself* as being, what it *claims* for itself, how it *seems* being a subject; on the other hand, there is what I *know* or *grasp*. Notice what this means. It means that, since I grasp the metaphysical state of affairs, I must be able to free myself (in terms of what I grasp or understand) from the perspective of both my horizon and yours. Indeed, I must be able to free myself from the perspective of *any* horizon. I (we) must have a conception of a "space" in which our horizons, each representing itself as the preeminent horizon, i.e., as including all others, exist all together, side by side. A space of coordinate horizons. This is the conception we need, insofar as we are committed to (O).

The space of horizons—the space that contains your horizon and my horizon, side by side—is not, of course, the space of the world, the space in which you and I confront each other. It is not, in other words, *space*. The space of the world, space, is internal both to my horizon and to yours. Our horizons contain the same world and thus the same space, the space in which the world spreads out. That space, therefore, cannot be the space that contains these horizons. A horizon could not contain the space by which it is contained, the space in which it exists side by side with other horizons.

Nor can the space of horizons be identified with the communal horizon (Int.6). We who find ourselves together as insiders of the communal horizon thereby find ourselves with metaphysical equals (Others); thus, as insiders, we mutually grasp our position in the space of coordinate horizons. But this abstract structure is not the communal horizon; that is, it is not the indefinitely rich system of language-games by being on the inside of which we are thinkers, the engulfing context into which we were drawn, and on the inside of which we now find ourselves together—that is, with Others.

It is in a very different way that the space of horizons brings together the multiplicity of horizons. In this space all horizons are, as we said, side by side. At the same time, each horizon represents itself as including all the others. So the space of horizons cannot be incorporated into any single horizon's representation of things, that is, into (as we might put it) the structure of seeming that comes with being at the center of a horizon. No horizon, we might say, can *represent* the fact of its existing side by side with other horizons. But we all *grasp* the fact, that is, that our horizons exist side by side. I grasp the fact, and you grasp it. We grasp something here that we cannot represent.

Let me borrow an expression used by Wittgenstein. Each horizon represents itself like this: I have "no neighbors."[4] Yet we all grasp, we all know, that we have neighbors. Once again, we grasp something we cannot represent.

But then, it seems, we grasp something transcendent. Each of us grasps that there is something *outside* our own horizon. I grasp that there is something outside THIS. What? Your horizon. If your horizon exists side by side with THIS, with my horizon, it is outside my horizon. I represent your horizon as included by my horizon, but I grasp that it is outside my horizon. I grasp that our horizons are neighbors. And of course, the same goes for you, vis-à-vis my horizon. You grasp that our horizons are neighbors. And we both grasp that we grasp this, and so on. Our grasp of our neighborly status is mutual.

So you, who are present within my horizon and are part of the totality I call "the world," are at the center of a horizon which contains that same totality and that, while I represent it as included within my horizon, I

---

[4] See "Notes for Lectures on 'Private Experience' and 'Sense Data,' " reprinted in *Philosophical Occasions*, ed. James C. Klagge and Alfred Nordman (Hackett Publishing Co., 1993). Wittgenstein writes, giving voice to what he regards as a misguided philosophical thought: "You can't deny that there is my personal experience and that this in a most important sense *has no neighbors*." He follows this up with: "But you don't mean that it *happens* to be alone but that its grammatical position is that of having no neighbors." His point, I take it, is that in expressing the thought we imbue it with more than grammatical significance: we mistakenly suppose we are expressing some kind of important fact. Well, granting that it does not just "happen" to be the case that my horizon (my personal experience) "has no neighbors," does this not have more than "grammatical" significance? Is it not an important fact? What my death means to me, its significance, is (to anticipate our later discussion) closely bound up with this fact. Is what my death means to me, the significance to me of my death, merely grammatical?

recognize as existing *alongside*, and thus *outside*, my horizon. This recognition or grasp of things, which I cannot represent, is part of my attitude toward you, part of what is involved in my regarding you as a metaphysical equal.

The DH is transcendent. Thus we said that if my attitude toward you, my regarding you as a metaphysical equal, makes it rationally impossible to believe the DH, this attitude must be itself in some way transcendent. My attitude toward you must have, as we put it, a transcendent dimension. Perhaps we can now say what this is. My attitude toward you involves that I recognize the existence of something outside THIS, outside my horizon, namely, your horizon. In regarding you as a metaphysical equal, I recognize your horizon as outside my horizon.

We must, however, remark that although your horizon is outside my horizon, outside THIS, the relation that holds between your horizon and mine is obviously not the same as that which, if THIS were a dream, would hold between THIS and the wider horizon. A wider horizon is one into which I might emerge (4.6–7). I could not emerge into your horizon. Your horizon is outside mine in the manner not of a wider but, as we might put it, a disjoint horizon.

And my grasp of this side-by-side layout, this neighborly arrangement, constitutes the transcendent dimension in my attitude toward you. But of course not just in my attitude toward you. It is present in my commitment to (O), the proposition that I am with Others, which commitment pervades everything in my life. If everything in my life speaks against dream skepticism, this is because it speaks of something outside my life. Everything in my life speaks of the life of the Other.

6.10 Other Minds

The reader may have spotted an apparent inconsistency in our attitude toward other minds. (Note: an "apparent" inconsistency; later in the book we shall uncover a real inconsistency.) Dream skepticism is transcendent. In this respect it differs from other familiar types of philosophical skepticism, e.g., skepticism about the past, skepticism about the future (inductive skepticism), skepticism about the existence of the external world. Such immanent skepticisms, we explained (5.3), are independent of dream skepticism. This includes skepticism about other minds. Thus I might be unsure whether creatures other than myself have minds while sure that THIS is not a dream; or I might have no doubt that other creatures have minds but be uncertain whether THIS is a dream. Yet now we seem to be denying the second point. We seem, that is, to be asserting that insofar as I am committed to the existence of other minds, it is rationally impossible for me to believe that THIS might be a dream. If dream skepticism is rationally excluded by a commitment to the existence of other minds, it is not independent of skepticism about other minds.

To dispel the appearance of inconsistency, we must recall the duality in our conception of mind. Generally, we said, the phenomenal conception of mind (as we called it) dominates our reflections in the philosophy of mind (4.6). On the usual understanding, skepticism about other minds assumes this conception: it is skepticism about the occurrence of mental phenomena (states, events, etc.) in creatures other than myself. However, the commitment that makes it rationally impossible to believe the DH and thereby excludes dream skepticism, the commitment to (O), looks not to the existence of other mental phenomena, but to the existence of Others, of metaphysical equals. This invokes the horizonal conception of mind. What makes it impossible to believe the DH is not that I take you to be the locus of special inner phenomena, but that I take you to be the subject of a coordinate horizon.

On the usual picture, your mental phenomena (your states of experience, your feelings, etc.) go on, or occur, in you; mine occur in me. Skepticism gets a foothold with the thought that your mental states are not available to me in the way they are to you; nor are they available to me in the way that your behavior is available to me. In light of the asymmetry, the question arises of how I might justify my certainty that there are mental phenomena occurring in you. It seems compatible with how things are for me that there is nothing "mental" occurring in you or anywhere else in the world; it seems that, for all I can tell, my mind (the mind in me) is the only mind.

This issue, we said, is independent of whether THIS is a dream, whether there is a horizon wider than THIS. In particular, I might be a dream skeptic but have no doubts that there are mental phenomena occurring in you; that you are, in this sense, an other mind. However, I cannot be a dream skeptic if I regard you as a metaphysical equal, the subject of a coordinate horizon. Dream skepticism is compatible with taking you to be an other mind but not with taking you to be an Other. It is, in other words, compatible with the thought that there are mental phenomena going on in you, but not with the thought that you are the subject of a coordinate horizon.

The skeptic about other minds (as we are representing him) employs the phenomenal conception of mind: How do I know the world contains any mental phenomena other than my own? Note, however, that the conception of the horizon is implicit in the very contrast on which such skepticism is founded. Your mental phenomena (your mental states, etc.), I think, are not available to me in the way your behavior is. How so? Your behavior, as opposed to your mental states, is available in the form of phenomena that themselves appear; that is to say, appear from within my experience. Here, by "my experience," I refer not to a counterpart in me of the inner phenomena about whose existence I am meant to be uncertain in your case, but to the horizon from within which you and your behavior appear, and of which I am at the center. Hidden within our understanding of skepticism about other minds is another conception of mind, mind not as a phenomenon but as the horizon: the conception (let us say) of MIND, i.e., the horizonal conception of mind.

6.11 Skepticism and Solipsism

I would argue that skepticism about other minds (other mental phenomena) rests on a confusion. It is not this, however, but another kind of skepticism that we need to consider here. Even if we dismiss skepticism about other minds, there remains skepticism about other MINDS.

Insofar as I am committed to (O), I regard you as occupying the position at the center of (as the subject of) a coordinate horizon—a horizon that contains the world, the same world that is present within my horizon. In demonstrating *this* object to you, say, I take the object to be there for both of us: present within our respective horizons. The same, as we both grasp, holds from your standpoint: it is mutual. The picture is not of something going on in you and something going on in me being "directed at" one and the same object, but of one and the same object simply being there, out in the open, mutually available (shared) within both horizons. This is the picture that is called into question by skepticism about other MINDS. Perhaps nothing is shared—not because something other than the world (what else is there?) is present within other horizons, but because there are no other horizons (I am alone). No other MINDS. Might it be that THIS is unique, unreplicated, that my MIND is the only MIND?

Let us reflect on how solipsism comes into this. The first thing to remark upon is that solipsism is not itself a form of skepticism but a positive belief: my horizon is preeminent (it includes all others). If mine were the only horizon (if there were nothing for it to include), it would thereby be preeminent (it would include what there is to be included: nothing). Thus solipsism is compatible with other MINDS skepticism. But it is also compatible with a belief in other MINDS. From the standpoint of solipsism, if there are other MINDS, they are included in THIS, in my horizon (mine is the preeminent horizon). Yet it should be clear that unless solipsism is assumed, other MINDS skepticism cannot get started. Solipsism does not entail other MINDS skepticism, but it is what makes such skepticism possible, whereas insofar as I am committed to (O), to the existence of equal MINDS, I cannot be skeptical about the existence of other MINDS.

Thus my commitment to (O) is incompatible not just (as we have explained) with dream skepticism but with other MINDS skepticism. Note too, whereas solipsism is what makes dream skepticism (like other MINDS skepticism) possible, and thus is assumed by dream skepticism, it does not require the belief that THIS is a dream. I could not be a dream skeptic unless I take my horizon to include all others (if there are any); but that my horizon is in this sense preeminent does not entail the possibility of a horizon into which I might emerge.[5]

In sum, my commitment to (O), my being with Others, is what excludes both dream skepticism and other MINDS skepticism. Well, can I doubt that I am with Others? Can I even *think* it? I find myself with Others in finding myself an insider of the communal horizon, our system of language-games. All my resources for thinking come from this system. Insofar as I find myself thinking, I find myself an insider, and insofar as I find myself an insider, I find myself with Others (6.5). The thought that I might be alone, that my MIND might be the only MIND, is in a real sense unthinkable.

Yet it seems I can think it! Or rather, first it seems one way, then the other. When I reflect on my situation as an insider of our system of language-games, as a thinker, the situation in which I find myself, I find myself with Others: the existence of other MINDS is already settled. But is it not always possible (as in our reflections on dream skepticism) to step back from this engagement, to withdraw to the first person (6.6): to view everything—including the fact that I find myself a thinker, an insider of our system of language-games and thus with other MINDS—as falling within THIS, within my horizon? "Everything is within my life." Does not this thought speak to something that we all recognize?

Recall Wittgenstein's remark that the language-game "is not reasonable (or unreasonable). It is there—like our life."[6] But when it is "our life" that stands as ultimate, when we withdraw to the first person, the language-game is not there *like* our life but *within* our life, i.e., within THIS, within my life. The gestalt reverses itself. Now, it strikes me that the system of language-games, my status as thinker, all this is itself something within my life, within my horizon. What is ultimate, or primary, is not what is "ours" but what is "mine."[7] Viewed one way, the communal hori-

[5] We must be careful to distinguish the relation, on the one hand, between THIS and (given the DH) the "wider" horizon into which I might emerge, and, on the other, between THIS and (given the truth of solipsism) the horizons that would be "included within" it. Those at the center of the included horizons could not emerge into my horizon in the way I might (on the DH) emerge from THIS into the wider horizon.

[6] See above, Int.8.

[7] Thereby reversing the intention of Wittgenstein's dictum (*Investigations*, 656) that we should "Look on the language-game as the *primary* thing."

zon swallows up the personal; viewed the other way, the personal horizon swallows up the communal.

The thing to point out is that when the personal horizon dominates, other MINDS are included within mine. Thus other MINDS are not equal MINDS. To withdraw into the first person is, in effect, to withdraw into solipsism: it is to embrace the thought that my horizon is preeminent. And solipsism—though (as we observed in 6.10) it does not entail skepticism about other MINDS—is what makes other MINDS skepticism possible. Insofar as I view my MIND as preeminent, I am free to wonder whether whether there are other MINDS (whether mine is the only MIND, whether I am alone). For what blocks other MINDS skepticism—along with dream skepticism—is precisely my taking other MINDS as equal MINDS (my commitment to (O)). If this is removed, I am free to wonder whether mine might be the only MIND. And it is removed when I withdraw to the first person: when the personal horizon assumes dominance over the communal.

Thus, however deep and pervasive my commitment to (O), it is precarious, at the mercy of the ever-present possibility of withdrawing to the first person. But of course this too is always subject to reversal. Thus if I let myself be struck by the way that I simply find myself an insider of our system of language-games, on the way that I simply find myself thinking—including the very thoughts in which I withdraw first personally and thereby come to question the existence of other MINDS—the communal horizon reasserts its dominance. And from within the communal horizon I already find myself with Others, i.e., with equal MINDS. If I find myself with equal MINDS, there can be no question about the existence of other MINDS.

The upshot, it seems, is a permanent conflict or instability. Insofar as the communal horizon dominates, we are committed to (O). And in fact, as insiders of the communal horizon, this is how we live: with Others, with equal MINDS. We live in such a way that the possibility of other MINDS/dream skepticism has already been excluded and thus cannot be taken seriously. Yet in the midst of our life with Others there remains the unspoken option of pulling back, of withdrawing to the first person, from which standpoint things look different. Now it strikes us that "everything is within my life," including other MINDS. When in this way the personal horizon dominates (solipsism), both other MINDS and dream skepticism find an opening. This explains why if we honestly confront such skepticism our response may be ambivalent. At the same time that we (if we are not crazy, or posing philosophically) find it impossible to take seriously other MINDS/dream skepticism, an underlying uneasiness may remain: a sense of the always-available option of first-person withdrawal that makes room for such skepticism.

Perhaps it seems that the resolution of this conflict is obvious, in fact that we have already provided the resolution. Thus we observed (6.4, 6.9) that whereas my horizon claims to include yours, I know that your horizon, with equal right, makes the same claim. "It is the same for all of us." I take the preeminence of my horizon not as holding absolutely but only from the standpoint of my horizon, as holding only relatively. Insofar as I, as we, grasp the objective state of affairs, we are able to free ourselves from the perspective of our own horizon and form the conception of a space in which our horizons, each representing itself as all-inclusive, exist side by side, as coordinate horizons. Viewed in light of this conception, which we mutually grasp, the conflict disappears. Withdrawing to the first person is always open to us. But since the picture with which the withdrawal presents us, that in which my horizon is all-inclusive, is grasped as representing only the view from within my horizon, it is compatible with recognizing our objective metaphysical equality, the coordinate status of our respective horizons.

In thus resolving the conflict between solipsism and our commitment to (O), this suggestion leaves intact our response to dream/other MINDS skepticism. Is this not exactly the kind of resolution we are looking for? Now, I believe the points we have developed thus far are correct. The trouble is that they constitute not so much a resolution of the basic conflict as an elaboration of one side of it. We have, as it were, depicted solipsism from a partisan point of view whose aim is to integrate it harmoniously into our life from within the communal horizon, our life with Others. We have yet really to contemplate solipsism itself: to contemplate the difficult truth in solipsism, a truth that holds not just relatively but absolutely. This—in reflecting on the meaning of death—is something we shall attempt to do in the next part of the book. If we can become open to what death means to us, perhaps we can become open to the truth in solipsism.

PART TWO

Death

7. I Will Die

7.1 Dream and Death; Discovering the Meaning of Death

I will die. This is not a guess or surmise but something I know, a fact. Am I unique in this respect? Each of us has knowledge of the same first-person fact. Each of us knows: I will die.

Of course I do not know exactly when I will die, only that I will die. On the other hand, whereas I am fairly sure that I will not be dead by tomorrow, I am utterly certain that I will be dead one hundred years from now. It is also part of what I know that my death could come at any time.

I know that I will die, but I am not clear what it means. This may remind you of what we said about the dream hypothesis. In that case, however, we were careful not to speak of "knowledge." We said that I was certain the DH is false, not that I know it to be false; but also that, while certain it is false, I was not clear what the hypothesis means. And we are now saying, although I know that I will die, that I am certain of the fact, I am not clear what the fact means. In both cases, then, there is certainty about something whose meaning is unclear.

The reason for not calling my certainty "knowledge" in the death but not the dream case is the same as the reason for speaking of the "dream hypothesis" but not the "death hypothesis." Although I am certain the DH is false, there is in this case the possibility of a skeptical challenge about what justifies my certainty. No comparable challenge presents itself in the case of my certainty that I will die. I am a human being. Human beings, like all other animals, like all other living things, age and die. Everything I know about human beings, and about living things in general, points to this. It all points to death. Is there a problem about finding evidence to back up, or justify, the conviction that I will die? There is so much evidence I do not know where to begin—so much that it seems odd to speak of "evidence." In contrast, once its meaning is properly understood, we can see that nothing could ever count as "evidence" against the DH. Philosophy has to deal with an epistemological challenge in the case of dream. In this respect, we get off lightly in the case of death.

I know that I will die because I know that all living creatures die. But when we say that the meaning of death is unclear, we mean the meaning of (what for each of us is) *my* death is unclear. As in the case of the DH, our project is essentially tied to the first-person singular. Just as when I reflect on the possibility that THIS might be a dream I am thinking about my case, about my situation, so, when I reflect on the meaning of death, I am occupied with the meaning of my death. This is true whether or not I actually express myself in the first-person singular, whether I speak of "my death" or "our death," or simply of "death." But of course, at the same time that these reflections about the meaning of death are about the meaning of "my" death, they are not intended as a piece of autobiography. I see myself as reflecting on behalf of all subjects, as attempting to uncover truths that we all already know about death (an example of what in Int.5 we called the presumptuousness inherent in philosophical reflection). And certainly I (we) do already know what death means. How could my death *mean* something to me, if I did not know what it means? Yet this, what my death means, is just what I am not clear about, and want to get clear about. That is, it, what my (our) death means, is just what I want to bring to light, to become open to. I want to become open to something that I (we) already know.

Does this sound strange? There is no other way it could be. If I did not already know what my death means, I could not become open to it. You will, I hope, recognize that we are talking now of philosophically discovering something (see introduction). I, we (all of us), already know what death means. We already know it, but we are not open to what we know. So we must discover it, discover what we already know. Not, of course, *the fact that* we will die, but what that fact *means*. The fact of death, we might say, is already out in the open. The meaning of death, although we know it, remains hidden.

7.2 Being Disturbed by the Prospect of Death

One manifestation of the meaning death has for me is the way I sometimes react when I contemplate the fact that I will die: my reaction to, as we may put it, the prospect of death. The prospect of death can unsettle or disturb me in a way that nothing else can. (An eccentricity of mine? A peculiar weakness unknown to others?) This reaction is a reaction precisely to what is held up to me in the prospect. It is, in other words, a reaction to what the fact that I contemplate means to me: to the meaning to me of my own death.

To be sure, it is not true that every time my thoughts touch on the fact that I will die I become unsettled. It is not even usually true. I listen to a salesman's patter about life insurance. He is reminding me of the fact of death in a very practical way. Am I unsettled? Disturbed? Maybe a little, maybe not at all. And right now, in philosophizing about death, about the meaning of my death, I am completely undisturbed. Were I actually disturbed, unsettled (in the way we all know it is possible to be unsettled by the prospect of death), I would not be philosophizing about death, or anything else. I would not be able to philosophize about death. I would be, you might say, philosophically disabled.

It is one thing to contemplate, or think about, the fact that I will die, and something else for that fact to *sink in*. The fact sinks in when I am struck by its meaning (by what it means to me). So, it seems, in philosophizing about death, in trying to get clear about the meaning of death, I am not struck by the meaning of death. This is how it is: when I am trying as hard as I can to look right at it and get clear about it, I am not struck by the meaning of death, by what I am trying to get clear about.

Perhaps this is not entirely right. The suggestion is that we cannot be struck by the meaning of death without being disturbed—as if the meaning of death were something we could not handle. Is that necessarily the case? We are not apt to believe that a person who jokes or speaks lightly about his death is at that moment struck by what it means. (Yet people joke, etc., just to show us, or to show themselves, that they can handle the meaning of death.) No doubt a person who is struck by the meaning of death will not talk too much. The real question, though, is whether he can be totally calm. We might think that being calm means the meaning is not getting through. (If there are no ripples, nothing has broken the surface.) I am not sure about this. But I am sure that if someone claims that he cannot understand why a person who is struck by the meaning of death should be disturbed, either he is not being honest or he himself has never been struck by the meaning of death. Perhaps we can say that although it is possible to be struck by the meaning of death without being disturbed, being struck by the meaning of death is something that *warrants* being disturbed.

However that may be, let us focus on the case where, in being struck by the meaning of death, we are disturbed. Whether or not we can be struck by the meaning of death without being disturbed, it is certain that we can be struck by the meaning of death without being clear about the meaning of death.

When does this happen, that I am (we are) struck by the meaning of death? The usual occasion is when there is a real or imagined reason to think that death is close. But that is not the only occasion. A child, for no apparent reason, can be struck by the meaning of death. Anyone can be struck by the meaning of death. At any time. Or, for that matter, at no time. The fact that we know the meaning of death does not guarantee that we will be struck by what we know. All along, we all know what death means; but why the meaning strikes us when it does, or why it strikes at all, we do not know. The meaning of death decides (as it were) whether to strike and chooses its own time. Yet it is also true that when death seems close we are vulnerable.

Lots of things can disturb or unsettle us. We said that we are disturbed, etc., by the prospect of death in a way that nothing else disturbs us. In what way is that?

It is commonly said that we "fear" death. But again, we fear all sorts of things. If it is true that the prospect of death arouses fear in us, this fear is not like the fear of anything else. Dread, terror? The point is the same. Death inspires its own kind of terror, its own kind of dread.

Some philosophers seem to think (this is an ancient idea) that, insofar as we "fear" death, our reaction to the prospect of death is inappropriate to the prospect and hence either is based on confusion or is irrational. The argument is that the reaction could be appropriate only if the prospect involved that something bad is going to happen to us. But when might it happen? Before death and in dying, bad things may happen to us, but what happens to us at these times is not to the point. Thus our being bothered or disturbed, etc., by the prospect of death would survive knowledge that the run-up to death will be smooth, and the dying painless. Is it that we are disturbed by the prospect of what will happen to us after we are dead? After we are dead there is no "us" to which anything bad can happen. If what disturbs us is the prospect of what will happen after death, we are confused: we imagine ourselves being, after death, somehow still in the picture. Otherwise, it seems, our reaction is simply irrational.

Perhaps it will be objected that bad things *can* happen to us after we are dead (we may be ridiculed by people we took to be friends, say), that our accepting this does not entail having a confused notion of surviving death. Indeed, that such posthumous harm might befall us is something that it would be appropriate to fear. But it should be plain that the prospect of posthumous harm is not the basis of our peculiar reaction to the prospect of death. That reaction would be untouched by total assurance that there is no prospect of posthumous harm.

Now, as we said, the conclusion we are meant to draw from such reflections is that there is nothing in the prospect of death that warrants, or makes appropriate, our reaction to this prospect, and that in this sense our reaction is either based on a confusion or simply inappropriate: irrational. I do not draw this conclusion. I would say, what these reflections indicate is that we are not really clear what the prospect of death *is*, what it contains or involves. If we can get clear about this, there will be no further problem about showing that our reaction to the prospect is appropriate.

Or rather, if we can get clear what the prospect of death is, what it holds up to us, we will have done what can be done by way of showing that (or whether) our reaction to the prospect of death is appropriate. There is nothing we can do here except try to bring out in the open, to make explicit, what it is in the prospect of death that evokes our reaction. We bring this out, or try to bring it out, and then it has to speak for itself. It is like trying to get at what makes a particular joke or situation funny. What can we do? (Study Freud's theory of jokes?) All we can do, or try to do—this may not be easy; it requires a certain type of intelligence—is to bring out (draw attention to) what it is *in* the situation that makes it funny: what it is that makes us laugh. Similarly, all we can do is try to bring out what it is *in* the prospect of death that makes it awful: what it is in this prospect that disturbs, or bothers, us in the way that it does.

Notice, we have casually slipped something in here, by implication, about both the case of humor and death—an idea to which I shall just call attention and then drop. When we try to gain insight in certain areas, the usual contrast philosophers draw between subjective and objective collapses. Our insights can be expressed either way: subjectively or objectively. What makes us laugh is what makes the situation funny, and what makes the situation funny is what makes us laugh. Similarly, what disturbs (bothers, unsettles) us in the prospect of death is what makes death awful, and what makes it awful is what disturbs us. If we look for one we will not come up with anything different from what we would come up with if we look for the other. Looking inward, we might say, at ourselves (i.e., at our reaction to death), is no different from looking outward, at death itself.[1]

7.3 That the Prospect of Death Holds Up Something Not Just Awful but Incomprehensible; Death and Self-Deception

There is something else. It is not just the awfulness in the prospect of death that disturbs us in the peculiar way we are disturbed. When we are struck by the meaning of death, the fact of death, the fact that we will die, can seem not just awful but impossible. At the same time, it looms as a fact, and this, that death is both impossible and yet a fact, is something that we cannot comprehend. Death may strike us incomprehensible. Not so? Thus when the fact of death looms, we may react by thinking, "It cannot be." Yet it is a fact. It will be. What cannot be will be. Death, it seems, confronts us with an impossible, and therefore incomprehensible, fact.

---

[1] Ethical reflection, I believe, provides another example of this kind of subjective/objective collapse. Suppose we ask ourselves what is wrong about deceiving people. This sounds objective: it presupposes that deception is wrong (as it is). The point is that we could cast our question subjectively. We could ask, e.g., what it is that bothers us, or makes us feel bad, about deceiving others. What we are getting at, with these questions, is really the same.

This adds a further dimension to the impact that the prospect of death has on us. The incomprehensibility of death (that death presents itself as impossible and yet a fact) figures, along with the awfulness that faces us, as part of the chemistry of our reaction to the prospect of death; as a factor in why the prospect, when it sinks in, disturbs us in a way that nothing else does. So there are two things that we must try, eventually, to get clear about here: what it is in the prospect of death that makes death awful, and what it is that makes it seem impossible, i.e., something that cannot be—something that cannot be, and yet (as we know) inexorably will be.

Let us be clear that we are taking the words "it cannot be" in a literal way: to express a reaction to an apparent impossibility. There are other ways of taking these words. For example, sometimes when we say "it cannot be" we express surprise. I am told that I won the Sweepstakes. "It cannot be." I am surprised because, out of all those tickets, it is so wildly unlikely that mine should have been drawn. Or imagine that I know in advance that someone out of a huge crowd will be chosen to die and am surprised (and aghast) when I learn that my number has been drawn. But this kind of surprise is not essential to being struck by the meaning of death. How could it be? I already knew that I will die.

That is, I already knew: I will die sooner or later. Might I not be surprised at how soon it will be? Of course. But once again, this is not the relevant case. When it sinks in, the fact that I will die (the prospect of my death) can seem like something that "cannot be" without having even an approximate date attached it, hence without my being surprised at how close death is. (This simply reenforces the more general point that the relevant case does not involve surprise.) Death can seem like something that "cannot be" even when I suppose that it is not close.

Saying "it cannot be" is sometimes a way of expressing not surprise but the difficulty of coming to terms with something. In that case we mean, in effect: if only it would not be! And certainly it may be difficult to come to terms with the fact that we will die. But this, it would seem, is a reaction to the awfulness of death, whereas the point here is precisely that the prospect of death holds up something *else*, something that though bound up with the awfulness of death can nevertheless be distinguished from it, and to which our reaction is naturally expressed by the words "it cannot be." And not just naturally expressed by these words but literally expressed, since now we are taking the words "it cannot be" at face value, as we initially proposed. And this is how we shall continue to take the words, at face value—as giving expression to a glimpse of something in the prospect of death that makes the fact that we will die seem impossible, and thus a fact we do not comprehend.

There is in the prospect of death something we find hard to come to terms with. But there is also something that seems impossible, and this makes the undeniable fact of death incomprehensible. The prospect of death holds up to us something awful and incomprehensible.

We said that in the relevant case the words "it cannot be" do not express surprise that death is close, since the relevant case need not involve assigning a particular date to death and, more generally, need not involve surprise. However, apart from the question of surprise, there is something important in this regard about the closeness of death. For it is undeniable that death is more likely to seem impossible, something that "cannot be," when it seems close. Why should this be?

At one level the answer is that it is only when the prospect of death sinks in, only when we are struck by the meaning of death, that death seems impossible, and we are more apt to be struck by its meaning when we think death is close. But why is it that we are more apt to be struck by its meaning when death seems close?

This question relates, I think, to a familiar kind of self-deception about death. People say in a confessional mode, "Of course I know that one day (sooner or later, etc.) I will die, but somehow I do not believe it. Somehow I do not believe it will actually happen to *me*." We might call this the "not-me" phenomenon. It is a form of self-deception with which most of us are familiar. We do not straightforwardly claim not to believe that we will die. We say we know that one day we will die, but that we "somehow" do not believe it. We are, here, admitting to self-deception—yet without undeceiving ourselves.

The self-deceptive admission of self-deception is not essential to the basic self-deception that we engage in about death. We may leave it aside. There is another complexity that seems to affect self-deception about death. In the usual case of self-deception we profess that p, even to ourselves, but know that not-p. In the case of death, we profess that p *and* in fact to *know* that p (that I will die); we profess this even to ourselves. And we *do* know it. But a little part of us (as we say) believes that not-p; or at any rate does not openly face what we know—that is, does not openly face what we know and profess to know. So there is an extra layer here, which serves to disguise the self-deception. "How can you accuse me of deceiving myself about the fact that I will die when I tell you that I know that I will die?"[2]

---

[2] This sort of complexity is of course not restricted to the case of death. "I know I am not good enough to get that job," he tells others. And he knows it: he is not good enough. But this is not what he tells himself: he views himself as appearing "modest." Thus although what he tells others in fact accords with what he knows about himself, there is a layer of self-deception in between.

The thing is, whatever form it takes, whatever the complexity, we engage in self-deception about death to keep the meaning of death at bay. The motive for the deception is plain: the awfulness of death. But when we know that death is close, the deception is harder to maintain—unless we buttress it by a further self-deception; i.e., unless we refuse to believe what we know (that death is close). Once the usual defenses are down, the prospect of death can sink in: we are struck by what death means to us.

But for the most part, it seems, the "not-me" phenomenon prevails: we live in self-deception about death.[3] That is to say, we live knowing that we will die but "somehow" believing that it will not happen (to others yes, but not to me) and thus without being struck by the meaning of death. And when we are struck by the meaning death, the fact that we will die presents itself as "impossible." You could say, somewhat paradoxically, that it is only when the fact that we will die presents itself as "impossible" that we really believe that we will die.

7.4 Reacting to the Prospect of Death: A Text

Abstract assertions of the kind in which we have been indulging, philosophical assertions about death, generally fail to evoke a sense of how the prospect of death can actually affect us. We might get closer to the true potential impact of this prospect, and at the same time give some substance to our abstract assertions, if we had before for us the thoughts of someone being struck, overwhelmed, by the meaning of death—if we had a text, so to speak, of the dawning on someone of what death means. And we have such a text: in Tolstoy's remarkable novella *The Death Of Ivan Ilyich*. I shall quote extensively.[4]

Ivan Ilych is a typical career-minded official working his way up in the czarist legal bureaucracy. He is not overly serious or reflective, but he is affable, cultivates the right people, makes a reasonable (though after the first flush, ill-tempered and unrewarding) marriage, and achieves modest success in the provinces. Then out of the blue things take a decided turn for the better: he receives an appointment in Petersburg, several notches up the scale. Prior to moving his family, Ivan goes by himself to Petersburg to arrange for their new quarters. In the course of enthusiastically overseeing the decorations, he slips from a ladder and suffers a knock to his

[3] See Heidegger's discussion of "Being-towards-death and the Everydayness of Dasein," in *Being and Time*, section 51.

[4] All the quotations are from the Penguin Classics edition, 1960, trans. Rosemary Edmonds.

side. A seemingly trivial thing; but, as we gradually realize, it has terrible consequences—and just when everything was looking rosy.

Not right away, but after awhile: a funny taste in his mouth, an uncomfortable feeling in his side. And it gets worse, leading to irritability and renewed unpleasantness in his marital relations. He consults specialists, self-important types (a bit like himself, in his dealings with defendants), who speak impressively about "floating kidneys" and "blind intestines," but avoid giving him straight answers. He follows orders, takes pills, tries one cure then another, one doctor then another, oscillates in his moods, kids himself about his condition. And so on. There is, however, a steady deterioration—the gnawing ache, the ugly taste, the general loss of strength and appetite—that will not let itself be ignored, and which confronts him within his increasing sense of isolation from his work and social life, and from his unsympathetic family.

It drags on, with occasional ups—just to raise false hope—in a basically downward slide. (Is that not the usual, teasing profile of our decline?) So much is background. The passages that interest us (our "text") occur in sections 5 and 6. Ivan has rushed off with a friend to see a new doctor (a new doctor, a new hope). The doctor has diagnosed a trifling problem in the intestinal appendix. After the examination, recalling the doctor's words, Ivan feels optimistic: "Stimulate one sluggish organ, check the activity of another—secretion ensues, and everything would come right." He goes home, where a jolly social gathering is in progress; he seems to be in fairly good spirits (considering that that appendix-thing is always in the back of his mind), but he leaves the party early to retire by himself for the night. Alone in his room, he imagines that the improvement in the appendix has already occurred:

> Secretion, evacuation were stimulated: regular action re-established. "Yes, that's it!" he said to himself. "One has only to assist nature, that's all." He remembered his medicine, sat up, swallowed it and lay down on his back, watching for the medicine to have its salutary effect and stop the pain. "All I have to do is to take it regularly and avoid harmful influences. Why, I am better already, much better." He began to feel his side: it was not painful to the touch. "There, I really don't feel it. It's much better already." He put out the light and turned on his side . . . "The appendix is righting itself, secretion is occurring." Suddenly he felt the old familiar dull, gnawing pain, the same obstinate, steady, serious pain. In his mouth there was the same familiar loathsome taste. His heart sank, his brain felt dazed. "O God, O God!" he whispered. "Here it is again! And it will never cease." And in a flash the trouble presented itself in quite a different guise. "Intestinal appendix! The kidney!" he said to himself. "It is not a question of appendix or kidney but of life

and . . . death. Yes, once there was life, and now it is drifting away, and I can't stop it. Yes. Why deceive myself? Isn't it obvious to everyone but me that I am dying, and that it's only a matter of weeks, days . . . it may happen this very moment. There was light but now there is darkness. I was here but now I am going. Where?" A cold chill came over him, and he heard only the throbbing of his heart.

"I shall be no more, then what will there be? There will be nothing. Then where shall I be when I am no more? Can this be dying? No, I will not have it!" He jumped up and tried to light the candle, fumbled about with trembling hands, dropped the candle and candlestick on the floor and fell back upon the pillow.

Ivan tries to get control of himself. He reviews the stages of his illness (as if close scrutiny might reveal that it never really started). The knock, the early signs, the doctors . . .

"and all the time I got nearer and nearer to the abyss. My strength began to fail. Nearer and nearer! And now I have wasted away and there is no light in my eyes. [Something he has overheard someone else say of him.] Death is here, and I am thinking of an appendix! I am thinking of how to get my bowels in order, while death knocks at the door. Can it really be death?" Terror seized him again and he gasped for breath.

The days go by, and Ivan is wretched:

In the depths of his heart he knew he was dying but, so far from growing used to the idea, he simply did not and could not grasp it.

The example of a syllogism which he had learned in Kliezewetter's *Logic*: "Caius is a man, men are mortal, therefore Caius is mortal," had seemed to him all his life to be true as applied to Caius but certainly not as regards himself.

He goes on in this vein a bit—maybe you will recognize the "not-me" phenomenon—and then:

"If I had to die like Caius I should have known it was so, some inner voice would have told me. But there was nothing of the sort in me, and I and all my friends, we know that it was quite different in our case [the "not-us" phenomenon]. And here it is!" he said to himself. "It can't—it can't be, and yet it is! How has it happened? How am I to understand it?"

And he could not understand it, and tried to drive this false, errone-ous, morbid thought away and supplant it with other proper, wholesome thoughts. But the idea, and not the idea only but as it were the reality itself kept coming back again and confronting him.[5]

This completes our "text." There are several things in the text about which we shall comment, some right now, others later on.

First of all, despite what he says, Ivan always knew that he would (someday) die. When he says that it never seemed that the syllogism about Caius applied to *him*, Ivan, he is just giving expression to the "not-me" phenomenon. He always knew that he would die but "somehow" did not believe it. In other words, he deceived himself. *Now*, however, now that death is close, Ivan can no longer maintain the self-deception. So he no longer has a barrier to keep out the meaning of death.

But note, when Ivan says, "Why deceive myself?" the self-deception to which he refers is only indirectly that of the "not-me" phenomenon. The self-deception to which he directly refers concerns the fact that now his death is close. Others have seen it, and he himself has known it for some time, but only at this point does he admit it to himself. Only at this point does he undeceive himself about the meaning of the pain and the other changes that have occurred in him: I am dying. These changes are of course recent; hence Ivan's self-deception about the meaning of the changes (of the fact that he is dying) is recent. There is, however, a sense in which he has *always* deceived himself about death—not about its closeness (it was not always close) but about the sheer fact, the fact that: I will die. This prior, basic self-deception, the deception that is motivated by the awfulness of what death means and which takes the form of his "somehow" not acknowledging that the syllogism about death applies to himself as well as Caius, is threatened by his knowledge that he is actually dying, that death is close. So he employs, as it were, a further self-deception to protect the basic deception and thus keep the meaning of death from getting through.

That is, Ivan refuses to admit to himself what he has known for a relatively brief time, that he is dying, and thereby enables himself not to believe what he has always known, that he will die. Insofar as he manages to hang on to the later, basic self-deception, he is safe: he will not be struck by the meaning of death.

On this analysis, the text contains a less than obvious complexity. Ivan undeceives (and therefore has deceived) himself at two levels. At one level, he undeceives himself about the meaning of the changes in his body: he admits what he already knew, that he is dying ("in a flash the trouble

---

[5] "When the commonplace "We must all die" transforms itself suddenly into the acute consciousness "I must die—and soon," then death grapples us, and his fingers are cruel." George Eliot, *Middlemarch* (Oxford University Press, 1996), chap. 52.

presented itself in quite a different guise"). And with this admission the basic, deeper-level self-deception collapses. Ivan can no longer enjoy the luxury of thinking of himself in a way he knows to be false: as an exception to the syllogism about death. So now he is struck by the meaning of death. When Ivan whispers "O God, O God," these words (they echo in the reader's head) compress all this complexity into a single charge. They are the cry of someone being struck by the meaning of death.

What then is the meaning by which Ivan is struck? The prospect of death has sunk in. What does the prospect hold up to Ivan? We do not learn. Ivan (Tolstoy) does not tell us. In the time that is left to him, Ivan comes to learn something about the meaning of his life (the last few sections of the novella), but not about the meaning of his death. He is struck by the meaning of his death without being clear about what he is struck by. What we must focus on right now is this: Whatever it is that Ivan is struck by, whatever his death means to him, it seems to render the fact that he will die not just awful but incomprehensible.

Thus, having admitted to himself that he is dying ("In the depths of his heart . . . "), "so far from growing used to the idea, he simply did not and could not grasp it." What he cannot grasp, I take it, is not the business of dying itself, but death, his death, the fact that: I will die. This fact means something to him that makes it, the fact of his death, seem impossible, and thus, since the fact remains a fact, incomprehensible.

Ivan (like the rest of us) has always "somehow" fancied himself exempt from the syllogism about death (the basic self-deception). But now that he admits that it is close ("here it is"), he can no longer deceive himself. He is no exception: I will die. Ivan is struck by what this means, and what it means seems to involve something impossible. "'It can't—it can't be, and yet it is. How has it happened? How am I to understand it?' And he could not understand it." He cannot understand it because, though *impossible*, it *will be*. A little later, he reflects (a quote not included above) on the triviality of the concern that led to the fatal knock: "Can it be possible? How terrible and how ridiculous! It cannot be! It cannot be, but it is."

What is so impossible here, beyond understanding? That he should have climbed a ladder to show the workmen how to hang the curtain? That he should have slipped and received a blow to his side? That this in turn should have caused funny things to happen in that damned appendix, or wherever? It is the sheer fact of his death that seems impossible to Ivan, the fact that: I will die. Now that he admits to himself that he is dying, he is struck by the meaning of his death. And what he is struck by makes the fact that he is dying seem both awful and impossible. It seems impossible and yet is a fact. Thus he cannot comprehend it.

7.5 Philosophical Reflection and Real-Life Disturbance

When the meaning of death gets through to us, this is what we are faced by, something awful and incomprehensible. Our question is: What is it about death that makes it awful? And in what way or sense is it impossible and thus (since it remains a fact) incomprehensible?

At the very end, after Ivan has come to realize something about the way he has lived, he experiences a release, and then (it all happens rather quickly) a revelation—a kind of mystico-religious vision—that there is no death: "In place of death there was light." This would suggest that, whatever it was in the prospect of death that evoked his earlier reaction, it was illusory. It suggests that, in some sense, the prospect of death is an illusion. It some sense, it is not a fact that I will die.

But who is to say that (assuming we go along with the account of his experience), once the activity of Ivan's brain ceases completely, light will continue to be present within his experience, that the light will not after all be replaced by death? Everything we know says that death will follow, and when there is death there will be no light. Death is not an illusion. It is a fact: I will die. The idea that death is illusory, that things will open up into light, is itself an illusion (or perhaps another form of self-deception).

Note, however, even if we were to agree that death is illusory, we might still want to get clear about what it is that is held up to us in this illusion (of death), what it is that disturbs us. In other words, we might still want to get clear about the content of the (supposed) illusion, about what death means to us. After all, if death is an illusion, it is not a *trivial* illusion.

So our aim would be unaffected: to get clear about what it is in the prospect of death that disturbs us, that strikes us as awful and incomprehensible. But it may not be clear why this aim should belong to philosophy.

One thing is clear: being disturbed by the prospect of death does not require philosophy. We do not need analyses, or arguments, or any other kind of intellectual preliminary in order to be disturbed by the prospect of death. (When Ivan says, "O God, O God," is that based on an argument?) What do we need? We are more likely to be disturbed when we believe death is close. Yet such a belief is not essential. Only one thing is essential: that we are struck by the meaning of death. And this happens when it happens. Philosophical reflection is required not to precipitate the disturbance but to understand it, to make clear to ourselves why we are disturbed: to make clear the meaning of death.

Notice, being disturbed by the meaning of death is not the same thing as being clear about the meaning of death. The disturbance is a symptom of the fact that the meaning is getting through. This, as we said, has no need of philosophy. But clarifying—analyzing—what gets through (if it does), getting clear about the meaning of death, this is a peculiarly philosophical enterprise.

It might be of interest to compare the disturbance in the case of death with the momentary disorientation that may be occasioned by the thought that THIS may be a dream. This too, we observed (3.5), is a real-life possibility. And like death disturbance, it does not require philosophical preparation. The role of philosophy is in both cases to analyze, to get to the bottom of, a disturbance that has its source outside philosophy.

In the dream case, the real-life question "Might THIS be a dream?" comes over us and then it goes. Why does it go? Not because we have established to our satisfaction that THIS is not a dream. Nor is it because, having been unable to satisfy ourselves, we have decided to put the question aside, to leave it unanswered, which is what generally happens when in philosophy we seek to justify our belief that THIS is not a dream. When in real life we actually wonder for a brief moment whether THIS is a dream, we take the question seriously. And precisely because we take the question seriously, it cannot survive. For, as we explained, the question is incoherent. It asks, in effect, whether I might emerge from the context of which I am the subject (the one at the center), the context that contains the whole of what I call "the world" plus the infinity of egocentric space and time, into that very same context—as if I might enter a room by leaving it. The confusion implicit in this question (the confusion of standpoint) cannot survive for very long in an intact mind that is seriously raising the question. The question simply disintegrates and leaves us nothing to answer.

But although the momentary disorientation itself, the panicky coming and going of the thought that THIS is a dream, is a real-life phenomenon that does not depend on philosophical reflection but can occur in the middle of everyday life, our analysis of what is going on in such a case, which employs the results of our reflections on the DH, obviously takes us into philosophy: into (we might say) the realm of metaphysics. Similarly, the analysis that we shall give of our reaction to the prospect of death, of the peculiar way in which this prospect can disturb us, will also draw upon metaphysical (philosophical) resources; in fact, the same resources as we have employed in the analysis of dream disorientation—of the peculiar way in which the DH can disturb us. In both cases there is a real-life disturbance that, at bottom, is metaphysical. And this, the underlying metaphysical disturbance that breaks into everyday consciousness, is what philosophy must seek to uncover.

Of course, we should expect that in some respects the dream and death cases are different. The disturbance in the dream case rests on a metaphysical confusion (a confusion of standpoint). When, however, we are disturbed by the prospect of death, that is, by what death means to us, although the source of the disturbance is metaphysical, there is no confusion. What is held up to us is something that is both awful and such that we cannot understand it. There is not confusion here but, rather, a glimpse of the truth. The prospect of death contains something awful and incomprehensible.

If this is correct, it follows that while in both cases the role of philosophical reflection and analysis is to disclose what is going on at the metaphysical level, the upshot is rather different. In the dream case we get insight into a mistake, a confusion; in the death case, on the other hand, we gain insight into something that is actually there, confronting us in the prospect of death. Philosophical reflection on death uncovers, I believe, a puzzle—a puzzle that is already there for us outside philosophy. Thus, whereas in the dream case the surface disorientation goes away of its own, without philosophy (philosophy only explains why it goes away), nothing—not even philosophy—will touch the puzzling character of death. This is a puzzle that never goes away.

8. The Subject Matter and "Mineness" of My Death

8.1 The Prospect of Death

The prospect of death holds up something that, when it sinks in, disturbs us in a way that nothing else does: something awful and incomprehensible. But what exactly is contained in the prospect of death? At a certain level of generality, the question is not difficult to answer. We may conceive of what is contained in the prospect of death as having two aspects. The first is that something that now *is* will *cease to be*—where the ceasing to be is not temporary but once-and-for-all. The second is that what will cease to be is in some way or sense *mine*. It is because it is "mine" that its ceasing to be is "my" death.

The prospect of death, then, holds up to us the once-and-for-all (we shall not always explicitly mention this) ceasing to be of something, a subject matter, that is mine. So there are two questions. What is held up as that which will cease to be: what is the subject matter of my death? What makes (constitutes) this subject matter, and hence my death, *mine*? In the present chapter we shall mainly consider the first of these questions. The question about the "mineness" of my death will be introduced here but not answered, since it spills over into the discussion of solipsism that follows. My thought is that if we can answer these questions, we will gain some insight into what it is that makes the prospect of death so disturbing, into its awfulness and incomprehensibility; we will, in other words, gain insight into the meaning of death.

Of course with my death all kinds of things will cease to be. But not everything that will cease to be can be included in the subject matter of (my) death. For example, my breathing will cease to be; the flowing of blood through my veins and arteries carrying oxygen to my brain, the activity of such-and-such valves in my heart, of such-and-such glands and organs in the rest of my body—all these activities and processes will cease to be. But it is not the cessation of these activities, etc., that is held up to me in the prospect of death. It is compatible with the prospect of death— of what is held up to me in this prospect—being just what it is that I should know nothing of what goes on in my body. Such ignorance is compatible with death having for me precisely the meaning it has. The activities and processes in my body, then, are not the subject matter whose ceasing to be is held up to me in the prospect of my death. They are not the subject matter the prospect of whose ceasing to be is so disturbing, the subject matter of death. Let us pursue this briefly.

We may assume there is some set of biological processes—involving my heart, lungs, brain, central nervous system, and so on—that is essential to the human being I am remaining alive, the set of essential life processes (call it "E"). When E ceases, I die. Insofar as I do not know what E includes, then, there is a sense in which I do not know what death is.[1] Yet E, whatever it includes, is not the subject matter of my death. For it is not the cessation of E that is held up to me in the prospect of death. Remember, we are concerned with what death means—that is, what *my* death means *to me*. Whatever this is, it is not the cessation of a set of processes about which I may or may not know. You could say, knowing what death means is compatible with complete ignorance about what (in the present sense) death is.

When E ceases, the human being that I am will cease to be a living human being. The human being that I am will be a dead human being. Yet E is not the crucial subject matter. It is not the subject matter the prospect of whose ceasing to be disturbs me in the peculiar way that I am (or may be) disturbed by the prospect of death. E is not the subject matter of my death.

Perhaps it will be objected that if this were correct, if the prospect that so disturbs me were not the prospect of the E ceasing to be, then, were I to learn (say) that I have serious heart disease or cancer of some vital organ, this would not disturb me. But it certainly would disturb me, and in precisely the peculiar way that I am (or may be) disturbed by the prospect of my death.

The question, though, is not just whether the prospect of (say) heart failure in the near future would disturb me in the peculiar way that the prospect of death disturbs me (of course it would), but whether this prospect would disturb me *as such*. Here, once again, the possibility of igno-

---

[1] In fact, the question (which we shall not discuss) of what E includes is difficult. The issue complicated by the interdependence of the relevant processes, and the possibility of artificial intervention. Thus, in the absence of artificial intervention, the heart needs the lungs, and the lungs the heart, and both need the brain stem, which in turn needs the heart and lungs. And (roughly) the upper brain, including the neocortex, needs all of these, whereas they do not need the upper brain. On the other hand, without the upper brain there is no awareness or consciousness. Moreover, a mechanical ventilator can maintain the function of the lungs. Hence there is the possibility of a conscious human being relying on a ventilator; and again, the possibility of a permanently unconscious human being not relying on a ventilator (though needing other forms of artificial support). Which of the processes are the "essential" ones?

rance is relevant. It is only because I happen to know what it signifies, or indicates, that the prospect of my heart's ceasing to function, of this functioning ceasing to be, disturbs me. What does it signify? Death. My death. That is to say, the prospect of the functioning of my heart ceasing to be signifies that something *else* will cease to be. The prospect of heart failure does not disturb me as such but only because it signifies that the subject matter which is the subject matter of death will cease to be—if only we could say what this is.

Think about the following. You suspect—the blood coughed up on the handkerchief, the lump you nervously finger each day—that something is wrong; that is, wrong inside you, inside the human being that you are. Why are you upset? Because of the blood or surface lump itself? Does the blood, etc., disturb you as such? No, it is because of what it signifies. What? Maybe an internal lesion or growth. Then would the lesion, etc., disturb you as such? The lesion itself? Picture a slight tear in some tissue; or a small protuberance in an artery; or a tiny dark spot on an X-ray. Is *that* what gets to you? It is what the lesion, or whatever, signifies. What does it signify? That maybe the problem inside you is, or will become, more widespread; that maybe such-and-such organ will be involved. But again, what is so disturbing? The threat to the organ itself, to the crucial set of processes itself? Or is it what this, in turn, signifies? What does it signify? It signifies cessation of something else, of the crucial subject matter. But what is that?

Notice, we keep talking about what such-and-such "signifies (indicates)." This is signification in a causal sense. The prospect of heart failure, for example, disturbs me because it signifies the cessation of something else, of the crucial subject matter. Why does heart failure have this kind of significance for me? Heart failure, the failure of my heart, signifies the ceasing to be of the crucial subject matter in that the crucial ceasing to be (that of the crucial subject matter) would be a causal (natural) consequence of heart failure. The crucial ceasing to be, the ceasing to be whose prospect peculiarly disturbs us, is at the mercy of the world; so our knowledge of the crucial ceasing to be is at the mercy of our knowledge of the world.

Recall Ivan's words when he undeceives himself: "And in a flash the trouble presented itself in quite a different guise. 'Intestinal appendix! The kidney. It is not a matter of appendix or kidney but of life and . . . death.' " In one sense, of course, it *is* a matter of the appendix, or whatever. That is to say, it is a matter of the set of essential biological processes ceasing to be. This matters. But it matters only because, as a causal consequence, something *else* will cease to be. It is the ceasing to be of the "something else" that *really* matters. It is the "something else" that is the subject matter of death.

8.2 I Will Cease to Be

With death, my life will cease to be. My life is the subject matter of my death. This sounds right, but what do we mean in this context by "my life"? One thing should now be clear: we cannot mean "my life" in the biological sense, i.e., in the sense of some ongoing set of biological processes or phenomena. This (as we have just seen) is not the subject matter whose cessation is held up to me in the prospect of death. The subject matter of death keeps eluding us. If it is not the ceasing to be of my (biological) life that is held up in the prospect of death, what could it be?

It may seem that the answer is obvious: I will cease to be. I now exist and, with my death, I will cease to be. What will cease to be with my death, the subject matter the prospect of whose ceasing to be peculiarly disturbs me, *is* me, the entity that I am. I am the subject matter of my own death. How does Ivan express it? "I shall be no more." Could there be a more direct, or simple, or natural answer to our question? What should *my* death mean to me, what should the prospect of my death hold up to me, if not that *I* will cease to be? Thus the subject matter of my death is "mine" in the most complete way possible, that of identity. It is "mine" in the way of *being me*.

The problem with this thought is not that it is false—it seems clearly true—but that it is not clear in what sense it is true. The difficulty becomes apparent if we reflect on the use of the first person here. In 2.5 we distinguished two uses of the first person: the referential and the positional. For example, in "I have been writing all morning," the "I" is used referentially, to refer to a certain human being, JV. Compare this with my saying (in a philosophical vein), "JV is the human being that I am (that is me)." Here, we said, the first person is used positionally. It functions not as a singular term but to convey or express a position within THIS, within the subject matter of the DH. What I mean is that JV is the human being at the center (who occupies the subject position) of THIS. So there are these two uses of the first person. The question is: How do I use "I" when, thinking of death, I say that "I will cease to be."

There is no way to take the first person positionally here. The positional use of the first person presupposes a reference to some entity or individual of which we then say (using the first person positionally) that that individual occupies the subject position, the position at the center of THIS. In "I will cease to be," the presupposed reference would have to be achieved by the initial "I." However, there is in that case no use of the first person left over that might count as positional. It would seem, then, that the "I" in "I will cease to be" must be referential.

But to what does it refer? We have asked this kind of question before—in trying to make sense of the thought, "I am dreaming" (2.4, 4.3). In that case, the reference, we said, is to a certain human being, to JV. It would seem that in "I will cease to be" I refer by "I" to that same human being, to JV, i.e., the human being that I am (the one at the center of THIS). On this interpretation, however, "I will cease to be" fails to capture what faces me in the prospect of death. The ceasing to be of JV, the human being that I am, is simply a more extreme case of the ceasing to be of E, the processes on the part JV essential to keeping him alive. In both cases, the cessation in question guarantees my death; but in neither case is the relevant subject matter that whose ceasing to be is held up in the prospect of my death.

The subject matter of my death is that the prospect of whose ceasing to be peculiarly disturbs me when I contemplate the prospect of death. What peculiarly disturbs me, however, is not the prospect of JV, the human being that I am, ceasing to be. In fact, I know that the human being in question will not cease to be but will survive (as a corpse, a dead human being). I, the human being that I am, will die; but I, *this* human being, am not the subject matter of my death.

Note, all that is required to see this point is to appreciate the possibility of the human being's surviving the subject matter whose ceasing to be is held up in the prospect of death. The point would hold even in a world where, in fact, creatures die by suddenly vanishing without a trace. In such a world, the human being that I am would not survive the subject matter the prospect of whose ceasing to be is peculiarly disturbing. Nonetheless, the ceasing to be of that human being (its vanishing) would not be the crucial ceasing to be. If from the perspective of such a world I were to contemplate the prospect of my death in a world where (like the actual world) the human being that I am does not vanish with death, this prospect would seem no less disturbing than the prospect that faces me in the world where I will vanish. Indeed, the prospect of my death would seem no less disturbing than in a world where (unlike the actual world) the human being that I am somehow remains forever intact.

These reflections may suggest that we have chosen the wrong type of object as the reference of "I," namely, a human being, a bodily thing, a material part of the world. If we take the "I" to refer not to a human being but to a soul, an immaterial part of the world, we can grant that the ceasing to be of JV is not the crucial ceasing to be and still maintain that I am the subject matter of my death, since the entity that I am is not JV, the human being. I am a soul. That is to say, it is a soul, not a human being, that occupies the subject position (is at the center) of THIS, of my horizon.

Let us suppose that there is a soul, S, that figures at the center of my horizon. Is it not the prospect of death compatible with the immortality of S? Might I not, while completely assured of S's continued existence, find myself faced by the peculiarly disturbing ceasing to be that is my death? Imagine that God tells me that the future of this soul, S, is guaranteed. Yet, it seems, there may remain a question mark over *my* future. The prospect of death may still loom for me. Just as the human being might survive the ceasing to be of the crucial subject matter, so might the soul. If I am an immaterial part of the world (if it is an immaterial part of the world that is at the center of THIS), it is not the cessation of that part of the world that is held up to me in the prospect of death. I may be a soul, but a soul is not the subject matter of my death.

8.3 Death and the Stream of Mental States

The subject matter of death continues to elude us. It is not the set E of biological processes, biological phenomena, essential to my remaining alive (so it is not my life in the biological sense); nor is it the entity that I am, the one at the center of THIS, whether we take it to be the human being (a biological entity) or the soul, a material or immaterial part of the world.

Let us return to E. I believe that my death would follow as a causal consequence of the cessation of E. Moreover, I believe that the continuation of E would have as a causal consequence the continued being or existence of the crucial subject matter, that whose ceasing to be is my death. Causally speaking, then, the continuation of E (whatever exactly E includes) is necessary and sufficient for the continued existence of the subject matter of my death. This yields, at least, an indirect characterization of the subject matter of death: it is such that as long as certain processes in my brain (and body) continue, it will remain in existence, and as soon as these processes cease, the crucial subject matter will also cease to be.

Now here it may strike us that two things converge. At the same time that we are looking for something that fits our indirect characterization of the subject matter of death, we may have a growing sense that we are, in our attempt to characterize this subject matter, neglecting something that is obviously required, viz., a reference to "consciousness," or "mind." Thus it may occur to us that my mental (conscious) states, or rather, the ongoing stream of such states—the stream of my experiences, beliefs, feelings, intentions, memories, etc.—fits our indirect characterization of the subject matter of death; that is, that the continuation of certain processes in my brain is causally necessary and sufficient for the continuation of the stream of my mental states, the stream of consciousness. The obvious suggestion, then, is that this stream of mental states, of consciousness, is the subject matter of death.

We can, I think, evaluate this suggestion without settling the issue of whether my mental states are themselves states of my brain. Thus we can leave open the possibility that, as many philosophers claim, my mental states are a class of such states; a class distinguished from other states of my brain by the fact that (to use the current jargon) they have representational content. In any case, it may be said, the notion of representational content is essential to the suggestion, since, whether my mental states are states of my brain or states of my soul, no series or succession of states could count as the subject matter of my death unless it possessed the right kind of continuity, and the right kind of continuity in this case could derive only from the content of the states in question. What I now do will be (or may be) represented in memory at a later stage of the stream, just as what I have done is now represented; what I now intend to do will, when I do it, be represented as something that I intended; and so on. Philosophers often speak in this regard of "psychological continuity." The stream of my mental states is not just any series or succession of states, but a psychologically continuous series. The suggestion, then, is that the subject matter of death is a psychologically continuous series of states; that it is the prospect of this psychologically continuous series coming to an end, ceasing to be, that so peculiarly disturbs me.

Thus we might say that the subject matter of my death is my mental stream. By my "mental stream," we mean a psychologically continuous series or succession of mental states. These states, the states in the series, are "mental" in that they have representational content. The psychological continuity of the series, the continuity that constitutes the mental series a mental "stream," derives from the states in the series having the right content.[2]

In the same vein, we might say that the subject matter of my death is my consciousness, or my experience—i.e., that my consciousness/experience is the subject matter whose ceasing to be is held up in the prospect of my death. Would this not be a natural thing to say? But again the question is: What do we mean my "consciousness," my "experience." On the present suggestion, we mean a certain stream of mental phenomena, my mental stream.

So, our characterization of the subject matter of death now includes a reference to mind (consciousness, experience), or the mental. Note that

---

[2] Here and elsewhere in the present chapter we touch on ideas that are relevant to the philosophical topic of personal identity, to which, of course, death is relevant. We shall discuss personal identity at length in part 3.

the conception of mind we are employing here is that which we earlier called the phenomenal conception of mind (4.6). What is the crucial subject matter? My mental stream: a series of states or phenomena that have representational content and are, by virtue having the content they have, psychologically continuous.

I think that if in our reflections on the subject matter of death we manage to focus our attention exclusively on the conception of a series of states with representational content—if, that is, we keep focused exclusively on this conception and do not allow in anything extraneous—it will be evident that we have not properly conceived the subject matter of death. The phenomenal conception of mind, you might say, does not give us what we need to conceive the subject matter of death.

The best way to ensure that we extrude from our reflections here everything except what strictly belongs to the conception of a stream of mental states, of states with representational content, is to consider the stream from the standpoint of a godlike observer looking into my head or soul and reading off the content of the states as they succeed one another. From this standpoint, it is hard to suppress the thought that the stream might continue right through my death. Or considered from my standpoint, when I contemplate what is held up to me in the prospect of death, i.e., what this prospect means to me, it seems possible that I should be facing precisely *that*, precisely what is held up in the prospect of death, and yet that I have reason to believe that the series of states with representational content occurring in me will continue. It seems that, for any such series now occurring in me, the series that the godlike observer could read off, new states with content appropriate to preserving the psychological continuity of the series might just keep accumulating, adding on to the series, that such states might keep adding on to the series after I die—like a thread that runs through my life and then out of it again on the other side, that continues on when the crucial subject matter (whatever that is) has ceased to be.

Assume there is occurring in me such a stream as we have described. Could not God (a godlike observer) assure me that it will continue after I die—that (for all we need say) it will continue forever? This would not guarantee the continued existence of the crucial subject matter. It is compatible with what God assures me that there should remain the same prospect of the awful, incomprehensible ceasing to be: the same prospect of the total once-and-for-all shutting down, the complete blackout, that will be my death. This prospect could remain, just as it could remain were God to offer me a guarantee that a particular human being, or a particular soul, will remain endlessly in existence.

There are two points to bear in mind here. The first concerns causation. If the foregoing is correct, the subject matter of death can no more be identified with a stream of mental states occurring in me than with the activity in my brain, etc., that is causally necessary and sufficient for the continued occurrence in me of the stream. But we believe that, in fact, the activity in my brain is causally necessary and sufficient for the continued existence of the crucial subject matter, the subject matter of death. It follows that the continued activity in my brain is causally necessary and sufficient for the continued existence of the crucial subject matter and for the continued occurrence of the mental stream. Yet—this is the first point—it does not follow that the subject matter of death *is* the mental stream. We have just seen that, whatever it is, it is not the mental stream.

The other point concerns the possibility of a godlike perspective on my mental stream. To call attention to such a possibility is a way of dramatizing what philosophers often call the "external" or "third-person" perspective. Thus we imagined how the stream would present itself to someone "looking into" my head (or soul) and reading off the content of my mental states—as perhaps someone might read off the content of the inner states of a computer. When the stream is considered in this way, we said, there seems to be no reason why it might not continue right through the crucial cessation, the cessation that is held up to me in the prospect of death.

Suppose, however, we adopt the "internal" or "first-person" standpoint. Instead of imagining "looking into" my brain or soul, we imagine how it is for me in "looking out"; in other words, how it is for me when I am simply occupied with what is going on in my experience—when, that is, I am occupied with the bit of the world that appears from within my experience. It may now seem impossible that the stream of my mental (experiential) states should survive my death. On the contrary, it may seem that the continuation of the experiential stream would plainly be equivalent to the continuation of the crucial subject matter. As long as the experiential (mental) stream continues, the crucial subject matter continues.

But there is a confusion here. When we consider my situation from the internal (first-person) perspective, we in effect consider the world as it appears from within my experience. Thus—and we cannot but be at some level aware of this—we introduce the horizonal subject matter, i.e., my experience in the horizonal sense, into our reflections. At the same time, given our philosophical preoccupation with the phenomenal conception of mind (experience), we misconceive this subject matter as a stream of states. Insofar as in our reflections we obscurely intend the horizonal subject matter, we correctly grasp that as long as "my experience" continues, the crucial subject matter continues. Yet insofar as the phenomenal conception of experience dominates our reflections, insofar as we confusedly regard the experiential horizon as a stream of experiential states, we arrive at the mistaken view that the crucial subject matter (that whose ceasing to be is held up to me in the prospect of death) is a stream of mental (experiential) states.

The confusion just described cannot arise when we consider my experience purely from the external perspective. The picture from the internal perspective is the picture of how things are from within my horizon (this is the sense in which the perspective is "internal"). From the external perspective (when we "look into" my head or soul), my horizon does not figure at all. This is why from external perspective we are able to adhere to the conception of my experience as a stream of states; why, then, there is no possibility of confusing the horizon with a mental stream. By adopting the external perspective—by keeping the horizon out of the picture and thus eliminating the possibility of misconceiving it as a stream of phenomena—we allow the mental stream to present itself unambiguously as a stream of phenomena. Thus presented, it is evident that the stream might continue through the cessation of the crucial subject matter, that therefore it cannot be regarded the true subject matter of death.

But we have yet to identify this elusive subject matter, the true subject matter of death.

8.4 The World and the Subject Matter of Death

What is the subject matter whose ceasing to be is the crucial ceasing to be, the subject matter of death? It is not a set of biological processes, or a human being, or a soul, or a stream of mental states. There seems to be nothing—nothing in the world: no substance or phenomenon or stream of phenomena, physical or mental, material or immaterial—whose ceasing to be is the ceasing to be that matters, the ceasing to be that is held up to me in the prospect of death. Strange. On the one hand the prospect of death is a prospect in which it seems that nothing will cease to be. Yet it is also a prospect in which it seems that everything will cease to be.[3]

You know where this is heading. The subject matter of death—that which the prospect of death holds up as ceasing to be; that the prospect of whose ceasing to be is so peculiarly disturbing—is the same subject matter as that which emerged in our reflections on the DH, viz., THIS, my horizon (the personal horizon): the horizon of which I (JV, the human being) am at the center and to which the whole of what I call "the world" and the infinity of egocentric space and time are internal. The subject

---

[3] "The Big Ending, though no one knows what, if anything, is ending and certainly no one knows what is beginning. It is a wild celebration of no one knows what." Philip Roth, *The Dying Animal* (Vintage, 2002) p. 148.

matter of death and the subject matter of the dream hypothesis are one and the same.

The subject matter of death has more than one name. What will cease to be? My consciousness, my experience, my life. That is to say, my consciousness, experience, life in the horizonal sense. A plurality of names (guises), one subject matter: the personal horizon. This is what is held up to me in the prospect of death, the ceasing to be of my (the personal) horizon.

"When I die, this will be no more." What (I ask myself) will be no more? THIS will be no more. Not the human being (soul) that I am, or something going on in that entity. Not a part of the world, material or immaterial, but that from within which the world appears, the horizon of the world, my horizon.

What appears from within my experience—which may include myself—is (or so we may assume) part of the world. But that from within which the world appears, including the bit that is myself, this is not anything occurring in myself. It is not anything occurring anywhere, in any part of the world. It is not, as we said, part of the world but the horizon of the world. It, THIS, is the subject matter of death.

I know that I will die. I know this, we might say, in both the biological and metaphysical sense. That is, I know that I am a living creature and that all living creatures die. Death in the biological sense. I also know that the existence or being of THIS, the personal horizon, depends causally on what is going on in my brain. I know that when my brain shuts down, there will no longer be such a thing as THIS, as my horizon, that the crucial subject matter will no longer be. The cessation of the crucial subject matter, of my horizon, is death in the metaphysical sense.[4] When I die biologically, I will die metaphysically: there will cease to be such a thing as THIS. It is death in the metaphysical sense that is in the first instance disturbing. The prospect of my biological death is disturbing only because of what it means causally, viz., my metaphysical death, the ceasing to be of THIS.

How do I know this? I know, e.g., what happens when I fall sleep, or when I am put under deep anaesthesia. And I know that what happens when I fall asleep, or am put under deep anaesthesia, is a consequence of an altered state of my brain. What happens? Looking back on it, there is a gap or blank in my past: a blank within the past of THIS. Then what

---

[4] The distinction between biological and metaphysical death is closely related to the distinction that we drew 8.1 between what my death "is" and what it "means," i.e., what is held up to me in the prospect of death. The subject matter of biological death is a certain set of processes going on in me; the subject matter of metaphysical death is what is held up as ceasing to be in the prospect of death, that whose ceasing to be peculiarly disturbs me.

would happen if my brain ceased to function entirely—not just an altered mode of functioning, but a complete once-and-for-all cessation of activity? Based on the occurrence of past gaps, gaps within the past of THIS, I know what would happen. There would be, as it were, a once-and-for-all gap.

Of course a once-and-for-all gap is not a *gap*. A period of time can figure, retrospectively, as a "gap" only from within the horizon. (Once the horizon has ceased to be, there is nothing with respect to which a gap might be defined.) Death is once-and-for-all, but it is not a gap; it is the once-and-for-all ceasing to be of that which makes a gap possible. I know that sooner or later the once-and-for-all ceasing to be will arrive. I know this because I know that the ticking of my brain is all that stands between me and the once-and-for-all ceasing to be, and I know that sooner or later the ticking of my brain will cease.

To repeat: the subject matter of death is the subject matter of the DH. But note, the DH, since it entails the possibility of a world outside THIS, is a transcendent hypothesis, a hypothesis about what holds outside THIS. Thus, if THIS is reality, that fact is a transcendent fact. In contrast, that I will die (metaphysically) is not a transcendent fact. That THIS will cease to be is not a fact about what holds outside THIS. It is compatible both with there being something outside THIS (with THIS being a dream) and with there being nothing outside THIS (with THIS being reality). However, though it is not a transcendent fact, the fact of death has its subject matter in common with the transcendent fact that THIS is reality: both are facts about THIS, about the personal horizon.

Thus the fact that I will die (in the metaphysical sense[5]) leaves the totality I call "the world" untouched in the same way that the fact that THIS is reality leaves that totality untouched. For, once again, the fact of death concerns not the ceasing to be of anything *in* that totality, but the ceasing to be of THIS, the horizon of the totality.[6] This is why, no matter where we look, we are unable to find anything in the totality with which to identify the subject matter of my death.

With death, THIS will no longer be. Then what will there be? It seems that the answer must be that "everything" will be. That is to say, everything in the world will remain as it is. Something will cease to be, but what ceases to be is such that it will leave everything—everything in the world—as it is.

---

[5] We shall henceforth understand this qualification without noting it.

[6] Of course the biological fact that I will die, that the human being that I am will cease to be alive, will constitute a difference in the totality: certain things will cease to be (occur) in the human being that I am. Unless otherwise indicated, by "the fact that I will die" we shall henceforth understand the metaphysical fact.

Let us cast our minds back to what we said in 4.6 about the subject matter of the DH, viz., that it "adds nothing" to the world; so it could be "subtracted" while leaving the world as it is. The subject matter of the DH, we said, is not nothing (it is something), but it is nothing in itself— i.e., nothing apart from something being present from within it (4.5). In contemplating the prospect of death, we answer "everything" to the question "What will there be?"; we thereby recognize that death will subtract nothing from the world. It is a ceasing to be of something that is nothing in itself; a ceasing to be that therefore leaves everything in the world as it is.

But is it not also the case that when I contemplate my death and ask, "What will there be?" I am inclined to give precisely the opposite answer—just as Ivan does? Ivan thinks: "I shall be no more, then what will there be?" He answers: "There will be nothing." Does he mean that the world will cease to be? If we consider the ceasing to be that really matters to him, this will leave the world as it is. Clearly, Ivan does not mean that the world (the bed on which he suffers, his house, his family, and so on) will cease to be. Then what does he mean when he says, "There will be nothing"? What do I (we) mean when I say this?

Recall the mutual dependence between the existence of the horizon, the subject matter of the DH, and facts of presence/appearing (4.5, 4.6). Facts of presence, we said, hold only from within this subject matter, only from within the horizon. So if there were no horizon, there would be no such facts. There would be a sheer absence of presence. What would that be like? Not like silence, or darkness. These are, if you think about it, limiting cases of presence. A complete absence of presence is not "like" anything and thus cannot be imagined (there is nothing to imagine). It is a big zero, an unimaginable blank. An unimaginable nothingness: NOTHINGNESS. If there were no horizon, nothing would be present, and if nothing were present, there would be NOTHING. The world, we may assume, would still be there, just as it is. But it would not be present, or appear in any way. There would be NOTHING. On the other hand, if nothing were present—absolutely nothing—there would be the unimaginable blank, in which case there would be no horizon. No such thing as THIS. If there were NOTHING, there would be no such thing as THIS.

It is the dependence in the first direction that is relevant right now. Contemplating death, we say (with Ivan), "There will be nothing." What do we mean? Not that there will be no such thing as the world. On the contrary, the world will, we may suppose, remain as it is. What will no longer be is THIS, that from within which the world is present/appears. In that case, there will be NOTHING. Is this not what we (and Ivan) mean—that there will be NOTHING? Everything in the world will be just as it is, but there will be NOTHING.

This is how it is with death. Looked at it one way, it makes a difference that is not a difference. Looked at it another way, it makes the greatest difference of all.

8.5 The "Mineness" of My Death and the Horizonal Use of the First Person

The second aspect of the meaning of death, i.e., of what is held up to us in the prospect of death, is, we said (8.1), the "mineness" of the subject matter that will cease to be—that which we have now identified with the subject matter of the DH, viz., THIS, my horizon (the personal horizon). The mineness of my death is the mineness of my horizon. The question is: In what sense is my horizon "mine"? In what does its "mineness" consist?

Each of us has his "own" death. Insofar as it "is" at all, Heidegger says in *Being and Time*, "by its very essence, death is in every case mine."[7] Heidegger is talking here about what we called death in the metaphysical sense (8.4). Death (in this sense) is in every case mine. But what makes it mine? (In what does its mineness consist?) Heidegger does not tell us. If we say, what makes my death mine is that the horizon whose ceasing to be is my death is *my* horizon, this takes us nowhere—except back to the question of what makes my horizon mine?[8] The questions "What makes my death mine?" and "What makes my horizon mine?" are the same question.

The subject matter of death, my horizon, has, as we have observed, many guises. It is my life, my experience, my consciousness. Let us now draw attention to another guise of this subject matter. The subject matter of death is, in a certain sense, "myself." Not, we know, in the sense of being the human being that I am, JV, but in the horizonal sense, i.e., in the sense of being my horizon. Just as there is a horizonal conception of my experience, and so on, there is a horizonal conception of the self. The horizonal conception of the self is not the conception of an entity or an individual, but of the subject matter in virtue of being at the center of

---

[7] *Being and Time*, p. 284.

[8] In *Being and Time*, the question of what makes my death "mine" is the question of what makes Dasein's Being "mine." Heidegger says again and again that Dasein's Being is in each case "mine." So the "mineness" of death is the "mineness" of Dasein's Being. However, I can find no place in *Being and Time* where Heidegger tells us in what the mineness of Dasein's Being consists. In pointing out that "mineness" is essential to Dasein's Being, Heidegger tells something about Dasein's Being, but he does not tell us what the mineness essential to Dasein's Being is. Yet if we do not know this, we do not understand something that is essential to death, viz., as he puts it, "that it is in every case mine."

which a certain entity, a certain human being (JV), is myself (in the positional sense), i.e., the human being that I am.

The horizonal conception of the self, then, is not the conception of an entity. Nor is it—we are anticipating here ideas that will be discussed in part 3—the conception of the position by occupying which a certain entity is myself (= the one that I am), i.e., what we earlier called the positional conception of the self (2.5). So far from being the positional conception, the horizonal conception of the self is the conception of the subject matter within which the positional conception of the self is defined.

Thus the horizonal conception of the self is a conception of the same subject matter that is the subject matter of the DH and death. It is the subject matter that (as Heidegger says) "is in every case mine." But this takes us no closer to answering our question about the "mineness" of this subject matter. Maybe the answer seems obvious: my horizon is "mine" by virtue of the fact that *I* am the one who occupies the position at its center, the subject position. But now we have come around in a circle (a circle that will keep plaguing us). Thus, as we pointed out, the subject position—the position by occupying which a particular human being is the one that I am (myself)—is a position defined by reference to my horizon: it is by virtue of being at the center of *my* horizon, that JV is the human being that *I am*. So if our question is, "By virtue of what is my horizon "mine"?"," we cannot answer by appealing back to the fact that the human being that I am is the one at its center. It is precisely by being the one at its center that that human being is the human being that I am. We shall call this the "circle of the first person."

The "my," then, in "my horizon" cannot be understood as referring possessively to the human being that I am. You could explain the "mineness" of my hand, or my car, or my children in some such way as this, but not the "mineness" of my horizon. If a certain human being is the one that "I am" by virtue of being at the center of my horizon, it cannot be by virtue of belonging to that human being that I am that the horizon is "mine."

Is it not possible to include myself, the human being I am, in the scope of "how things are for me," in other words, to withdraw in reflection to a point where the very human being that I am is there *for me*? When the words "for me" are used to express this kind of reflective withdrawal, they have (I believe) the sense of "within my horizon." The reflective thought that includes JV within the scope of how things are "for me" is a thought about how things are from within my horizon. Thus the "me" in "for me" cannot—on pain of getting caught up in the circle of the first person—be understood as referring to JV, to the human being that I am.

In trying to explain the "mineness" of horizon, we encounter a use of the first person that must be recognized as other than its familiar referential use. Nor, it seems, can this use of the first person be identified with what we called the positional use of the first person: the use to express or convey the position by occupying which a certain human being is the one that "I am" (2.5). If in a philosophical context I think, "JV is the human being that I am," I use the first person not to refer once again to JV (not, in other words, by way of stating an identity), but to convey the position at the center of my horizon (that by occupying which JV is the one that "I am"). Clearly, the "my" in "my horizon" is not used in this way, i.e., positionally. Taken as a whole, the expression "my horizon" functions as a singular term for the horizon within which the subject-position is defined. How the could the "my," which figures as part of the singular term and thus by way of specifying the subject matter to which the term as a whole refers, convey a position within that same subject matter?

Notice, the question of what makes my horizon "mine" has emerged as the same question as that about a particular use of the first person, the use in "my horizon (consciousness, experience, life)." This is a third use of the first person, that is, a use that cannot be identified with either the referential or the positional use. How are we to understand it? If we do not understand it, we do not understand the "mineness" of my horizon; and if we do not understand the "mineness" of my horizon, we do not understand the "mineness" of my death.

We have, you may recall, already remarked upon the third use of the first person—in discussing dream skepticism. (See the end of 6.7.) If when I raise the DH I ask myself whose dream it would be, the answer is that it would be "mine." This use of the first person, we argued, is neither the referential nor the positional use. We called it the "horizonal" use of the first person.

If THIS were a dream, the dream would be mine. Not your dream but my dream. When THIS ceases to be, the death that will be will be my death. Not your death but mine, the death that peculiarly disturbs me. And so it is when we turn to the self. What makes a particular human being me, the one that I am, is that he occupies the position at the center of my horizon. Not your horizon but mine. In all these cases we are directed to something, to a horizon, that is mine. But what makes the horizon "mine"? How, in other words, are we using the first person when we refer to the subject matter of the DH, to the subject matter of death, to the subject matter by being at the center of which a certain human being is me (the one that I am), as something that is "mine"?

Well, as we said, we are not using the first person referentially or positionally but "horizonally." So far, however, this is nothing more than a bit of terminology. We need an explanation of the horizonal use of the first person. We need, that is, to know what makes my horizon "mine," in what the "mineness" of my horizon consists. The problem is, it may seem that there cannot be an explanation. For what could make my horizon "mine" except that the horizon in some way belongs to the entity that is me, the one that I am? But, we know, if we appeal to this, we introduce the circle, since the explanation of what makes the entity in question the one that "I am" is that it occupies a certain position within my horizon. There seems to be nothing by reference to which we might explain what makes my horizon "mine."

Is there then nothing by virtue of which my horizon is mine? My death is, after all, not your death. Your death is the ceasing to be of your horizon; my death is the ceasing to be of mine. So there must be a difference between your horizon and mine. (Otherwise there would be no difference between your death and mine.) There must then be something that accounts for this difference, something that makes my horizon "mine," hence some way of explaining the horizonal use of the first person. But what is it? In what does the "mineness" of my horizon consist?

9. Solipsism

9.1 My Horizon and the Horizon

My hand is "mine" in that it is literally part of me, my body, the human being that I am. My car is "mine" in that it belongs (in a legal sense) to me, to the human being that I am. My children are "mine" in the sense of being my offspring. In these and similar cases, the "mineness" of something is explained by reference back to me, the human being that I am, JV. If we ask about that human being, JV, what makes him the human being that "I am," the explanation refers back to my horizon: JV is "me," the human being that "I am," by virtue of being the one at the center of my horizon. So far, so good (though we have yet to consider what it is to be "at the center," etc.). If, however, we go on to ask what makes my horizon "mine," we seem to be at a loss. There is nothing to refer back to, in the way that in explaining what makes my car, etc., "mine" we refer back to me, and in explaining what makes me "me" we refer back to my horizon. We may be tempted to say that what makes my horizon "mine" is that I, the one that I am, am at its center—but of course now we are caught in a circle (the circle of the first person). When we get back to my horizon, we are, it seems, as far back as we can go.

It follows that the explanation of what makes my horizon "mine" will have to conform to a different pattern. It will not be by reference to something else that we explain the "mineness" of my horizon. What is the explanation? What makes my horizon "mine"?

In essence, I believe, the explanation is simple. (Simple but difficult.) What makes my horizon "mine" is that, in a sense, my horizon is *the* horizon.

In fact, in discussing the subject matter of the DH and death, we have often spoken of "the horizon." But this may be regarded as elliptical for "the horizon that is mine." Thus, for example, if we say that a certain human being is the one that "I am" by virtue of occupying the position "at the center of the horizon," we mean "at the center of the horizon that is mine." What we are now talking about is not an ellipsis but a straightforward replacement. The idea is that the "mineness" of my horizon consists in its uniqueness: in its being (in some sense) *the* horizon. If this is right, the horizonal use of the first person is a disguised use of the definite article.

In this way, we are all solipsists. What makes my horizon "mine" is that it is the horizon. Thus the "my" in "my horizon," i.e., the horizonal "my," is really a stand-in for the definite article. Is this not a simple solution to the problem we have raised, a way out of the circle of the first person? Solipsism is the solution to our problem.

There are two general points to enter in advance of taking up the flurry of questions and objections with which this "simple solution" is apt to be greeted. First of all, when we say that solipsism is the solution to our problem, we do not mean that the fact that it is a solution, etc., is a "reason" for accepting solipsism. There is a style of philosophical argumentation from which I would wish to distance myself here. Philosophers sometime argue for a "view" (or "theory," etc.) on the basis that, if we accept this view, we can solve such-and-such problem. (If we accept phenomenalism, we can solve the problem of the external world; if we accept functionalism, we can solve the mind-body problem; and so on.) It seems to me that this kind of indirect reasoning goes against the spirit of philosophy, that in philosophical reflection we should accept only what itself seems true (including what we find ourselves rationally forced to accept as true[1]).

In any case, I do not think we need an indirect reason for accepting solipsism to be true. I think we already know it to be true. We know it, and thus we believe it—but we have to become open to what we know. We have, in other words, to discover philosophically this truth that we already know, the truth of solipsism.[2]

The second point concerns the relation between solipsism and our reflections on death. The "mineness" of my death is the "mineness" of the subject matter of my death—the "mineness" of the subject matter the prospect of whose ceasing to be is so disturbing—in short, the "mineness" of my horizon. And this "mineness," we are now saying, consists in the fact that my horizon is in some sense *the* horizon; it consists in the truth

---

[1] See Int.6.

[2] Russell somewhere (I cannot recall the reference) expresses amused surprise at the naiveté of a correspondent who informs him in a letter that not only has she become convinced of the truth of solipsism, she cannot understand why "all philosophers" are not solipsists. Russell is amused at the way this person, like a confused child, fails to appreciate how the content of what she says (if not the fact that she communicates it in a letter) betrays her own belief in the falsehood of what she says. I cannot comment on the philosophical beliefs of Russell's correspondent, but I would say that a philosopher who believes that the expression, or communication, of a belief in solipsism automatically displays childlike confusion not only is very far from a true philosophical grasp of solipsism, he is not open to his own beliefs, to his own solipsism.

of solipsism. The point is that there is no better way to grasp the truth of solipsism than by reflecting on death. Death puts us in touch with the truth of solipsism, our own solipsism, in a way that nothing else does. Thus it must not be anticipated that we shall be able to arrive at an understanding of the "mineness" of my horizon, the sense in which "my" horizon is "the" horizon, and then, as it were, use that understanding to throw fresh light on the topic of death, since it is only by reflecting in a particular way on death that we are brought to recognize the fact of our solipsism and thereby arrive at whatever understanding we manage to obtain of the "mineness" of my horizon.

Just as it is by reflecting on the DH that the horizon comes into view, so the "mineness" of the horizon, the truth in solipsism, can become clear to us if we reflect in the right way on death. Dream and death. Each lends itself to a philosophical discovery, to becoming open to something we already know.

Once again, we are saying that solipsism contains the solution to the problem about the horizonal "my," to the problem of what makes my horizon "mine." Of course, one may wish to object that solipsism itself is problematic. How can a problem be a solution to a problem? There is a lot to talk about here.

On its horizonal use, the first person—e.g., the "my" in "my horizon"—is a stand-in for the definite article. What makes my horizon "mine" is (to repeat) that it is, in a certain sense, *the* horizon. This is, I am saying, not just a "view" or "theory" in philosophy, it is, something— something nontrivial—we actually believe. We (I, each of us) actually believe that, in a certain sense, my horizon is "the" horizon. In what sense? In what sense are we solipsists?

The solipsist (the solipsist in each of us) wants to say that my horizon is "the" horizon in the sense that it is *alone*. Aloneness is the essence of solipsism. In what sense "alone"? Clearly, I (we) do not believe that mine is the one and only horizon (life, consciousness, experience). My horizon is alone, not in the sense that it is the only horizon, but in the sense that (borrowing Wittgenstein's image once again) it has no neighbors. That is, my horizon includes all others (see 6.9–11). It is not the only, but the preeminent, horizon and thus stands alone. (It is one thing to think "I am alone" when you look up and notice everyone has left the room; it is another thing to think this when you find the room full of people.)

So the thought is that my horizon is "the" horizon, unique, in the sense that it is the preeminent, the all-inclusive, horizon. Herein consists the "mineness" of my horizon: it is the horizon that includes all other horizons and therefore has no neighbors. My horizon stands alone. This is something we all know—each for himself. The aloneness is ours, something we live with. We all know, and hence believe, the truth in solipsism. We are all solipsists.[3]

9.2 The Solipsism of Wittgenstein's Tractatus

It will not escape the reader that we are here directly contradicting what we said in chapter 6 by way of responding to dream skepticism. As an insider of the communal horizon (our system of language-games), I find myself committed to (O). That is to say, I find myself with Others, metaphysical equals: subjects of coordinate horizons: horizons that are not included in mine but stand alongside it, as neighbors. Thus the commitment to (O), which pervades my life, amounts to antisolipsism. This commitment, as we explained, is what makes it rationally impossible to take dream skepticism seriously. In effect, we (I) dismiss the DH because we are antisolipsists. How then can we now say that we all know (and thus believe) the truth in solipsism?

This is the way we live, committed to (O): with Others. With Others—yet alone. If my aloneness entails taking my horizon to be preeminent (if that is what makes my horizon "mine"), it is not obvious how these things might be reconciled, since our togetherness entails taking our horizons to be coordinate. If the "mineness" of my horizon consists in the truth of solipsism, how can I (as it were, antisolipsistically) regard *my* horizon as situated in a space of coordinate horizons? Unless we are wrong in supposing that our aloneness, our solipsism, conflicts with our commitment to (O), our life with Others. Let us pursue this thought by considering the statement of solipsism in Wittgenstein's *Tractatus*.

In at least two respects, our statement of solipsism is very close to Wittgenstein's. The solipsist, as we have represented him (and remember, we are the solipsist), is occupied with THIS, the subject matter of the DH, the subject matter of death, i.e., with the horizonal subject matter, with something that is not part of the world but the horizon of the world. The solipsist of the *Tractatus* is occupied with this same subject matter. Wittgenstein calls it the "philosophical self." He says we must distinguish the self in this sense from the self studied in psychology, and more generally, from the "self" in any sense in which the self is regarded as part of the world. The philosophical self, he says, "does not belong to the world:

---

[3] The usual version of solipsism (see, e.g., the chapter on solipsism in Russell's *Human Knowledge* [Simon and Schuster, 1948]) says that, apart from my mind, everything (including other minds) that exists exists only in my mind, that therefore my mind is the only mind, the only entity, that exists on its own. Thus I am (my mind is) alone. The contrast between the usual version of solipsism, which no one believes, and the version that I am saying we all believe will become clear as we proceed.

rather it is a limit of the world" (5.632). Again: "The philosophical self is not the human being, not the human body, or the human soul, with which psychology deals, but rather the metaphysical subject, the limit of the world—not a part of it" (5.641). The "limit" of which Wittgenstein speaks, the "metaphysical subject" or "limit of the world," is, I think, the subject matter that emerged in our reflections on the DH: that to which the world and the infinity of space and time is (in the way that it is) internal. This subject matter—THIS: the horizon or limit of the world—is the subject matter with which the solipsist of the *Tractatus* is concerned.[4]

The second respect in which our account of solipsism resembles Wittgenstein's is that we are taking solipsism to be not just an eccentric philosophical "theory" but a truth (a truth that we all know). Thus Wittgenstein remarks that what the solipsist means is "quite correct." It is correct, i.e., true—"only [he continues] it cannot be said, but makes itself manifest" (5.62). Now here, it seems, we get a divergence from our conception of solipsism.

Why (or in what sense) is it the case that, although what he means is true, the solipsist cannot say (or think) what he means? It is, I take it, for the very reason that what the solipsist means is a fact that makes itself manifest. If a fact, or truth, makes itself manifest, then it must be manifest. Now, something cannot be manifest on its own but only from only from within a horizon (only from within consciousness in the horizonal sense). In short, a fact of manifestness, like a fact of presence/appearing, requires a horizon. So a fact that "makes itself manifest," a fact or truth that cannot hold without being manifest, is a fact that requires a horizon. Thus the fact that the solipsist means, since it makes itself manifest, is a fact that requires a horizon.

It follows that if there were NOTHING, if no fact of presence held, the fact that the solipsist means would not hold. For if there were NOTHING, there would be no horizon from within which that fact might hold (4.5).

A fact that makes itself manifest, we just said, is a fact that cannot hold without being manifest: if it holds, it cannot but be manifest that it holds. Consider the fact that the object present to me right now is a cup. We may take it that the fact in question is manifest. Yet it is not a fact that makes itself manifest. For clearly, it need not have been manifest. It might have come as a surprise that *this* is a cup. That this or that

---

[4] Identifying Wittgenstein's "limit" of the world, the metaphysical subject, with our horizonal subject matter requires us to think very carefully about the point of the analogy Wittgenstein draws between the metaphysical self and the eye with its visual field (5.633–1 of course the eye, though it does not appear in the visual field, *does* belong to the world. It would seem that the proper analogue of the metaphysical subject is not the eye (as the passage actually suggests) but the visual field.

object is present can always come as a surprise. What cannot come as a surprise, however, is that *something or other* is present, that *some* fact of presence holds, that (as we might express it) there is SOMETHING, not NOTHING.

The fact that there is SOMETHING, not NOTHING, is a fact that makes itself manifest; but it is not a fact that makes itself *hold*. A fact, a truth, that makes itself hold would be a fact, etc., that cannot but hold, a necessary fact or truth, whereas a fact that makes itself manifest, since it requires a horizon from within which to hold, is not a necessary truth. It is contingent that there is SOMETHING, not NOTHING. However, given that there is SOMETHING, not NOTHING—given, in other words, that there is such a thing as my horizon—it is necessary that this fact, since it makes itself manifest, is manifest.

From this you can see that the fact in question does not depend for its being manifest on my being in any way occupied with that fact; otherwise its being manifest would not be ensured by the mere fact that there is SOMETHING, not NOTHING. Whether I am probing tomatoes at the supermarket, nagging my kids, chasing a bus, daydreaming, philosophizing—it does not matter. It cannot come as a surprise to me that there is SOMETHING, not NOTHING. This fact cannot but be already manifest.

This means that if I *do* occupy myself with this fact if I actually think it (or say it), my thinking (saying) what I think will, inevitably, be redundant. It will just repeat what is, and could not but have been, already manifest. It will be an empty kind of thinking—like retracing words already written out for us. Is there not a sense in which such thinking does not really *think* anything, and more generally, a sense in which a fact, or truth, that makes itself manifest "cannot be thought (said)"?

There is also a sense, obviously, in which a fact that makes itself manifest "*can* be thought (said)." Indeed, this is presupposed by the very account we have given of the inevitable redundancy, the sense in which such a fact "cannot be thought (said)." For the redundancy is a redundancy that arises precisely in our thinking (saying) the fact in question.

Notice, it is not just that if I think "There is SOMETHING (not NOTHING)," what I think will inevitably be manifest; it will, inevitably, *already* be manifest. The inevitable manifestness of what I think comes at me, so to speak, in the present perfect tense. Compare this with Descartes' thought, "I am thinking." The idea (at least, this is how Descartes is usually represented) is that, when I think "I am thinking," I cannot doubt the truth of what I think. Why? It is not quite enough (as many commentators seem to suppose) that my thinking what I think guarantees its truth. Truth, as such, is compatible with doubt. My thinking what I think not only guarantees, but, we must say, makes manifest the truth of what I think. It would, however, be misleading to describe the thinking of "There is SOMETHING" in this way, i.e., as making manifest the truth of what I think. Such a description would miss the perfective character of the manifestness of this truth: the fact that the truth of what I think inevitably is, when I think it, "already" manifest. For it "already" holds and, in holding, makes itself manifest.

And if the truth of what I think is, inevitably, already manifest, then, as we remarked, there is a sense in which if I actually think (say) it, I do not really think, or say, anything; a sense in which what I think or say cannot be thought or said. This, I believe, is Wittgenstein's point when he says that what the solipsist means, that is, what we mean, though correct, "cannot be said." If we say (think) it, what we say (think) will, inevitably, be looking back at us. It will, inevitably, be manifest—not because our saying (thinking) it makes it manifest, but because the very fact or truth that we mean (and in some sense say, or think) makes itself manifest, and thus, since it already holds, is already manifest.

What the solipsist wants to say makes itself manifest. What is it that he wants to say? What is it that we all want to say, that we all mean here, but, since it makes itself manifest, cannot say? It is, Wittgenstein tells us, that "the world is *my* world" (5.62). Again: "What brings the self into philosophy is the fact that 'the world is my world' " (5.641). This is the fact or truth that makes itself manifest and thus cannot be said. This, according to Wittgenstein, is the truth in solipsism.

"The world is my world." That is: the totality of things building out around me, and including me (the human being or soul that I am)—all *this*,[5] let us say—is *mine*. In what sense "mine"? (Do I own it all?) The clue to answering the question lies in the statement that what brings the self into philosophy is the fact that "the world is my world." The "self" here is the "philosophical self": not part of the world, not the human being (or soul) then, but a "limit" of the world, the metaphysical subject: THIS, my horizon. The world, all *this*, is "mine" in the sense of being present within the horizon that is mine. Such is the fact that makes itself manifest, the solipsistic fact. When I am in philosophical reflection struck by this fact, by the fact that it is within *my* horizon that the world is present, the subject matter which cannot but already have been known to me, my horizon, comes to light for me (is brought into philosophy). It comes to light as the horizon of all *this*, as the horizon of the world. "The world is my world."

---

[5] That to which we refer here by the words "all *this*" is thus to be understood as including not just the totality of whatever is present, but the larger totality, the world, of which what is present is a tiny part.

9.3 Solipsism and Self-Consciousness

It is on this interpretation immediately intelligible why Wittgenstein thinks that what the solipsist means "cannot be said." The fact that all *this* (the world) is mine, i.e., present within my horizon, is, if anything is, a fact that makes itself manifest. And if it makes itself manifest, it is, inevitably, already manifest. Thus if I think (say) it, what I think will inevitably be an empty retracing of what is already manifest. I look around and tell myself, "All *this* is present within *my* experience (horizon)." Is that news? Could it have come as a surprise?

Imagine I am engrossed in something. It could be something trivial, like watching two raindrops slipping down a window pane and wondering which one will win the race. Am I thinking about myself? Or about my experience? Am I thinking that this is going on within my experience (horizon)? I might be—but not if I am engrossed in the raindrops. Yet, however engrossed I am in what is going on, the fact that it is within my experience that it is going on cannot come as a surprise. However engrossed I am in the world, the fact that the world is my world (Wittgenstein's solipsistic fact) cannot but already have been manifest.

No doubt, this interpretation of Wittgenstein will be contested—not to speak of the questions that it leaves unanswered.[6] Our aim here, however, is not to settle textual issues but to seek a way out of the apparent conflict between the aloneness of our solipsism and the togetherness of our life with Others (metaphysical equals), our commitment to (O). In this respect, the present interpretation may seem to give us what we need. If the solipsistic thought is that the world is "mine" in the sense of being given from within my horizon, there is no conflict. Why should it not be the case that what is given (present) from within my horizon is also given from within your horizon? Thus the world is both "mine" and "yours." In other words, we have no reason to suppose that my horizon and yours are anything but coordinate horizons from within which the world is equally present; no reason, then, to suppose there is a conflict in this regard.

Yet we might wonder whether, in thus accommodating our metaphysical equality, the present interpretation leaves out the essence of solipsism: my aloneness. For it gives us no reason to suppose that my horizon is preeminent, or again, to suppose that it is the only horizon, or that I am the only subject (the only one at the center of a horizon). In what sense, then, might I be "alone"? In the *Notebooks* Wittgenstein says, "Mine is

[6] See below, note 16.

the first and only world!."[7] But what is to prevent this "first and only world" from being "yours" as well? Why, that is, could not the "first and only world" be present within both your horizon and mine, where these are coordinate horizons?

O.K. Let us put solipsism aside for a moment and focus on Wittgenstein's idea that the "mineness" of the world is a fact that makes itself manifest and therefore cannot but always already be manifest. It cannot, in other words, but always already be manifest that the world is given from within a subject matter that is "mine": from within my consciousness (horizon). In that case, there is another, more basic fact, a presupposed fact, that cannot but always etc. be manifest, that is to say, a fact that makes itself manifest, viz., the fact that there is such a subject matter as my consciousness (my horizon). Thus from within my consciousness its existence, the existence of my consciousness, cannot but always already be manifest. I believe that when philosophers discuss self-consciousness—when in particular they assert that consciousness is necessarily self-consciousness—what they have in mind is precisely this, the manifestness of the existence of my consciousness (horizon).

There are two points to keep in mind here. One is that, on the present conception, self-consciousness is not an act of first-person thinking. It is not an act, or event, of any kind, but a fact. The other point is that, like Wittgenstein's fact about the "mineness" of the world, self-consciousness is a fact that makes itself manifest. Or rather, it is the manifestness of a fact that makes itself manifest. Given that there is SOMETHING, not NOTHING, given that there is such a thing as my consciousness, its existence, i.e., the existence of my consciousness, cannot but already be manifest, and this fact of manifestness—which is a fact about the fact of the existence of my consciousness—this metafact is self-consciousness.

It follows that any actual thinking of the fact of the existence of my consciousness will be, like the thinking of Wittgenstein's solipsistic fact, redundant and in that sense unthinkable. Just as the "mineness" of the world is (in this sense) unthinkable, so is the existence of the subject matter by being given from within which the world is "mine." This provides the key to a well-known puzzle about self-consciousness.

It seems undeniable that the world's being given from within consciousness (experience) is, for us, more than just a primitive or blank registering of what is there but is self-conscious. This is the source of the philosophical idea that consciousness—that is, our consciousness—is necessarily self-consciousness. But what does it mean? Usually, it is taken to mean that, necessarily, I am conscious of every act of consciousness, starting

[7] The entry for 2.9.16 *Notebooks 1914–1916*, ed. G. H. von Wright and G.E.M. Anscombe, trans. G.E.M. Anscombe, 2d ed. (Basil Blackwell, 1979), p. 82e.

with my consciousness of the world. In that case, since our consciousness is necessarily self-conscious, for every act of consciousness there must be another, higher-order, act of consciousness, and thus an infinite regress of such acts.[8] Yet there is no such regress. On the contrary, it seems perfectly obvious that I may be engrossed in what is happening within my experience without any relevant act of self-consciousness, without thinking, e.g., "This is happening in my experience"—without thinking any first-person thought whatever.[9] Such is the puzzle.

The philosophical mistake is to conceive of self-consciousness as an act, viz., as a bit of first-person thinking. Suppose I think, "This is happening within my consciousness." If we identify self-consciousness with this (act of) thinking, the necessity of self-consciousness demands another such thinking. And so on. The whole conception is wrong. Self-consciousness consists not in an act of first-person thinking, in a thinking directed at an act of consciousness, but in the manifestness of a certain first-person fact: that there is such a subject matter as my consciousness (my horizon). Given that there is such a subject matter, the fact of its existence makes itself manifest and thus cannot but always already be manifest. Self-consciousness is the metafact that consists in manifestness of the fact that there is such a thing as my consciousness, i.e., the manifestness of the existence of my consciousness.[10] Thus, like Wittgenstein's fact about the "mineness" of the world, the fact that there is such a thing as my consciousness, that it exists, is unthinkable.

Note, the manifestness of the fact that there is such a thing as my consciousness (self-consciousness) is itself a fact: a metafact. Yet this does not generate a regress. If, on the back of the first, we posit a second fact of manifestness, it immediately collapses back into the original (so it is not really a "second" fact).

Assume that it is manifest that p. The attempt to get a regress started here will assert that *that* fact, i.e., the manifestness of the fact that p, is

---

[8] For an exposition as well as historical references (that go back to Aristotle in *De Anima*), see Brentano's discussion of the problem in *Psychology from an Empirical Standpoint*, book 2, chap. 2.

[9] On one of Kant's formulations of self-consciousness, the necessity is not that the "I think" is always thought but only that, as he puts it in the B version of the *Transcendental Deduction* (B131), "it must be possible for the 'I think' to accompany all my representations." Since the necessity is only that the "I think" be possible, not actual, this might seem to avoid the regress. However, if consciousness is necessarily self-conscious, it is not clear how the mere possibility of an accompanying "I think" could suffice. If you need light to fix your watch, will you be satisfied with the possibility of turning on a light?

[10] Cf. Sartre's discussion of the "pre-reflective cogito" in the introduction to *Being and Nothingness*. It was only after arriving at the ideas developed in the present section that I felt that I finally understood what Sartre was getting at: the sense in which the pre-reflective cogito is *pre*-reflective.

itself manifest—which manifestness will, in turn be manifest. No, it is not like that with manifestness. The manifestness of the manifestness of the fact that p is simply the manifestness of the fact that p. The regress cannot get going.

In this respect, manifestness may be compared with truth. If it is true that p, we can, if we wish, assert that it is true that it is true that p. Have we asserted a further truth? Are there two truths here? (Does every truth generate an infinite regress?) If we think about thinking that p, this is a further thinking. If we then think about that thinking, we have yet another thinking. Each act of thinking in the hierarchy refers to the previous thinking. In contrast, the manifestness of the manifestness that p, like the truth of the truth that p, is just the manifestness (truth) that p. You could say that manifestness, like truth, stays one and the same. It does not give rise to a hierarchical series of referentially linked elements, in the way that thinking does.

9.4 Kripke on the Solipsism of the Tractatus

The solipsism of the *Tractatus*, as we have interpreted it, concerns the horizonal subject matter (the metaphysical self, or the limit of the world); moreover, it expresses a fact or truth. Yet, as he explained, the fact that it expresses is not the fact of solipsism: it fails to capture the aloneness of solipsism. But if it fails to capture the aloneness of solipsism, it fails to capture solipsism and thus cannot extricate us from the conflict between *solipsism* and our commitment to (O), our life with Others. Let us consider a different interpretation of Wittgenstein's solipsism.

Saul Kripke, in the postscript of his book on Wittgenstein, suggests that in the *Tractatus* (and the later writings, too) Wittgenstein held the purely negative view of the self that occurs in Hume.[11] Hume tells us that when he looks for what he calls *myself*, all he comes across is this or that "impression"; he never observes the special persisting thing philosophers call the "self," the entity to which all the impressions are supposed to belong. He concludes there is no such thing, that the idea of a "self" in the sense of a persisting "something" to which all my impressions belong, is a philosophical invention.[12]

We might imagine Hume thinking,

(H) There is just all *this*: these impressions [no owner].

[11] *Wittgenstein on Rules and Private Language* (Basil Blackwell, 1982).
[12] See *A Treatise of Human Nature*, book 1, section 6.

According to Kripke, something like (H) expresses Wittgenstein's view as well. The only significant difference is that Hume's epistemology of impressions (and ideas) is foreign to Wittgenstein. In Wittgenstein's case, the reference of "all *this*," might include impressions, but primarily it would refer to the world. So Wittgenstein's thought would be,

(W) There is just all *this*: the world [no owner].

In (W), the "just" has the same exclusive force as in (H).

Hume, we might say, is denying the existence of an owner subject (like a Cartesian soul). There is no problem reading this into the *Tractatus*. The rejection of an owner subject is, I think, what Wittgenstein is getting at when he asserts that "There is no such thing as the subject that thinks or entertains ideas" (5.631). (We shall, in Wittgenstein's case, speak of an "entertainer subject.") What are "ideas" in this context? Since the *Tractatus* does not employ a sense-data ontology,[13] by "ideas" we may understand simply things that are present (whatever they are; that is, whether they are part of the world, sensations, images etc.). The point is to deny that there is an entity that stands in some special relation to these things: that of entertaining them. There are "ideas," things that are present; but there is nothing, no entity, related to these things in such a way that it might be said to "entertain" them. They are just present.[14]

Perhaps we are overlooking something—the metaphysical subject, the limit or horizon of the world. Do not the things that are present (ideas) stand in a special relation to the horizon? For what is present is present from within the horizon. One might suggest that being "present from within" is just another name for the relation of "entertaining (owning),"

---

[13] Or so I would maintain; I realize that some dispute this.

[14] Consider, e.g., the following from the "Notes for Lectures on 'Private Experience' and 'Sense Data,'" *Philosophical Review* 77 (July 1968), reprinted in *Philosophical Occasions*:

What is seen *I* see" (pointing to my body). I point at my geometrical eye, saying this. Or I point with closed eyes and touch my breast and feel it. In no case do I make a connection between what is seen and a person. (p. 297)

But the point is that I don't establish a relation between a person and what is seen. All I do is that alternatively I point in front of me and to myself. (p. 299; cf. pp. 282, 311)

In pointing to himself, he points to a human being; but the human being does not have the special relation to what is seen that an entertainer subject is supposed to have. That is, there is just "what is seen," the things that are present. He can say, "I see these things," but the "I" here will not stand for an entertainer subject. (Does it not, then, stand for the human being? How does the human being, the person, fit in here?) Remarks in a similar spirit can be found in the *Blue and Brown Books* (Harper and Row, 1965), mainly after p. 57 (see, e.g., pp. 67, 69, 74). See also *Philosophical Remarks* (Blackell, 1975), p. 100, and the references in Kripke, *Wittgenstein on Rules and Private Language*, pp. 123–24. What Strawson calls the "no ownership" theory (*Individuals* [Methuen, 1961], chap. 3, section 3) is basically the same idea, viz., the absence of an entertainer subject.

that the metaphysical subject, the limit or horizon, etc., is really the entertainer subject.

This is a mistake. Being present within my horizon is not like being inside a box. Presence within a horizon is not a relation. A relation needs relata: it needs things (objects, items, entities) between which to stand. But something can serve in the role of a relatum, something can (as it were) hold up one end of a relation, only if it is something in itself—which is precisely what the horizon is not. The horizon, as we explained (4.5–6), is nothing in itself. Objects that are present from within my horizon may be related in such-and-such ways to one another, and to me (the human being that I am, who is part of the world); but they are not "related" to that within which they are present, to the horizon (the metaphysical subject).

Wittgenstein denies that there is an entertainer subject. But there remains the metaphysical subject, the limit/horizon from within which all *this* is present, and without which there would be NOTHING. Right after asserting that Wittgenstein means to deny the existence of a "subject" (pp. 122–23), Kripke qualifies his assertion by noting a "deviation" from Hume that "comes in the suggestion in 5.632 that in some sense it may be legitimate to speak of a subject after all, as a mysterious "limit" of the world, though not an entity in it" (see also note 12, pp. 130–31.) To say that it "may in some sense be legitimate to speak of a subject . . . " is an understatement. It is impossible to understand the *Tractatus* without the metaphysical subject.

Consider the following as a statement of solipsism:

(Neg) There is just all *this*: the world [no horizon]

Not only is there no entertainer/owner of all *this*, there is no metaphysical subject either. What is there? There is just all *this*. (Neg), I believe, captures the spirit of Hume. But it does not represent Wittgenstein in the *Tractatus*. Thus he says that if he wrote a book called *The World as I Found It*, he would report on his body and would say which parts are subordinate to his will, "this being a method of isolating the subject, or rather of showing that in an important sense there is no subject; for it alone could *not* be mentioned in that book" (5.631). The "subject" here is the metaphysical subject, the limit or horizon of the world. Is it not evident that the "important sense" in which "there is no such subject," i.e., no horizon, is that the subject is not part of the world—not that there simply *is* no such subject?[15] The existence of such a subject is, after all,

---

[15] This might be a good place to remark that none of these conceptions of a subject that we have been considering in this section—neither that of an owner/entertainer, nor that of a "limit" or horizon of the world (the metaphysical subject)—is the conception of a subject

presupposed by what the solipsist (for Wittgenstein) means: that the world is my world; i.e., that the world is internal to my horizon. A denial of the horizon would leave the solipsist without the subject matter of his unsayable/unthinkable fact. There would be no such fact, nothing for the solipsist to mean.

Kripke's apparent dismissal of the metaphysical subject might seem to get some support from the remark in 5.64 that "solipsism, when its implications are followed out strictly, coincides with pure realism. The self of solipsism shrinks to a point without extension, and there remains the reality coordinated with it." The "self of solipsism" is plainly the philosophical self: the metaphysical subject, i.e., the limit of the world. What is "pure realism"? If we assume it to be the view expressed above by (W), then, given that Wittgenstein says solipsism coincides with this view, it will follow that he is committed to saying there is no self of solipsism, no metaphysical subject.

There is, however, another way to understand the passage in question. The horizon or limit of the world, the self of solipsism, is nothing in itself and thus adds nothing to the world (4.6). Solipsism "coincides with pure realism" in the sense that "reality"—which in this context means the world—is no way increased by being internal to the self of solipsism, that is, to my horizon. This is how I would interpret 5.64.

The self of solipsism adds nothing to the world, just as death takes away nothing from the world (8.4). For what death "takes away" *is* the self of solipsism, not part of the world but the horizon or limit of the world.

9.5 Negativism

Let us put aside the question of what Wittgenstein means in the *Tractatus*[16] and consider (Neg) in its own right. The thought behind (Neg) is:

---

that we have been using (and will continue to use): the conception of "the one at the center" of the horizon.

[16] Having completed our discussion of solipsism in the *Tractatus*, we should point out that it is only half the story; that (it seems to me) there are in the *Tractatus* two separate ideas that go under the name "solipsism," both of which might be encapsulated in the slogan that "the world is my world." There is, first, the idea we have discussed in the text, that the world is present within my horizon. We might call this "subject solipsism." But there is also something we might call "logic solipsism." Thus in 5.6 Wittgenstein says, "*The limits of my language* mean the limits of my world," and in 5.61, that "Logic pervades the world; the limits of the world are also its limits." This prepares the way for the statement of logic solipsism in 5.62: "what the solipsist *means* is quite correct; only it cannot be *said* but makes itself manifest. The world is *my* world: this is manifest in the fact that the limits of *language* (of that language which alone I understand) mean the limits of *my* world." Re-

there is just all *this*—there is nothing that owns/entertains it; nor is there a horizon from within which all *this* is present. Hume, if we forget about his phenomenalism[17] and the fact that he does not explicitly employ the horizonal conception of the self, would (I think) have endorsed (Neg). The question is whether (Neg) captures the aloneness of solipsism. We shall focus on the denial of the horizon.

(Neg) does not, of course, deny that there is such a thing as me, the human being that I am. He is (I am) part of all *this*: part of the world. What (Neg) denies is that there is anything *from within which* the world (including the human being I am) is present, a limit or horizon of the world, a metaphysical subject.

If there is just the world, if there is no such thing as a horizon of the world, there is no possibility of generating a multiplicity of horizons. There is, we might say, no possibility of all *this* being given more than once. For given "more than once" could only mean: given from within more than one horizon. If there is no horizon, there is no possibility of a multiplicity from within which all *this* might be repeated. So there is (I tell myself) the unrepeatable all *this*—and that's it. It may seem that there could be no greater form of aloneness.

But is it really aloneness? What is it that is alone? Certainly, if there is no horizon, there is no possibility of a multiplicity of horizons. The question, however, is *why* there is no such possibility. If (Neg) is true, the reason there is no possibility of a multiplicity of horizons is that there is no horizon at all. In that case there is nothing that might be "the only" horizon: nothing that might be "alone." What we have here is not solipsism but, as we shall call it, "negativism."

---

member, in 1.1 we are told that the world is "the totality of facts, not of things." But when in 5.461 Wittgenstein says that the "philosophical self is not the human being," that it is "the limit of the world—not a part of it," it would seem he means exactly the *opposite* of what he has told us in 1.1. For whereas it is quite natural to think of the self as a human being, a "thing," it would never occur to us to think of the self as a *fact*. In 5.62, however, it is clear that he has reverted to his conception of the world in 1.1, as the totality of facts. What he means here is that logic sets the limits on what can be a fact, and thereby on what can be part of the world in the sense of 1.1. Solipsism enters by virtue of the fact that my only understanding of logic comes from language, i.e., from the logic built into language, and I only have the language I have—the one of which I find myself a speaker/thinker. To repeat, this language, *my* language, with its built-in logic, is all that I have. (Contrast this with the later thought that all I have is what I have from within *our* language.) Thus, while the world as the totality of things is "mine" in the sense that it is present from within the horizon that is "mine," the world as the totality of facts is "mine" in the sense that what can be part of that totality is fixed by the logic of the language that is "mine," the language of which I find myself a speaker and which is all that I have.

[17] The view that whatever belongs to all *this* is either an impression or a construction of impressions.

You could put it like this. The possibility of counting presupposes that there is something to be counted. The solipsist counts horizons. He has something to count, but he counts only one. If, on the other hand, there is no horizon, there is nothing to count. The negativist has nothing to count. Whereas the solipsist starts and stops counting at one, the negativist cannot start counting.

Negativism, then, cannot capture the "aloneness" of solipsism. There is another point. Negativism has no way to conceive of the independence of the world. Objects that are part of the world are objects that exist independently of being present within experience (1.7).[18] If there is no such thing as experience (in the horizonal sense), there is nothing by reference to which some objects versus others have the independence that constitutes them part of the world (the totality of independently existing objects and phenomena); no way, then, of distinguishing within all *this* between what is and is not part of the world.

In fact, insofar as the negativist limits what he is prepared to recognize philosophically to all *this*, he implicitly transcends his own limits, since the fact of presence, the demonstrative availability of that to which he limits himself, already implicates the horizon. The world, all *this*, is present within my horizon. This is the fact that, as Wittgenstein says, makes itself manifest. The negativist, then, like all of us, cannot but know this fact—which means he cannot but know of the subject matter whose existence he denies. He cannot but know this, but he is not open to what he knows.

Yet negativism remains philosophically tempting. For once we have taken account of the human being (and the soul), there seems to be nothing left in the world that could be the metaphysical subject. And there *is* nothing in the world that could be the metaphysical subject. There is just the world, which is present: all *this*. In this way, we pass (with Hume) right over the fact that that fact itself, the presence of the world, implicates something *else*—not a special part of the world but the horizon of the world, something that is nothing in itself.

---

[18] It is worth noting that phenomenalism does not deny this kind of independence but claims to provide a reductive analysis of it—in terms, say, of hypotheticals about sense-data or impressions, etc.

10. Death and the Truth of Solipsism

10.1 Solipsism and My Life with Others

Solipsism is not an eccentric philosophical "view" but a fact, a truth—a truth that each of us knows and hence believes, a truth about THIS, about my horizon: the subject matter of the DH and death. But what exactly is the content of this truth? It is not that mine is the only horizon. This might capture the aloneness of solipsism, but it is not something I believe. Nor is it that the world is present from within my horizon: that (as Wittgenstein puts it) the world is my world. This is something I believe, but, since it is compatible with believing that the world is your world (present from within your horizon), it does not capture the aloneness of solipsism. Is it then that the world is present *only* from within my horizon? This would capture the aloneness of solipsism, but, once again, it is not something that I believe. I believe the world, the same world that is present from within my horizon, is present from within your horizon, from within all horizons.

What, then, is the content of solipsism? The answer—the answer we gave back in 9.1—is not that my horizon is the only horizon, but that it is the preeminent horizon: the horizon that includes all others. In this sense, it stands by itself (it has no neighbors). The trouble is, whereas this may capture our aloneness, the question of truth, and belief, returns yet again. I am committed to (O): I regard other subjects as Others, as metaphysical equals, i.e., as being each at the center of a horizon coordinate with mine. This commitment, which comes with insidership of the communal horizon and thus pervades my life, is the direct antithesis of the belief in the preeminence of my horizon (see 6.11). The commitment to (O) is, in effect, a commitment to antisolipsism.

The antisolipsism of my commitment to (O) generates the conception of a space in which all horizons, since they are coordinate, exist side by side—as neighbors. I cannot, we said (6.9), represent this space, but I grasp its possibility. Of course, solipsism (in the present sense, which sense we shall henceforth assume) cannot tolerate such a space. Solipsism, we might say, negates the space of horizons. Yet it allows for the existence of other horizons. Your horizon, like mine, contains the world (and space and time). The same independently existing totality is internal to both, and in principle any part of that totality, including the human beings we

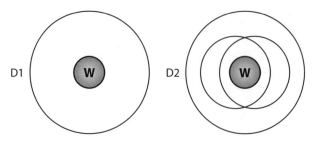

Figure 10.1

are, can be present, or show up, within either. Our horizons, on the other hand, are not part of the world. You, the subject, can appear within my horizon, but your horizon cannot appear from within mine. Thus solipsistic preeminence is expressed by saying not that my horizon "contains" all others but that it "includes" all others. Insofar as the world is internal to my horizon (insofar, i.e., as my horizon contains the world), my horizon contains you (the human subject). Insofar as my horizon is preeminent, it includes your horizon; but while my horizon contains you, the human being at the center of your horizon, it does not contain (but includes) your horizon.

Solipsism, then, regards the world as equally internal to all horizons. The preeminence of my horizon derives not from the fact that the world is exclusively internal to it, but from the fact that all other horizons are included by it. My horizon (my experience, my consciousness, my life) not only contains the whole of the world, it includes all other horizons. By virtue of containing the world, my horizon is in no way singled out among horizons; by virtue of including all others, however, my horizon stands alone. It is the all-inclusive horizon.

Perhaps we can summarize and bring together these interconnected points with the help of some diagrams. In figure 10.1, let the shaded circle W stand for the world, and the other circles for horizons. The fact that a horizon-circle encloses W depicts the fact that a certain horizon contains the world; the fact that one horizon-circle encloses another depicts the first horizon as including the second. The boundary of a diagram is always the outer horizon-circle (this is the rule for individuating diagrams). The outer horizon-circle is always my horizon.

We can think of D1 as diagramming Wittgenstein's solipsistic fact, that the world is my world (that the world is present within my horizon). In D2, other horizons enter the picture. Since the outer horizon-circle stands for my horizon, my horizon represents itself as preeminent, as including all others. D2 diagrams solipsism as we are understanding it.

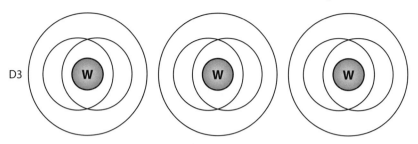

Figure 10.2

Suppose I want to depict the situation from the standpoint of your horizon. I have, it seems, no option but to use the same diagram (D2) again.[1] But this is not a problem. I simply let the outer circle stand for your horizon. I know the structure of things from within your horizon: it is the same as the structure from within my horizon. "It is the same for you as for me."

Now suppose I wish to depict the space of horizons (our metaphysical equality), the space in which all our horizons exist side by side. It would seem that, for a three-horizon space, the diagram must be as depicted in figure 10.2. However (by our rule), D3 is not *a* diagram, i.e., a single diagram. Since, if we depict horizons at all, a single diagram will always have an outer horizon-circle (the world appears within a horizon, not a horizon within the world), it is obvious that there is no way of incorporating the side-by-side layout of the space of horizons in a single diagram. What we represent in a single diagram will (by the rules) always have "my" horizon as outer, as including all the others. Here we have a diagrammatic expression of our inability to represent the space of horizons, i.e., to represent our metaphysical equality. We cannot represent our metaphysical equality (the space of horizons), but, once again, we grasp it. It is our grasp of our metaphysical equality that, as we explained (6.8), makes it rationally impossible to believe the dream hypothesis.

D3, to repeat, is not a single diagram but, in effect, three diagrams, each representing anew, as in D2, the truth of solipsism. D3, we might say, gestures diagrammatically at the space of horizons, which is something we grasp inasmuch as it is implicit in our life with Others, implicit in our commitment to (O). The problem is that what we thus grasp and are committed to is incompatible with the truth represented in D2, the truth that we all know, the truth of solipsism, that my horizon includes all others.

---

[1] Cf. Kant in the A version of the third Paralogism: "It is obvious that, if I wish to represent to myself a thinking being, I must put myself in his place, and thus substitute, as it were, my own subject for the object I am seeking to consider" (A353–54).

10.2 Relativized Solipsism

It may occur to the reader that we have been over this ground before, and, in fact, that we have already indicated the resolution of the conflict. When I withdraw to the first person, my horizon represents itself as including yours: it claims preeminence. But I accept that you can withdraw in the same way, that your horizon with equal right makes the same claim to preeminence (see 6.4, 6.9). I thus conceive of the preeminence of my horizon not as holding absolutely (without qualification), but as holding only relatively, i.e., from within my horizon. That is, I free myself from the perspective of my horizon and form the conception of a space in which all horizons, each representing itself as all-inclusive, each claiming preeminence, exist side by side, as coordinate horizons. Viewed in light of this conception, the conflict disappears. It is always open to us to withdraw to the first person. At the same time, however, since we grasp that the solipsistic picture with which we are thereby presented is always relativized to a given horizon, we are able to combine this picture with a recognition of our metaphysical equality, of the coordinate status of our respective horizons (see 6.11).

Solipsism (solipsism proper), viz.,

(S) My horizon is preeminent,

may be distinguished from relativised solipsism,

(RS) My horizon is preeminent for me (from within my horizon).

The idea is that we are solipsists only in the sense that we take (RS), not (S), to be true. For everyone, it seems like this: my horizon is preeminent. For everyone, it seems that (S) is true. And we all know this; i.e., we all know that for everyone it seems that (S) is true. But no one believes (S). No one, in other words, takes his horizon to be preeminent in an unrelativized way, that is, as preeminent *period*. No one, then, believes (S). What we all believe, and know that we believe, is (RS). Thus what we all believe, our "solipsism," is compatible with our commitment to (O), with our life with Others.

Solipsism exercises a pull on us; however (this is the idea), it does not pull us all the way to believing (S). Its pull consists in the fact that (S) seems true. But we recognize this seeming for what it is, a "mere" seeming: something that holds only from within my horizon. We do not believe (S). Rather, we believe (RS). If we believed (S), we would refuse to relativize it. The solipsist, you could say, declares himself, declares his solipsism, by his refusal to relativize, by refusing to add "for me" to the expression of how things seems from within his horizon, to the claim to preeminence of his horizon.

But suppose it is not like this. Suppose our actual belief—if we are open to it—will not tolerate any kind of watering down or qualifying of what is expressed by (S). What do I, what do we, actually believe? What do I (we) know? What is the truth about the inclusiveness of my horizon? It is that my horizon (my life) is the all-inclusive horizon (that my life is the all-inclusive life). Not merely all-inclusive *for me*, but all-inclusive *period*. If this is how it is, our solipsism stands in conflict with our commitment to (O).

Moreover, if this is how it is, then, if we represent ourselves as prepared to relativize, we misrepresent ourselves. We misrepresent ourselves to ourselves. We know, and thus believe, that (S) is true. If we say that all we know is the relativized truth expressed by (RS), we are not open to what we know. We are not open to our own solipsism.

I think that what is expressed by (S) is something we all know and hence believe, that we are unrelativized solipsists: solipsists. However, we are not open to what we know. In part, this is because of our commitment to (O), which pervades our lives. But whatever the reason, given that we are not open to our solipsism, we are in this respect in a position to discover something that we already know: to make a philosophical discovery. To become open to the truth of solipsism is to make a philosophical discovery.

Notice, living with the commitment to (O) is not thereby being philosophically open to the fact that we live this way; thus our commitment to (O) is also something we may discover philosophically. The conflict that emerges between our solipsism and our commitment to (O) thus breaks out, as it were, within philosophical discovery. But it is an unequal conflict.

All philosophical discovery, as we observed earlier, presupposes resistance (see Int.4, Int.7). One source of resistance is our engrossment in the world. Resistance from this source is common to all philosophical discovery. Thus it is present in the case of the "discovery" of our commitment to (O). In the case of solipsism, however, there are other sources of resistance. There is, for one thing, the peculiar nature of the subject matter of solipsism: the peculiar nothingness of the horizon. But there is also, as just remarked, the way we live, that is to say, the all-pervasive commitment with which our solipsism stands in conflict, our commitment to (O).

Now in the nature of the case, these assertions (which is all we have so far: assertions) about solipsism will, if they are true, be resisted—which can hardly be offered in support of the assertions. What is required is something else, something simple. We must become open to, we must philosophically discover, the truth of solipsism.

Earlier (Int.4) we compared philosophical discovery with undeceiving ourselves. Although the kind of truth we discover, as well as the source of the resistance to the discovery, is different in the two cases, there is the same phenomenon of becoming open to something we already know.[2] Self-deception protects itself—by more self-deception. But if we are trying to get someone to see that he is deceiving himself, it will not help to point this out. Then what can we do? What *do* we do? We draw the person's attention to certain facts, viz., facts that entail or evoke or suggest—facts that, in one way or another, point to the fact that he is deceiving himself. Of course the person already knows these facts too, as well as what they point to. He may, however, continue to resist. Resistance to undeceiving yourself is always a possibility.

It is basically the same in the philosophical case. To become open to what we already know, we draw attention to, we confront, facts that point to what we already know—where these facts themselves (as well as what they point to) are things we already know and, as such, are subject to continued resistance. To become open to what we already know, we have to become open to what we already know. You could say, the facts that we confront invite us to be open—if they are the right facts. But, given the resistance, in the end *we* have to be open, i.e., to *let ourselves* be open. What are the "right" facts in the case of our solipsism, the facts that invite us to be open to this truth that we already know?

10.3 Solipsism and the Meaning of Death

Actually, there is just one fact. It is the same fact that occupies Ivan (7.4.). Or rather, it is at one remove from this fact. Philosophically, we have to start where Ivan leaves off. When Ivan undeceives himself about what is happening to him, that he is dying, the basic self-deception about death (the "not-me" phenomenon) falls away. When that happens, he becomes open to the fact that he will die. He becomes open to a fact that he, like all of us, already knows. This is where we have to start, with the fact to which Ivan becomes open: I will die. The fact of death, our own death, can (if we let it) open us up to solipsism, to our own solipsism, in a way that nothing else can. But in order for that to happen, we have to be open to the meaning of this fact, to the meaning of death.

---

[2] Roughly, the truths in the self-deception case are personal, and in the philosophical case they are impersonal; in self-deception, the source of the resistance is that the truths to which we become open are something we do not want to be true, whereas (as indicated above in the text) this kind of motivation is irrelevant in the philosophical case.

What confronts us in the prospect of death is, we said, the ceasing to be of something that is "mine." Of what? Not this or that part of the world, like the human being that I am, or a stream of his states, but the horizon of the world: that from within which things are present, including the human being that I am, etc. (8). If that from within which things are present ceases to be, nothing will be present. There will be a complete absence of presence. What will there be? Not silence and darkness but a complete, unimaginable blank. NOTHING. The world will remain, but there will be NOTHING (4.5). This is what the prospect of death holds up to us, the meaning of death:

(N) There will be NOTHING.

The idea is that by letting ourselves be open to (N), to what death means to us, we may become open to the truth of solipsism.

There are two points on which everything depends. The first is that in order to express or capture what death actually means to us, we have to leave (N) as it stands—without any relativizing qualifications. If we relativize (N), that is, if we replace it by,

(RN) There will be NOTHING for me,

then we shall simply fail to capture what death means to us. The NOTH-INGNESS of death is absolute. It does not admit of relativization. Second, if this is right, if it is the unrelativized (N) and not (RN) that expresses what death means to us, then, similarly, it is the unrelativized (S), rather than (RS), that expresses our solipsism. These things go together. If the NOTHINGNESS of death is absolute, so is our solipsism. Let us consider each of these points in turn.

What does death mean to us? It means: there will be NOTHING. Not NOTHING *for me*, but just plain NOTHING: NOTHING *period*. Is that not so? Try to imagine that you have just learned that you are dying, that death is close. There will be NOTHING. Are you inclined to add "for me"? It is I not the doctor who is dying, but the NOTHINGNESS that confronts me does not seem to be particularly "mine." It is just NOTHINGNESS.

When we contemplate the NOTHINGNESS that faces us in death, the unrelativized (N) seems to capture perfectly, and fully, what we are faced by: the meaning of death. In contrast, the relativized (RN) seems somehow to diminish or detract from this meaning. If we want to capture in an honest way what death means to us, its full radical impact, we have to leave (N) as it is, unrelativized. Any pulling of punches, any drawing back from the recognition of absoluteness, and we will fail to capture the meaning of death. That is, we will fail to capture what death, when we confront it, *actually* means to us.

Recall Ivan's reaction when he becomes open to the meaning of death. He says: "I shall be no more, then what will there be?" The answer that comes back is unqualified, absolute: "There will be nothing." Not, "There will be nothing for me," but simply, "There will be nothing." Nothing? Will not the world still be there, just as before? Of course, "nothing" here means: NOTHING. Everything (the world) will be there, just as it is, but there will be NOTHING. And, I put it to you, this means exactly what it says, that there will be NOTHING. Not NOTHING for me, but NOTHING. NOTHING period. I also put it to you that you already know this. The true answer to what faces us in facing death, the answer you already knew, is the unqualified answer. What faces us (you, me) is: NOTHING.

We are not finished with this yet (see below, 10.4), but let us turn to the second point: the connection between the fact that the NOTHING-NESS that faces us in facing death cannot be relativized and the unrelativized, or absolute, character of our solipsism.

It is implicit in our commitment to (O), in our life with Others, that other horizons are coordinate with mine, that they exist side by side with mine, as neighbors in a space that I cannot represent but nonetheless grasp (the space of horizons). Within each horizon there is SOMETHING, not NOTHING; if there were NOTHING, there would be no horizon (4.5). Since the other horizons in the side-by-side space of horizons are not included within my horizon but are its neighbors, they are in a real sense "outside" my horizon (6.9). Hence my death, the ceasing to be of my horizon, can in no way affect the fact that within other horizons there is SOMETHING; which is just to say, it can in no way affect the fact that there *are* other horizons. From this it follows that the NOTHINGNESS of my death must be relativized NOTHINGNESS, i.e., NOTHINGNESS for me (for my horizon), not absolute NOTHINGNESS. If it were absolute NOTHINGNESS, NOTHINGNESS period, it could not be the case that the situation with other horizons would be independent of the ceasing to be of my horizon. Conversely, if it is the case that my death means absolute NOTHINGNESS, then it cannot be the case that the other horizons exist as genuine neighbors, as coordinate with my horizon, but must rather be included within my horizon, since if they did exist as coordinate with mine, the NOTHINGNESS of my death would not be absolute.

The side-by-side structure of the space of horizons cannot, it seems, handle absolute, i.e., unrelativized, NOTHINGNESS. The side-by-side structure entails that each horizon stands and falls by itself, independently of its neighbors. Each has, so to speak, a separate destiny. Thus the fact that there is NOTHING for my horizon leaves the other horizons as they were. I think to myself: There will be NOTHING for me, but not yet for you. Or perhaps, there will be NOTHING for you, but not yet for me. Horizons drop off one by one, piecemeal fashion. It should be obvious that in formulating this thought we have to employ the relativized (versus absolute) conception of NOTHINGNESS. It is always NOTHINGNESS for you, or NOTHINGNESS for me, etc., that we mean, never NOTH-INGNESS period. If it were NOTHINGNESS period, we would be calling into question, all at once, the whole thing—the whole space of horizons.

Absolute NOTHINGNESS, you might say, knows nothing of divisions or partitions, of separateness, of "one by one," and so on. At one swoop it obliterates the space of horizons, the space in which we make sense of our metaphysical equality, our life with Others—our commitment to (O). Making sense of these things presupposes that we conceive of death in terms of relativized NOTHINGNESS.

Here is an image that may help us see the point. When I die my light goes out. Does this mean there is no more light, that when my light goes out there simply is no light? Anywhere? No light period? Absolute darkness? Or does it mean just that there is no light for me? Relativized darkness.[3] Consider the implications of the thought that there is simply no light. What about other lights? If these lights are "outside" mine, then the darkness consequent on my light going out could only be relativized darkness: no light (darkness) *for me*. So, to turn this around, if my light going out means that there is no light *period*, that there is absolute darkness, it follows that there are no lights "outside" my light (other lights illuminate only within my light).

When my light goes out there will be: no light. This is, if we do not push it too far, an apt image for the meaning of death. When I die there will be: NOTHING. If when my light goes out there will be no light, there are no lights "outside" mine; similarly, if when I die there will be NOTHING, there are no horizons "outside" mine. But, since mine is not the one and only horizon, what about other horizons? They are all included by my horizon. Mine, as the solipsist says, is the all-inclusive horizon.

10.4 Qualifying the NOTHINGNESS of Death

Insofar as we refuse to relativize (N), we refuse to relativize (S): in effect, we embrace solipsism. I expect that most people will accept that (N) and (S) are connected in this way; but then they will add that, of course, since solipsism (in our sense) is false, there must be some way of relativizing or qualifying the NOTHINGNESS of death.

---

[3] Bear in mind, though, that darkness is only an *image* for NOTHINGNESS. If we drop the image, we will have to acknowledge that the difference between darkness and NOTH-INGNESS is "greater" than that between darkness and light: darkness, since it presupposes the horizon, presupposes that there is not NOTHINGNESS.

Now, you cannot rationally force (by means of an argument) someone to recognize that (N), and therefore (S), express truths that we already know and hence believe. It is a matter, ultimately, of letting ourselves become open to these truths. On the other hand, in claiming to uncover here a commitment to solipsism, perhaps it is we who are not yet open to the truth about what death means (see Int. 5). More specifically, perhaps we have overlooked a way of viewing this meaning that allows us to relativize it, or if not to relativize it (the meaning itself), to make sense of a picture in which a multiplicity of subjects face, each for himself, his own death: some way, in other words, of viewing the meaning of death that softens the hard edge of its apparent absoluteness and thus to reconcile the pull of solipsism with our commitment to (O), our life with Others. We shall now consider five suggestions to this effect. Seeing why in each case the suggestions fail may, in fact, help open us up to the unrelativized truth about the meaning of death.

1. The first suggestion requires us carefully to distinguish the asserting of (RN) from the content of what is thereby asserted. Someone might acknowledge that, if we wish to express what death means to us, we will, like Ivan, use (N) rather than (RN). Nonetheless he might maintain that it is (RN) rather than (N) that captures what death means to us. He would explain this by pointing out that asserting (RN) seems trivial—whereas if anything is not trivial, it is what death means to us. He will, however, insist that although the asserting (RN) seems trivial, its content, the fact itself, is not trivial. Is it trivial that there will be NOTHING for me?[4]

This suggestion exploits Wittgenstein's idea of a fact that makes itself manifest. The fact that the NOTHINGNESS I face is "mine," that with death there will be NOTHING "for me," is, like the fact that the world is "mine," a fact that makes itself manifest, a fact the saying or thinking of which cannot but repeat what is already manifest, and in that sense "cannot be said (thought)." This is why asserting (RN) seems trivial. But we need not for that reason deny that (RN) expresses what death means

---

[4] Philosophers sometimes try—in the spirit of later Wittgenstein—to dismiss solipsism by arguing that the only way it can come out true is if its content reduces to something trivial. (See, e.g., Gareth Evans, *The Varieties of Reference* [Oxford University Press, 1982], pp. 233–35. David Pears maintains that this view of solipsism, which he apparently endorses himself, and which he says Wittgenstein builds on in his later philosophy, is already present in the *Tractatus*; see *The False Prison* [Oxford University Press, 1988], vol. 1, chap. 7, and vol. 2, chap. 10.) I am inclined to doubt that anyone would on reflection want to characterize as trivial a statement intended to express what death means to us, i.e., that the only true statement of what death means to us is a trivially true statement. So I would say that once the connection between what death means to us and solipsism is clear, perhaps it will no longer seem that solipsism, if true, must be trivial.

to us—which is not trivial. The triviality lies not in the fact that (RN) expresses but in our saying (asserting) or thinking this fact.[5]

The suggestion runs into difficulty as soon as we ask how we are to understand the "for me" in (RN). For we cannot understand it in the way we understand the "my" in Wittgenstein's proposition that "the world is my world." The world is "my" world, we explained, in that the world is present from within my horizon. But if NOTHINGNESS obtains, there is no such thing as my horizon; there is nothing from within which anything might be present. There is nothing, then, by reference to which the NOTHINGNESS might be "mine." The suggestion is to relativize the NOTHINGNESS of death to a given horizon. But with NOTHINGNESS we lose the horizon; we lose the subject matter to which NOTHINGNESS is meant to be relativized.

2. Perhaps the intention is to relativize the NOTHINGNESS of death not to my horizon but to the human being at the center of my horizon, the human being that I am. In that case, we have misinterpreted the "for me" in (RN). It means not "within my horizon" but "for the human being that is at the center of my horizon." On this interpretation, (RN) would seem to express a truth. When there is NOTHING, there will be no horizon; but the human being that I am may still be there—and for *him*, for that human being, there will be NOTHING.

The problem with (RN) on this interpretation is that, while true, its truth is derivative; and that from which its truth derives is the fact of unrelativized NOTHINGNESS, the very fact that is creating our difficulty. Let us accept, when my horizon ceases to be, there will be NOTHING for the human being that I am, the one at the center of my horizon. But why is that? The answer would seem to be that, since the horizon of which I am at the center will no longer be, there will be NOTHING. Not, yet again, NOTHING for the human being that I am, but NOTHING period. So, very quickly, we have come back around to unrelativized NOTHINGNESS. In facing death, the human being that I am faces NOTHINGNESS. He faces NOTHINGNESS because he is the one at the center of my horizon, and when my horizon ceases to be there will be NOTHING. And here NOTHING means just that: NOTHING: NOTHING period.

3. Might we not insist that NOTHINGNESS for me, i.e., for the human being that I am, does not reduce in this way to absolute NOTHINGNESS

---

[5] We may detect a certain irony about this suggestion. Wittgenstein uses the idea of a fact that makes itself manifest to explain solipsism. And here we are, using the same idea in an attempt to save ourselves from solipsism. But then Wittgenstein's conception of solipsism is not our conception.

but has it own meaning—that "NOTHINGNESS for me" is an irreducible relation between NOTHINGNESS and a particular human being? But if we stick to this, we shall, I think, fail to capture what death actually means to us. Imagine that, facing death, I am assured that a week after my death God will endow the human being I am, this same human being (JV), with life. In that case, the human being in question will be at the center of a horizon, and hence it will not be true that there is NOTHING "for this human being." Yet it seems that I am faced by death. I might think: "Fine, this human being (JV), the one I am, will have a life, but it will not be my life. There will no longer be such a thing as my life (horizon)." And if, like Ivan, I were to ask myself, "What will there be?," the answer would be the same as with Ivan: "There will be NOTHING." Granted that (given what God has assured me) "for this human being" it will *not* be the case that there is NOTHING (the human being in question will be at the center of a horizon); all the same, I would say: there will be NOTHING.

4. This much in the foregoing proposal seems correct. If we ask who is faced by death when "I am faced by death," the answer is that it is I, this human being, the one at the center of my horizon. In facing death, I (JV, the human being that I am) face death from within my horizon, i.e., from within the horizon of which I, this human being, am at the center. I face death from within my horizon, and in facing death I face NOTHINGNESS. So I face NOTHINGNESS from within my horizon. Each of us faces the NOTHINGESS of death in this way, for himself, i.e., from within his own horizon.

Here, you might think, we have a way of relativizing the meaning of death to a horizon. We may agree that (N) as opposed to (RN) expresses or captures what we face in facing death, that it captures what death means to us. At the same time we know that in each case, what we face is faced from within a separate horizon. In this way, the meaning of death is always relativized to a horizon, to the horizon from within which it is faced.

This way of relativizing the meaning of death, however, does not resolve the difficulty. It is rather a way of stating the difficulty. The suggestion depends on distinguishing *what is faced* in facing death from the *facing* of what we face, etc. It is the facing versus what is faced that is relativized, i.e., that is qualified as being "from within my horizon." We can say then both that the NOTHINGNESS I face in facing death is faced from within my horizon, and that what is faced is unqualified, unrelativized NOTHINGNESS. But in that case the difficulty is still there. For the difficulty consists precisely in the fact that the unrelativized character of what each of us faces is (as we explained in 10.3) incompatible with its being faced more than once, from within a multiplicity of horizons; incompatible, in other words, with the fact that it is faced by *each* of us. What each of us, each from within his own horizon, faces is not NOTHINGNESS "for me" (from within my horizon), but just NOTHINGNESS. How could that be? How could absolute, unrelativized NOTHINGNESS be multiply faced?

Notice, if this is right, it totally undermines our earlier reconciliation of solipsism and the commitment to (O). The idea was that while each horizon claims preeminence, we may view these claims as in each case holding only from within, and in that sense always relativized to, a given horizon (10.2). If, however, the meaning of death is absolute, then so is our solipsism (10.3), i.e., the claim to preeminence made by each horizon. Yet it seems impossible that a multiplicity of such claims be valid. (Compare: each ticket holder claims to be the winner. Can each claim be valid?) That is, it seems impossible that a multiplicity of horizons should each validly claim for itself something that can hold only once.

5. It may be suggested, finally, that although what death means to us is absolute NOTHINGNESS, this very absoluteness is merely a matter of how, in facing death, things seem to us. What death means to us is: NOTHINGNESS period. So, in facing death, this is how things seem to us: there will be NOTHINGNESS period. But at the same time we recognize that this absoluteness (which we highlight by adding "period")—that which is part of how things seem—is mere seeming. Thus, whereas what death means to us is absolute (unrelativized) NOTHINGNESS, we do not believe that what we are faced by is absolute. We believe, rather, that its seeming absoluteness is mere seeming.

If what death means to us, that is, how things seem to us in facing death, conflicts with what we believe, on which side should we come down? In a way, the question answers itself. If we believe that p, we have already come down on the side of p. Let me elaborate on this.

Belief is itself a form of seeming. If I believe that p, this is how things seem to me: that p. If, however, we regard something as a matter of "mere" seeming, that means we do *not* believe it. Thus it is incoherent to assert "p, but it merely seems that p," since by "p" we express our belief that p. (The point is closely related to Moore's famous paradox about belief.) In other words, although belief is a form of seeming, when seeming takes the form of believing we cannot regard it as mere seeming. (We cannot, you might say, distance ourselves from our own beliefs.) In contrast, it is unproblematic to regard perceptual seeming as mere seeming. At the same time that an object looks red to me, I may regard its seeming this way as mere seeming. Hence I may believe about an object that seems (looks) red that it is not red.

Now this much is clear: if what death means to us can be regarded as mere seeming, then, although its NOTHINGNESS seems absolute, it is possible to believe that it is not absolute. I wonder, though, whether, when the meaning of death hits home, when we are genuinely open to what death means, we *can* regard this as a matter of "mere seeming."

The question is not whether "mere seeming" might be part of the content of how things seem in facing death, but whether, granted that the content of how things seem (of what death means) to us is that there will be NOTHING period, we can regard this as (believe it to be) mere seeming. I would say that if someone thinks that the unrelativized character of what he is faced by in facing death, i.e., the unrelativized character of what death means to him, is a matter of mere seeming, then the meaning of death is not getting through to him. This person is not yet open to what death *actually means* to him. He is (in this respect) like someone who persists in deceiving himself, who is not open to what he knows about himself.

There is no way to get between what death means to us, when we are open to what it means, and what we believe about death. What death means to us is nothing less than the truth for us about death; which is to say, it is what we believe about death. When its meaning hits home, what death means is: absolute NOTHINGNESS. If this is what death means to us, we believe it, and if we believe it, we cannot regard it as mere seeming.

11. The Awfulness and Incomprehensibility of Death

11.1 The Awfulness of Death

There is something in the prospect of death (in what we face in facing death, in what death means to us) that is awful; but not just awful—incomprehensible. The combination of awfulness and incomprehensibility, if we are open to it, is what gives the prospect of death its peculiar impact. Nothing unsettles or disturbs us in the way the prospect of death does.

Death (the prospect of death) is awful in that it is the prospect of absolute NOTHINGNESS. What makes it incomprehensible is that the coming to pass of this NOTHINGNESS seems impossible, as if it were something that could not come to pass. If the NOTHINGNESS held up in the prospect of death cannot come to pass, why should it disturb us? Because we know it will come to pass. It will be. That it will be is a fact. Something that cannot be, will be. The prospect of death confronts us with an impossible fact. It is not surprising that we cannot comprehend it. Who can comprehend an impossible fact?

We have yet to explain the impossibility of death; but let us first briefly consider the other aspect of death: its awfulness.

What is it in the prospect of death that makes it awful? It is, as we said, the absolute NOTHINGNESS by which we are faced. Actually, something else comes in here, which we have mentioned but not sufficiently emphasized, viz., the once-and-for-all character of what faces us in facing death. Someone who is going to be put under deep anaesthesia faces NOTHINGNESS, but not the NOTHINGNESS of death. In facing deep anaesthesia, I project ahead to a time when the NOTHINGNESS that I now face will appear retrospectively as a gap in my life. I cannot, of course, look *into* the gap but only ahead to a time when I can look back on the gap. In the case death there is no possibility of a retrospective view of the NOTHINGNESS I face; no possibility, in other words, of viewing it as a "gap." It is NOTHINGNESS once and for all. Final NOTHINGNESS. The dying man thinks (if he can think): "This is it. It will be all over, and it will never be again."[1]

---

[1] This is, I believe, the source of nostalgia. In nostalgia we are struck by the fact that some important event, or period of our life, is finished—that it will be "never again." These

The finality of death, its once-and-for-all character, presupposes it NOTHINGNESS, since it is precisely the NOTHINGNESS that is once and for all. Henceforth when we speak of the NOTHINGNESS of death we shall take it to include the aspect of finality—which is obviously essential to the awfulness of death. In fact, in everyday consciousness, and everyday chat, it is often the aspect of finality that is prominent. "You have only one life," "You only live once," "Life is not a rehearsal," and so on. These are commonplaces. How rarely we are struck by what they mean.[2]

In facing death, we face absolute (and final) NOTHINGNESS. But, one might ask, why is *that* awful? Why should the prospect of NOTHING-NESS disturb us in the peculiar way that it does? I understand the urge to ask such a question, but in a real sense there is no answer. Think back to what we said about humor (7.2). If someone does not find a situation funny, we point out to him the things in, or about, the situation that make it funny. If the person says he does not see why *that* makes the situation funny, there is nothing more we can do. (You cannot "prove" to the person that such-and-such makes the situation funny.) Similarly, if someone asks what makes (the prospect of) death awful, we may draw his attention to, and attempt to evoke, the fact of absolute once-and-for-all NOTH-INGNESS. If the person says he does not see why that makes death awful, there is nothing more we can do (except, of course, more of the same). If he does not find it awful, he does not it awful.

However I would say that if someone does not find the NOTHING-NESS we face in facing death awful, there is something is wrong, some-thing missing in this person. (A similar point holds in the case of humor, but the humor case is more complicated; we shall drop the analogy now.) Either that, or the person is in fact not open to what death means, to its NOTHINGESS. (Just repeating the formula, "With death there will be NOTHING" is not sufficient.) The point is not that, if we are open to the meaning of death, necessarily we ourselves will be disturbed or unsettled. Maybe some people can take it all in and stay calm. (Maybe that is the way to be—to see the awfulness but remain calm.) But if we do take it in, if we are genuinely open to what death means, i.e., open to the fact that there will be absolute and final NOTHINGNESS, then, unless something is missing in us, we cannot but see the awfulness of this prospect.

---

little "never agains," the "never agains" within my life, are premonitions of the big "never again," that of my life itself.

[2] Autobiographical footnote: My first serious thought about death came at age eight and related to the aspect of finality. It occurred to me, lying in bed one night, that when I was dead I would be dead "forever," or as it presented itself to me, "forever and ever and ever . . . ." I recall being so overwhelmed by this thought (it can still get to me) that I got out of

Thus being open to what we face in facing death, while it does not entail actually being disturbed, does—we have noted this before (7.2)—entail appreciating that what is faced warrants being disturbed. You cannot criticize someone for being disturbed in the face of death (as if this were some kind of shortcoming); but we might wonder about someone who is unable to appreciate that the prospect of death warrants being disturbed.[3]

There is a familiar line of thought that can be represented as follows: "Why should I find death, the prospect of NOTHINGNESS, awful? When the NOTHINGNESS is realized, it is not something I will experience. I will no longer be around to experience anything." What does this mean, "I will no longer be around to experience anything"? It means: there will no longer be such a thing as my experience (life), my horizon. That is, there will be NOTHING. But precisely this, that there will be NOTHING (once and for all), is what makes the prospect of death so awful. So if someone tells us that since we will no longer be around, there can be nothing awful in the prospect of death, the reply is that the prospect of "no longer being around" is what is awful. Perhaps you do not find it awful. But the fact that you will "no longer be around, etc." cannot serve as a reason for not finding the prospect of death awful. Once again, that is just what makes the prospect of death awful.

In some ways this resembles an idea that came up in our discussion of the DH, viz., that "it would not matter" if THIS were a dream (6.2). The reason "it would not matter" is that the fate of everything that matters is internal to THIS, to my horizon, internal, that is, to the subject matter of the DH. How could it matter whether there is anything that transcends the horizon of everything that matters? If THIS were a dream and I emerged from THIS, the horizon into which I would emerge would displace THIS, the horizon of everything that matters. How could that matter, if everything that matters is internal to the horizon that would be displaced? Yet we might feel that precisely *that*, the possibility that the horizon of everything that matters should be displaced by a horizon from whose standpoint everything that matters would no more matter than what happened in my dream of last night—that precisely this would, if it were a serious possibility, matter; that in fact it would matter in a way about which we might wish to say that "nothing could matter more."

---

bed in confusion and wandered into the living room where I surprised my parents, to whom I was unable to explain why I had gotten up or what I wanted.

[3] Might there be a whole culture in which people not only react with equanimity but see nothing awful about the NOTHINGNESS of death? In that case, either the "whole culture" is not open to the NOTHINGNESS of death (that could happen), or there is something wrong with the "whole culture": it is, in a certain way, blind (that could happen too). I

Similarly, if someone says that since the prospect of NOTHINGNESS is a prospect whose realization we will "no longer be around to experience" the prospect is not awful, the response is that it is precisely in being the prospect of our "no longer being around," i.e., the prospect of final NOTHINGNESS, that the prospect of death is awful. Thus we might say about the NOTHINGNESS that faces us in facing death what we said about the possibility that THIS is a dream, viz., that although in one way "it does not matter," in another way "nothing could matter more."

When the stakes get sufficiently high, it can seem either that nothing is at stake, or that incomparably much is at stake.

Let us consider again the ancient conundrum about fearing death (7.2). Is it rational to fear death? The assumption is that it is rational to fear an evil (harm) only if it is one that we will suffer. But when will we suffer the evil of death? Not before we die. (The evil of death is not to be confused with the evil of dying.) And after we die, we are no longer around to suffer an evil. If you say, it is possible for an evil to befall someone when he is no longer around, this—though in itself correct—is irrelevant; for if death is an evil, it remains so in the absence of posthumous evil.

So we are meant to conclude that it is not rational to fear death. In fact, this conclusion seems to me correct: it is not rational to fear death. However, it is not in any way irrational or confused to be disturbed by the prospect of death. At any rate, being disturbed by the prospect of death is (as we put it) warranted. What we face in facing death is NOTHINGNESS, and this prospect is awful; and, being awful, it warrants being disturbed. It might be better if—fully grasping its awfulness—we were not disturbed, if we were able to regard the awful prospect of NOTHINGNESS with composure. But you cannot deem it a weakness, or a shortcoming, or a piece of irrationality or confusion, if someone is disturbed by the prospect.[4]

Again, it is not rational to fear death in that death entails once-and-for-all NOTHINGNESS, and once-and-for-all NOTHINGNESS excludes the possibility of future suffering on my part. It does not, however, follow that the prospect of death is not awful or that it is not rational

---

would not, however, wish to extend these remarks to the case of humor. Here is one place where the parallel seems to run out.

[4] Another well-known conundrum about death is: Why should we be disturbed by the endless NOTHINGNESS that the prospect of death holds up, when the endless NOTHINGNESS before we were born does not trouble us at all? The key to answering this question lies in the simple fact that the past NOTHINGNESS is past, that it cannot be a "prospect" and hence cannot have the "finality" that looms with death. However, getting clear about what this involves requires getting clear about the past/present versus future temporal asymmetry—something that, although it will come up again in the book, we shall make no attempt properly to discuss.

to be disturbed by this prospect, since it is precisely the prospect of once-and-for-all NOTHINGNESS that is awful, and thus warrants our being disturbed.[5]

11.2 The Two Forms of the Impossibility of Death

What faces us in facing death is not just awful; it is incomprehensible. Recall Ivan, when he admits to himself that he is dying and becomes open to what the fact that he will die means:

> In the depths of his heart he knew he was dying but, far from growing used to the idea, he simply did not and could not grasp it . . . . "And here it is!" he said to himself. "It can't—it can't be, and yet it is! How has it happened? How am I to understand it?" And he could not understand it.

Ivan cannot understand it. Why? Because it seems impossible: "it can't be." Then why not rejoice? Because it will be. As he says: "it can't be, and yet it is." "It can't be": it is impossible. "And yet it is": it will be. It is both impossible and a fact. An impossible fact. How could Ivan, how could anyone, understand this, an impossible fact?

Philosophers sometimes say that "impossibilities," e.g., contradictions, cannot be understood. But they mean, really, that, since a contradiction cannot be true, we cannot understand what it would be for a contradiction to be true, a fact. Of course, there is a sense in which we do understand the contradiction: we understand in what it consists. Otherwise we would not be in a position to judge that it cannot obtain. This holds for impossibilities quite generally. In the case of death, too, we grasp in what the impossibility consists. The problem is that, despite the impossibility, it will come to pass. It is only because we understand in what the impossibility consists that the fact that it will come to pass is incomprehensible. You could say that it is only because we comprehend the impossibility of death that death is incomprehensible.

That I will die, that this is a fact, needs no philosophical explanation. It may not be clear, however, why the fact should seem impossible, i.e., in

[5] It might occur to us that death, the fact that we will die, is an "evil" in the following sense, that since the prospect of death, the NOTHINGNESS that faces us, is awful, the fact that we will die means we have to live our lives under the shadow of something awful. One might think it would be "better" if we did not have to live our lives this way. (It might be better if man never fell from grace.) I do not believe this is *obviously* true (I can think of reasons one might wish to deny it), but it may be true. I am not sure what to say about this—except that if we did not live our lives under the shadow of death, what we call "living our lives" would be different in ways that we cannot really envision.

what the seeming impossibility consists. The impossibility can assume either of two forms. One form, to which we have already drawn attention, relates to solipsism: the absolute NOTHINGNESS of death reflects (and thus puts us in touch with) the truth of solipsism, the fact that my horizon is the all-inclusive horizon; but this contradicts the way we live, with Others (metaphysical equals). How can it be true both that other horizons are coordinate with mine, that they exist side by side in a space of horizons, *and* that the ceasing to be of my horizon entails absolute NOTHINGNESS?

The other form of the impossibility relates to something that emerged in our reflections on the dream hypothesis, viz., that the world and the infinity of egocentric space and time are internal to the subject matter of the DH; internal, that is, to THIS, my horizon. But the subject matter of the DH is the subject matter of death. If whatever is temporal is internal to this subject matter, to my horizon, it cannot itself be temporal but must, rather, be conceived as being outside time. Yet in confronting the fact that I will die, I confront the fact that my horizon will *cease to be*. How is that possible? How, if it is not itself temporal, if it is outside time, can my horizon (my life, my consciousness) "cease to be"?

11.3 The Temporal Impossibility of Death

We shall first consider the impossibility concerning time. I will die. My horizon, THIS, will cease to be. But whatever is present, past, or future—whatever is either *now,* or before or after *now*—is internal to subject matter of the DH (see 1.6), internal to THIS. In that case, THIS, my horizon, cannot be conceived as existing *now,* or in the past or future. It must be conceived as outside time, nontemporal. Yet what I face in facing death is the ceasing to be of this very subject matter, my horizon. The subject matter that is the subject matter of death is, it seems, such that cannot be the subject matter of a ceasing to be. However, this is just what death is, a ceasing to be. The subject matter of death is, it seems, such that it cannot be the subject matter of death.

Obviously, the same kind of problem might be raised about the "coming to be" of my horizon. At one time, there was no such thing as my horizon. And now there is. So it, my horizon, "came to be." How could this happen if my horizon cannot itself be conceived as temporal? Thus it may seem "impossible"—and therefore, since it is a fact, incomprehensible—that such a thing as THIS, my horizon (life, experience), has come to be and thus now is. Incomprehensible, like death. And awful too, but in a positive way: awesome, we might say. (The wonder that there is such a thing as THIS, that there is SOMETHING not NOTHING.) But we shall focus on the case of ceasing to be, the case of death.[6]

Just as the whole of the world is, in the relevant sense, internal to THIS, to my horizon, so whatever is happening *now*, and whatever happened or will happen before and after *now*, the entire history of the world, present, past, and future, is internal to my horizon. Let us be clear, this does not mean that it has the status of an internal object, i.e., that it exists only from within my horizon, but that it is internal to my horizon in the way or sense that things are internal to a dream (1.7). My horizon is, in this sense, the horizon not just of the world, but the horizon time and hence of the history of the world. The history of the world is internal to my horizon despite the fact that most of this history occurred, or will occur, when there was, or will be, no such thing as my horizon.[7] Of course, this

---

[6] In a certain respect, the case of death is easier to think about. The reason is, the impossible "ceasing to be," that which is my death, seems like a datable event. There will be (impossibly) a certain moment in time when my horizon ceases to be. Ivan: "and all the time I got nearer and nearer to the abyss. My strength began to fail. Nearer and nearer!" To what is he getting "nearer"? Something that cannot properly have a date and thus to which he cannot get "nearer"—but to which, nevertheless, he is getting "nearer." At the other end, there is the same impossibility; but there is no question of a datable event (we are of course not talking about the biological event of birth). The impossible "coming to be," the coming to be of my horizon, is a gradual "coming to be." Gradual, but that makes it no less temporal, and thus, given the nontemporal character of my horizon, "impossible."

[7] Notice, if we fail to distinguish relevant sense or kind of internality, if we view the world and time as internal to my horizon not in the way that something is internal to a dream but in the way that something that exists only from within my horizon is internal to my horizon, then, since what I call "the world" and "time" would come into being with my horizon and cease to be when my horizon ceases to be, there will be—in addition to the problem of understanding how you and I live in a common world and time—a special problem about how to make sense of the fact that the world was there before there was such a thing as my horizon, and, indeed, since the existence of my horizon depends (causally; we shall come back to this in the next section) on my brain and hence on all sorts of things having happened in the world, that had the world not been there before, etc., there would have been no such thing as my horizon. Schopenhauer, who I think fails to distinguish the relevant kind of internality, states this predicament as a problem about "the first time":

> Thus we see, on the one hand, the existence of the whole world necessarily dependent on the existence of the first knowing being, however imperfect it be; on the other hand, this first knowing animal just as necessarily dependent on a long chain of causes and effects which has preceded it, and in which it itself appears as a small link. These two contradictory views, to each of which we are led with equal necessity, might certainly be called an *antinomy* in our faculty of knowledge. (*The World as Will and Representation*, trans. E.F.J. Payne [Dover, 1969], vol. 1, p. 30)

In other words, there could be no time before the first knowing subject (the "first horizon"), and yet that first knowing subject, dependent as it on the existence of an animal, could not have existed in the absence of a prior chain of conditions. Schopenhauer's solution does not eliminate the problem: if whatever is present, past, or future is internal to my horizon, my horizon must be outside time. How can it be true, then, that, as death reminds us, this subject matter will cease to be and therefore will at some future time no longer be?

11.4 Consciousness and Causation

The impossibility of death can assume other guises, depending on the guise assumed by its subject matter. Thus, under the guise of consciousness (in the horizonal sense), the fact that this subject matter is causally maintained by the activity of my brain may seem impossible. The impossibility of death is that something that is nontemporal will cease to be; the impossibility of the causation of consciousness is that something that is nontemporal is caused to be.

Let us begin by recalling something we noted in discussing the DH. If THIS, my consciousness (in the horizonal sense), were a dream, the brain on whose activity it would depend would not be *my* brain, the brain up here in this head. The brain up here (I touch my head) is awake; it is not a dreaming brain. The dreaming brain would be a transcendent brain, a brain that belongs to the world of the wider horizon, the world outside THIS (see 4.3). But of course we dismiss the DH. There is no wider horizon, no transcendent world. The world that spreads out around the human being I am, and includes that human being, is the only world. It is the brain of that human being, my brain, whose activity maintains THIS, my consciousness.

---

to this antinomy is to maintain that "time with its whole infinity in both directions is also present in the first knowledge. . . ." Accordingly,

the past out of which the first present arises, is, like it, dependent on the knowing subject, and without this it is nothing. It happens of necessity, however, that this first present does not manifest itself as first, in other words, as having no past for its mother, and as being the beginning of time; but rather as the consequence of the past according to the principle of being in time, just as the phenomenon filling in this first appears as the effect of previous states filling the past according to the law of causality. (ibid., p. 31)

This will not satisfy us. It may explain why it appears to the philosophically innocent subject, including the first subject, that the advent of his horizon was preceded by an infinite time. However, the philosopher who wants to accept Schopenhauer's account of the matter will not be able to take at face value the appearance of a prior temporal and causal order unless he somehow pulls the wool over his own eyes and hides from himself the philosophical account he wants to accept. If I view past events as part of a history that exists only from within my horizon, I cannot accept that such events might be causally responsible for, and hence prior to, the existence of that same horizon (the same "knowing subject").

The fact that the activity of my brain maintains my consciousness is a causal fact, roughly analogous, say, to the fact that the activity of the fan overhead maintains certain air currents in the room. This means that my horizon must be itself "in time," temporal, in the same sense that the phenomena (the activity, events, processes, etc.) in my brain that maintain my horizon in existence are temporal. Only what is temporal can figure as a term in the causal relation. However, since whatever is temporal, "in time," is internal to THIS, internal to my horizon, my horizon cannot itself be included "in time," and thus cannot stand to anything in a causal relation. So it may—and I think it sometimes *does*—strike us as impossible that my consciousness, THIS, should be causally dependent on what is occurring now in my brain. Yet the causal dependence is a fact. If now my brain were to cease functioning in the right way, there would be NOTHING. There would no longer be such a thing as THIS, as my consciousness.

In the B version of the "Paralogisms," Kant writes:

> The subject of the categories cannot by thinking the categories acquire a concept of itself as an object of the categories. For in order to think them, its pure self-consciousness, which is what was to be explained, must itself be presupposed. Similarly, the subject in which the representation of time has its original ground cannot thereby determine its own existence in time. And if this latter is impossible, the former, as a determination of the self . . . by means of the categories, is equally so. (B421–22)

If we equate Kant's "subject of the categories" with our horizonal subject matter, THIS, it becomes clear what Kant is getting at when he says that the subject cannot "acquire a concept of itself as an object of the categories" for the reason that "it must itself be presupposed," and for the same reason cannot "determine its own existence in time." The subject, the horizon (on this reading), is "presupposed" in the sense that whatever is a possible object of the categories, or has its existence determined "in time," is internal to it; so it, the subject, cannot itself be an object of the categories, or be determined "in time."[8] In the case of the category of

---

[8] Accordingly, the contrast at the heart of Kant's transcendental idealism—the contrast between the transcendental object X *as it appears* versus *as it is in itself*—presupposes the horizonal subject matter; for it is only from within this subject matter (from within consciousness, experience, in the horizonal sense) that there can in the first place be such a thing as appearing; hence that there can be a contrast between the X as it appears (it appears as the world in space and time) and the X as it is in itself (apart from the way it appears, about which we, in the nature of the case, know nothing). If one takes Kant in this way (I would not claim it is what he explicitly means), the horizonal subject matter is there all along,

causation, the two points come together: that the subject, as the horizon of whatever is "in time," cannot itself be determined "in time," entails that it cannot be made an object of the category of causation. As we said, only what is "in time" can stand in a causal relation.

Kant, however, appears oblivious to the underlying problem. How can we avoid supposing that the subject of the categories depends for its existence on what is happening in my brain? What is happening in my brain is, of course, part of what is happening in what I call "the world," i.e., in the totality of things to which I apply the categories and whose history has unfolded and will continue to unfold in the infinity of time before and after *now*. All this, the world and its history, whatever is (as Kant puts it) "determined in time," is internal to my horizon, the subject of the categories. Yet it seems that my horizon, the subject, etc., is causally dependent for its existence on what is going on in a certain little bit of the world; on what is going on in that little bit that is my brain. Not so? If right now my brain ceased to function, what would happen? There would be NOTHING. Would the Kantian "subject of the categories" survive the NOTHINGNESS that would be consequent upon the shutting down of my brain? Since its being depends causally on certain things happening in my brain, the Kantian subject would cease to be. But here the subject of the categories appears as (in Kant's phrase) "an object of the categories," in particular, as an object of the category of causation. The problem is, if the Kantian subject depends causally for its existence on what is happening in the brain, it must be temporally related to what is happening in the brain: that in which the representation of time has its original ground must itself be determined in time.

Let me quote another philosopher in this regard. Wittgenstein, in the *Investigations* (412), speaks of the "feeling of an unbridgeable gulf between consciousness and brain-processes," and then he wonders why this feeling "does not come into the considerations of our ordinary life." When, Wittgenstein asks, does the feeling actually occur?

> It is when I, for example, turn my attention in a particular way on to my own consciousness, and, astonished, say to myself: THIS is supposed to be produced by a process in the brain!—as it were clutching my forehead.—But what can it mean to speak of "turning my attention on to my own consciousness"? This is surely the queerest thing there could be! It was a particular act of gazing that I called doing this. I stared fixedly in front of me—but not at any particular point or object. My eyes were wide open, the brows not contracted (as they mostly are when

---

unannounced, unacknowledged, as an essential element in the framework of transcendental idealism. (See below, 20.3.)

I am interested in a particular object). No such interest preceded this gazing. My glance was vacant; or again like that of someone admiring the illumination of the sky and drinking in the light.

I clutch at my head and stare with eyes wide open. At what? At nothing in particular. My gaze is vacant, or as if I were "drinking in the light." The point, I take it, is that when I engage in the queer business of "turning my attention on to my own consciousness," there is nothing to attend *to*. I just stare vacantly, etc. No wonder I am "astonished" at the thought that that to which I attend—"THIS," "my own consciousness"—should be the product of what is happening in my brain. There is nothing there, nothing to which I might be attending. I have hold, as it were, of nothing, and I am considering the possibility that "it" is the product of a brain-process. This is, indeed, "the queerest thing there could be."

The manic little performance that Wittgenstein describes is meant to expose a peculiar kind of philosophical confusion wherein we work ourselves up into a false puzzlement. I see the matter rather differently. To begin with, I do not believe that the puzzlement or astonishment to which Wittgenstein refers is essentially philosophical. Anyone at anytime may be struck, and then puzzled (astonished), at the thought, "THIS, my consciousness, is the product of a brain-process." There is no need for philosophical argumentation or analysis to prepare us for this thought, or to make it seem puzzling. Our puzzlement is not, in this case, like that with which we respond, say, to Zeno's paradoxes about motion, or Russell's paradox about classes, or Goodman's paradox about "grue." In these cases, we have first to work through a seemingly correct argument, or piece of reasoning, whose consequence we then find puzzling (see Int.9). The puzzlement to which Wittgenstein draws our attention does not depend on any such philosophical preparation. We are, without the benefit of analysis or argumentation, simply struck by the thought that "THIS (my consciousness) is the product of things happening now in my brain." And we are puzzled. Our puzzlement is, I believe, like Ivan's puzzlement when he confronts the impossibility of death. Why are we puzzled? It is in both cases because we know that the thought by which we are struck ("I will die," "THIS is the product of things happening now in my brain") is true; that is, because we know it is true despite seeming impossible.

Nothing guarantees that we will actually be puzzled by this "truth" or "fact" about consciousness; just as nothing guarantees that we will be puzzled about death. But if death strikes us (in the way it strikes Ivan) as incomprehensible, it will not be because we have worked through a philosophical argument. It will be because, despite knowing that death is a fact, it seems impossible. Similarly, we do not need arguments in order to be puzzled by the causal dependence of our consciousness on the brain.

We are puzzled (if we are) because, while knowing the dependence to be a fact, it nonetheless seems impossible.

There is, however, more than a similarity between the puzzlement about death and the puzzlement about the causation of consciousness. The puzzlement is in both cases about the same subject matter, and at bottom it is the same puzzlement. The subject matter is in both cases THIS, my horizon, the subject matter of the DH.[9] In one case, it is puzzlement at the fact that THIS, my horizon (consciousness), will cease to be; in the other case, it is puzzlement at the fact that it is maintained in existence by what is happening in my brain. In both cases the fact seems impossible. What lies behind the sense of impossibility in both cases is that the subject matter in question is the horizon of whatever is temporal. Whatever is "in time" is internal to it. Thus it seems impossible that the subject matter "itself," THIS, should cease to be (that I will die), or that it should stand in a causal relationship to something happening in the world (that it should be the product of, be maintained in existence by, what is going on in my brain).

Consider again Wittgenstein's description of what happens in "turning my attention on to my own consciousness." I am astonished, puzzled. "How could THIS (my consciousness) be the product of a brain-process?" I "stare fixedly in front of me, but not at any particular point or object." A "vacant" gazing, like "drinking in the light" from the sky. Now, in a way, this is an apt description. It is apt because what I refer to by "THIS," by "my consciousness," is not something I might pick out, or demonstrate. In other words, there is nothing about which I might judge that *this* is my consciousness: that *this* is THIS. Anything about which I might make a demonstrative judgment would be present within THIS, within my consciousness (in the horizonal sense). Anything to which I might in this way turn my attention would be present from within my consciousness and thus could not be my consciousness (the argument from internality). The vacant staring expresses a kind of futile yearning to "take in" the horizon. It is the best we can do. But it is out of place. What kind of behavior would not be out of place? What kind of behavior would be appropriate to the object of reference? No kind of behavior. (The best we can do is not good enough.)

Wittgenstein wants to create the impression that when, staring vacantly, I am puzzled at the idea that "THIS (my consciousness) is the product of a brain-process," I refer by "THIS (my consciousness)" to nothing. In a way, he is right. But it is not that there is nothing to which I refer (which is Wittgenstein's point), but that that to which I refer is nothing. That is

---

[9] Thus, from our standpoint, it was very obliging of Wittgenstein to have employed here the capitalized "THIS."

to say, it is nothing apart from there being something present within it—nothing in itself. Consciousness, which as the horizon of time is outside time and thus outside the scope of causation, is nothing in itself.

11.5 The Solipsistic Impossibility of Death

Let us consider now the second form assumed by the impossibility of death. Death means: there will be NOTHING. Not, remember, NOTHING for me, but NOTHING period. The reason it seems that that this (in Ivan's words) "can't be," is that the absoluteness of what I am faced by conflicts with what is implicit in my commitment to (O), viz., that other horizons are coordinate with mine. We are metaphysical equals: our horizons exist side by side, as neighbors in a space of horizons. This means that when I die, when my horizon ceases to be, its ceasing to be will not touch the being of other horizons. For Others everything will be the same. Do I not believe this? Would I not, in fact, say that I *know* it to be the case? But, as we explained (10.3), the picture that is presupposed here, that of horizons being extinguished piecemeal fashion—of NOTHING-NESS for you, of NOTHINGNESS for me—is at odds with the absoluteness of the NOTHINGNESS that I face. Insofar as the NOTHING-NESS I face is unrelativized, absolute, it will not accommodate the picture of separate horizons dropping off one by one.

My light will go out. *My* light, not *your* light. Yet how can this be, if what I am faced by is simply: *no* light. Not no light for me versus no light for you—but simply no light. This is the solipsistic impossibility of death. Just as the absoluteness of the NOTHINGNESS of death reflects the truth of solipsism, the solipsistic impossibility of death reflects the impossibility of solipsism.

The solipsistic impossibility of death is present even where we seem to be denying the solipsistic implications of what we face in facing death. We think (with Ivan): "There will be NOTHING." But then we may wish to add: "It is like that (the same) for everyone." This generalization seems to strike exactly the right note. Is it not the case that everyone faces the same thing here, that we are all in the same boat? In fact, however, the solipsistic impossibility is hidden within the seemingly antisolipsistic thought, i.e., within the generalization that "It is like that for everyone." The generalization contains the impossibility. It is, you might say, an impossible generalization.

"It is like that for everyone." Like *what* for everyone? Well, we all face absolute NOTHINGNESS. Insofar as our thought concerns what it is like *for everyone*, its import is general. Insofar as it concerns *what it is like* for everyone, it concerns absolute NOTHINGNESS. Both elements are essential to our thought: it is a thought that generalizes the facing of absolute NOTHINGNESS. The problem is that absolute NOTHINGNESS cannot be generalized. If the NOTHINGNESS we all face is absolute, it cannot be what we all face. There cannot be more than one absolute NOTHINGNESS (10.3). Our thought is a thought that generalizes what cannot be generalized. It is an impossible generalization.

Each of us casts a shadow. This would not naturally be taken to mean that there is some one shadow that we all cast (that we all cast the same shadow), but that, for each of us, there is a shadow that he casts. You cast your shadow, I cast mine. Similarly, the thought "It is like that for everyone" does not mean that there is one NOTHINGNESS for all of us—a single death that we all face. There is not one death but many, and each of us has to face his own death: his own NOTHINGNESS. This is how we understand the thought in which we generalize the facing of NOTHINGNESS. Yet if the NOTHINGNESS we face is absolute, the thought is incoherent.

My facing absolute NOTHINGNESS cannot, it seems, be one among many such facings. A multiplicity is no more possible in this respect than a multiplicity of horizons each of which is the all-inclusive horizon. These are, in fact, the same impossibility. Then how can I generalize what I face? How can I, in effect, generalize my solipsism?[10] How can I think, "It is the same (like that) for all of us"? Yet that is what I think. It is what we all think, and mutually know that we think. The thought, "It is the same for all of us" is, in fact, a perfect expression of our togetherness. We are together as a community of solipsists—together, one might say, as an impossible community (a community founded on an impossible generalization). What could better serve to bond us than a mutual grasp of the fact that we are all caught up in the same predicament?[11]

11.6 The "Aloneness" of the Dying Subject

The dying subject is alone. Let us consider our attitude toward an Other for whom death is close. The dying Other, let us assume, knows the score.

---

[10] There is an analogous puzzle, which we shall not discuss in this book, about the temporal present. What do we mean by "now," the temporal present? We mean: the time at which things happen (become, are actualized, etc.). Or perhaps: the time from whose standpoint everything has the value or importance it has. *The* time? Does everything happen (is everything actual) all at once? Again, is the importance of what happens fixed once and for all, from the standpoint of just one time? No, it is always like that. How can it *always* be like that? How can each time be *the* time, etc.? "It is always like that." An impossible generalization.

[11] Here, perhaps, we have something worthy of being called a "metaphysical foundation of ethics."

Why does his situation move us in the way that it does? If the Other is someone we care about, we shall "lose" him; but let us abstract away from this. The question is why we are moved on the Other's behalf. It is not simply because of what is happening to him. What is happening to him might be happening without his knowing it, hence without his being faced by death, by absolute, once-and-for-all NOTHINGNESS—in which case we would not now be moved in the way that we are. We are moved in the way we are because of what the Other is facing.

Of course the dying Other not only faces the awful prospect that we all face, but unlike the rest of us he has to deal with it *now*. Clearly, the temporal immediacy of what he faces figures in our attitude toward the Other. Our time will come as well, but now is not our time. It is his time now. The Other has to deal now with the awful prospect of NOTHING-NESS, and we do not.

Nor is there anything we can do for him, that is to say, anything that matters. "No one," Heidegger writes, "can take the Other's dying away from him. . . . Dying is something that every Dasein must take upon itself at the time. By its very essence, death is in every case mine, insofar as it 'is' at all."[12]

What would it be to take away the Other's dying? Why is it impossible? Heidegger is not talking here about the biological process of dying, but about death in what we called the metaphysical sense (8.4). The impossibility of taking the process away, of transferring it to ourselves, is like the impossibility of transferring to ourselves the particular phenomenon of the Other's breathing, or digesting.[13] This is impossible, but it is not the relevant impossibility.

What would it be to take the Other's death (in the metaphysical sense) away from him? It would not be (as Heidegger notes) to die in his place; for the death that is then faced is not his but mine. Then what would it be? What is it, exactly, that is supposed to be impossible here?

I cannot take over the Other's horizon. That is, I cannot occupy for the Other, the dying human being, the position at the center of his horizon, the horizon that will soon cease to be. Of course, I cannot do this even if the Other is not dying. One subject cannot take over another's horizon. The reason is that the Other's horizon, like my horizon, is nothing in itself. That which in the case of the dying Other will cease to be, and whose ceasing to be means there will be NOTHING, is in its own way nothing. So there is nothing, no re-identifiable entity—like a house, or a piece of land—that might be occupied first by one subject

---

[12] *Being and Time*, p. 240.

[13] It is the impossibility of transferring what Strawson, in Individuals (chap. 1, part section 7) calls "dependent particulars."

and then by another. There is nothing, then, that I might take over from the dying Other.[14]

In facing and having to deal now with this absolute, NOTHINGNESS, the dying Other is alone. He is alone and he knows that he is alone, and we know it, and we know that he knows that we know, etc. We are "with" the dying Other in his aloneness. Yet it is *he* who is dying, dying now, and he is alone in this. Such is the aloneness of the dying Other.

Are we not alone as well? We too have to deal with our own death. The fact remains, though, the dying Other has to deal with death *now*, and we do not. He has to deal now with something that we have yet to deal with. This fact, the fact that NOTHINGNESS is closer for the dying Other than in our own case, highlights something that has been implicit through our discussion of the aloneness of death. It highlights the picture of separate NOTHINGESSES, one for each of us. And yet the absoluteness of the NOTHINGNESS that the Other faces, that each of us faces—an appreciation of which is essential to our attitude toward the Other—excludes this picture. This is the solipsistic impossibility of death. It is present inside our attitude toward the dying Other.

Consider the situation from his standpoint. Being surrounded by Others will not relieve the dying subject of his aloneness; on the contrary, it may serve to heighten his sense of being alone. Thus, eyeing those around him he might think, "It is *I* who am dying, not *they*." The metaphysical meaning of this thought is: It is *my* horizon, not *theirs*, that will soon no longer be. This contrast between "my" horizon and "their" horizons is essential to the dying subject's sense of aloneness: the other horizons will remain; mine will cease to be. I am the one who is "leaving."[15]

Earlier (chapter 9) we discussed the aloneness of solipsism. The aloneness of the dying subject, we must be clear, is not the aloneness of solipsism. In fact it is at odds with the aloneness of solipsism. For, as we just explained, the picture required to understand the aloneness of the dying man is not that of my horizon including all others, of having no neighbors, but that of my horizon existing side by side with others, of coordinate horizons (neighbors). The lights go out one by one, and right now it is my turn. (The jumpmaster has called my number.) *My* turn, not

---

[14] Compare this with the more familiar question (which we shall discuss in the next part of the book) of whether I might take over—come to find myself in—an Other's body. Here the problem concerns not the possibility of re-identifying that which I take over, viz., the body of the Other, but of re-identifying myself, the reference of "I," in that body.

[15] Max Brod, in his biography of Franz Kafka, reports that, when he was very close to death, Kafka asked his doctor, who had moved away from the bed to attend to something, not to leave him. The doctor assured him, "But I am *not* leaving you," to which Kafka "answered in a deep voice, 'But I am leaving you.' " *Franz Kafka: A Biography* (Schocken Books, 1963), p. 212.

their turn![16] My turn for what? For NOTHINGNESS, i.e., for NOTH-INGNESS period. This is what I, not they, immediately face: absolute NOTHINGNESS. The contrast between myself and Others, the fact that the finger points at my horizon not theirs, presupposes the space of coordinate horizons. But the absolute character of the NOTHINGNESS faced from within these horizons, and faced up close from within the horizon of the dying subject, this reflects the aloneness of solipsism and thus will not tolerate the space of coordinate horizons—the very thing in terms of which we understand the subject's aloneness in dying.

In dying I am on my own. The awful NOTHINGNESS is faced up close now not by you but by me, i.e., from with my horizon—the horizon whose ceasing to be is close in time. The "mineness" of my death is thus the "mineness" of my horizon. In what does this "mineness" consist? It consists, we said, in the fact that my horizon is "the" horizon (9.1); that is to say, in the fact that it is the all-inclusive (preeminent) horizon. This fact or truth, the truth of solipsism, comes into the open when we reflect on what we face in facing death: it comes into the open when we become open to the absoluteness of death. Death, as Heidegger says, is in every case "mine." Death is in every case "mine" in that it is faced from within, and is the ceasing to be of, a subject matter that is "mine"; a subject matter whose "mineness" consists in a fact to which we become open by reflecting on, once again, death. But if the "mineness" of my death consists in the truth of solipsism, the generalization that death is in every case "mine" is in effect the generalization of solipsism. It is an impossible generalization.[17]

Thus the impossibility present in the aloneness of the dying man merely dramatizes something that is already there for the living man: the general solipsistic impossibility. In fact, the impossibility is implicit in the very philosophical project of analyzing the impossibility. For example, in developing the idea about the absolute (unrelativized) character of the NOTHINGNESS that faces us in facing death, we have expressed ourselves in the first-person plural as often as the first-person singular. We have regularly (as in the last sentence) spoken of what faces "us" in facing death, how things are "for us," and so on. Yet the idea has been that what we (there we go again) face, the NOTHINGNESS, is absolute, that if we try to represent what we (!) face here in terms of relativized NOTHING-NESS, we fail to capture what we actually face, what death actually means

---

[16] "Why does it have to be *me*?" thinks the dying subject. Funny: first the "not me" phenomenon, then the "why me?" phenomenon.

[17] How is it that Heidegger, who probes the meaning of death so deeply, does not see the impossibility? It is, I believe, because he neglects to ask in what the "mineness" of my death consists; that is, as we remarked in 8.5, to ask in the first place in what the "mineness" of Dasein's Being consists.

to us. Moreover, were I painstakingly to restrict myself to the first-person singular, this would achieve only the most superficial disguise of the problem. For all the while that I would be formulating things in the first-person singular, I would be addressing what I thus formulate to *you*, i.e., to a community of metaphysical equals, a community whose members are "with" me, and for whom I know what I formulate holds true in the same way it holds true for me.[18]

We might compare this with the predicament that afflicts the philosophical attempt to take seriously the hypothesis that THIS is a dream (6.6, 6.8). No matter how secretive we are about this, how isolated the circumstances of our philosophizing, we address the attempt to Others, to metaphysical equals. Yet if the hypothesis we attempt to take seriously were true, those we address would not be my metaphysical equals. Similarly, when we formulate the point that what we face in facing death is absolute NOTHINGNESS, we address Others, metaphysical equals. I take myself, then, to be addressing subjects who face exactly what I face. Yet if the NOTHINGNESS I face is absolute, those I address cannot be metaphysical equals. I alone face absolute NOTHINGNESS.

A big difference between the dream and death case is that, you might say, in the dream case the predicament is philosophically welcome: it makes clear why it is that we do not, that we cannot, take the DH seriously. Nothing like this applies in the death case. Are we looking for an explanation of why we cannot take seriously the fact that we will die? We do not take the DH seriously, but we take death seriously. We know that we will die.

11.7 The Puzzles of Death and the Causation of Consciousness

Death confronts us not just with awfulness but impossibility—at the same time that we know that it is a fact. Ivan: "It can't be—yet it is." Thus, when (if) the meaning of death gets through to us, death may seem (as it seems to Ivan) incomprehensible.

Similarly, it is a fact that our consciousness is caused by what is going on in our brains. Yet this may strike us as impossible, as an impossible fact. So here too is something we cannot comprehend.

[18] In his book *Past, Space, and Self* (MIT Press, 1994), John Campbell writes about death that: "The problem is not the expectation of pain and suffering that may be associated with death; it seems to be even more fundamental than that. Death is the end of everything, and that is what is terrifying" (p. 155). Insofar as it characterizes the meaning of death in an absolute, unrelativized way, this, it seems to me, is exactly right. (What death means is not the end of everything "for me," but simply the end of everything.) Yet the characterization is, in effect, addressed to a community of metaphysical equals. We, all of us in this commu-

The impossibility of death takes either of two forms. One form is as a temporal impossibility. What will cease to be with my death is THIS, my horizon, the subject matter that emerges in our reflections on the DH. But since whatever is in time is internal to it, this subject matter itself, my horizon, is outside time and therefore cannot cease to be. The second form is the solipsistic impossibility of death. When THIS ceases to be there will be NOTHING. In facing death, I face NOTHINGNESS—not NOTHINGNESS somehow qualified or relativized, but just NOTHING-NESS: NOTHINGNESS period (absolute NOTHINGNESS). This, as we explained (chapter 10), entails solipsism. The problem is, what I face can be generalized: we all face the same thing. If what I face is absolute NOTHINGNESS, this generalization is impossible (it amounts to generalizing solipsism). What I face is something impossible, something that cannot be: a generalizable absoluteness. Something that cannot be, yet (as we know) something that will be.

If THIS, my consciousness (the horizon under a different guise) is outside time, it is outside the scope of causation. My consciousness, however, is causally maintained by the activity of my brain. (If there were no such activity there would be no such thing as THIS, as my consciousness in the horizonal sense.) Wittgenstein's muddled philosopher exclaims: "THIS is supposed to be produced by a process in the brain!" I do not think this philosopher is muddled. He may not be clear about the source of his puzzlement, but he is right to be puzzled. The causation of consciousness is an impossible fact.

These impossibilities, notice, all concern THIS, the personal (my) horizon. Thus our analysis of the impossibilities of death and the causation of consciousness presupposes our earlier reflections on the DH in which this problematic subject matter, the horizonal subject matter, comes into view. On the other hand, we do not need philosophical reflection in order to react to the fact of death, or the causation of our consciousness, with incomprehension. We do not philosophize ourselves into puzzlement about death or consciousness as we philosophize ourselves into, say, Zeno's paradoxes about motion, or Russell's paradox about sets, or Goodman's puzzle about "grue." The puzzlement, the lack of comprehension, simply comes over us (if it does; there is no guarantee). It comes over us without any philosophical buildup or preparation. (See Int.9–1.)

This is because in these cases, as opposed to the more familiar philosophical puzzles wherein arguments, etc., are essential to our being puzzled (the intraphilosophical puzzles, as we called them), the source of the puzzlement is extraphilosophical. Thus the role of philosophy is different

---

nity, face the same thing. Is there not a problem here? If the characterization accurately represents what we all face in facing death, how can *we all* face it?

here from its role in the intraphilosophical puzzles. In the latter case, since philosophy creates the puzzles, it takes upon itself the obligation of solving the puzzles. In the extraphilosophical case, philosophy enters not by way of creating the puzzles but (as we have been attempting to do) by way of exposing their elements, of articulating or analyzing the puzzles.

Of course, analysis figures in the intraphilosophical cases as well: (if you want to solve a puzzle, you have to analyze it). The thing about the extraphilosophical puzzles is that they are there for us in any case, independently of philosophy; they do not have philosophical solutions. In analyzing these puzzles, the aim is simply to understand the puzzles—to understand ourselves.

Insofar as the extraphilosophical puzzles are already there for us, we already know they are there. Just as we already know of the problematic horizon. We know the puzzles are there, and we know of the horizon, but we are not yet open to what we know. Allowing, via our reflections on the DH, the horizon to come into view, analyzing by reference to the horizon the puzzles in which it figures—these are ways of becoming open to what we already know, ways of making a philosophical discovery (see introduction).

The general picture, then, is one in which we have, independently of philosophy, an implicit grasp of certain puzzles. In one way or another, the puzzles all relate to personal horizon. We need philosophy to bring the horizon into view and to analyze the puzzles. But whether we do this or not, the puzzles are there and may break into everyday consciousness as blank incomprehension in the face of something we know to be a fact. The role of philosophy, once again, is not to solve the puzzles (they have no solutions), but to uncover the horizonal subject matter and, by reference to this subject matter, to analyze and thus understand the puzzles. But the puzzles will, I think, remain, with a potential to trouble us extraphilosophically, whether we understand them or not.

PART THREE

The Self

12. Imagination and the Cartesian Self

12.1 *What Is "the Self"?*

The subject matter of the DH, that which would be a dream if THIS were a dream, is the subject matter of death, i.e., the subject matter whose ceasing to be is my death. When we now ask "What is the self?" you are no doubt expecting the same answer yet again, and in fact I believe that, in a sense, this is the answer. The horizonal subject matter, that which emerged in our reflections on the DH and whose ceasing to be is my death, assumes, as one of its guises, the guise of the self. You will note I say that "in a sense" this is the answer. Qualifications are necessary. The self is a complex topic.

Thus simply identifying the self with horizonal subject matter would clash with the fact that we have a conception of the self on which, as Descartes appreciates, the self is that to which we refer in the first-person singular, that to which each of us refers by "I." When I refer by "I," I refer to a certain human being, or perhaps a soul, in any case to a part of the world and not to the horizon, THIS, the subject matter to which the world, including the bit that I am, is internal. One may wonder, then, in what sense the horizonal subject matter is the self. Perhaps, for the moment, we may settle for the neutral statement that without explicit reference to the conception of the horizonal subject matter, to the horizonal conception of the self, we will not sort out the complex philosophical topic of the self.

12.2 *The Cartesian Argument*

Let us assume, with Descartes, that the everyday use of the "I" is referential, and that what we refer to in using the "I" is an entity in the world. Descartes, as is well known, argues (in the second meditation) that whatever this entity is, its existence cannot be doubted. It is indubitable then that I exist. The next question for Descartes is: What is this entity to which I refer in the first person and whose existence is indubitable? What am I? Descartes' answer to this question is also well known. I am a soul, an immaterial substance. For Descartes this entails that I am a nonspatial substance.

Now although off and on we have paid a certain lip service to this answer and have tried to keep it in play, like most philosophers these days I share the prevailing anti-Cartesian *Weltanshauung*. This says: there are no immaterial substances (in Descartes' sense). Why? Is it just a prejudice? The vague thought (which I doubt if I could improve on very much) is that there is no room for immaterial substances in a "scientific" picture of the world. There is room, certainly, for all sorts of strange things like quarks and gluons and neutrinos. But (apart from the fact that they are not in the philosophical sense "substances"), quarks and the others are not to be compared with Cartesian immaterial substances. They exist inside the boundaries of the everyday object. Thus in whatever sense they might be said to be "immaterial," they are not, in contrast to the Cartesian soul, nonspatial.

A *Weltanshauung* is not an argument. Here is an anti-Cartesian argument. I conceive of myself as being, say, "near" this thing, and "far" from that thing; again, this thing is "over here," that thing "over there." The details are constantly changing, constantly being adjusted, but the implicit conception of myself, the background of my engagement in the world, is constant. And clearly it is part of this conception that I take myself to have spatial position. How could anything be "near" what has no spatial position? What could "over there" mean apart from a spatial standpoint? It seems clear, then, that I do not conceive of myself as an immaterial thing.

The conception we have of ourselves as spatially oriented, as living and acting in space, is obviously fundamental. I do not think we will allow the Cartesian to persuade us that it is a *mis*conception. But the Cartesian might maintain that our spatial orientation is, in a certain sense, indirect; that, strictly speaking, the required point of reference is established not by *my* spatial position (strictly, I have no spatial position), but by the position of the body to which I am causally linked ("my body"). It is via reference to the position of this body, then, that things are "here," "over there," and so on.

Yet if we reflect for a moment on what spatially oriented life is actually like, this is hardly more convincing than the idea that we have no such life at all. I want my hat. Where is it? It is "over there." Can anything get between me and what establishes the position by reference to which the hat is "over there"? I *am* what establishes that position, the point of reference. That is, the spatial point of reference is established not by something *linked* to me, but by *me*. Insofar as that which establishes the spatial point of reference must be itself something spatial, I myself must be something spatial.

We shall not pursue this any further.[1] However conclusive the argument may be, there is a powerful argument on the other side, an argument that purports to show that I am not a material substance, not a bodily thing. Let us assume that I am a bodily thing, a human being. The argument that I have in mind (the Cartesian argument) has as its premise that being a bodily thing is not part of my essence, that being bodily is not essential to my being (existing). Hence,

(CP) I might exist without being bodily.

The conclusion is meant to follow straightaway:

(CC) I am not a bodily thing.

This is all there is, really, to the Cartesian argument.[2] Of course, Descartes wants to say more. He wants to say not just that I am not a bodily thing, not a material substance, but that I am an immaterial substance. This requires that, assuming that I am a substance of some kind, if I am not a material substance, I must be an immaterial substance. Let us give him this and focus on the argument for (CC), that I am not a bodily thing.

If someone provides us with a seemingly good argument for a proposition we do not believe, it is not sufficient to counter with an argument that the proposition in question is false; we must try to expose a mistake in the argument for the proposition. (Otherwise we may be left with a paradox.) But it might be said that the Cartesian argument is not a seemingly good argument, that on the contrary it is an obviously bad argument. Consider the following: It is possible that I exist without being bearded; therefore, I am not a bearded thing (I do not have a beard). The premise is true but, as it happens, the conclusion is false. Clearly, this form of argument is not valid. Since the Cartesian argument is of the same form, it is not a formally valid argument.

So much is undeniable. Nonetheless, the Cartesian argument is valid. That is, even though (CC) does not follow by virtue of the form of the

---

[1] See Gareth Evans's discussion of self-identification in *The Varieties of Reference*, especially sections 7.1, 7.3.

[2] Let me quote, without comment, the relevant passage from *Meditation VI*:

Because I know certainly that I exist, and that meanwhile I do not remark that any other thing necessarily pertains to my nature or essence, excepting that I am a thinking thing, I rightly conclude that my essence consists solely in the fact that I am a thinking thing. And although possibly (or rather certainly, as I shall say in a moment) I possess a body with which I am very intimately conjoined, yet because, on the one side, I have a clear and distinct idea of myself inasmuch as I am a thinking and unextended thing, and as, on the other, it is certain that this is entirely and absolutely distinct from body, and can exist without it. (*Philosophical Works of Descartes*, vol. 1, p. 190).

argument, it follows from (CP) that I am not a bodily thing. It follows because of what it is to be a bodily thing.

If X is a bodily thing, whatever else X is, X is a essentially a bodily thing; that is, being bodily is essential to X's being (existing) at all. You cannot say about something, e.g., this pen, that although it is a bodily thing, it might not have been a bodily thing. If it, this pen, were not a bodily thing, there would have been no such thing as this pen: the hypothesis of the pen's not being a bodily thing is equivalent to the hypothesis of its simply not being, not existing. In contrast, being a bearded thing is not essential to what is bearded: something that is bearded need not have been bearded. I am bearded; but I need not have been bearded.

Let us accept that the Cartesian argument is valid (though, as we said, not formally valid).[3] Assume that (CP) is true, that it is possible that I should exist without being a bodily thing. If I were a bodily thing, then being bodily would be essential to my being, my existing. The hypothesis that I exist without being a bodily thing would therefore be equivalent to the hypothesis that I do not exist. In other words, if I were a bodily thing, (CP) could not be true. Hence if, as we are assuming, (CP) is true, (CC) follows: I am not a bodily thing.

12.3 Imagination and Proof

This means that our final assessment of the Cartesian argument rests on whether we think (CP) is true. Why should we think it possible that I exist without being bodily? Here again, there is a well-known argument. I can, it seems, imagine existing without being bodily. If I can imagine this, then, the idea is, it is possible that I might exist without being bodily.[4]

Is the possibility of my existing without being bodily supposed to *follow* from the fact that I can imagine existing without being bodily? Many philosophers challenge the inference from imaginability to possibility. I can (it seems) imagine going to sleep and waking in the eighteenth century. Does it follow that this is possible? On the other hand, you can hardly claim that when a possibility is at issue the appeal to imagination is out of place, as if imagination had no role here at all. If we reject the notion that imagination supplies a premise from which the possibility "follows" (from which it can be "inferred"), perhaps we should look for an alterna-

---

[3] Of course, the Cartesian argument rests on the essential/accidental contrast (we have used the contrast before; 1.2, 4.1), which is itself a large philosophical topic. It is, however, a topic I hope we can avoid. Although the basis of the contrast may not be clear, it seems to me that even those who are skeptical about it have an intuitive grasp of the contrast and find no difficulty applying it.

[4] See, e.g., W. D. Hart's *The Engines of the Soul* (Cambridge University Press, 1988).

tive. It may be that imagination can prove (establish) a possibility without purporting to offer an argument for the possibility.

Notice, when we assert that "we can imagine" its being the case that p, we are already in the domain of possibility. We assert, in effect, that it is *possible to imagine* its being the case that p. What gives us the right to make such an assertion—to move like this into the domain of possibility?

Suppose we understand this as asking how we establish, or prove, the possibility in question: the possibility of imagining its being the case that p. Well, one might say, we actually *do* it. We establish the possibility of imagining its being the case that p by imagining its being the case that p. This is a way of proving, or establishing, a possibility. It is not, however, a proof by *argument*. It is, rather, what we might call a proof by *exhibition*. I say to you that I can tear a London phone directory in two with my bare hands. You are doubtful. So I do it, I tear the directory in two. This is not an argument for, but an exhibition of, the possibility that I asserted. In exhibiting the possibility I prove (establish) it. Similarly, one might suggest, if we imagine its being the case that p, we exhibit the possibility of imagining this, and in exhibiting the possibility we prove it—not (once again) by argument but by exhibition.

A proof by exhibition is defeasable. It can always turn out that we have not done what we represent ourselves as doing, and hence that we have not exhibited the possibility in question. When I claim that I can tear a directory in two, you may suspect a trick. In that case, you will watch me very closely. In being offered a proof by exhibition, it pays to be on our guard.

This applies as much in the case where the exhibiting proceeds via imagination as any other—except that in this case "watching closely" will not help. Yet we are not altogether without means. We may probe, ask questions, consider things in new ways (which is liable to involve further imagining), and so on. Suppose, for example, someone tells us he can imagine being in two places at once. We ask him to tell us more, to describe what he imagines. He can imagine, he says, being at the same time in London and Paris. More details, please. He can imagine seeing, up close, Big Ben on one side and the Eiffel Tower on the other. But now we will point out that, since what he imagines might be realized without his being simultaneously in London and Paris (the Eiffel Tower, say, is moved to London), he is not entitled to describe what he imagines as "being in two places at once."

Another kind of mistake, which arises through carelessness, is that we may simply imagine the wrong thing. In the Arthurian tale, the Green Knight, having been decapitated, picks up his living head, puts it under his arm, and walks off. We will say that we can imagine how this is for him. Do it. What do you imagine? You imagine (most likely) carrying your head under your arm, like, say, you would carry a football. What you may have overlooked in imagining this is that since your living head (never mind how it stays alive) with your eyes is under your arm, the visual perspective of what you imagine should have its point of reference next to your body, under your arm, and not above your shoulders. Is that how you imagined it? It is not so easy to imagine.

But we might improve in this respect. We might work up to being able to imagine what at first we are unable to imagine. In the present case, I start by imagining someone else carrying me under his arm. Then I imagine away the rest of my body. So now it is someone else carrying just my head. From this it seems a small step to imagining that the "someone else" is the headless me, JV without his head.

Another example. It seems impossible to imagine all-around (360-degree) visual experience. We know that, if my sense organs were supplemented by further visual sensors connected to the visual center of my brain (which was enhanced so that it could integrate the new information with that from my two eyes), then, physiologically, I would be equipped for all-around visual experience. However, this by itself makes it no easier actually to imagine all-around visual experience. But again, we might work up to, or at least in the direction of, imagining such experience— e.g., by looking at 360-degree photography and trying to block out what lies to either side, or by trying to extrapolate from the difference between the visual field with one eye closed and both eyes open.

Philosophical claims about what we "can imagine" are meant (I think) to include not just what we can now, limited as we are, imagine, but also what we might one way or another work up to; they are meant to transcend inessential limitations on what we can imagine. Of course this introduces a new element of uncertainty. When is a limitation inessential? Each case has to be studied as it comes along. Here, as before, there is no substitute for further reflection and imagination.

In the end, by whatever means a possibility is (or is claimed to be) exhibited, there is no guarantee against being fooled, or being careless. How could there be? (In the case of imagination, we may fool ourselves.) But that is not a reason for rejecting the method of proof by exhibition; it is just a reason for being careful, for being on our guard.

12.4 Exhibiting Possibilities in Imagination

The Cartesian thinks the truth of (CP) can be established by arguing from what I can imagine, viz., existing without being bodily. Against this it is objected that, from the fact that we can imagine a given state of affairs, it does not follow that the state of affairs is possible. The suggestion is that there is an alternative way to conceive of the role played by imagination in this regard: its role is not to supply a premise from which we infer (CP), but to exhibit the possibility expressed by (CP). We put imagination to the service not of a proof by argument but a proof by exhibition.

How exactly does this work? So far we have observed that, in imagining its being the case that p, I exhibit the possibility of imagining its being the case that p. In imagining existing without being bodily (assuming that that really is what I do, that there are no mistakes or tricks here), then, I exhibit, and thereby prove, the possibility of imagining existing without being bodily. So far so good. However, it must now strike us that there is a gap between what I have exhibited, and thus proved, and what the Cartesian wants to prove. I have, by imagining what I imagine, proved the possibility of imagining existing without being bodily; but what the Cartesian wants to prove is the possibility of existing without being bodily.

Perhaps it now seems that, when it comes to exhibiting possibilities, imagination is no different from anything else. We make it the case that p, thereby creating an actuality. In doing this, we exhibit the possibility of no more than the actuality we create: its being the case that p. So, one might think, in imagining its being the case that p (in making it the case that we imagine this), we exhibit the possibility of no more than our imagining its being the case that p; for this is the only actuality we create, our imagining its being the case that p.

The implicit principle here might be expressed by saying that an exhibited possibility cannot transcend the actuality by means of which it is exhibited. When we imagine its being the case that p, the relevant actuality is our imagining its being the case that p. Hence the possibility we thereby exhibit can be no more than that of our imagining its being the case that p. If we suppose the exhibited possibility is the possibility of the state of affairs itself, the possibility of its *being* the case that p, this would violate the principle. The exhibited possibility would transcend the actuality by means of which it was exhibited.

Now this may sound convincing when it is set out in an abstract and general way. Yet once we start thinking in terms of particular examples, it does not hold up. If we deny that imagination can exhibit possibilities that transcend its own actuality we miss the essential thing about imagination—which is precisely the way it exhibits possibilities transcending its own actuality. One or two simple examples should suffice to bring out the point.

Suppose the possibility is that of two circles intersecting. We draw two intersecting circles. In doing this, we create the relevant actuality and thereby exhibit the possibility of two circles intersecting. Now suppose, instead, we imagine two circles intersecting. Will you want to insist that this exhibits no more than the possibility of imagining two circles intersecting? Is it not evident that, in imagining two circles intersecting, we exhibit not just the possibility of imagining two circles intersecting, but the possibility of two circles intersecting?

Another example. One way of exhibiting the possibility of having a pain in my thumb is by creating a state of affairs in which I have a pain in my thumb. I do this, say, by striking my thumb with a hammer. By creating the state of affairs, I exhibit its possibility. But could I not have spared myself the trouble (and the pain) by imagining having a pain in my thumb? In imagining having a pain in my thumb, I exhibit not merely the possibility of imagining this, but the possibility of having a pain in my thumb.

Now it may be that the examples we have chosen are in some way special, that the exhibiting of possibilities in imagination works only for some kinds of possibility. We shall consider this later. But the examples suffice to refute the general restriction envisioned above: that the only possibility exhibited in imagining its being the case that p is the possibility exhibited by the actuality of that very imagining, viz., the possibility of imagining its being the case that p. It seems clear that at least for some kinds of possibility, imagination exhibits possibilities that transcend its own actuality.

This is how a proof by exhibition works. We create an actuality that exhibits the possibility we wish to prove. Of course, we always have to remember our caveat: we are assuming that we really do create the relevant actuality (that there are no mistakes or tricks, etc.). In the case where I imagine the circles or a pain, I do not create circles or a pain. But I exhibit the relevant possibilities. The imagining is itself an exhibiting of the relevant possibilities. The imagining of an intersection or a pain exhibits no less than an actual intersection, an actual pain, the possibility of an intersection of circles, or a pain in my thumb. In this sense, the imagining might be described as actuality that transcends itself.

We have contrasted the use of imagination to supply a premise for an argument with its use to exhibit the truth of a proposition. Suppose that by imagining its being the case that p we exhibit and thereby prove the possibility of its being the case that p. Are we not, trivially, in a position to construct a corresponding argument or inference? Of course, we can do this with any proof by exhibition. If by drawing circles we exhibit the possibility of two circles intersecting, we may then argue: we can draw intersecting circles; therefore such intersection is possible. Similarly, if we imagine circles intersecting, we may argue that, since we can imagine it, the intersection is possible. Yet it must be obvious that what is doing the real work here, what establishes the possibility, is not the inference from the fact that we can draw or imagine the intersection, but the prior exhibiting of the possibility. The inference is window dressing. When we draw the inference, the possibility inferred has already been established.[5]

12.5 Imagination and Experiential Possibility

We may agree, then, as a general point about possibility and imagination, that we can exhibit, and thus prove, possibilities in imagination. In a way, by imagining and thus becoming open to them, we discover these possibilities. Yet the possibilities that get exhibited, and thus discovered, in this way are not really new to us. They are possibilities of which we already know. We already know of them, but until we exhibit them, until we become open to them and make them explicit to ourselves in imagination, we are apt to pass them by. So in exhibiting, in discovering (becoming open to), these possibilities, we discover what we already know. This should sound familiar. Discovering possibilities by exhibiting them in imagination is a kind of philosophical discovery.

I can imagine my hand suddenly disappearing—as in a cartoon film. Now it is there, now it's gone. Surely this exhibits some kind of possibility. Perhaps we will want to say that it exhibits a logical possibility; that is, that it exhibits the absence of a contradiction in the proposition expressing the state of affairs that is my hand's suddenly disappearing. And it does exhibit this. But there would seem to be another kind of possibility exhibited here, a kind of possibility the exhibiting of which is peculiar to imagination. Logical possibility is not, in this respect, peculiar to imagination.

In fact, logical possibility is exhibited in exhibiting *any* kind of possibility. Suppose we exhibit the possibility of wood floating by placing a piece of wood in water. This would be a case of exhibiting what we might call a "natural," or "causal," possibility. But would we not be entitled to say that it also exhibits a logical possibility (that of wood's floating)?

Logical possibility is not just another kind of possibility. Not only is it exhibited whatever kind of possibility we exhibit; there is a sense in which we *cannot but rely on* logical possibility. Take the example of natural possibility. We exhibit the natural possibility of wood floating by placing

---

[5] The method of proof by exhibition can, obviously, be used to establish an actuality as well as a possibility. If what is in question is whether there are F's, I may produce or demonstrate an F, thereby exhibiting (and thus establishing) the fact that there are F's. It seems to me that this is what is going on in Moore's famous "proof of an external world." Moore presents his proof as a proof by argument—from the premise "Here is a hand." But really, he is exhibiting the fact that a hand, hence an external object, exists. It is on the back of the unacknowledged proof by exhibition that Moore constructs his argument. Of course, this diagnosis does not touch the question of whether, if we needed a proof, Moore's "proof" would be of any use to us.

a piece of wood in water. There is an implicit, negative appeal here to natural law: the floating of wood does not conflict with any natural law. What kind of "conflict" is this? Natural? Natural *laws* are natural, but *conflict* (or absence thereof) with natural laws is logical (that wood floats does not contradict any natural law). In asserting a natural possibility, we appeal to natural law; but we rely on logic. We always, we cannot but, rely on logic. You could say that this is what logic is, that which "in thinking" we cannot but rely on.

This is true even where we appeal to logic itself. Let L be a logical principle or axiom. If we criticize a proof by observing that a particular step conflicts with L, we rely on logic (the "conflict" is logical). In appealing to logic, we rely on logic.

If the possibility peculiar to imagination is not logical, how shall we understand it? For example, what kind of possibility is exhibited by my imagining the sudden disappearance of my hand? Obviously it is not natural possibility. What conflicts with the laws of nature is not naturally possible, and the disappearance of a hand, just like that, would (or so we may assume) conflict with the laws of nature. Or I imagine myself flying by waving my arms. What I imagine is not naturally possible; so it cannot be the case that, in imagining what I imagine, I exhibit a natural possibility. Yet it seems evident that there is in these cases *some* kind of possibility—some kind of possibility other than logical possibility—exhibited in imagination.

What is exhibited in these cases is a way things might be, or develop, within experience: when we say that we "can imagine" such-and-such, we mean to describe a way things might be, or unfold, or play themselves out, within experience. That is, within experience in the horizonal sense. There is an implicit reference here to the experiential horizon. What we exhibit, or claim to exhibit, is a way things might be, or play themselves out, etc., from within this horizon. Let us say that in such cases the kind of possibility exhibited, and thus philosophically discovered, is an "experiential" possibility.

Often when we make claims about what we can imagine we use the "what it would be like" locution. Instead of saying we can imagine "its being the case that p," we say we can imagine "what it would be like if it were the case that p." This way of expressing ourselves brings a little closer to the surface the implicit reference to experience (the horizon). In effect, "what it would be like" is an ellipsis for "what it would be like within experience"; for it is only from within experience, from within the horizon, that there is such a thing as what we mean here by its being *like* something—and it is precisely this, what it would be "like," i.e., a way things might unfold or be played out within experience, that we claim to imagine.

It should be clear, then, why natural possibility is not exhibited in imagination. The limits of natural possibility are fixed by something that places no constraint on the possibilities of experience as such: on the ways things might be played out within experience. The limits of natural possibility are fixed by the actual nature (the actual inner structure, as described by chemistry and physics) of objects in the world. What is coherent, what makes sense, qua experience—i.e., as an unfolding or playing out of things from within experience—floats free of the actual nature of the world, and thus, since natural possibility is fixed by the actual nature of the world, it is not exhibited by imagining such a "playing out," etc.

The point holds, notice, even in the case where the imagined "playing out" is naturally possible. Wood burns—this is a natural possibility. But the possibility is not exhibited by my imagining wood burning. Again, although the intersection of two circles inscribed with chalk, say, is a natural possibility, the natural possibility is not exhibited by imagining two chalk circles intersecting. So far as what is exhibited in imagination goes, intersecting chalk marks might obliterate each other upon contact, making it naturally impossible to construct an intersection.

Yet it may not be correct to conclude that, logical possibility aside, the only kind of possibility exhibited by imagining circles intersecting is experiential possibility. It may be said that imagining the intersection exhibits a "geometrical" possibility. Or is geometrical possibility a species of experiential possibility? We are drifting into an area that lies outside the main focus of our concern. Suffice it to observe that, in common with experiential possibility, geometrical possibility does not depend on the actual nature or inner structure of the world in the way that natural possibility does; thus it is understandable that geometrical possibility should be exhibited in imagination, i.e., in exhibiting experiential possibility.[6]

12.6 Experiential Possibilities and Possibilities of Essence

Let us assume, for the moment, that I can imagine existing without being bodily. My imagining this would exhibit, and thus establish, the possibility of my existing without being a bodily thing. A proof by exhibition. A proof of what? Of what kind of possibility? A proof of an experiential possibility. The question now arises whether this is sufficient for the Cartesian conclusion (that I am not a bodily thing).

We need more details. I can imagine my hand's suddenly disappearing. This makes sense experientially. That is, it is a way things might be, or

[6] See Strawson's discussion of Kant's view of geometry in *The Bounds of Sense* (Methuen, 1996), part 5.

be played out (develop, unfold), within my experience. We may take it, however, that the sudden disappearance of my hand (just like that) is not a natural possibility. What I imagine, then, exhibits an experiential, not a natural, possibility.

Now, if it makes sense experientially that one of my hands should go, why not the other hand as well, and then my feet, and my legs and torso. It could be like this. I see myself in the mirror, i.e., the whole of the body I call "mine." The hands (my hands) disappear—I can see this by looking either down or in the mirror. Then, the feet and legs, and so on. Each time a part of my body disappears, the objects that were behind it become visible, either in the mirror or (perhaps) directly. The process continues until all that is left is my head. Of course, my head is visible only in the mirror. But there it is in the mirror, my head (JV's head). It is all that is left of my body. And then it goes too! So now, within my experience, things are like this: there is everything that was visually present before, either directly or in the mirror, plus a little more (say a bit of the wall that was previously obscured by my head); and included among the objects visually present is the mirror, in which bits of the room are visible, but not my body. The mirror is, in this respect, startlingly empty. My body is nowhere, in no way (i.e., direct or indirectly) present within my experience.

Have we not described a way things might develop, a way things might be played out, within my experience—an experiential possibility? You, the human being over there, might suddenly disappear within my experience. So why not *this* human being, JV, the one I am? Of course, just as you might disappear from within my experience, I, the human being I am, might disappear from within your experience. But that is not what we are talking about. We are talking about *me*, the human being I am, disappearing from within *my* experience. We can imagine this—JV, the human being I am, disappearing from within my experience. This is a way things might be, or develop (unfold), within my experience. It is an experiential possibility.

Notice, what we imagine here, the possibility we thereby exhibit, is not a natural possibility. It is, as we just said, an experiential possibility. It makes sense (you could say) experientially. Now, it would seem, the Cartesian does not need to establish a natural possibility. On the other hand, it may be that the experiential possibility does not give the Cartesian what he needs for his argument. That is to say, it may be that the experiential possibility of my body (the human being that I am) disappearing from within my experience is not the possibility that the Cartesian needs to reach the conclusion that I am not a bodily substance.

What the Cartesian needs to establish (for the premise of his argument)—and thinks we can establish by the appeal to imagination—is that being bodily is not essential to my being the entity that I am. If we can establish that I, the entity that I am, could exist without being bodily, it would follow that I am not essentially a body. And if I am not essentially a body, I am not a body, since, as we observed (12.2), if something is a body, it is essentially a body. Let us say that the possibility the Cartesian needs to establish, the possibility of my existing without a body, is a "possibility of essence."

The possibility of essence, the possibility that entails that the entity I am is not essentially a body, is established by the appeal to imagination only if it is exhibited in what I imagine. But this may strike us as dubious—for the same reason that natural possibility cannot be exhibited in imagination. What is exhibited in imagination is a way things might be, or be played out, within experience. The essence of the entity that I am, however, is obviously intrinsic to the entity I am and thus, like a natural possibility about that entity, cannot be exhibited in imagination. The essence of a worldly entity cannot be exhibited in imagination.

These reflections invite the question of whether, or how, exactly, what we are calling "a possibility of essence" is a distinctive kind of possibility. How, in particular, is it different from natural possibility? This is an interesting question; but in the present context, it is a side issue.[7] Insofar as a possibility of essence is, like a natural possibility, intrinsic to the entity—the substance—itself, the problem for the Cartesian is the same: a possibility of essence belongs to the substance independently of how things may play out or unfold within experience and therefore cannot be exhibited in imagination. Imagination cannot exhibit, and in this way prove, the essential possibilities of a substance. It can no more exhibit the essential possibilities of a substance than—assuming these are different—it can exhibit the natural possibilities of a substance.

12.7 The Paralogism of Imagination

Corresponding to the distinction between the referential and positional uses of the first person (2.5, 6.7), we may draw a distinction between the referential and positional uses of certain definite descriptions containing

---

[7] The difficulty of distinguishing essential from natural possibilities and necessities should not be underestimated. E.g., David Wiggins, in his paper "Essentialism, Continuity, and Identity," *Synthese*, 1974, has a go at formulating the distinction when he writes that "essentialist necessity arises at that limit where the removal of the feature in question destroys the bearer itself. Here, at this point, a feature is fixed to its bearer by virtue of being inherent in the very individuation of it" (p. 350). However, introducing the idea of destruction here may tip things too far in the direction of natural necessity. Suppose it were a law of nature that tomatoes that diverge from such-and-such range of shapes self-destruct. Would falling within the range of shapes thereby be a feature that belongs to the essence of tomatoes?

the first person. Consider, for example, the definite description "the entity that I am." Whereas the first person within this description functions positionally (to convey the position at the center of my horizon), the description itself may be used either positionally or referentially. Thus,

> (S) There might have been no entity that is the entity that I am,

is ambiguous. If we take the definite description referentially, (S) says of a particular entity (the one that I am) that there might have been nothing that is that entity, i.e., that that entity might not have existed (I might not have existed). On the other hand, (S) could be a way of formulating the possibility exhibited in imagining my body disappearing, viz., the possibility of there being no entity at the center of my horizon. In the latter case, "the entity that I am" is used not referentially but to convey the subject position within my horizon, the position at the center. It is used positionally, in the same way as the "I" inside the definite description.

Or consider,

> (S') The entity that I am might not have been the entity that I am.

If both occurrences of the definite description are referential, (S') is metaphysical nonsense (it denies the necessity of identity). If, however, we take the first occurrence as referential and the second as positional, (S') asserts about a particular entity, JV, that he might not have occupied the subject position within my horizon (that position might have been occupied by a different entity, or by none at all). This, we are saying, is a genuine experiential possibility.

The mistake analyzed in 12.6—that of mistaking an experiential for an essential possibility—may be encouraged by confusing the referential and positional use of definite descriptions such as "the entity that I am." Suppose that we formulate the experiential possibility of my body disappearing (the possibility that we exhibit in imagination) as:

> (C) The entity that I am might not have been a bodily thing.

If in reporting the exhibited possibility we take the definite description in (C) referentially, we shall take ourselves to have exhibited an essential possibility about the particular entity that I am, the possibility of that entity's not being a bodily thing. If we take the definite description positionally, we shall take ourselves to have exhibited the experiential possibility of there being nothing, that is, no bodily thing, at the center of my horizon. But whereas we have exhibited the experiential possibility, we have not exhibited the essential possibility. The danger is that we may confound the referential and positional readings of (C) and help ourselves to something from each. That is, we may derive the meaning of (C) from the referential reading of its truth from the positional reading. It is this confusion, which would deliver (CP), that we are calling the "paralogism of imagination."[8]

12.8 The Cartesian Reply

Let consider the following reply. Although it is in general true that imagination cannot exhibit essence, the case of the self, i.e., of *my* essential possibilities, is special. The reason is that it is within *my* experience that such possibilities are imagined and thereby exhibited. I imagine my body disappearing, bit by bit. This makes sense experientially. It is a way things might be, or unfold, within my experience, an experiential possibility. If the possibility were realized, there would be no such thing as my body; but by hypothesis there would be such a thing as my experience, since what I imagine is precisely that my body disappears within my experience. In that case, there must be such a thing as *me*, the entity that I am, that whose experience it is and within which my body has disappeared. The entity that I am, then, would exist without there being a bodily thing that I am. I would exist without being bodily. Thus, in imagining the disappearance of my body within my experience, we exhibit the fact that being bodily is (as Descartes maintains) not part of my essence. Contrary to what holds in the general case, here we have a case in which essence is exhibited in imagination. Such is "the Cartesian reply."

Certainly, if the entity that I am might survive the disappearance of my body, the entity that I am cannot be my body. So if we take the imagined possibility, the disappearance of my body (JV, the human being) within my experience, as entailing the possibility of the entity that I am surviving the disappearance of my body, it follows that the entity that I am is not a human being, a bodily thing. But the entailment is open to question. For it is not clear that, if the imagined possibility were realized, the entity that I am would have survived. It is not clear because it is not in the first place clear that, if the possibility were realized, there would be *any* entity that is the entity that I am.

When in the second Meditation Descartes asks "What am I?" he takes for granted that I am a substance of one kind or another, a material or an immaterial substance. He asks, in effect, which kind of entity it is that I am. In asking this question, however, he overlooks another question. Whichever kind of entity I am, what is it that makes *it*—that singles *it* out

---

[8] The terminology is of course inspired by Kant. We shall discuss Kant's paralogisms in a later chapter.

as—the one that "I am," the one that "is me"? Suppose I am a human being, a body. Then the particular human being that I am is *this* one, JV. Why him? Why not *that* one? By virtue of what is *this* one *me*? Similarly, if we assume that the entity that I am is immaterial, a soul: what is it about *this* particular soul as opposed to all others that makes it, this one, *me*, the soul that *I am*?

Now, however we answer Descartes' question, i.e., whatever kind of entity we suppose ourselves to be, this further question (which Descartes does not ask) is a meaningful question: What is it that makes a particular entity in the world (one versus all the others) "me," the one that "I am"? The answer we have given to this question makes reference to the horizonal subject matter, the subject matter of the DH and of death, i.e., to the personal horizon: my experience (consciousness, life). The answer we have given (it is only an outline-answer) is that the entity that I am is the one who occupies a certain position within my horizon (see 2.5, 8.5). The one "I am" is, as we put it, the one who occupies the subject position, the one who is at the center, of my horizon. Whether it is a human being or a soul (I assume it is a human being), it is the fact that the entity in question is at the center of my horizon that singles it out, that makes it "me," the one that "I am."

Of course we have yet to consider the content of the positional conception of the self, i.e., in what "being at the center, etc." consists. But let us concentrate on the general point that it is by virtue of occupying a certain position within my horizon that a particular entity, a particular bit of the world, "is me." If what makes a particular entity "me" is that it occupies a certain position within my horizon, this opens up the possibility of there being nothing that occupies that position, of there being no entity that "is me," the one that "I am." Generally, one might say, it is of the nature of a position that it can be unoccupied.

In fact, given our anti-Cartesian bias—given that there are no immaterial substances—it is precisely the possibility of an empty subject position, of there being nothing that is "me," that we exhibit in imagining the disappearance of my body. On the other hand, if for the sake of argument we leave open the question of whether there are such substances, we cannot claim to have exhibited this possibility; for, presumably, if the subject position were occupied by a soul, this would not show itself in what we imagine. My body looks and feels a certain way. I have a sense of my body. Is this true of my soul? A soul, it would seem, has no way of showing itself in what we imagine. If there are souls, then, imagining my body disappearing within my experience would not exhibit the possibility of there being no entity that I am; a soul, an immaterial substance, might be there without showing itself.

Our aim now, however, is not to argue that a human being occupies the subject position within my horizon but to undermine the Cartesian argument that it is a soul. (If we can do that, we are entitled to feel comfortable going along with what otherwise seems evident: that I am a human being.) The Cartesian, as we are representing him, argues that in exhibiting the possibility of there being nothing within my experience that is my body, we exhibit the possibility of the entity that I am existing without there being any bodily entity that I am; that therefore this entity, this substance (the one that I am), must be immaterial. Surely, though, if we accept that souls (being what they are, etc.) have no way of showing themselves in imagination, then, so far as what we imagine is concerned, there is no difference between the position at the center of my experience being occupied by a soul and its being empty, not being occupied at all. Thus, imagining the disappearance of my body within my experience cannot be said to exhibit the possibility of the entity that I am existing in the absence of my body, which possibility would entail that I am a soul, since what we have imagined could equally be said to exhibit the possibility of there being *no* entity at the center of my experience (no entity will do as well as a soul), and hence to exhibit the possibility of there being no entity that I am.[9]

Perhaps we will be accused of overlooking an essential part of the Cartesian reply. Since what I imagine is my body disappearing within my experience, if what I imagine were realized, by hypothesis there would remain such a thing as my experience. But how could this be unless I, the entity that I am, remain? Unless the entity that I am remains, there is nothing by reference to which the experience within which my body has disappeared, the experience we imagine to have nothing at its center, could be "my" experience.

The foregoing argument rests on a mistake. The mistake is to assume that my experience (in the horizonal sense) is "mine" by virtue of being owned in some way by me, the entity that I am. My wallet (my arm, my son) is "mine" in that (in one way or another) it belongs to me, the entity (the human being) that I am. If we take this as our model for understanding the "mineness" of my experience (horizon), we shall find ourselves, once again, caught in the circle of the first person (8.5, 9.1). For we began by asking what makes a particular entity (a particular human being or soul) "me," the one that "I am," to which our answer was that it is the one at the center of my experience (horizon). We cannot now hope to

---

[9] By the same token, as long as souls are reckoned as part of the world, imagination cannot exhibit the absence of an entity at the center. For the Cartesian, imagination has a diminished role in philosophizing about the self—despite the fact that he is the first to appeal to it here.

understand what makes my experience "mine" by saying that it is the experience that belongs to me, the entity that I am. No, we need a different model. What makes my horizon (experience) "mine" is that, in a real sense, it is *the* horizon—i.e., the preeminent horizon, the horizon that includes all the others. To understand the "mineness" of my horizon, we must become open to a truth that we already know, the truth of solipsism (chapters 9 and 10).

The mistake may also be described in terms of our use of the first person, viz., as the mistake of assimilating the use of the first person in "my experience (horizon)" to its use in "my wallet (arm, son, etc.)." In the latter, "my X" is equivalent to "the X that belongs to me," wherein the first person is used referentially. (It refers, say, to a particular human being.) The "my" in "my horizon (experience)," however, is not referential but, we said, functions as a stand-in for the definite article. Of course, the whole expression "the horizon" is referential. It refers to the subject matter that has been occupying us all along: the subject matter of the DH, and of death, that to which the totality I call "the world" and the infinity of space and time is internal. The definite article itself, however, simply gives expression to the fact that the subject matter referred to is, in a certain respect, unique. It is the preeminent horizon, the horizon that includes all others (and thus has no neighbors).

The use of the first person in "my horizon (experience)" is what we have called the horizonal use of the first person (8.5). In effect, just as the paralogism of imagination confounds the positional and referential uses of the first person, the Cartesian reply mistakes the horizonal for the referential use of the first person. This mistake conspires, as it were, with imagination to create the illusion of the Cartesian self. Thus if we formulate the possibility exhibited in imagination as that of "there being no bodily thing at the center of my experience," and if (mistaking the horizonal for the referential use of the first person) we take in this context the "my" in "my experience" as referential, we are apt to conclude that I must be an immaterial substance, a soul.

13. Metaphysical Possibility and the Self

13.1 Metaphysical Possibility

Let us put aside, once and for all, the Cartesian idea of the self as an immaterial substance. (We never believed it anyway.) I am a human being. That is, it is a human being—an entity that is essentially bodily and therefore could not but be bodily—that is at the center of my horizon (that occupies the subject position). The possibility that we exhibit in imagining the absence of an entity at the center of my horizon (experience), an entity that I am, does not contradict this truth about the essence of the entity that I am. What we exhibit, rather, is a way things might be, or develop, within my horizon, an experiential possibility—which does not touch the essence of the entity that in fact occupies the subject position within my horizon. That entity is essentially a human being, a bodily thing.

In imagination we can exhibit experiential possibilities. But we cannot in this way exhibit possibilities of essence. Nor, as we have several times noted in passing, can we exhibit natural (causal) possibilities. Let us now consider another type of possibility that transcends what can be exhibited in imagination: metaphysical possibility.

The term "metaphysical possibility" has acquired a confusing variety of uses in recent philosophy. Sometimes it is meant to be contrasted with "epistemic possibility"; sometimes it is meant as synonymous with "de re possibility"; sometimes it is meant more or less in the way that we shall now explain. On this use, which we shall henceforth assume, it signifies compatibility with certain well-known "metaphysical" principles, e.g., the principle of universal causation, the principle that nothing can come from nothing, the principle of sufficient reason. Such principles are traditionally regarded as holding of the world with a kind of necessity that entails that, if the principles are known, they are known a priori (i.e., independently of experiential evidence); thus they are regarded not as natural (causal) laws but rather as a distinctive class of propositions of peculiar interest to philosophy. We shall (without going into this) follow tradition here. Just as a state of affairs is deemed naturally (causally) impossible or possible according to whether or not it contradicts some natural law or other, so it may be deemed metaphysically impossible or possible according to whether or not it contradicts a metaphysical principle. Let us consider some examples.

Suppose we look out in the garden and discover to our surprise that where yesterday a rosebush stood, today there is an azalea shrub. A rosebush can blossom, wither, change color, die, but it cannot turn into an azalea: this is naturally impossible.[1] Our assumption will be that one replaced the other. How? Well, someone or something put one in place of the other. We may not learn who or what this was, but we will insist that some such story is true. We will insist, in other words, that the replacement did not "just happen." This would contradict the principle of universal causation and thus be metaphysically impossible.

Or suppose we plant two very similar azalea shrubs next to each other. One thrives, the other dies. We assume there was some difference in the makeup of the shrubs, or in the soil in which they were planted, or that something befell one plant but not the other, and so on. We would not countenance the hypothesis that absolutely everything concerning the two plants was the same. This conflicts with the principle of sufficient reason. It is, in our sense, a metaphysical impossibility that there should be simply no reason why the fate of the two shrubs should differ as it does.

In neither of these cases is there a self-contradiction in the states of affairs described (they are both logically possible). Moreover, both make sense experientially. In both, that is, we can describe a way that things might unfold within experience, an imaginable possibility. Of course the states of affairs in question are causally (naturally) impossible. The point, however, is that they are "more" than this. They contradict in each case a general metaphysical principle (the principle of universal causation, the principle of sufficient reason), a principle that we know—or so we are assuming—a priori. Although these states of affairs are experientially possible, they are not just causally but metaphysically impossible.[2]

---

[1] Perhaps it will also be considered essentially impossible. See note 7 of the previous chapter.

[2] Consider what is currently known in the philosophy of mind as the "principle of supervenience." Suppose I now believe that p and then change my views: I come to believe that not-p. The principle of supervenience says that there must have been some change in me—let us assume, in my brain. Again, if I believe that p, and you believe that not-p, there must be some difference between you and me, i.e., between my brain and yours. The point, to stay with the case of belief, can be summarized by saying that the content of a belief "supervenes" on a state of the brain: there cannot be a difference in belief content unless there is some difference in the brain. Since this is put forward a priori, the impossibility is intended as more than causal (natural) impossibility. The principle of supervenience is a special case of the principle of sufficient reason, the impossibility of a difference in content without a difference in the brain, a special case of metaphysical impossibility. It is a special case, etc., in that it depends on both the principle of sufficient reason and the brute causal fact that it is because of what is happening in the brain that things are as they are within consciousness/

An experientially possible state of affairs may be causally impossible yet metaphysically possible. Suppose it is our practice to talk to one of the azaleas every day (always the same one) while ignoring the other. The one we talk to is the one that thrives. Here we have an experiential possibility that does not run afoul of the principle of sufficient reason. Yet if we stipulate that our socializing with one plant rather than the other is the only difference between them, the case is (I take it) naturally impossible.

13.2 Metaphysical Possibility and the Self

Experiential possibility, we have observed, does not guarantee natural (causal) possibility. Nor does it guarantee metaphysical possibility. Let us see how this applies to our reflections on the self.

We argued (12.8) that it is a mistake, a mistake induced by treating the horizonal use of the first person as referential, to suppose that in imagining the disappearance within my experience of my body, we exhibit the possibility of the substance that I am, myself, continuing to exist in the absence of my body. On the other hand, it seems, we do in this way exhibit the possibility of my experience continuing to exist in the absence of my body. So if the imagined possibility were realized, there would be such a thing as my experience (horizon), but no such thing as my body.

Notice what we just said: if the imagined possibility were realized, there would be such a thing as my experience, but no such thing as my body. But *could* this be realized?

First one hand goes, then the other, then my feet, and so on. Finally just my head is left—it is visible in a mirror. And then it disappears too. The empty mirror, along with the rest of my immediate "environment," is, as we imagine this, present within my experience (horizon). So there is such a thing as my experience; but there is no such thing as me, the human being that I am. Not even my head. Now here is something that, when we ran through this before, we failed to ponder: if my head goes, so does my brain. Yet it is my brain that causally fixes how things are within my experience. It is my brain that maintains my experience, the horizon, in existence. (When its activity ceases, there will no longer be such a thing as my experience.) It is my brain, then, that maintains in existence the subject matter presupposed in what we are imagining: the subject matter within which it is being imagined that my brain disappears.

Recall the puzzlement about the causation of consciousness (11.4), that is, about the fact that THIS, my consciousness (horizon), is maintained

---

experience. When this brute causal fact is added to the principle of sufficient reason, the result is the principle of supervenience.

in existence by what is going on now in my brain. This fact, we said, may (given that the horizon is outside time) strike us as "impossible" and, therefore, since it is nonetheless a fact, incomprehensible. In the present context, we are drawing attention to the same "impossible fact"—except that now we are ignoring its "impossibility" and are keeping our eye, so to speak, just on its factness, on the fact that it is a fact. It is because of what is going on now in my brain that there is such a thing as my experience, my consciousness (in the horizonal sense). Will anyone deny this?

In that case, there is an incoherence implicit in what we imagine in imagining the disappearance within my experience of my body with its brain. The state of affairs imagined, that in which my body, etc., disappears, could not be realized within my experience, since if it were realized there would be no such thing as my brain, and if there were no such thing as my brain, there would be no such thing as my experience (horizon) from within which the state of affairs might be realized; for, once again, it is my brain that keeps my experience in existence. We have, you could say, lost the subject matter within which the imagined possibility, the disappearance of my body (brain included), is supposed to be realized. Remember, an imagined possibility is an experiential possibility: a way things might be or develop within my experience. How could something be realized within my experience if there is no such thing as my experience?

It might be said that, given that the dependence of my experience on my brain is causal, the foregoing merely exposes a hidden causal impossibility in the realization of the imagined state of affairs; and a causal impossibility is something we can take in our stride here. After all, we are already accepting that experiential possibility is compatible with causal impossibility. Thus we are already accepting that, despite being causally impossible, the cartoonlike disappearance of my body within my experience, (horizon) makes sense experientially. It would seem that the further impossibility, the further incoherence, we have uncovered is just more of the same.

But not only can we imagine my body, including its head and brain (my head and brain), disappearing within my experience, we can imagine the same for any body, for any entity in the world. Whatever entity X you might propose as a candidate for maintaining my experience, we can imagine X disappearing within my experience. So, with a little ingenuity, we can imagine things transpiring within my experience in a way that leaves nothing that might maintain my experience, my horizon, in existence. Let S be this more radical state of affairs. Now, that my experience should be maintained in existence by something other than my brain may or may not be causally possible. However, that there should be such a thing as my experience, and yet nothing—not my brain, or some other brain, or an organism of some other kind, or perhaps a nonorganism (a machine or whatever), but simply nothing—by which my horizon is maintained, this state of affairs, S, goes beyond causal impossibility. It is metaphysically impossible. Thus, as before, what we imagine is incoherent; but this time metaphysically incoherent. S presupposes the existence of a subject matter, my horizon, whose existence is excluded by what we imagine; excluded, that is, not just causally but metaphysically.

The important point here for our reflections on the self is that, despite being metaphysically impossible, there is no problem imagining S obtaining within my experience, and in imagining S obtaining within my experience, we imagine an experiential possibility. In imagining S, then, we exhibit as experientially possible a state of affairs that is metaphysically impossible, a state of affairs that, metaphysically speaking, could not be realized.

13.3 The Logic of the Self

Experience has its own kind of possibility and impossibility, its own "logic" or way of making sense. The logic of experience is different from the logic of concepts (language-games). It is, I believe, what philosophers often mean by "phenomenology," and what we ourselves shall mean by this term when we come to discuss in more detail the positional conception of the self.[3] In investigating the logic of concepts (which of course, like everything, depends on our grasp of logic proper), we draw upon that grasp of things that we have acquired as insiders of our system of language-games, as insiders of the communal horizon; in investigating the logic of experience, phenomenology, we draw up that grasp of things that we have as subjects of experience, as positioned, so to speak, at the center of a personal horizon.

But in light of what emerged in the foregoing section, we may wonder why the logic of experience should be of interest to philosophical reflection on the self. That a human being should vanish bit by bit, as if composed of soap bubbles, is not naturally possible. Yet I can imagine myself vanishing in this way within my experience. It is an experiential possibility even though, causally (naturally) speaking, it is impossible. Again, I can

[3] This use of the term "phenomenology," where it refers to uncovering of possibilities and necessities peculiar to experience (in the horizonal sense), is Husserl's use (in, e.g., *Ideas* and *Cartesian Meditations*). Heidegger's use of the term is more general, embracing roughly all of what we are calling "philosophical discovery": the discovery of, the becoming open to, what we already know. (See *Being and Time*, introduction 2, 7.C.). Thus the truths of phenomenology, in Husserl's sense, constitute only part of what is discoverable by phenomenology in Heidegger's sense, i.e., of what is (in our sense) philosophically discoverable.

imagine satisfying myself from within my experience that there is *nothing* in the world that supports the existence of my experience, even though, it seems, what I thereby imagine is metaphysically impossible. If we can exhibit in imagination possibilities about the self that are not only causally but metaphysically impossible, metaphysically unrealizable, what interest could imagination have for our understanding of the self? In imagination we exhibit experiential possibilities. If our philosophical aim here is to understand the self, why we should pay attention to a kind of possibility that is so wildly out of line with what can actually come to pass?

Why? Imagination is our method for exploring, for discovering, what makes sense from within the experiential horizon, for exploring, etc., the kind of possibility peculiar to experience (in the horizonal sense). It is, in other words, our method for exploring a kind of possibility peculiar to the subject matter of the DH and death: the subject matter that is "mine" in a way that nothing else is, and by occupying a certain position within which a particular substance, a particular human being (*this* one, JV), is "me," the human being that "I am." And this subject matter, my experience (horizon), simply *is* the self.

Or rather, it is the self on a certain conception of the self: the horizonal conception of the self. And—or so we are maintaining—unless, by letting the horizon come into view (by becoming open to it), we have acquired an explicit conception of this subject matter and thereby made it available to philosophical reflection, we will never sort out the complex topic of the self. For it is only by reference to the self as horizon that we can explain what makes a particular human being "myself" (the one that "I am"). We are talking then about what, once we have hold of it philosophically, is evidently the deepest, the most fundamental, conception of the self.

Hence the fact that the kind of possibility exhibited in imagination, experiential possibility, outreaches what is metaphysically possible does not diminish the interest of imagination for the philosophical topic of the self. On the contrary, it helps define the topic. It defines the topic precisely as having an essential reference to a subject matter whose peculiar logic, whose peculiar kind of possibility, outreaches metaphysical possibility. This, to repeat, is what the self, on its most fundamental conception, *is*. It is a subject matter with its own kind of possibility or way of making sense, and imagination, as we said, is our method for exploring this kind of possibility. We have no other. The logic of the self, we might say, belongs to the logic of experience, to phenomenology. Imagination, then, is our method for exploring the logic of the self.

Why should we pay attention to imagination, to experiential possibility, in trying to understand the self? This is in my view like asking why we should pay attention to causal possibility in trying to understand nature.

Nature is the subject matter whose peculiar kind of possibility, whose "logic" or way of making sense, is not experiential or metaphysical but causal. The self, for its part, is the subject matter whose way of making sense, whose peculiar kind of possibility, is not causal or metaphysical but experiential.

13.4 Naturalizing the Self

Of course, if we are not philosophically alive to the subject matter in question, i.e., if we have not yet made explicit to ourselves the horizonal conception of the self, this point about imagination and the self will not register. If, further, we have rejected the Cartesian conception of the self (the self as an immaterial substance), our attitude toward imagination as a philosophical method for investigating the self may become downright hostile. What I have in mind here anticipates a view, or attitude, about the self that we shall encounter later on, when we discuss the so-called problem of personal identity; but it might be worth introducing the view right now.

Some philosophers, having rejected the Cartesian conception of the self, accept in its place a "naturalistic" conception of the self, a conception of the self as the human being. Such philosophers are apt to question the relevance of the familiar kinds of philosophical thought experiments in this area. What are these "thought experiments"? Well, we tell some scientifically far-fetched story, typically about my brain—the brain gets divided, or copied, or transplanted, or whatever—and then we try to imagine what it would be like for *me*, if the story were realized. This is how in philosophy we explore the self: by imagining how under such-and-such circumstances things would be, for me, for myself. We explore the self, you might say, by first-person imagination.

The thing is, once we accept that the self is the human being, it may seem that no purpose could possibly be served by this use of imagination. Human beings, after all, constitute a natural (biological) kind. The philosophical study of the self, whatever else it is, must be appropriate to the study of a natural kind. Thus, while it need not restrict itself to the methods a scientist would employ, neither can it contravene these methods. Would a scientist be interested in what we can imagine about a natural kind? Would this not be in spirit totally at odds with the scientific study of a natural kind? The games philosophers like to play with imagination and the self, the exploration of experiential possibility, none of this, it may seem, has anything to contribute here.

The "naturalizing" of the self leaves no place, obviously, for immaterial substances. Descartes asks, "What am I?" to which the naturalizer (as we shall call him) answers: I am a member of a natural (biological) kind—not a soul, or any other exotic entity, but an animal creature, a human being. This answer, the answer that the naturalizer gives to Descartes' question, is the correct answer. But there is a further question here to which, as far as I can see, the naturalizer, like the Cartesian, has no answer. Given that I am a human being, what is it that makes the particular human being that I am the one that "I am"? What is it that makes *this* human being, JV, "me"?

The reason the naturalizer cannot answer this question is that (like the Cartesian) he lacks, philosophically, a grasp of the horizonal conception of the self. The substance that I am is, certainly, a member of a natural kind, a human being. But if we wish to capture explicitly what makes that particular substance, that particular human being, the one that "I am," we must make reference to a subject matter that cannot be conceived under a natural kind, or as in any sense part of nature; not because this subject matter must be conceived as an immaterial part of the world, which would make it foreign to a "scientific" picture of the world, but because anything I might include in the world, and hence in nature, is internal to this subject matter; not, in other words, because this subject matter is a "queer" part of the world, but because it is the horizon of the world, that from within which the world appears, and thus cannot itself be included in any picture of the world.

The naturalizer, we said, will dismiss as irrelevant to our understanding of the self the appeal to imagination. (How can imagination teach us anything about the essence or causality of a natural kind? About the nature of a natural kind?) So he will dismiss as irrelevant the kind of possibility that is exhibited in imagination, experiential possibility. Were the naturalizer philosophically in touch with the subject matter to which this kind of possibility is peculiar, that is, were he philosophically in touch with the subject matter that is, in the most fundamental sense, the self, he would, I think, regard the appeal to imagination here somewhat differently. The naturalizer lacks an explicit, philosophical conception of the self as the horizon; he lacks the horizonal conception of the self. But the subject position, the position whose occupancy makes a particular human being the one that "I am," is defined by reference to the subject matter of this conception: the subject position is the position at the center of my horizon. Insofar, then, as the naturalizer lacks the horizonal conception of the self, he lacks the positional conception of the self; and insofar as he lacks the positional conception of the self, he lacks the conceptual means to answer the question of what makes a particular human being "myself," the one that "I am."

Notice, in thus challenging the naturalizer, we need not deny that human beings, the natural kind of which we are members, stand out in various ways from other natural kinds. We can, with the naturalizer, recognize that human beings possess all sorts of capacities that set them apart from other creatures: a higher form of intelligence, the use of language, rationality, self-consciousness. Of course, the naturalizer may have trouble integrating these capacities into his naturalistic view of things. Or maybe not; it is beside the point right now.[4] The point is, whatever special capacities human beings possess as members of a natural kind, these capacities, precisely because they belong to the kind, will not provide an answer to the question that we are saying the naturalizer cannot answer, the question of what makes a particular human being (a particular member of that natural kind) "me," the one that "I am." I look around at my fellows. All, like me, are intelligent in the way that human beings are; all, like me, are rational, possessed of self-consciousness, and so on. But *not* all *are* "me." Only *this* one, JV, is "me." What makes *him*, versus any of the others, "me"? Clearly, not the fact that he is intelligent, or rational, or self-conscious, etc. These things are true of all of us.

We may summarize this by saying, whereas the naturalizer gives the right answer to Descartes' question, viz., that I am a human being, he cannot, in a certain way, back up his answer: he cannot tell us what makes a particular human being the one that "I am." Not only that. Without the horizonal, and hence the positional, conception of the self, the naturalizer cannot, in my view, correctly explain or analyze the mistakes that may prompt us to give the *wrong* answer to Descartes' question; the mistakes (discussed in 12.7 and 12.8) that may prompt us to suppose I am not a bodily thing, not a human being, but a soul, an immaterial substance.

---

[4] I am making things easy for myself here by working with a very general account—the minimal essence (as I see it)—of what the naturalizer wants to maintain, without discussing details of what actual philosophers who might qualify as naturalizers maintain. A few examples of publications that I would place in this category are Bernard Williams, "Personal Identity and Individuation," in *Problems of the Self* (Cambridge University Press, 1973); David Wiggins, *Sameness and Substance* (Oxford University Press, 1984); Richard Wollheim, *The Thread of Life* (Harvard University Press, 1984); Mark Johnston, "Human Beings," *The Journal of Philosophy*, 1987; Kathleen Wilkes, *Real People* (Oxford University Press, 1988); Paul Snowdon, "Persons, Animals and Ourselves," in *The Person and the Human Mind*, ed. Christopher Gill (Oxford University Press, 1990), and "Persons and Personal Identity," in *Essays for David Wiggins*, ed. Sabina Lovibond and S.G. Williams (Blackwell, 1999).

14. Preliminary Reflections on the Positional Conception of the Self

14.1 Nagel's Puzzle about "Being Me"

The positional conception of the self is the conception of a position, namely, a position within THIS, the personal horizon (my horizon): the subject matter of the dream hypothesis and death, that to which the totality I call "the world" and the infinity of space and time are internal. We have thus far characterized this position, the subject position, as being the position "at the center" of my horizon. The main idea is that it is by virtue of occupying the subject position that a particular entity, a particular human being, is "me," the one that "I am." Thus the picture contains three elements: the entity that I am; the position by occupying which that entity is the one that I am; and the subject matter, my horizon, within which this position is defined. But what exactly is the position? What is it to be "at the center" of my horizon? We have yet to spell out the content of the positional conception of the self.

JV is the one at the center of my horizon. He is the one that I am. Yet it is possible (experientially) that there be no one at the center, or again, that it be someone other than JV (this will be important when we get to the topic of personal identity). There is a sense, then, in which "the human being that I am might not have been the human being that I am": the human being that I am, JV, might not have occupied the position at the center of my horizon. (On this reading, we take the first occurrence of "the human being that I am" as referential, the second as positional; see above, 12.7.) This possibility, though it may be in various ways problematic, does not contradict the necessity of identity. It is an experiential possibility, one that can be exhibited in imagination. It is, then, a possibility peculiar to the horizonal subject matter and is in that sense part of the logic of the self.

Notice, the fact that a particular human being, JV, occupies the subject position—the fact that he is "myself," the one that "I am—this is a fact that, like the fact that a particular object is now present or appears in such-and-such way, can hold only from within a horizon. If you take away the horizon, there can be no fact of presence or appearing; similarly, in the absence of a horizon, there can be no "fact of self." Yet a fact of self is a fact about a particular human being. Just as a fact of appearing, e.g., the fact that this cup appears thus-and-so, is a fact about a particular cup, the fact that JV is "myself," the fact of self, is a fact about a particular human being. Thus, like the fact of appearing, it is a fact about the world. It is a fact about the world that holds only from within a horizon.

This resolves, I think, a puzzle that Thomas Nagel raises about "being me":

> If we suppose "being me" to be any objective property whatever of the person TN, or any relation of that person to something else, the supposition quickly collapses. We are bound to include that property or that relation in the objective conception of the world that contains TN. But as soon as it has been made an aspect of the object TN, I can ask again, "Which of these persons am I?" and the answer tells me something further. No further fact expressible without the first person will do the trick: however complete we make the centerless conception of the world, the fact that I am TN will be omitted. There seems to be no room for it in such a conception. . . . But in that case there seems to be no room for it in the world. For when we conceive of the world as centerless we are conceiving of it as it is.[1]

There seems to be a fact about JV that is not a fact about the world: that he is the one who is "me." However, given that JV is an object in the world, this seems impossible. Given that JV is an object in the world, any fact about JV is thereby a fact about the world. It seems, then, that we are required to deny either that JV is an object in the world or that there is such a fact as the fact that JV is the one who is "me." This, as I understand it, is Nagel's puzzle.

Once we distinguish the horizonal and positional conceptions of the self (which requires that the horizonal subject matter has philosophically come into view for us), and in these terms grasp the nature of a fact of self, the puzzle disappears. The object that I am, JV, is part of the world. So the fact that JV is the one that "I am," the one who is "me," is a fact about an object in the world. It is, however, a fact about JV, about an object in the world, that holds only from within a subject matter that is not part of the world. It is a fact about the world that, like the fact that this cup appears thus-and-so, holds only from within a horizon.

14.2 Individual Essence; Frege on Our "Particular and Primitive" Mode of Self-Presentation

Let us consider how we might answer the question of what makes a particular entity in the world "me" if we lack an explicit grasp of the horizonal conception of the self and thus are not philosophically prepared to regard

---

[1] *The View from Nowhere* (Oxford University Press, 1986), pp. 56–57.

this question as a question about a position within the horizon, i.e., as a question about the positional conception of the self. Of course we can always think of or devise features F possessed uniquely by the human being that I am. I am the only one sitting at this time at this table. But that is not what makes (constitutes) the human being in question, JV, "me." JV might have been sitting at a different table; a different human being might have been sitting at this table. Would it follow that JV would not have been me, that the other human being would have been me? Perhaps the problem is that in framing F we have employed singular references ("this time," "this table"). However, it is a trivial exercise to construct perfectly general descriptions expressing features uniquely possessed by JV, but whose possession is clearly *not* what makes JV *me*. JV is (we may assume) the one and only human being with a scar on the bridge of his nose and an ink smudge on the inside of his left thumb who, wearing a slightly threadbare grey sports jacket with a pen in the vest pocket, etc., has ever sat in a café writing about the self. Is that what makes JV me, the one that I am? It should be clear that such idiosyncratic general features, though in fact uniquely satisfied by JV, do not have the right counterfactual implications. Had JV not had the scar, etc., he would still have been me; and had the man at the next table satisfied in all its trivial detail the above general description, he still would not have been me.

There are, we may agree, features that are essential to JV, the individual—e.g., being a human being, a bodily thing—which, being essential, have counterfactual implications. But these features are not what we are looking for. If they were what make a particular human being "me," the whole human race would be me.

In this way we arrive at the idea of a feature that is not only essential but also individualizing, at the idea of an "individual essence." Being a human being is essential to JV; but this is not his individual essence. It is not what makes JV the very individual he is and not another individual.

What is my (JV's) individual essence? Clearly, it is not itself an individual—like a little nugget ensconced in JV. A nugget could in principle be transferred to another individual. Different individuals, then, might, at different times, be identical with JV. It would seem that JV's individual essence must be something general, a property or characteristic or feature, etc. However, what is general is in principle shareable by different individuals at the same time. So, right now, individuals other than JV might be identical with JV.

Insofar as it is nontransferable, JV's individual essence would have to be like something general; yet insofar as it is nonshareable, it would have to be like an individual. This means, although we might refer to JV's individual essence, it could not be expressed (put into words) by a purely predicative expression (a pure predicate), since a pure predicate can, in principle, be true of any number of individuals. We are clutching at straws. The idea of something that qua nontransferable resembles something general but that qua nonshareable and thus inexpressible resembles an individual, this is an idea we would have nothing to do with were we not desperately trying to solve a problem.

In any case, individual essences will not solve our problem. Suppose that JV has an individual essence. JV, then, has an inexpressible feature that makes him, JV, the particular individual he is. But this is not what we are looking for. What we are looking for is not something that makes a particular individual, JV, *that particular individual*, but something that makes a particular individual, JV, *me*, the one that *I am*.

What makes a particular individual, a particular human being, "me," the one that "I am"? If we want an answer to this question, we had better forget about individual essences, inexpressible features. We had better forget about essences altogether. If we want to understand the self, the conception we need is not the conception of an essence—not, more generally, the conception of a feature intrinsic to a particular individual in the world—but of a position occupied by an individual; a position, i.e., within to THIS, within my horizon, within that to which the world (including the individual that I am), is internal.

What makes JV "me" is not anything intrinsic to JV but his occupying a special position within my horizon, his being at the center—which, as we shall see, is a matter of his figuring a certain way within my horizon. Spelling out the way of figuring, i.e., spelling out the phenomenology of the subject position, is spelling out the positional conception of the self. It might be of interest to compare this with a well-known pronouncement by Frege on the self:

> Everyone is presented to himself in a particular and primitive way, in which he is presented to no one else. So, when Dr. Lauben thinks that he has been wounded [an example Frege has previously introduced], he will probably take as a basis this primitive way in which he is presented to himself. And only Dr. Lauben himself can grasp thoughts determined in this way.[2]

In one respect, this is close to our view of the matter. On Frege's view, what makes JV "me" is the primitive way in which JV is presented to himself (myself). What is the fact of JV's being presented in a certain way if not the fact of JV's figuring a certain way? So far there is agreement between Frege's view and our own.

---

[2] "The Thought," reprinted in P. F. Strawson, ed., *Philosophical Logic* (Oxford University Press, 1967), pp. 25–26.

The question is why Frege thinks that self-presentation is "particular and primitive" (hence that there is no possibility of spelling it out). Notice, to begin with, just because a mode of presentation is individuating (e.g., appearing at a particular time to occupy a particular place), it does not follow that it is a plausible candidate for what makes JV "me." Moreover, assuming we have identified a mode of presentation that is a plausible candidate, we cannot—without entering the circle of first person—say that what makes JV "me" is that he is the only one present in that way to myself, i.e., to the individual who is myself (me). Yet, if, to avoid the circle, we appeal simply to the way in which the relevant individual is presented, then, whatever that way is, nothing can prevent others from being self-presented in precisely that way (and thus being "me"). A way of being presented (a way of figuring) is in this respect like a property: it is shareable.

It is this problem that Frege seeks to avoid by stipulating that my mode of self-presentation is "particular and primitive." He is, in effect, stipulating that my mode of self-presentation is unshareable (hence inexpressible). But this cannot be stipulated. Insofar as a mode of presentation might plausibly be regarded as making a particular individual "me," it is, like a property that might be regarded as essential to a particular individual, shareable.

Frege's idea of a "particular and primitive" mode of presentation is, really, the phenomenological counterpart of an individual essence: an individual essence is a property that is both unshareable and essential; my mode of self-presentation is both unshareable and what makes a particular individual "me." If we balk at individual essences, phenomenological counterparts of these will not seem like much of an improvement. However, what needs to be contested here is not just whether there is such a thing as an unshareable way in which JV presents himself, but whether it is anything like this that makes JV the individual that "I am." It may strike us that, so far from being "particular and primitive," what makes JV the individual that "I am" is in a real sense *the same for all of us*— and not just the same for all of us, but *graspable* by all of us. Thus it is something that we can reflect upon philosophically, and attempt to spell out, and hence express or put into words.

Why does this not lead to the absurd conclusion that all human beings are "me," the human being that "I am"? Because what is the same for all of us—the way of figuring or being presented, the position (as we are calling it)—is in each case a way of figuring within a horizon, and in each case a different horizon. What makes JV the human being that "I am" is that he is presented in a certain way, that he occupies a certain position, within my horizon. He is at the center. It is the same for you: you are at the center of your horizon. Each of us is *the one at the center*, and in this sense we each occupy *the same position*; but in each case the position, the same position, is a position within a different horizon.

"It is the same for all of us." I know this, you know this, we all know it. And we all know that we know, and so on—just as we all know, mutually, that the same world is there within each of our horizons, and that these horizons are coordinate (that we are metaphysical equals).

You could say that Frege is led to the notion of a "particular and primitive" mode of self-presentation because the subject matter by reference to which the positional conception of the self is defined, my horizon, is not explicitly (philosophically) available to him; this, despite the fact that the horizonal conception of the self is presupposed by his own philosophical idea of a mode of presentation, hence by his own philosophical idea of a mode of self-presentation.

Generally, if in our philosophical reflections on the self we lack an explicit conception of the horizon, if this subject matter has not come philosophically into view, then, even if we get the detailed phenomenology of the subject position right, its meaning will elude us: we will have formulated the content of the positional conception of the self, but we will not conceive of what we have formulated as the content of the position at the center of my horizon, i.e., as the content of the positional conception of the self.

14.3 My Body and Me (the Human Being That I Am)

Our question, viz., "What makes a particular human being 'me'?" might also be formulated as the question, "What makes my body 'mine'?" For example, in our reflections on the Cartesian self, we imagined "my body" disappearing from within my experience. Could we not have conducted these reflections in terms of "the human being that I am," and have imagined the disappearance within my experience of "the human being that I am." Philosophically, the point would have been the same. We have in fact, without comment, been assuming some such equivalence.

But perhaps it deserves comment, since although at the same time that I am tempted to identify myself—i.e., the human being that I am—with my body,[3] the identification may (as philosophers have pointed out) seem problematic.[4] Of course, we can acknowledge that the expression "my

---

[3] Thus Merleau-Ponty, in drawing the contrast between my body and an "external object," observes that "I am not in front of my body [in the way an external object may be in front of my body], I am in it, or rather I am it." *The Phenomenology of Perception*, trans. Colin Smith (Routledge and Kegan Paul, 1962), p. 150.

[4] See, e.g., Bernard Williams, "Are Persons Bodies?" in *Problems of the Self* and David Wiggins, in *Identity and Spatio-Temporal Continuity* (Basil Blackwell, 1967), part 4.

body" is not always used in a way that would tempt us to make the identification. Sometimes, for example, we use the expression contrastively. ("My body is O.K., but my face is a wreck.") When the philosopher asserts, "I (the human being that I am) am my body," there is no part of my body, inside or out, back or front, top or bottom, that he means to leave out; so there is nothing called "my body" with which to contrast the human being that I am. We might dub this philosophical use the "all-in" as opposed to the contrastive, use of "my body."

But even on the all-in use, which we shall henceforth take for granted, there are countless things we can say about the human being that, it seems, we cannot correctly say about my body. I (the human being that I am) am drinking a cup of coffee. Is my body drinking a cup of coffee? (Or planning to leave the café? Or thinking about philosophy?) Yet if on this basis we suppose there are two entities here, two bodily things, it is unclear how they are related, since, for example, they fill out precisely the same space and are composed of precisely the same assemblage of microentities. And if they are two bodily things, why is it nonsense to suppose that we might add up their weights?[5]

I think we can avoid getting entangled in this little knot of tricky questions. There is a relatively clear and uncontroversial sense in which "I (the human being that I am)" and "my body" are equivalent, and this is the sense that bears on our present concern. In whatever way my body figures within my horizon (experience), so does the human being that I am; and in whatever way the human being figures, so does my body. My body and the human being that I am—whether you conceive of them as one or two, as identical or materially coincident—are, as we shall put it, "phenomenologically equivalent." Thus the spelling out of the positional conception of the self, of the phenomenology of the subject position, can take the form either of spelling out the way in which a particular human being figures within my horizon, or the way in which a particular human body (all-in) figures within my horizon.[6] We may speak, in the first case, of what makes a particular human being the one that "I am (me)"; in second case, of what makes a particular body "mine." It does not matter. The phenomenological spelling out will in each case be the same.

Suppose the idea is that what makes a particular human being the one that "I am" is that it figures perceptually within my horizon in a distinctive way. We note, for example, that the human being in question is the human being whose face can be seen only in a reflective surface. Could

---

[5] See Williams, "Are Persons Bodies?"

[6] This assertion, in fact, needs to be qualified. It holds for what we shall later call "perceptual centrality" and "centrality of feeling" but not—at least not entirely—for "centrality of will."

we not reformulate this in terms of a particular human body? "My" body is the body whose face can be seen, etc. In one case, we spell out what makes a particular body "mine," in the other, what makes a particular human being the one that "I am." But in both cases, the phenomenology is the same. My body and myself (the human being that I am) are, as we said, phenomenologically equivalent. The equivalence will give us a certain leeway in our reflections on the phenomenology of the subject position: we may express the points we wish to make as points about either the human being or the human body.

And one point leads to another. The phenomenology of the subject position, whether in terms of the human being or the human body, is inexhaustible. So of course our attempt to spell out the phenomenology of the subject position, and thereby the positional conception of the self, will be incomplete. It follows from the nature of the enterprise that there is always more to spell out. Frege says that the way I am presented to myself (the way, as we would put it, I am presented within my horizon) is "particular and primitive." This would mean that we cannot even begin to spell it out (14.2). But just the opposite seems true: there is no end to spelling it out.

14.4 The Multiplicity of the Phenomenology of the Subject Position

We just mentioned in passing, and by way of illustration, that the body within my horizon that is "mine" is the perceptually central body. But when we look into the question of what makes a particular body "mine," a particular human being "me," i.e., when we ask about the way of figuring within my horizon by virtue of which a particular human being (human body) is the one at the center and is thereby "me" ("mine"), it emerges that the question has not one but three answers, that there are three kinds of centrality. The human being (body) that is "me" ("mine") is the one that is perceptually present in a unique way (perceptual centrality); is the one that is the locus of feeling (centrality of feeling); and is the one whose movements figure as willed (volitional centrality). The phenomenology of the subject position thus has a three-part multiplicity. We shall comment on each part separately in the next chapter. In the present chapter, we shall confine ourselves to a few general observations about the implications of this multiplicity.

Consider the case where no human being figures in any of the three ways. If within my horizon no human body is perceptually central, or is the locus of feeling or will, then, quite simply, no human body is "mine" (no human being is "me"). On the other hand, although at least one of the ways of figuring is necessary, it is not the case that all three must hold.

JV's body might never be the locus of feeling and yet be "mine." The same is true with respect to perceptual and volitional centrality. (I might be blind or paralyzed from birth.) However, if *no* human body figures within my horizon in *any* of the three ways, no human being occupies the subject position: no human body is "mine" (no human being is "me").

From these remarks, you might get the impression that the three ways of figuring, the three kinds of centrality, are independent of each other. This is not entirely true. It is an important fact about the phenomenology of the subject position that will is not independent of feeling.[7] Where feeling is completely absent—where there is no sense of my body at all— the possibility of the movements of my body figuring within my experience as willed is absent as well. There can be bodily feeling without will, but not will without feeling.

Note, we are not talking here about numbness—the sort of thing you get, say, with local anaesthesia. Numbness itself is (or involves) a kind of feeling. We are talking about the more extreme possibility of a total loss, a sheer absence, of feeling. If this happened to your arm, could you move it (in the normal way)? It is not that if you tried to move it you would fail. You could not even *try* to move it. Without feeling, there is, so to speak, nothing at which the will might aim. Feeling is what makes the body "visible" to the will. And if something is not visible, you cannot aim at it.

A particular human body could not be "mine," we are saying, unless it possessed at least one of the three kinds of centrality. But of no one kind can we say that it is necessary. On the other hand, apart from the dependence of will on feeling, each aspect of the phenomenology of the subject position seems individually sufficient for being "me." Any body that figures perceptually within my experience in the way JV's body now figures, or that figures as the locus of feeling, or will, would thereby be "my" body; the human being whose body it is would be "me." Hence it is correct to say of each of these ways of figuring that it "makes" a particular human body "mine" (a particular human being "me").

This fact of individual sufficiency is what lies behind a familiar kind of philosophical puzzlement about the self; for it seems to have the consequence that the self might fragment in the sense of spreading itself over different bodies. Thus philosophers sometimes ask questions like the following. "Could I will to move that arm over there which is not part of my body?" "Could I feel things in that arm?" Strange questions—we hardly know what to make of them.[8] We shall discuss such questions at

---

[7] See Brian O'Shaughnessy, *The Will* (Cambridge University Press, 1980), vol. 1, chap. 7, section 4.

[8] See, e.g., Arthur Danto's "What We Can Do," *The Journal of Philosophy* 60 (1963), and "Basic Actions," *American Philosophical Quarterly* 2 (1965).

various points as we go along. For the moment, let us simply observe that, were the phenomenology of the subject position not comprised of a multiplicity of individually sufficient ways of figuring, the questions would not so much as occur to us.

14.5 The Standing/Operative Ambiguity

There is a further complication that we need to take account of in advance, viz., an ambiguity that potentially affects all our statements about what makes a particular human being (body) "me" ("mine"). Consider the statement that if a particular human body figures in any one of the three relevant ways within my horizon, that body is "my" body. The ambiguity relates to whether the "figuring" here is understood in the *operative* or in the *standing* sense. In the first case, the figuring is identified with a particular datable happening or holding of some fact. In the second case, this kind of identification is impossible. Perhaps we can illustrate the distinction with a different example. Suppose I refer by name to someone in the café and you ask me to whom I refer. I point, "That man over there, the one who looks angry." In this case we may suppose that the man's "looking angry" is a particular datable happening or occurrence. He "looks angry" in the operative sense. But suppose—without being able to point out the man, because, e.g., he is not in the café—I say, "You know, the guy who usually complains about his bill, the one who looks angry." I may have in mind no particular occurrence of his "looking angry." I mean something typical or characteristic of the individual to whom I refer. This is how the individual figures with us, how we typically think of him: as the man who "looks angry." He "looks angry" not in the operative but in the standing sense.

That someone "looks angry" in the standing sense ("$looks_s$") is a fact of a different level from the fact that he "looks angry" in the operative sense ("$looks_o$"). Obviously, X could not looks angry unless there are times at which he $looks_o$ angry. If it is true at t that X $looks_o$ angry, then, there is at t a manifest fact that is X's $looking_o$ angry. However, from its being true at t that X is someone who $looks_s$ angry, it does not follow that there is a manifest fact that is X's $looking_o$ angry at t. More generally, there is no time particular t_1 such that, from its being true at t that X $looks_s$ angry, it follows that there is at t_1 a manifest fact of X's $looking_o$ angry at t_1; although, of course, if it is true at t that X is someone who $looks_s$ angry, it follows that there are times at which X $looks_o$ angry.

These points, which are meant to capture the gist of the relation between the standing and operative levels, can be generalized from $looking_s$ and $looking_o$ to $appearing_s$ and $appearing_o$, and thence to $figuring_s$ and figuring$_o$. Consider the generalization to figuring. Being the body which within my experience is the locus of feeling and will, these are ways my body figures (but not, as we shall stress, appears) within my experience. The thing is, my body figures$_s$ as the locus of feeling and will even when, as it happens, it does not figure$_o$ in these ways.

We have said about the several aspects of the phenomenology of the subject position, about the ways of figuring with my experience that make a body "my" body, that while figuring in any of these ways is individually sufficient for JV's body being "my" body, there is no one way such that figuring in that way is necessary; but that if JV's body is "mine" it must figure in at least one of the relevant ways. Perhaps it is now clear that the talk of "figuring" here is to be understood in the standing versus operative sense. Right now, say, in order that JV's body be "mine," it must figure$_s$ in one of the three ways; but it need not figure$_o$ in any of the three ways.

Even in the ordinary course of events there are times when my body does not figure$_o$ in one or the other of the relevant ways. I am studying a person coming toward me in the distance, or I am walking along looking in shop windows. Need my body at such times appear$_o$ within my experience in any particular way? Notice, at such times my body is still the body that appears$_s$, and in that respect figures$_s$, in the way that makes it "my" body.[9] That is, at such times, the relevant way of appearing remains a standing way in which my body appears within my experience. It is just that at such times that way of appearing is not operative. Again, if I am lying perfectly still staring at the sky, need my body at that moment figure$_o$ as an object of will? Yet it still figures$_s$ in that way. That is, it figures$_s$ as the body whose actions figure$_o$ within my experience as willed.

It might seem that the case with feeling is different. I do not always perceive my body, or use it in action. Do I not, however, always (when awake) have a sense of my body? This is certainly the normal state of affairs. However, we know that it is possible through local anaesthesia to create numbness in some part of one's body. But let us contemplate the extreme possibility of not just numbness but the sheer absence of feeling throughout my body (the possibility of "super anaesthesia"): the possibil-

---

[9] Commenting on Hume's famous inability to "catch *myself* at any time without a perception" and to "observe anything but the perception," Gareth Evans remarks that "there is something in Hume's point. . . . For what we are aware of, when we know that we see a tree, is *nothing but a tree*." (*The Varieties of Reference*, p. 231.) Note, first, that Evans's point applies only to visual appearing (to that particular way of figuring within experience); and second, that even with this restriction understood, it overlooks the standing/operative distinction (thus at the same time that I am focused entirely on the tree, my body continues to figure within my horizon as the body that visually appears$_s$ in such-and-such way). Of course, these remarks may be irrelevant to what Hume is getting at in the passage in question, viz., as we explained earlier (9.4), his Negativist view of the self.

ity of my body not figuring$_0$ within my experience as the center, or locus, of feeling (of any kind whatever). Yet even in the extreme situation of super anaesthesia my body could figure standingly, i.e., figure$_s$, as the center of feeling.[10] This standing way of figuring would then still be part of what makes my body "my" body.

The whole of my body, imagine, has been super anaesthetized while I remain awake. Not only will my body not figure$_0$ within my experience as felt or sensed, the movements of my body (such as they might be) cannot figure$_0$ within my experience as willed. Of course my body might still appear visually within my experience in the unique way it does, in the way that makes it "mine." Imagine we subtract this as well. Not only is there a complete absence of feeling, and hence will, my body can no longer appear within my experience. Here we have a situation philosophers like to talk about, that of total sensory deprivation (SD). In an SD situation, my body does not figure$_0$ within my horizon (experience) in any way at all. So it does not figure$_0$ in any of the three ways that we are saying comprise the phenomenology of the subject position, the ways of figuring within my horizon that make *my* body "my" body.

Yet there is no reason to suppose that, even in this extreme situation, the total SD situation, my body might not continue to figure$_s$ within my experience in the ways that make it mine. I might know all the facts about my situation. Why not? Would I not then know that *my* body is submerged in the tank? Even in the SD situation, the body in question, JV's body, would be the body within my experience that appears$_s$ and feels$_s$ thus-and-so, and whose actions figure$_s$ as willed. Thus even in the SD situation, JV's body would be "my" body (JV would be the human being that "I am"). By hypothesis, it would not figure$_0$ as "mine"; but it would figure$_s$[11] as "mine," i.e., in the ways that make it "my" body.

14.6 Causal Centrality

It is worth considering whether our three-part phenomenology of the subject position is complete, whether there are other ways of figuring within my horizon that, while not individually necessary, are individually sufficient for a particular human body being "mine." P. F. Strawson, in the

[10] The distinction we are drawing between figuringo and figurings as the center of feeling corresponds, roughly, to the distinction Merleau-Ponty draws between "the customary body and the body at this moment" (*The Phenomenology of Perception*, p. 82), as well as (at least in terms of motivation) to Brian O'Shaughnessy's distinction between "the short-term and long-term body-image" (*The Will*, vol. 1, chap. 7, section 5).

[11] Henceforth we will omit the subscripts, unless confusion is possible or special emphasis is appropriate.

chapter "Persons" of his book *Individuals*, draws attention to certain facts that he says "might be said to explain why, granted that I am going to speak of one body as *mine*, I should speak of *this* body as mine."[12] Examples Strawson gives of such facts are that there is just one body whose eyelids must be open if the subject of visual experience is to see, and on the position of whose body and the direction of whose head and eyeballs what is seen is causally dependent (pp. 90–91), summarizes facts of the relevant kind as follows:

> for each person there is one body which occupies a certain *causal* position in relation to that person's perceptual experience, a causal position which in various ways is unique in relation to each of the various kinds of perceptual experience he has; and—as a further consequence that this body is unique for him as an *object* of experience. (p. 92)

Since our present concern is solely with the phenomenology of the subject position, i.e., with the way or ways of figuring within my experience that make a particular body "mine," we shall not raise questions about "persons," "experience," "subject of experience" etc. but shall reformulate the question in our own terms. The question is whether the special causal position of my body, its causal centrality, is part of what makes a particular human being (body) "me (mine)."[13]

Of course, the movements of my body affect how things appear within my experience in a unique way. Thus if I turn my head, what I see is affected in a way that is not affected by your turning your head. But notice, what affects the content of my experience is my turning my head, and generally what I do with my body. The body that is causally central is already "mine." It is already "mine" in that it is the body whose movements figure within my experience as actions, as willed (I turn my head, etc.). My conception of myself as causally engaged in the world presupposes the conception of a certain human being as active, and that I already conceive of the human being (body) as myself (mine). The "mineness" of the body that is causally central within my experience derives not from its causal centrality but from its prior status as the locus of will.

Let us approach the matter from a different direction. Might there not be a situation in which the way things appear (visually, say) within my experience depends causally not on the position and condition, etc., of

---

[12] *Individuals*, p. 93.

[13] Note that Strawson alludes here not just to the fact that "my" body is the one on which the ways things appear within my horizon (experience) is causally dependent, not just, i.e., to the causal centrality of that body, but to the special ways in which, as a consequence of its causal centrality, that same body itself appears within my experience. In our scheme of things, this is a separate aspect, or part, of the phenomenology of the subject position, viz., the aspect that we are calling "perceptual centrality."

JV's body, but on that of another body, and yet in which JV's body (not the other body) is (as in fact it is) the one that is "mine"? Can I not imagine that, say, when you shift your place, or turn your head, things change in a systematic way within my experience, but that when I move around or turn my head in a different direction, it makes no such difference experientially? It might be thought that the fact that we have described the situation as one in which things change within my experience when "you" shift "your" place but not when "I" move around, and so forth, begs the question of whether causal centrality is part of what makes a particular body "mine." But we are simply putting it forward that the situation as described is an experiential possibility, that this is a way things could be within my experience (horizon). Judge for yourself. Is it not an experiential possibility? Can you not imagine this sort of thing happening within your experience?

One might wonder how it would work. Suppose the relevant "information" is transmitted from the brain in X's head to the brain in JV's head. But then would not the way things appear within my experience depend more directly on that brain than on the brain in X's head? If we stipulate that the causal dependence be "direct," it would be JV's body that is "mine."

Wait. We have not thought things through properly. In the imagined situation, what X's brain registers would be the causal upshot of what is happening in the rest of X's body, including X's nervous system and sense organs. All of that gets transmitted to the brain in JV's head. This, on reflection, seems to have the consequence that, rather than JV's body, it is X's body that is "my" body. Consider the aspect of perceptual centrality, the peculiar way that (in the actual situation) JV's body shows up visually, say, within my experience. In the imagined situation, because of the fact that what is happening in JV's brain is causally parasitic upon what is happening in X's body, X's body would appear within my experience in exactly the way that, in the actual situation, JV's body appears. Would this not, when it comes to settling which body is "mine," override the fact that the way things are within my experience—including the perceptual centrality of X's body!—is directly causally dependent on JV's brain rather than on X? If the view within my experience is (so to speak) the view from X's brain, then X, i.e., X's body, will be perceptually central. And if X's body is perceptually central, X's body (including X's head) will be "my" body.

What I am trying to evoke (by these admittedly hard-to-keep-straight reflections) is the recognition that purely causal facts about a particular body are—once we have isolated them from facts of will—not really ways in which that body *figures* within my experience and, therefore, that they fall outside the phenomenology of the subject position: they are not in themselves facts that can settle, or determine, which body is "mine." Think about the way the body I call "mine" figures perceptually (when it does) within my experience. (Do this, of course, in your own case.) The body in question is not only present, demonstratively available, it presents itself—that is, it appears—in a certain way. If we hold this constant, it does not seem to matter how we play around with the causal facts that operate behind the way the body in question appears within my experience. Given that it appears in the way it appears, it, *this* body, is "my" body.

It should be evident now that we need not have troubled ourselves supplying, and working out the consequences of, a plausible causal story to support our initial intuition that the way things appear within my experience might depend on a body other than that which is "mine." For it does not matter what causal story we supply. Consider a story in which the dependence on X's body is direct, i.e., in which the brain in JV's body makes no causal contribution to the way things appear within my experience, yet in which things appear exactly in the way they do now, in the actual situation. In that case, despite the fact that the way things appear is causally dependent on X's body, since the way things appear includes the centrality within my experience of JV's body, it is JV's body, not X's body, that is "mine."

You may say, this cannot be: the location and attitude, etc., of X's body are different from those of JV's body. So, if the way things appear within my experience were to depend on X's body, how could the way things appear be exactly as it is in the actual situation? This is not just a causal but a metaphysical (in the sense explained in the previous chapter) impossibility. But the point is precisely that it is only what makes sense experientially that matters. This is what settles the question of whether a particular body is "my" body. If a body figures in the right way within my experience, then, whatever the causal story, that body is "my" body.[14]

It turns out, then, that it might not be *my* brain that causally determines how things are within *my* experience. For the question of which brain is

---

[14] Quassim Cassam maintains in this regard (with a supporting quote from Wittgenstein) that the "question "What makes a given body *my* body?" is simply illegitimate, for there is no independent "I" whose ownership of a particular body can be in question." See his *Self and World* (Oxford University Press, 1997), p. 67. Now I agree about there being no independent "I" who owns my body (see 9.4–5). However, it is not by virtue of its being owned by a particular entity that my body is "mine," but by virtue of the way this body figures within my horizon (experience). The trouble is that this subject matter, the horizon, is not explicitly taken up in Cassam's discussion: the horizon has not come philosophically into view. So, given that a Cartesian soul has been ruled out as the "owner," it seems that there is no answer to the question of what makes a given body "my" body, that the question is illegitimate; for the answer—and does not the question cry out for an answer?—presupposes the very subject matter that has not been uncovered, that remains philosophically out of view.

"mine" is settled independently of what causally determines how things are in my experience. My brain is the brain of the body that is mine, the brain of the human being that I am, and which human being/body this is settled phenomenologically, that is, on the basis of which human being/ body standingly figures in the right way within my experience. Which brain is "my" brain? The first instinct is to point to the one "up here." Where? In "my" head—the head of the body that is "mine." Well, what makes that body "mine"? Does the answer have anything to do with the causal role of its brain? Could I not definitively answer the question of which body is "mine" without even knowing that I have a brain? What makes my body "mine" is that it figures in a certain way within my experience.

14.7 Causation and the Phenomenology of the Subject Position

Notice, at the same time that the causal role of my body is not part of the phenomenology of the subject position, it is because of what is happening in my body, in its brain, that things are within my experience as they are, including the very fact that the body in question figures in a way that makes it "mine." Given that there is more than one way of figuring within my experience that makes a particular body "mine," an unsettling possibility comes into view. Causally speaking, the world might conspire to bring about a state of affairs that does not makes sense in terms of the phenomenology of the subject position.

Phenomenologically (experientially), it makes sense that at a given time no body figures as "mine," but not that more than one body figures "mine." Assume JV's body figures perceptually just as it does. Can I imagine a different body, X's body, simultaneously figuring within my experience as the locus of feeling, or (which presupposes the later way of figuring) as the body whose movements figure as willed?

The issue here is not whether, as Wittgenstein suggests in the *Blue Book*, I can feel things (like pain) in another's body.[15] For one thing, we are not interested in the kind of peripheral case that Wittgenstein seems to have in mind,[16] but in a case in which the whole locus or space of feeling within my experience, my whole body image (as they say), is another's body. This seems impossible. I cannot imagine it. Why? Because any body I imagine as the space of feeling within my experience would, for that reason, *not* be *another's* body; it would be my body. The impossibility that interests us—that simultaneously one body should figure within my experience as the locus of feeling and another as perceptually central: that two

---

[15] *The Blue and Brown Books* (Harper Torchbooks, 1958), p. 68.
[16] Like that where your body and my body are joined at the hand. Ibid., p. 54.

bodies both should simultaneously figure within my experience as "my" body—takes this as given.

But the relevant impossibility is still not properly defined. It would seem that two bodies might *share* my body space (image), that my body space might be split into two parts, each of which is a complete and distinct human body whose movements figure within my horizon as willed. It could not, of course, be the case that each is perceptually central within my horizon in exactly the way that JV's body is perceptually central; but we can imagine that, perceptually speaking, the positions are symmetrical and similar enough to the position of JV's body so that this is not a problem. If this were possible, i.e., experientially possible, each body would be "mine" more or less in the way each of JV's arms is "mine." However, the case that interests us now, the case that we are saying is experientially impossible, is not this case, in which two human bodies share the same kind of centrality, but the case where each of two human bodies monopolizes a different kind of centrality, so that there is competition between them for status of being "my" body.

Let us reflect on this. I imagine pointing to a body, Body Two, which is distinct from the body whose arm points, Body One. So Body One, since its pointing movement figures within my horizon (experience) as willed, figures as "my" body. But this same body, the body whose pointing movement figures as willed, Body One, would also, thereby, figure as perceptually central. (Imagine yourself pointing and this will be clear.) So far, then, it is Body One that is undisputedly "my" body. If we are to suppose that, in addition, Body Two is "my" body, this must be because it, as opposed to Body One, is the body that figures within my experience as the locus of feeling. But we have already allocated will to Body One, and the body whose movements figure within my experience as willed, as active, is precisely the body that figures within my experience as the locus of feeling. (As we remarked in 14.4, in the total absence of feeling, you cannot even *try* to act.) In that case it is after all Body One, the perceptually central body, not Body Two, that figures as the locus of feeling and is therefore "my" body.

In sum, a state of affairs in which more than one body simultaneously figures within my experience as "mine" is experientially incoherent, impossible. The problem is that if the way things figure within my experience is determined causally by events in a brain, from a causal standpoint, nothing, it would seem, prevents a setup in which the following is true: there occur independent sets of conditions (involving brains and nervous systems, supplemented by some fancy technology) such that, simultaneously, one set determines that Body One figures within my experience as perceptually central, while another that Body Two figures as the locus of feeling and will. Then both Body One and Body Two would, impossibly, figure within my experience as "my" body.

The logic of the self is phenomenological. Causation, on the other hand, knows nothing of phenomenology—but goes its own way. Given the brute causal dependence of phenomenology on what happens in the brain, more generally on what happens in the world, it follows that the world has the causal potential to subvert the logic of the self. This idea (we shall take it no further at present) will be important in our discussion of personal identity.

14.8 Orientational Centrality

Another possible addition to our three-part phenomenology of the subject position concerns what might be called "orientational centrality." The idea is implicit in some well-known philosophical discussions of the self. Husserl, e.g., in the fifth of his *Cartesian Meditations*, writes that "my animate bodily organism . . . has the central 'Here' as its mode of givenness; every other body, and accordingly the 'other's' body, has the mode 'There.' "[17] Note, the fact that my body is given (figures) as the central "Here" is not itself a fact of spatial orientation—like, say, the fact that the coffee cup is "right here" but is presupposed by the fact about coffee cup: it is by reference to the central "Here" that the coffee cup is "right here." Thus a few pages later Husserl describes "*my* animate organism" as "the zero body, the body in the absolute Here."[18] An object that is "right here" is not the zero body. The zero body is, rather, that by reference to which an object is "right here."

For our purposes, the suggestion is that figuring as the zero body—i.e., as the reference point presupposed by facts of spatial orientation—is one the ways of figuring that makes a particular human body "mine" (a particular human being "me"). Causal facts about my body do not need a horizon but hold on their own and thus, as we have observed, fall outside the phenomenology of the subject position. In contrast, the fact of my body's orientational centrality (of its figuring as the zero body) is a fact with phenomenological import, a fact about how a certain body figures within my experience. It is therefore at least a candidate for inclusion within the phenomenology of the subject position.

Yet it cannot be included. The reason is, the fact that a certain body figures as "mine" is itself a condition of there being facts of spatial orientation, hence of my body's figuring as the zero body. Unless a certain body

[17] *Cartesian Meditations*, section 53.
[18] Ibid., section 55.

figured as "mine" (unless a certain human being figured as "me"), there would be within my experience no facts of spatial orientation, and thus no fact of a particular body's figuring as the reference required by such facts, as the zero body.

The point is familiar. For an object to be "here" is for the object to be near me, i.e., near the human being that I am (near my body). It is by virtue of being near not just any object or body but the body that is "mine" that, within my experience, another body is "here." So unless within my experience a certain body were "mine," nothing within my experience would be "here," since there would be nothing by being near that anything could figure in this way. There would then within my experience be no such fact as the fact a particular object is "here." The same holds, of course, for an object's being "over there," "up ahead," "yonder," "back there," and so on. In criticizing Descartes' view of the self, we remarked that spatial orientatedness requires that the entity that I am be a bodily thing (12.2). The present point is that the bodily thing required by spatial orientatedness be the entity that "I am," the body that is "my" body. The body that figures as the ultimate reference point presupposed by facts of spatial orientation, as the zero body, could not figure that way unless it already figured as "mine." Thus if our question is what makes a particular body "mine," the answer cannot be that it figures within my horizon as the zero body. This, i.e., figuring as the zero body, cannot be regarded as part of the phenomenology of the subject position.

14.9 The Sense in Which the Positional and Horizonal Conceptions of the Self Are "Always in Play"

Insofar as the fact of X's figuring within my experience as "right here," "back there," "up ahead" etc., implicitly involves a reference to the body that is "mine" (the human being that is "me"), the obtaining of such a fact implicitly brings into play the positional conception of the self. The same holds, of course, if I actually think that X is "right here." My thought, like the fact that is thought, will implicitly bring into play the positional conception of the self. Yet it will not be a first-person thought. The expression of a first-person thought contains a term or a verb ending with first-person reference. This is not essential to the expression of an orientational thought. In thinking, "X is right here," the only reference is to X, not to myself. On the other hand, implicit in what I think about X is a reference to myself, to my body (the human being that I am); otherwise X would not figure within my experience as "right here." An orientational thought implicitly brings into play what a first-person thought explicitly brings into play: the positional conception of the self.

Obviously, not all non-first-person thoughts bring the positional concept of the self into play, e.g., purely general thoughts, or thoughts about abstract objects; or unless the objects are conceived of perspectivally or demonstratively, singular thoughts about objects in the world. Yet even in these cases, there is a sense in which the positional conception of the self is in play.

In thinking a first-person or orientational thought, we explicitly or implicitly bring the positional conception of the self into play. There is, however, a sense in which that conception is *already* in play. It is not just that we already grasp the conception, but that when we bring it into play, we are already *drawing upon* the conception. A sense in which we are, in fact, *always* drawing upon the conception.

What sense is this? We are always drawing upon the positional conception of the self, the conception is always (already) in play, in that it is, in fact, always the case that some body figures within my experience as "my" body (that some human being figures as the human being that "I am"). The holding of this fact is a constant within my experience, a permanent feature of life from within the horizon. Thus even when nothing explicitly or implicitly brings the positional conception of the self into play, the fact in question holds: there is always a body that figures within my experience as "my" body.

This does not mean that there is always within my experience a body that feels$_o$ or appears$_o$ in the special way that makes a body "mine," or that that there is always a movement of that body that figures$_o$ within my experience as willed. When we say that the positional conception of the self is always in play, or that we are always drawing upon this conception, we mean that there is always a body that figures$_s$—figures in the standing (versus operative) sense—within my experience as "my" body.

We shall say that the positional conception of the self is always in "background play." Being in background play, note, must not be confused with being implicitly in play. If I think "X is right next to me," this thought brings the positional conception of the self explicitly into play. If I think "X is right here," this brings the conception implicitly into play. But either way, the conception was already in play, i.e., in background play. It is *out of* background play that the first-person and orientational thoughts explicity or implicitly bring the conception *into* play. The positional conception of the self can be brought into play, implicitly or explicitly, only because it is already in background play.

If the positional conception of the self is always in background play, the horizonal conception must likewise always be in background play, since the positional conception is the conception of a position within my horizon. But there is a difference. The positional conception of the self is always in play in the sense that a certain phenomenological fact, the fact that JV's body figures$_s$ in such-and-such a way, always holds from within my horizon. There is no such fact with which the being in play of the horizonal conception of the self can be identified. The being in play of the horizonal conception is a fact that holds, not because of the way this or that entity figures from within my horizon, but simply because there is such a thing as my horizon.

There is also this difference. The horizonal conception of the self is not just always in background play; it is inevitably in background play. Given that there is such a thing as my horizon, my experience (consciousness, life), the conception cannot but be in background play. There is no comparable inevitability in the case of the positional conception of the self. Thus, as noted, we can imagine its being the case that there is no body that figures as "my" body: not just that (as in the sensory deprivation case) no body figures$_o$ as "mine" but that the subject position within my experience is empty, that no body figures$_s$ as "mine." What we thereby imagine may not make sense causally, or metaphysically, but we can imagine it (it is an experiential possibility). We do not, however, in imagining this emptiness, imagine a situation in which there is no such thing as my experience. How could that be, when the emptiness we imagine is an emptiness at the center of my experience?

Note, from its ceasing to be the case that a body figures$_s$ within my horizon as "my" body (if this could be realized), it does not follow that I would cease to grasp the positional conception of the self. I would grasp the conception, but it would cease to be in background play. There is more to the conception's being in play than my grasping it; for the conception to be in play a human being must actually figure$_s$ as "me," as the one at the center of my horizon. If the conception were not in play (if no human being figured as "me"), life would be different from within my horizon.

It is not, we said, because of the way this or that entity figures from within my horizon that the horizonal conception of the self is in background play but simply because there is such a subject matter as my horizon. Perhaps the reader will recognize here the metafact that we earlier (9.3) identified as self-consciousness: the manifestness of the fact that there is such a subject matter as my consciousness (horizon). That there is such a subject matter, a horizon that is "mine" in a way that nothing else is "mine," is, like Wittgenstein's "mineness" of the world, a fact that makes itself manifest and thus cannot but always already be manifest. Given that the existence of my consciousness, the horizon, is manifest, the horizonal conception of the self is in play. That is to say, in background play. The conception's being in background play is one and the same as the always-already-given manifestness of the existence of my consciousness, the fact of self-consciousness.

It does not follow, of course, that I am always thinking to myself that there is such thing as my consciousness (my horizon). There is, you might say, no *need* to think this. The fact whose manifestness constitutes my self-consciousness is always already manifest. Therefore, as we explained (9.3), if I actually do think it, my thinking inevitably comes too late: it is redundant or empty. In this sense, the fact of the existence of my consciousness is, like Wittgenstein's fact about the "mineness" of world, an unthinkable fact.

15. The Phenomenology of the Subject Position

15.1 Perceptual Centrality: The Visual and Tactual Appearing of My Body

The phenomenology of the subject position, we said (14.4), has three parts. There are three ways a human body (being) figures within my experience, at least one of which is necessary and each of which is sufficient for its being "mine (me)": perceptual centrality, centrality of feeling, and volitional centrality. We shall begin with perceptual centrality, the special way my body appears within my experience. Mine is not the only body that appears within my experience. But, the idea is, it has a way of appearing that distinguishes it from all other bodies, a way of appearing that in fact makes it "mine."

The perceptual centrality of my body is the unique way of appearing within my experience of my body, i.e., the unique standing way in which my body appears (appears$_s$), within my experience. For of course my body does not appear$_o$ in the relevant way at all times. In fact, not only is the unique way my body has of appearing not always operative, it might drop out of the phenomenology of the subject position altogether, or never in the first place be part of the phenomenology of the subject position. In the first case, the body that is mine ceases to appear$_s$ in the unique way that makes it "mine" and yet continues to figure$_s$ as "my" body. Assume, for the moment, that only visual appearance matters. Suppose I become blind. My body need not straightaway cease to figure$_s$ in the unique visual way that makes it "mine."[1] But this might happen after awhile. The self might, so to speak, become something less than it was. Or suppose I am born blind. In that case, my body never has a chance to appear (figure) in the unique visual way, etc. In either case, whether the impoverishment of the subject position is a development within my experience or original, it is possible that a certain body figures within my experience as "mine"; for it is possible that the body figures in one or both of the other ways that make a body "mine," as the center of feeling and/or the center of will.

---

[1] As before, where the context makes clear what is intended, we will not always employ subscripts.

What is the way of appearing that makes my body "mine"? So far, we have alluded only to the visual appearing of my body. We may, I take it, dismiss more or less out of hand the suggestion that my body has a way of tasting, smelling, or sounding that could support the kind of counterfactual conditionals implicit in saying of a way of appearing that it "makes" a particular body "mine." However, the case of tactual appearing is not so obvious. In addition to visually appearing in a special way, does not my body also have a special way of appearing tactually?

Generally, what appears tactually is a bodily thing, part of the world. The thing itself is present and appears within my experience. This is as true of my body as any other: my body appears tactually within my experience. The question is whether there is a tactual way of appearing that is part of the phenomenology of the subject position, a way of tactual appearing that makes my body "mine."

Note, what appears tactually is the bodily thing, not bodily sensations. The sensations occur at the edge of my body-space, in my fingers (say), whereas the thing that appears, unless we are talking about my body itself, appears outside my body-space. I am feeling for a certain box in a dark closet. "*This* is it." What I demonstratively refer to here are not sensations in my fingers but the object I was looking for, the box. (Might I have been looking for sensations?) It is the box that I pick out, that is tactually present/appears.[2] True, unless making contact with the box caused sensations in my body (fingers), the box would not be present/appear tactually. It is via tactual sensations that objects in the world, like the box, tactually appear. However it is the box (versus the sensations) that tactually appears/is present within my experience.

Given that it is via tactual sensations that a bodily thing is tactually present, there is a potential duality for attention. Thus when the box tactually appears I can fix my attention either on it or on the sensations in my fingers. In contrast, it is not via visual sensations that the world visually appears. Visual sensations are, presumably, visual phenomena that occur only in our experience and are not part of the world—e.g., flashes, sparklings, splinterings, "seeing stars," fuzziness, brightenings, dimmings, visual explodings. On this understanding, visual sensations are something of a rarity. Typically, the world is visually present and appears without the accompaniment of any such phenomena. The potential duality that exists for attention in the tactual case is by and large absent in the visual case.

---

[2] A question we shall not discuss here is whether, when I touch an object, the "felt resistance" can be reduced to tactual sensation or, more generally, to bodily sensation, or whether it should be regarded as itself a distinctive way in which bodies are present within my experience (viz., as offering resistance).

There are, to be sure, well-known philosophical arguments that have the conclusion that what is visually present is never the world but always an internal object, a visual sense datum. But although I would not wish to make light of such arguments,[3] they do not constitute a reason for supposing the presence of visual sensations in experience. An argument for visual sense data is not an argument for visual sensations. Sensations are items that occur within my experience *along with* items that count as part of the world. (Thus I can switch my attention from one to the other.) They are one side of a duality that can be made out within my experience. However, if the arguments for visual sense data are correct, no such duality results. On the contrary, visually speaking, the whole experiential field (which we naively suppose to be occupied by objects in the world) would be usurped monolithically by a display of sense data. In this sense, we would be just where we were before—as far as ever from being presented with the kind of duality that would allow us to distinguish an element of sensation within experience.

To repeat, arguments for visual sense data are not arguments for visual sensations. I am not sure we can imagine what it would be like if within our experience there were nothing but visual sensations. But this much is clear, it would be nothing like what the arguments for sense data would have us imagine. It would be utterly disorienting and strange, whereas the arguments for sense data would have us suppose that things would be just like they actually are.

Perhaps we can return now to our question about tactual appearing and the phenomenology of the subject position. My body can appear tactually within my experience. I feel with my hand, say, to determine whether my beard needs trimming, or whether the swelling on the back of my head has receded. In such cases, my body, or a part of it, appears tactually within my experience. The question, however, is not just whether my body can appear tactually but whether this way of appearing is part of the phenomenology of the subject position, part of what makes a particular body "my" body.

It may seem evident that the answer to this question is affirmative. I touch my face. Could *this* be anything but *me*? Anything but *my* body? But we have to untangle the contribution of my body's tactual appearance from the fact that it figures within my experience as the locus of feeling, and again, from the fact that its actions figure as willed. When I touch

---

[3] The most famous is the so-called argument from illusion. Another, more powerful (it seems to me) argument, a causal argument, is that to which I refer in *The Puzzle of Experience* as the "problematic reasoning." We shall consider the causal argument later on; in the present context it would simply be a distraction.

my face there is feeling (sensation) in my fingers, and also in my face. These feelings are located within a felt body-space (body-image) that already fixes the tactually present body as "mine." If we wish to determine whether the ways my body tactually appears play a role in the phenomenology of the subject position, we must be careful to factor out the contribution of bodily feeling in this respect. Given the inevitable attendance of feeling when my body tactually appears, and given that this feeling itself plays a role in the phenomenology of the subject position, it would be easy to mistake what is really due to feeling for a contribution made by tactual appearance.

A similar consideration applies in the case of will. When I feel (touch) my face, I feel (sense) in my face and fingers. But I not only feel (sense) in my fingers, I act with my fingers—and hand and arm. The actions of my fingers and the rest figure within my experience not just as things that happen but as actions, as willed. In that case, the body whose fingers, etc., they are figures as "my" body. Its face is "my" face. Thus its face is "my" face quite independently of the way that that face tactually appears within my experience.

There are, of course, differences between feeling and will to take account of here. Whereas an object cannot tactually appear unless there is feeling (sensing) in my body-space, it can tactually appear without action on my part. (An object may, e.g., rub against my body when I am lying motionless on my back.) On the other hand, if we think of the way we explore the world tactually, it should be obvious that will enters the picture. The point is, insofar as object's tactual appearance depends on what I *do*, the relevant movements of my body thereby figure as "mine." Thus if we ask whether a certain way of appearing tactually makes a body "mine," we shall have to be careful to separate out not just the contribution made in this respect by bodily feeling, but the contribution made by bodily will.

And once we have done this, it seems clear that there is no way my body has of tactually appearing within my experience that makes it "mine." It seems, rather, that all the ways my body appears tactually are ways that other human bodies might appear. I feel (touch) my forehead. How does it appear tactually? How (as we say) does it feel?[4] It feels slightly moist and smooth. But no one could suppose that this is part of what makes it "my" forehead. My beard feels (tactually appears) rough. Is that what makes it "mine"? Could not the beard of another have exactly the same tactual appearance?

---

[4] Note, in addition to "feel (touch)" and "feel (sense)," here we have a third use of "feel" (= "tactually appear").

De facto uniqueness, we know, is not sufficient. The unique way of appearing that makes a body "mine" must generate counterfactual possibilities. For example, if a forehead other than JV's were the unique forehead with the right tactual appearance, the body of that forehead would be "mine." This is obviously not the case. Our foreheads, yours and mine, might exchange tactual appearances while remaining just what they are, "yours" and "mine." The tactual appearance of my body is not part of what makes my body "mine." It is not part of the phenomenology of the subject position.

True, when (say) I feel my forehead, there can be no question but that it is "mine." Its "mineness," however, derives not from the way my forehead tactually appears but from the fact that it is the forehead of the body whose movement of touching the forehead figures within my experience as willed; and of the body within my experience in whose fingers and forehead things are felt, the forehead of the body, etc., that figures as the locus of sensation. These ways of figuring within my experience—figuring as the locus of will and sensation—are ways of figuring within my experience that not only are de facto unique (within my experience) to my body but make that body "mine." These ways of figuring are part of the phenomenology of the subject position.

15.2 Perceptual Centrality: The Visual Appearing of Myself

My skin has a very particular shade of pinkish tan. Is this what makes the arm in question "my" arm? Maybe no one else has exactly the same skin color. It does not matter. We can construct the same sort of counterfactual-exchange argument that we just employed in the case of tactual appearance.

But then color does not exhaust the ways in which my body visually appears. In his book *The Analysis of Sensations*, Ernst Mach offers (in the course of trying to explain the gulf between "physical and psychological research") the following observations accompanied by the picture reproduced in figure 15.1.

> I lie upon my sofa. If I close my right eye, the picture represented in the accompanying cut [above] is presented to my left eye. In a frame formed by the ridge of my eyebrow, by my nose, and by my moustache, appears a part of my body, so far as visible, with its environment. My body differs from other human bodies—beyond the fact that every intense motor idea is immediately expressed by a movement of it, and that, if it is touched, more striking changes are determined than if other bodies

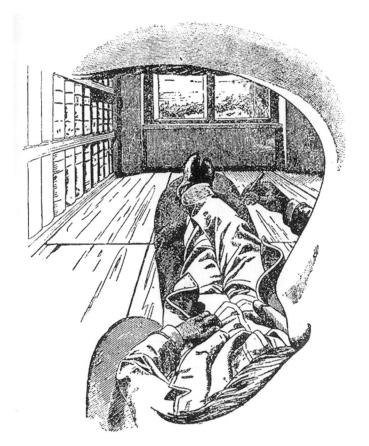

Figure 15.1

are touched—by the circumstance, that it is only seen piecemeal, and, especially, is seen without a head.[5]

The crucial statement here is that "my body differs from other human bodies . . . by the circumstance, that it is only seen piecemeal, and . . . is seen without a head." Mach's picture is meant to illustrate this statement. It pictures a way my body can be seen, i.e., a way it can visually appear, within my experience. So my head does not, except very peripherally, appear in the picture. The idea that we are to extract from this is not that a body would not be "mine" unless it appears within my experience in the way pictured (who knows, I might never lie down, or I might only lie

[5] *The Analysis of Sensations*, trans. C. M. Williams (Dover Publications, 1959), pp. 18–19.

down in the dark; or then again, I might be blind), but rather that appearing this way suffices for its being "my" body. Precisely in this way?
Perhaps we could say that the way of appearing pictured is representative
of the *kind* of way of appearing within my experience that makes my
body "mine."[6] Understood thus, Mach's picture may, I think, claim to
convey or illustrate part of the phenomenology of the subject position
(the perceptual centrality of my body).

Leaving aside for now the sort of science fiction possibility mentioned
in 14.6 (where the brain in one head is collecting its visual information
from the eyes and brain in another head), it might be objected that if, for
example, I were lying on my stomach above an illuminated depression,
another's body might be positioned in such a way that it appeared in the
way the body pictured in Mach's picture appears. But is that so? What
about the inner ridge of the eye and the side of the nose, etc.? (And suppose Mach had included, as he might have, some of his shoulders and
more of the upper part of his chest.) More importantly, we must bear in
mind that it is not just one particular way of appearing that is relevant.
Mach's picture, we said, should be taken as representative of a "kind" of
way of appearing. There is, in fact, a whole system of pictures that might
be employed in this regard. (I hope we can get away without supplying
further examples.) Think of the countless ways my body appears from
within my experience—of the countless positions I adopt and activities I
pursue in the course of normal life. Of course, a bit of another's body
may, because of the way it appears within my experience, be mistaken for
my own (and conversely). So we may contrive a situation in which I am
mistaken. But this is a peripheral case. Could we devise a whole system
of setups and arrangements that would make sense of another's body
appearing within my experience in the multifarious interconnected ways
in which my body appears?

Or let us turn this around. If any such system succeeded, i.e., if in fact
another body displaced in an ongoing way JV's body as the perceptually
central body within my horizon, the other body would simply be "mine."
Given the multiplicity of the subject position, the other body might have
a rival for this status (there might be conflict), but it would have the same
claim to being "mine" that JV's body has. Imagine going about your everyday business, with a body showing up visually in your experience in
the countless, smoothly and systematically connected, ways your body

---

[6] We are overlooking the fact that Mach makes no reference here to the horizon. Yet
without this reference, the statement that my body is *the* human body seen only piecemeal,
etc., is patently false. The same can be said of your body—of (more or less) every human
body. What is true is, my body is *the* human body seen only piecemeal, etc., from within
my experience.

shows up. Is there anything, really, that might convince you that that body is not your body? (This kind of question will be raised again, when we discuss the "science fiction" cases.)

15.3 Perceptual Centrality: Views of Myself

Mach's picture should be considered, we said, as a representative of the kind of way of appearing within my experience that makes a certain body "my" body. But there is an ambiguity in this statement. My body's "way of appearing" may mean either a particular *view* of my body, of myself (the human being that I am), or an *aspect* of such a view. An aspect of a view of my body is an *apparent feature* of my body—an apparent feature of my body *in* that view of it.

Consider a different example. Here is the cup. The idea is that, if we speak of the "way the cup appears," we may mean either a view of the cup or an aspect of a view of the cup, i.e., an apparent feature of the cup in our view of it. An apparent feature of the cup, etc. (an aspect of the view) is something we might express. Thus we might say that the cup looks "old," or "yellowish," or "shiny," or "misshapen," or whatever. A view of the cup, however, while it can be described, cannot be expressed.

When we describe X, we use words to say about X what we take to be true of X; when we express X, we use words to put X into words. Everything can be described, but not everything can be put into words, that is to say, expressed. The cup, like everything else, can be described. But there is no such thing as expressing the cup. You can put an apparent feature of the cup into words, but not the cup itself. In describing the cup, we use words that express its apparent features; we use these words to say about the cup what we take to be true of it. So in describing the cup, its apparent features are expressed but, once again, not the cup. What would it be to "express the cup"?

A view of the cup is, in this respect, like the cup itself. It is not something that can be expressed. We can describe it all right, but there is no putting it into words. We can express this or that apparent feature of the cup, i.e., this or that aspect of a view of the cup, but not the cup. Here is where pictures come into their own. A view of an object cannot be expressed, put into words—but it can be pictured. (To say a picture is worth a thousand words does not go far enough.) This is what pictures are all about. Views of objects are what pictures are made for.

Of course, in picturing a view of an object, we picture apparent features of the object. But we must get the priority right. It is the features that are pictured in picturing the view, not the view that is pictured in picturing the features. The picture as such aims at the view. What we should say, strictly, is not that a picture pictures apparent features of an object, aspects of the view of the object, but that aspects of the picture picture aspects of the view. The picture as such pictures the view, aspects of which are pictured by aspects of the picture. This way of speaking properly aligns aspects with aspects.

Objects appear in experience both tactually and visually. Thus objects have both apparent tactual (it feels rough, round) and visual (it looks orange, round) features. So far, the tactual and visual cases are similar. If, however, we consider not apparent features of objects but views of objects, the two cases are different. Tactually, as opposed to visually, there seems to be no such thing as a view of an object. The point here is not just the utter triviality that tactually we do not see objects, but rather that there is no tactual counterpart to what in the visual case we call a "view" of an object. Consider our statement that the "way X appears" may mean either an apparent feature of X or a view of X. This statement holds only if we are talking about the way X visually appears.

This is what lies behind the conclusion reached in 15.1, that tactual appearing is not part of the phenomenology of the subject position. The way of appearing that makes a particular body "mine" is, we said, a "way of appearing" in the sense not of an apparent feature of that body but of a (kind of) view of it. Since there is no such thing as a tactual view of a body, the relevant way of appearing is not tactual but visual, viz., a view of the kind represented in Mach's picture. But let us consider more carefully the assertion that there is no such thing as a tactual view of a body.

One point is that objects do not present themselves tactually in the global, wide-screen way that they do visually.[7] Objects appear tactually bit by bit. Thus—except in the case of something very small—we cannot tactually determine the contour of an object all at once but must move our fingers over its surface. Suppose our vision were restricted so that objects appeared only to one eye through the tiny orifice of a closely fitting mask that we were not able to remove. We would then have to "move around" an object visually to determine its color. To determine its size and shape visually, we might in addition have to employ mathematical reasoning. However that may be, this much is plain. If we were thus visually restricted, we could not, visually, gain a view of an object.

However, the ability to take in an object in a global way is not sufficient for having a view of it. Imagine our tactual capacities augmented by an

[7] In this respect, I think O'Shaughnessy is correct to maintain that there is no "sensory field" in the tactual case. See *The Will*, chap. 6. See also Michael Martin's "Sight and Touch," in *The Contents of Experience*, ed. Tim Crane (Cambridge University Press, 1992). Martin, although he follows O'Shaughnessy in denying a tactual field analogous to the visual, distances himself (correctly, I think) from O'Shaughnessy's conception of the visual field in terms of visual sense data.

elastic tactile film, or net, attached to the fingers of one hand, which attachment we could spread over an object, or a part of it, to gain an impression of its shape. If we were thus equipped, more of an object's tactually apparent shape would be disclosed within our experience; but we would still not in this way gain a "view" of the object.

To see the point, compare the view of my body pictured in Mach's picture with the way my body might be disclosed within my experience were my tactual capacities enhanced in the manner just described. That my body presents within my experience the view in Mach's picture is, we are saying, part of what makes it "mine." Imagine I cover with my tactile cling film precisely the part of JV's body that appears in Mach's picture and thereby determine that it has such-and-such tactually apparent shape. Now imagine I cover another body in same way. It might turn out on this basis that the other body has the very same shape. Would that make it "my" body? Yet, we said, the fact that it presents the corresponding view within my experience makes JV's body "mine." I think the conclusion we ought to reach here is that we cannot identify its tactually apparent shape with a "view" of my body.

In that case, taking in an object in a global way, though necessary, is not sufficient for being presented with a view of the object. What more is needed? What do we have in the visual, but not the tactual, case that enables the way an object appears visually (but not tactually) to constitute a "view" of the object?

A view presupposes a point of view. And that point cannot be a point on the surface of the object of which the view is a view. A point on the surface of X may, certainly, be included *in* our view of X. But for that very reason it cannot be the point *from* which X is viewed. A point of view must in this sense be "detached" from the object of which we have the view.

Now an object can appear tactually within our experience only if we are in contact with the surface of the object. So in this case, it seems, we cannot get the kind of detachment that is necessary for a point of view. And without a *point of view* there is no *view*.

Tactually, we might say, an object appears at different points on its surface to have such-and-such features or qualities. At one point it appears smooth and flat, at another rough and curved. And so on. (Of course, "point" in this context is not to be understood in the mathematical sense, but means something like a small portion of the surface.) Given our actual capacities, the tactually apparent features of an object are disclosed to us, so to speak, point by point. If our capacities were augmented by, say, the acquisition of a tactile film, then the tactual disclosures within our experience would be much more extensive. An object would appear to have such-and-such features not at different "points" but (let us say) at different "areas" or "segments" of its surface. But, for all that, we would remain at (on) the surface of the object and thus, no matter how extensive the tactual disclosures of its features, we would not acquire the kind of detachment necessary for a point of view on an object. And, as we said, without a point of view there is no view.

An object may tactually appear within my experience one way or another, but the "way of appearing" will not be a view of the object; it will simply be a feature that the object appears to have. Tactually, then, there is no such thing as a "view" of an object. Reflection would, I submit, reach a similar conclusion (though in each case on different grounds) for the hearing, smell, and taste. We have no audial, olfactory, or gustatory views of objects, although objects appear as having features relevant to each sense. Views of objects, including ourselves, are thus limited to visual views. The only view of myself from within my experience is visual.

Yet, at least in the tactual case, this seems like a contingent limitation. We can imagine a different augmentation of our capacities from that contemplated above. A view presupposes a point of view and thus a certain "detachment" from the object of which it is a view. Suppose we develop "remote touch." We become sensitive to waves (perhaps, heat waves) emanating from objects in patterns analogous to light waves. So, in passing by an object, we might get different tactual "views" of the object. We might also acquire a tactual view of ourselves. What makes a particular body "mine" would in that case include not just a certain kind of visual, but a certain kind of tactual, view of that body from within my experience. As things are, however, there is no such thing as a tactual "view" of my body, or any other. As things are, then, there is a visual but not a tactual component to the phenomenology of the subject position.

This points to an underlying contingency in the positional conception of the self. The contingency stems from the fact that the content of the positional conception of the self is phenomenological, and the relevant phenomenology—the ways of figuring within the horizon in virtue of which a particular human being is "myself," the phenomenology of the subject position—depends (causally) on the powers or capacities, hence on the biology, of human beings. If the biology were different, the phenomenology would be different, and if the phenomenology were different, our self-conception might be different.

However, while the phenomenology of the subject position depends causally on our biology, insofar as our interest is in our self-conception, biology is irrelevant. It is not in terms of biology that we gain insight into what makes a particular human being (body) "myself" ("mine"). Whatever makes JV the human being that "I am," this is something I already grasp. What I already grasp are not facts of biology, but the special ways in which a certain human being (body) figures from within my horizon, the phenomenology of the subject position—which is there to be investigated quite independently of the underlying biological facts.

15.4 Centrality of Feeling: Figuring as the Space of Feeling

My body is the body that figures within my experience as the locus or (as we shall sometimes say) space of feeling. Figuring within my experience as the space of feeling is not merely unique to my body; it is, like the kind of visual appearance (view) represented in Mach's picture, part of what makes my body "mine," part of the phenomenology of the subject position. (Could any body that figures within my experience in this way, be anything but *my* body?) Yet, unlike perceptual centrality, figuring as the space or locus of feeling is not, as we shall explain, a way of appearing within my experience. Generally, not all ways of figuring within my experience are ways of appearing within my experience.

My body, JV's body, is a human body, and a human body is a body. My body is one among many bodies. From within my experience, however, it is unique. As a body, my body—like all bodies—*occupies* a space; from within my experience, however, my body uniquely *figures as* a space, the space of feeling. My body is both of these things: the self-same object both occupies, and figures within my experience as, a space. And this object is my body (myself, me, the human being that is me). My body occupies (I occupy) a space just like any other body. Yet my body figures within my experience in a way no other body figures.

The space that my body occupies is a space that any object, any body, could occupy. It in no way belongs to my body. The space that my body figures as, on the other hand, is, as Merleau-Ponty puts it, a space to which other bodies "have no access."[8] For there is no way of "having access" to the space that my body figures as (versus occupies) except by figuring within my experience as that space, the space of feeling; but any body that figured in that way would, for that reason, *be* "my" body. Figuring in that way, as the space or locus of feeling, is part of the phenomenology of the subject position, part of what makes my body "my" body. Yet the space occupied by my body is a space to which, in a sense, any body has access: any body, can, like my body, occupy this space. My body's access to the space of feeling within my experience is not by occupying it, but by figuring as that space.

---

[8] "My visual body is certainly an object as far as its parts far removed from my head are concerned, but as we come nearer to the eyes, it becomes divorced from objects, and reserves among them a quasi-space to which they have no access." *The Phenomenology of Perception*, p. 92.

Let us now point out a difference between this way of figuring within my experience—as the space or locus of feeling—with the way of figuring represented in Mach's picture. In the picture, my body visually appears within my experience in a way your body does not. The picture represents a kind of view of a human body that makes the body in question "mine." Of course my body visually appears in other ways as well, in ways that your body might appear within my experience. That is to say, not all the ways in which my body visually appears from within my in experience are part of the phenomenology of the subject position.

Hence the possibility of a certain type of comparison exists in this regard. We can compare the ways of visual appearing (the kinds of view) that make my body "mine," i.e., that belong to the phenomenology of the subject position, with other ways in which my body might visually appear from within my horizon, ways in which it could happen that bodies that are not "mine" might appear. In fact, where there are ways of appearing, the possibility of such comparisons seems to hold quite generally. If an object appears a certain way, it will in principle always be possible to specify alternatives, that is, similar but different ways of appearing. Ways of appearing, it would seem, always come as part of a set, or range, of alternative possible ways of appearing.

No such principle holds in the case of figuring within my experience as the locus, or space, of feeling. There is no way of a body's figuring within my experience that is similar to, and thus that can be compared with, figuring as the space of feeling other than that way of figuring itself. There is, in other words, no way of figuring that is similar to yet different from figuring as the space of feeling. So we have no relevant set of alternatives, no possibility of comparison. Think about it. What might the alternatives be? What might be ways of figuring within my experience that are similar to yet different from figuring as the space of feeling? We draw a blank here.

Consider the way of appearing, the view, within my experience that is represented by Mach's picture. It is easy to imagine alternatives, e.g., the head-on view, way of appearing, of my body that would show up in a mirror. I can, as it were, hold up this view and compare it with Mach's view, and note that the latter way of appearing, but not the former, is a way of appearing that makes my body "mine," that it is part of the phenomenology of the subject position. Can I do this with the way of figuring that is my body's figuring as the locus, or space, of feeling? Can I hold up an alternative, i.e., a similar but different, way of figuring within my experience about which I can then judge that, in contrast to the first way of figuring, the second way is not part of the phenomenology of the subject position? There is nothing to hold up, no second way of figuring to place alongside figuring within my experience as the space of feeling. This is a way my body has of figuring within my experience that has no alternatives. (It takes up the whole page.) What follows? It follows that this way of figuring is not a way of appearing.

My body appears within my experience as having such-and-such visual and tactual features, and in such-and-such views—which, as we noted, are restricted to visual appearing. But it does not *appear* within my experience as the space, or locus, of feeling. My body's figuring within my experience as the space of feeling is not a way of appearing.

Generally, the possibility of making comparisons presupposes a range of alternatives, i.e., of similar but different cases. (We compare shapes with shapes, colors with colors, but not shapes with colors.) But a range of alternatives is just what we lack in the case of figuring as the space of feeling. Comparisons are not possible here. The way my body visually appears within my experience is different from that of all other bodies. The point is, in figuring as the space of feeling, my body's way of figuring within my experience is not just different but *incomparably* different from that of all other bodies.

This point relates to the familiar assertion (in philosophy) that I know, or am aware of, my own body in two very different ways. I know my body "from the outside"—in the same way I know other bodies, say, your body—but also "from the inside." My body is the only body I know "from the inside." What are these two ways of knowing my body?

I know my body "from the outside" in that it appears (visually and tactually) within my experience. It appears in a way, in a view, that no other body appears; yet although my body is the only body that appears in that way, it is not the only body that appears within my experience. It is not, we might say, the only body that figures within my experience as a body that appears within my experience. My body is, however, the only body that figures within my experience as the space of feeling, and this, this way of figuring within my experience, is what we mean when we say I know my body in a way that I know no other body, that I know my body "from the inside." In this respect, there is nothing, no body, with which to compare my body.

15.5 The Centrality of Feeling: The Sense in Which the Space of Feeling (My Body-Space) Is a "Space"

The space of feeling is not literally a *space*. If it were literally a space, it would be something that any body can occupy. But no body, including my own, can occupy this space. (My body has access to the space of feeling by figuring as that space, not by occupying it.) Again, there is such a thing as the space of feeling only from within my experience. This cannot be said of what is literally a space.

Of course, since it exists only from within my experience, the space of feeling within my experience, my body-space, is not an external object. An external object, like my body, exists independently of whether it is present within my experience. It follows that my body-space cannot be identified with my body. My body *figures as* that space; but we cannot say that it *is* that space. Thus a part of my body might disappear while my body-space remains intact (the phantom limb phenomenon); conversely, it is compatible with my body remaining intact that part of my body-space might disappear. Note, too, whereas a part of my body-space might disappear, this is not possible with what is literally a part of space. My body might disappear, but not the space occupied by my body. In sum, the space of feeling within my experience, my body-space, is neither the space my body occupies nor my body itself, the external object.

External objects, objects whose existence is independent of presence within experience, contrast with internal objects, objects whose existence is exhausted by their presence within experience. Hence, internal objects exist only from within experience. Might we then view the space of feeling within my experience, my body-space, as a kind of internal object?

The two main examples of internal objects (at any rate, the examples philosophers usually mention) are afterimages and sensations. Clearly, the space of feeling is unlike an afterimage. An afterimage is an object, or item, that seems to have a location outside the space of feeling within my experience, i.e., outside my body-space. Thus we may say of an afterimage that it seems to be "on the wall," "hovering over the door frame," etc. In fact, since it exists only within my experience, an afterimage is not at any point in space. Afterimages are not located in space; yet, insofar as they seem to be located in space, they have a kind of spatiality. But then, insofar as the space in which they seem to be located is outside my body-space, there can be no question of identifying my body-space with anything like an afterimage.

The obstacle to identifying my body-space with a sensation is, in a way, just the reverse. Sensations—pains, tingles, itches, aches, tickles, and so on—are always located inside my body-space, inside the space of feeling. This space, then, cannot be a sensation. A sensation cannot be located inside a sensation.

A tingling sensation (say), like an afterimage, exists only from within my experience; but unlike an afterimage, it exists within my body-space (the afterimage exists within my experience but outside my body-space). Since my body-space exists only from within my experience, with sensations, in contrast to afterimages, there is a double internality. An afterimage, although it exists within experience, is in a real sense "nowhere": it is not in my body-space nor in space (it only seems to be in space). A sensation, on the other hand, is "somewhere," and, moreover, just where it seems to be. Not at a particular point in space, but at a particular point in the space of feeling within my experience, at a particular point in my body-space.

The space of feeling within my experience, my body-space (or, as it is often called, my body-image)—the space that cannot be identified either with my body or with the space occupied by my body but which my body figures as—this space, we have said, is neither an external nor an internal object. In fact, since it exists only from within my experience, it is not literally a space. That is, it is not part of space proper. Perhaps, then, we should ask what justifies speaking here of a "space" at all.

The only justification could be that, despite the fact that my body-space exists only from within my experience, in certain respects it resembles space proper. Thus what we should expect to find are partial analogies, partial similarities, between my body-space and space proper. Let us briefly mention three such analogies.

The first concerns "connectedness." In the case of space proper, connectedness consists in the possibility of continuous movement from any one part to any another. There may be obstacles, but in principle these could be overcome. All the parts (and the parts of such parts) of space proper are connected.[9] Is there not an analogous connectedness in the case of the parts of my body-space?

Imagine a tickle in the palm of my left hand and, simultaneously, a tickle in the palm of my right hand. Each hand occupies its own bit of space proper, and from each of these bits of space it is possible to move to the other. We could connect them by a string. Of course, movement along the string would be movement in space proper, not in my body-space. But we can imagine a sensation moving in my body-space. We can imagine, say, the tickle in my right hand moving continuously up my left arm, across my chest, down my left arm, etc., until it reaches the sensation in the palm of my right hand. This is the body-space analogue of connectedness.

Notice, when we refer to the imagined movement as "up my arm," "across my chest," and so on, we are not referring to, or describing, a movement on the surface of my body—like a fly crawling over me. We refer to my body by way of referring to parts of my body-space, in order to describe a movement in my body-space.

As we said, we can expect to find only a partial analogy here. Connectedness in body-space is not connectedness in space. In the case of space,

[9] In this context, we have of course left the dream hypothesis behind us. But it might be worth recalling that if THIS were a dream, although the parts of the space outside THIS, outside the dream, would be connected with one another, they would not be connected with the parts of the space spreading out around me, since, as we explained (1.5), there would be no such thing as a continuous movement from inside to outside the dream.

any two parts not only are connected, they must be connected: it must be possible (in principle) for a single object to move continuously from one part to the other. There is no corresponding guarantee in the case of my body-space. Thus we can imagine a band, or corridor, of nonfeeling cutting across (as it were) the space of feeling. We can imagine, say, a band of nonfeeling just below my elbow, say, and encompassing a cross-section of my body-space at that point. In that case, the continuous movement of the sensation from the palm of my left hand, up my arm, etc., would be interrupted at this point, and whether or not we are prepared to count as the movement of "the same sensation" a sensation-movement that begins on the other side of the gap, we would have lost the possibility of a continuous movement. Clearly, the break, the discontinuity, would be inside my body-space.

Again, assuming it is infinite, for any part of space proper, no matter how inclusive, there will always be further part with which it is connected. Imagine a sensation moving in my body-space in a certain direction. It cannot keep moving endlessly in that direction. Viewed this way, my body-space, like a part of space of proper, is finite. On the other hand, there is no further body-space, no space outside my body-space, that stands to my body-space in the way a further part of space proper always stands to any given part of space proper. (Other body-spaces are not accessible from within mine.) So there is no possibility of a movement that starts inside my body-space and continues to a point outside my body-space. On this basis, my body-space resembles an infinite space, like space proper.

A second (partial) analogy between space proper and body-space relates to "positionality." In any part of space proper there is, given that there are objects located at some of the positions within that space, the possibility of establishing a unified system of positions. Insofar as we have a unified system, items located at different positions can be related to one another. Thus the bodies in this room all occupy positions within the room and thereby stand to each other in various spatial relations. For example, they are at such-and-such distance from one another, or lie on the same straight line, or between objects on the same line. Similarly, we locate sensations at positions in body-space, in my right calf, my left knee, at the center of my back, and so on. And by virtue of their positions, the items (sensations) thus located stand, at least in a vague and rough way, in various relations. Thus it would be unproblematic to describe the tingling in my foot as "closer" to the feeling in my calf than to the ache in my shoulder, and that the feeling in my calf is "between" the tingling and the ache.

However, the vagueness of these characterizations is not a matter of laziness on my part—as if, were I to apply myself, I might be able to achieve greater precision. In body-space, the relations are (we might say) essentially vague. Whereas in space proper we can measure distances between items, line them up, calculate angles, etc., we have no way of measuring the distance between the items dispersed in my body-space; nor can we really place them on a straight (or curved, or any other shaped) line, or calculate angles, and so on.[10] Certainly, we can draw lines and measure distances *on* my body. Hence we can draw lines, and measure the distances, between the points on my body to which I refer by way of referring to the sensations in my body-space. But, we know, my body-space, the space of feeling within my experience, cannot be identified with my body. Nor with the space my body occupies. My body-space is not the space my body occupies but the space it figures as—a space that exists only from within my experience.

Third, the essential vagueness that affects distance in my body-space is even more pronounced with respect to size and shape; accordingly, any analogy that we might draw in this respect will be even weaker. Yet there is an analogy. My head, say, occupies a certain measurable volume of space, and this volume has a definite shape. If my head grew bigger, it would occupy a greater volume of space, and the increase could be measured. If my head changed its shape, we could devise (with diagrams, say) a way of precisely representing the change.

Now, such changes in my head, and in the space occupied by my head, would not entail corresponding changes in the part of my body-space that we refer to via my head. They would not entail that I feel my head to be larger, or a different shape. Yet it does not seem wild to suppose that, if my head did grow larger, or change its shape, there would be a change in how things felt, a change that I would be prepared to describe as a change in the size and shape of the relevant part of my body-space. What would the changes be? In the case of size, I might say that it has "expanded." By how much? Of course this is just what I cannot say. Did my head, to begin with, feel a particular size? All I can say is that it feels "larger." In the case of shape, I would be equally at a loss. My head does not feel this as opposed to that shape—it just feels the way it feels.[11] Yet it seems we can imagine its feeling a "different" shape.

In fact, the kind of essentially vague changes we are imagining in a part of my body-space could occur without any change in the relevant part of my body, or in the space occupied by that part of my body; just as there might be changes in my body without any change in the relevant part of my body-space. This highlights, once again, that we are dealing with different "spaces."

---

[10] See O'Shaughnessy, *The Will*, pp. 198, 224.
[11] See ibid., p. 224.

15.6 Centrality of Feeling: The Ontological Dependence of My Body-Space on My Body

I remember as a graduate student hearing one of my teachers remark that if there is a pain in your hand and you put your hand in the oven, it does not follow that there is a pain in the oven.[12] The point, as I understood it (and still do), is not that an oven is not the sort of thing that can suffer a pain, but that a sensation is not the sort of thing that is literally located in a part of the body. If it were, its location would be transitive in the following sense: if X is in Y and Y is in Z, X is in Z. A marble you are holding in your hand is literally "in (on the surface of, or perhaps enclosed by)" your hand. Thus, if a marble is in your hand and your hand is in the oven, there is a marble in the oven. The fact that this kind of transitivity does not hold in the case of sensations means that a sensation is not literally "in" this or that part of my body; in particular, in the part of my body to which we refer in locating the sensation.[13] In that case, where is it? It is in my body-space, in the space of feeling within my horizon (experience).

How then can it be that we refer to the location (place) of a sensation by pointing or otherwise referring to a place, etc., in/on my body, which is in space proper? How, i.e., if the space of feeling, that wherein the sensation is located, exists only from within my experience and is thus not part of space proper? I have this pulsating ache. "Where?" "Around here." I outline an area on my right shoulder. This is, after all, how we indicate "the location (place) of a sensation": by pointing, or somehow referring, to a place in/on the body. There is no other way. Yet the place of the sensation is not literally in/on my body but within my body-space.

It might be said that locating sensations by reference to my body is just part of the language-game (concept) of sensations. But then precisely this, this feature of the language-game, may seem puzzling. That is, once we

---

[12] It was either (I am not sure) Robert Coburn or Fred Siegler. This was back in the 1960s. The argument has been discussed by Ned Block in "Mental Pictures and Cognitive Science," *Philosophical Review*), 1983, and Michael Tye, "A Representational Theory of Pains and Their Phenomenal Character," in *Philosophical Perspectives*, vol. 9, ed. J. Tomberlin (Ridgeview, 1990). (I am indebted to James Tartaglia for drawing these papers to my attention.)

[13] O'Shaughnessy gives the nice example of a cyclist with a toothache to make the point (*The Will*, p. 183). We could develop this as follows. Imagine the cyclist has just gone by. Now, as part of some investigation, there might arise the need to establish the precise path traversed by the cyclist's head, or jaw. In principle we could do this, and perhaps mark out the path by a suspended piece of wire. Then we could run our fingers over the wire and say that the person's jaw moved "right along here," that at time t it was "right here," and so on. Would we wish to say this sort of thing about the person's toothache, the pain in his jaw?

reflect that the space in which sensations are located, the space of feeling within my experience, my body-space, cannot be identified with either my body or the part of space proper occupied by my body, it may seem puzzling that a sensation should be located via a reference to my body, that our language-game offers us no other way of locating a sensation.

Here we must recall that although my body occupies a bit of space proper, it figures within my experience as the space of feeling; this is part of what makes it "my" body. There is an obvious sense, then, in which the space of feeling within my experience, my body-space, *depends* on a body: if there were no body that figured as the space of feeling within my experience, there would be no space of feeling within my experience. Why? Because that space, my body-space, just is the space within my experience that a particular body figures as—and, in thus figuring, is "my" body.

Maybe an analogy will help us grasp the kind of dependence that is involved here. Suppose, in a given performance of "Hamlet," there is no actor playing the character of Fortinbras. Then, in that performance, there is no Fortinbras. Without an actor playing the character in a performance of the play, the character cannot occur in that performance. Yet the actor and the character in the performance of the play are not one and the same: the actor has a life outside the play. The dependence of my body-space on my body has a similar structure. If within my experience there is no body figuring as the space of feeling (and thereby as "my" body), then, within my experience, there is no space of feeling. Without the body figuring as the space, there is no space of feeling. Yet my body-space and my body are not one and the same: my body-space, in contrast to my body, exists only from within my experience.

In light of the foregoing, we might say that my body-space is "ontologically dependent" on my body. My body is the particular entity in the world that figures as my body-space. It, this worldly entity, figures as my body-space though my body-space, since it exists only from within my experience, is not itself part of the world. Insofar as my body and body-space are related in this way, my body-space is ontologically dependent on my body. My body-space, then, is ontologically dependent on the very object that, by virtue of figuring as that space, figures as "my" body. The self-same space, my body-space, both confers "mineness," and is ontologically dependent, on my body.

My body-space, moreover, is the space in which sensations are located. Given, then, the ontological dependence of my body-space on my body, if there were no such thing as my body, there would be no space in which to locate sensations. Perhaps what may otherwise seem puzzling— viz., that despite the fact that sensations are not literally located in my body, they are located by reference to my body; indeed, that there is and can be no other way of locating of a sensation—perhaps, this will now make sense.

The point about ontological dependence may also provide some insight into the much discussed phantom limb phenomenon. I have a pain, say, in my right forearm. Without telling me what they are up to, the doctors put me to sleep and amputate the arm at the elbow. When I awake, and before apprising me of what has happened (I am on my back and cannot see), they ask me how the pain is. "It is still there." "Where?" "Right where it was before." "Show us." "Right here." In saying this, I innocently point with my left hand to a place occupied by nothing but bed covers, etc.

In what way am I mistaken, or under an illusion? I believe my arm is still whole. I am mistaken about that. Am I mistaken about the pain? Surely not about the fact that there is a pain. It might be thought, however, that I am mistaken about its location. No. I will be surprised to learn that there is now nothing where part of my arm was before, but the pain, as I report, is "right where it was before." Would I, when I learn about my arm, retract this? ("Well, that is where the pain was the last time I looked.") Where is the pain? It is just where it feels to be (where else?): at a certain point in my body-space.[14]

But note, whereas learning about my arm would not affect my judgment that the pain is "right where it was before," I would be reluctant to repeat my pointing gesture, etc. I would not now point to the place where, had it not been amputated, my forearm would have been and assert that the pain is "right here." In the phantom limb case, the body that figures within my experience as the space of feeling, my body, is diminished; thus the space that my body occupies is diminished. However, the space that my body *figures as*, my body-space, is (or so we may imagine) undiminished. This, we know, entails that my body and my body-space cannot be identified. Then why the reluctance to point? The purpose of pointing in this case would be to indicate the location of the pain, and that was always (and still is) in my body-space. If my body-space is not my body, why should the absence of part of my body embarrass the pointing?

True, the purpose of pointing would be to locate the sensation by indicating a part of my body-space. But given the ontological dependence of my body-space on my body, there is no way to indicate a part of my body-space by pointing except by pointing to a part of my body; to the part, viz., that figures in my experience as the part of my body-space I wish to

[14] Even so-called referred pain is where it feels to be; the surprising thing about referred pain is not the location of the pain in my body-space but the location in my body of the cause of the pain.

indicate. If that part of my body is missing, then, of course, I cannot by pointing to *it* indicate the relevant part of my body-space. And there is, in this regard, nothing else to which I might point.

We might say that in the phantom limb case, whereas my body-space remains intact, the loss of part of my body deprives me of demonstrative access to a part of my body-space. More generally, I am deprived of direct referential access to the relevant part of my body-space. Thus I could not indicate where the pain is by saying that it is "in my right forearm." Of course, we are not totally without resources in this regard. For example, I might ask you to imagine that I still had my arm and that it was in such-and-such position, and then (pointing) add that "this is where I would point to show you where the pain is," or indicate the location in my body-space by reference (say) to the elbow of the imagined arm.

15.7 Volitional Centrality: Acting/Will and the Phenomenology of the Subject Position

Let us turn now to the third part, or aspect, of the phenomenology of the subject position: will. The general idea is that certain of my movements figure from within my experience in a way that the movements of no other human being figure, viz., as "willed," as "actions," i.e., as "actively done by me," and that by virtue of figuring in this way the movements in question are "mine," i.e., movements of the body that is "mine," of the human being that is "me." Of course, there are many questions here. What is "will"? What is to it "do" something, to "act"? When I act with my body, something happens, but "acting" is not (as they say) a "mere happening"? What is it then? What kind of a phenomenon is "acting"? If it involves something more than a "mere happening," what is the "something more"? Philosophers agonize about these and related questions, about (we might say) the metaphysics of will. Our concern here is limited to the phenomenology of will, to the way of figuring within my experience that makes a bodily movement "mine," and thus a certain body "mine," in other words, to will (action, active doing) insofar as it is part of the phenomenology of the subject position.[15]

The movements of a certain human body (human being), JV, figure within my experience as willed, as actions. To be an action, to be willed, just is to figure in this way. That JV's movements figure this way, as willed,

[15] A discussion of some of the metaphysical issues about will, such as the problem of free will, was, for reasons of length, dropped from the original version of the present work. I hope to publish this material elsewhere.

makes JV (JV's body) "me (mine)." An action need not figure within my experience as willed. Your actions do not figure within my experience as willed, as actions. Certainly I take—directly, without any inferring or interpreting, etc.—the movements of your body to be, by and large, actions. This means that I take your movements to figure within your experience as willed. Notice: I take your movements as actions; from within my experience, they do not actually *figure as* actions, as willed.

Can it be denied that, from within my experience, my movements figure in a way that is utterly different from the way your movements figure? You and I simultaneously reach for the cup. Your action appears (visually) within my experience. So, let us assume, does mine. And they differ in the way they appear, in the kind of view I have of them. But is there not a further difference? My action but not yours figures within my experience as willed, as an action.

In this example, your action, like mine, appears within my experience. It is on the basis of its figuring within my experience in this way, on the basis of the way it appears within my experience, that I directly take your movement to figure within your experience as willed; hence, that I take it to be an action. But whereas your action appears within my experience, and whereas on that basis I take it to figure within your experience as willed, it does not figure within my experience as willed.

What about my actions? Do I directly take my actions to figure within my experience as willed, as actions? No. Neither, obviously, do I take my actions to figure as not (other than) willed. There is no "taking" in my own case. My actions *simply figure* within my experience as willed, as actions. And so they are actions. This (we are saying) is all there is to being an action: figuring as willed: figuring as an action. And figuring this way makes an action (the bodily movement that thereby is an action) "my" action and thus the body (human being) whose movement it is "my" body (the human being that "I am"). This is how will enters the phenomenology of the subject position.

As before, since the phenomenology defines the positional conception of the self, it has counterfactual implications. In the actual case, JV's body is the body whose actions figure within my experience as actions (willed). So it, JV's body, is "my" body (JV is "me"). Had it been a different body whose actions figured within my experience as willed, then that body would have been "my" body. I would have had a different body. What does this mean? Not, clearly, that JV would have had a different body, but that a different human body would, by virtue of the fact that its actions figured within my experience as willed, have occupied the subject position within my experience, that a different human body (human being) would have been "mine (me)."

15.8 Volitional Centrality: The Phenomenology of Will

Let us start with the point that figuring within my experience as willed, as active, is not a way of appearing—any more than figuring within my experience as the space of feeling, as my body-space, is a way of appearing. A way of appearing, we said, can always be compared with other ways of appearing, and the possibility of comparison presupposes a range of alternatives (15.4). We can compare, then, the way my body and your body appear within my experience. In the case of my body's figuring as my body-space, the space of feeling, there are no alternatives. From within my experience your body does figure as the space of feeling in a different way from the way my body figures as the space of feeling; it simply does not figure as the space of feeling. The difference here is, as we put it, incomparable. The same incomparability exists in the case of will. Your actions and my actions can both appear within my experience, and thus differ in the way they appear. But they do not differ in the way they are willed, since from within my experience, your actions do not in any way figure as willed. Your actions and mine are in this respect incomparably different.

But what is it to figure as willed? I reach for the cup. The movement appears visually within my experience and figures as willed. Can we say anything about the difference between these two ways of figuring within my experience?

There is a certain possibility of continuity in the appearing of an action that is absent in the case of will. We might formulate the difference like this. Whereas it is always at least possible that, within my experience, the appearing of a bodily action "unfolds out of" the prior appearing of my body, or some part of my body, there is nothing out of whose prior figuring as willed the willing, the acting, might unfold. On the contrary, it belongs to figuring as willed that what figures this way figures as "breaking into" my experience—out of nothing. For example, it is possible that my arm first visually appears motionless and then, without any break or discontinuity in the appearing of my arm, appears as reaching. Of course, when I act in this way my arm need not appear at all within my experience. But it is hard to deny that it might have appeared and hence that the possibility for this kind of continuity must be there. After all, the action is a movement of my body, and my body does not spring into being when I act. Hence the relevant part of my body might appear within my experience both before and during my action, in which case the appearing of my action would (as we are expressing it) unfold out of the appearing of my body.

Seeking an analogous continuity in the case of will, we might suppose that, for any bodily movement *m* on my part that figures as willed, there is a prior such movement, a prior action, out of which *m*'s figuring as willed unfolds. But clearly, there need not be any relevant action prior to m. I am sitting motionless, inactive; then I reach for the cup. There is no movement out of whose figuring as willed the figuring as willed of my act of reaching unfolds.[16]

You could say, the only such movement that there must be in this case is *m* itself. But *m* cannot serve as something out of whose figuring as willed *m*'s figuring as willed unfolds—unless we suppose that *m*'s figuring as willed might unfold out of itself.

But now it might strike us that the idea of "unfolding out of itself" is just what we are looking for, that it captures perfectly the phenomenology of will. In that case, the phenomenology of will is radically different from the phenomenology of the appearing of an action. If in figuring as willed, *m* figures as unfolding out of itself, this is evidently at odds with the potential for continuity that must exist in the case of *m*'s appearing. What "unfolds out of itself" within my experience constitutes something new, something that "breaks into" my experience.

Perhaps there is a way of repairing the analogy between appearing and will. Suppose I deliberate about whether to reach and decide to act, to reach, in a few seconds' time. So, now I intend (mean, aim, etc.) to reach. What is this—intending to reach? It might be said that, phenomenologically, intending is akin to doing. For what we intend is precisely to do something, to act. In intending to reach (say) for a particular ball, I, the human being that I am, figure within my experience as "heading toward" the performance of an action, a reaching for the ball. Now clearly, this is not a way in which the human being that I am *appears* within my experience. Intending is a way of figuring that belongs, phenomenologically, not to the sphere of appearing but to that of will. Just as the appearing of my act of reaching unfolds, or may unfold, out of the appearing of my body, the suggestion is that my action's figuring as willed may unfold out of the

---

[16] No doubt the example is artificially simple. We have chosen a single, easily individuable movement (the movement of my arm) that, in the context assumed, can be described as figuring within my experience as willed. If you think of what I do with my body in walking, or writing, or sawing a plank, or eating a sandwich, or loading groceries at the supermarket, and so on, it is not obvious how, or whether, we can divide up my activity up into individual movements that can be described in this way (figuring as willed). But the phenomenological point remains. However we divide up my activity on a given occasion, or if we take it as a whole, insofar as we have individuated something that figures within my experience as willed, we have individuated something whose figuring as willed is independent of any prior figuring as willed. So, for the purposes of getting the phenomenology right, it will not matter if we stick to our simple example.

figuring of the human being that I am as "heading toward" reaching, out of intending to reach.

The analogy fails. Whereas, for any bodily movement, there must exist the possibility of its appearing out of the prior appearing of my body, there need be no prior intending. Without first intending to do so, I reach out. Just like that. Without "heading toward" acting, I simply act. This makes sense phenomenologically. It is a possibility that belongs to the phenomenology of will.

More fundamentally, in whatever way it is akin to acting, intending to act is not acting. In "heading toward" reaching, the reaching movement does not yet figure as willed. How could it? There *is* no such movement. The fact of will, that the movement of my arm figures as willed, this is not more of the same but something new within my experience. Thus there is in this respect no continuity but rather a break within my experience. Willing, that is to say, a movement's figuring within my experience as willed, does not unfold out of anything prior within my experience. It unfolds out of itself.

Again, in reaching, my arm (let us assume) first appears as not moving, then as moving. This is a change in the way my arm appears. But if first I intend to move my arm and then move it, this most certainly is not a change in my intentions. Rather, I have *ceased* intending. I *act*. That is to say, the movement of my arm figures within my experience as willed. This active way of figuring is not a different way of intending but (as we said) something new.

Figuring as willed is figuring as self-unfolding. But this is not sufficiently precise. Recall the cartoonlike disappearance of parts of my body imagined in 12.5. I am looking at my arm. I intend to reach for the cup. But I do not succeed in doing this. My arm suddenly disappears. Out of the blue. Now consider the possibility of my arm suddenly reaching out in the same out-of-the-blue way that it might suddenly disappear. I am about to reach when, surprisingly, my arm reaches out. In this case, the movement of my arm does not figure as willed, as active. Yet it might not be evident why the movement should not be said to figure as "self-unfolding."

One might suggest, in the sudden, out-of-the-blue case the movement is not something I actively do. Exactly. But this just means that the movement does not figure within my experience as an act, as willed, which is what we are trying to capture. Is it perhaps the suddenness of what happens within my experience that disqualifies it as willed? No, however suddenly my arm might move out of the blue, I might act, will, just as suddenly.

What is the difference between the two cases of "self-unfolding"? To answer the question we need to look away from the cases themselves and reflect on the attitudes, or ways of being (as we shall call them), that are possible, that make sense, in each case—phenomenological possibilities in which they are embedded.

Intending is an attitude, a way of being, that has its own phenomenology. In intending, there is a way that I, the human being that I am, figure from within my horizon: a way that is, for example, manifestly different from my appearing from within my horizon. Intending is an attitude, a way of being, in which I "head toward" something. Toward what? Toward action, toward doing something. Intending makes sense only where the prospect in view is the prospect of acting, the prospect of something figuring as willed. Thus we can distinguish the kind of self-unfolding essential to the phenomenology of will by saying it is the kind of self-unfolding toward which the attitude of intending makes sense. Might I *intend* an out-of-the-blue extending of my arm? If that were the prospect, would the attitude of intending, that way of being, make sense (phenomenologically)?

Notice, just as in order to grasp the phenomenology of intending we must see that intending is an attitude that makes sense only as an attitude, a way of being, toward acting, toward figuring as willed, in order to grasp the phenomenology of will, in particular, to grasp the kind of self-unfolding that this involves, we need to see that the kind of self-unfolding we are trying to grasp is that toward which the attitude of intending makes sense. Of course, moving back and forth this way between the phenomenology of will and intending will not yield a conventional-style "analysis" or "definition" of either will or intending. But that is not our aim. Our aim is to gain some insight into the phenomenology of will, and the aim is served by placing the latter in a picture of interdependent elements. I do not think we can expect more than this. Giving an "analysis" of will, that is, identifying independent elements that then noncircularly *add up* to the particular way of figuring within experience that we are calling "figuring as willed," presupposes a kind of atomism that is foreign to phenomenology—to that of will or anything else.

But there is more to the picture. Imagine that the same kind of out-of-the-blue arm moving, the kind that cannot be intended, repeats itself in a few seconds, and then again, and again, at regular intervals. So now I expect it to happen in about two seconds. This time we cannot say that I am "surprised," or that the event occurs "out of the blue." I expect it. What exactly do I expect? An appearing (and, perhaps, certain sensations): I expect that my arm will move and the movement will appear within my experience. Expecting is a way of being that makes sense here. Expecting makes sense, but not intending. In fact, precisely because expecting makes sense, intending does not makes sense. And if intending were in order, expecting would be out of place. These are ways of being that, phenomenologically speaking, seem to get in each other's way.[17]

Thus we might distinguish the kind of self-unfolding that does not belong to the phenomenology of will by saying that it is the kind toward which the attitude of expecting makes sense.

Consider the possibility of surprise. It does not make sense (phenomenologically) that, when I straightforwardly act, this should come as a surprise. Reaching with my arm may have all sorts of surprising aspects and consequences, but it cannot surprise me that I *act*, that the movement of my arm figures within my experience as willed.[18] However, if the movement figures in the other self-unfolding way, the way that contrasts with the kind of self-unfolding that characterizes figuring as willed, this fact may be surprising. It need not be surprising (if it starts happening regularly, it will not be surprising); but there is in this case the possibility of surprise. So we can say, to distinguish the kind of self-unfolding that does not belong to the phenomenology of will, that there is in this case the possibility of surprise.

Let us briefly observe how these points about surprise fit into, and make sense within, the larger phenomenological picture. Surprise presupposes the attitude of expecting: we can be surprised at something only if it contradicts an expectation (either a specific or a general expectation). Now, toward something that figures as willed, and only toward this, the attitude of intending makes sense (phenomenologically). But if intending makes sense, expecting does not, since, as we remarked, these attitudes get in the way of each other. And surprise presupposes expecting. Hence where something figures willed, surprise does not make sense phenomenologically.

Again, in the case where surprise makes sense, it also makes sense that we should have the attitude of "waiting to see" whether the event in question happens. Is this an attitude I can maintain toward my own actions, i.e., toward what figures within my experience as willed? I can, of course, wait to see whether you will act. Indeed, I might be on tenterhooks about

---

[17] Of course it is also true that if I intend to φ I in some sense expect to φ (believe that I will φ). We might speak of a "practical expectation." The relevant contrast is between an expectation that is independent of, and that which is parasitic upon, intention. Whereas a practical expectation is parasitic upon intention, the incompatibility of expectation and intention alluded to in the text assumes that we are talking about expectation that is independent of intention. (If we were striving for an "analysis" here, this would land us in circularity.)

[18] Can I not "surprise myself" with a bold or foolhardy, etc., action? Of course we talk this way, and in doing so we point to a real possibility. But however real the possibility is, surprise at my own actions *differs* from surprise at the actions of others—just as feeling sorry myself, knowing myself, lying to myself, differs from feeling sorry for others, and so on.

whether you will act. Might I be on tenterhooks about whether I will act? Phenomenologically, waiting to see is a kind of "holding back." How can one simultaneously "hold back" and *act*? "Holding back" is at odds with acting—at odds with the phenomenology of will.

Or consider surprise and, as we might express it, the absence of will. It would seem that if figuring within my experience as willed cannot come as a surprise, neither can refraining from acting, or simply not acting. What can come as a surprise, however, is that I have lost the ability to act. But it is important here to separate two different cases.

Case One: Something has gone wrong in my nervous or muscular systems affecting my hand. I do not realize this: everything feels normal. I then try to perform some simple action and discover that I cannot do it. I am surprised. Case Two: I have (for whatever neurological reasons) no feeling in my hand. My hand just dangles there, like dead meat. This part of my body is, at least temporarily, lost to my body-space. So I cannot act with it, I cannot (say) close my fingers. In this case, however, there is no surprise. I already know that the possibility of acting is lost to me. The knowledge is reflected in the fact that, in such a case, I cannot (as we earlier remarked) even *try* to act.

What lies behind the difference between these two cases is that whereas phenomenological facts about my body, facts about how my body figures within my experience, are as such apparent within my experience, causal facts about my body, not being phenomenological facts about my body, are not as such apparent within my experience. Thus if (Case Two) part of my body becomes lost to my body-space and is thereby beyond the scope of my will—that is, such that its movements cannot figure within my experience as willed—this fact cannot but be apparent within my experience: I know in advance that I cannot act with the relevant part of my body. In contrast, assuming my body-space remains intact, a causal breakdown in a bodily system that supports action (Case One), not being as such something that figures within my experience, is not as such apparent within my experience. This means I may not know in advance that I have lost the ability to act. I may be surprised.[19]

[19] Hume's man who is "suddenly struck down with a palsy in the arm or leg . . . . [and who] endeavors, at first, to move them" is surprised that he cannot do so. Hume's point is that whether I have "power" over this or that limb of my body is not something that is apparent a priori within my experience. (Such a "power" is not, as Hume says, something of which I am "conscious": "We learn the influence of our will from experience alone.") This seems correct, if the point is confined to knowledge of my "powers" insofar as they depend on causal facts about my body; at least, causal facts that do not affect my body-space. But once we bring my body-space into the picture and take account of the way this limits what can figure within my experience as willed, it seems we have the basis for a kind of negative a priori knowledge about my "powers." *An Inquiry Concerning Human Understanding*, section 7, p. 77.

OK. We have focused in some detail on a narrow set of interconnected possibilities and impossibilities. I hope it will be evident that we could easily expand the compass of our reflections to include such things as choosing, acting for a purpose (reason), deliberating, being unsure what to do, worrying about what to do, deciding what to do, changing one's mind, carrying out (or failing to carry out) a decision, giving up a decision, giving in to (resisting) temptation, regretting what one has done, and so on. For example, only what figures as willed can be purposeful (have an end or reason in view), or be decided or deliberated upon. Again, if I confidently believe that φ'ing is impossible, or if I believe that I will φ, I cannot deliberate about whether to φ, or make up my mind to φ, or change my mind about whether to φ. This network of possibilities/impossibilities—which exists only from within the personal horizon—informs practical life. And at the very center of the network, at the center of practical life, is will, active doing.

In sum, to get clear about will, about active doing, is to get clear about a certain way of figuring within the personal horizon. And to get clear about this, about the phenomenology of will, is to get clear about the place of will in a network of possibilities, etc., internal to the personal horizon, about the place of will within practical life.[20]

15.9 Volitional Centrality: The "Mineness" of My Actions

Our problem was to distinguish the self-unfolding essential to will from that which is foreign to will. Perhaps we might speak of "active" versus "nonactive" self-unfolding. In the active case, it makes sense (phenomenologically) to maintain the attitude of intending, but not expecting; hence surprise does not make sense here. In the nonactive case, expecting and therefore surprise make sense; hence intending does not make sense. Of course, as we stressed, remarks of this sort cannot claim to provide an "analysis" of will; our aim is rather to adumbrate an encompassing phenomenological picture of which will is the core element. The relevance of these reflections to the phenomenology of the subject position is straightforward: this way of figuring within my experience, figuring as willed, as actively self-unfolding, and so on, is what makes a movement "my" movement, i.e., a movement of my body, of the human being that I am. My bodily actions are "mine" simply by virtue of being movements

---

[20] It is, we might say, to get clear about the place of will within what John McDowell (in his book *Mind and World* [Harvard University Press, 1994]), has called "the space of reasons." I discuss McDowell's views on action in the material alluded to in note 15.

that figure within my horizon as willed—by virtue of being, from within my horizon, actions.

Does this not seem right? Could any movement that figures within my experience in the way *this* movement figures—any movement, that is, that figures in the actively self-unfolding way that we have been trying to capture by reference to its place in practical life—fail to be "mine," a movement of "my" body? In that case, the body (the human being, JV) whose movement it is, is "mine (me)." Figuring as the locus of will is, clearly, part of the phenomenology of the subject position.

It is also true that a movement might be "mine" by virtue of the way it appears within my experience. Notice the difference in priority here. My body is "mine" because it is the body whose actions, or movements, figure within my experience in a way that makes them "my" actions, viz., as willed (self-unfolding). In the case of appearing, it is the other way around: my movements appear in a way that makes them "mine" only if they appear as the movements of the body whose way of appearing makes it "mine."

A movement that figures within my experience as willed, as an action, is thereby "mine." Your movements cannot figure this way within my experience. They can, however, appear within my experience. Thus if our limbs are entangled in the right way, I might, on the basis of the way it appears within my experience, mistake a movement of your body for a movement of my body. Now we said that, in terms of appearing, what makes a certain body "mine" is its appearing within my experience in a unique kind of view (the kind of view represented by Mach's picture). If its way of appearing within my experience is to make a movement "mine," and thus exclude the sort of mistake just envisioned, the movement must appear, that is, come into view within my experience, as a movement of the uniquely appearing body. In coming into view as a movement of the uniquely appearing body, it comes into view as a movement of "my" body.

I close my hand. Let us assume that this movement, this action, appears within my experience in a way that makes it "my" action. The same movement at the same time figures within my experience in a totally different way, as actively self-unfolding, as willed; and this other way of figuring, this too makes the movement "mine." The action is "mine," so to speak, twice over: by virtue of appearing in a certain way, and, entirely independently of the way it appears, by virtue of figuring as willed.

How does my body-space come into this? The will, as we have observed (14.4), is confined to my body-space: only the movement of what figures as part of my body-space can figure within my experience as willed. But what figures as part of my body-space is thereby part of "my" body; its movement is thereby "my" movement. So, if the movement also appears within my experience in a way that makes it "mine," these three ways of figuring within my experience, the three parts of the phenomenology of the subject position, dovetail in a single movement, a single action.

In order that there be a space of feeling within my experience, there must be a body that figures as that space, as my body-space; and whichever body it is, that body is *eo ipso* "my" body. My body-space, as we put it, depends ontologically on my body (15.6). Compare this with the way my actions depend on my body-space. Here it is a matter of what makes sense phenomenologically (i.e., in terms of how things figure within my experience). It makes sense that a movement figures within my experience as willed only if it is the movement of something that figures within my experience as part of my body-space. Just as my body-space depends ontologically on my body, so, we might say, my will depends phenomenologically on my body-space.

Any body may appear within my experience; but only one body figures within my experience as the space of feeling; and, by virtue of thus figuring, the body in question is "my" body. In this sense I have special way of knowing my body: whereas I may know any body from the outside, it is only my body that I know from the inside (15.4). Anyone, including me, can know my body from the outside (my body can appear within anyone's experience); I alone, however, know my body from the inside (only from within my experience does my body figure as the space of feeling). Now, given the phenomenological dependence of my will on my body-space, we may extend this point to will. We may say that whereas I can know anyone's actions, including my own, from the outside (anyone's actions can appear within my experience), it is only my own actions that are known from the inside (only my actions figure within my experience as willed).

The duality of access to my own actions and thereby to my body (to myself) i.e., via appearing and via figuring as willed, becomes clear when we reflect on the use of demonstratives in this regard. Whatever appears within my experience must be present within my experience, and whatever is present must appear in some way. Consider our device of emphasizing the demonstrative. So far, the device has been intended to highlight the fact that the object of reference is here and now present within experience. Now, it would seem to be a condition of demonstrative reference in general that what we refer to is immediately available within experience. Being present is obviously a way of being immediately available within experience. But is there not another way?

Imagine that the arms of four of us (who are similarly dressed, etc.) are confusingly intertwined. At precisely the same moment, each closes the fingers of his right hand. I might, on the basis of how things appear within my experience, wonder: "Am I doing *this*?" Now imagine I close my eyes. Is it not still possible for me to make a demonstrative reference to a particular action? But this time, it seems, I cannot wonder: "Am I doing *this*?"

In the first case, we are assuming that the condition of immediate availability is satisfied by the fact that the particular action to which I refer is present (and thus appears) within my experience. By hypothesis, there is no such fact of presence in the second case. Yet is undeniable that in the second case I refer demonstratively to a particular action. It follows that availability for demonstrative reference can consist in something other than a fact of presence. It can consist in a fact of will, that is, in the fact that something figures within my experience as actively self-unfolding, as willed. This is how it is in the case where my eyes are closed: the availability for demonstrative reference consists in a fact of will. Let us say that in the first case I use the demonstrative as a "demonstrative of presence ($this_p$)," and in the second case as a "demonstrative of will ($this_w$)."

Consider now the epistemic asymmetry noted two paragraphs back. It is possible to wonder, "Am I doing $this_p$?" but not, "Am I doing $this_w$?" What explains the difference?

Where an action is picked out by a demonstrative of presence, it is picked out on the basis of the way it appears. As we have observed, there are any number of ways an action may appear within my experience, and not every way is such as to make it "my" action. Thus we have the possibility of uncertainty and mistake. Where an action is picked out by a demonstrative of will, on the other hand, the way of figuring on the basis of which the action is picked out, viz., figuring as willed, is incomparable: there are no relevant "ways" of figuring. Either an action figures within my experience as willed or it does not, and if it does, that makes it "mine." Hence there is no room for uncertainty or mistake.

Notice how the two kinds of access, the inside and outside knowledge (awareness), can come apart even in the case where the access is to the same action. Our arms are entangled. I may be unsure whether I am doing $this_p$. Yet I cannot be unsure whether I am doing $this_w$. Still, it may turn out that $this_p = this_w$. My action, the same action, is known within my experience in two ways, from the outside and from the inside. And just as my action is known in these two ways, so is the body, the human being, whose action it is. I know myself from the outside, as the one who appears within my experience in such-and-such a way, and from the inside, as the one whose actions figure within my experience as willed.[21]

---

[21] Consider the following passage from Schopenhauer:

To the subject of knowing, who appears as an individual only through his identity with his body, this body is given in two entirely different ways. It is given in intelligent perception as representation, as an object among objects, liable to the laws of these objects. But

15.10 Volitional Centrality: Phenomenology and Causality

Let us, in concluding this chapter, reemphasize the point that our interest here is strictly phenomenological: that we are trying to capture the phenomenology of will, of active doing, about a way that certain worldly events figure from within my experience. The idea is, to the extent that we succeed in capturing this, we capture what will is, since the phenomenology of will is (we are saying) all there is to will. Insofar as a bodily movement figures from within my experience as willed, as actively self-unfolding, it is willed. In this respect, it is exactly like the presence/appearing of an event: insofar as an event figures as (say) visually present/appearing, it is present/appearing. These, like will, are simply ways of figuring within my experience (horizon).

My hand, say, is present within my experience; it appears a certain way. This fact about my hand is a fact that needs a horizon: a fact that holds only from within experience. Without the horizon, there are no such facts. Of course, the fact of my hand's existence remains, but not the fact of its presence, or the fact that it appears this or that way. It is the same with a fact of will, the fact (say) that this movement of my hand figures as willed, as actively self-unfolding. In the absence of a horizon, there could be no such fact. The movement might exist (occur), but not the fact of its being willed. Facts of will, like facts of presence and appearance, need a horizon.

In this sense, a fact of will is not a fact about the intrinsic nature or character of the worldly event—the complex biological event that is the bodily movement—that figures as willed. Thus it is fundamentally different from facts about the causal history of this event. The causal history of a worldly event does not need a horizon from within which to hold. Causal facts are, in this respect, like facts of worldly existence (occurrence): they hold on their own, apart from any horizon. Facts of will, on the other hand, like facts of appearing/presence, hold only from within a horizon. Yet, insofar as they hold of worldly entities, they are facts

---

it is also given in quite a different way, namely as what is known immediately to everyone, and is denoted by the word *will*. (*The World as Will and Representation*, vol. 1, p. 100).

When Schopenhauer speaks of my body being "given in intelligent perception etc.," he refers to the fact that my body appears within my experience. Since any object can appear within my experience, insofar as my body is given in this way, it is "an object among objects." But Schopenhauer also says that my body is "given in a quite different way." The obvious implication is that, with respect to this other way of being given, my body is not just "an object among objects"; rather, no object other than my body is given (within my experience) in this way. What is this way? This is where will comes in: my body is the body whose actions figure as willed.

about the world: they are facts about the world that hold only from within a horizon.

Thus the fact that the movement of my hand is willed, an active doing, is compatible with any causal history we might wish to assign it. It is open to assume that the movement is the outcome either of a perfectly continuous development of phenomena in which everything that happens has a set of causally sufficient conditions, or of a development of phenomena containing causal gaps. For the fact of its being willed is a fact about how the movement figures from within my horizon, a phenomenological fact, whereas the fact of its causal history, its development out of prior bodily events or states, does not belong to its phenomenology.[22]

Notice, finally, if we accept that there are biological conditions causally sufficient for the event that is my action, for the event that figures as willed, it seems we must also accept that there are conditions causally sufficient for the fact that the event figures this way. Thus, once we have a sense of the phenomenology of will—of the potentially disruptive, developing-out-of-itself way of figuring within my experience that is at the center of practical life—it may occur to us that causally speaking, a bodily movement of mine figures this way only because of what is going on in my body, in my brain: that the phenomenology of will, the phenomenology in which a particular bodily event figures within my experience as actively self-unfolding, etc., itself develops causally out of what is going on in that same body, my body. But this phenomenology is part of what makes a particular movement, and hence the human body whose movement it is, "mine." The fact then that a certain body figures within my experience in a way that makes it (the body) "mine" develops causally out of events in the brain of that body, the body that is "mine" by virtue of the way it figures within my experience.

Such is our situation. The phenomenology of the subject position, by virtue of which a certain body (human being) is "mine (me)," floats free of causation: its content is investigated by imagination without any reference whatever to its causal source. Yet it has such a source (in the brain of the very body that is "mine")—to the investigation of which imagination, the method of phenomenology, is totally foreign.

---

[22] Although we shall not pursue this, the bearing of the remarks in the present section on the problem of free will should be obvious. But let me say, in case this occurs to anyone, I do not regard the phenomenological conception of will as offering an obvious "solution" to the problem.

16. The Uses of the First Person

16.1 Introduction

At scattered points throughout our discussion of the self (e.g., 12.7, 14.1–2), and at earlier points in the book (e.g., 2.4, 2.6, 6.7), we have been required to state and explain certain ideas about the first person. But given the piecemeal way in which the ideas have emerged, it may not be evident how they combine with each other. We shall now attempt to draw things together, to arrive at a unified view of the matter, and, in light of this, to address some of the troublesome questions philosophers have raised about the first person.

Some philosophers (e.g., Locke, Kant, and Wittgenstein) distinguish two uses of the first person. We have gone one better and have distinguished three uses: the referential, the positional, and the horizonal. We shall take up each of these three uses in turn. But let us, in advance, try to dampen the incredulity that may greet the suggestion that the "I," the first person, has more than one use.

One might say: When I use "I," I refer to myself, to the person or human being that I am. That is the long and short of it. There are not two or three—or five or six—uses of "I"; there is just one use.

In part, I agree with this simple reaction. There is just one object or individual to which I refer by "I"—a particular human being, JV. It does not follow, however, that this is the only use of "I"; for it does not follow that all uses of the "I" are uses in which I refer to something.

Certainly there is a referential use of "I." The referential use, which is the central everyday use, is one of the three uses of "I" that we have distinguished. Moreover, in using "I" to refer, there is, for each of us, just one object (one human being) to which we refer. We do not, in this respect, have a selection of two or three objects to choose from (an "inner" and an "outer" object, say). This would be an implausible—in fact, incoherent (since it leaves room for the possibility both that I am F and that I am not F)—view of the first person. In any case, it is not our view. When we say that there are three uses of "I," three uses of the first person, we do not mean that there are, for each of us, three different objects to which we may selectively refer by "I." We mean, rather, that in addition to the referential use, which use it seems obvious that we all grasp, we all (no doubt, less obviously) grasp two further uses of the first person, two nonreferential uses, viz., the positional and horizonal uses of the first person.

Moreover, granting that there is (for each of us) just one object referred to by "I," the nonreferential uses of "I" actually play a role in the referential use. If we reflect on the referential use, we uncover the positional and horizonal uses of the first person: they lie buried within our grasp of the referential use. Thus we will not achieve a full understanding of the referential use of the first person unless we bring out into the open, and examine in their own right, the deeper, nonreferential uses of the first person.

16.2 *The Referential Use of the First Person*

The referential use of the first person is, as we said, the central everyday use of the first person, the use that we initially (by what can seem like a near miracle) catch on to in learning the language. "I want that one," "I have eaten too much," "I need a haircut," "My foot is swollen," "There is a scratch on my arm," "I am tired," "I am sitting in the wrong seat," "I have gained ten pounds," "I have a pain in my knee (my knee hurts)," "I see rain clouds," "I am raising my arm," "I am thinking about Vienna," and so on. In all such cases, I use "I" to refer—to refer to the human being that I am. This seems (to me, at least) obvious.

Yet it is sometimes denied. G.E.M Anscombe, in her paper on this topic, arrives at the conclusion that the solution to various perplexities about the first person is that " 'I' is neither a name nor another kind of expression whose logical role is to make a reference, *at all.*"[1] Her point is not that there are *some* uses of "I" that are nonreferential, but (I take it) that *the* use, *the* logical role (as she calls it) of "I," i.e., *the* familiar everyday use, is nonreferential. It will be clear that I am in agreement with a number of points that Anscombe makes on this topic, but, it seems to me, there must be other ways of dealing with the perplexities of the first person. For if anything in this whole difficult area seems plainly true, if anything deserves to be regarded as a datum, it is that the everyday use of the "I" is referential.

Actually, we do not have to take this as a datum. There is a simple argument to which we may appeal here (the argument from contradiction). If I utter, "I need a haircut," another person may contradict me: "He has not gained ten pounds." How should we make sense of the fact that the Other straightforwardly contradicts what I assert—not, mind you, something implied by what I assert, or something that can be figured

[1] "The First Person," in G.E.M. Anscombe, *Collected Papers*, volume 2, p. 32.

out on the basis of what I assert, but what I assert—if he and I do not refer to the same object? In such a case, "I" and "he" referentially intersect. The same possibility exists with "I" and "you," "I" and proper names, demonstrative expressions and definite descriptions referring to human beings. These multifarious intersections carry the same message: the basic everyday use of "I" is to refer, to refer to a human being.[2]

It might be thought that whereas Anscombe is mistaken about the use of "I" for certain types of everyday case, for other cases her view is correct. Suppose I assertively use a sentence of the form "I am F." One case that might be thought to fit Anscombe's view is where there is an epistemic asymmetry between my basis for asserting "I am F" and that of another person who, referring to me, asserts, "He is F." In "I need (he needs) a haircut," both my assertion and that made by the Other are based on observation of me, the human being that I am. But the argument from contradiction does not depend on I/Other epistemic symmetry. I do not (it is often pointed out) normally base my knowledge of my bodily sensations, or of what I am doing with my body, or its attitude, or again, my knowledge of how things are visually within my experience, on observation of my body and its situation; whereas the Other may have nothing but observation of my body (me), etc., to go on. In such cases there is an epistemic asymmetry. Yet if I assert, say, "I have my legs crossed," "I am raising my arm," "I feel a pain in my knee," "I see rain clouds," it is open to the Other, on whatever basis, to contradict me in the third person. The epistemic asymmetry in such cases does not affect the symmetry of reference.

The second type of case that might be thought favorable to Anscombe's view relates to Wittgenstein's distinction between "the use of 'I' as object" and "the use of 'I' as subject."[3] The idea would be that where "I" is used as object, "I" is referential; where it is used as subject, however, Anscombe's view holds. But what is the distinction between the use of "I" as subject and its use as object?

Some examples. "I need a haircut," "My foot is swollen," "I have gained ten pounds," illustrate the use of "I" as object. "I am raising my arm," "I feel a pain in my knee," "I see rain clouds," illustrate the use of "I" as subject. Taking these sentences as having the form "I am F," the distinction may be explained as follows. Where "I" is used as object, it is possible that I know that someone is F, while being unsure whether it is *I* who am F, whereas such uncertainty is not possible where "I" is used as subject. In the latter case, I cannot, as Sidney Shoemaker expresses it,

---

[2] The point is something of a theme in chapter 7 of Gareth Evans's book, *The Varieties of Reference*.

[3] See the *Blue and Brown Books*, pp. 66–7.

"misidentify" the one who is F: my use of "I" is "immune to error through misidentification."[4]

But even when used as subject, "I" is referential. "I have a pain in my knee"/"JV does not have a pain in his knee"; "I see rain clouds"/"JV does not see rain clouds." In both cases, there is a contradiction. In both cases, "I" refers to the same human being as "he."

16.3 Reference and the Use of "I" as Subject/Object

Let us stay with Wittgenstein's distinction. What one would like to understand is why, given that both cases are referential, "I" should be immune to error through misidentification when it is used as subject but not as object. Wittgenstein says that the object case involves "the recognition of a particular person," whereas "there is no question of recognizing a person" when I report that I have a pain. Only in the object case has "the possibility of an error been provided for."[5] Where there is no question of recognizing, i.e., identifying, someone, there can be no question of *mis*identifying anyone. This is, I take it, Shoemaker's view as well.[6]

It seems clear that if I assert something of the form "I am F," whether there is immunity to error through misidentification depends on the content of "F." This suggests that the relevant identification (recognition) is of someone *as F*. Thus if I assert, "I have a swollen foot," or "I need a haircut," I must identify (recognize) someone as having a swollen foot, or as needing a haircut; but if I assert, "I am raising my arm," or "I feel a pain . . . " or "I see rain clouds," there is no question of identifying (hence no question of misidentifying) anyone as raising his arm, or feeling pain, or seeing. It may now seem that Wittgenstein's distinction amounts to nothing more than our earlier epistemic asymmetry: there is in the subject case no question of identifying (recognizing), etc., in that I know what I know in this case (versus the object case) without observation.

---

[4] "Reference and Self-Awareness," *The Journal of Philosophy* 65, 19 (October 3, 1968), p. 556. Note, if I am sure that either you or I see rain clouds (and hence that someone sees rain clouds) but am unsure whether *these* are rain clouds, I will be unsure whether it is I who see rain clouds; yet "I see rain clouds" illustrates "I" used as subject. To preserve Wittgenstein's point, we may stipulate that uncertainty (error) introduced by uncertainty about the *object* of seeing, thinking, or whatever, is irrelevant; that the relevant uncertainty must concern seeing, thinking, etc., itself. Thus, presumably, I could not be sure that someone is seeing (something or other) but be unsure whether I am the one who is seeing. (And for these purposes we may take "seeing" to include cases of visual hallucination; to include any case in which something appears visually within my experience.)

[5] *Blue and Brown Books*, p. 67.

[6] See part 2 of "Reference and Self-Awareness."

But Wittgenstein is getting at something prior to the epistemic asymmetry. The epistemic asymmetry relates to my basis for asserting "I am F," i.e., for deeming it true that I am F, whereas Wittgenstein's asymmetry relates not to my basis for making an assertion but to my basis for using "I."

Reference in general has a precondition: you cannot refer to something unless you have already in some way "fixed on" or "singled out" the object; but this in turn presupposes that the object is available to be fixed on, etc., that it is in some way given. The point is most evident in the case of demonstrative reference. Suppose, nodding in the direction of someone we have never seen before, I say, "He (that man) looks like JFK." It is a precondition of my use in this case of "he (that man)" that the object of reference be in some way given, available for me to fix on. Were the object not given, reference could not get started.[7] The precondition of givenness is not confined to demonstrative reference. Generally, it seems, we cannot refer to an object unless the object is available for reference, that is to say, in some way given. In the case of demonstrative reference, the prior givenness consists in the object's presence within experience. But, in the general case, the prereferential stage setting can be satisfied without the object's being present. There is after all such a thing as an object's being "given in memory," or "given in thought." In one form or another, though, reference presupposes availability for reference: givenness.

It might be suggested that what distinguishes the use of "I" as subject (versus object) is that in this case the general precondition of givenness does not hold.[8] When I assert, "I see rain clouds," or "I feel a pain in my knee," or "I am raising my arm," the reference does not require that the human being to whom I refer by "I" is in any way given. I simply refer by "I" to the human being. Think how different this is from the case where you assert of me, "He (that man) feels pain . . . ," or "He sees . . . ," or "He is raising his arm." There is an evident asymmetry here—not just in the basis for deeming true what is asserted about the human being that I am, but in the basis for the reference to this human being. However, is it not the same with the use of "I" as object? In order to assert, say, "I need a haircut," I must (assuming I rely on myself) in some way observe, JV, the human being that I am. But this pertains to my basis for deeming it true that I need a haircut, not to my basis for using "I." If we confine our attention strictly to my use of "I," this would seem as independent of the givenness of JV as my use of "I" in "I feel a pain. . . ."

---

[7] See *The Puzzle of Experience*, 4.7.

[8] Cf. J. David Velleman in his paper, "Self to Self." "Genuinely reflexive thoughts don't rely on an antecedent specification of their target: they just point to the subject, at the center of the thought." *Philosophical Review*, January 1996, p. 60.

It now looks as if the asymmetry in our basis for reference serves to highlight something distinctive not about the subject versus object use of "I," but about first-person reference as such. As in all reference, first-person reference requires that we single out the object to which we refer. This singling out of the object is reflected in our referential intention. What distinguishes first-person reference is that our referential intention does not, as in the general case, presuppose the givenness of the object singled out. But we have yet to explain the difference within first-person reference between the use of "I" as subject and object.

Let us try a different tack. Let us attempt to spell out the content of a first-person referential intention. I mean, one might say, to refer to "a certain human being." This, however, is silent on a crucial aspect of my intention. To *which* human being? The words "a certain, etc." indicate that the content of my referential intention is definite without actually telling us in what the definiteness of the intention consists. Should we say, then, that I mean to refer to "the human being that I am"? But the task we have set ourselves (that of spelling out the content of my intention in first-person reference) is precisely that of spelling out the content of my intention in referring to the human being that *I am*. What progress can it make toward fulfilling this task if we say that I mean to refer to the human being that I am?

Yet the task need not stump us. It is the task that has engaged us in the previous two chapters of the book, the ever-incomplete task of spelling out the phenomenology of the subject position, the content of the positional conception of the self. Insofar as we manage to spell out the phenomenology of the subject position, we spell out who or what I mean to refer to in using "I." Thus, whereas the singling out of the object, the referential intention, differs in other-person reference from case to case, in first-person reference it is always the same. Moreover, whereas the intention in other-person reference may have to be formed, as it were, on the occasion of reference, in first-person reference, there can be no need for an on-the-spot formation of a referential intention, since the object of reference is always already singled out. We might say, whereas other-person reference may have to wait upon something else, first-person reference always has what it needs. It waits only upon itself.

Recall the sense in which the positional conception of the self is always in play. It is, we said, always in background play: there is always within my experience, within my horizon, some human being figuring as the one at the center (14.8). That is to say, there is always some human being (body) figuring$_s$ in this way, figuring in the standing (versus operative) sense. (The idea, remember, is not that at every moment some movement of the human being that I am figures$_o$ as willed; or that at every moment his body figures$_o$ as the space of feeling; or that at every moment he figures$_o$ as perceptually central, i.e., in the kind of way represented by Mach's picture). Insofar as someone always figures$_s$ in one or more of these ways, the positional conception of the self is always in background play; and insofar as the positional conception of the self is always in background play, first-person reference always has what it needs: we are in this sense always ready, always set up, for first-person reference.

All that is missing is to bring the positional conception of the self out of background play into play (14.8). In other words, all that missing is simply to refer: to refer to the one who already figures$_s$ as the one at the center of my horizon—to refer, that is, with precisely this intention.

If we are set up for first-person reference, are we not thereby set up for other-person reference? The self/other contrast is correlative: if something figures within my experience as myself, as "me," something must always figure as other, as "not-me." But there is an important difference here. In the first-person case, I mean to refer to "the one" who figures at the center of my experience. This has the definiteness necessary for a referential intention. It should be clear, however, that there is no such thing as "the one" who figures within my experience as *not at the center*. There are indefinitely many things. In other-person reference, what I mean to refer to is not simply *not-me*, but *this or that* not-me. The mere fact of there being, correlative to me, something that is not-me does not of itself suffice for the content of a referential intention: it does not of itself set me up for reference. There is more to "do." What? From within the domain of the not-me, I must select something. I must fix on the particular not-me to which I shall refer.[9]

This is why we may have the feeling of being "closer" to first-person reference than to other-person reference, as if there is nothing that could ever insert itself between us and our use of "I." Of course this feeling also depends on the fact that what sets me up for first-person reference is simply figuring$_s$, i.e., figuring in the *standing* sense, as one at the center of my experience; that it is totally irrelevant whether, on the occasion of reference, I happen to figure operatively in this way, whether, on the occasion of reference, I happen to appear$_o$ as perceptually central within my experience, or figure$_o$ as the locus of feeling or will—which, if it were not irrelevant, would constitute a potential *obstacle* to first-person reference. (The only potential obstacle is the more radical experiential possibility that we have several times remarked upon, the possibility of emptiness at the center: of there being, not just at a given time, nothing that figures$_o$ within my horizon as "me," but of there being in a standing way nothing

[9] Cf. Anscombe: "With names, or denoting expressions (in Russell's sense) there are two things to grasp: the kind of use, and what to apply them to from time to time. With "I" there is only the use." "The First Person," p. 32.

that figures as "me.") Thus there is no intrinsic difference between first-person reference in the extraordinary situation of total sensory deprivation and the ordinary situation, where (or so we may assume) at the moment of reference it is at least true that my body figures₀ as the locus of feeling. First-person reference no more relies on this in the ordinary situation, where it is available, than in the extraordinary situation, where it is not available.

Perhaps we can now explain the distinction between "I" used as subject and "I" used as object, taking our examples to be of the form "I am F." Where "I" is used as object, e.g., "I need a haircut," "My arm is scratched," it could happen that I am sure someone is F while being unsure whether it is I. Where "I" is used as subject, e.g., "I have a pain in my knee," "I am raising my arm," this is not possible. The use of "I" as subject is (in Shoemaker's phrase) immune to error through misidentification. Thus which use it is seems to depend on the content of "F" in "I am F." Yet the distinction concerns not the predicate but the use of "I." How could this be?

The answer is, by its being the case that the content of "F" connects with the positional conception of the self, the conception that is brought into play (out of background play) by first-person reference: the conception whose content is one and the same as the content of our intention in first-person reference. Figuring within my experience as the locus of feeling and will are ways of figuring that make a certain body "mine," a certain human being "me." If I assert, "I feel a pain in my knee," or "I am raising my arm," the body, the human being, whose knee is it, whose arm it is, is that which figures within my experience as the space of feeling, as the locus of will. But then that human being, that body, the one via whose knee a position in the space of feeling within my experience is identified, the one whose arm movement figures within my experience as willed, that human being is *eo ipso* "me" (his body is *eo ipso* "my" body), the human being I mean to refer to by "I."

Compare these examples with "I need a haircut" or "My arm is blue." Here there is no connection between the predicative content of what I assert and the positional conception of the self, i.e., between the predicative content of my assertion and the content of my first-person referential intention. The state of a certain human being's hair or skin is not part of the phenomenology of the subject position; not part, then, of the positional conception the self. In contrast with being the locus of will or the locus of feeling, these things are not part of what makes a certain human being (body) "me (mine)." Thus, whereas there is no possibility of being sure that someone figures as the locus of will or feeling while unsure whether *I* am the one who acts or suffers, there is a corresponding possibility in the case of needing a haircut or the color of my arm. In such cases, the use of the first person is not immune to error through misidentification.

In both the subject and object cases, within my horizon things are like this: some human being (someone) is F. In the subject cases, given the connection between being F and the content of the positional conception of the self, there is no question but that *I* am the one who is F; there is no question because, given the content of the positional conception of the self, there is no difference between *someone's* being F and my being F. In the object cases, being F is not similarly connected with the positional conception of the self. Thus the question of whether I am who is F may arise. The "possibility of an error has been provided for."

16.4 "I Am Thinking . . . / I See . . . "

"I see rain clouds," "I am thinking about Vienna." These cases exemplify the use of "I" as subject. Can I be unsure whether it is *I* who see, whether it is *I* who am thinking? Yet they differ in an obvious respect from "I am raising my arm," or "I feel pain in my knee" (which also exemplify the use of "I" as subject). In both the seeing/thinking and the feeling/acting cases, there is a way (call it "W") things are within my horizon that makes true the relevant sentence of the form "I am F." In the feeling/acting cases, W necessarily includes the fact that some human being figures within my horizon in a way that makes him "me"; so, given W, there can be no question but that *I* am the one who is F. In the seeing/thinking cases, however, the human being that I am figures only incidentally in W (only if I happen to be looking at, or thinking about, myself). In our seeing example, W, i.e., the way things are within my horizon, is such as to make it true that I see rain clouds. So W will include rain clouds visually appearing within my horizon. In the thinking example, W will include the city of Vienna presenting itself in some way or other. Clouds, a city. In neither case need W include the human being that I am. Thus our explanation of immunity to error through misidentification in the feeling/acting cases does not work for the seeing/thinking cases.

At this stage we may be tempted to suppose that what Anscombe says about the use of "I" in general holds true for the seeing/thinking cases. The reasoning would be that since the question "Is it I who see . . . /am thinking . . . ?" can arise only if "I" is used referentially, if "I" is not used referentially, the question cannot arise—so there is no possibility of being mistaken whether it is I, etc. Yet it is undeniable that in the thinking/ seeing cases "I" referentially intersects with "he." If I assert "I see . . . / am thinking . . . ," it is open to the Other to contradict me: "He does not see . . . /is not thinking . . . ." Does not the Other refer by "he" to a certain human being? Then the fact of the contradiction entails that by "I" I refer to the same human being.

But now the question arises of what function first-person reference might serve in the thinking/seeing cases. Since in these cases W—the way things figure from within my horizon—does not (except incidentally) involve the human being that I am, why in asserting "I see . . . /am thinking . . . " should I refer to that human being? Why should a human being come into this, when, it seems, no human being need figure in what makes my assertion true?[10]

Note, even where in these cases W does involve the human being that I am, the way he figures will not be analogous to the way the human being figures in the feeling/action cases. In the latter, the human being figures as the locus of feeling/action within my horizon. But when the human being that I am figures visually or in thought, it is not as the locus of seeing, or the locus of thinking. The reason is simple: there is, phenomenologically, no such way of figuring, no such thing as the "locus" of seeing or thinking. There are just objects (which may include the human being I am) appearing visually within my horizon, or figuring as objects of thought. In contrast, then, to the feeling/action cases, there is nothing that could be part of the phenomenology of the subject position (the positional conception of the self). There is of course a way, or kind of way, of visually appearing within my horizon that is part of the phenomenology of the subject position (the way represented by Mach's picture). However, to figure as perceptually central is not to figure as the *locus of seeing* but rather as *seen* in a certain way.

What (once again) is the function of the first-person reference in "I see . . . /am thinking . . . "? Consider the corresponding question in the case of "he." The Other's understanding of "I/he" is the same as mine. Just as I understand how the Other uses "he," when he refers to me, the Other understands how I use "I." All this is mutually grasped. The Other understands then that W need not involve the human being that I am. So, just as we are asking why by "I" in "I see rain clouds" I should refer to the human being that I am, i.e., what the point of such reference could be, we might ask why the Other should refer to that human being in "He sees

---

[10] Anscombe remarks about the seeing/thinking cases that they have the "character of being far removed in their descriptions from the descriptions of the proceedings etc. of a person [human being, body] in which they might be verified." Ibid., p. 35. However, whereas I regard this as posing a problem, or question, about the use of "I," she takes it as a reason for regarding these cases as "not the ones to investigate if one wants to understand 'I' philosophically." It seems to me that, given their problematic character, they are precisely the cases we need to investigate.

rain clouds." For the same W that makes true what I assert makes true what the Other asserts.[11]

Let us reflect further on what I and the Other mutually understand. The Other understands—and of course I understand that he understands: we are together all the way—that JV, the human being who figures thus-and-so within his (the Other's) horizon, the human being who, let us say, right now appears within his horizon, is, like himself, at the center of a horizon, and that, in virtue of being at the center of a horizon, JV figures within that horizon as the human being that "I am." We, who are equals, whose horizons are mutually grasped as coordinate, mutually take each other to figure, each for himself, as being at the center of a horizon and thus as always having in background play the positional conception of the self; that is, as always being (as we put it) set up for first-person reference.

You could say, we—we human beings—are a community of "I" users. In each case, the "I" user, the human being, is at the center of a horizon. Notice, however, it is not the horizon but the human being at the center that appears within the horizon of an Other. There is no way a horizon (either its existence or how things are from within it) can become known to an Other except via the words and behavior of the human being at its center figuring somehow within the Other's horizon. This whole mutually grasped structure of things—the side-by-side space of horizons each with an "I" user, a human being who can appear within other horizons, at its center—is part of what we pick up in picking up the use of "I." It should be obvious, then, that mastering the use of "I" is not an isolable linguistic feat, mastering just another bit of language. On the contrary, it cannot be separated from being drawn into the system of language-games as a whole, i.e., from becoming a thinker, a self-conscious subject.

To repeat, there is no way to know how things stand from within another horizon except via the words and behavior of the human being at its center figuring some way from within our horizon. (How else could it be?) This fact too, that our only access to each other's horizon is via the way we figure from within each other's horizon, is part of what we mutually grasp. Wittgenstein remarks that the best picture of the soul is the human body.[12] Perhaps we could say, the best picture—or rather, the *only* picture—of an Other's horizon is the human being at the center of the horizon.

---

[11] Of course the Other's *basis* for asserting what he asserts is not my basis for asserting what I assert. W is what makes true what the Other asserts, not his basis for asserting it; and this is the same for both of us.

[12] *Philosophical Investigations*, p. 178.

This suggests a response to the question about the function of first-person reference in the seeing/thinking cases. When I say, "I see rain clouds," my use of "I," by referring to the human being who is at the center of the horizon from within which rain clouds visually appear, identifies the relevant horizon, the horizon from within which the fact of appearing holds. If the Other knew only that from within some horizon rain clouds appear, there would be an unanswered question. He would not know from within which (whose) horizon it is asserted that rain clouds appear. My use of "I" answers this question.[13] Such is the function of the "I" in these cases.

If the Other asserts, "He does not see rain clouds," he refers by "he" to the same human being that I refer to by "I." There is referential intersection. Both the Other and I refer to the same human being, the one at the center of the relevant horizon. Given that the horizon is thus identified, I assert that from within it rain clouds visually appear, whereas the Other contradicts this.

It is no objection that the Other may identify the relevant horizon *without* my actually referring to myself—e.g., if I say, "Look, rain clouds," or point and say "Rain clouds." Or perhaps the Other merely sees me looking at the sky. He knows, let us assume, that I, JV, see rain clouds (that rain clouds appear visually within the horizon of which JV is at the center) and thus does not need a first-person reference on my part to identify the relevant horizon. Nonetheless, if I assert "I see rain clouds," it remains true that my first-person reference identifies a horizon (the one of which JV is at the center). It does this whether or not, in the particular context, it needs to be done. If, in choosing a team, I utter X's name at the same time that I point to X, does it follow from the fact that my utterance is redundant that it does not identify X as the one I want? The redundancy of a function does not entail that it cannot be fulfilled.

Or consider the situation where I use "I see rain clouds" in soliloquy. There is, there can be, no need to identify the relevant horizon for myself. The reason is that the relevant horizon is "mine," and the fact that it is "mine" makes itself manifest (the meta-fact of self-consciousness; 9.3). Still, if I do use "I" in the soliloquy situation (and what can stop me?), my use will be the same use that I picked up in becoming a speaker, a thinker (hence someone who can engage in monologue), viz., to refer to the human being that I am, the one at the center of my horizon. I will

---

[13] We can imagine a linguistic practice wherein "Rain clouds visually appearing" is understood to express how things are from within some horizon while leaving open (no matter who utters it) which horizon. Identifying the horizon, by pointing or naming or the use of the first person, would then be a separate task.

pointlessly refer to that human being and thereby pointlessly identify the relevant horizon as the one of which he is at the center.[14]

Let us return to the immunity to error through misidentification. I can know that someone needs a haircut, or weighs 70 kilograms, but be mistaken about whether I am the one. Why can I not be wrong about whether it is I who feel/act or see/am thinking? In the feeling/acting cases, the human being that I am, figures in W, and moreover figures precisely in a way that makes him the human being that "I am," viz., as the locus of feeling/will. However this explanation does not work in the seeing/thinking cases, since in these cases the human being that I am need not figure in W in any way at all. (And if he does figure, it will not be in a way that makes him "me," i.e., as the locus of seeing/thinking: there is no such way of figuring.) Whether the human being in question figures in W is irrelevant to the immunity, etc., in these cases. Yet I can no more be mistaken whether it is I that see/am thinking than whether it is I that feel/act.

In the seeing/thinking cases, that it is I that see/am thinking is settled independently of the particular way things figure from within my horizon, thus independently of what appears visually or is given in thought. It is settled by the fact that it is from within *my* horizon that things appear, which fact is manifest (the meta-fact of self-consciousness). The only question is whether the one at the center of my horizon is me, the one that I am. But this is not a real question. Why? The answer is that occupying the position at the center of my horizon, i.e., figuring in the right way from within my horizon, is precisely what makes someone "me" (the positional conception of the self).

Notice, when we say that in the seeing/thinking cases, the fact that it is I who see/am thinking is settled independently of the particular way that the human being that I am figures from within my horizon, we are talking about the way he operatively figures (14.5). When, on the other hand, we say that figuring in the right way from within my horizon is what makes someone "me," we mean figuring standingly in the right way. Operatively, in the seeing/thinking cases, the human being that I am need not figure in any way at all from within my horizon.

Let us conclude with a general observation about Wittgenstein's distinction between "I" used as object and subject in sentences of the form "I am F." Concerning the subject use, we have distinguished between the "I feel/act" and "I see . . . /am thinking" cases. In both the subject and object

---

[14] Peter Geach writes that "The use of 'I' in such soliloquies is derivative from, parasitic upon, its use in talking to others; when there are no others, 'I' is redundant and has no special reference; 'I am very puzzled at this problem' says no more than 'This problem *is* puzzling.' " *Mental Acts* (Routledge and Kegan Paul, 1957), p. 120. I agree, the use of "I" in soliloquy is redundant. But this is not a reason to say that it "has no special reference."

uses, however, "I" is referential: it refers to the human being that I am. But as we move from the object use (e.g., "I need a haircut," "I weigh 70K") through the feeling/acting to the seeing/thinking cases, there is a progressive disengagement of the human being to which "I" refers. This may be seen in the way the human being that I am in each case instantiates the predicative part of "I am F."

In, e.g., "I weigh 70K," the human being simply instantiates the grammatical predicate. In "I feel pain in my knee," the human being instantiates the predicate by operatively figuring in a certain way from within my horizon (as the space of feeling). In "I see rain clouds," the human being instantiates the predicate neither by simply instantiating it nor by figuring within my horizon in a particular way. Rather, he instantiates the predicate simply by occupying the position at the center of my horizon. Notice, this means only that he standingly figures from within my horizon in a way that satisfies the positional conception of the self, not that he operatively figures in any particular way; it means only, in other words, that the positional conception of the self is in background play (14.8). Hence we may gain the impression that, when I see rain clouds, the human being that I am does not come into it at all. But of course he does: he is there at the center of my horizon (where he always is), i.e., at the center of the horizon from within which in this case rain clouds appear.

16.5 The Positional Use of the First Person

The central everyday use of "I"—which covers both Wittgenstein's object and subject use—is referential: to refer to the human being at the center of my horizon.[15] However, inside (as it were) the referential use of the first person lie two further uses of the first person, which we have called the positional and the horizonal uses. These come to light when we attempt to spell out what is involved in our grasp of the everyday referential use of the first person. A grasp of the nonreferential uses of the first person is implicit in our grasp of the referential use.

Suppose we start with the thought that when I refer in the first person I refer to the human being that I am, and then ask, "What makes *this* one, JV, 'me' (the one that 'I am')"? The answer—or so we are maintaining—is that he, JV, is the one who occupies a certain position within my horizon: he is the one at the center. Being "me," the one that "I am," is being the one at the center of my horizon. The point is that in these reflections on the referential use of the first person we use the first person in a way that is not referential. Thus when we ask what makes JV "me," etc., we

---

[15] Here I agree with Evans, *The Varieties of Reference*, pp. 217–18.

are not asking about JV and a particular human being what makes these one and the same, identical—as we would be if "me" were referential. There is nothing that makes (constitutes) X and Y identical: X and Y simply are or are not identical. There is, however, something that makes JV "me," the one that "I am," viz. his figuring as the one at the center of my horizon. Here the use of "me" and "I" is not referential but positional (see 2.5).

Hence if (in the right philosophical context) I assert "JV is me," we may take "is me" as replaceable by "figures as the one at the center of my horizon," i.e., as a predicate, whereas were an identity intended, we would have to take it rather as comprised of the "is" of identity plus a singular term. To spell out the meaning of the predicate is to spell out the phenomenology of the subject position, i.e., the positional conception of the self (chapter 15).

Consider the following passage from the Anscombe paper cited above:

> If I am right in my general thesis, there is an important consequence, namely, that "I am E.A." is after all not an identity proposition. It is connected with an identity proposition, namely, "This thing here is E.A." But there is also the proposition "I am this thing here" [which is not an identity proposition]. (p. 33)

Anscombe's general thesis is that "I" is not a referring expression. "E.A." in "I am E.A." is a referring expression; but unless "I" is also a referring expression, "I am E.A.," is not an identity proposition. Thus her general thesis has the consequence "I am E.A." is not an identity proposition.

But what if we reject her general thesis? We may still accept that "I am E.A." is not, as Anscombe intends it, an identity proposition. That is, we may accept that, while its central everyday use is referential, there is a philosophical context (when we are reflecting on the self) in which "I" is used positionally. Since "I am E.A." would assert an identity only if "I" were used referentially, if it is used positionally in "I am E.A.," the latter does not express an identity.

Of course, "I am E.A." *might* be used to assert an identity. Imagine Anscombe talking to someone who has studied her paper "The First Person." They are, in fact, talking about that paper, about what Anscombe argues, and so on; but the person, who has never seen Anscombe before, does not realize that it is Anscombe, E.A, to whom he is speaking. In such a situation Anscombe might, to clear things up, say to the person, "I am E.A.," in which case she would assert an identity. But this stands in obvious contrast to what Anscombe intends when she draws the consequence of her thesis that "I" is not a referring expression. I think that, in this case, Anscombe is in fact using "I" positionally.

A fact of identity about a worldly object, e.g., a human being, is, in a certain respect, like the fact that the object exists: it is a fact that needs nothing but itself, a fact that holds on its own (4.5). Let me switch to my own case. Although I can imagine everyday contexts in which I might use "I am JV" or "JV is me" to assert an identity, the fact that I have in mind in reflecting philosophically on the self is not an identity. The fact I have in mind is not a fact that holds on its own, but a fact that needs consciousness, the personal horizon. That is to say, it is a fact that holds only from within consciousness, only from within my horizon. So it is not a fact about JV's identity.

If "I am JV" does not assert an identity, "I" must be used in some way other than referentially, other than, e.g., the way it would be used in "I am thinking about Vienna," "I feel pain in my knee," "I have gained ten pounds," or the way it would be used to set straight someone who does not realize that he is speaking to JV. In what way is that? As we said, it would be used positionally. Assuming the positional use of the first person, the meaning of "JV is me (the one that I am)" is: JV figures as the one at the center of my horizon. The "is" in the expression "is me," then, is not the "is" of identity, nor is "me" a singular term; rather the whole expression "is me" functions as a predicate.

Similar remarks apply to Anscombe's other example: "I am this thing here." Given a certain philosophical context—as when we are struck by the fact a particular object in the world is *me*, the thing that *I am*[16]—this would not express an identity. On the other hand, imagine that in the dark someone who is with me touches an object that he is unable to identify. "What is this thing here?" I can feel his hand touching my knee. "It is me." The use of the first person in this case is referential. I assert, for the benefit of the Other, an identity between a certain object in the world and the human being that I am. In the philosophical case, on the other hand, what I assert is not an identity but the fact that the object in question figures within my horizon in a way nothing else does, that it occupies the position at the center. In this case, my use of the first person is not referential but positional.

Notice, we said that in the situation where I tell the Other "It (the object you are touching) is me," I assert for his benefit an identity between a certain object in the world and the human being that I am (who is me). Now consider this *last* sentence, i.e., the sentence in which we offer a philosophical comment on the nonphilosophical use of "It is me"; in particular, consider our use of the phrase "the human being that I am (who is me)." Here, in effect, we provide a gloss on our everyday referential

---

[16] Cf. Nagel on "being someone," *The View From Nowhere*, chapter 4, section 1, discussed above in 14.1.

intention in using the first person. When we use "I" we mean: the human being that I am. But suppose we now pursue this and ask about the use of "I" in our rendering of the everyday first-person referential intention. That is, when we say philosophically, "In the everyday case, by 'I' we mean: the human being that I am," how do we use "I" in "the human being that I am"? Here the use of "I" is not referential but positional. This brings out what we meant at the beginning of the present section when we said that the positional use of "I" turns up "inside" its referential use.

Therefore, if by "This thing is me" I assert an identity, my assertion depends on my grasping a first-person thought that is not a first-person identity; for my referential intention in using "me" is to refer the human being who is me—that is to say, to the human being who figures at the center of my horizon. But I could not have an intention with this content without grasping positional use of the first person. Thus, a grasp of the positional use of the first person is implicit in the intention with which we refer in the first person, and implicit in our assertion of a first-person identity is a first-person thought that is not an identity.[17]

16.6 The Horizonal Use of the First Person

The first person is characterized by a nested structure: just as the positional use of the first person turns up inside the referential use, so the horizonal use turns up inside the positional use of the first person, and hence inside the referential use. Thus having in our philosophical commentary on the everyday use formulated our everyday referential intention by saying that in using "I" I mean to refer to the human being that I am, wherein we use "I" positionally, if we now seek to explicate the positional use of "I," the use we employ philosophically to express our everyday referential intention, we shall arrive at the thought that the human being to which I refer, the human being that I am, is the one at the center of my horizon. And here, with the words "my horizon," we encounter the third use of the first person: the horizonal use (see 6.7, 8.5).

Clearly, the "my" in "my horizon" is not yet another positional use of the first person, as if by "the horizon that is mine" we might mean: the horizon that is at the center of my horizon. On the other hand, the attempt

---

[17] This is the more or less the opposite of Gareth Evans's view. Evans maintains that if I have the thought about myself that "I am F," I must not only grasp for some object δ what it would be for $<\delta$ is F> to be true, "I must also have in mind what it would be for $<\delta = I>$ to be true." *The Varieties of Reference*, p. 210. I would claim that my grasp of this last thought, the identity, *in turn* depends on my grasping a thought that can only be expressed by means of the positional use of the first person; hence on my grasping a thought that is *not* an identity.

to view the "my" in "my horizon" referentially leads into a circle. If I point and say, "That is my car," I mean that the car to which I point belongs to me, the human being that I am. When we reflect philosophically on the self, we seem to hanker for an "owner" (9.4), and thus may be ready to suppose that there is some entity that stands to my horizon in a relation analogous to that in which the human being that I am stands to my car. But what might this entity be? If we leave aside the Cartesian soul, there is, it seems, nothing but the human being. Which human being? The one that "I am," of course. Which one is that? It is the one who figures at the center of my horizon. The circle, i.e., the circle of the first person (8.5, 9.1), is now complete.

Nor can we avoid the circle by positing a Cartesian soul to serve as the owner of the horizon. Ownership by a soul will make the horizon "mine" only if the soul is *me*, the soul that "I am"—which raises the question of what makes one soul rather than any other "me," the one that "I am." Once again, the answer refers us back to my horizon.

What makes my horizon, THIS, "mine"? Something very simple: the fact that it is *the* horizon (9.1). Not, as we explained, the one and only horizon, but the horizon that includes all other horizons: the preeminent horizon. Insofar as it includes all others, it has (in Wittgenstein's phrase) no neighbors, but stands by itself, alone, and its "mineness" consists in this, in the fact that it stands alone.

Taken as a whole, the expression "my horizon" is referential. It refers to THIS: the subject matter to which the totality I call "the world" and the infinity of space and time are internal: the subject matter of the DH: the subject matter of death: the subject matter of this book. But within the expression "my horizon," the expression "my" does not function referentially. Unlike the "my" in (say) "my car," the possessive "my," it does not refer to an owner. It simply expresses aloneness, and thus, despite the grammatical analogy with the possessive "my," it does not refer at all.

We may take "my car" as equivalent in meaning to "the car that belongs to me," and the latter, which contains a referential use of the first person, to "the car that belongs to the human being who is me," wherein the referential has given way to the positional use of the first person; again, we may take "the car that belongs to the human being who is me," as equivalent to, "the car that belongs to the human being at center of my horizon," wherein the positional use of the first person has given way to the horizonal use of the first person. At this point we have run out of uses of the first person. Yet there is a further step, viz., to replace the horizonal use of the first person by the definite article. Whereas the first three moves leave behind a residual use of the first person, with this last move the first person has disappeared without residue. We are left instead with the definite article, an expression of our aloneness, and thus have escaped from the circle of the first person.

We have escaped from the circle—into a puzzle: the puzzle of solipsism. Let us be clear, our actual grasp of the first person does not contain a circle. Rather, when in philosophy we reflect on our grasp of the first person, when we try to explicate what we grasp, we are (or may be) led via a mistaken grammatical analogy (with the everyday, referential use of the possessive "my") to represent what we grasp as containing a circle. In fact, what lies buried inside our grasp of the first person is not a circle but solipsism, which is not a creature of philosophical reflection but is already there for us (whether we become open to it or not). The fact of solipsism is already there is for us, and with the fact comes a puzzle, the puzzle of solipsism. So the puzzle too is already there for us, inside our grasp of the first person.

The puzzle, as we have presented it, is that at the same time that my horizon includes all others and thus is preeminent (stands alone), I know that it is the same for all of us, that we are metaphysical equals, each at the center of a horizon coordinate with the others. I, all of us, live with this knowledge, committed to (O). (This, we said, is what makes it rationally impossible to accept dream skepticism; 6.8.) Yet we also live with the truth of solipsism, the aloneness or preeminence of my horizon, an aloneness that we can no more relativize away than we can relativize away the absolute character of the NOTHINGNESS that faces us in death—which, as we explained (chapter 10) entails the truth of solipsism. Our horizons are, impossibly, both coordinate and each for itself all-inclusive (chapter 11). Such is the puzzle implicit in our grasp of the first person.[18]

The puzzle can be brought out in another way. Our grasp of the first person is acquired in the course of being drawn into our system of language-games, the communal horizon. In fact, as we remarked (16.4), this grasp is not an isolable linguistic competence but is inseparable from our

---

[18] Gareth Evans is right when he remarks that "the solipsist thinks he can say: I am that object such that when it is in pain something frightful is to be expected" (Ibid., p. 324). Insofar as this expresses what the solipsist would mean in using "I," the solipsist escapes the circle of the first person. The trouble is, as Evans (in effect) notes, in order to avoid the patent falsehood that no one else's pain is frightful, the solipsist must add "by me" to the words expressing his first-person referential intention, which, Evans says, renders what he means "tautologous." But Evans introduces solipsism at the wrong level. What the solipsist (each of us) thinks is: I am that object within my horizon such that, etc. This is not false but nontautologously true. At this stage, the threat of the circle remains—which is where solipsism comes in: my horizon is the horizon (not the only, but the all-inclusive, horizon). And now we have arrived at the underlying puzzle. To be sure, Evans regards solipsism as a philosophical mistake. So he would regard the puzzle as a symptom of the mistake. I regard solipsism as a truth we all know, and the puzzle as something that is there for us in any case, whether we expose it philosophically or not.

grasp of the system as a whole, from our insidership in the communal horizon. I was drawn into this system and now find myself an insider. The system is all that I have. I have no resources for thinking, for grasping or formulating anything, except the resources with which the system provides me.[19] But insofar as I find myself an insider of the system, of the communal horizon, I find myself with Others, committed to (O) (see Int.6, 6.4). Thus while my grasp of the first person rests on solipsism, on the preeminence of the personal horizon, it is inseparable from insidership in the communal horizon, from within which I find myself part of a community of metaphysical equals. My (our) grasp of the first person, it seems, both rests on solipsism and entails a way of being that is incompatible with solipsism.

There is a further, related conflict we might mention here. The conflict in this case takes the form not of a contradiction between two truths but an oscillation, or ambivalence, between two images or pictures representing the respective claims to dominance of the personal and communal horizons. Solipsism, whose truth comes into the open when we reflect on the meaning of death, offers us a picture in which all other horizons are included within mine, the personal horizon. But from where do I acquire the means to conceive of this picture? Somehow they must derive from resources provided by the communal horizon, the system of language-games, that of which I find myself an insider. (What else do I have?) Here the picture is one in which the communal horizon is dominant. From this perspective, it is as if my horizon (my life, my consciousness) were a creature of the communal horizon. Yet the picture can be reversed at a stroke. True, my only resources for conceiving the personal horizon, the truth of solipsism, are resources acquired in the course of being drawn into the communal horizon, and thus coming to find myself with Others. But does not (I ask myself) everything, the whole process of being drawn into the communal horizon, develop from within my horizon? With this thought, the gestalt changes. The communal horizon—with myself and Others standing as equals within it—remains, but it has been swallowed up solipsistically within THIS, within my horizon.

Of course nothing can stop the gestalt from reversing again. Every reversal is, in turn, reversible. Does not this oscillation—which we have described in an abstract, jargonistic way, drawing upon the results of our prior reflections, upon an ever-accumulating pile of philosophical baggage—resonate with something that we all sense in a simple and direct way outside philosophy? My life and that of Others are internal

---

[19] NB: the system on the inside of which I *find* myself. I did not *choose* to be an insider of this system, to have the resources for thinking that I have. See *The Puzzle of Experience*, 8.8. (The influence of Wittgenstein here should be evident.).

to something "bigger than all of us." Yet everything is within my life. A sense of this conflict does not require the benefit of philosophical analysis or argument. The conflict makes itself known before we ever attempt (if we ever do attempt) to articulate it philosophically. Do you not recognize the conflict that we are talking about here? Did you not already know about it?

17. What Makes First-Person Reference First Personal?

17.1 The Meaning of the Question We Are Asking

The question entitling the present chapter is the question that has most exercised philosophers in recent discussions of the first person. But perhaps it will not be immediately clear what the question is getting at.

The central everyday use of the first person is, as we stressed in the previous chapter, referential. It is referential, and that to which we refer is a human being. You call from the next room, "What are you doing?" I reply, "I am looking for my keys." In using "I," I refer to a certain human being, to JV. The reference would be the same if I answered, "I am thinking about my book," or "Nothing, I have a headache," or again if I were not talking to anyone else but simply asked myself, "Where did I leave those keys?" These would all be examples of the everyday referential use of the first person, of first-person reference. The philosophical question, "What makes first-person reference first personal?" arises when we note a certain inadequacy in the way we just characterized the referential use of "I"; when, that is, we note that, with respect to the above examples, although in each case the reference is first personal, this does not in fact follow from our characterization of first-person reference.

Let the example be, "I am looking for my keys." In using "I" here, I refer to a certain human being, to JV. Now, JV is the human being that I am. Thus it follows from the fact that in using "I" I refer to JV, that, in using "I," I refer to the human being that I am. However, from the fact that I refer to the human being that I am, it does not follow that I refer first personally. We can readily think of situations in which I refer to that same human being, JV, the one that I am, but do not refer first personally. So, clearly, it is not sufficient to characterize first-person reference simply as reference to the human being that I am. The question arises, then, as to what more is required for first-person reference, what more, that is, beyond the fact that I refer to the human being that I am. What more is required to make first-person reference first personal?

The cases philosophers usually mention, by way of getting us to focus on this question, are cases where I use a proper name not realizing that I am the one called by that name; or where I use a definite description not realizing that I am the one who (let us suppose) uniquely satisfies that description; or where I refer demonstratively, not realizing that I am the one to whom I thus refer. The last type of case makes the point in a particularly vivid way. For example, seeing myself darkly in a mirror, I think, "This man looks dangerous," not realizing that the man I see is myself. Or again, I am crowded together with others, our limbs crossed in such a confusing way that, when I judge "This arm is sun burnt," I fail to realize that "this arm" is my arm, that I am sun burnt.

Now it would be easy enough to exclude such cases by stipulating that, in first-person reference, I must use "I" or "me" or "my" or "myself," or some equivalent expression. It is obvious, though, that whereas this move would enable us to reformulate the initial question, it cannot claim to answer the question, to explicate for us in what the first-person character of personal reference consists. For the rationale behind the stipulation is precisely that, used referentially, the expressions in question are used to refer first personally. Thus, instead of asking what makes first-person reference first personal, we might have formulated our question as: What is it about the referential use of "I," "me," "my," and so on, that makes it first personal?

17.2 Following the Rule for the Use of "I"

An answer that looks to the latter formulation of the question appeals to the fact that the relevant expressions are governed by a certain rule. It is because we who have learned the language appreciate this fact and, in using the expressions, mean to use the expressions in accordance with the rule, that our use of the expressions is first personal.

One point is obvious: if we appeal to the rule for the use of the first person by way of trying to explicate first-person reference, first-person reference must not figure in the content of the rule. Suppose we state the rule as follows:

(FP) An utterance of a sentence of the form [φ is F] is true just in case the person who utters [φ is F] is F.

Then we might say that what makes the referential use of "I," "me," etc., first personal is that we appreciate that "I" is an instance of φ, i.e., that "I" is governed by (FP); and further, in using "I," we mean to use it in accordance with (FP). We may abbreviate these two points by saying that, in using "I," we *follow* (FP). Clearly, it will be said, in using demonstratives we do not follow (FP); nor in using ordinary proper names or definite descriptions (unless they happen to contain a first-person expression).

Thus even where, in using a demonstrative, etc., I refer to the human being that I am, my reference will not count as first personal.

Now, as we remarked, if this suggestion is to provide the kind of insight we are seeking into the nature of first-person reference (if it is to tell us what makes first-person reference first personal), the content of (FP) must be, as indeed it appears to be, free of first-person reference. The difficulty, however, is that first-person reference comes in here in another way, not as part of the content of (FP) but in the condition that we "follow" (FP); and this undermines our attempt to explicate the nature of first-person reference in terms of following a particular rule.

"I am looking for my keys." My use of "I" is first personal in that I appreciate that "I" is governed by (FP)—hence I appreciate that the utterance of "I am looking for my keys" is true just in case the one who utters it is looking for his keys—and mean to use "I" in accordance with (FP). But what is meaning to use "I" in accordance with (FP) if not meaning that *I* use "I" in accordance with (FP)? Generally, meaning (intending) to use an φ in accordance with a rule, following the rule for φ, is self-directed: I mean *my* use of φ to accord with what the rule for φ requires. Or we might say, my "following" a rule entails seeing *myself* as acting in accordance with—seeing myself as bound by—the rule. It is the element of self-directedness, with its implicit first-person reference, that distinguishes following a rule from merely acting in a way that conforms to a rule; thus we cannot explicate first-person reference in terms of following a rule.

Does this not prove too much? In order to learn how to use "I," we must have learned to follow (FP). But if following (FP), or any other rule of language, itself involves implicit first-person reference, how did we manage in the first place to learn how to use "I"? As we have described it, the use of "I" seems to be what makes possible the learning of language, and thus somehow prior to learning language; yet we know that it is learned in learning language.

Here we need to remind ourselves of the fact that mastering the first person is not, as we expressed it, an isolable linguistic competence but is rather inseparable from being drawn into the communal horizon, the system of language-games (16.4). Just as we gradually become insiders, we gradually acquire a grasp of the first person. However, since our gradually becoming insiders just is our gradually becoming rule followers, there can be no question of our having to grasp the first person prior to learning language, prior to becoming rule followers. You might as well require that we learn language prior to learning language, that we follow rules prior to becoming rule followers.

Let us drop this line of reflection and focus on a more specific problem with the present suggestion. The suggestion, once again, is that what makes a referential use of φ first personal, is that in using φ the user follows (FP). It may be pointed out that as the rule is stated, following (FP) could not of itself be what makes the difference between reference simpliciter and first-person reference. As stated, (FP) lays down that (an utterance of) [φ is F] is true just in case the person uttering [φ is F] is F. But is not something more required if the reference by φ is to be first personal? Must not the person who uses φ not only take the object to which he refers to be F but *take himself* to be that object, the one that is F?

Anscombe, in her paper, describes a language community whose practice of self-reference brings out the point nicely.[1] Each member of the community has his own (different from all the others) letter α publicly displayed on his back and chest; and each gets used to seeing α in a certain characteristic way (when he looks directly down, in a mirror, etc.) Each, moreover, has privately displayed (on the inside of his wrist) the letter "A." Finally, each member of the community is taught the following rule: he has reason to accept [α is F], just in case he has reason to accept "A is F." We could fuss about more with the details, but the basic idea should be clear. Despite the overt similarity, there is a fundamental difference between the use of "A" and our use of "I." Although each member of the community uses "A" to refer to the person who is in fact himself, he does not use "A" to refer first personally. The point is that if our grasp of "I" were exhausted by the fact that in using "I" we follow (FP), then our use of "I" would resemble the use of "A." That is to say, we would, in using "I," refer to ourselves, but the reference would not be first personal.[2]

Why not? What is missing? Anscombe says that our use of "I" involves self-consciousness—this is what is missing in the case of "A."[3] But what are we to understand by "self-consciousness" in the present context? What is the self-consciousness of first-person reference? It is not the metafact of the manifestness of the fact that there is such a thing as my horizon (9.3). Nor (equivalently) is it the fact that the positional conception of the self is always in background play (14.9). For whereas the positional conception of the self is always in background play, and the metafact of self-consciousness always holds, it is obviously not the case that we are always referring to ourselves in the first person.

---

[1] "The First Person," pp. 24–25.

[2] Ibid., 32–33.

[3] Ibid., p. 25. Similarly, John Campbell, in his book *Past, Space and Self*, imagines a community whose speakers have no use of the first person, no self-conscious sense of themselves, adopting a rule like (FP) without thereby becoming self-conscious. His point, I take it, is that the lack of self-consciousness would not of itself be a bar to their adopting the rule, and that therefore there must be more to our grasp of the first person than the grasp of such a rule: viz., as Anscombe says, self-consciousness (pp. 111–13). See also Nagel, *The View from Nowhere*, pp. 57–60.

Yet it seems that Anscombe is right: the use of "I" is, in *some* sense, self-conscious. (This is what distinguishes it from the use of "A.") In what sense? The answer to this seems straightforward. If someone uses φ to refer first personally, then, in using φ, he means to refer to himself. That is to say, he means to refer to himself *as himself*. This is what we do in using "I," and what the members of the community Anscombe describes do not do in using "A."

It would seem, then, that we should reformulate the rule (FP) as follows:

> (FP') An utterance of a sentence of the form [φ is F] is
> true just in case the person who utters [φ is F] is F and means
> by φ to refer to himself as himself.

The problem is obvious. The reason the rule requires that the user of φ means to refer to himself "as himself" is to ensure that, from his perspective, the user means to refer to: *myself*. In effect, first-person reference is built into (FP"), into its content. Not only, then, is the remainder of the rule redundant, it is apparent that we cannot appeal to the rule to answer our question, that is, to explain what makes first-person reference first personal.

17.3 Inner First-Person Reference

If we eliminate the redundant part of the rule, we are left with the idea that what makes first-person reference first personal is that, in referring to myself, I mean to refer to myself; that this, the fact that my referential intention is to refer to myself, is what makes first-person reference first personal. Of course, this is no improvement over an answer that appeals to (FP').

If we are to make progress here we need an explication of the *inner* first-person reference—the inner "myself," i.e., the first-person reference that crops up inside my referential intention in first-person reference; an explication that does not yet again introduce first-person reference. At this point the dialectic may start to have a familiar ring. Our explication of the inner "myself" will take the form of a definite description. So we will say that by "myself" I mean: the so-and-so. What content shall we assign to "the so-and-so"? If we omit the first person entirely, if we employ purely general terms in the definite description that expresses what I mean by "myself," the prospects seem hopeless: either we shall fail to capture anything peculiar to me, or we shall capture only some trivial or eccentric feature of myself (14.2). Maybe, then, by "myself" I mean—as Frege says—something primitive: an unshareable and therefore inexpressible mode of presentation, something that cannot be put into words and that I alone grasp (14.2). Not, mind you, a little self-atom, but something general. General and yet unshareable! This is not the way forward.

There is another possibility. It is obvious why we must exclude the first person from the definite description by which we explicate the inner "myself." But is there any reason not to make use of demonstratives? Of course it will not do to say that by "myself" I mean *this* human being. The human being to whom I demonstratively refer may indeed be myself; but in thus referring to him, I do not express what I mean by "myself": any human being can be, for me, an object of demonstrative reference. Perhaps, though, there is something X uniquely related to the human being who is myself, such that we can capture the inner "myself" via a demonstrative reference to X.

An example of what I have in mind is found in Anscombe's paper. Having observed that "I am this thing here" is not an identity (see 16.5), she offers us the following account: "this thing is the thing, the person . . . of whose action *this* idea of action is an idea, of whose movements *these* ideas of movements are ideas, of whose posture *this* idea of posture is an idea."[4] Why does Anscombe conceive of her demonstrative references as references not to actions or movements or postures, but to "ideas" of actions, etc.? She wants, I take it, to guarantee that she singles out the right person. A demonstratively available action (say), an action that I pick out as "this action," might turn out to be your action; but, presumably, an idea that I pick out as "this idea of action" could not turn out to be your idea.

Let us assume, for the moment, Anscombe's demonstrative method of singling out the person who is "myself" yields the right results. It singles out the right human being. But can it be thought to capture, or express, what I mean by "myself"?

Roderick Chisolm, commenting on the same passage from Anscombe, writes:

> She thus attempts to explicate *her* use of the first person pronoun in terms of the demonstrative "this." It is clear that she cannot explicate *my* use of "I" in this way, and I think she might concede that she cannot grasp my "I"-propositions at all. Indeed, how would we report her view if we did not have access to direct quotation?[5]

Chisolm, if I understand him, is objecting to the very fact that Anscombe employs a demonstrative in explaining her use of "I." As "I" users, we all grasp the same thing: not *my* use, but *our* use, or *the* use, of "I." Thus,

---

[4] "The First Person," p. 33.
[5] *The First Person* (The Harvester Press, 1981), p. 21.

since that is what you grasp too, I grasp your use (= our use). If we all grasp this, must it not be possible to express what we—you and I, all of us—grasp? Yet Anscombe's statement of what she grasps in using "I" applies only to her own case. Certainly the particular items (the ideas) that she refers to, that she picks out, have nothing to do with what the rest of us grasp in using "I."

Chisolm's objection might be put in the form of a dilemma. If we are trying to express what another grasps in using "I," we cannot actually *use* the demonstrative. For if we actually use the demonstrative, if we actually refer demonstratively, what we thereby pick out has relevance only to our own case. On the other hand, if we simply describe another's situation in general terms, or just *mention* the demonstrative that he uses, we at most indirectly characterize what he grasps and thus do not actually express what he grasps. So if what another grasps in using "I" can only be expressed by using a demonstrative, only he can express it. No one else can express it. How, then, if we cannot express it, can it be true that we grasp what another grasps? This seems to lead to Frege's conclusion that we cannot grasp what another grasps in using "I." But this is wrong. I grasp what you grasp (what we all grasp) in using "I."

I hear from the next room S exclaim, "This is hot." I understand (grasp) how it is for S. How? There is something demonstratively available within S's experience that feels hot. Or I could say, there is something that S picks out by "this" that feels hot to him. Either way, one might argue, my words get at how it is for S only indirectly; only, that is, in general terms ("there is something demonstratively available"), or by mentioning S's words ("this"). I have not actually expressed, put into words, how it is for S. Suppose then I say, here is how it is for S: this is hot. But now the argument may be that, since I use (versus mention) "this," I actually make a demonstrative reference. This means I pick out something other than what S picks out. And if I pick out something other than what S picks out, I cannot claim to express, or therefore grasp, how it is for S.

Something is amiss here. Suppose I say or write,

(Dm) Here is how it is for S: this is hot.

Here, it seems, I use versus mention the demonstrative. Do I, in thus using the demonstrative, make a demonstrative reference? In that case, it would seem that I, trying to express how it is for S, actually assert about something present to me that it is hot. This is implausible.

Our mistake is that we are allowing ourselves to be sraightjacketed by the logician's use/mention distinction, and thus are failing to appreciate that we may use (versus mention) language in a way that enables us to *take the part of* an Other, to express or put into words how things are from within his horizon, without thereby *taking over* his semantic commitments; his commitments, i.e., to reference and truth. When S says, "This is hot," I understand how it is for him, from within his horizon. I must therefore be able to express how it is for S. There is no bar to my doing this—it is what I do with the embedded sentence in (Dm). I use the sentence in a semantically neutral way, simply to put into words how it is for S, without actually referring to anything, or asserting anything.[6]

The problem with Anscombe's view does not, as Chisolm maintains, derive from the supposed impossibility of grasping what another grasps in using a demonstrative, but rather from an unclarity in the particular demonstrative reference that Anscombe makes. She says that by "I am this thing here" she means that this thing here, E.A., is the person of whose action this idea of action is an idea. To what does she refer by "this idea of an action"?

Let us consider things from my perspective. Perhaps, in using the first person, I refer to: the human being who is aware of *this* object. But then everything depends on the kind of object I pick out. It will not work, obviously, if I pick out an ordinary object like a table, since anyone could be aware of the table. Nor, for much the same reason, will it suffice to say that I mean: the one who performs *this* bodily action. (At least not if my basis for using the demonstrative is purely visual.) The action to which I demonstratively refer might turn out to be your action.

Anscombe introduces "ideas" into her account to avoid this type of problem. Her thought is that whereas *this* action might turn out to be your action (our limbs are crossed, etc.), the action of which *this* idea of action is an idea could only be my action. But what is picked as "this idea of action"? Is there *anything* to be picked out above and beyond the action itself, the particular action?

Some philosophers argue that, strictly speaking, ordinary objects and events in the world are never demonstratively available, that the only objects that are demonstratively available are sense data, internal objects (objects whose existence and presence within my experience are one and the same). With awareness of sense data, it might be said, it is guaranteed that "the one who is aware" is myself.

---

[6] Without entering into details, we can, perhaps, glimpse how this possibility—the possibility of using language in a semantically neutral way; the possibility that we are saying is inherent in our being together as insiders of a system of language-games—might be what lies behind the frequently noted phenomenon of failure of substitutivity in indirect discourse. (The suggestion is, at the level of logical form, encapsulated by the theory of indirect discourse proposed by Donald Davidson in his paper "On Saying That," in *Inquiries into Truth and Interpretation* [Oxford University Press, 1984].) You could say, given our togetherness as insiders, etc., failure of substitutivity is already explicable. Would it not be strange if there were not some such deeper explanation of the phenomenon, that is to say, if the seeming deviations from basic logical principles were just a brute, inexplicable quirk at the surface of language?

On this view, knowledge of the existence the external objects becomes problematic. Thus reference to the human being as "the one who is aware of *this*" becomes problematic—unless we invoke some kind of reductionism about the object of first-person reference.[7] Such issues need not detain us, since Anscombe's view about the first person does not depend on endorsing the view that sense data stand between us and external objects. It is clear, then, when she speaks of "this idea of action," she does not mean to refer to a sense datum. But this simply increases the mystery of what she does mean. I move my arm. I know what it would be to refer to my action, but I cannot for the life of me discern anything I might pick out as "this idea of action." There seems to be nothing to pick out but the action, the action itself, and not some "idea" of it. Yet if what I mean is the action itself, we lose the guarantee that the action in question is "mine," and hence that the one who acts is myself.

However, we have so far been assuming that, in using "this idea of action," our demonstrative reference is visually based. Let us consider the possibility of picking out the action by what we called a "demonstrative of will" (15.9). In that case, the action—$this_w$ action—could not (as we explained) turn out to be your action. In explicating the inner "myself," then, we might avail ourselves of demonstratives of will. What do I mean by "myself"? I mean: the one whose action $this_w$ is.

Of course, in order to mean "myself" I do not need to be acting; I can mean "myself" even if I have lost the capacity to act. But there is a more fundamental point. The reason $this_w$ action could not turn out to be your action, the reason the "mineness" of the action is guaranteed, is that figuring as willed is part of the positional conception of the self. If we simply help ourselves to this guarantee without making explicit the conception of the self from which it derives, then, although we may have hit upon a sure-fire way of singling out the human being that I mean by the inner "myself" (by the "myself" inside the expression of my first-person referential intention), we shall not understand why or how this should be so.[8] On the other hand, once we have philosophically taken hold of the positional conception of the self, there is no need to appeal in our attempt to explain what makes first-person reference first personal to the guarantee provided by the demonstrative of will; we already have (as we shall see) our explanation.

[7] Thus Russell asserts that we can define "I" as "the biography to which 'this' belongs." By "this" he conceives of himself as picking out a sense datum, and by a "biography" he means a construction over time out of sense data. See *An Inquiry into Meaning and Truth* (George Allen and Unwin, 1940), chap. 7, esp. pp. 108, 113.

[8] A similar point will apply if we attempt to rely on the guarantee that would be provided by a demonstrative reference to a sensation ("I am the one whose sensation *this* is"), i.e., to something located in my body space.

17.4 *Attitudes* de Se

But before getting into that, let us consider briefly a different suggestion. It emerges not in direct response to our question but as a kind of by-product of a "theory" about the objects of belief and other so-called propositional attitudes. The theory says we should conceive of the objects of belief and other propositional attitudes not as propositions (as the nomenclature implies) but as properties of the subject, of (say) the believer. It is then held out as a point in favor of the theory that it can explain certain aspects of first-person belief that are otherwise difficult to explain. Perhaps, then, since first-person belief involves first-person reference, it can explain what makes first-person reference first personal.

Versions of the theory have been propounded by Roderick Chisolm in *The First Person* and David Lewis in his paper "Attitudes *De Dicto* and *De Se*."[9] We shall draw on Lewis's version. The basic idea is that in *all* belief the subject *self-ascribes* (as Lewis puts it) a property. Take a belief that we would naturally consider to be about something quite distinct from myself, say the belief that lead is heavier than tin. What is this about? About lead and tin. Lewis would of course not deny that in some sense this is correct; but he also suggests that, in believing that lead is heavier than tin, I self-ascribe a certain property. I self-ascribe the property, viz., of inhabiting a world in which the proposition that lead is heavier than tin is true. So we are required to make an adjustment in our usual conception of what is involved in believing that p. Instead of conceiving of ourselves simply as being related to the proposition that p (let us agree that this is our usual conception), we must conceive of ourselves as having, as self-ascribing, the property of inhabiting a world in which p is true.

How the theory works out in detail, how on its own terms it deals with certain fairly obvious difficulties—that is, apart from the fact that it may feel wrong right from the start; and apart from whether, more generally, philosophical insight in this area is apt to be furthered by the project of assigning to propositional attitudes some uniform kind of "object"—this need not concern us. (Nor shall we worry about the metaphysics of possible worlds that Lewis employs.) Let us turn immediately to the application of the theory to first-person belief.

In all belief, according to Lewis, we self-ascribe a property; but the property we self-ascribe need not, as in the lead and tin example, be a property that has the form: inhabiting a world in which it is true that p. It need not be what Lewis calls a property that "corresponds to a prop-

---

[9] *Philosophical Review*, vol. 88 (1979); reprinted in David Lewis, *Philosophical Papers* (Oxford University Press, 1983). (All page references are to the latter.)

osition" (or as we shall say, a "propositional property"). A propositional property, if it holds of one inhabitant of a world, automatically holds of all inhabitants. Clearly not all properties are, in this sense, propositional. I am now seated. The property of being an inhabitant of a world in which JV is seated is a propositional property; thus it holds of all the inhabitants of our world. This is obviously not true of the simple, nonpropositional property of being seated. The idea, roughly, is that in first-person belief I self-ascribe a nonpropositional property.[10] If I believe that I, JV, am seated, I self-ascribe the nonpropositional property of being seated. If, on the other hand you believe that JV is seated, you self-ascribe the propositional property of being an inhabitant of a world in which it is true that JV is seated.

It is possible, however, to believe something about myself without thereby self-ascribing the relevant nonpropositional property. We can imagine circumstances in which I believe that JV is standing but that I am seated. For Lewis, this means I self-ascribe the propositional property of being an inhabitant of a world in which it is true that JV is standing and at the same time self-ascribe the nonpropositional property of being seated. Or consider the following example of John Perry's that Lewis discusses.[11]

A chap called "Rudolph Lingens" is wandering in a library suffering from amnesia. He happens upon the complete biography of Rudolph Lingens that contains, among other things, a description of the library he, RL, is in as well as the fact that RL is in it at such-and-such time, etc. The point is, whereas reading from this amazing book RL can come to know any true proposition about RL, and in that sense come to know everything about himself, there still is something fundamental he does not know about himself. He does not know: I am RL, the subject of this biography. Since it seems that, for Lewis, the knowledge RL lacks about himself cannot be propositional, how should we conceive of it? Lewis's idea is that the beliefs that constitute RL's knowledge about himself are self-ascriptions of propositional properties, i.e., properties of the form: being an inhabitant of a world in which it is true that RL is such-and-such. The knowledge RL lacks, on the other hand, would be that expressed by the self-ascription of the nonpropositional property of being RL, the subject of this biography.

Perhaps we now have a way of answering our question about first-person reference. Given that S refers to the human being who is himself, we can distinguish the case where the S goes on to self-ascribe a propositional property (S refers to himself in the context of self-ascribed proposi-

---

[10] Lewis, *Philosophical Papers*, sections 3–4.
[11] See Perry's "Frege on Demonstratives," *Philosophical Review* 86 (1977).

tional property), and the case where S goes on to self-ascribe a nonpropositional property (S refers to himself in the context of self-ascribing a nonpropositional property). What makes first-person reference first personal? In first-person reference, the subject not only refers to the human being who is himself but refers to himself in the context of self-ascribing a nonpropositional property.

But what new insight have we actually gained here into the nature of first-person reference? Has not the whole burden simply been shifted to the idea of "self-ascription" about which nothing has been said at all? Self-ascription figures in Lewis's account like a conceptual black box. When Anscombe distinguishes the use of the first person by the fact of self-consciousness (for her, remember, the use of the first person is not referential), she then attempts to clarify what "self-consciousness" involves. Lewis, however, never asks what "self-ascribing a property" involves.[12] He just uses the concept as a kind of primitive in his theory about the "objects" of the belief. Now, as we said, we are not concerned with the merits of Lewis's particular theory or his project in general. But insofar as the theory claims to sort out certain questions about the first person, we must be careful not to walk away with the impression that it has answered our question, that we now understand what makes first-person reference first personal.

Consider again the situation of RL. By reading the biography of RL, RL comes to believe, say, that on such-and-such date RL is wandering in the largest library in the United States. So he self-ascribes the property of being an inhabitant of a world in which it is true that RL is on such-and-such date wandering in the largest library, etc. However, he does not self-ascribe the property of being in the largest library, etc. But why not? He, RL, is RL. And he, RL, believes that RL is in the largest library in the United States (i.e., he self-ascribes the property of being an inhabitant of a world in which RL is in the largest library, etc.). Now, since he has been reading RL's biography, this is not just some chance, isolated bit of information relating to RL that he has come to believe. His belief that RL is in the largest library, etc., is a belief about RL—just as, if on the basis of reading Boswell's biography of Samuel Johnson you believe that Johnson lived just off Fleet Street, you have a belief about Johnson. But then RL believes about the human being who is himself that he is in the largest library in the United States. In that case, why does RL not self-ascribe the property of being in the largest library, etc.?

The answer to this question must, it seems, have something to do with what "self-ascribing" is. But what, exactly? Or to restate the question directly in the first person, and in general terms: What more is necessary

---

[12] The same for Chisolm and what he calls "direct attribution."

for self-ascribing a nonpropositional property than believing about the human being who is myself that he has that property? There is no answer to this question in Lewis's discussion. (The question is not raised; if self-ascription is treated as primitive within the theory, it cannot be raised.) But it should be evident that the question about self-ascription and our question, that is, the question of what makes first-person reference first personal, are the same question. So it should be evident that we do not get an answer here to our question.[13]

17.5 First-Person Reference and the Positional Conception of the Self

Perry's example highlights the point of our question: What makes first-person reference first personal? RL refers to himself, i.e., to the human being that he is, but his reference is not first personal. The missing element in RL's conception of his situation is precisely what makes first-person reference first personal. What is missing?

RL builds up a conception of a particular human being who, as it happens, is RL, himself. What he does not know is: RL is me (I am RL). This means, he does not know that: RL is the one at the center of THIS, of my horizon. The knowledge that RL lacks is, therefore, not knowledge of an identity. It is knowledge in which the positional conception of the self comes into play. Were RL to make the relevant discovery and think, "RL is me (I am RL)," his use of the first person would not be referential but positional.

Here, I believe, we have the answer to our question. In referring first personally I refer to the human being that I am. But in referring, I conceive

[13] Consider Perry's view in "Frege on Demonstratives" (see especially section 3). Perry introduces a distinction between a *thought*, conceived as an object plus an incomplete Fregean sense, and a *role*, which is basically a function that takes us from contexts to objects. One and the same thought can be apprehended, and hence believed, via different roles. We might suppose that there is an I-role (this is my way of putting it, not Perry's—I hope I am not misrepresenting him). In the context of me (so to speak), of JV, the I-role has me, JV, as its value; in the context of you, it has you as its value. And so on. The role remains constant over all first-person beliefs. When in the library situation RL believes about RL that he is in the largest library in the United States, the relevant thought, viz., that comprised by RL and the incomplete sense expressed by "is in the largest library in the United States," is not apprehended via the I-role (but via some other role). So although the thought is the same as that which RL would believe in the corresponding first-person belief, it is not believed first personally, since it is not apprehended via the I-role. Now, Perry's view may or may not make a contribution to the semantics for sentences containing first person expressions; but, as with Lewis's proposal, we must not imagine that it answers the question of what makes first-person reference first personal. It is, in this respect, subject to the same kinds of objections that we raised (17.2) to the attempt to answer the question by reference to the semantic rule for "I." Thus our so-called I-role would fit exactly the role via that Anscombe's community of A-users apprehend thoughts about themselves.

of that human being, the object of reference, in a particular way: I conceive of him as the one at the center of my horizon. Thus the positional conception of the self figures in my referential intention. That is to say, in referring, I bring the positional conception into play. This is what makes my reference first personal.

When I refer to myself first personally, I refer to myself (as Anscombe puts it) with self-consciousness. We took the point to be that I not only refer to myself, i.e., the human being who is myself, I refer to myself "as myself" (17.2). How are we to understand this talk of "self-consciousness," of referring to the human being who is myself "as myself"? Here, again, we must look to the content of my referential intention in referring to the human being who is myself. In referring to the human being who is myself, I mean to refer to: the human being that I am, the human being who is myself. But does not this answer to our question about first-person reference simply repeat what we already assume in asking the question?

No. The use of the first person that occurs inside the expression of my referential intention is not the referential but the positional use of the first person. Thus, in stating the content of my referential intention, we may replace the "is myself" by a predicate expression. In referring first personally, I refer to: the human being who figures at the center of my horizon (who occupies the subject position within my horizon). Having this intention in referring to myself is referring to myself "as myself," referring to myself "with self-consciousness." Having a referential intention in which the positional conception of the self is play, this, once again, is what my makes reference first personal.

In a sense, the positional conception of the self is always in play: it is always in background play (14.9). That is, it is always the case that some human being figures standingly within my horizon as the one at the center, as occupying the subject position. What makes first-person reference first personal is that, in referring, we bring the positional conception of the self into play. We bring it into play out of background play. Think again about RL's situation. RL believes of himself that he is in such-and-such library, etc. But his way of conceiving of himself in this belief, his referential intention, does not bring into play the positional conception of the self. He of course has this conception of himself, but it remains in background play.

17.6 The First Person and Emptiness at the Center

The positional conception of the self is always in background play. Yet we have noted a sense in which it *need* not be in play; i.e., in which it need not be in play *at all*—even in background play. We can imagine that within my horizon, within my experience, there is nothing that figures at the center. Not, let us be clear, just that there is nothing that figures$_o$, but nothing that figures$_s$, at the center: that there simply never has been anything at the center, occupying the subject position within my horizon. We can, you might say, imagine a standing emptiness at the center, an experience (horizon) in which the subject position is standingly unoccupied, in which therefore there is no one who is "me." This, as we explained, may not be causally or metaphysically possible, but it makes sense experientially, as a way things might be from within my experience (12.5–6; 13.2).

Within such an experience there would be no referential use of the first person. For the referential use of the first person is a use in which the intention is to refer to the one at the center of my experience. If no one figures$_s$ at the center of my experience, if the subject position is standingly unoccupied, there is nothing to be intended by a first-person referential intention. Right now there is a cup in front of me on the table, but there is no plate. I am sure of this. Can I refer to "the plate in front me"? I can utter the words, I can pretend to refer. But can I, in uttering the words, *mean* to refer to a plate in front of me? Could that (given what I believe) be my referential intention? Such an intention would not make sense as an intention. It would be, we might say, a meaningless intention. Similarly, from within an experience, a horizon, in which the subject position is unoccupied, the intention to refer to the one occupying that position—to the one that "I am"—would be a meaningless intention. From within such an experience, there would be no referential use of the first person.

One of Anscombe's arguments for her view that the "I" is not referential turns, in effect, on this possibility of emptiness at the center. She says that in the situation of complete sensory deprivation, I cannot have a thought about "this body," since there is no body to pick out demonstratively. In such a situation "the possibility will perhaps strike me that there is none. That is, the possibility that there is then nothing which I am."[14] Yet, the possibility of using "I" would remain. (How else could I be thinking that there may nothing that I am?) There is, it seems, no way to make sense of this residual use of the "I" on the assumption that "I" is referential.[15]

The problem, in our terms, is that given emptiness at the center, there is no object for a first-person referential intention. Any such intention would be a meaningless intention. Accordingly, if we insist that the use of the first person is referential, there is, it seems, no way to account for the residual possibility of using the first person—or rather, Anscombe reasons, the only way to account for it would be to suppose the object of first-person reference is not a body, a human being, but a soul. "Thus," she says, "we discover that *if* 'I' is a referring expression, then Descartes

[14] "The First Person," p. 34.
[15] Ibid., pp. 31, 34.

was right about what the referent was."[16] Of course, this is meant to be a reductio of the assumption that we use the first person to refer.

Perhaps (since they do not exist) we can leave souls out of this. When we speak of "emptiness at the center," we mean that there is no human being at the center of my horizon. Note that Anscombe contemplates an ordinary situation of sensory deprivation. In such a situation no human being figures$_o$ at the center of my horizon. But given that this is compatible with a particular human being figuring$_s$ at the center of my horizon, it does not itself preclude the referential use of the first person. (See above, the last two paragraphs of 14.5.) By "emptiness at the center" we have in mind the more radical situation of standing emptiness at the center, etc. In this case, there is no possibility of using the first-person referentially.

Hence whatever use of the first person might survive emptiness at the center, it is not the referential use. Even so, Anscombe's conclusion—that the everyday use of the first person is not referential—does not follow. All that follows is that the use of the first person that survives emptiness at the center would not be the everyday use.

Then what might it be? What use, or uses, of the first person are possible in a situation in which there is nothing that is "me," i.e., in which there is emptiness at the center of my horizon? *These* very uses are possible: the uses we make of the first person when speak of "there being nothing that is 'me' " and of "emptiness at the center of my horizon," that is, the positional and horizonal uses of the first person. I could not refer first personally (there is nothing to refer to); but the possibility of using the first person—positionally and horizonally—would still be there.

Recall the nested structure of the first person (16.6): the positional use inside the referential, the horizonal inside the positional. You could say that whereas in the radical situation of emptiness at the center the outermost nest of this structure would not exist, the inner two nests would remain. Thus although there would be no possibility of forming a first-person referential intention, the thought "Nothing is me," wherein the first person occurs positionally, would be a possible thought (it is precisely my knowing the truth of "Nothing is me" that excludes the referential intention)—and this thought, in turn, being equivalent to "Nothing occupies the position at the center of my horizon," implicates a grasp of the horizonal use of the first person.

From within a horizon whose subject position is empty, then, the possibility of both the positional and horizonal use of the first person would remain. There would, however, be a difference concerning the respective

---

[16] Ibid. p. 31; see also p. 32. Notice, the stipulation is unnecessary from our standpoint, since when we speak of "emptiness at the center" we mean this to entail the absence of a Cartesian soul at the center as well as a bodily subject.

conceptions of the self. Since nothing would figure at the center of my horizon, the positional conception of the self would no longer be in background play. On the other hand, since the emptiness is emptiness at the center of my horizon, the existence of my horizon is presupposed, and given the existence of my horizon the horizonal conception of the self inevitably remains in background play. For, given the existence of my horizon, the fact of its existence is manifest; and this metafact of manifestness, the fact of self-consciousness (9.3), entails the being in play—i.e., the being in background play—of the horizonal conception consciousness (14.9). The being in background play of the horizonal conception of consciousness is thus built into what we imagine in imagining emptiness at the center of my horizon. It is, in fact, built into whatever we imagine when we imagine a way things might be from within my horizon.

It is worth remarking, finally, that when we speak here of the possibility of emptiness at the center and hence of the positional and horizonal uses of the first person surviving into this situation, we are talking about the logic of the self. Thus we have in mind experiential possibility, the kind of possibility that is exhibited in imagination (see chapter 13). No one is claiming that these things are causally or metaphysically possible. The distinction between experiential and causal/metaphysical possibility will be important in our discussion of the self in time, to which we now turn.

18. Temporalizing the Self

18.1 Introduction

So far in our reflections on the self and the first person we have abstracted away from the dimension of time. Thus, in discussing Descartes' question "What am I?" our focus was entirely on *what* I am (a soul?, a human being?) without raising the question of *when* I am supposed to be whatever kind of entity it is that I am. In fact, since Descartes' question asks about the essential nature of the entity that I am, in a sense there can be no question of "when" it is that I am what I am. Where *e* is the entity that I am, if *e* entity exists at all, *e* has the essential nature it has. Take away its essential nature and you take away the entity itself, the entity that I am.

Of course, assuming the answer to Descartes' question is "I am a human being," I can now truly assert "I am a human being"; and if I can now truly assert this, it must now be true that I am a human being. In that case, trivially, I can truly assert, "I am now a human being." But this must not be understood in the manner of, e.g., "I am now a senator," or "I am now a member of the Chamber of Commerce." That is, "now" used in the answer to Descartes' question is not meant as: now *versus some other time* in my existence. The use of "now" in the answer to the Descartes' question has no temporally contrastive force. It is, we might say, a gratuitous use of the present tense.

Thus the absence of temporal considerations from our reflections on Descartes' question makes perfectly good sense. But time, as an explicit theme, was absent also from our reflections on the positional conception of the self. Here, taking it as given that I am a human being, we sought to answer the question, "What makes a particular human being 'me,' the human being that 'I am'?" In our attempt to work out the answer to this question, to work out the phenomenology of the subject position (the positional conception of the self), temporal considerations, tense did not play a contrastive role. We asked simply what makes a particular human being "me," not what makes that human being *now* (versus at such-and-such time *in the past/future*) "me." Similarly, when in discussing the horizonal conception of the self we asked "What makes my horizon 'mine'"? the contrast between present, past, and future did not weigh in our reflections at all. The question was not what makes my horizon *now* (versus at such-and-such time *in the past/future*) "mine," but simply what makes my horizon "mine."

However, while in all three cases we abstracted away from temporal considerations, it does not follow that such considerations are irrelevant to the cases themselves, or that the cases are alike with respect to time. In the case of Descartes' question, time is irrelevant: given that the entity that I am has at one time a certain essential nature, there is no possibility that that same entity might, at another time, have a different essential nature. In contrast, in the case of what makes a particular human being "me," it will be clear that tense is not irrelevant. The role of tense in the positional conception of the self is at the heart of the so-called problem of "personal identity," the problem of my identity through time. Finally, in the case of the question of what makes my horizon "mine," here again temporal considerations drop out—but not because we are, as in the case of Descartes' question, concerned with the essential nature of some worldly entity. The reason in this case is, as we shall explain, utterly different from that which makes time irrelevant in the case of Descartes' question.

We may say that the question of what makes a particular human being "me" has a temporalized form, whereas the question of what makes my horizon "mine" cannot be similarly temporalized. In the remainder of the present chapter we shall try to give a preliminary account of this difference: first, of how temporal considerations enter the question of what makes a particular human being the human being "me," the one that "I am"; and second, why such considerations are alien to the question of what makes my horizon "mine." The ideas we introduce here will be developed further in later chapters. But we should note in advance that our interest will be confined to the way temporal considerations affect questions about the self. In some cases, our explanations will entail, or require for their understanding, particular views about time—and of course we shall have to provide the necessary clarifications; but there will be no serious attempt in this book to deal with the topic of time as such. Thus, for example, though we shall make great use of the contrast between past/present/future, we shall not try to answer the question of what this contrast means to us, or the question of whether it is reducible to conceptions of temporal order, or again, the question of whether facts to whose expression tense is essential are in some sense subjective, or mind-dependent. All such questions will be left on one side.

18.2 Tense and the Phenomenology of the Subject Position

Assuming then that Descartes' question has been settled—that what I am is a human being, a member of that natural kind—there is, we know, the further question of what makes a particular human being "me," the one that "I am." He is the one who occupies a special position within my horizon (experience): he is the one at the center. Spelling out what being "at the center" involves, i.e., spelling out the positional conception of the self, is a matter of spelling out the phenomenology of the subject position: the distinctive way, or ways, the human being in question figures within my horizon (see chapter 15). So far, as we said, our discussion of these matters has abstracted away from tense. Our question has never been what makes a certain human being the one I *now am* (versus *was*, or *will be*), but always, without any temporal contrast in view, what makes a certain human being the human being that *I am*, the one who *is me*.

Perhaps, it will seem that our question could not have been other than it was. For what point could there be in introducing temporal contrasts, tense, into our account of the phenomenology of the subject position unless there were a possibility that the human being I now am is not the same (the numerically identical) human being as the human being that I was/will be. But, it may be said, there is no such possibility. JV is the human being I now am. It is nonsense to suppose that this human being, JV, might at some time in the past have been a different (numerically distinct) human being, or that he, JV, might become a different human being at some time in the future.

This objection depends on confusing the referential and positional uses of first-person definite descriptions (see 12.7). Consider, for example:

> (1) The human being that I am might become in the future, or have been in the past, a different human being.

If we take "the human being that I am" referentially, then, it is used to refer to JV. In that case by (1) I would assert that JV, that very human being, might become, or have been, a different human being. Here we have nonsense. On the other hand, if the definite description is used positionally, what I assert is that a human being other than JV might come to be, or have been in the past, at the center of my horizon (might in the future occupy, or have occupied in the past, the position within my horizon that makes a particular human being "me"). This, it seems, makes sense.

Or consider:

> (2) A human being other than the human being that I am might become, or might have been in the past, the human being that I am.

In (2), if both occurrences of "the human being that I am" are taken referentially, we get nonsense. If, however, we take the first occurrence referentially and the second positionally, what I assert is that a human being other than the particular human being that I am, other than JV, might in the future come to be at the center of my horizon. Once again, this seems to make sense.

That is to say, it makes sense experientially: as a way things might unfold or develop within my experience (horizon). It is, as we explained (12.5), a possibility that I can exhibit in imagination. I can imagine a human being other than JV coming to occupy the subject position within my experience at some point in the future; I can imagine a human being other than JV having occupied this position in the past. Let us try to convince ourselves that this is the case, that these are possibilities that can be exhibited in imagination.

Recall our earlier example. I can imagine that bit by bit the human being who figures at the center of my experience, JV, vanishes and that nothing takes his place, that the subject position within my experience becomes empty, unoccupied (12.6). I can, in this sense, imagine its being the case there is no one who is "me." This, we agreed, is an experiential possibility. It makes sense as a way things might be, or develop, within my experience (horizon). Having exhibited to ourselves this possibility—the possibility of there being no human being at the center of my horizon—it would seem to require only a small step of imagination to reach the further possibility of there being at some future time a *different* human being, a human being other than JV, occupying the position at the center of my horizon, and thus being the human being that "I am."

In this respect, what holds for the future holds for the past. If I can imagine someone X, someone other than JV, occupying the subject position within my horizon at some point in the future, I can imagine X being the one at the center, occupying the subject position within my horizon at some point in the past. For what I would imagine is exactly analogous to what I would imagine if, having imagined X occupying the subject position within my horizon at some point in the future, I imagine, from that future standpoint, that it was JV who occupied the subject position at a certain time in the past. That is, just as I can imagine from X's standpoint in the future JV figuring as the human being who at such-and-such time in the past was the one that "I am," so I, JV, can imagine, from my actual standpoint in the present, someone other than JV figuring in this way, i.e., as the human being who at such-and-such time in the past was one that "I am." I can imagine, in other words, someone other than JV now figuring as the human being who was then (at such-and-such past time) the one at the center of my horizon, who was then the human being that "I am."

What point (we asked) could tense have in our exposition of the phenomenology of the subject position? In light of the experiential possibilities to which we have drawn attention, the answer should be obvious. The point of employing tense is simply that these possibilities—that a human being other than JV should now figure as the human being who *was* then (at such-and-such past time) at the center of my horizon; that a human being other than JV *will* (at such-and-such future time) figure this way within my horizon—are (although we had previously ignored this fact) possibilities to which tense is essential: tensed possibilities.

Clearly, given the past and future tensed possibilities, there is also a present tensed possibility. There is, in other words, a point (in this philosophical context) to saying about JV that he figures as the human being who is *now* at the center of my horizon, that he is *now* the human being that "I am." This is not a gratuitous use of the present tense. Generally, then, there is a point to employing tense in spelling out the phenomenology of the subject position. There is a point to employing tense, etc. because the way or ways of figuring within my horizon by virtue of which a certain human being is "me," the one that "I am," are tensed ways of figuring within my horizon. The phenomenology of the subject position is, we might say, a tensed phenomenology.

In what follows, we shall treat the positional "I am (is me)" as if it were tense-neutral and introduce tense separately, via a temporal indicator or tensed verb. Thus in,

> (3) JV figures within my horizon as the human being who is *now* the one that "I am,"

the tensed character of JV's way of figuring within my horizon is (as we shall understand this) expressed not by "am" in "I am" but by the temporal indicator "now": JV figures as the human being who is now the one that "I am" (at the center of my horizon). Similarly, in,

> (4) JV figures within my horizon as the human being who was (at such-and-such past time) the one that "I am,"

and,

> (5) JV will (at such-and-such future time) figure within my horizon as the human being who "I am,"

we shall understand the positional "I am" as tense-neutral, and the vehicle of tense to the relevant verb: in (4), the verb "was"; in (5), the verb "will figure." Although admittedly this is artificial—since the way of figuring is of itself in each case essentially tensed—it will enable us to keep track of the element of tense and to spot nuances and difficulties that might otherwise pass us by.

18.3 The Tense Asymmetry in the Phenomenology of the Subject Position

Let us now remark upon an important asymmetry: tense enters twice in the past and present cases, whereas in the future case it enters only once. Thus when we say in (4) that "JV figures, etc.," we mean that JV *now* figures within my horizon as the human being who *was* the one that "I am" (at the center of my horizon). Similarly, in (3) we mean that JV *now* figures as the human being who is *now* the one that "I am." (5) is different. We cannot say about JV that he *now* figures within my horizon as the one who *will* (at such-and-such future time) figure at the center of my horizon. What might this way of figuring be? There is a present way of having in the past figured at the center of my horizon, but no present way of figuring in the future at the center. The only future-related possibility is simply that of figuring in the future at the center of my horizon, i.e., as asserted in (5), that JV will figure as the one that "I am."

Consider the way JV now figures within my horizon, that is, his way of figuring by virtue of which he is now the one at the center, the one that "I am": his way of appearing visually, and his figuring within my horizon as the space of feeling and the locus of will. It is not, we know, necessary that at this moment JV's body actually figures within my horizon as the space of feeling, or that some movement of his body actually figures as willed, or that his body actually appears visually within my horizon. What is in question is JV's figuring within my horizon in the standing, not the operative, sense: his figuring$_s$, not his figuring$_o$, as the one at the center of my horizon. Yet, as we observed (14.5), JV could not figure$_s$ as the one at the center of my horizon unless there were particular times at which he figured$_o$ as the one at the center. His figuring$_s$ as the one at the center is parasitic upon his figuring$_o$ as the one at the center. This is where the tense asymmetry becomes relevant.

Consider the case of action. A movement of JV's body, a movement of JV's arm, say, might right now figure$_o$ within my horizon as willed, as an act. In that case, there is a particular movement of JV's that now figures$_o$ as willed. Suppose, instead, I intend to move my arm. I intend to do this in precisely ten seconds, in a very specific manner. But however specific, however detailed, my intention, there is no relevant movement that might now figure$_o$ within my horizon as willed. Why not a particular future movement? There is no particular future movement. There will be such a movement (or so we may assume), but there is no such movement now.

I carry out my intention. I move my arm. Now I look back on it. When I acted, the movement of my body *then*, at that past time, figured$_o$ within my horizon as: now willed. And now? *Now* it figures$_o$ within my horizon as *then* willed. Like any past event, this action of mine, this movement, is "there" as a potential object of thought (reference). Thus it, that same event, can figure now within my horizon. And given how it figured then, at the past time, viz., as now willed, it can now figure as then willed. In a sense, the movement can figure now just as it figured then: it can figure in a way that holds everything constant—everything, that is, except tense.

In sum, looking to the past, there is now, as in the case of the present, something that now figures as willed: in the case of the present, it now figures as now willed; in the case of the past, it now figures as then willed. Looking to the future, on the other hand, there is nothing that now figures as willed: there is no particular action, say, such that I now mean to perform "it." When we look to the future, you could say, nothing looks back.

The asymmetry that has emerged in the phenomenology of the subject position is an instance of a more general temporal asymmetry to which philosophers have often called attention between past/present versus future. (We alluded to it at the beginning of 1.6.) There is a large issue here, into which we shall not enter, about whether the asymmetry is intrinsic to the being of events or is in some sense subjective; that is, expressed in our terms, whether the contrast between past/present versus future belongs to events independently of their figuring from within the personal horizon, or whether, like (say) the contrast between self and other, it is a contrast that exists (that makes sense) only from within the horizon. We shall simply take the contrast at face value and ignore the question of its metaphysical status.

Bearing this caveat in mind, we may assert that whereas singular reference to events in the present/past seems unproblematic, in the case of future events there is nothing to which to refer, no relevant object of reference.[1] Thus thought about future events, even when expressed in terms of definite descriptions, is implicitly general. (This is one place where Russell's theory of descriptions has a genuine purpose to fulfill.) Suppose I watch you act. You move your arm. Your action now figures as now appearing a certain way within my horizon. Consider the temporal standpoint before you act: although I may now anticipate that you will act in a particular way, there is now no act that might figure, one way or another, within my horizon. Hence there is nothing, no act, that *now* figures as

---

[1] The asymmetry is central to Gilbert Ryle's paper, "It Was to Be," in *Dilemmas* (Cambridge University Press, 1953). Again, Donald Davidson seems to have the asymmetry in mind when he writes "that the event whose occurrence makes 'I turned on the light' true cannot be called the object, however intentional, of 'I wanted to turn on the light.' If I turned on the light, then I must have done it at a precise moment, in a particular way—every detail is fixed. But it makes no sense to demand that my want be directed to an action performed at any one moment or done in some unique manner." "Actions, Reasons and Causes," in *Essays on Actions and Events* (Oxford University Press, 1980), p. 6.

something that will figure etc. However, switching our perspective to the later time, now that you have acted, now that your action has appeared within my horizon in the way that it did, it can *now* figure within my horizon in that same way—but with a shift in tense. It can now figure as *then* appearing within my horizon.

Let us summarize these points as they apply to the phenomenology of the subject position. JV *now* figures$_s$ both as the one *now* at the center of my horizon, and as the one who in the past *was* at the center, but not as the one who *will be* the one at the center; rather it is simply true, or so we may assume, that JV *will* figure$_s$ as the one at the center. This asymmetry of tense in the phenomenology of the subject position derives from the corresponding asymmetry in the relevant operative figuring$_s$ of JV within my horizon, which is, in turn, a special case of the more general asymmetry between the present/past versus future.

18.4 Tense and the Horizonal Self

I, JV, am a human being. It is metaphysical nonsense to suppose that this human being, JV, might have been in the past a (numerically) different human being, or that he might become such in the future. We can, however, give sense to the possibility that a human being other than JV in the past was "me," or that a human being other JV might be "me" in the future. That is, it makes sense experientially (as a way things might be or develop from within my experience) that, in the past, a human being other than JV occupied the position at the center of my horizon, or that a human being other than JV will occupy this position in the future. The phenomenology of the subject position is, as we put it, a tensed phenomenology. In contrast, as we remarked (18.1), tense plays no comparable role in the case of the horizon itself, i.e., the horizon from within which the subject position is defined: my horizon (the personal horizon), the horizonal self. Thus whereas there is a point to qualifying the question of what makes a certain human being "me" with a reference to the past, present, or future, such a qualification has no point when we ask what makes my horizon "mine." What might the point be? Might it be the case that, say, the horizon (experience, consciousness, life) that is now "mine" was "yours" in the past, or will be "yours" in the future?

What makes my horizon "mine" is not that it is owned by one human being rather than another, so that at different times it might have different owners, but that it is, in a certain sense, *the* horizon: it is the horizon that includes all others. If my horizon were "mine" by virtue of being owned by a particular human being, the human being would have to be the one who is "me"—which would raise the question of what makes him "me."

We would find ourselves, once again, caught in the circle of the first person. To break out of the circle we must recognize that rather than my horizon being "mine" by virtue of being owned by the human being who is "me," the human being who is me is "me" by virtue of his position within my horizon; while, for its part, the "mineness" of my horizon consists not in its having this or that relation to something else but, as we said, in its being the all-inclusive horizon. It is the truth of solipsism that makes my horizon "mine."

But the question is still there: Why is tense irrelevant? Why might not the horizon be "mine" now but not "mine" in the future? Or "mine" now, but not "mine" in the past?

The short answer is this. When it was not "mine," there was no "it," no horizon, to be either "mine" or not "mine," and when it will be not "mine," it will simply not be. It either is or is not, and insofar as the horizon is, it is "mine." It cannot undergo a change from being "mine" to not "mine," or being not "mine" to "mine."

In fact, it cannot undergo a change of *any* kind. Remember, we talking not about this or that "ordinary," philosophically unproblematic object but about a subject matter that, with reflection, becomes ever more confounding, ever more problematic, viz., the subject matter that first emerged in our reflections on the DH: the subject matter that contains the totality I call "the world" with its infinity of egocentric space and—the important thing in the present context—time. Whatever is before and after *now* is internal to this subject matter. This means that the horizon itself is neither now, nor before or after now; neither present, past, nor future. The horizon itself is the horizon of time. Then when is it? It is not at any time. It is, as we put it, outside time (see 1.6, 3.1).

A change from the horizon's being "mine" to being not "mine" would be an event, an event of which the horizon itself is the subject. Suppose there is a future event, say, of which the horizon is the subject. Then that event, qua future event, would be internal to my horizon, which means that the subject of the event would be internal to my horizon as well. But we are supposing that the subject of the event *is* my horizon. How could my horizon be internal to my horizon, internal to itself?

It would not be amiss to remind ourselves here that the internality of present/past/future to my horizon is not the internality of an internal object, like an afterimage. It is an internality that is of a piece with internality to a dream. From within a dream, the world does not exist only from within the dream but has the same independence that it has in reality. Thus from within a dream, we draw the same contrast between the world and an internal object that we draw in reality. Similarly, from within a dream, time does not exist only from within the dream, but stretches as endlessly out of the past and into the future as it does in reality.

The fact of death will serve to highlight the difference between the two kinds of internality. I will die: there will be NOTHING. When there is NOTHING, there will be no such thing as my horizon. As I contemplate death, then, I know there will be a time, in fact an endless time, in which there is no such thing as my horizon. In terms of being internal to my horizon, we can make sense of this. The infinity of future time, which as future is internal to my horizon, includes an infinity of time when there will be no such thing as my horizon. In terms of the internality of an internal object—the internality of something that exists only from within my horizon—however, the same thought would be incoherent. Were it the case that time exists only from within my horizon, the looming fact of NOTHINGNESS would entail that there will be no time after my death.

Insofar as the infinity of time is internal to it, my horizon is outside time. My horizon, then, in contrast to the human being that "I am," the one who figures at the center of my horizon, cannot be the subject of an event that is present, past, or future. Thus, whereas there is a possibility (an experiential possibility) of someone other than JV having been "me" in the past, or being "me" in the future, there is no corresponding possibility of a different horizon having been "mine" in the past, or of a different horizon being "mine" in the future. Any such past or future would entail the occurrence of an event of which my horizon is the subject. And, once again, there can be no such event. My horizon, the horizonal self, is outside time.

Have we not glossed over a obvious difficulty? Included in the infinity of time internal to my horizon is an infinity of time when there will be NOTHING, no such thing then as my horizon. This, we said, provided we are not confused about the kind of internality involved, is coherent. However, if there will be a time when there is NOTHING, when there is no such thing as my horizon, there must be a time when there ceases to be such a thing as my horizon. And what is this "ceasing to be" if not an event, a future event, that befalls my horizon, that is, a future event of which my horizon is the subject? And here, it seems, we have exactly what we said there cannot be, something that—unlike the fact of future NOTHINGNESS—is incoherent, viz., a future event of which my horizon is the subject. If all future events are internal to my horizon, my horizon cannot be the subject of a future event.

You will no doubt recognize where we have arrived: at the temporal puzzle of death (11.3). The self as horizon, my horizon, since it contains whatever is temporal, is outside time. Being outside time, the horizon cannot cease to be, since its ceasing to be would be an event of which it, the horizon, is the subject. But inasmuch as I know that I will die, I know that my horizon (my consciousness, my life) will cease to be: this is what my death is, the ceasing to be of my horizon. What is outside time and therefore cannot cease to be will cease be. This puzzle, the temporal puzzle of death, is thus implicit in our explanation of why the question of what makes my horizon "mine," in contrast to the question of what makes a certain human being "me," cannot be temporalized. But the puzzle, if we are right, is not created by our explanation. The puzzle is there for us in any case—whether or not we philosophize about the time and the self, whether or not we philosophize about anything at all.

19. The Problem of Personal Identity

19.1 The Special Philosophical Problem of Personal Identity: The Problem of First-Person Identity

My existence in time is not that of an event. I, JV, the human being that I am, do not "occur at" this or that time. I "exist at" times, i.e., at different times, and thus "exist through" time. I, the human being that I am, the one who is sitting now in the café penning these lines, existed at the time of (say) JFK's assassination. I remember that day, in Chicago, hearing about the assassination from a stranger who just got on the elevator with me. I, JV, existed then, at that time, and at the time of countless other past events. And I, JV, the same human being, will, or so we may suppose, exist at the time of countless events in the future.

The uninterrupted existence through time of an entity of a given kind entails the identity through time of that entity. I, JV, am an entity of some kind or other. So there is such a fact as the fact of my identity through time. This fact, the fact of my identity through time, is, it would seem, simply the fact of the identity through time of the entity—of whatever kind entity it is—that I am.

What could be more straightforward? For we know what kind of entity I am. I am a human being. My identity through time, then, must consist simply in the unbroken existence through time of that same human being, the human being that I am.

Yet philosophers often present the fact of my (our) identity through time as raising a special problem, and therefore as meriting philosophical reflection. I allude to the so-called problem, or set of problems, commonly known as the "problem of personal identity." The problem of personal identity is a problem about my identity through time. But, as we said, my identity through time would seem to be nothing more or less than the identity through time of JV, the human being that I am; nothing more or less, then, than the identity through time of a particular human being. What could the special problem, or problems, possibly be?

We might consider weird cases of biological metamorphosis. The human being that I am starts to acquire the characteristics of another species. At a certain stage it might be difficult to say whether we still have a human being, hence whether it is the same human being. But this problem, such as it is, could be raised about a mouse, or a camel, about a creature of any species. It can hardly be thought to be the special problem that philosophers mean by the "problem of personal identity."

A biological species is a natural kind. Perhaps the special philosophical problem of personal identity concerns not the fact that I am a member of a natural kind, a human being, but the fact that I am a "person." But what is a person? And is it obvious that persons are not, as such, a natural kind? These are difficult questions. It seems to me that the answer to the second is negative, but I am not sure what the complete answer to the first should be. Presumably, the kind in question will be defined in terms of having certain capacities. The central capacity, as suggested by Locke's famous definition of a person, would be that of being able to think and reason with self-consciousness.[1] In that case, it seems hard to rule out a priori the possibility that members of a species other than human beings might have the right capacities and thus count as persons. But then what should we say about such creatures, including human beings, at the point in their development before they fully acquire the capacities? Or suppose a creature fully acquires the capacities but then, through injury or disease, loses them? Or is born defective and never develops them? Or, since a creature that can reason and think about itself with self-consciousness must have self-conscious beliefs about itself and about its past and future, what shall we say if that creature acquires, perhaps overnight, a whole new set of such beliefs whose content is incompatible with its prior set of beliefs? Once again, difficult questions.

Difficult, but in my view they still fail to capture the specialness of the special philosophical problem about personal identity—although the last question, insofar as it introduces the idea of the subject having self-conscious beliefs about itself, indirectly points to what makes the problem special. In order that the specialness of the problem should become fully apparent, in order that we should properly catch hold of what distinguishes this problem about identity through time from all other problems and puzzles about identity through time, we must, I think, not only recognize that the subject whose identity is in question has self-conscious beliefs about itself, about its past and future, we must grasp these beliefs in a way that directly and explicitly reflects the fact of their self-conscious self-directedness. This means, simply, that we must grasp the beliefs in terms of their first-person content, as beliefs about *myself*, about *my* past, and *my* future.[2]

---

[1] Thus Locke defines a person as "a thinking intelligent being, that has reason and reflection, and can consider itself as itself, the same thinking thing, in different times and places; which it does only by that consciousness which is inseparable from thinking, and, as it seems to me, essential to it," *An Essay Concerning Human Understanding*, book 2, chap. 27, section 11.

[2] Accordingly, the reference to self-consciousness in Locke's definition of a "person" should be viewed not so much as specifying a capacity that distinguishes a particular kind of substance (persons) from other kinds of substance, but as indicating the particular orien-

We said that the problem of personal identity is a problem, or set of problems, about my identity through time. It should be clear now that this formulation is meant to be taken very strictly. The problem of personal identity, the philosophical problem, we might say, is essentially a problem about *my* identity through time. It is thus a problem that can be exhibited only in first-person reflection; only, that is, in self-conscious reflection on my identity through time—reflection on my identity through time as *my* identity through time. If the problem is not this, it is not anything.

There are, of course, difficult and interesting questions about identity through time that are completely independent of the first-person perspective—for example, the well-known puzzle about the ship of Theseus. When reflecting on the identity of a ship through time, the first-person perspective is irrelevant. But do not suppose that solving the puzzle about the ship of Theseus, or some puzzle about the identity through time of a church, or a club, or a nation (or any of the other kinds of entities that philosophers like to mention in this regard), will solve, or even cast light on, the special philosophical problem of personal identity.

Nor, as should be apparent from what we have already said, are we denying that there are interesting questions, etc., about the identity through time of persons that are independent of the first-person perspective. S has suffered total loss of memory. Is he still a person? The same person? If we decide that S cannot be punished now for what he did earlier, is that because we think he is no longer a person? If a person dies is he, the dead human being, still a person? And so on. To grasp or appreciate such questions, we are not, it seems, required to adopt the first-person perspective. Yet they are, in some sense, questions or problems about the "identity of persons," about "personal identity." In some sense—but not the sense that interests us. Our question, our problem, is a problem that can be entered only via the first-person perspective. Our problem is the essentially first-person problem of personal identity, the problem (as we might call it) of *first*-person identity.

No one is insisting that we take an interest in this problem, i.e., in this problem or set of problems, rather than the non-first-person problems about the identity through time of persons. But wherever we direct our interest, the first-person problem—the problem implicit in Locke's famous chapter on identity, and explicit in Kant's *Paralogisms*—this problem, the special philosophical problem of personal identity, will still be there. What point could there be in turning our backs on the problem?[3]

---

tation—that of the first person—required to enter the special topic of personal identity. More on Locke below (19.3).

[3] Thus, it seems to me, even when philosophers explicitly claim to eschew the first-person perspective in discussing the problem of personal identity, if you reflect carefully on the

The problem of first-person identity is heralded by Descartes' procedure in the *Meditations*. Thus Descartes, in the second Meditation, claims to prove his own existence, that "I exist," before asking "What am I?" The order is important, since it suggests that it is possible philosophically to engage in first-person reflection about myself (self-conscious, self-directed philosophical reflection) while leaving open the answer to the question of what kind of entity I am, the ontological question. It suggests, you might say, that in philosophy the first person offers us a domain of refection that is independent of ontology, an autonomous domain of reflection (a point encapsulated in Kant's remark that the sole text of rational psychology is "I think").

In any case, it is the essentially first-person problems that will occupy us here. These, as we shall see, divide into two kinds. One concerns the entity to which I refer by "I": the entity at the center of my horizon, the entity that occupies the subject position within my horizon. The other concerns my horizon, the horizon by figuring at the center of which a certain entity is the one I refer to by "I." We cannot pretend to consider all the problems that might be included here. Yet I would expect that, although the principle on the basis of which we are organizing our discussion may not be familiar, the problems that we shall discuss will seem familiar enough and will, moreover, be recognized as being at the heart of the special philosophical problem of personal identity, the problem of first-person identity.

19.2 Imagining Myself Persisting through a Change of Human Beings (Bodies)

Let us begin with a problem, or puzzle, about the identity through time of the entity at the center of my horizon, the entity that I am. This entity, we know, is a human being. Thus my identity through time, it would seem, must consist in the identity through time of that human being, JV. Perhaps it is not obvious why, or how, the first-person perspective should give rise to a special problem here. The special problem, we said, concerns

---

examples they use, it becomes evident that what gives the examples their edge, and thereby accounts for the special character and philosophical interest of the problem under discussion, is the fact that, however things are officially described, we *grasp what is going on* in the examples as something that might happen to *me*, that is to say, in the first person. With this in mind, the reader might wish to study, e.g., Bernard Williams's remarks about the "third personal" presentation of the thought experiment in his paper "The Self and the Future," in *Problems of the Self* and Derek Parfit's repeated emphasis, in part 3 of *Reasons and Persons* (Oxford University Press, 1986), on the "impersonal" nature of his "reductionist" view of personal identity. (We shall examine Parfit's view below.)

my identity through time. If JV, the human being, is the entity that *I am*, in what should *my* identity through time consist if not the identity through time of that same human being, JV?

The problem emerges in light of a claim philosophers often make about imagination. I can, it is claimed, imagine myself at some point in the future "having," or "being in," a different body. Not just a body that looks different from the way my body, the body of JV, looks (such a body could in fact be JV's body), but a numerically distinct human body, including the brain: a human body that materially coincides with a human being other than, that is, numerically distinct from, JV, the human being that I am. Thus (in the typical scenario) I can imagine myself waking up, going to the mirror and discovering a different human being (a human being other than, numerically distinct from, JV) looking back at me. In imagining this, it seems I imagine finding myself having, or being in, the body of a different human being.

In that case, who, or what, do I mean here by "myself"? By hypothesis (this is part of the story), it seems it must be the one who wakes up. Then it must be a human being. When I awake from sleep, the one who awakes is the one who has been asleep, and the one who has been asleep is a human being. Which human being, then, is the one who wakes up? Whoever it is, he, it seems, is the one I mean by "myself."

Which human being is it? It is not JV. First of all, JV is not (in the story—if you follow it) the human being who wakes up. Second, how could JV find himself having, or being in, the body of a different human being? JV is a human being. How could a human being have, or be in, any body but the body of the human being that he is?

It seems we must suppose that it is the other human being that wakes up and discovers that he has a different body. But this is equally nonsense. The human being who wakes up, the other human being, simply has the body he has, the body of the human being he is. We can no more suppose that he, the other human being, has a different body than we can suppose that JV, the human being I am, has a different body.

When I imagine finding myself having, or being in, the body of a different human being, I imagine my identity having persisted through a change of human bodies—of complete human bodies—i.e., through a change of human beings. But what has persisted? Myself. I imagine *myself* having persisted through a change of human beings. It seems impossible to make sense of this on the hypothesis that *I am* a human being. How could the "myself" that finds itself in the body of a new human being, that persists through a change of human beings, itself *be* a human being? How could a human being persist through a change of human beings, or find itself in a new human being?

Of course, you might say, that is the point. The fact that I can imagine finding myself "having," or "being in," the body of another human being shows precisely that I am *not* a human being. Then what am I? A soul? This at least seems to make sense of what I imagine when I imagine finding myself in a new body: I imagine the soul that I am finding itself, myself, in a new body. But we do not want to go this way. I am not a soul. I am human being. This is the puzzle. I am (or so we are supposing) a human being; but what I can imagine about myself, about what might happen to me in the future, seems to entail that I am not a human being. What I can imagine about myself seems to entail that I am not what I am.

We know how to solve this puzzle. It is a matter of being clear about the temporalized phenomenology of the subject position, the temporalized positional conception of the self (18.1–2). What I imagine when I imagine finding myself at some future time "having" or "being in" (as the philosophical claim would express it) the body of a different human being is a different human being, a different human body, occupying the subject position within my horizon, the position at the center: the position by virtue of occupying which a certain human being is "myself," the human being that "I am." Thus the imagined state of affairs does not depend on imagining the persistence, the identity through time, of JV or any other human being. Nor of a soul. It does not, more generally, depend on imagining the persistence of any entity, of any object in the world, whatever.

What in this case holds for the future holds equally for the past. Just as I, without thereby imagining the persistence of any object in the world, can imagine having in the future the body of a different human being, I can imagine having had the body of different human being in the past: I can imagine that a different human being occupied the position at the center of my horizon and thus was "me (myself)," the one that "I am."

JV, the human being, is the human being that "I am." That is to say, explicitly temporalizing the statement, JV is *now* the human being that "I am." But I can imagine a future in which a human being other than JV will be the human being that "I am" (or a past in which a human being other than JV was the human being that "I am"). I can imagine that, in a sense, *my* identity persists through a change of human beings. In what sense? Not, obviously, in the sense that I imagine JV, the human being that "I am," persisting through the change. I do not imagine JV, I do not imagine *any* entity, persisting through the change. I imagine "my identity persisting," etc., in the sense that I imagine a human being other than JV occupying in the future the position within my horizon that JV now occupies, the position at the center of my horizon, the position by virtue of occupying which a certain human being is "myself," the human being that "I am."

19.3 Locke's View of Personal Identity

It is compatible with the temporalized phenomenology of the subject position that at different times different human beings should occupy the subject position within my horizon; that the human who used to occupy this position, or who will occupy it, is not the one who now occupies the position; that therefore the human being who used to be "me," or who will be "me," is other than the human being who is now "me," the one that "I am." Thus what we can imagine in these cases under the description of "having" or "being in" a different body, etc., does not force the conclusion that I am a nonbodily substance, a soul. Of course, neither does it exclude this conclusion. But notice, if we assume that it is not a body but a soul at the center of my horizon, hence that there is a temporalized phenomenology of the subject position in the case of souls, we are, as in the case of bodies, free to imagine that this position has different occupants—in this case, different souls—at different times. There is, it seems, no kind of substance whose identity through time is necessary for first-person identity through time.

Neither is it sufficient. If it is the way of figuring within my horizon that makes an entity "back then" the one I was, or the way an entity will figure in the future that makes it the one I will be, then precisely *that*—and not the persistence of some entity—is what suffices for first-person identity. There is, it seems, no kind of substance, bodily or otherwise, whose persistence is either necessary or sufficient for first-person identity.

Anyone who has read chapter 27, book 2 of Locke's *Essay* should recognize this negative conclusion about first-person identity as that at which Locke arrives. Personal identity consists, he says—crystallizing a great deal of reflection and argumentation in which the point has emerged, and will continue in the ensuing discussion to emerge, again and again—"not in the identity of substance, but . . . . in the identity of consciousness."[4] Good. Of course we shall now be curious about Locke's positive conception of first-person identity, about what he means here by "identity of consciousness." What is it for Locke in which my identity through time consists yet which is compatible with the nonidentity through time of the substance (human being or soul) that I am?

Locke says about the sameness (identity) of consciousness in which personal identity consists that "as far as this consciousness can be extended backwards to any past action or thought, so far reaches the identity of that person." (section 11). Such talk of consciousness "extending," or again "reaching," to past actions, etc., which occurs in a number of places

---

[4] *An Essay Concerning Human Understanding*, book 2, Chap. 27, section 19.

in chapter 27,[5] may suggest that by "consciousness" Locke means some kind of ongoing mental stream, a stream of consciousness, a stream that at different times can accompany different substances (human beings or souls)—as, employing a spatial analogue, the same river at different places runs alongside different cities—and which in this sense can be said to "persist through" numerically distinct substances. My identity out of the past or into the future, my personal identity, would then consist in the identity of a particular stream. A past action accompanied by the relevant stream would be "my" past action; and the substance, the human being or soul, whose action it was would be the human being who used to be "me"; and so on.

This merely raises a new version of our old question. A past action is "mine," the substance that performed it is the one who used to be "me," just in case the action was accompanied by a particular stream of consciousness. Which stream? It would have to be the stream that is "mine." But which stream is that? Just as earlier we were required to deal with the question of makes a particular human being "me," we now have the question of what makes a particular stream of consciousness "mine," Obviously, on pain of circularity, we cannot say that what makes the stream "mine" is that the substance that it accompanies is "me."

In any case, the suggestion is plainly at odds with the spirit of Locke's position. Consider what he says about souls (spirits, immaterial substances):

> Let anyone reflect upon himself, and conclude that he has in himself an immaterial spirit, which is that which thinks in him, and, in the constant change of his body keeps him the same; and is that which he calls *himself*: let him also suppose it to be the same soul that was in Nestor or Thersites, at the siege of Troy . . . but he now having no consciousness of any of the actions either of Nestor or Thersites, does or can he conceive himself the same person with either of them? Can he be concerned in either of their actions? attribute them to himself, or think them his own, more than the actions of any other men that ever existed? (Section 14)

Are those past actions, the actions associated with Nestor, *my* past actions? Locke is trying to get us to see here that if this question is taken in an essentially first-person way, the basis for settling it—that is to say, what makes (constitutes) the past actions "mine" or not—is independent of

---

[5] It is one the dominant metaphors of Locke's discussion; see, e.g., sections 10, 14, 16. Related to the "extending back" metaphor is Locke's description of consciousness as something that can "go along with the substance" (section 16), or again as something that can be "annexed to" a substance (section 25).

any question about the identity through time of a soul. Even if we assume that my soul is identical with Nestor's, those past actions are not "my" past actions. By the same token, we can imagine, wildly but compatibly with the assumption of a nonidentity of souls, that those actions of Nestor's have what makes past actions "mine," that they are "my" past actions. So again, whether there is soul identity through time is irrelevant. If the question concerns the past actions of a particular soul, soul identity through time is not irrelevant; but then the question is no longer being understood in an essentially first-person way.

Just as soul identity through time is, for Locke, irrelevant to what makes a past action "mine," so is the identity through time of a stream of consciousness. Could we not on Locke's behalf more or less repeat the above quoted passage substituting references to streams for references to souls? If, as things are, I became completely convinced that the stream of consciousness flowing through me now is the very same stream that accompanied Nestor's actions, I would no more regard those actions of Nestor's as "mine" than I would regard as "mine" the actions of anyone else. On the other hand, Locke would say, I can imagine those actions being "mine" compatibly with any assumption whatever about the identity through time of this or that stream of consciousness. I can do this, in fact, with JV's action of, say, an hour ago. Compatibly with those actions being, as they are, "my" past actions, I can accept that my present stream of consciousness does not flow out of the stream that accompanied the earlier behavior of JV, but, say, is an independent ongoing stream into which the earlier stream has flowed. I can accept this (or some other totally fanciful story) because what makes a past action "mine" has nothing to do with the identity through time of an ongoing stream.[6]

So it is not just that there is no substantial entity (human being or soul) whose identity through time constitutes "my" identity through time, i.e., my first-person identity through time, there is no ongoing stream (process, series of events) either. There is, more generally, nothing *in the world* whose identity through time constitutes "my" identity through time; nothing *in the world* whose identity through time and relation to a particular past action constitutes the past action "my" past action.

Then how should we understand Locke's idea that what constitutes (makes) a past action "my" past action is that my consciousness "extends back" to the action? The clue lies, I think, in the following passage:

> [i]t is plain, consciousness, as far as ever it can be extended—should it be to ages past—unites existences and actions very remote in time into

---

[6] Unless, of course, we confusedly smuggle into our conception here something that belongs not to the conception of a stream of consciousness as such, an ongoing mental stream,

the same *person*, as well as it does the existences and actions of the immediately preceding moment: so that whatever has the consciousness of present and past actions, is the same person to whom they both belong. Had I the same consciousness that I saw the ark and Noah's flood, as that I saw an overflowing of the Thames last winter, or as that I write now, I could more doubt that I who write this now, that saw the Thames overflowed last winter, and that viewed the flood at the general deluge, was the same *self*,—place that self in what *substance* you please—than that I who write this am the same *myself* now whilst I write (whether I consist of all the same substance, material or immaterial, or no) that I was yesterday. (section 16)

The form of Locke's argument is clear. I cannot doubt that it is I who do this now, or who see this now. Thus if I have the "same consciousness" of a past action as of what I am doing right now, or of a past seeing as of what I see right now, there is no doubting that it was I who did it, or saw it: my consciousness "extends back" to that action or seeing. The question concerns what Locke means by the "same consciousness." How, or in what sense, could I have the "same consciousness" of a past as of a present action, etc.?

The answer to this question (of which I believe Locke, though he is not philosophically in a position to formulate it, cannot be totally unaware) refers us to the way an action or something seen figures from within my consciousness: to have the "same consciousness" of X present and past is for X, present and past, to figure in the same way from within my consciousness—in the same way, that is, apart from tense. If a past action now figures within my consciousness in the same way as *this*$_w$ action figures, i.e., if the past action *now* figures as *then* willed, my consciousness extends back to that action: it was I who did it. Similarly, if a past event or object now figures from within my consciousness in the same way as *this*$_p$ object, etc., figures, i.e., if the object in the past *now* figures as *then* visually appearing, my consciousness extends back to the seeing of the object: it was I who saw it.[7]

Notice that Locke—and so far we have gone along with this—treats the cases of action and seeing as if they were the same. In fact, there is an important difference. In contrast with the action case, the subject in the case of seeing—the one who sees—figures only indirectly. The action, that which figures within my consciousness as willed, is thereby "mine," and the one who acts is thereby "me." Figuring as the locus of will is part of

---

but rather to the conception of what actually does make a past action "mine." Here the reader might recall our discussion of death and the mental stream in 8.3.

[7] The subscripts indicate that we are using what in 15.9 we called demonstratives of will and perceptual demonstratives.

the phenomenology of the subject position. However, as we observed (16.4), there is no comparable way of figuring in the case of seeing: no "locus" of seeing. There is a way of visually appearing (a way a human body can visually appear) from within my horizon that is part of the phenomenology of the subject position; but to figure in this way, as perceptually central, is to figure not as the locus of seeing but as seen in a certain way. In any event, as we explained, to be the one that sees it is not necessary to be seen, to appear visually from within my horizon. Then what makes it the case that it is I who now see, or who saw then? And how does the human being come into this?

I see the Thames overflowing. This means simply that the event now figures as now visually appearing from within my consciousness (horizon). But assuming the human being, JV, does not visually appear, how does *he* come into this? JV, the human being, comes in by being the one who standingly figures at the center of my consciousness, the horizon from within which the event of overflowing now figures as now visually appearing. Apart from tense, the case of past seeing is exactly the same. If the event of overflowing *now* figures as *then* visually appearing within my consciousness, it was *I* that saw the overflowing. The human being, the one who sees, comes in by being the one who now figures as then figuring (standingly) at the center of my consciousness. This, we know, leaves open the (experiential) possibility that that human being, the one who saw, was other than JV. Suppose that is the case. Then although in one sense it was I that saw the overflowing (the overflowing now figures as then visually appearing from within my horizon), in another sense, it was not I (the human being that then figured standingly at the center of my horizon is other than the one who now figures at the center).

19.4 Persistence and the Horizon

I can imagine myself persisting through a change of human beings and hence can imagine a different human being "me." This is a way things might develop within my experience, an experiential possibility. But remember, it does not follow that such a development is causally or metaphysically possible (see 13.2). Let us, however, leave this qualification aside for now (it will become important later) and consider further the experiential possibility in its own right.

One thing that may occur to us is that whereas imagining finding myself in the body of a different human being does not depend on imagining the persistence of any object in the world, it does depend on imagining the persistence of my horizon, the subject matter to which the world is internal. For it is only insofar as I imagine a certain human being occupying—

in the future (say)—the position at the center of my horizon that I imagine finding "myself" in the body of that human being. So it would seem that I must imagine my horizon persisting through to the relevant future time.

It is true, when I imagine finding myself at some future time in the body of a different human being, I imagine a certain human being at that time occupying the subject position within my horizon. Yet this cannot require that I imagine my horizon persisting through to that time, since in this respect there is *nothing to imagine*. As the horizon of time, my horizon (consciousness), the horizonal self, is outside time (18.4). Whatever is temporal, hence whatever might be said to "persist through time," is (in the relevant sense) internal to my horizon. There is no such thing as my horizon "persisting through time." There is nothing then to imagine here, nothing that might count as imagining the persistence of my horizon through time.

I, the human being that I am, JV, persist; but my horizon does not persist. Rather, I persist within, at the center of, my horizon. So when I imagine my persistence, or imagine something that entails my persistence, the horizon is presupposed. Say I imagine performing an action of a certain kind. This means, I imagine something figuring within my horizon as willed. The same is true if I intend to perform an action of a certain kind, or remember performing a particular action. In the case of the past, the action now figures within my horizon as then willed. In the case of the future, I now intend that there will be within my horizon an action that figures as willed. The horizon is always presupposed.

I can imagine the persistence, the identity through time, not just of my body, of the human being that I am, but of any object in the world. I cannot, however, imagine the persistence of the horizon. It should be clear now that, when I imagine the persistence of an object X, or imagine something that entails the persistence of X, the horizon comes into this in a different way entirely—not by being, like X, itself imagined to persist, but as "that within which" X is imagined to persist, as (we could say) the horizon of persistence.

Of course the point is not confined to imagination. After all, in imagination I imagine ways things might be, or develop, within my experience (my horizon). So once again, the horizon is presupposed. I anticipate seeing X, or I remember seeing X. In the first case, I anticipate that X will visually appear within my horizon. In the case of memory, X now figures as having appeared within my horizon.

Notice the difference here between memory and anticipation (expectation): between, one might say, looking forward and backward within my horizon. Anticipation is a form of imagination; remembering is not. Memory looks to the past. A particular event, or an object on a particular occasion, now figures within my horizon as having figured then in such-

and-such way. In the case of anticipation, which looks to the future, there are no particular events or occasions that might now relevantly figure within my horizon. We can, so to speak, quantify into memory but not anticipation (this is another example of the past/future asymmetry that we discussed in 18.3).

Finally, we should remind ourselves that past events, whether or not they involve me, are in a certain way (in the way things are internal to a dream) internal to my horizon. They are internal to my horizon in this way simply by virtue of being past, before *now*. But obviously not every-thing in the past *now figures* within my horizon, in the way that an event, or an object on a particular occasion, that I now recall now figures within my horizon. Suppose I recall an event E that I previously witnessed: E now figures within my horizon as having visually appeared in a certain way. Then two things are true: E now figures within my horizon as having appeared, and, simply by virtue of being past, E is internal to my horizon. Unless E were internal to my horizon, it could not now figure within my horizon as having appeared, etc.

19.5 Remembering; The Past-Self Ambiguity

I, JV, the human being that I am—like any other part of the world— persist within my horizon, the subject matter to which everything tempo-ral, hence everything that persists, is internal and which therefore cannot "itself" be conceived as persisting. What distinguishes JV from everything else that persists is that he persists in the subject position, at the center of my horizon. JV now figures within my horizon both as the one now at the center and as the one who has all along been at the center. That is, JV now figures within my horizon as the one who now appears and has all along appeared in a certain kind of way (the kind of way represented by Mach's picture); and as the one who now is and has all along been the locus of will and feeling.

In saying that JV now figures within my horizon as the one who has all along been at the center, we mean that he now standingly figures this way, that he now figures$_s$ as the one who now is, and has all along been, at the center. This depends, in turn, on there being the right past-directed operative figurings. Unless JV now figured$_o$ within my horizon as having on particular past occasions figured$_o$ as perceptually central and the locus of will and feeling—i.e., unless, JV now figured$_o$ as having in the past figured$_o$ in those ways that comprise the phenomenology of the subject position—JV would not now figure$_s$ as the one who has been all along at the center, as the one who has all along been "myself."

Such past-directed figuring$_s$ are what we mean by "remembering (recollecting)." Under this heading we include, of course, not just past-directed figurings$_o$ of figurings$_o$ that comprise the phenomenology of the subject position. Otherwise I could not remember *you* acting on some past occasion. Assume I witness (see) you act, and now remember you acting as you did. Your past action now figures$_o$ within my horizon as then appearing$_o$ a certain way. Hence you too now figure$_o$ as then appearing$_o$ a certain way. In remembering my own actions, the case is different. Neither my actions nor myself, JV, need now figure$_o$ as then appearing$_o$ in any way (since they need not then have appeared in any way[8])—although I, JV, now standingly figure within my horizon as the one who was then at the center, hence as the one who then standingly appeared in a certain way. The essential thing in remembering my own actions is that my actions now figure$_o$ within my horizon as then willed, which is a way that your actions cannot figure$_o$ within my horizon. (Henceforth we shall employ subscripts only where there is a potential for ambiguity.)

The past, we might say, is not only internal to my horizon—it is, or may be, available from within my horizon. In memory (remembering), a past event, or an object on a past occasion, now figures within my horizon as having then figured in some way. This is the essence of memory: the present figuring within my horizon of things past.

Suppose that on the basis of having seen you act, I say that I "remember you doing such-and-such." I might also have said that I "remember seeing you do such-and-such." Have I in the first case neglected to report something—e.g., that a certain event (a "visual experience") occurred in me?[9] No, I report exactly the same thing in both cases: not that at the relevant past time something, a seeing-event, occurred in me, but that your action, and thus you, now figure within my horizon as then visually appearing.[10]

Or, to take a more complicated example, I remember seeing you on a certain occasion seeing X. This means that you and X now figure within my horizon as then visually appearing: appearing as related to each other in such a way that I take it that X appears visually within your horizon. Whereas it is essential to my remembering my seeing you seeing something that you now figure within my horizon as having visually appeared on the relevant occasion, it is not essential to my remembering my seeing something (in the present case, your seeing X) that I, the human being I am, now figure within my horizon as having visually appeared in any way

[8] My actions, although they may appear from within my horizon, do not, as actions, figure as appearing but as willed: figuring as willed is not a way of appearing. See 15.8.

[9] In order to focus on the interesting point, we are excluding the possibility that my memory is tactually or audially, etc., based.

[10] Gareth Evans makes basically the same point in his discussion of memory but uses a totally different framework of analysis. See *The Varieties of Reference*, p. 240.

on that occasion. This contrast brings out that a past seeing is "mine" not by virtue of *what* on the past occasion visually appeared within my horizon, but simply by virtue of its being within my horizon that something then visually appeared.

Let us, confining ourselves to those present figurings, those rememberings, that involve the past-tensed phenomenology of the subject position (e.g., remembering doing or feeling something), now consider more carefully a potential ambiguity on which we have several times remarked in the course of our discussion.

I squeeze a ball. The movement of my hand now figures within my horizon as now willed. Since figuring as willed belongs to the phenomenology of the subject position, the fact that the movement figures this way within my horizon makes the human being whose body moves this way the human being that "I am." Let us shift our perspective to a later time at which I remember that act. The same movement that then figured within my horizon as now willed, now (at the later time) figures within my horizon as then willed. Given that the movement now figures in the way that it does, there can be no question but that the human being who acted was "myself": no question but that it was *I* who acted, *I* who made the movement.

Yet we know there is also a sense in which—keeping fixed the way the movement now figures within my horizon—it might *not* be *I* who acted. What sense is that? It is possible that the human being whose movement now figures within my horizon as then willed is not the human being whose movements now figure as now willed; possible, in other words, that the human being who *now* figures within my horizon as *then* at the center, as *then* "myself," is not JV, the human being who *now* figures as *now* at the center, as *now* "myself." This is something we can imagine, an experiential possibility.

So there is a potential ambiguity here: keeping fixed the way a certain past action now figures within my horizon, there is a sense in which it could not but be the case that "I did that," and a sense in which it is possible that the action was not "mine," in which it might not be the case that "I did that." It could not but be the case that the human being who was *then* "myself" is the human being who performed the action. But, since it might be the case that that human being, the one who performed the action, is not the human being who is *now* "myself," it might be the case that the human being who is now "myself" is not the human being who performed the action.

Let us call this the "past-self ambiguity." It should not be hard to appreciate how failure to grasp the past-self ambiguity might engender philosophical confusion and false conflicts about memory and the self. Recall the possibility of finding myself in the body of another human being

(19.2). Suppose we rule out souls. One might reason that, if I found myself in the body of another human being, I, the human being that I am, could not correctly claim as "mine" the actions performed by the human being JV. Yet if we are struck by the way the actions of JV would now figure within my horizon, it might seem impossible to deny that these actions are "mine." Once we are clear about the past-self ambiguity, the conflict is resolved. JV's actions now figure within my horizon as then willed. In that sense, they are "mine." On the other hand, since in the imagined situation a human being other than JV is now at the center of my horizon, is now "myself," the human being who is now "myself" did not perform JV's actions. In this sense, JV's actions are not "mine."

Consider memory of my past actions. If I remember (remember correctly, truly, etc.) squeezing the ball, how—one might ask—could it fail to be the case that I did what I remember doing? Yet it might also occur to us that the truth of the claim "I remember squeezing the ball" need not entail that JV, the human being that "I am," squeezed the ball. Again, the past-self ambiguity may affect our reactions here. It is possible that the past action now figures within my horizon as then willed, and thus is "mine," even though it was performed by a human being other than JV, the human being who is now at the center of my horizon.

Of course, the latter interpretation will occur to us only in philosophical reflection. It does not belong to our everyday understanding of claims of the form "I remember Φing." The everyday claims entail not just that the act of Φing now figures within my horizon as then willed, but that the human being who performed the action, the one who now figures within my horizon as then at the center, is the same human being who now figures within my horizon as now at the center (the one that "I am").

This relates to an idea, due to Sidney Shoemaker, that has been prominent in recent discussions of personal identity: the idea of "quasi (q)-memory."[11] The idea concerns (as I understand it) not so much a special kind of memory as a special language for expressing memory claims. In this language, "I q-remember Φing" entails everything entailed by our present "I remember Φing" except that it leaves open whether it was I who Φ'd. That is to say, it entails that the past action of Φing now figures with the characteristic phenomenology (i.e., as then willed) while leaving it open whether the action is "mine."

Except for tense, the phenomenology of a past action of mine—the way a past action of mine now figures within my horizon—replicates the way

---

[11] See "Persons and Their Pasts," *American Philosophical Quarterly*, October 1970, especially sections 2 and 3. The idea of q-memory plays a crucial role in Derek Parfit's views about personal identity. See his "Personal Identity," *Philosophical Review*, January 1971, and *Reasons and Persons*, section 80.

the action figured in performing it. As Shoemaker puts it, my past actions are remembered "from the inside." His idea is that although in the actual world memories of actions that have the from-the-inside phenomenology are always memories of my actions, in a world where, say, I (for whatever science fiction reason: brain transplants, division, etc.) sometimes "found myself in the body of another human being," memories of actions might have precisely this phenomenology without its being true that it was *I* who acted, without its being true that the actions were "mine." In such a world, we would have reason to use the language of q-memory.

The thing to notice is this: although as things actually are we have no use for the language of q-memory, the actual phenomenology of our memories of past actions, according to Shoemaker, allows for such a language. It allows for it in that a claim to q-remember an action, which claim is meant to leave open whether the action is "mine," is meant to express the actual phenomenology of memory of our own past actions. So this phenomenology must itself leave open, or be neutral about, whether the actions are "mine," and our belief that the actions are "mine" must depend on a belief about the identity of the agent which belief is independent of the phenomenology of the memories, viz., the belief that I was the agent.

Gareth Evans, in his book, attacks precisely this aspect of Shoemaker's view. Evans's argument rests on the idea that a spontaneous everyday claim to remember performing an action expresses *knowledge* that it was I who performed the action. (Shoemaker, as far as I can see, would not contest this.) Such claims, Evans maintains, are based not on *reasoning* about myself and the world but simply on the phenomenology of the remembering of the action I claim to remember. If the phenomenology of the remembering left open whether it was I, then, since the claim to remember performing the action is based simply on the phenomenology, the claims to remember would not, as they do, express knowledge.[12]

Introducing the concept of knowledge here raises a number of issues—not only about the concept itself but, more fundamentally, about how in memory we relate to the past. (This will occupy us later, in chapter 21.) About knowledge, let us simply point out that knowing (if that is the right word) it was I, JV, who Φ'd might, in fact, be based on something that leaves open the possibility that it was not I, JV, who Φ'd. It depends on the kind of possibility involved. We shall come back to this shortly.

Evans concludes that "If a subject has, in virtue of the operations of his memory, [the right kind of] knowledge of the past states of a subject, then that subject is himself" (p. 245). In our terms, if my past states, in particular my past actions, now figure within my horizon in the right way, the

---

[12] *The Varieties of Reference*, pp. 244–45.

identity of the subject is not left open: those actions are "mine." This seems correct. On the other hand, given that (as we have explained) it is compatible with my past actions now figuring as they do—compatible with the phenomenology of my remembering the actions being what it is—that the human being who performed those actions is *not* JV, is *not* the one that "I am," can we not appreciate what Shoemaker is getting at in supposing that the phenomenology of remembering a past action leaves open the identity of the subject, leaves open, in other words, whether the action is "mine"?

By now the point should be obvious. Behind the conflict, in the form that we have presented it, lies the past-self ambiguity. When this is exposed, the conflict disappears. In one sense, the phenomenology of remembering my past actions leaves it open whether the remembered actions are "mine"; in another sense, it does not leave this open. What is left open by the phenomenology is whether the human being whose past actions now figure within my horizon as then willed is the human being who now figures within my horizon as now at the center, as now the one that "I am." What is not left open is whether the human being whose actions now figure as then willed now figures as then the one at the center, as then the one that "I am." In this sense, there is no question but that the remembered actions are "my" actions.

19.6 Possibility, Personal Identity, and Naturalizing the Self

But even with respect to what is left open by the phenomenology of remembering an action, viz., whether it is "mine" in the sense of having been performed by JV, we may suppose that I know it was JV, and moreover that this knowledge might be based exclusively on the phenomenology of the remembering, the very phenomenology that leaves it open that it was not JV. How could this be? How could knowledge that it was JV be based exclusively on something that leaves open the possibility that it was not JV?

The answer is that the possibility left open by the phenomenology of remembering is a possibility left open by the temporalized phenomenology of the subject position, i.e., an experiential possibility, and this, we know, is compatible with not just causal but metaphysical *im*possibility. Something that makes sense as a way things might develop within my experience (something I can imagine) need not make sense in terms of the laws of nature, or the principle of sufficient reason (chapter 13). In a case where an experiential possibility is metaphysically, and thus causally (naturally), impossible, it is unrealizable.[13] In such a case, where an experiential possibility cannot be realized, the fact of the possibility can hardly be thought a bar to knowing something, that is, to knowing something that would be falsified if the possibility were realized.

For example, I can imagine finding myself in another body. The challenge is to explicate the possibility in a way that does not conflict with the assumption that I am a human being. Our explication was that I can imagine a human being other than JV occupying in the future the position at the center of my horizon, the position now occupied by JV. Yet it may not be clear whether what I have imagined, while it represents an experiential possibility (a way that things might develop within my experience), is a metaphysical/causal possibility. It is not clear, then, whether it is a realizable possibility.

Let the story be as follows: I go to sleep, wake up, go to the mirror, and find a different human being looking back. Note, I *find* a *different* human being looking back. I find a different human being at the center of my horizon. There is a lot going on here, a lot built into this description of things.

The human being I find, etc., the one at the center of my horizon, is a "different" human being. Different from (other than) whom? Different from JV. But I do not just find a human being—call him X—*who is* other than JV—I find X *to be* other than JV. This implies that X's occupancy of the subject position within my horizon was not expected, or at any rate that it contradicts how I remember things being. If someone finds a "different" human being at the center, etc., he must remember how things were. Who is this "someone"? It is I. Who am I? The one at the center. And who is that? By hypothesis it is X. So it is X who is doing the remembering, and hence the "finding." That is, X now figures as the human being who is now at the center of my horizon, who is now "myself," whereas JV now figures as the human being who was at the center of my horizon, who was "myself." This, as we said, is presupposed by my "finding" what I find. It is only against the background of such a remembering, of JV's now figuring within my horizon as the one who was in the past at the center, that there could be such a thing as my "finding" a "different" human being to be the one now at the center.

The problem is that, so far as we have described the case, there is no way to make sense of this remembering; no way, i.e., to makes sense of it metaphysically. Remembering, the fact that something past now figures within my horizon as then being thus-and-so—this cannot come from nothing. There must be something, something in the world, that accounts

---

[13] What is causally possible is thereby metaphysically possible; what is metaphysically possible (e.g., that I should now jump thirty feet in the air) need not be causally possible.

for the fact of the remembering (this is the principle of sufficient reason speaking), that is, for the present figuring within my horizon of something past. What accounts for the remembering, we must suppose, is the brain of a human being. (Is there something else?) But the only brain to which we can appeal in the present case is the wrong brain. It is not JV's brain (this, for all we know, has been destroyed), but the brain of the human being *now* at the center of my horizon, the brain of the new human being: a new brain, X's brain. How could this new brain, which had nothing whatever to do with the adventures of JV, account for the fact that JV's past actions now figure within my horizon as then willed? How could this new brain, which is completely unrelated to the past life of JV, ever account for the fact that JV now figures within my horizon as the one who was in the past at the center, who was then "myself"?

In sum, whereas JV's now figuring within my horizon as the one who was in the past at the center is essential to what I imagine in the case as described (otherwise we cannot account for the element of surprise), the same description of the case renders such figuring, such remembering, metaphysically impossible.

Of course we might alter the description in a way that gets around this difficulty. We might include in the story something intended to explain how the currently available brain, the brain inside the human being who now figures within my horizon as now at the center, could make metaphysical sense of the fact that JV now figures as the one who in the past was at the center—e.g., that JV's brain has been transplanted into the body of this human being, or that the brain of the other human being has been somehow modelled on JV's brain. The point is that *even without* any such alteration of the original description, i.e., even as a description that cannot be realized, the description makes sense experientially. Thus it may happen that, while we fix on its experiential possibility, the metaphysical impossibility and hence unrealizability of the case described slips right past us.

This tendency of experiential possibility, imaginability, to transcend metaphysical possibility provides further ammunition for the naturalizer's view of the self. The naturalizer, as we represented him in 13.4—prior to introducing time into our discussion of the self—maintains that the answer to Descartes' "What am I?" question is that I am a human being, a member of that natural (biological, animal) kind. In investigating a natural kind, imagination may suggest possibilities, but it cannot establish the inherent properties of the kind. We have no right to suppose, then, that just by imagining things about human beings we can learn what it is for an entity to be a human being, to be a member of that natural kind. Nor, the naturalizer will say, is this point affected by the introduction of time, that is, when we turn from asking what it is for an entity to be an entity of such-and-such natural kind to asking what is for an entity of that kind to persist through time. Given that I am a human being, my identity through time is nothing more or less than the identity through time of the animal entity that I am. Imagination has nothing to tell us about what makes such an entity one and the same through time. It has nothing to tell us then about my identity through time.

Thus the naturalizer concludes that the philosophical investigation of personal identity need pay no special attention to what I can imagine about my past or future.[14] As far as the philosophical question or topic of personal identity is concerned, what I can imagine about my future is either irrelevant or misleading. Is not the same conclusion dictated by our own reflections on imagination and personal identity? Imagination has a way of getting metaphysically out of control. If what I can imagine about my past/future identity, if what makes sense experientially in this regard, may part company with what is metaphysically and hence causally (naturally) possible—if, then, it may diverge from what is realizable, i.e., from what can actually come to pass—what possible value or interest could it have in a serious attempt to understand my identity through time?

I do not think our reflections warrant such a negative assessment of the role of imagination in this regard. On the contrary, at the same time that they point up the potential divergence between experiential and metaphysical/causal possibility, between what can be imagined and what can be realized, our reflections place imagination at the heart of the philosophical question of personal identity. Our view, as should be apparent from the discussion in chapter 18, is that if you take away what I can imagine about my identity into the future, you take away personal identity as a special topic for philosophical reflection. That is to say, if the possibilities exhibited in first-person imagination, first-person experiential possibilities, are not relevant to it, there is no special philosophical question, no special philosophical problem, of personal identity.

The naturalizer, we said (13.4), misses philosophically the subject matter of the DH and death, the subject matter to which what I call "the world" and the infinity of ego-centric space and time are internal, the horizonal subject matter. Since it is by reference to this subject matter, my horizon, that the positional conception of the self is defined, that we spell out the phenomenology of the subject position, the naturalizer lacks an explicit philosophical grasp of the positional conception of the self. Thus although he has an answer—by our lights, the correct answer—to Descartes' question about what the entity is that I am, he has no answer (any more than Descartes has an answer) to the question of what makes the particular entity that I am the one that *I am*. For, if we are right, there is

[14] See the references cited in note 4, chapter 13.

no answer to this question except by reference to a particular way of figuring within my horizon; except, i.e., by reference to the phenomenology of the subject position.

There is of course a sense in which my identity through time cannot diverge from JV's identity. JV now figures within my horizon as the one now at the center, and his identity, JV's identity, cannot diverge from JV's identity (the necessity of identity). But the temporalized phenomenology of the subject position leaves open the experiential possibility that a human being other than JV might in the future occupy within my horizon the position now occupied by JV, in which sense my identity through time can diverge from JV's identity. Insofar as the horizonal and hence the positional conception of the self remains philosophically hidden from the naturalizer, this possibility, this sense in which my identity through time can diverge from JV's identity, will also remain hidden from him.

But if this possibility is merely an experiential possibility—if it makes sense as a way things might unfold within my experience, as something I can imagine about myself, without being metaphysically possible and thus realizable—why, one might wonder, should the philosophical investigation of personal identity attach any significance to it? It is as if in our investigation of personal identity we had allowed ourselves to get sidetracked into an autonomous sphere of reflection, a sphere with its own logic or rules, its own way of making sense. Within this sphere we are insulated from the constraints of metaphysical and causal possibility; in working out its logic, we need appeal only to imagination. Now, you might say, there may be such a self-contained sphere of reflection, and if there is, we are free to investigate it. But you might then wish to add that if the philosophical investigation of personal identity, of our identity through time, belongs to this sphere, it is not the serious business we initially supposed it to be. Rather, it is a harmless but trivial little game, a free-for-all in which we are allowed to imagine about ourselves whatever we please, without ever having to consider whether what we imagine might actually come to pass.

Apart from the disparaging tone, I would accept most of this: the philosophical investigation of personal identity, of my identity through time, does belong to an autonomous sphere whose logic we work out in imagination, and so on. In fact, we entered this sphere before we got to the question of my identity through time (personal identity). We entered it when we raised the question of what makes JV as opposed to any other human being "me," the one that "I am." But now ask yourself: Is *this*, the attempt to answer the question of what makes a particular human being the one that "I am," a trivial game? That is, does the *question* strike you as trivial? Then how could the attempt to answer the question be thought trivial? Yet, if we are right, the answer takes the form of spelling out the distinctive way that a particular human being figures within my horizon, in other words, of spelling out the phenomenology of the subject position; and our method here, we know—the method by which, generally, we explore the logic peculiar to the horizonal subject matter, by which we explore what makes sense as a way things might be or unfold within my horizon (experience) and thereby draw the boundaries of experiential possibility—our method here, to repeat, our method of testing what makes sense experientially, is imagination (see Section 12).

It is no accident that in reflecting on the topic of personal identity, philosophers commonly have recourse to what we can and cannot imagine. Remove imagination, and, in a real sense, the self is philosophically out of reach, lost to us as a topic for philosophical reflection. Of course, speaking generally now, in appealing to what we can imagine, it is easy to feel uncertain, or at a loss, and indeed to lose our way (see above, 12.3–5). But will anyone who has (more than just briefly, but for a period of years) seriously engaged in philosophy claim that he has never in the course of his reflections had some possibility/impossibility exhibited to him via an imagination-based thought experiment, that he has never in this way had some philosophical conviction shaken and perhaps overturned? This method of proceeding is part of the philosophical enterprise. Dismissing the method on the basis of difficulties and uncertainties inherent in it and therefore part of the exercise, is, it seems to me, a misplaced attempt at rigor. (Philosophy is philosophy, not science.)

However, we have seen that imagination, our method for exploring and spelling out the phenomenology of the subject position, and thereby answering the question of what makes a particular human being the one that "I am," can exhibit possibilities, experiential possibilities, that, when we look into them, do not make sense causally or even metaphysically. This remains true when the phenomenology of the subject position is temporalized, i.e., when we consider the possibilities that bear on my first-person identity through time. Here too we shall uncover possibilities— i.e., experiential possibilities—that are metaphysically/causally impossible and thus unrealizable.

If someone asks why unrealizable experiential possibilities about myself and my identity through time should be of interest to the philosophical investigation of personal identity and, more generally, the philosophical investigation of the self, there is not much we can do beyond pointing out what we have just pointed out. The unrealizable possibilities are implicit in the phenomenology of the subject position. They are, you might say, located within the territory at the center of my horizon, and this is the territory that we must investigate if we wish to get to the bottom of the first-person puzzles about the self, and the self in time. Why are the merely experiential possibilities of philosophical interest? They come with this territory.

One last point. We have drawn attention to cases where experiential possibility transcends metaphysical/causal possibility. There are also, we shall see, cases of transcendence in the opposite direction: states of affairs that make sense causally and hence metaphysically, but which are nonetheless *impossible*, experientially impossible. That is to say, there are things that might happen to me, JV, the human being that "I am," that are causally and metaphysically possible and yet are not imaginable, that do not make sense as ways things might develop within my horizon. With respect to these cases, and in contrast to cases of the first kind, we may find ourselves confronted by a kind of puzzle about first-person identity through time, by a puzzle about first-person identity, that has no resolution.

20. Time and the Horizon

20.1 The Oneness of the Horizon

A certain human being, JV, not only now figures within my horizon as now at the center, he now figures as the one who has all along figured at the center. Moreover, although he does not now figure at the center in the future (the past/present versus future asymmetry), I anticipate that he will figure at the center. In this sense I live not only in the present but looking ahead within my horizon, and looking back: I live in the future and past as well as the present. And in both directions, up ahead in the future and back in the past, it is always with JV—either as anticipated (future) or as remembered (past)—at the center, always with JV in the subject position.

In contrast to JV, who persists at its center, the horizon cannot be properly conceived as persisting, as identical through time. The horizon is not just something else that persists but is, as we put it, the horizon of persisting—and therefore cannot itself be conceived as persisting (see 19.4). The horizon is outside time.

Does this not conflict with what we have said about memory and anticipation? If, for example, I now remember seeing X on a certain past occasion, X now figures within my horizon as then visually appearing. In remembering seeing X, my horizon is presupposed as "that from within which" X now figures as then visually appearing. Similarly, if I now anticipate encountering X, my horizon is presupposed as that "that from within which," as I anticipate, X will appear. Must it not be true then that, in the first case, my horizon existed at the time of the past encounter and hence, since it exists now, that it has persisted from that time to now, and in the second case, that, if what I anticipate is realized, my horizon will exist at the time of the future encounter and hence will persist from now to the time of that encounter? Insofar as they presuppose the existence of my horizon, memory and anticipation must, it seems, presuppose its persistence.

What confuses us here is that we have no standpoint to conceive of, or reflect on, the horizon except that from within it, and from within the horizon its temporal structure is inescapably presupposed. Thus, inescapably, I am in reflecting on my horizon provided with a temporal structure to which I can, if I wish, relate the existence of my horizon, viz., the very temporal structure internal to it. I am, then, inescapably provided with the option of relating the existence of my horizon to the present, past, or future. I have this option despite its being the case that—precisely because whatever is in time (whatever is present, past, or future) is internal to my horizon—my horizon exists outside time. The mistake is to suppose that in thus *relating* my horizon to the present, past, or future, I thereby *locate* my horizon in time. Since whatever is in time is internal to my horizon, my horizon, as we said, cannot be located in time.

We are, I think, independently familiar with the possibility of relating to time things that, strictly, have no place in time. We can, for example, correctly assert that mathematicians have known of the existence of irrational numbers for centuries. Numbers (let us agree) do not exist in time. But the inescapable temporal structure of the horizon (past/present/future) is, inescapably, available when we think about numbers—which enables us to relate numbers to time. Relate to time, but not locate in time.

Similarly, despite the fact that it exists outside time, it is not incoherent to conceive of my horizon as existing in the past or future, thereby relating its existence to time. Of course, the extratemporality of my horizon derives not, as in the case of numbers, from being abstract (numbers are regarded as abstract entities), but, once again, from the fact that whatever is temporal is internal to my horizon.

If I regard X as persisting through time, I regard X as something that can undergo change, as something to which things can happen: as a possible subject of an event (18.4). It should be clear that regarding something as a possible subject of an event locates it in time, i.e., in the temporal structure internal to my horizon, and therefore that I cannot coherently regard my horizon as the potential subject of an event. However, it should also be clear now that the fact that my horizon now exists, or did or will exist, does not of itself entail this kind of incoherence. For thus relating my horizon to times internal to my horizon does not entail that my horizon persists from one such time to another.

Whereas memory and anticipation presuppose the existence of my horizon, death reminds us that there is an infinity of time internal to my horizon when there is no such thing as my horizon. This, as we explained (18.4), is not problematic. What makes death problematic, in a way that neither anticipation nor memory is problematic, is that it seems to convert my horizon into the subject of an event. For it is not just that the time of my death is, like the time of an anticipated event, up ahead, in the future internal to my horizon; my death *is* the future ceasing to be of my horizon. And what could this be if not a future event of which my horizon, the subject matter that contains everything in time and is thus itself outside time, is the subject?

But even if its being outside time means that I cannot conceive my horizon as persisting, as identical through time, is it not *one and the same* horizon that exists at different times, in the past and future? The extratemporal existence of my horizon can be related to the present, past, and future internal to my horizon. In this way, we can make sense of the thought that my horizon exists now, and has existed and will exist. Note: my horizon (life, consciousness, experience) now exists, has existed and will exist. What is *my* horizon, *my* life, etc., if not *one* horizon, *one* life? Is it not this single horizon, this single life, that is presupposed when I raise a question about the identity through time, the persistence, of an object in the world (including the object that I am), e.g., when I wonder whether the object that now figures as now present within my horizon is the same as the object that now figures as present on such-and-such past occasion? Perhaps, then, although it cannot be conceived as persisting, as identical *through* time, we can, insofar as it is always one and the same horizon that exists at different times, give a sense to saying that my horizon, my life, is identical *over* time. Let us dwell on this briefly.

I remember, or anticipate, seeing X. X now figures as having appeared in the past, or I anticipate that X will appear in the future. My horizon is presupposed as "that from within which" X now figures as having appeared in the past, or as "that from within which" will appear the future. When I look back or ahead in time, the times to which I look back or ahead are times internal to my horizon. The horizon, my horizon, which is outside time, is always already given, presupposed. And it, my horizon, is "one." A single subject matter. Insofar as my horizon, my life, is always already given, always already presupposed, there is a oneness that is always already given, an identity that is presupposed, viz., its identity, its oneness: the oneness of my horizon.

Of course, when we say that my horizon, hence the oneness of my horizon, is presupposed, we do not mean that whatever happens there must be (exist) such a subject matter as my horizon, such a oneness as its oneness. My horizon may cease to be. In fact it is certain that it, with its oneness, will cease to be (death). In which case, there will be no looking back or ahead from within it. Nor will the world appear from within it. There will be no "it" from which anything might appear. There will be NOTHING.

If, on the other hand, there is not NOTHING but SOMETHING, if the world now figures as now appearing and having appeared, and if I now anticipate its future appearing, there is such a subject matter as that from within which it now appears, and so on. There is, in short, such a subject matter as my horizon, my life. Given this subject matter—the subject matter that is nothing in itself (nothing, i.e., apart from the fact of something appearing from within it) but to which the totality I call "the world" and the infinity of time and space are internal; the subject matter of the DH and death; the subject matter that is presupposed by any question about the persistence or identity through time of an entity in the world (including the entity that is myself)—this subject matter is one, a single subject matter.

20.2 Skepticism about the Oneness over Time of My Horizon

Or can skepticism insert itself even here? On what basis do I exclude the hypothesis that the horizon presupposed by any question about identity through time (persistence), my horizon, is not really, over time, a multiplicity of horizons (the multiplicity hypothesis; MH)?

Our first reaction may be that, since the presupposed subject matter is precisely that to which the present, past, and future are internal, the kind of skepticism suggested by this question cannot get started. The hypothesis of a multiplicity of horizons over time, the MH, is incoherent. When I look back or ahead in time, the past or future time to which I look is internal to the very horizon from within which I look, the horizon that is now "mine." For example, if I remember seeing X, X now figures within my horizon as having appeared; if I anticipate seeing X, I anticipate seeing X from within my horizon. What is remembered and anticipated, as well as the remembering and anticipating, are internal to the same presupposed horizon. There is, it seems, no way for the MH to get off the ground here.

There is, however, a thought that aims to undermine our confidence on this point. It is that whereas the MH is incoherent if we consider it from the standpoint of a given "now," we grasp the possibility of a standpoint that abstracts away from the standpoint of any given "now"—the possibility of a temporally absolute standpoint (such as is sometimes attributed to God). From the absolute standpoint, things happen at particular times, but nothing is past, present, or future. Whereas the oneness over time of my horizon, its oneness out of the past and into the future internal to my horizon, is presupposed from the standpoint of any given "now," nothing guarantees this oneness from the absolute standpoint. Thus, from the absolute standpoint, nothing guarantees that the horizon whose oneness over time is presupposed from the standpoint of each of the series of "nows" is one and the same at different times. Let us elaborate on this idea.

One thing to point out is the way that the temporal present "dominates" the past and future. If I remember seeing X, X *now* figures from within my horizon as having appeared in the past; if I anticipate seeing X, I *now* anticipate that X will appear in the future. Memory and anticipation involve a present looking back or ahead from within my horizon. When I look ahead to the future, or back to the past, I look ahead or back not only from within my horizon, from within my horizon I look ahead or back from the standpoint of the present, of *now*.

I live, as we put it, in the past and future as well as the present. But I live in the past and future from the standpoint of the present. For example, what has happened and will happen, not only what is happening now or is about to happen, is important to me; but the past and future have the particular importance that they have from the standpoint of *now*, the present. Just as I have no standpoint on my horizon except that from within my horizon, from within my horizon I have no standpoint on the time internal to my horizon and the unfolding temporal series except the standpoint of the temporal present. Thus from within the inescapably presupposed horizon, the standpoint of the temporal present is inescapably presupposed.

The present, *now*, dominates the past and future. Moreover, it is *always* like that. Past and future times are not *now*, but they have had, or will have, the same dominating status. One "now" usurps another. And each makes its own claim to dominance. So the whole structure of an inescapably presupposed temporal standpoint, that from which the importance of everything is arbitrated, this keeps repeating itself. "It is always like that."[1] Is it not always like that? Is there not a difficult truth about time here that we all recognize?

And from the standpoint of any given "now," the presupposition that renders the MH incoherent holds true. Thus from the standpoint of any given "now," when I look back or ahead, to the past or future, the past or future to which I look—no matter how far back or ahead I look—is internal to the same horizon as the horizon from within which I look, my horizon. From the standpoint of any given "now," then, the MH is incoherent.

However, the thought is, when we abstract away from the temporal present and consider what holds absolutely, the MH no longer seems incoherent. There seems to be no reason why the horizon whose identity over time is presupposed from the standpoint of one "now" might not be other than the horizon whose identity over time is presupposed from the standpoint of another "now." Over the series of "nows" there might be a series of horizons, each of which is "my" horizon.

For example, at t, when I anticipate seeing X, it is incoherent, i.e., incoherent from the standpoint of *that* "now," to suppose that the horizon

---

[1] We are passing by a potential puzzle here: the temporal analogue of the impossible generalization that we encountered in our reflections on death and solipsism. See above, 11.5.

from within which X will (at t+1) appears is other than that from within which X then (at t) figures as anticipated to appear.[2] And at t+1, when X appears, it is incoherent from the standpoint of *that* "now" to suppose that the horizon from within which X then appears is other than that from within X earlier (at t) figured as anticipated to appear. Yet although from the standpoint of each of these "nows" the MH is incoherent, from the absolute standpoint, that which abstracts away from the temporal present, the possibility of a multiplicity of horizons remains open. It thus seems possible that, from the absolute standpoint, the horizon from within which (at t) I anticipate that X appears (at t+1) is other than that from within which X (at t+1) actually appears, which makes room for the skeptical question: How do I know that the horizon whose identity over time is presupposed from the standpoint of the "now" at t is identical with the horizon whose identity over time is presupposed from the standpoint of the other "now" at t+1?

Let us accept that the absolute version of the MH is coherent. It is coherent but, if you think about it, we do not—or rather, we cannot—take the hypothesis seriously. It is, in a certain sense, an empty hypothesis.

The point here is not that the absolute version of MH lacks experiential content, which of course it does. Since there is no way a replacement of horizons could show up within my horizon, the absolute version of the MH leaves the past, present, and future exactly as it is. Thus, for example, if I anticipate meeting X in ten minutes, the hypothesis that my horizon will be replaced, that the meeting will be realized within a different horizon, makes no difference whatever to what I anticipate. The distinctive emptiness of the absolute version of the MH derives not from the absence of experiential content but from the absoluteness of the hypothesis; that is, from the fact that it avoids the incoherence entailed by the presupposed oneness over time of my horizon, the oneness presupposed when I contemplate the past or future from the standpoint of "now," by appealing to a standpoint that abstracts away from the temporal present and thus from the past/present/future structure internal to my horizon.

The problem is that this standpoint is not available to me. There is, for me, no looking that is not a looking from the standpoint of "now," a looking structured by present, past, and future. You might say that while I grasp the possibility of a standpoint from which this structure plays no role, and thus I grasp as coherent the possibility expressed in the absolute version of the MH, the standpoint in question is not a standpoint that I can *occupy*; that the only standpoint I can occupy is that from within my

---

[2] Note, X, the person, can figure this way, but not the encounter with X, the event. There is as yet no such event: nothing to figure one way or another. Here, of course, we are assuming the past/present versus future asymmetry.

horizon, the standpoint from which the unity over time of my horizon is—looking ahead to the future and back to the past—always presupposed. The only standpoint I can occupy, then, is a standpoint from which the MH is incoherent.

It is as if I first had the dizzying thought that maybe my horizon, my life, is not a single life, a single horizon, but a series of horizons, etc., seamlessly replacing one another—and then caught myself up with the realization that the thought is empty, that it cannot be taken seriously.

It might be of interest to compare the MH, in its absolute form, with the dream hypothesis and with the hypothesis that everything doubled in size last night (see 6.1). As in the case of the DH, the possibility envisioned by the MH does not concern what is internal to my horizon. Yet, like the doubling hypothesis, and in contrast to the DH, the MH is not transcendent. That is to say, it does not envision the possibility of a wider horizon (with its own world and space and time). Whereas the emptiness as well as the peculiar empirical content of the DH derives from its transcendence, the emptiness of the doubling hypothesis derives from the fact that, though it confines itself to the world internal to my horizon and is thus an immanent hypothesis, it contrives to exclude the possibility of any appearance of the world that might bear on its truth value. The absolute version of the MH, on the other hand, envisions a possibility that neither transcends nor is internal to my horizon but (as the hypothesis that "my horizon" is really a multiplicity of horizons) concerns "the horizon" itself. Its peculiar emptiness, then, derives neither from transcendence nor from contrived immanence, but from its reliance on a standpoint that I cannot occupy, on a standpoint that is unavailable to me.

20.3 Kant's Third Paralogism: The Self "in Time" and the Self That "Time Is In"

If the MH is empty, so is its denial, the proposition that my horizon (consciousness) remains identical over time. One thinks, "However I imagine things developing, it is always *for me*," but at the same time may have the feeling that he is not really thinking anything. It does not explain the absence of content to observe that anyone who has the thought can (in Kant's phrase) attach the "I think"—precisely because *anyone* can do this for himself, whereas I am trying to think something here not about anyone but about *myself*, i.e., about *my* consciousness. The absence of content is that of a thought whose coherence depends on a standpoint that I cannot occupy. The standpoint I inescapably occupy, that in which I live, is the standpoint from within my horizon (consciousness). This fact of inescapability condemns the hypothesis of a multiplicity of horizons to emptiness.

It is what creates the sense that in thinking that it is always "for me," we are not really thinking anything.

This view of the matter may provide some insight into what is going in Kant's Third Paralogism, which deals with personal identity. (We shall confine ourselves to the A version of the Paralogism.) Kant's objective here is to expose the source of a fallacy that leads to the Cartesian conclusion that I am a soul, an immaterial substance.[3] The idea is roughly this. It seems that our identity through time cannot be doubted, that it is absolutely certain. Since the identity of a bodily substance over time is not certain in this way, we conclude that our identity through time is that of a soul, an immaterial substance. Our mistake is that whereas there is an identity that is certain, it is not the identity of a substance. It is not a substantial but only what Kant calls a "formal" identity. Drawing the Cartesian conclusion depends on mistaking this formal for a substantial identity.

In fact, the formal identity, that which is certain, might hold through a multiplicity of souls. It is

> only a formal condition of my thoughts and their coherence, and in no way proves the numerical identity of my subject. Despite the logical identity of the "I," such a change may have occurred in it as does not allow of its identity, and yet we may ascribe to it the same-sounding "I," which in every state, even in one involving a change in the [thinking] subject, might still be the thought of the preceding subject and so hand it over to the subsequent subject. (A363–64)[4]

---

[3] When we referred earlier to the Paralogisms (11.4), our interest was not with the fallacious inference, but with a certain puzzle about consciousness (viz., a puzzle about the causal dependence of my consciousness on my brain). At that point in our reflections, time had not yet entered as an explicit theme.

[4] Kant elaborates on this in a well-known footnote (A364) in which he compares the possibility of one soul passing on to another its thoughts, or representations, with that of the transfer of momentum from one body to another. In this way, he says, "the last substance would then be conscious of all the states of the previously changed substances, as being its own states, because they would have been transferred to it together with the consciousness of them." It will be clear (in the next chapter) that I regard as misguided this way of conceiving our consciousness of the past; but the point of the analogy remains. Of course, referring back now to the quoted text, a question arises about what *my subject* is supposed to be, that *it* should allow of a change (replacement) of soul substances. How is Kant using the expression "my subject" in this context? Clearly, he cannot by this expression simply *be referring* to the substance that I am; for in that case, his point would be that the fact of my formal identity through time is compatible with one soul substance becoming a different soul substance, which is absurd. The way out of this particular difficulty (which there is no reason Kant could not accept) is to treat "my subject" as positional rather than referential. Kant's point might then be stated by saying that it is compatible with my formal identity through time that at different times different soul substances occupy the subject position within my horizon—which, we know, is not absurd but represents an experiential possibility.

Thus even if the Cartesian is right about what I am (a soul), the certainty of my identity through time would not guarantee the identity through time of a soul substance.

We might compare this with the mistake diagnosed earlier as the "paralogism of imagination" (12.7). In the latter case, we infer that I am a soul not by mistaking a formal for a substantial identity, but, in effect, by mistaking a position within my horizon for a substantial entity. Our implicit grasp of the positional conception of the self enables us to imagine a different human being occupying the subject position within my horizon. So it is "me" in the imagined situation. But who is this "me"? Whoever it is, we suppose, it is the same substantial entity, myself, as the one who imagines being in the situation. Since that entity cannot be the human being (the imagined situation contains a different human being), we infer that it must be a soul. The inference, as we explained, is fallacious: whereas the position remains the same, it can be occupied by a multiplicity of substances.[5]

Where our analysis appeals to the positional conception of the self, Kant's analysis appeals to a conception of my "formal" identity through time. In both cases, however, there is something whose singleness is compatible with a multiplicity of substances but which we mistake for an identity of substance: in our case, the position at the center of my horizon; in Kant's case, my formal identity.

But what is my formal identity? Here is the key passage:

> Now I am an object of inner sense, and all time is merely the form of inner sense. Consequently, I refer each and all of my successive determinations to the numerically identical self, and do so throughout time, that is, in the form of the inner intuition of myself. This being so, the personality of the soul [my identity through time] has to be regarded not as inferred but as a completely identical proposition of self-consciousness in time; and this, indeed, is why it is valid *a priori*. For it really says nothing more than that in the whole time in which I am conscious of myself, I am conscious of this time as belonging to the unity of myself; and it comes to the same whether I say that this whole time is in me, as individual unity, or that I am to be found as numerically identical in all this time. (A362)

I am not sure about everything in this difficult passage, but a few points seem fairly clear.

One point—this is part of his transcendental idealism, as applied to the self—is that Kant draws a distinction between myself as I am in myself and myself as I appear. As I am in myself, I cannot be placed in time. Time

---

[5] See also 19.2–3.

is part of the form of the way I, like everything in the world, appear; or in this case, part of the way I "inwardly" appear. I inwardly appear "in time." I not only inwardly appear in time, time, Kant says, being the form of inner sense, is "in me," and thus "belongs to the unity of myself." Insofar as I inwardly appear in time, that is to say, insofar as I am conscious of myself in time, I am conscious of the unity of myself. My formal identity through time, my identity of person, is precisely this unity of myself of which I am conscious in being conscious of myself in time.

But what is the self whose unity it is? What is the self that "time is in"? The self as it appears in time, i.e., the self in time, is (in the terminology of transcendental idealism) the "phenomenal" self. This cannot be what we are looking for. How could the self that *time is in* be the self that *is in time*?

The self in time, the phenomenal self, contrasts with the self as it is in itself, the "noumenal" self. Of the noumenal self, the self as it is in itself, we know nothing; we know only how it appears within consciousness: it appears (this is part of it) as temporal, as being in time. This suggests that when Kant says that the whole of time is "in me," that it belongs "to the unity of myself," by "me" or myself" he does *not* mean the noumenal self, the self as it is in itself. If we know nothing of the self as it is in itself, we have no right to assert that the whole time is "in" it. Kant, it seems, must be employing a further conception of the self here. In fact, this further conception is required by the whole contrast between phenomenal and noumenal and thus could not be identified with the noumenal conception of the self (we shall come back to this). Let us call the self that "time is in," the self to which time "belongs," the "transcendental self."

One might wonder why the phenomenal self, myself as I appear (versus am in myself), should be restricted to myself as I "inwardly" appear. In one place Kant acknowledges that I also appear outwardly (as an object of outer sense), viz., as a man, a human being (B415). So it would not, for Kant, be incorrect to accept the naturalist answer to the "What am I?" question: I am a human being. This is not what I am in myself; but I appear as, and thus exist in time as, a human being. Let us henceforth take the phenomenal self to be the human being. The real problem for Kant concerns the transcendental self: not the self, the "me," as I appear (whether inwardly or outwardly), i.e., not the self "in time," but the self that "time is in," the self to whose unity time "belongs."

The problem is, as philosophers have pointed out, it sounds as if the existence of time depends on my existence. P. F. Strawson is typical in this regard when he accuses Kant of an "extreme subjectivism in which the source of *all* the structural features of the world is declared to be in *our* subject, 'the subject [here Strawson is quoting Kant, B422] in which the representation of time has its original ground'."[6] Let us consider this charge.

The "me," the self, that "time is in" is, we said, neither the phenomenal self, i.e., the human being/soul, nor the noumenal self, but (as we are calling it) the transcendental self. The question thus becomes: What is the transcendental self? My answer is that it is the horizonal self, my horizon (consciousness, life). On this reading of Kant, you do not get the extreme subjectivism of which Strawson complains.

Of course, if we suppose that time exists *only from within* my horizon, that it has the status of an internal object (like an after image, or sensation), Strawson's complaint is justified.[7] But we know from our reflections on the dream hypothesis that what is internal to my horizon is not thereby an internal object; that what is internal to my horizon includes, in fact, the whole of the world with its infinity of space and time (see 1.5–7). It includes, in other words, what I take to exist independently of my horizon, i.e., to exist whether or not it figures within my horizon. This after image, say, is internal to my horizon; but for that reason it is *not* part of the world. It has only a fleeting, marginal existence that stands in contrast to the independent existence of the world with its infinity of space and time. Yet the whole of the world with its infinity of space and time is internal to my horizon—internal to my horizon, i.e., in the way things are internal to a dream (1.7).

We can now address our earlier question about my "formal" identity through time. Kant's idea is that we mistake my "formal" identity through time for that of a substance. The inference to a persistent Cartesian soul depends on this mistake. The question is: What is my "formal" identity through time?

---

[6] *The Bounds of Sense*, p. 173. Compare this with Kant's statement (A129) that "all the objects with which we can occupy ourselves, are one and all in me, that is, are determinations of my identical self." Adrian Moore, commenting on this passage in his book *Points of View* (Oxford University Press, 1997, p. 125), remarks that "Here the idealism reaches its point of greatest intensity," and goes on in the next paragraph to say that the idea that " 'all objects etc. are in me' ... seems plainly false." Perhaps. But if (anticipating the suggestion we shall make shortly) we identify the self to which Kant here refers, the transcendental self, with the horizonal self, our evaluation of the Kantian statement may alter. Thus whereas it may be "plainly false" (in fact nonsense) that the world, the totality of "objects with which we can occupy ourselves," is *in me* in the sense of being in the bit of the world that I am, it is, I would say, a philosophical truth that the world, including the bit that I am, is internal to my horizon.

[7] And, to be sure, there are places where Kant invites the complaint. For example, shortly after the passage from A362 quoted above, in remarking on the difference between my own consciousness of my identity of person and the view of myself from the standpoint of another's consciousness (from which standpoint I am an object only of "outer" versus "inner" intuition), he says, "just as the time in which the observer sets me is not the time of my own

Kant describes it as the "completely identical proposition of self-con-sciousness in time," which "is why it is valid *a priori*." He goes on to assert that "it really says nothing more than that in the whole time in which I am conscious of myself, I am conscious of this time as belonging to the unity of myself; and it comes to the same whether I say that this whole time is in me, as individual unity, or that I am to be found as numer-ically identical in all this time." This is bewildering. How should the grasp of a trivial, strict identity, i.e., of something of the form "A = A," be equivalent to the grasp of the proposition that the whole of time is in me, or that I am to be found as numerically identical in all this time?

The strict identity would be: I = I. Or: I am myself. This, how-ever, contains no reference to time. Kant's allusion to "the same-sound-ing 'I' " suggests something different. We are self-conscious subjects, and, by hypothesis, it is our identity through time that is at issue. Self-conscious subjects are "I" users. Thus, even in the case where one soul replaces another (each passing on its thoughts to its successor), the result will be a subject who can refer to himself as "I." So, it will always be "I (myself)." The mistake is to conclude on this basis that it is always the same substance.

But notice, you too refer (to yourself) by "I." By the same reasoning, then, we might conclude that you and I, in fact that all of us, are the identical substance. Such reasoning is evidently fallacious. In fact it seems *too* evidently fallacious. I do not believe that this is the fallacy in the paralogism of personal identity.

Consider Kant's assertion that in the whole time in which I am con-scious of myself, I am conscious of this time as belonging to the unity of myself. It is, apparently, this "unity of myself" that is the problematic identity. That is, in being conscious of myself, I mistake "the unity of myself" for the identity of a substance through time. But how, if the prob-lematic identity is not what is expressed by "I = I," or what follows from the ever-present possibility among self-conscious subjects of first-person reference, should we understand this "unity of myself"?

The "myself" here, as we have already pointed out, is not the self "in time" but that which "time is in." It is my horizon (consciousness), the transcendental self. Thus we are not talking about the identity though time of this or that worldly entity, but about the identity (the oneness or unity) over time of the subject matter from within which questions about identity through time of worldly entities arise: the oneness or unity over time of my horizon (20.1–2). Whereas the infinity of time, the time before and after *now*, is "in me" in the sense that it is internal to my horizon,

---

but of his sensibility, so the identity which is necessarily bound up with my consciousness is not therefore bound up with his" (A363).

my consciousness, I, the human being that I am—i.e., the human being who by figuring at the center of my horizon is "me"—am "in time." The self in "in time," the Kantian phenomenal self, is the worldly entity, the human being, at the center of my horizon; the self that "time is in," the transcendental self, is my horizon, the subject matter by being at the center of which the human being in question is "myself." The identity, then, that we mistake for a substantial identity is the identity over time of the transcendental self, i.e., of my horizon.

Now, we saw (20.2), this turns out to be an empty identity. Of course, so is the identity "I = I," as well the identity that we express in asserting that the subject is always "myself." But the source of the emptiness is different in each case. The first identity is empty in that it is true by virtue of its form. The second is empty in that its truth is guaranteed by the rule for using "I." The emptiness of the hypothesis of the oneness of my horizon over time, on the other hand, derives from the fact that—like its contradictory, the multiplicity hypothesis—coherence of the hypothesis depends on a temporal standpoint that we grasp but cannot occupy: a standpoint that abstracts away from present-dominated time, from the structure of past/present/future, that is, from time as we know it from within the horizon. Thus, when I look ahead, or look back, the same horizon (consciousness), that from within which I look and of which I am at the center, is inescapably presupposed as the horizon from within which the past or future to which I look is remembered or anticipated as unfolding. The oneness of my horizon (the unity of myself) over time, the oneness that in the Kantian paralogism we mistake for an identity of substance through time, is this inescapably presupposed sameness or unity, that of the horizon to which not just the present but the infinity of past and future, the infinity of time, is internal.

Perhaps now, in concluding, we can briefly explain our earlier statement that the transcendental self, so far from being identical with the noumenal self, i.e., with the self as it is in itself, is required by the very contrast between the noumenal and phenomenal, the contrast at the core of Kant's transcendental idealism.[8]

The central thought of transcendental idealism is that there is something that shows itself, that appears, from within experience. In the nature of the case, we know this "something" only as it appears, not as it is in itself. And it appears as the world, the totality of objects in space and time. Time, for Kant, is the form, or a form, of this appearing. That is, the "something," the X about which we know nothing of how it is in itself, this appears as being in time. It appears as being in time, but we can have no right to assert that it—as it is in itself—is in time.

[8] The point was anticipated both in Int.8 and in chapter 11, note 8.

If I judge of an apple, say, that it looks (appears) red, my judgment is already about a worldly object, hence already about what Kant would call an appearance. Clearly, then, we need to distinguish two levels of appearing: the transcendental level, at which the "something," the X, appears as the world and thereby in time; and the empirical level, at which this or that object in the world (which is itself an appearance, an appearance of the X) appears as looking red. At both the transcendental and the empirical level, however, a fact of appearance presupposes the horizon. Just as only from within experience in the horizonal sense can an object that is part of the world look red, only from within the horizon can the "something," the X, appear as the world—as that of which the red-looking object is a part. Only from within the horizon, then, can the X that appears as the world, as that of which the red-looking object is a part, appear as in time.

The point should now be clear. The Kantian transcendental self is the horizonal self. It is the subject matter that is presupposed by the phenomenal/noumenal contrast, that is, by the contrast between the X as it appears and the X as it is in itself, and hence by the contrast between the phenomenal and the noumenal self. How then could it *be* the noumenal self?[9] The concept of the noumenal self, on this reading, is one element in the conceptual system that is Kant's transcendental idealism. The concept of the transcendental self, on the other hand, is the very framework of the whole system, the framework of transcendental idealism.

---

[9] Henry Allison, in his book *Kant's Transcendental Idealism* (Yale University Press, 1983), argues that unless a distinction is drawn between the transcendental self and the noumenal self, Kant's view in the Paralogisms becomes incoherent (pp. 287–90). It should be clear that I am in agreement with this general assessment of the Paralogisms. However, since the horizonal conception of the self plays no part in Allison's analysis of Kant, his analysis differs from the analysis offered here, as does his suggestion about how to make sense of the Paralogisms (pp. 290–93).

21. My Past

21.1 The Availability in Memory of Past Events

In the same way that the world is "my" world, the past is "my" past: whatever has happened before *now* is, like the world, internal to my horizon. However, this temporal form of Wittgenstein's solipsism is not what we mean by "my" past in the present context. We mean not everything that has happened before *now*, but only, as one might put it, a personal selection of this—my "personal past." The principle of selection is this: an event belongs to my past, i.e., to my personal past, just in case it is not only before *now*, and hence internal to my horizon, but is, within my horizon, available to memory. Obviously, this raises new questions: questions about memory. Some of these questions are, others are not, relevant to the problem we are going to discuss in this chapter. The answers to the questions that are relevant to our problem will be implicit in our discussion of the problem; for the problem we are going to discuss is precisely a problem about memory.

We live in the past and future from the standpoint of the present. The present, as we put it (20.2), dominates the past and future. But although the past and future are equally internal to my horizon, they do not (obviously) have the same meaning: we fear what will happen, not what has happened. We have hopes for the future, not for the past. We regret what we have done, not what we will do; feel relief that trouble is past, not that it is future. And so on. Looking ahead to the future and looking back to the past are both internal to the horizon; but they are not the same kind of "looking."

Behind this difference lies the basic past/future asymmetry (18.3). In contrast to past events, there is (or so we are assuming) no possibility of singular reference to future events. The point is not that it is hard to discern the events that lie ahead (in the future)—as if they were obscured by mists—but that there are no events lying up ahead to be discerned (no events over which to quantify). When we look to the future, nothing—as we put it—looks back. Thus a thought about a future event, even when expressed in terms of a definite description, must be implicitly general.

Of course there is no shortage of philosophers who reject any such interpretation of the past/future asymmetry.[1] But the problem we shall be discussing depends on the assumption not that we *lack* potential objects of singular reference in the case of future events, but that we *have* such objects in the case of past events. If you think the future and past are symmetrical, you will think that, at least in principle, the problem we shall discuss affects the future case as well. We shall, however, continue to assume the asymmetry and will therefore assume that the problem affects only the case of past events. Let us, before getting into details, try to indicate the general nature of the problem.

Past events are, we are assuming, available in such a way that we can make singular reference to them. When we talk here about the availability of past events for singular reference, we are talking about memory, that is, about the way that past events are available in memory for singular reference. We may, certainly, make singular reference to past events that are not themselves available in memory. I can refer, say, to the assassination of Caesar and to the First World War. I have learned facts about these past events and may remember these facts. In reporting these facts I make singular references to the events in question. Yet there is no possibility of my remembering the events themselves. The events are available for singular reference; but they are not available in memory. Events that are not available in memory are, *eo ipso*, not available *in memory* for singular reference.

Let us focus now on events that are available in memory for singular reference. Straightaway we encounter an ambiguity: the availability may be either actual or potential. That is, we may mean the availability for reference that an event has *in* the very remembering (recollecting) of the event, or the availability it has in virtue of the fact that it *can become* available in this way. Henceforth, when we speak of the availability "in memory" of an event for singular reference, we shall mean actual, realized, availability for singular reference. If we mean that an event is available to become (actually) available in memory, we shall say that the event is available "for" or "to memory." For example, we may suppose that what I am doing now will, from within my horizon, be available for memory ten minutes from now. It will be thus available even if I do not actually recall what I am now doing, even if I never think of it again. In other words, ten minutes from now what I am doing now will, within my horizon, be available to memory, for memory, even if it never becomes available in memory.

---

[1] See, e.g., A. J. Ayer, "Fatalism," in *The Concept of a Person* (Macmillan, 1964), and more recently, D. H. Mellor, *Real Time II* (Routledge, 1998), pp. 21–23.

This is still pretty rough, but it will suffice to identify our problem. Our problem is a problem about the availability of an event, not for or to, but in memory; that is, a problem about the availability of an event in memory for singular reference. It is, I believe, a problem that anyone who thinks philosophically about memory must come to grips with. But we shall present it via our particular way of characterizing memory (19.5)—as if, indeed, it were a problem peculiar to our characterization.

In memory we are related to the past, to past events, and, we are assuming, the way we are related puts us in a position to make singular references to these events. In what way are we related? However exactly we answer this question, the answer, it would seem, must respect the following basic truth about memory, that in memory our relation to the remembered event, to the past event, can only be indirect. Our relation to the past event can only be indirect for the simple reason that a past event is *past*: that it is not *now* occurring. In a real sense, *it*, the event itself, is not available as an object of thought. At any rate, it is not available in the direct way that (as we shall spell out) our earlier characterization of memory seems to require. What is available in that way, what is strictly speaking now there, available for me to fix on in thought, is not the past event itself, but something that *represents* the past event. Our characterization of memory seems to ride roughshod over this basic, undeniable truth about memory and the past. It seems to imply, absurdly, that the remembered event is now there—as if it were, after all, not past but present. Or as if it were in some funny way both past and present. This, in general terms, is the problem.

21.2 The Argument from Pastness

Let us consider, in terms of our earlier account, how past events are available (for singular reference) in memory. There are two primary ways in which worldly events are available in memory. An event may now figure as having appeared within my horizon, or, in the case of my own actions, it may now figure as having been willed. In the latter case, the figuring of my body (or parts of my body) as (part of) my body space, the space of feeling, may also come into the way the event figures. Then too, since an action of mine may visually appear within my horizon, an action may, it seems, be available in memory in three ways.

Perhaps it would be more accurate, phenomenologically, to characterize the threefold availability of a past action, not as three ways of being available in memory, but as three aspects of a single availability. For example, I climb a rope. We may assume that the movements of my body figure as willed, that they are associated with certain hard-to-describe feelings (tension, pressure, strain, rubbing, etc.) in my arms and legs and other parts of my body, and finally that, in some partial and fragmented way, certain bits of my body and the rope and the surroundings appear visually within my horizon. In that case, we may suppose that if I recall climbing the rope, the availability in memory of my action (activity) within my horizon will have three aspects to it. In contrast, suppose you watch me climb the rope. Within your horizon, the same event of climbing will, if you recollect it, be available in memory only via one of these three aspects, that is, as visually appearing in a certain way.

Events other than my actions—events generally, not just the actions of others—are available in memory only as having appeared. Memory in such cases is a matter of past appearing. This includes, of course, in addition to past visual appearing, past tactual, audial, olfactory, and gustatory appearing. In remembering, say, a particular occasion of eating a pizza, I may remember the way it tasted and smelled. And so on. However, in the case of events other than our own actions, it is (for those who are not blind) past visual appearing that is the central form of memory; and it is this form of memory, visual memory—what we commonly mean when we say that we "remember seeing" something—that we shall henceforth have in mind.

What is the problem? I remember the train arriving at the station this morning. I remember it coming into view. I remember pressing the button to open the door, getting on, and the way things were in the train as I got on. (Let us keep things simple.) So there is a certain event, the arriving of the train at such-and-such time and place, and certain other events, including actions on my part, that I now recall. These events are, we shall assume, now (actually) available in memory. How do the events now figure within my horizon? The arrival of the train now figures—or rather, the train on that past occasion now figures—as having visually appeared in a certain way, and my actions on that occasion figure as willed. The arrival of the train (the train on that occasion) and my actions are, within my horizon, past, before *now*: they belong to the past internal to my horizon. And in that past, back then within my horizon, they figured, respectively, as visually appearing, or as willed.

The problem concerns the fact that the events in question not only *then* figured within my horizon as appearing and willed, but that they *now* figure as having then figured in these ways. Clearly, this is essential to my now actually remembering the events, to their now being (actually) available *in* memory. It is not sufficient that the events occurred, or that at the time of their occurrence they figured in certain ways within my horizon. The latter is compatible with my having totally forgotten the events, with their having in fact become totally and irrevocably unavailable to memory.

But even assuming that the events in question are now available to memory, this is not sufficient for my actually recollecting them. If it is to be the case that the events are now, within my horizon, available *in* memory, they must now—not just *then* but *now*—figure in certain ways from within my horizon. It must be true that they now figure as having then figured in certain ways. Otherwise there is nothing in which the fact of their now being actually recollected might consist, nothing that might distinguish their having occurred and as a consequence now being within my horizon available to memory, on the one hand, and, on the other, their now being actually given within my horizon, that is to say, their now being available *in* memory. And precisely this is what may strike us as problematic. For the past event is, qua past, not now occurring. If it is not now occurring, how can *it*, that very event (the event itself), *now* figure within my horizon in any way at all?

It is at this point that we may be tempted to say that it is something else, something related to the remembered event, that now figures within my horizon and is thereby now available, etc. Thus it is common in philosophical reflection on memory to suppose that what is actually available in memory is not the remembered event itself but a representation, perhaps an image, of the event.[2] Right now, for example, as I remember the arrival of the train this morning, as I remember my actions in getting on the train, what is available is not the event of the train's coming into the station, not my act of pushing the button that opens the train door—how could *those* events (the past events "themselves") *now* be available?!— but a representation of the events in question. It is only in some indirect way, i.e., only via the immediate availability of a representation, that past events are available in memory.

We might point out that, on our assumption about the past/future asymmetry, this argument for the indirect availability of past events (the argument from pastness) has no analogue in the case of future events. The reason is not that future events are directly available but that, on our assumption, there is in the future case nothing to be available, directly or indirectly. In this case, the argument seems to call not for indirectness of reference but, in the case of apparent singular reference, generality.

What about objects and events in the present? There are well-known philosophical arguments whose conclusion is that *these* objects, the objects *now* directly available—experientially present—within my horizon, and therefore now in existence, are not worldly (external) objects but

---

[2] The idea goes back (at least) to St. Augustine: "It is in thee, my mind, that I measure times . . . the impression, which things as they pass by cause in thee, remains even when they are gone; this it is which, still present, I measure, not the things which pass by to make this impression." *Confessions*, trans. E. B. Pusey, book 11 (Henry Regnery, 1948).

sense data or impressions, or whatever. Notice, though, it is not an assumption of such arguments that the objects about which we are meant to conclude that they are only indirectly available (the worldly objects) necessarily no longer exist; whereas, in contrast, this assumption is what the argument for the indirect availability of past events, i.e., the argument from pastness, is all about.[3] Hence I suspect that, whether they accept the argument or not, most philosophers would agree that the argument from pastness—and on this basis, some version of representationalism—is on stronger ground than arguments for representationalism that are restricted to the present. Turning the point around, we might say that "naive realism" seems more attractive in the case of the present than the past, that it is easier to believe (philosophically) in the direct availability of presently existing external objects and events than the direct availability of past events, or the direct availability of objects that no longer exist.

It is, so to speak, the very pastness of the past that provides the argument for the conclusion that, in memory, events are only indirectly available for singular reference; and thus for the view that it is not "the events themselves" but something else—an image or representation of the events—that is directly available in memory.

21.3 Being Open to the Availability of the Past

Yet the situation is not completely one-sided. There is a way of reflecting on the past that seems, at a stroke, to subvert the argument from pastness. This way of reflecting proceeds not by exposing a mistake in the argument, or by providing a counterargument, but rather, simply by opening us up to a truth that contradicts the conclusion of the argument from pastness; that is to say, by opening us up to something we already know— by enabling us to make a philosophical discovery. Thus what we philosophically discover in this case, contradicts the conclusion of a philosophical argument (the argument from pastness). Philosophy at odds with itself.

In fact, not only does the discovery contradict the conclusion of the argument, the discovery is *possible* only *in the face of* the argument. Philosophical discovery presupposes resistance (see Int.4). It presupposes that something hides or covers over, or distracts us from, what we already know. (Otherwise, why should we have to "discover" it?) In the present case, the resistance is supplied by philosophy itself—in the form of an argument. Unless we first engaged in philosophical reasoning or argu-

---

[3] Perhaps, since this might occur to someone as an exception, we should point out that Russell's famous time-lag argument appeals not to the *necessity* of the external object's no longer existing, but only the *possibility* of its no longer existing.

ment, and thereby let philosophy cover over what we already know, we would not be in a position to discover, to become open to, what we already know, viz., that the past is there for us to refer to.

How do things stand outside philosophy with respect to the past? Well, we simply refer to the past. Are we, as we go about our everyday business, closed off from the truth, the fact, that the past is there to be referred to? No, we simply refer to the past. There is no question of being closed off from anything. What closes us off from what we know is philosophical reasoning (the argument from pastness), whereas in everyday life the reasoning never occurs to us. Are we then, in everyday life, *open* to the truth about the past, to the fact of its immediate availability? No. The necessary resistance, the resistance that is presupposed by openness and in the present case derives from the reasoning, this is, once again, lacking. We are, it seems, neither open to what we know nor closed off from what we know. We just go about our business in the way that we do, knowing what we know in the way that we know it—simply referring to things in the past.

The knowledge of our relation to the past is, as we go about our everyday business, in our possession. Yet to become open to and in this sense discover what we know, what we already know, we need philosophy. In the present case, we need philosophy in two respects: first to create, and then to overcome, the resistance presupposed by the discovery.

Suppose that I am, right now, convinced by the argument from pastness. On the basis of the argument, then, it seems evident that past events are not themselves directly available for singular reference, that what is directly available is only an image or representation of a past event. For example, I now recall getting on the train this morning. So, being convinced by the argument, I tell myself that it cannot be that very past action of mine, the event itself, that is available now in memory for singular reference, but only an image, a representation, of that event.

Hold on. In saying—in thinking, telling myself—that *that* action, *that* event, my getting on the train, is not now itself directly available for singular reference, I seem to have precisely what I am telling myself that I do not have: the direct availability for singular reference, the direct availability in memory, of the past event. If in telling myself what I am now telling myself the event of my past action were not directly available, I would not be telling myself what I am telling myself. Yet what I am telling myself is that the action, *that* action, is not directly available.

It is as if in applying to myself the conclusion of the argument from pastness I catch myself out. I catch myself doing precisely that which, if the conclusion of the argument were true, I could not be doing: making a singular reference to a past event. I catch myself making a singular reference to a past event in applying to myself a philosophical conclusion which, when applied to myself, entails that I cannot be making a singular reference to a past event. Let us be clear, catching ourselves out like this, catching ourselves making a singular reference to a past event in the process of applying to ourselves the philosophical conclusion that such reference is impossible, this is not an *argument* that past events *are* directly available in memory for singular reference. It is a way of jogging ourselves, of opening ourselves up to the fact of such availability; a way, in other words, of opening ourselves up to what we already know.

In the face of a philosophical argument, we make a philosophical discovery. We make a philosophical discovery that contradicts the conclusion of the philosophical argument. Indeed, as we said, without the argument, without the resistance to overcome, there would be no discovery. Our discovery in this case is, as we said, a discovery that we make in the face of a philosophical argument.

Let us back up to the point where, convinced by the argument from pastness, I reflect on my past action of getting on the train. We represented me as reflecting on "that action (then)." But, one might object, this representation of my thought does not require us to assume (as we did) that I make a singular reference to my past action, hence that the action is available for such a reference. There is Russell's alternative—one to which we ourselves appealed in the case of future events. If a putative singular reference to a future event may be understood as a general thought to the effect that there will be just one event of such-and-such kind, why not suppose an analogous reading in the case of past events?

The past case would differ in that here (or so it is being claimed) we *do* have an object available for singular reference: not the past event but a memory image of it. The general thought in this case would be that there was just one event, an action on my part, that the directly available image represents. Accordingly, when in reflection I think, "that action (then) is not directly available for singular reference," this may be understood as the thought that there was then just one event that is represented by this image (now), and that the event is not now directly available for singular reference.[4]

It seems to me that if this were right, my own past actions, and the events I have witnessed, would be foreign to me; i.e., foreign in a way they are clearly *not* foreign to me. What kind of foreignness is that? I contemplate, say, a photo of a man. I wonder who he was. It would seem that I am sure of at least this: that there is, or was, a man whom the photo represents. Other than that, and what I can glean from the photo itself, I

---

[4] Note that we must employ the past tense along with the quantifier. If we say that there *is* just one event that this image now represents, we undermine the point of introducing generality here.

know nothing about the man in the photo. What is this man to me? I know there is (was) such a person. But for me, i.e., from within my horizon, he is, or was, just someone-or-other-out-there-in-the-world. Perhaps this being just someone-or-other, etc., will indicate the kind of foreignness that we are trying to evoke here. Is there anything like it in recollecting a past action of mine, or a past event that I have witnessed?

It may seem obvious that what explains the absence of such foreignness in the recollection case is that there once was an event present visually within my experience. However, in the photo case, too, we may suppose the man (in the photo) was once present, etc. The prior presence of the man within my experience is compatible either with his figuring or with his not figuring as just someone-or-other-out-there-in-the-world. What accounts for the difference? There is foreignness if, despite the fact that the man was once present, he is now lost to memory in the sense that he is no longer even potentially available for singular reference. Insofar as the man *is* thus available, then, I take it, he will for that reason *not* figure as just someone-or-other, etc. Similarly, it is precisely because they are available for singular reference that, in recollecting them, my past actions, and past events that I have witnessed, do not figure in this way, that they do not have this kind of foreignness.

Suppose that I know that I got on the train this morning; suppose, further, that the action is represented by a current image. If what the action is for me is just some-action-or-other-back-then-in-the-past represented by this image (as in our example, the man is for me just-someone-or-other-out-there-in-the-world represented by this photo), would we want to say that I am *recollecting* it? Am I in recollecting my past actions and events I have witnessed estranged from these things, estranged from my own past? If you really take this in, the idea is so implausible, so manifestly at odds with how it actually is in personal memory, that contemplating the suggestion can only have the effect of undermining its intention. It can only have the effect, i.e., of opening us up to what we already know: that the role in which we are trying to cast the image is in fact filled by the event that the image is supposed to represent; that however images come into the story, it is the event itself that is referentially available.

Perhaps we have omitted something, that the image of the past event comes with a "sense of familiarity."[5] But unless this is just a disguised way of alluding to the fact of the event's direct availability in memory for singular reference, it will not give us what we know we have in remembering a past event. For you could attach a feeling of familiarity even to the

---

[5] See, e.g., Russell in *The Analysis of Mind*. A memory image, he says (p. 161), is one that we trust, and "the characteristic by which we distinguish the images we trust is the feeling of *familiarity* that accompanies them."

case where I consider the picture of a man who is, for me, just someone-or-other-out-there, etc. It could be someone who died long ago, whose yellowed picture I come across fingering through a pile of old photos in a second-hand shop. The man might nonetheless "seem familiar." Would it not be manifestly implausible to suggest that it is like this in the case of recollecting one of my own past actions or an event that I have witnessed?

Here is another line of thought. The alarm goes off: "*This* noise (now) is unbearable." A bit later, after the alarm has stopped: "*that* noise (then) was unbearable." The first thought, it would seem, is a paradigm example of a thought involving singular reference to an event. I pick out an event, a noise, and judge it to be unbearable. Simple. In contrast, the second thought, on the present suggestion, turns out to contain an unexpected complexity. What I pick out is not a noise but a noise-image, and what I judge to be unbearable is not what I pick out. Rather, I judge that there is just one noise that is such that it both is represented by what I pick out and is unbearable. Does this seem right? Could anyone really believe that as I move in an ordinary case from *this* noise (now) to *that* noise (then), such a new complexity suddenly enters the picture? What could seem smoother, less like a jump or break, than the transition from the present- to the past-directed thought? The past-directed thought is just as simple as the present-directed thought. The past event is just as available *now*—looking back—for singular reference as it was *then*, when it was a temporally present event.

Or are we to say that the complexity enters only after a certain period of time has elapsed? How long? Might we not still have referential hold of, say, *that* noise an hour ago or yesterday, *that* noise last week, last year? Or does the complexity enter gradually? These stories are all equally implausible. And their implausibility serves, I think, to open us up, once again, to what we already know: to the fact that past events—not images or representations of past events, but the events themselves—are in memory directly available for singular reference.

21.4 Memory Images

But how *do* memory images come into the story? Surely images play a role in memory. It might seem, in fact, that they play an essential role, that without images we would not remember doing or witnessing anything, that nothing would be available in personal memory.

It does not follow, of course, that whenever we think or talk about an event in our personal past (which is, after all, not something we go in for only occasionally), we have at that moment a more or less detailed, corresponding memory image. I tell you what I did this morning: worked, went to the supermarket, bumped into so-and-so, witnessed a minor traffic accident, and so on. It is not likely, or at any rate necessary, that as I casually report these humdrum events, perhaps half thinking about something else, there is for everything I report a corresponding image. Yet what would it be if there were *no* relevant images? Could I, if there were no relevant images, be telling you—telling you in the way that I am, that is to say, telling you *on the basis of present recollection*—about what happened this morning? Without images, it seems, there would be no recollection: the events in question would not be available now in memory.

We can agree, images are essential to the availability in memory of past events. But in whatever way they are essential, whatever role we assign to the image in memory, we must not lose sight of the fact that the past event, the event itself, is directly available. Then what shall we say about the image? Is it directly available? Or is it merely the vehicle of the event's availability?

There is such a thing as fixing on and describing a memory image. And not just describing the image as an image *of* such-and-such. A memory image may, it seems, be described *as an image*. Thus we say that our memory of an event has "faded," or that it is "confused," "patchy," "indistinct," and so on. The event is not indistinct. What is indistinct? It must be the image that is indistinct. Yet we do not *infer* that this is so. The image itself, it seems, is directly available.

This creates a problem. For we cannot suppose that the image is directly available in addition to the event, as if, when I recollect the event, two things are directly available. But if just one thing is directly available, and if it is the image, it follows that the event could not be directly available. The event, it seems, would be blocked off by the image. No, the event itself is directly available in memory. Then, once again, what shall we say about the image?

I now recollect seeing a man reading a newspaper as I got on the train. That, the man reading a newspaper, the event itself (if we may call it an "event"), is now directly available in memory. Do I now have a memory image of the event? Of course. Suppose I try to fix exclusively on it, i.e., on the image as opposed to the past event of which it is an image. This seems impossible. I can fix on the image but, in fixing on the image, I thereby fix on the event. There is no duality here. If I have an ordinary picture (a photo, say) of an event that I recollect, I can fix on the picture independently of the event: the picture is directly available in experience, the event is directly available in memory. But within memory itself there is no comparable duality. Thus if I try to go back and forth between my memory image of the man reading and the event, if I try to fix first on one then on the other, I seem to stay fixed on the same thing. But what is it that I stay fixed on? Is it the past event or the present image of the past event?

We know, as before, that it is the event—which leaves us with no account of what the image is doing here.

Perhaps the image and the event are both directly available, i.e., directly but not independently available (available in such a way that we can go back and forth between them). But how? If they are not independently available, how can both be directly available? Would not one "get in the way" of the other? The idea that the image and event are nonindependently yet directly available seems like the phenomenological equivalent of the metaphysical impossibility of two physical objects (simultaneously) filling out exactly the same space.

Of course if we suppose that the image and the event are identical, there is no problem. But we cannot suppose they are identical. If the item we call the memory image of an event were identical with the event, then it could not be the image of the event. An image must be distinct from that of which it is an image. Something cannot be an image of itself.

Right here, I think, with the idea that a memory image must be a distinct item, i.e., an item distinct from the event of which it is an image, we touch on the crucial point. Insofar as a "memory image" is essential to the direct availability in memory of an event, it is not really an *image* of the event. That is, it is not an image of the event in the way, or sense, that an ordinary picture (like a photo) of the event would be an image of the event. An ordinary picture of X is an item distinct from X that represents X. If we conceive of a memory image as a representation of the event, hence as an item distinct from the event, we are, I think, using a false conception of a memory image.

A memory image is neither an item (entity) identical with, nor an item distinct from, the event (or object) of which it is an image. It is not in the first place an *item*—something that might be identical or not identical with the event of which it is an image. So it is not something that might be held up alongside, or get in the way of, the event of which it is an image. It is, rather, the concrete fact of the event's availability: the event's now figuring within my horizon in the particular way that it does. In our example, my getting on the train this morning now figures within my horizon—figures in a particular way—as then willed; the man reading a paper now figures, in a particular way, as then appearing. These particular concrete ways of figuring within my horizon are not inner items distinct from the events in question. The only relevant items are those very events themselves, figuring in the particular ways that they figure.

This, if it is right, makes clear why a memory image is essential to the direct availability in memory of an event. The direct availability of a past event must take some form or other. The memory image is (like a Fregean mode of presentation) simply the particular form the availability takes, the particular concrete way in which the past event is available. And this is not a further item, i.e., an item in addition to the past event whose particular way of being available is the memory image of the event.

Thus if we say that a memory image is "confused" or "indistinct," etc., we do not thereby qualify an item distinct from the event. Nor, obviously, do we qualify the event. We qualify the way the event now figures within my horizon. We are saying, in effect, that the past event now figures within my horizon only confusedly or indistinctly, that it is only confusedly or indistinctly available.

Consider what philosophers call "sense impressions." This cup in front of me is present from within my experience. So, it seems, I must have a sense impression of the cup. But what is that? If we suppose the impression is an inner item that represents, and is therefore distinct from, the object, then, since the impression is directly available, it will "get in the way" of the object: it will be the impression, not the cup, that is directly available in experience. Yet is it not the cup that is directly available? Is not *this* the cup?

An impression is, indeed, essential to the direct availability of the cup. It is not, however, a further item (in addition to the cup), but the particular way in which the cup now figures (visually appears) within my experience. It must appear some way or other—this is why an impression is essential; but its way of appearing is not a further item. The only relevant item is the object itself, the cup, appearing in the way that it now does within my horizon. Similarly, in recollecting seeing the cup, the only relevant item is the cup, figuring in the particular way that it now figures within my horizon. Of course there is a difference. In perception the cup now figures as now appearing. In memory, it now figures as then appearing.

21.5 Letting the Past Be Past

Are we not sometimes fooled in memory? A memory image may be of nothing; there may be no past event answering to the image. We may be fooled in perceptual experience too. An impression too may be of nothing: it can seem that an F now appears within my horizon when there is no F, no relevant external thing. Yet in such a case, the case of hallucination, it would seem that there is *some* demonstratively available item, *this* item, which, let us assume, I mistakenly take to be an F. If the item is not an external object, it must, it seems, be internal (an object that exists only from within my experience). Would not the same sort of thing be true in the case of memory? Would it not follow then that, in the case of memory hallucination, there occurs an internal object, an item that exists only from within my horizon and that I (possibly) mistake for an event from my personal past, i.e., for an event that now figures within my horizon as then figuring in some way or other?

What we have in the offing here is a version of the so-called argument from illusion and the corresponding version of the argument for the case of memory. The argument purports in both cases to demonstrate that all that could ever be directly available within my horizon is an internal item or object. In neither case, however, does this follow. We can accept that, in the perceptual case, there is on the odd occasion an internal object, or item, within my horizon that I mistake for a presently appearing external thing. Again, we can accept that sometimes in case of the memory there occurs an internal item that I mistake for a previously appearing event. We can, in other words, accept that there is the occasional internal item that I confusedly take for part of the world, or for part of my personal past. But from the possibility of confusing the internal and external, it simply does not follow that what is directly available is *always*, and *only*, something internal. It gives us no reason, then, to call into question what we all know: that by and large it is the world that now figures within my horizon as now appearing, that by and large it is events from my personal past that now figure as then appearing, and so on.[6]

Thus the fact that a memory image is essential to the recollection of an event from my personal past does not provide any argument for the conclusion that events from my personal past are only indirectly available in memory. On the contrary, once we are clear what a memory image *is*— a particular concrete way in which a past event or object now figures from within my horizon—it cannot escape us that I live with past object and events directly available from within my horizon; just as I live with present objects and events directly available from within my horizon.

Of course, events from my personal past are not now occurring. If they were now occurring, they would not be past. Events now occurring may, like the world around me, now figure as now appearing within my horizon (experience); or in the case of my own actions, they may now figure as now willed. Past events cannot now figure as now appearing, or as now willed. If they figured in these ways, they would be occurring now and hence would not be past. How do past events now figure, how are they now available, within my horizon? They now figure as then appearing, as then willed. They figure—there is no mystery about this—just

---

[6] The point is due to J. L. Austin. See *The Puzzle of Experience*, 5.2. It is the essence of what, in the recent literature on perception, is called the "disjunctive view" of appearances. See Paul Snowdon, "Perception, Vision and Causation," *Proceedings of the Aristotelian Society* 81 (1980/1); John McDowell, "Criteria, Defeasibility and Knowledge," *Proceedings of the British Academy* 68 (1982).

in the way they do, in the way we all know they do. They are available in the way they are available, in the way we all know they are available.

I hope it will not seem pretentious to say that behind these empty assertions there lies a philosophical point. It is that we must learn, philosophically, to let past events be what they are. We must learn to let past events be past.

This is exactly what the argument from pastness will not let past events be. We get it into our heads that past events themselves cannot now be directly available in memory for the reason that, as past, they are not now occurring; that therefore the only thing that could *now* be directly available in memory is a representation of a past event. In effect, we treat as a reason for saying that past events cannot now be directly available, etc., what is only a reason for the trivial thought that past events are not present events: that past events are past. It is as if we wanted the past to be present, and then, realizing it cannot be like this, showed our displeasure by refusing to recognize the kind of being that the past actually has (the kind of being we know it has).

21.6 Moving from Inside to Outside the Sphere of Phenomenological Reflection

Perhaps we can appreciate now that there was always something precarious about the argument from pastness. In formulating the argument, we remain, one might say, entirely within the sphere of (temporalized) phenomenological reflection: the sphere in which we reflect on how the world with its temporal structure figures from within my horizon. When we reflect in this way, the direct availability of the past cannot (if we are open to how things are from within my horizon) escape us. But then the argument from pastness, since it proceeds entirely inside this sphere, has no way, really, to gain a foothold except by placing an incoherent condition on the availability of the past, a condition that in effect turns the past into the present. Hence only a relatively minor shift in our thinking, a slight jog, is needed to let ourselves become open to the incoherence and thereby to expose the mistake in the argument.

The argument from pastness seeks to establish not that the past is not available in memory, but rather, on the assumption that it is available, that it is not directly available. We might compare this with the well-known time-lag argument. The time-lag argument starts with the point that an event that is demonstratively available (present) within my experience—*this* event—must be occurring *now*. It then appeals, first, to the general fact that how things are within my experience is the causal upshot of events brought about in my nervous system and brain by other things happening in the world, and second, to the fact that since light travels at a finite speed, there is time-lag between the occurrence of an external event and the consequent events in my nervous system and brain. If we accept that the presence of *this* within my experience is the causal upshot of what is going on in my brain, it seems to follow that the demonstratively available item cannot be the external event.

Both arguments aim to force us to accept a certain indirectness of availability, in one case of past events, in other of external events. The argument from pastness proceeds, as we remarked, entirely inside the sphere of phenomenological reflection. The time-lag argument, since it starts with the point that what is demonstratively available must be occurring *now*, starts inside this same sphere. Yet in appealing to facts about the physiology of perception and the transmission of light, and to the general fact that how things are within my experience is determined causally by what is happening in my brain, etc., the argument moves outside the phenomenological sphere—into (as we might call it) the sphere of worldly reflection: the sphere wherein we ask not how the world *figures from within the horizon*, but simply how the world is. Moreover, in appealing to the idea that the facts disclosed in the phenomenological sphere are causally fixed by facts disclosed in the sphere of worldly reflection, it draws attention to a point of brute contact between the two spheres.

An argument for the indirect availability of the world that (like the argument from pastness) remains completely inside the phenomenological sphere would rest on the following thought: that no part of the world, such as the cup, can be directly available within my experience—for the simple reason that it is an *external* part of the world. How, one might ask, could anything that exists independently of my experience be present within my experience? Only something whose existence is exhausted by its presence within my experience, an internal object, could be thus directly available. This argument, which is intended to parallel the argument from pastness, might be called the "argument from externality."

The argument from externality can, if anything, be overthrown more decisively than the argument from pastness—just by opening up to how things actually are now from within my horizon. If, in the face of the argument from externality, I open up to how things are, what do I find? I find what I already knew I would find, the cup (the world). Objects in the world are, spatially, at a distance from the human being that I am. But they are (just as that human being may be) present within my horizon, and in that way they are directly available within my horizon. Similarly, events in my personal past are at a temporal distance from events happening now, in the present. They are at a temporal distance from those events; yet they are directly available—not, of course, in the way that events present within my experience are directly available, but in their own way, in the way (how else?) that past events are directly available.

Both the argument from pastness and the argument from externality remain entirely inside the sphere of phenomenological reflection. In both cases, we accept a false premise (if we do) because we allow ourselves philosophically to become closed off from what we know. Thus refuting the argument is in each case simply a matter of letting ourselves become open to what we already know. If there is a correct argument for the conclusion that these arguments seek to establish—that in one case the past, and in the other currently existing objects and events, are not directly available—it must be an argument that, like the time-lag argument, moves from inside to outside the sphere of phenomenological reflection.

In the case of currently existing objects, etc., there is in fact an argument that, since it depends on less, is more fundamental than the time-lag argument, viz. "the causal argument." The causal argument, like the time-lag argument, assumes that how things are within my experience is the causal upshot of a chain of events in the world, starting with the reflection of light by an object and culminating with what happens in my brain, but dispenses with the fact that light travels at a finite speed. Thus, for purposes of the causal argument, we can assume that light travels instantaneously (that there is no time-lag).

Roughly, for any given object I might directly fix on in experience, e.g., *this* object—the object which, were I not engaged in this particular line of philosophical reflection, I would unhesitatingly assert to be a cup—it is possible that I remain fixed on it, while the relevant external object, the cup, is somehow eliminated; for whereas in the actual situation the cup is involved in the causal chain responsible for how things are now in my experience, the elimination of the cup is compatible with holding constant the current state of my brain, in which case the object on which I am fixed, *this* object, would remain the same. So *this* object, since it can survive the elimination of the external object, cannot be the external object, the cup. It should be clear that the causal argument can be generalized for any external object.[7]

On the one hand, the causal argument seems to survive all attempts to refute it, that is, to expose a mistake in the argument.[8] Yet if in the face

---

[7] For a more careful presentation and discussion of the causal argument, see my *The Puzzle of Experience* (there the causal argument is called "the problematic reasoning").

[8] See ibid., chaps. 2, 4–8. In the last few years, I have read, and discussed in conversation, suggestions about possible mistakes in the causal argument that I did not think of in writing *The Puzzle of Experience*; but I do not believe any of these seriously undermine the argument. Of course there is no closing the book on possible mistakes. Let me stress that it is the exposing of a mistake that is required here. For example: however powerful, however convincing, Kant's transcendental argument that we cannot but take the objects of experi-

of the argument—at the very moment when it exercises its grip—I let myself become open to how things actually are within my experience, all I find is the cup, the world (which is what I always knew I would find). The argument remains, but it comes up against something that overturns its conclusion.

In the case of the arguments that fall entirely inside the phenomenological sphere, philosophical openness uncovers a false premise, a mistake *in the arguments*. Openness cannot in this way help us in the case of the causal argument, since the crucial premise moves outside the phenomenological sphere. We may overturn the conclusion of the argument, but the argument itself is untouched. Thus the very object within my experience that the argument demonstrates to be not part of the world turns out, when I open up to my experience, to be part of the world. Yet as we said, the argument itself remains. Here we have a real puzzle (the puzzle of experience).

It is not hard to construct a memory version of the causal argument. In this case, the premise that moves outside the phenomenological sphere is that how things are in memory is the causal upshot of a chain starting with a past event and culminating with what is happening right now in my brain as I recollect the event. Of course there are differences with the perceptional case. First, the memory chain is "longer" than the corresponding perceptual chain. Thus, if what I remember is seeing such-and-such event, the memory chain will include, in addition to the perceptual chain, the chain that leads to the laying down of memory traces in my brain, and the activation of these traces when I recollect the perceived event. Then too, the memory version of the causal argument cannot have the same form as the perceptual version. In the perceptual case, the causal argument appeals to the possibility of holding constant the current state

---

ence to be part of the world; or Heidegger's phenomenological exposition of the kind of "Being" we have (our way of carrying on, of living)—which according to Heidegger is typically missed in philosophy (philosophy, you could say, never in the right spirit cottons on to the fact that there *is* such a subject matter as our Being)—in particular, the fact that it is essential to our Being that we are in-the-world "alongside" the familiar things of everyday life, that it is therefore essential to the kind of Being we have that it simply leaves no room for a question about whether or not the world is directly available; to repeat, no matter how powerful, etc., these philosophical views are, they merely *oppose*, they do not *refute*, the causal argument (which, as we said, requires exposing a mistake in argument). As long as the causal argument stands, such transcendental arguments and phenomenological expositions only exacerbate the basic puzzle.

Another point worth registering here concerns the disjunctive view of appearances (see note 6 above). Although this view may expose the weakness in the argument from illusion, which proceeds within phenomenological sphere of reflection, it poses no threat whatever to the causal argument, where the phenomenological sphere is left behind. (The point is implicit in chapter 5 of *The Puzzle of Experience*.)

of my brain while eliminating the relevant object. There is no such possibility in the memory case; for in this case the relevant object, i.e., the relevant event, is past. What would it mean to *eliminate* the past event?[9] Nor is the relevant possibility that the past event need never have occurred; for then there would be nothing to remember.

We may state the memory version of the causal argument as follows. If how things are for me in memory is the causal upshot of a chain the last stage of which is comprised of events now occurring in my brain, what is now directly available in (personal) memory is the immediate causal upshot of events now occurring in my brain. For how things are in memory cannot be unrelated to what is directly available in memory. On the contrary, how things are in memory is in part constituted by what is thus available. It follows that what is directly available in memory cannot be a past event. If past events were directly available in memory, then, given that how things are for me in memory is in part constituted by what is directly available, events in the past would have to be included in the causal upshot of what is happening now in my brain. What is happening now in my brain would, absurdly, have to be causally responsible for what happened in the past.

The memory version of the causal argument, it seems, reduces to absurdity the assumption that past events are directly available in memory. If from the inside, looking back, what is directly available is fixed causally by what is happening now in my brain, how could it include past events? Yet if in the face of the argument I open up to how things actually are in memory—if (say) I open up to how things are now when I recollect getting on the train this morning—my getting on the train now figures within my horizon as then willed. This is all that is there from within: the past event. The past event, the event itself (not some representation of it), is directly available in memory.

21.7 The Puzzle of Memory and the Puzzle of Experience

In fact, our statement of the memory version of the causal argument suggests a more essential way of stating the perceptual version of the argument. Quite simply, if what is present within my experience is the causal upshot of what is happening in my brain, it cannot be the world that is present. Currently existing (occurring) objects and events in the world are

---

[9] There is more to this point here than may at first be evident. It touches in fact on what is at the root of the ontological asymmetry between present/past and future (an asymmetry to which we have several times alluded, but which we have not properly discussed).

in general no more the causal upshot of what is happening in my brain than are events in the past.

We are confronted, then, by two analogous puzzles: the puzzle of the past and the puzzle of experience. In each case, a philosophical argument creates the resistance presupposed by a philosophical opening up.[10] That is, by closing us off from what we know, the argument creates the possibility of our becoming open to what know, the possibility of making a philosophical discovery (see Int.9–10). But then this discovery, this opening up, overturns the conclusion of the argument. So we have a philosophical argument creating the possibility of a philosophical discovery that overturns the conclusion of that same argument, the argument that set us up to make the discovery. Yet in each case—this is why there is a puzzle—the argument seems correct.

If the arguments are correct (I take them to be correct), we cannot blame the resultant puzzles on philosophy. Both the puzzle of experience and the puzzle of memory are brought to light and articulated in philosophical reflection: the arguments—the reasoning and the analysis on which it depends, as well as the turnabout openness in the face of the arguments—all belong to philosophy. The situation here is thus quite different from that in which philosophical reflection is led astray by an ambiguity or unclarity. Recall our distinction between intra- and extraphilosophical puzzles (Int.9). In the case of intraphilosophical puzzles (e.g., Zeno's paradoxes of motion, or Goodman's "grue" paradox), philosophy itself introduces a mistake into our reflections; so it must assume responsibility for exposing the mistake, i.e., solving the puzzles. In contrast, where the puzzles rest on truths and correct reasoning, their source is extraphilosophical. Here there are no solutions. The role of philosophy is that of uncovering the elements of a conflict that is there for us in any case, whether or not we manage to articulate it philosophically. The puzzles of death and the causation of consciousness (chapter 11) are examples of extraphilosophical puzzles, as are, or so we are now claiming, the puzzles of experience and memory.

As if to confirm their extraphilosophical reality, the underlying puzzles in these cases have, without any philosophical preliminaries or softening up, a way of breaking into everyday consciousness. This takes the form of an undeniable fact suddenly striking us as impossible, i.e., as impossible and yet a fact and therefore uncanny, incomprehensible (see 11.3–11.5).

---

[10] Of course, philosophically, we need not just roll over and accept the arguments. In each case, there are objections—which we are not going to consider here. I have discussed objections to the perceptual causal argument in *The Puzzle of Experience*. Some of the discussion will apply equally to the memory case. Then too, I suspect most people will feel that the latter argument requires less defense than in the perceptual case. As we remarked earlier, naïve realism seems more compelling in the case of the present than that of the past.

Such bafflement, if it comes over us (there is no assurance that it will), derives from an implicit extraphilosophical grasp of the same puzzle that philosophical reflection brings into the open.

Thus it may strike us that, whereas a part of the world, an independently existing entity, may be as close to me in space as you please, the idea that it should have invaded my experience, entered the space that is "mine" in the way nothing else is—that (in other words) *this* object should be the worldly object itself—this (in the right frame of mind, may seem impossible; and yet, of course, we know it is so. Again, while it is unproblematic that a certain event should have happened only moments in the past, that *it*, that very event, should be right *now* there for me to think about, may seem impossible, though we know it to be the case. Such thoughts give expression (in an admittedly dressed-up and philosophically knowing way) to an extraphilosophical puzzlement. What strikes us as incomprehensible is the fact of the direct availability of the world, and the past. The fact strikes us as incomprehensible in that, at the same time that it seems impossible, we know that it is (like death, like the causation of our own consciousness) a fact.[11]

We are, outside philosophy, acquainted in at least a rough way with the fact that how things are within experience, and within memory, is the causal upshot of what is going on in our brains, that in this sense we are causally entrapped in the world and its past (tied, as it were, to a brain). I do not think that this view of ourselves as causally entrapped is a philosophical invention. It belongs to our picture of the world, the picture that we absorbed in the same way, and at the same time, that we were drawn into the communal horizon (our system of language-games). It is also the case that the world and its past are (and are unreflectively known by us to be) directly available from within the personal horizon. The fact of our entrapment, however, entails that what is directly available is the causal upshot of the events in the world/past—which means that what is directly available cannot actually be part of that world/past. The same world/past that is directly available causally entraps us and thus is not directly available.

One could say that, from within the personal horizon, we live, we are, in the world and the past. Yet given that the world and the past are causally responsible for how things are from within the horizon, it seems we cannot be in the world or the past. It seems we cannot be where we actually are.

---

[11] Notice: whereas the arguments from pastness and externality (21.2, 21.6) reach the philosophical conclusion that the past/world is only indirectly available, that therefore it must be something else (an image, etc.) that is directly available, there is no conclusion, only incomprehension, in the case of our extraphilosophical puzzlement—a puzzlement that is

Of course this is not everyday consciousness speaking. The foregoing analysis is not the concern of everyday consciousness—or, for that matter, of science. It is, if anything is, the concern of philosophy. But whereas the analysis is the concern of philosophy, its elements are grasped extraphilosophically. Thus the puzzle is there, and has the potential to disturb us, outside philosophy.

21.8 The Puzzle of Memory and the Problems of First-Person Identity

The argument that underlies our extraphilosophical puzzlement about memory rests on the awkward fact that straddles the spheres of worldly and phenomenological reflection, viz., the fact that the way things are for me now in memory is the causal upshot of what is happening now in my brain: the causal-phenomenological fact. In contrast, the special problems of first-person identity that we considered earlier were both formulated and resolved inside the sphere of phenomenological reflection. Thus, for example, it was in terms of the temporalized phenomenology of the subject position that we explained how to make sense of the possibility of finding myself in a different body (19.2); and again in these terms that we explicated the past-self ambiguity, thus reconciling the conflicting philosophical intuitions about the possibility of q-memory (19.5). The causal-phenomenological fact is a foreign element in this context. By introducing it, we throw our reflections on first-person identity into disarray and we get caught up in a different problematic entirely.

It belongs to the (temporalized) phenomenology of the subject position that my past actions are directly available in memory. Since the problems of first-person identity arise within the context of this phenomenology, in discussing the problems of first-person identity the direct availability of my personal past is not open to question but must, rather, be taken as given—which it was in our discussion of personal identity. If we introduce into the picture the causal-phenomenological fact (the fact that the present state of my brain determines causally how things are for me now in memory), we seem driven then to the absurd conclusion that the present state of my brain causally determines which actions in the past are "mine," as if my personal past were at the mercy of changes that might now be brought about in my brain.

Or should we conclude that what is directly available in memory is, after all, not the past event itself, not part of my personal past, but only

---

based on our implicit grasp of an impossibility (that philosophy may spell out for us) of what we know to be a fact. Puzzlement is not an argument.

a representation of it? But if we accept this conclusion, we will at the same time know (and thus be in a position philosophically to discover) that what now figures within my horizon as (say) then willed is nothing short of my action, the event itself. We will, in other words, get entangled in the puzzle of memory. And when that happens we lose sight of the problems with which we were engaged, the problems of first-person identity. Everything has its place. The discussion of first-person identity is the wrong place to introduce the causal-phenomenological fact.

The point can be illustrated by reference to a passage in Locke's discussion of personal identity. Locke does not explicitly consider the causal-phenomenological fact about memory, but he does consider what is, in effect, a consequence of the fact, viz., the possibility (as he puts it) of "consciousness of past actions" being "transferred from one thinking substance to another." What does Locke say about this possibility? Instead of openly grasping its implications, he retreats behind our ignorance of the "nature of thinking substances." Thus he says that

> the fact that the possibility is not realised by us will, till we have clearer views of the nature of thinking substances, be best resolved into the goodness of God; who as far as the happiness or misery of any of his sensible creatures is concerned in it, will not, by a fatal error of theirs, transfer from one to another that consciousness which draws reward or punishment with it.[12]

This fails to confront the difficulty. What Locke has in mind is not the relatively trivial possibility of my misremembering what you did as what I did, or my confusedly taking something that I imagined doing as something I actually did. These possibilities of mistake and confusion are realized all the time (apparently not offending against the goodness of God). The transfer of consciousness to which Locke alludes does not involve a mistake or confusion. It is the more radical possibility that actions performed in the past by another subject might retroactively be transferred to my consciousness; that is to say, that the *actions themselves* (versus representations of the actions) might now come to figure from within my consciousness in the way that the past actions of JV now figure, viz., as then willed, and thus that they might now come to be "my" past actions (actions to which, as Locke puts it, my consciousness extends back).

The difficulty here is not something God can avoid. Rather, that there is something here that God can avoid, this is the difficulty. For if God can avoid another's actions retrospectively becoming "mine," such transfers must be in the first place possible. It would seem, in other words, to be in God's power to create right now out of the actions of others a new per-

---

[12] *Essay,* book 2, chapt. 27, section 13.

sonal past for me—not just the illusion of a new past, but an actual new past. The problem, the puzzle, is that whereas the absurdity of this result requires us to suppose that what is available in memory is confined to representations of past events, we know and thus can become philosophically open to the fact that the events themselves are directly available.

Locke professes ignorance of the means, on the grounds that they would involve the obscure workings of a "thinking substance," by which such a transfer of consciousness might be realized. Well, we could devise a story about the brain: a story that exploits the fact that how things are from within my consciousness is causally fixed by what happens in my brain (the literature on personal identity abounds with such stories). In any case, ignorance here is not the point, which concerns not the means of such a transfer but the mere fact of its possibility; for this is what leads to the absurdity and thereby, as we explained, to the puzzle: the puzzle of memory. Of course the puzzle is a topic that merits philosophical reflection; what I am trying to get across right now, however, is that if our topic is first-person identity, the puzzle takes us into a different sphere and therefore should be regarded as a distraction.

22. My Future

22.1 My Future versus the Future

We shall begin by briefly reviewing the main points about the self and the future that have emerged in our reflections thus far, and adding a few preliminary explanations that will be relevant in what follows.

Just as my past does not include everything in the past internal to my horizon, since that includes everything in the past (everything before *now*), so my future does not include everything in the future internal to my horizon, since that includes everything in the future (everything after *now*). But whereas the past and future are equally internal to my horizon, there is a fundamental asymmetry here. Past events have an availability lacking in the case of the future—not because future events lie behind a veil but because in a real sense (or so we are assuming) there *are* no future events. Past events are not occurring now (they are past). Future events are not occurring now (they are future). But these truisms omit the difference: the way in which past (versus future) events "are." You can give an example of an event that is not now occurring because it is past, but not an example of an event is not now occurring because it is future. (You may think you can, but what you really have in mind is a kind of event.[1])

If the mistaken philosophical temptation in the case of the past is that of denying what is there, in the case of the future it is that of inventing what is not there. We must learn to grant the past its own way of being. We must learn to grant the future its own way of not being.

This observation applies, of course, to the personal future, to my future, since it is part of the future. I expect, say, to meet with X tomorrow; I intend to use the occasion to give him a certain book. There is, now, as I look to the future, no event individual that is my giving the book to X— in the way that, after our meeting, there will then be an event individual that is my past giving, etc. (though, obviously, since it will be past, it will

---

[1] I realize, of course, that there is lot to say about this. One possibility that needs to be explored here is that, if, say, in 1999 we talk enough about "the millennium party" that we are planning for next year, we create an entity or individual somewhat in the way that a fictive entity is created; but when the year 2000 arrives and we have our party, *that* event cannot, it seems to me, be identified with the future-fictive entity about which we have been talking. How could a real event ever be identical to a fictive event?

not be then occurring). So there is no event individual of which it might be true that I now anticipate or intend that very event. X now exists, as does the book. But there is no act individual of giving X the book, hence no act individual of which it is true that I intend to perform *that* very act. Rather, I now anticipate that there will be an event of such-and-such kind, a meeting with X; and I now intend to perform on that occasion an action of such-and-such kind, a giving of a book to X.

Similarly, if I now imagine the meeting, there are no event individuals of which it is true that I imagine those very individuals, no relevant event individuals for me to fix on in imagination, in the way that, after the meeting, there will be such individuals for me to fix on in memory. (The asymmetry holds even if we suppose that I imagine things being exactly as they turn out, and as I later remember them.) The people and objects involved are there to be fixed on in imagination, but not the events. In imagining X behaving thus-and-so on the anticipated occasion, in imagining myself doing this or that, I construct and thereby exhibit a possible way things might unfold within my horizon. X, the person, already figures within my horizon, as of course do I, JV, the one at the center. Not so the imagined events (actions). They are constructed by way of exhibiting future possibilities, i.e., possibilities that might turn out to be my future.

My future includes: (1) everything that will be done by me (every action that will be my action); (2) everything that will happen to me; (3) everything that will happen within my experience. Notice, to harp on the point, this statement must be taken in a certain way: "my future" is not a singular term referring to an already existent collection of events. If I wonder, say, what "my future" holds in store, I am wondering not what events are included in the particular collection of events that are, so to speak, headed my way, but simply what I will do, what will happen to me, and so on.

(1) A future action will be "mine," done by "me," just in case it will be done by the human being who figures at the center of my horizon, the one who occupies the subject position. But this is ambiguous (the analogue of the past-self ambiguity discussed in 19.5). It may mean an action that will be done by the human being who now figures at the center, by JV, or an action that will be done by the human being who will then, at the time of the action, figure at the center of my horizon. Of course, outside a philosophical context, the possibility that these might diverge never occurs to us. But the possibility is implicit in the temporalized phenomenology of the subject position.

The future-self ambiguity also affects (2). That is, when we speak of what will "happen to me" we may mean either what will happen to the human being who now figures at the center of my horizon, to JV, or what will happen to the human being who will then figure at the center—where, once again, this leaves open the experiential possibility that the human being who will then figure at the center, as the one that "I am," is other than JV, the one who now figures at the center of my horizon.

In the case of (3), where we have in mind what will appear from within my experience, there is no future-self ambiguity. The future-self ambiguity depends on the existence of a possibility implicit in the (temporalized) phenomenology of the subject position, in the positional conception of the self, viz., that at some point in the future the human being who figures then at the center of my horizon may be other than the human being who is now at the center. However, when we consider what will appear within my experience, the conception of the self that is in play is not that of a position within my horizon but that of the horizon itself, the horizonal conception of the self—which, in contrast to the positional conception of the self, does not provide for any such ambiguity.

22.2 My Future and My Brain: Jumping over Death

In chapter 21 we considered the implications of the fact (the causal-phenomenological fact) that the way things now figure from within my horizon, in both the present and the past, is causally determined by what is going on now in my brain. Since there are now no future events to figure from within my horizon (nothing to quantify over in this regard), there is, in the case of my future, no causal-phenomenological fact. There is, however, the related and equally problematic fact that it is the activity of my brain that causally ensures the existence of my horizon (experience, consciousness, life) itself. Let us call this the "causal-horizonal fact." We are causally entrapped, it seems, not just from within but from without the horizon. The causal-phenomenological is what lies behind the puzzles of experience and memory; the causal-horizonal fact is what lies behind our earlier puzzle of the causation of consciousness (11.4).

These two facts are more than just related; they are inseparable. Their inseparability derives not from the worldly side of the facts (that which does the causing), but from the phenomenological/horizonal side. Insofar as there is such a thing as my horizon, as THIS, there must be a phenomenology, a way things figure from within it, and insofar as things figure one way or another, there must be a horizon from within which they thus figure; there must be such a thing as THIS (4.5). On the worldly side of the facts, i.e., on the side of the brain, there is no comparable kind of inseparability. There is, in other words, nothing in the world like the horizon's need for a fact of presence, or, in the other direction, the need that a fact of presence has for a horizon.

Yet the brain and its activity are causally responsible for the inseparable facts. This causal relationship is a brute given with which we must come to terms philosophically. Descartes' causal straddling of the material and the immaterial is a straddling internal to the world. The causal straddling of the worldly and the phenomenological/horizonal, since it puts the world on one side of the causal relation, is more extreme—and in its own way, more problematic—than the Cartesian straddling.

Although the facts are inseparable, we shall sometimes, to highlight one or the other, speak of them separately. But to emphasize their inseparability we shall also speak of the "causal-phenomenological/horizonal fact (causal-HP fact)."

It is worth asking why philosophical thought experiments about personal identity commonly make reference to the brain. Experiential possibility (what we can imagine) outstrips not just causal but metaphysical possibility (chapters 12, 13). This is illustrated by the possibility of imagining finding myself at a future time in the body of a different human being. The experiential possibility of finding myself in a new body thus places no constraints either on the outward appearance of the new body or on the character or identity of its (the new) brain. It is thus compatible with the assumption that the brain of the human being who will occupy the subject position within my horizon is a brain that could in no way account for a future memory of what I am now doing or have done (in fact with the assumption that there is no relevant brain at all!), and hence, as we have observed, with the causal and even metaphysical impossibility of something essential to what I imagine, viz., my *finding myself* in the body of a new human being (see 19.6). In such a case what we imagine, though experientially possible, is, as we expressed it, unrealizable.

This explains the point of including reference to the brain in philosophical thought experiments about personal identity. It is to ensure that, however causally wild the story may be, there is some account of how the imagined experiential possibilities might be realized; to ensure, in other words, that the thought experiments do not fly in the face of the principle of sufficient reason, i.e., that they are not metaphysically impossible and thus unrealizable.

So, for example, in the case of finding myself in the body of a new human being, we might suppose that I (JV, the human being now at the center etc.) am put to sleep and that my brain is transferred to the body of a different human being (whose brain has been removed). An even wilder story, causally speaking, would be that some kind of total blueprint of my (JV's) brain is made, that my brain is destroyed, and the information on the blueprint is fed into the living brain of a different human being from which all the stored information has somehow been removed. This may be complete causal nonsense; but the assumption seems to account metaphysically for the experiential possibility of "finding myself" in a new body.[2]

Or does it? We cannot be too careful here. In the story by which we mean to ensure metaphysical possibility, we may have unwittingly included something that undermines the possibility we mean to ensure.

Consider the story in which a blueprint is made of my brain, my brain destroyed, and the information represented on the blueprint is fed into another brain. This is meant to explain how it might come to pass that I find myself in the body of a human being other than JV, that a different human being comes to occupy the position at the center of my horizon. But what about the causal-horizontal fact that the existence of my horizon depends on the activity of JV's brain, my brain—the brain that in the story gets destroyed? We have described a state of affairs that not just causally but metaphysically entails absolute, once-and-for-all NOTH-INGNESS: my death. As far as *my* future is concerned, it does not matter what happens to the information represented on the blueprint of my brain. My future is the future of the human being at the center of my horizon.[3] If there is no such thing as my horizon, there is nothing of which anything might be at the center; there is no such thing as my future. And after my death there is no such thing as my horizon: no such thing, then, as my future.

Given the causal-phenomenological fact and that the other's brain would be exactly like JV's brain, we are entitled to imagine it would be for the other exactly as it would have been for me. So we imagine the other human being occupying in the future the position at the center of my horizon. We imagine his body being my body, and thus my future continuing in this other body. All this makes sense experientially, as a way that things might develop from within my horizon. The trouble is, we have jumped in imagination to the future-related experiential possibility of finding myself in the body of another human being and, in doing so, have jumped *right over* the metaphysical implications of the intervening destruction of my brain, viz., the absolute once-and-for-all NOTHING-NESS that is my death: the ceasing to be of the subject matter from within which alone there is such a thing as my future. We have, in imagination,

---

[2] This is often the mark of science fiction: the reader is given a description of a mechanism that is supposed to account for a certain surprising event, thereby satisfying the demand for metaphysical possibility, i.e., that there be some account of how the event comes to pass, even though the mechanism described is causally absurd.

[3] We may ignore the future-self ambiguity here, since the statement is true in both interpretations of "my future." Note: my future is the future of a human being, the one at the center of my horizon. It is not the future of my horizon. My horizon is that to which the future, including my future, is internal. The horizon "itself" is outside time and thus has no future.

jumped over my death, the ceasing to be of my horizon, and thus over that which removes the metaphysical possibility for which our causally far-fetched story about blueprints and brains was meant to provide. You can jump over death in imagination, but you cannot jump over death. (Of absolute and final NOTHINGNESS there is no other side.)

Notice, if we alter the story so that my brain continues to function normally, there will be no death; everything will be for me—from within my life—as it otherwise would. However, there will (according to the story) also be *another* life, *another* horizon, from within which the same past will be available as from within my life. This, as we saw in the previous chapter may raise a puzzle about memory, but horizonally speaking it is coherent. That is to say, there is another subject at the center of another horizon whose past is shared with mine—but it is separate horizon, a separate life.

Here is another thought experiment.[4] I am about to undergo major brain surgery. I not only take in what is happening now, I project ahead to waking up after the operation in this same bed, and to recollecting then what is now happening. OK. I, JV, am anesthetized and operated on, and then I wake up. Let us now project into JV's postoperative situation. Things are more or less as previously anticipated. But then the surgeon arrives to inform me that during the operation a problem arose that threatened the functioning of my brain. Fortunately, a duplicate had been created and was quickly put in place, whereupon the original brain, having been removed, ceased to function. So, JV is at the center of my horizon (JV is "me"), and the same past is available from within my horizon as would have been available had everything gone smoothly.

In fact, we may be tempted to say that, from my point of view, nothing distinguishes this situation from one in which everything has gone smoothly. Yet the horizon of which JV was at the center is no more. Death has intervened. This will hit us if we adopt the preoperative standpoint. I, JV, am faced by an operation during which my brain will cease to function. The shutter will come down. I am (am I not?) faced by absolute once-and-for-all NOTHINGNESS, death—despite the fact that the human being now at the center of my horizon, JV, will continue to live and to be at the center of a horizon from within which he will have access to my past. JV will be at the center of a horizon, but the horizon will not be THIS, my horizon.

Let us stay with this example. The temporal present, we said, dominates (20.2): I live in the past and future, but always from the standpoint of the present. And from the standpoint of the present, my horizon, one and the

---

[4] I am not sure where I first got this example from; in any case, it is of a type with which philosophers will be familiar.

same horizon, is always presupposed as that from within which past events figure, and from within which future events will figure. This means that when I look to the past or future, there can be for me no real question (but only, as we explained in 20.2, an empty question) about the oneness of my horizon, the horizon to which the past and future are internal. Thus when, in our example, we imaginatively project into JV's postoperative situation, there is no question but that, from the standpoint of *that* "now," the available past is internal to the horizon of which JV then is at the center. From the standpoint of any "now," looking back and ahead, the oneness of my horizon is presupposed. It is only when we contemplate the situation of JV from the standpoint of the preoperative "now" that we realize JV is faced by absolute and final NOTHINGNESS, and therefore that the horizon, the life, from within which JV will postoperatively look back *cannot* be not that from within which he now (preoperatively) faces the future. This will be lost on us if we simply jump in imagination to the postoperative situation. In jumping to the postoperative situation, we will, in imagination, jump over death.

Of course, whereas looking ahead (like looking back) presupposes the oneness of my horizon, this does not secure me against death. I intend to meet with X this evening. What I intend is intended as something that, if it occurs, will figure from within my horizon. But this no more guarantees that there will be such a thing as my horizon than it guarantees that I will act in the manner intended.

In our thought experiment, looking forward, there is a sense in which I will continue to live: JV, the human being at the center of my horizon, the one who is "me," will continue to live (with a new brain). Yet I, the same human being, am facing death in that I am facing absolute and final NOTHINGNESS, the ceasing to be of the horizon of which I, JV, am at the center. Something will continue to be; something will cease to be. The human being now at the center of the horizon will continue to be; the horizon of which I am now at the center will cease to be. In the biological sense I will live, but there will be NOTHING. In the sense that peculiarly disturbs us, I will die.

How can it be that between the pre- and postoperative situations everything is held constant and yet two discrete lives, two discrete horizons, are involved—horizons as discrete, as separate, as your life and mine right now? It is not as if we had some way of counting lives (horizons) independently of counting subjects. Moreover, in the thought experiment the subject remains the same: JV is at the center of the horizon before and after the operation. We can make sense, say, of being transported while asleep from one house to another, however indistinguishable the two environments may be. This is because we know how to count houses on their own, in themselves. But my horizon, the subject matter of the DH, that to which the whole of the world and the infinity of space and time is internal, is nothing in itself, i.e., nothing apart from something being present from within it (4.5). When one reflects on the thought experiment in this light, the notion that separate lives (horizons) are involved seems empty—like the multiplicity hypothesis (20.2).

Unlike the latter case, however, where the hypothesis a multiplicity is nothing more than an arbitrary whim, the story in the thought experiment contains something that forces us to accept that it is a different life in the postoperative situation. Imagine that in the preoperative situation I am fully apprised of the relevant facts. I know that my brain will cease to function. This means, given the causal-horizonal fact, that I am faced by absolute once-and-for-all NOTHINGNESS: death, the ceasing to be of my horizon. But I also know that JV, the human being at the center of my horizon, will acquire a new brain. This, given the causal-horizonal fact, entails that, postoperatively, JV will be at the center of a horizon. Since the horizon from within which I looked forward will cease to be, there seems to be no escaping the conclusion that the postoperative horizon must be a different horizon. However things will be from within that horizon, it will not be my horizon.

22.3 Parfit on My Future Self

It may help us better grasp the meaning of these ideas if we apply them to one or two well-known and influential recent views about the self and the future. Let us first consider Derek Parfit's claim that what "fundamentally matters" to me when I consider my future is not my identity into the future but "psychological continuity." What matters is not whether the particular individual that I am will exist at the future time in question—i.e., whether I, JV, will persist until then—hence whether there will then be someone who is identical (one and the same) with me, JV, but whether there will be someone then who is psychologically continuous with me now.

Tomorrow I will remember a lot of what happens to me today. I will, let us assume, remember doing what I am now doing, seeing what I am now seeing. The following day I will remember a lot of what happens to me tomorrow, but a little less of what happens to me today. Generally, if on any given day, a subject remembers enough of what happened to him on an earlier day, there is (in Parfit's terminology) "psychological connectedness" between the subjects on these days. A subject, on any given day, is "psychologically continuous" with a subject on any earlier day just in case he is either psychologically connected with that subject or is psychologically connected to subjects who are in turn (possibly via still further links of psychological connectedness) psychologically connected with the subject on the earlier day. Since psychological connectedness is not transitive (if A is psychologically connected to B and B to C, it does not follow that A is psychologically connected to C), a subject with whom I psychologically continuous need not be one with whom I am psychologically connected. I can be psychologically continuous with a subject none of whose actions, etc., are now potentially available to me in memory.[5]

Parfit's claim, to repeat, is that when I look to the future, what matters is not whether I, JV, will still exist, but whether there will be someone who is psychologically continuous with me.[6] There are, however, several other aspects of his view to take account of if we are to evaluate the claim.

First, Parfit maintains (on what he says are basically empirical grounds) that we have no reason to believe in the existence of anything like Cartesian souls, immaterial substances.[7] The correct ontology, on Parfit's view, is "reductionist": it recognizes only human beings along with their brains, and the states/events that are of/in these bodily entities—including, since it is in terms of the content of such states/events that psychological continuity is defined, mental states/events. The only facts, then, in which my identity into the future might consist are facts about my body and brain and mental states, etc.; for (as he repeatedly stresses) if there are no further relevant entities, there *are* no further relevant facts.[8]

Second, acknowledging that it is the brain that is the usual cause of our mental states and their content, Parfit holds that, so far as concerns psychological continuity, hence so far as concerns what fundamentally matters when we self-interestedly contemplate the future, it is irrelevant what causes the states whose content constitutes psychological continuity in a particular case.[9] Moreover, third, he thinks that this content is not essentially first personal but, rather, "impersonal," that it can be formulated in terms of the language of q-memory (q-intention), etc.[10] This is important for Parfit in that, if the content of the states constituting psychological continuity were essentially first personal, it would, he thinks (he has in mind Butler's famous circularity objection to Locke's view of

---

[5] Parfit, *Reasons and Persons*, section 79.

[6] Ibid., chapter 13.

[7] Ibid., sections 81, 82, 88.

[8] Reductionism is a recurrent theme of chapters 11 and 12 in ibid. Here is an example of a synoptic statement of the view: "On the Reductionist View that I defend, persons exist. And a person is distinct from his brain and body, and his experiences. But persons are not separately existing entities. The existence of a person, during any period, just consists in the existence of his brain and body, and the thinking of his thoughts, and the doing of his deeds, and the occurrence of many other physical and mental events" (p. 275).

[9] Note, however, that Parfit always assumes there must be *some* cause; the point is that any cause will do. In other words, Parfit recognizes the requirement of (as we have called it) metaphysical possibility.

[10] Ibid., section 80; see also above, 19.5.

personal identity[11]), turn out that psychological continuity presupposes my identity through time, i.e., personal identity, which would undermine the claim that what matters to us is psychological continuity as opposed to personal identity.

Finally—this comes with his reductionism—Parfit argues that there are possible situations in which, unless we believe that my identity through time is constituted by that of the identity through time of a "separate entity," i.e., an entity apart from the body and the brain and its states (which separate entity could only be a Cartesian soul substance), there is simply no answer to the question of whether *I* would still exist or not (there is "no fact of the matter"), of whether a certain subject would be *me*; no answer, in other words, to the question of personal identity.[12] However, if in such cases there is (will be) a subject who is psychologically continuous with me, we may say that I "survive" as that person. Survival, since it is defined in terms of psychological continuity, can be a matter of degree. So, clearly, it is a distinct relation from identity.

This is where Parfit's claim about what matters comes in. In situations where it has no answer, there is no point agonizing over the identity question. Nevertheless, Parfit thinks that it would be rational in these situations to have a special attitude toward the future psychologically continuous subject, that even where there is no saying whether it is (will be) "me" or not, we have a self-interested reason for wanting that subject to continue to exist (i.e., a reason for wanting there to be a subject who is psychologically continuous with me). This, according to Parfit, shows that it is really survival (in his sense) and not personal identity that fundamentally matters to us.

To support the claim, Parfit discusses the possibility of teletransportation. My brain is blueprinted and the information on the blueprint is sent electronically to Mars, where it is fed into the brain of a waiting replica of the rest of my body. So my replica on Mars will be in possession of a replica of my brain. At the moment the process is completed, my brain (here on Earth) is destroyed. If I am now about to undergo this process, how should I regard it? Will it be me who finds himself on Mars?[13]

---

[11] Ibid., p. 219.

[12] Two main examples: the spectrum cases and the split-brain case (the latter of which we shall take up in section 23).

[13] The destruction of my brain is included in the story to avoid the complication of what Parfit calls the "branch line" case (section 97). If my brain is not destroyed, while everything else in the story remains the same, then (as we observed earlier), whatever we say about my replica on Mars, things will continue for me on Earth just as they otherwise would have done, in which case, it seems, there can be no question of my having been teletransported to Mars.

The first point to make here is that the question of whether it will be "me," etc. is ambiguous. Whoever it is, the human being who figures at the center of my horizon is, by virtue of thus figuring, "me." In this sense (the positional sense), if the human being on Mars, whoever he is, figures at the center of my horizon, he will be "me." However, in another sense, since by hypothesis that human being will not be JV, the human being now at the center of my horizon, he will not be "me." This much is clear.

But notice what we said: *if* the human being on Mars figures at the center of my horizon, he will be (in the positional sense) "me." Given the prior destruction of JV's brain, there will, as I look forward, no longer *be* such a thing as my horizon. Absolute and final NOTHINGNESS, death, will intervene. If there is no such thing as my horizon, there is nothing of which anyone by being at the center of which might be "me." So it will not be JV on Mars, nor, since there will be no such thing as my horizon, will it be the one at the center of my horizon. There is, it would seem, no sense in which it will be "me" on Mars.

What is Parfit's view of this case? He thinks, first, that the hypothesis that "it will be me" versus the hypothesis that "it will not be me" are not competing hypotheses; for he thinks that there is no fact as to whether it is "me" or not. Given that the brain on Mars will replicate my brain, psychological continuity is guaranteed (though it will not have its usual cause). Once we have taken this into account, plus the other facts entailed by the description of the case, we have exhausted the relevant facts. There is not, in addition, a fact to the effect that it will be, or will not be, me on Mars. The only way we could give content to such a fact would be if, in addition to the bodies, brains, and states thereof, referred to in our description of the case, we suppose there is a further, separate entity that is me, an entity (a Cartesian soul) about whom we might then wonder whether *it* will be connected to the relevant human body on Mars.[14]

However, second, despite maintaining that there is no genuine answer to the question of whether "it will be me," and despite conceding that it might be difficult to overcome the thought that I am about to die, and thus difficult to avoid being fearful, Parfit thinks it would be irrational to be fearful. On the contrary, he thinks that if, say, a conventional spaceship journey were more expensive, it would be positively rational to prefer teletransportation as a mode of "traveling" to Mars.[15] He thinks these things because he thinks that, given that the one on Mars will be psychologically continuous with me (hence that I will survive as that person), I have in this case all that *ever*—even in cases where the question about personal identity is unproblematic—fundamentally matters to me, viz.,

[14] See ibid., pp. 242–43, 279–80, 285–87.
[15] Ibid., p. 285.

psychological continuity. If I am fearful in the case described, this rests, irrationally, he says, on the assumption that something very important will be missing in this case. The fear is irrational in that the "something" in question could only be the persistence of a separate entity (a Cartesian soul); but, since there is no such entity, this is *always* missing.[16]

Now, we may agree with Parfit that, insofar as the prospect of teletransportation includes the destruction of my brain, my reaction to this prospect (my fear, if that is the word for it) cannot properly rest on the assumption that a special separable entity, a special immaterial part of the world, a soul, will no longer exist, since there is in the first place no such entity. Yet there is in this case something that will no longer be, that will cease to be, and the prospect of whose ceasing to be may ground my reaction. Insofar as the prospect that I face includes the destruction of my brain, it includes the prospect of absolute and final NOTHINGNESS—which entails the ceasing to be of THIS, my horizon. The prospect I face is the ceasing to be not of a special immaterial part of the world, but of that to which the world is internal; the ceasing to be of the subject matter by being at the center of which a certain entity in the world is "me." The prospect I face is the ceasing to be of that whose ceasing to be is my death (see section 8).

Is this ceasing to be something that does not "fundamentally matter"? We may think, "How could it matter?" or then again, "What could matter more?" We are talking about the ceasing to be of that to which everything that matters is internal—which is why it may strike us that its ceasing to be could not matter. But is it not precisely the internality of whatever matters to *it*, to this subject matter, that makes *its* ceasing to be matter in the way that it does? This is a ceasing to be that matters incomparably, in a way nothing else matters (11.1).

Parfit maintains that, if things were realized in the way we imagine, I would have what "fundamentally matters." His stated reason for this view is that my replica would be psychologically continuous with me. But, we might wonder (as Parfit himself seems to appreciate), what good to me is psychological continuity if in the meantime my brain has been destroyed, and thus my death has intervened? Parfit, I suspect, is under the spell of the dominance of the postteletransportation "now." Given that from the standpoint of any "now" the oneness in both directions of my horizon is presupposed, regarding things retrospectively from the standpoint of the later "now" creates the illusion that teletransportation preserves what in fact matters, matters incomparably, viz., that THIS, my horizon, still exists. It encourages the philosophical mistake of jumping

[16] Ibid., p. 280.

in imagination over that over which there is no jumping, the absolute and final NOTHINGNESS of death (see above, 22.2).

22.4 Nozick's "Closest Continuer" Theory

There is something else that plays a role in Parfit's view of the teletransportation case. Parfit, as we have remarked, thinks that the content of the memories in terms of which psychological continuity is defined is "impersonal." This way of thinking about memory invites us to adopt in our reflections on personal identity the external or third-person perspective; that is, to reflect on the subject's situation as if we were "looking into" his head or mind, reading off the content of his thoughts and memories, etc., in the way we might read off data that has been fed into a computer, as opposed to the perspective in which we "look out" at the world as it is for the subject, from within his horizon (see 8.3). However, if we do this, if we abandon the first-person perspective, we abandon the perspective from within which death means what it means. So it will not be surprising if, having adopted this perspective, we are not fully sensitive to the implications that death has for our reflections, and thus proceed as if we might jump over death.

Yet at the same time Parfit relies on the first-person perspective. It is not easy to disentangle what is going on here. The illusion that arises when we focus on how things will be retrospectively for my replica presupposes the first-person perspective. But given how he uses it, Parfit's reliance here on the first-person perspective operates to the same effect as adopting the external perspective—which turns us away from the meaning of death. What I mean is this. If we adopt the external perspective, it is the perspective itself that interferes with our being open to the meaning of death. We are, so to speak, in the wrong perspective. This is not what happens in Parfit's case. When we follow his reflections on the teletransportation case, we are in the right perspective; however, in that perspective, we allow ourselves to fall under the spell of the dominance of the retrospective "now" and thus to get distracted from the prior fact of death.

Of course, no philosopher who gets involved in reflections about death and what matters to us can completely exclude the first-person perspective; yet if he sees himself (philosophically) as reflecting from the external perspective, this may hold sway and in fact dictate the upshot of his reflections. An example of what I am getting at here occurs in Robert Nozick's discussion of personal identity.[17] Although throughout the discus-

[17] *Philosophical Explanations*, chap. 1.

sion we are in fact required to reflect first personally, the view of personal identity at which Nozick arrives, his "official" view (as it were), depends upon intuitions that are foreign to the first-person perspective.

Nozick begins the presentation of his view—he calls it "the closest continuer theory"—by rejecting two principles that, he says, underlie the view of personal identity developed in several papers by Bernard Williams.[18] It will suffice for our purposes to mention just the first principle: where x is an entity of a certain kind, nothing can be essential to the identity of x over time except what is intrinsic to x. In particular, whether or not there is at any time *another* thing, y, of that kind cannot be essential to the identity of x. What, we might ask, could be more intrinsic to a thing than its own identity? Only what is intrinsic to a thing, then, can be essential to its identity. Let us call this the "intrinsicality principle."[19]

The intrinsicality principle, Nozick claims, is false. To support his claim, he invites our judgment about the following case. Suppose, when the members of the Vienna Circle leave Austria and Germany, three of the original twenty end up in Istanbul, where they continue to meet and discuss philosophy, holding to their old philosophical program. The other members are presumed dead. Would not the Istanbul three be entitled to regard themselves as the Vienna Circle (now in exile). But then it comes to light that nine of the original members have made it to the United States, where they too have continued to meet, etc. It now looks like the Istanbul three are, after all, not the Vienna Circle, but just an offshoot; that their American colleagues are the Vienna Circle.[20] So, "Whether or not a particular group constitutes the Vienna Circle depends on what other groups there actually are."[21]

What lies behind the verdict favoring the American group is, Nozick thinks, the fact that it is the *closest continuer* of the Vienna Circle. Note, "closest" means closer than all others: there are no ties for closest. And the "continuing" of x by y requires more than just some sort of qualitative similarity between x and y: there must, according to Nozick, be real connectedness, causal or counterfactual, between x and y. A third point is that y's being the closest continuer of x is only necessary, not sufficient, for the identity over time of x and y (things that cease to exist may nonetheless have closest continuers): y might be the closest continuer of x but without being close enough to *be* x. Finally, assuming that x contin-

---

[18] See Bernard Williams, "The Self and the Future," "Personal Identity and Individuation," and "Bodily Continuity and Personal Identity," all reprinted in his *Problems of the Self*.

[19] For a detailed discussion of the principle, see Harold Noonan's *Personal Identity* (Routledge, 1989), chap. 7.

[20] Nozick, *Philosophical Explanations*, pp. 32–33.

[21] Ibid. p. 33.

ues, the question of which object is its closest continuer may be complex: first, it may involve more than one factor or dimension; and second, these may be given different weightings. The point about complexity may be illustrated by reference to the Vienna Circle example.[22] Not only the number of original members is relevant to whether a later group is the Vienna Circle, but, we may suppose, whether the later group adheres to the original philosophical program. Maybe we would give more weight to numbers; at a certain point, however, should the numbers be sufficiently close, we might favor a smaller group if it is unique in maintaining the original program.

Good. Perhaps the closest continuer theory gives us some insight into the identity over time of groups, institutions, political entities, and on. Perhaps, in these cases, the intrinsicality principle fails. But what does this have to do with personal identity, that is, with first-person identity, *my* identity over time? Why should we suppose the logic of personal identity is like that of a club, or a sewing circle, or a bunch of philosophers who share a few dogmas? For that matter, why should it be like that of an artefact? Or a natural substance? Why should it be like anything but itself? In the other cases, the intrinsicality of identity may be an issue. In the case of (first-) personal identity, it is irrelevant.

The philosophical topic of personal identity stands alone. To approach the topic properly, what is required is not that we reflect on this or that type of entity in the world, but that we back up philosophically until we are able take in the subject matter to which the world is internal, the horizon of the world, my horizon, and are thus in a position to work out the phenomenology of being at the center of this subject matter. But let us consider what happens when the closest continuer theory is applied to my identity over time, or, more to the point right now, to the teletransportation case. Nozick does not consider exactly this case. He does, however, consider a case that is essentially the same; so, in what follows, we shall treat his view of this case as if it were intended for the teletransportation case as described above.[23]

---

[22] Nozick uses the ship of Theseus example for this purpose. Ibid., pp. 33–34.

[23] Ibid., p. 39. The case Nozick actually considers is this: As I am dying, my "brain patterns" are transferred to a blank brain in another body by a process that simultaneously removes them from my brain; when the transference is complete, "the old body [including my brain] expires." A few pages later (p. 41), Nozick considers cases involving the recording and transmitting of information from the whole of a human being—cases involving, possibly, the dematerialization and rematerialization of the human being—to distant places. Although in all these cases Nozick seems prepared to accept that I might continue, it seems to me that the idea of "dematerialization," etc., raises fundamentally new issues (about the identity of the dematerialized human being); we shall therefore leave the latter cases to one side.

First of all, it emerges as a general point that he takes the chief constituent factors or dimensions of personal identity to be psychological continuity and bodily continuity (continuity of the human body with its brain). These continuities are, as continuities, subject to degree. In the teletransportation case, there is zero bodily continuity (since JV's body, including his brain, dies, or is destroyed) along with complete psychological continuity (since all the information in JV's brain is transmitted to the waiting brain on Mars). However, given that there are no other candidates, it is Nozick's view that not only would the human being on Mars—the one whose brain will be the recipient of the information from JV's brain and who will thus be psychologically continuous with me—be my closest continuer, he would be close enough to be me. This is, he says, "a way a person can continue on."

Might I not grant that the one on Mars will be my closest continuer and yet wonder whether it will be "me"? There is, as we saw in discussing Parfit, an ambiguity in such questions: Will the one on Mars be JV, the one now at the center of my horizon? We know it will not be JV. In the case described, JV dies on Earth and a replica is created on Mars. Perhaps it will be "me" in the sense that the replica on Mars will be the one at the center of my horizon? However, in this sense too, it will not be "me." Anyone who figures at the center of my horizon is thereby "me"; but given that JV's brain will be destroyed, there will be absolute and final NOTHINGNESS, hence no such thing as my horizon. The one on Mars will figure at the center of *a* horizon, *a* life, but it will not be *my* life, *my* horizon.

Of course, Nozick would not say that I, JV, will be the human being on Mars; but he would, I take it, say that in an important sense the human being on Mars will be "me." He will be "me" in that he will be my closest continuer. Let us grant that the human being on Mars will be my closest continuer. But if we think that this suffices in the circumstances described to make him "me," we have in our reflections jumped over the fact of absolute and final NOTHINGNESS, of death. Once death has intervened, nothing can count as a way of being "me."

Parfit, we said, at the same time that he attempts to provide (via the idea of q-memory/intention) an impersonal account of my psychological continuity with future subjects, relies on the first-person perspective in his reflections on what "fundamentally matters" to us. However, he seems in these reflections to fix on the retrospective view of the subject with its presupposed oneness of the horizon to which the subject's past is internal. This has the effect of reinforcing the tendency of the impersonal standpoint to overlook the meaning of death (its absolute and final NOTHINGNESS). Once we remove the illusion created by fixing on the subject's retrospective view, we are left with a naked tension between the impersonal account of psychological continuity and the first-personal perspective in our reflections on what fundamentally matters to us.

There is, I now wish to point out, a hint of the same tension in Nozick's discussion. Right from the outset it is assumed that the problem of personal identity is simply an instance of a perfectly general problem, or question, about the identity of things—of entities of any and all kinds—through time. Thus, in formulating an account of personal identity, Nozick is happy to take his cue from what, we may agree, are correct intuitions regarding the identity through time of a group or social entity. The point is that to the extent that we are guided in formulating our account of personal identity by intuitions about the identity of a group, etc., we abandon the perspective appropriate to grasping the meaning of death. Having abandoned this perspective, it will not be surprising if we arrive at an account of personal identity that like the closest continuer theory, allows for the possibility that my life might exist (so to speak) on both sides of my own death, as if my own death were something I might jump over.

Yet, as we said, a philosophical discussion of personal identity will be hard-pressed to avoid appealing to the first-person perspective—even where, as in Nozick's case, the discussion derives its primary orientation from examples to which the first-person perspective is alien. Thus, although the closest continuer theory of personal identity owes nothing to this, the appeal to the first-person perspective constantly insinuates itself into Nozick's discussion. This is particularly evident when the discussion turns to what we "care" about in contemplating our future.[24]

Let us fasten on just one point. Nozick says that what we, I, care about is "continuation rather than merely that some qualitatively similar entity will exist." This requires, he says, some kind of causal or subjunctive connection between "aspects" of the earlier and later "self." So far, there is nothing obviously first personal here; nothing that could not be maintained about the identity over time of social group, or an artefact, or a natural substance. But then, apropos of our caring about our own identity into the future, Nozick says that it is "as if your later self knows you now, and so (except in special cases) views you as its closest predecessor. Connecting with the later continuer is a way of not sinking into oblivion."[25] What I care about, it seems, is that the right connections will hold, ensuring that a later self will view me as his closest predecessor and that therefore, in this way, I will not sink into oblivion. So this, my not sinking into oblivion, is what I ultimately care about in contemplating my future.

[24] Ibid., pp. 62–70.
[25] Ibid., p. 66.

But what is it that I want not to sink into? What do we mean here by "oblivion"? Suppose I hold a golf ball in my hand. Oblivion for this golf ball might take the form of its disintegrating into a pile of dust, which is then dispersed. Something like this would also be, indeed it will be, oblivion for my brain and the rest of me. But when I contemplate the "oblivion" I ultimately care about, that which I do not want to "sink into," although the disintegration, etc., of my brain will have this oblivion as a consequence, the oblivion cannot itself be identified with the disintegration of my brain. What is the oblivion I, that we, peculiarly care about?

We know what it is. It is the oblivion that consists in there being, absolutely and once-and-for-all, NOTHING, hence no such thing as my life, my horizon. The oblivion I ultimately care about is my death, the meaning of which is solipsistic and thus bound up with our grasp of the first person. It is precisely this oblivion, the oblivion of death, that, if in our reflections on personal identity we adopt a stance that looks away from the first person—for example, the kind of stance assumed in the reflections by which we arrive at the closest continuer theory of personal identity—we are apt to jump over.

23. My Future: The Puzzle of Division

23.1 Personal Identity and Possibility (Review)

There are, as we have explained, states of affairs that make sense as ways things might develop within my experience (horizon) despite being not just causally but metaphysically impossible; states of affairs, that is, that are experientially possible (we can imagine them) but which conflict not only with the laws of nature but with the principle of sufficient reason. Experiential possibility is a guarantee neither of causal nor of metaphysical possibility.

The temporalized phenomenology of the subject position (the horizonal conception of the self) is framed in terms of experiential possibilities and thus is not constrained by causal/metaphysical possibility. I can, for example, imagine finding myself in someone else's body (his brain included) even though, if we think it through, this is metaphysically and therefore causally impossible, since, in terms of the story, there is no way—not even a causally wild or impossible way—to account for the fact that I "find myself" in the new body (19.6). As it stands, the story, while it makes sense experientially, describes a metaphysically impossible state of affairs.

Hence the reference to the brain in philosophical thought experiments about personal identity. The brain figures in both the facts that comprise what we called our causal entrapment in the world: the causal-phenomenological and the causal-horizonal facts (21.7,22.2). The thought experiments may be causal nonsense, but reference to the brain in this context represents an attempt to render them at least metaphysically respectable.

Consider the story about blueprinting my brain, etc., in the teletransportation thought experiment. Is it casually possible to make a blueprint of the brain and input this into a blank brain? Could there be a blank but living brain? What exactly would such "blankness" be? If the aim is simply that of achieving metaphysical possibility, awkward questions like this may be turned aside. The story in the teletransportation case aims to account for the possibility of "finding myself" in a replica body on Mars. The story may not make sense causally, but the aim of the story is to satisfy not the laws of nature but the principle of sufficient reason.

However, as we observed, such stories have a way of backfiring. Instead of securing metaphysical possibility they may in fact produce metaphysical impossibility. In the teletransportation case, the story involves not just that my brain is blueprinted on Earth and the information transmitted electronically to a blank brain on Mars, but that (since otherwise, though I would acquire a replica on Mars, my life would simply continue on Earth) at the time of transmission my brain is destroyed. The blueprinting of my brain, etc., accounts for the possibility of "finding myself" in the new body; but the destruction of my brain metaphysically entails death, absolute and final NOTHINGNESS, i.e., the ceasing to be of the horizon by being at the center of which a human being is "me"—which excludes the possibility of "finding myself" anywhere (22.2).

But notice, notwithstanding the various complexities and pitfalls in this area, we have not yet uncovered anything genuinely puzzling, i.e., anything that we have not been able to sort out. Thus, to take just this example, I do not believe we are confounded by the teletransportation thought experiment. On reflection we know what to say about this case (at any rate, this is what I would say): that there is no important sense in which the one on Mars is "me." We shall now consider a possibility that seems in contrast to be genuinely puzzling, a possibility that seems to confront us with an incoherence that there is no sorting out.

23.2 The Possibility of Division

It makes sense experientially that, at some future time, I should "find myself" in the body of another human being. I can imagine this. We may, at first, be unclear what is imagined here; but once we are in explicit possession of the temporalized phenomenology of the subject position, such puzzlement can be resolved (19.2). What do I imagine? I imagine that another human being figures at the center of my horizon, that at some future time a human being other than JV occupies the subject position within my horizon. This does not, we know, guarantee the metaphysical possibility of what I imagine. For example, if my brain is destroyed, it is not sufficient to suppose that a replica of my brain is created in the body of another human being. But what if we suppose that my brain itself, JV's brain, the brain of the human being who occupies the subject position within my horizon, is transplanted to the body of another human being? I would find myself in his body. This may not be causally possible, but here, it seems (unless we are overlooking something—which can always happen), we have described a case that satisfies the principle of sufficient reason. We have, in other words, described a case that is not just experientially but metaphysically possible.

Of course we are relying (as, in effect, philosophers always do in these discussions) on the causal-HP fact, the fact that my brain causally maintains my horizon (the causal-horizonal fact), my life, and how things are from within it (the causal-phenomenological fact). As long as my brain keeps going in the normal way, so long, and no longer, will there be such a thing as my horizon; so long, and no longer, will things continue to appear, to develop or unfold temporally, from within my horizon. So if I am about to undergo an operation in which my brain will be transplanted, I may anticipate that what I am doing now, what now figures as willed, will when I awake after the operation then figure as having figured as willed (as something I have done), that what I see now will then figure as having figured as visually appearing, and so on—just as what I did and saw yesterday now figures as having then figured in these ways.

The brute causal relationship embodied in the causal-HP fact is what creates the possibility that philosophers exploit in certain thought experiments about division or fission.[1] The brain is a bit of physical stuff. It is not just a lump of homogenous stuff, but a structured and enormously complex entity. One of the salient facts about the brain's structure is that, above the stem, it is divided into two hemispheres. The hemispheres have largely different functions, which are integrated via connections between the hemispheres. But although they have different functions, the hemispheres are capable of functioning independently, so that a human being can survive with "half a brain."

What would it be like for such a person? It depends on which half of his brain has survived—but here the kind of thought experiment to which I refer takes liberties. It is assumed that, despite the various asymmetries between the two halves of the brain, each half has the potential to function as a complete brain, hence that whereas in ordinary circumstances each half of the brain, connected as it is to the other half, makes a coordinated but different contribution to maintaining my life and how things are and develop from within it, if (this is the assumption) the need arose, each half could maintain my life on its own. Perhaps, to account for this (to keep the thought experiment within the bounds of metaphysical possibility; a point that is usually overlooked), we might build in the no doubt causally nonsensical assumption that, prior to being separated, the two halves are augmented so that each has the full capacity of the original whole brain. Thus if each half were transplanted into the skull of a separate human being, the result would be two human beings, transplant twins (as we might call them), each with a half a brain that has the capacity of a completely functioning brain and which is, at least initially, exactly similar to his twin's brain.[2]

---

[1] Due originally, I believe, to David Wiggins (see his *Identity and Spatio-Temporal Continuity*, section 4.3), and since discussed by many philosophers.

[2] There is a different type of case that we shall not discuss here, viz., one in which the separated halves continue to live in the body of the same human being, using the same

The thought experiment is this. I am about to undergo deep anaesthesia. I am told that after I am asleep, my brain will be first augmented and then bisected; and then each half will be kept going and transplanted into the skull of a different human being. My body, JV's body, will then be destroyed. The thought experiment asks me to look forward in a first-person way. I am, in light of what I know about the brain and my life, that is, in light of the causal-HP fact, to contemplate my future. How do things look? What is my future? That is: What will happen to me?

One thing seems fairly clear. This case is not like the case where I know that my brain will be destroyed and a replica brain created in another body. In the later case, assuming that I keep my reflective orientation essentially first personal and, further, do not let myself fall under the spell of the dominance of a future "now," I see myself confronted by absolute and final NOTHINGNESS, by death. In the present case, where my brain is not destroyed but augmented and divided—i.e., augmented, divided, and kept going until each half is transplanted into a new body, taking with it the full capacity of my original brain (henceforth we shall take all this for granted when we speak of "division," or of my brain being "divided")—it seems clear, given that each half of my brain, the brain that maintains my life, not only will keep going but will have the wherewithal of my now intact brain, that whatever else is true, there will not be NOTHINGNESS. On the contrary, each half brain will on its own ensure that there is within my horizon SOMETHING not NOTH-ING, i.e., that there *is* such a thing as my horizon, my life (consciousness, experience). If each half brain ensures that there is SOMETHING not NOTHING, how could it be true that there is NOTHING, no such thing as my horizon?

It seems clear that division makes sense metaphysically if not causally. Yet what its realization would mean for my life, my horizon—what it would mean, i.e., that there will be two entities in the world, two completely functioning brains, each in a separate human being and each maintaining my life and the development within it—this is utterly unclear. To what exactly am I supposed to look forward? Can I look forward to *two* separate lives, each of which is *my* life?

---

nervous system and sense organs. This is usually called the "brain bisection" case and in fact does not qualify as a philosophical thought experiment. There are well-known actual approximations of the case in which subjects suffering from epilepsy have had the nerve fibers connecting the two hemispheres of their brains severed. Although the purpose the surgical procedure was not (of course) brain research but to try to control the fits of the person with epilepsy, it later came to light that, under certain ingeniously designed test conditions, subjects who have undergone the procedure evince behavior that we might be tempted to describe (tendentiously, no doubt) as expressing "bisected consciousness." Philosophers, for their own purposes, have been quick to note the potential implications of such experiments. See, for example, Thomas Nagel's "Brain Bisection and the Unity of Consciousness," *Synthese* 22 (1971).

Let us put this aside for now and consider, rather, the question that usually occupies philosophers in reflecting on division, viz., the question that we originally raised. I am about to undergo division. Who will I be? Will I be R, the one with the right side of my brain, or will I be L, the one with the left side? Or will I be both? Or neither?

23.3 Parfit on Division

The "Who will I be?" question raises a well-known puzzle (the puzzle of division). The puzzle of division is sharply formulated by Parfit.[3] I am facing division. Who will I be? There seem to be three main possible answers, each of which, Parfit argues, is unacceptable.

(1) By hypothesis, there is no reason to say that I will be R as opposed to L, or L as a opposed to R. For, by hypothesis, the two halves of the transplanted brain have precisely the same capacities: at the time they are transplanted, they are, in effect, exactly similar brains.

(2) Will I be, then, both R and L? Here the familiar logic of identity comes into play. Identity is a one-one relation (it is transitive and symmetrical). Hence if a = b and c = b, it follows that a = c. So if I = R (R is me), and I = L (L is me), it follows that R = L. But this is evidently false. Consider, e.g., what is visually present to R (within R's experience). L, we may suppose, is visually present and appears in a way that R does not. From L's point of view, on the other hand, R is visually present and appears in a way that L does not. So already, it seems, we have a difference between L and R that entails that I cannot be both.

(3) Might I be neither? If am neither, this means that I have ceased to be. Yet if, looking ahead, I ignore L and concentrate on R, it seems obvious that R would be me, that what will happen to R is what will happen in my future; and similarly if, looking ahead, I ignore R and concentrate on L, it seems obvious that L would be me, etc. In each case, considered separately, it seems that I continue to be. So far then from having a reason to think I will cease to be, it seems that I have double reason to think I will continue to be. How, as Parfit expresses it, could a double success count as a failure?

If we suppose that I am an entity separate from any bodily thing, that I am a soul substance, then we might suppose that I will be (identical with) one or the other, R or L (or perhaps, that I will be associated with R, or associated with L). However, we know that Parfit, on empirical grounds, rejects the idea that there are such substances (22.3). Hence this answer is excluded. In sum, if we accept that apart from bodies (human

[3] See his paper, "Personal Identity," and *Reasons and Persons*, pp. 255–56.

beings) and brains there is in the division case no relevant entity that I might be, there seems to no satisfactory answer to the question of who I will be.

Parfit's view about this case is, for the most part, implicit in our earlier exposition of his general position. Given that the half brains transplanted into R and L each possess the wherewithal of my present whole brain, R and L will be psychologically continuous with me. Indeed, I will be as closely psychologically connected and therefore continuous with each as I am connected and continuous with myself yesterday. In Parfit's terminology, I will "survive" as each, as R and as L. I survive as each, but it is not true of either R or of L that I will *be* that person.

Survival has a different logic from that of identity. Identity is a one-one relation: transitive and symmetrical. Survival is transitive but not symmetrical. Again, survival, since it is defined in terms of psychological continuity, is a more-or-less relation. Identity, on the other hand, is an all-or-nothing relation. Thus (thinking about the first point of difference), whereas the logic of identity excludes my being identical with both R and L, there is no reason I might not survive as both R and L. However, though they are distinct relations, in the actual world identity shadows survival: whenever x survives as y, $x = y$.[4] This is because in the actual world the cause of psychological continuity is always accounted for by the fact of a single brain remaining in a single human being. Hence in the actual world there is no problematic branching of psychological continuity such as occurs in the division thought experiment.

To repeat, it is not true of R that I will be R, and not true of L that I will be L. Note, it does not follow that it is false of R and false of L that I will be that person. Parfit's view, rather, is that in the division case there is no "fact of the matter," i.e., no fact one way or the other about my identity in the future. If it were false of R and false of L that I will be that person, there would in each case be a relevant negative fact of identity (a fact of nonidentity). According to Parfit, however, once we have taken into account the facts about bodies and brains along with the facts about psychological continuity and survival, we have taken into account all the relevant facts: there is no relevant "further fact"—positive or negative—about my identity.[5]

Nonetheless, we have, Parfit thinks, taken account of what fundamentally matters to me when I contemplate my future. For what fundamentally matters to me is not whether there will in the future be someone who is me, but whether there will be someone who is psychologically

---

[4] *Reasons and Persons*, p. 262.

[5] The point is made, and argued for, again and again by Parfit, but for a clear and uncompromising summary statement, see ibid., pp. 279–80.

continuous with me: whether I will have a survivor. Parfit's reasoning here is that if what fundamentally matters is my identity in the future, then, since there is no one of whom it is true that I will that person, I ought to regard what I am facing as just as bad as death. But this, he says, is hard to believe:

> My relation to each resulting person contains everything that would be needed for survival. This relation cannot be called identity because and only because it holds between me and *two* future people. In ordinary death, this relation holds between me and *no* future person. Though double survival cannot be described in the language of identity, it is not equivalent to death. Two does not equal zero.[6]

You could put the argument like this: If my identity into the future were what matters, I would regard division as the equivalent of death; since I would not regard division in this way, it cannot be my identity that matters.

The puzzle of division, then, as Parfit conceives it, is that there is a question about my future identity that has no answer. He solves (or dissolves) the puzzle by replacing the identity question with a related question about my survival. The latter question has an answer. I will survive as both R and L. What justifies the replacement is, of course, not simply that the survival question has an answer. The thought is rather that it is my survival versus my future identity that, in any case, "fundamentally matters" to me.

One difficulty in evaluating Parfit's response to the puzzle of division is that he employs more than one conception of death. In the passage just quoted, he seems to understand death as the negation of survival. Thus he says, "In ordinary death, this relation [survival] holds between me and *no* future person." On this conception, my death consists in there ceasing to be anyone with whom I am psychologically continuous. Facing division, then, is not facing death, since in facing division I am faced by a state of affairs in which there are *two* future persons with whom I am psychologically continuous. On the other hand, sometimes Parfit seems to conceive of death as there ceasing to be any entity with which I am identical. Thus, in the run-up to the quoted passage he says that if I conceived of division in terms of identity, I ought to regard it as being as bad as death. Again, he asserts that the question "Am I about to die?" may be empty.[7] But it is precisely concerning the identity versus survival question that Parfit holds there may be no fact of the matter and thus that the question may be empty.

[6] Ibid., p. 278.
[7] See, e.g., ibid., pp. 277–79.

Now, apropos of the identity conception of death, we may (as Parfit acknowledges) find it incredible that anyone should view the question of his imminent death as an empty. Apart from this, there is the difficulty we encountered in our initial discussion of death (chapter 8). Whatever entity you consider, the continued existence of that entity seems compatible with my death. There seems be no entity in the world, material or immaterial, whose ceasing to be constitutes my death.

But the survival conception—that my death consists in there ceasing to be anyone with whom I am psychologically continuous—also seems wrong. There is no reason why there should not be people psychologically continuous with me after I die. This, we argued, is what happens in the teletransportation case (22.3–4).

Parfit, without explicitly distinguishing between them, makes use of both these conceptions of death. And neither captures what death is: what we are actually faced by in facing death. The question of what we are faced by, of what death actually means to us, has not been addressed. This happens (if I may venture a generalization) all the time in philosophical discussions of personal identity. Death plays a central role in these discussions (how could it not?). Statements about death (statements, e.g., to the effect that if such-and-such were the case, that would mean my death) are constantly on offer and used to draw conclusions about personal identity. Yet the question of what death actually is, of what I actually face in facing death, this question is not openly addressed.

Facing division, according to Parfit, is not facing death. Facing division is facing double survival, and double survival is not death. This seems right. But what is death? What is it that I do *not* face in facing division but face in facing death? You know our answer to the question. What I face in facing death is not, as such, the fact that there will be no one (no entity in the world) with whom I am identical, or again, the fact that there will be no one with whom I am psychologically continuous, but the fact that there will be NOTHING: absolute and final NOTHINGNESS. The subject matter of my death, then, that whose ceasing be is my death, is not the particular entity in the world that I am, the human being (or soul) at the center of my horizon, my life, but my horizon itself, the subject matter to which the world, including the entity that I am, is internal: the subject matter which, given that there will be NOTHING, will, thereby, no longer be.

But this criticism of his conception of death is not our main point about Parfit's response to the puzzle of division. Has Parfit solved the puzzle? If we expect a solution to provide a straightforward answer to the identity question (Who will I be?), Parfit's response is, by his own reckoning, not a solution. However, insofar as it provides a reason for replacing the identity question with a question that has an answer, the response might claim to dissolve the puzzle. And, in fact, Parfit says that on his view, the reductionist view, the problem about division disappears.[8]

I wonder whether this is necessarily a good thing, to devise a view on which the problem (the puzzle) disappears. What does it actually accomplish? I imagine myself facing division. I ask myself: Who will I be, R or L? Suppose, adopting Parfit's view, I dismiss the question as empty. I remind myself that I will survive as (be psychologically continuous with) both R and L. So I am facing double survival, not death. I have what fundamentally matters, not just once but twice. The trouble is, without knowing exactly why, I still seem to find the prospect of division puzzling. That I will survive as both and R and L, and thus have twice over what fundamentally matters, this does not help. It is not that I fear for my future, but that I do not know what to make of my future. Indeed, the doubleness of that by which I am faced and which is meant to supply twice over what matters, the doubleness my future, precisely this is what is puzzling. My life will simultaneously go to the right and to the left. It will be twice. Can I, can anyone, make sense of this?

Parfit says about division that "I should regard it as about as good as ordinary survival" (p 279). Why do I not regard it as about *twice* as good as ordinary survival? The reason is that I do not know how to regard it at all. If doubling something does not make sense, neither does doubling its goodness.

To repeat, Parfit's response to the puzzle of division is not (it is not meant to be) a solution of the puzzle; rather, in rejecting the identity question (Who will I be?) as empty and replacing it with a question (Who will I survive as?) that has an answer (both R and L), it claims to dissolve the puzzle. This seems to me unsatisfactory—not because it fails to solve the puzzle, i.e., to answer the question about my future identity; nor because (as critics of Parfit often maintain) my future identity *is* what matters; nor because in fact it fails to dissolve the puzzle—but because it does not get to the bottom of the puzzle. The puzzle, the real puzzle raised by the division thought experiment, so far from having been solved or dissolved, has not yet been disclosed.

23.4 *Other Responses to the Puzzle of Division: Nozick and Lewis*

Before explaining this, however, let us briefly consider two other responses to the puzzle of division. The first is that which Nozick offers in the context of his closest continuer theory (22.4). The essence of Nozick's view is that I will be the one who most closely continues me—where conti-

[8] Ibid., p. 259.

nuity depends on the existence of causal or subjunctive connections between my physical/psychological "aspects" and those of my continuer. In the teletransportation case, you recall, Nozick's theory delivers the result that I will be the one on Mars. Notice, we are talking about identity here (not some other relation, like survival): the closest continuer of me, assuming he is close enough, *is* me. If my closest continuer will be on Mars, *I* will be on Mars.

Suppose there is more than one person who is close enough to be me. How do we decide which is closer, and thus is me? This is not the problem right now. The problem concerns, rather, the fact that being closest means being closer than all others. My closest continuer must in this respect be unique. It follows that if there is a tie, if the future candidates for being me are not just individually close enough to be me but equally close, no one will be me. I will no longer be. I will no longer be, despite the fact that there will be two people each of whom, had the other one not existed, would have been me.

A tie of this sort is, of course, what we get in the division case: R and L are not just sufficiently close to be me, they are, in the nature of the case, equally close. It follows on the closest continuer theory that I will no longer be—which is the conclusion that Nozick draws.[9] The problem, which is not lost on him, is that it now sounds as if I am facing death; but facing division is not facing death. Thus Nozick observes that whereas if one of two candidates were eliminated, this would have the result that I would unproblematically continue to be, I would not for that reason be desperate to secure the elimination of R or L: desperate, i.e., in the way that I would be desperate to extricate myself, if I could, from a situation in which I was faced by death.[10]

In facing division I face no longer being; yet, it seems, facing division is not facing death. What is the difference? Does facing death involve something more than, something in addition to, facing no longer being? Or is facing death just different? Here, once again, one wants to ask: What do we face in facing death? What is death?

Nozick, like Parfit, does not directly address this question. Rather, he offers a view that, without telling us what death is, attempts to explain why our attitude toward division differs from that toward death. In division, but not death, we have, he says, what we "care" about. What we care about is our continued identity. The closest continuer relation is the "best realization" of this, it is what "our continued identity comes to." Hence,

---

[9] *Philosophical Explanations*, p. 63.

[10] E.g., as he points out (ibid., p. 64), I would not now pay a lot of money to eliminate all but one of my future continuers.

we will care especially about our closest continuer when there is one, for that then will stand in the best realized relation of continuing us; while also when there is a tie among continuers close enough to be us singly, we will care especially about these . . . since they then best realize our continued identity.[11]

This, Nozick thinks, explains the difference in attitude:

How is the tie case to be described on this view? I do not view a tie as like death: I am no longer there, yet it is a good enough realization of identity to capture my care which attaches to my identity.[12]

But now the question about death cries out for an answer. What is death? We may agree, I would not view a tie as like death. So we may agree, I would not view division as like death. In that case, though, it is hard to take seriously the claim that a tie, which we get with division, entails my no longer being there. Could anything be more like death than my no longer being there?

OK. We are hammering away at this point about death—the same point we made in connection with Parfit. Despite the central role played by the concept of death in philosophical discussions of personal identity, the concept tends to be just used without ever being properly examined. However, as in the case of Parfit, this is not the main point of our criticism. The main point is, once again, that what is really puzzling in the prospect of division remains out of view. Let us accept that Nozick's account provides a straightforward answer to the identity question—I will be neither R nor L, and thus will no longer be—as well as an explanation of why I nevertheless do not view division as death. But not only does it leave unanswered the question of what death is, it leaves the prospect of division as puzzling as ever.

Consider. In facing division I face a split in which each of the two parts claims to include everything in my life, the whole of it my life. Or rather, each is my life. Can we make sense of this? Does it help to be told that I will be neither R nor L, that there will no longer be anyone who I am? This is simply a consequence of the logic of identity, whereas the impossibility contained in the prospect of division comes from elsewhere. It is, as we shall see, independent of the logic of identity. Again, does it help, i.e., help diminish our puzzlement, to explain why, despite the fact that I will be neither R nor L, despite the fact that I will not be, I should care in a special way about R and L, thereby distinguishing my attitude toward division from my attitude toward death? No. What is puzzling is not why

[11] Ibid., p. 67.
[12] Ibid., p. 68.

I regard the doubleness that faces me in division differently from death, but how in the first place there could ever be such a doubleness. What is puzzling, you might say, is not the difference between division and something else, but the sheer prospect of division itself: the sheer prospect of my life doubling.

The other response to the puzzle of division that we shall mention is due to David Lewis.[13] Lewis's response, in contrast to that of Parfit and Nozick, does not raise the question about death. For Lewis thinks that in facing division I can look forward to being R and to being L, and thus that I am not facing death. How is this possible, given that R and L are not identical? Have we not, yet again, run up against the logic of identity? The possibility is provided for by the fact that, in a sense, I am *already both*. My twoness emerges with division; but it is there prior to division. Prior to division I am, you might say, occupied by two persons. (Lewis's view is sometimes called the "multiple occupancy thesis.") How does this work? In what sense is it true that, prior to division, I am already both R and L?

Lewis depends here on the idea that we can view persons as four-dimensional (space-time) aggregates of person-stages.[14] The stages of such an aggregate, or "continuant person," are all related to each other by "the I-relation," which is not identity but the relation that relates all and only the members of a single continuant. In the case of person continuants it is the relation of psychological continuity and connectedness ("the R-relation"). My person-stage today and my person-stage yesterday, though obviously not identical (the same person-stage), are R-related and therefore part of the same continuant person. Your person-stages belong to a continuant person too. But the stages of your continuant and mine have no R-relationship to each other. Thus your continuant and mine are not identical (in the familiar sense). Lewis—like Nozick, and unlike Parfit—believes that what matters to us when we contemplate the future is our identity. What this comes to, on the person-stage analysis, is that I am concerned that there be in the future person-stages that are R-related to my present stage; that, in other words, the person continuant to which my present stage belongs still exists.

Let us not balk at the metaphysics of space-time continuants and just consider how Lewis uses this to deal with the puzzle of division.[15] Who will I be? My present stage is R-related to the person-stages of R and, equally, to the person-stages of L. Hence my present stage and those of R belong to a single person continuant, and similarly in the case of L. But

[13] "Survival and Identity," in David Lewis, *Philosophical Papers*, vol. 1.
[14] Ibid., pp. 58–61.
[15] Ibid., pp. 61–62.

since not all the stages of R and L are R-related, these continuants are not identical. My present stage—as well as all the stages that prior to division are R-related to it—belongs then to two distinct person continuants, R and L. Moreover, these continuants both exist prior to division. This gives us the sense in which, prior to division, I am "both" R and L.

Lewis is aware that there is a problem here. He says that, if we consider the situation from the predivision standpoint, we "demand to say that only *one* person entered the duplication center; that his mother did not bear twins; that he should have only one vote; and so on . . . Counting at a time, we insist on a person who will fission [who faces division] as one." It is only after division that we count two. First we count one, then we count two. To reconcile our inclination to count in this way with the truth (as he sees it) that prior to division there are two person continuants, Lewis draws attention to the possibility of a different way of counting continuants. This depends not on the relation of identity but on the relation of identity-at-a-time (tensed identity).[16] Continuants C1 and C2 are identical-at-t just in case both exist at t and their stages at t are identical. Counting in terms of tensed identity, it turns out that (where T1 is prior to division) R and L are identical-at-T1, and that (where T2 is after division) R and L are not identical-at-T2. This result, presumably, accords with what we "demand to say" about the division case—one person before, two after—while leaving room for the truth that, in terms of identity, there are two person continuants all along.

It is not difficult to feel dubious about the notion of tensed identity. Of course we make judgments of identity at different times. So far, however, time enters only as the standpoint of our judgments, not as part of their content. Lewis claims that, in fact, we sometimes count in terms of spatially "tensed" identity. For example, two roads, A and B, come together at a certain point. Standing in one place we might say, "Here A are B are different roads," in another place, "Here A and B are the same road." Are A and B identical or not? They are not identical. The point is that it is also true that, while they not identical-at-P2, A and B are identical-at-P1. Why could we not use a temporal analogue of this in describing division?

Questions about counting person continuants may have their own fascination, but there is no point in pursuing them here. Whether or not we are able to devise a rule for counting person continuants that keeps track of things in the division case, the real puzzlement about division will remain. And its source will remain undisclosed. Lewis's response to the

---

[16] It seems that, having removed tense by employing a four dimensional space-time picture, Lewis is now reintroducing tense by incorporating it within a new identity relation.

puzzle no more brings the source of our puzzlement to light than Parfit's or Nozick's response to the puzzle.

I am now facing division. The time is T1. According to Lewis, person continuants R and L are not identical. This is true at T1, as I face division, and at any other time. Yet it is also true (again, at any time) that R and L, though not identical-at-T2 (after division), are identical-at-T1 (prior to division). Fine. But what is my future? To what do I look in looking ahead? Does Lewis's way of conceiving things, or any other ingenious proposal for counting in the division case,[17] enable us to make sense of what I face in facing division?

I can, certainly, imagine my future as L. From L's point of view, there would be the "other person" R. Equally, I can think myself into the future as R, from whose standpoint there would be the "other person" L. Individually, separately, there is no problem. Each way of thinking myself into the future makes sense separately. The problem comes when I try to combine these separately coherent futures, i.e., when, looking ahead, I try to grasp what it will be for them both to be realized. Two futures both of which will be "my" future. It seems no easier to grasp this view of the future than a view of the present in which there are, right now, two lives both of which are "my" life.

23.5 The Puzzle of Division and the Identity-Framework

The puzzle of division is conceived—not just by Lewis but by all three of the writers we have been discussing, and quite generally in the philosophical literature on this topic—in terms of identity. Identity has a certain logic, and with identity comes counting. Counting what? Counting entities, of course. If x and y are identical, we count one; if x and y are not identical, we count two. Hence (appealing to the logic of identity), if x and y are not identical, there is no entity z such that z is identical with x and identical with y. In this case, then, it seems we must count three. And so on. It is within this framework of identity/entity/counting (the identity-framework) that philosophers generally present, and discuss, the puzzle of division. Who will I be? That is, with which entity, R or L, will I be identical? Should we count one, two, or three? The puzzles that arise when we contemplate such questions seem to present a challenge to the identity-framework.

[17] See John Perry's "Can the Self Divide?" *Journal of Philosophy* 63 (1972). Perry painstakingly guides the reader through the potential complexities of counting in the division case. But once again, as with the other authors we have mentioned in this regard, he does not (in my view) get at the source of our puzzlement about division; for the source of our puzzlement here has nothing to do with counting.

On Parfit's view, the identity-framework breaks down in the case of division. The question we raise in terms of the identity-framework, the identity question, has no answer. There are no facts, one way or the other, about my identity with R or L. This is why we are puzzled. Parfit suggests that we replace the identity question with a question about survival (Who will I survive as?). The survival question, he thinks, not only has an answer (I will survive as both R and L), it captures what matters to us. Nozick, on the other hand, thinks the identity-framework delivers an answer to the identity question: I will be neither R nor L: there will be no one who I will be. He sees the problem as that of explaining why my attitude toward this prospect differs from that toward death. Lewis too, thinks the framework delivers an answer to the question, provided that we conceive of the relevant entities as space-time continuants and explicate identity in terms of a relation between stages of continuants. It turns out that I will be, because I already am, both R and L. The problem for Lewis, which he solves by introducing a new identity relation (identity-at-a-time), is to explain our inclination to count only one prior to division.

These writers all assume that the puzzle of division arises within the identity-framework; thus in responding to the puzzle they are all, one way or another, occupied with the framework. My view is that what is puzzling about division comes from a different quarter entirely, from outside the identity-framework. The source of the puzzle has nothing to do with entities, or identity, hence with counting entities. So the puzzle will not be solved, or dissolved, by replacing the framework, or tinkering with it, or clarifying our attitudes in light of the framework. So long as in our reflections on division we are occupied with the identity-framework, the true source of our puzzlement will escape us. Not only will we remain puzzled, we will not understand why we are puzzled.

Let us consider how things look in the division case if we reintroduce into our reflections the temporalized phenomenology of the subject position—i.e., the positional (and thereby the horizonal) conception of the self. Who will I be? Will I be either R or L? Or both? Or neither? If we consider the entity that I am, viz., JV, the human being now at the center of my horizon, that entity will (by hypothesis) be neither R nor L. R and L, these human beings, will each have an augmented half of JV's brain. But it is JV, the human being, not his brain, that now figures at the center of my horizon. It is JV that is the entity that "I am," and there is no question of an identity between JV and either R or L. In this sense, there is no question of an identity between the entity I am and either R or L, no question of my being either of these human beings.

Yet there is a sense in which I will be R. R will figure within my horizon in the same way that JV now figures within my horizon. R will be the one at the center of my horizon: R will appear within my horizon in that peculiar range of ways represented by Mach's picture; R will be the locus of feeling and will. In short, R, the human being, will occupy the subject position within my horizon. R will be the one that "I am," not (as we might put it) in the identity sense, i.e., in the sense that the human being that I am will be identical with R, but in the positional sense, in the sense that R will occupy the subject position within my horizon, the position at the center.

Of course, all this applies equally in the case of L. So we may assert of L that L will occupy the subject position within my horizon, and in that sense, in the positional versus identity sense, that L will be the one that I am.

Notice, there is nothing in any of this that conflicts with the logic of identity. There is in particular nothing that entails that, despite the fact that R and L are distinct human beings, there is some one entity, the entity (human being) that I am, that will be identical with R and identical with L. What is entailed, rather, is that a human being other than the human being that I am, viz. R, will occupy in the future a certain position within my horizon, and similarly in the case of L. Insofar then as it appeals to the positional conception of the self, our analysis of personal identity seems to provide an answer to the "Who will I be?" question (I will be both R and L) without violating the logic of identity. We asked how things look in terms of our analysis. How do things look in light of our analysis? If we do not look too closely, it might look as the analysis solves the puzzle.

However, it does not solve the puzzle. It merely raises the puzzle in a new way. Yet there is a kind of progress here. Raising the puzzle in a new way may enable us for the first time to see the source of the puzzle. What is forced on us by the prospect of division, understood now explicitly in terms of the temporalized phenomenology of the subject position, is the prospect of my horizon doubling; that is to say, the prospect of there being individually complete and separate horizons, separate lives (in the horizonal sense)—as separate as your life and my life—except that in this case *each* life is *my* life. It is, I believe, this prospect of horizonal doubling rather than any difficulty about the identity or counting of entities, this prospective doubling of my life, that is the underlying source of our puzzlement in the division case. And there seems to be no way out of it. Deal with the problem of identity and counting entities any way you want, the real problem here, the problem about the doubling of my horizon, will remain.

23.6 Horizonal Doubling versus Splits within the Horizon

But what exactly is the problem? In essence, the problem is simple. It is that when I look ahead it seems that the horizon, my horizon (my life), *cannot* double, that there is a kind of impossibility contained in the prospect of my horizon doubling. Yet, it seems, I know that if my brain is divided and the two (augmented) halves are transplanted into different human bodies, my horizon, my life, *will* double. Something will happen that cannot happen. This is what is held up to us in the prospect of division.

It is worth emphasizing that it is the doubling *of* my life, my horizon, that is in prospect, not a doubling *within* my life. Thus what I face in facing division is not anything like a splitting up of my visual field into two parts, or a splitting of my body space; nor is it the prospect of there being within my horizon a double subject: two human beings somehow sharing the center.

Consider a splitting of my body-space, the space of feeling, or of my visual space (my visual field). One part (say the lower part of my body) feels one way, the other part feels another way. The right half of my visual field looks one way, the right half another way. Obviously, this kind of split is not that by which we are faced in facing division. In fact, it presupposes the oneness of the subject matter that is doubled in division.

Or consider the way the experience of a brain-bisected subject is sometimes represented: as a functional conflict within a single horizon. When I am asked, say, what I see, the answer I am inclined to give by pointing clashes with my verbal answer. We can, it seems, imagine this ("Why is my mouth uttering these words?" "Why is my hand pointing to that?"): however otherwise perplexing, we can make sense (experientially) of this kind of alienated behavior. The conflict we thus imagine is the result of different parts of a single brain triggering responses in the absence of normal whole-brain integration (the corpus callosum has been severed). In the division case, however, the hypothesis requires that we have the equivalent of two functionally complete and individually fully integrated brains. Each augmented half of my brain will, after division, by itself maintain a life. Not a half life but a whole life. In this case there is too much to be contained within a single horizon. Metaphysically, the hypothesis in the division case entails not a split within my horizon but rather two horizons, two lives—each of which is *my* life.

In contrast to my visual field or my body space, it makes no sense that my actions should figure as *willed* in a split way. Suppose everything in the left half of my visual field looks fuzzy, and everything in the right half distinct. JV, the subject, insofar as he appears, might appear half fuzzy half distinct—a subject of split-appearing. Figuring as willed is also a way of figuring from within my horizon; but it is fundamentally different from appearing (15.8). From within my horizon, a given movement either figures as willed or it does not; it does not figure in one as opposed to another way of being willed. There are ways of appearing; so a given object may (in different parts) appear two ways at once. But there are no ways of willing. Thus there is no possibility of split-willing as there is of split-appearing.

What about the possibility of there being two subjects each of whose movements figure from within my horizon as willed? Each could not be *the* locus of will; but each might be *a* locus of will. And the two might cooperate: volitional partners. My body-space would be, as it were, spread over two human beings. Is this an experiential (versus metaphysical) possibility? Can we imagine it? Perhaps, as in the case of all-around visual experience, we might work our way up to imagining it (12.3). But once again, the imagined duality is internal to my horizon, which means that the oneness of my horizon is presupposed, whereas the prospect of division invites us to contemplate the doubling of this very subject matter, that whose oneness is presupposed when we imagine partners in will.

It precisely this—not the prospect of a duality within my horizon, but that of my horizon or life itself being doubled—that seems impossible. You may, in reflecting on the possibility of division, give up on identity in favor of survival (Parfit); or you may find a way of distinguishing our attitude toward division from that toward death (Nozick); or you may in this case devise a new way to count entities (Lewis). None of this helps: the prospect of my life doubling remains, and it does not make sense.

That is to say, it does not make sense experientially. I take it that, although it makes sense metaphysically, we do not really know whether it is (in principle) causally/naturally possible to separate and augment the two hemispheres of a brain, and to remove and transplant each into a new body. But we do know that it is experientially impossible. It may not be causally/naturally possible, but if my brain is divided, if each hemisphere is augmented so that it is has the capacity of my actual brain right now, if each hemisphere is transplanted into the body of a new human being, then each of these human beings will be at the center of my life, my horizon. My life will double. There will be two completely separate lives—as separate as your life and my life—each of which is my life. The conditions built into the thought experiment both establish the metaphysically possibility of division and entail a prospect that experientially does not make sense.

Compare the division thought experiment with that in which I find myself in the body of another human being. The latter, we argued, makes sense experientially (I can imagine finding myself in a new body); but when you look into it, it turns out to be metaphysically impossible. It is an experientially coherent metaphysical impossibility. In contrast, the prospect that I face in facing division, while it makes sense metaphysically, does not make sense experientially. The division thought experiment presents us with an experientially impossible metaphysical possibility:

with an outcome that does not make sense experientially, which violates the logic of experience, and yet which might be realized. This is the puzzle of division.

23.7 The Impossibility of Horizonal Doubling

However, we will not properly understand the puzzle until we make clear in what the experiential impossibility—that which appears to be metaphysically forced on us in the thought experiment—consists. Suppose someone says that he does not see anything impossible in the division case. He acknowledges, given the causal-HP fact and the conditions built into the thought experiment, that, if these conditions were realized, you could not *stop* the horizonal doubling, that there would be two separate lives, two separate horizons (R is at the center of one, L of the other). But (he asks) where is the problem? Can we not unproblematically adopt the standpoint of either R or L? Each horizon will in itself be as coherent, experientially, as my horizon right now.

Imagine I am now facing division. The incoherence arises not within either of the two horizons that will exist after division, but from within my horizon now, *looking ahead* to division. After the horizonal doubling has occurred, there will be no incoherence, since after division the only horizons from within which the incoherence might arise will be one or the other of the two separate horizons, and from within each of these everything will be perfectly coherent. They will just be two separate lives. The incoherence lies, rather, in the prospect of doubling, the prospect that faces me looking ahead, facing division. Thus to see the experiential incoherence, we must adopt the standpoint not of R or L, but of JV. We must adopt my standpoint before division looking ahead to division.

Imagine my situation facing division. I look ahead. I anticipate. What do I anticipate? The answer, it seems, must be that I anticipate there being two horizons, two lives, both of which are mine. Why both "mine"? Because as long as my brain keeps going in more or less the same way, there will be such thing as my life (the causal-HP fact), and the thought experiment provides—the augmenting and splitting of my brain—for my brain to keep going twice over. This makes sense metaphysically (if not causally). So it makes sense metaphysically (if not causally) that my life will keep going twice over, that my horizon will be doubled. But this is not an experiential possibility. An experiential possibility is a way that things might develop *from within* my horizon (my life, consciousness, experience). But it is not a way things might develop from within my horizon that my horizon itself should double. A doubling of my horizon is no more a way things might develop from within my horizon than is the ceasing to be of my horizon, my death.

Consider again the question what I anticipate in facing division. Perhaps we might give the following answer: I anticipate R and L, each with his new brain, going about his business—each at the center of a separate horizon to which, just as in the case of my horizon, the whole of the world and the infinity of time and space are internal. Where is the problem? What we are overlooking is the fact that (as we have more than once observed; see 19.4, chapter 20) the horizon from within which I anticipate the future, my horizon, is presupposed as the horizon from within which that which I anticipate will unfold. The same horizon, then, of which I anticipate that R will occupy the subject position is that of which I anticipate L will occupy the subject position. Yet it cannot be the same horizon. Given the splitting of my augmented brain and the causal-HP fact, there will be two horizons—each with its own subject and each of which is (impossibly) my horizon.

You could put it like this. When, given the conditions of the thought experiment, I anticipate R and L each at the center of a separate horizon, I carelessly include these separate horizons within my horizon. I fail to register the fact that, the horizon of which R (say) will be at the center will not be included within my horizon but, as the horizon from within which I anticipate, will *be* my horizon. Similarly for the horizon of which L is at the center. So, once again, we get the experientially impossible prospect of two separate horizons each of which is my horizon.

At the root of the impossibility of horizonal doubling is the presupposed oneness of my horizon. Looking back or ahead from the standpoint of any "now," a single horizon is presupposed: that to which I look, in looking back or ahead, is internal to the same horizon from within which I look back or ahead. Suppose, focusing on the case of the future, I anticipate an encounter with X. The encounter is anticipated as figuring from within the same horizon as that from within which I anticipate it. Similarly, for the special case where I anticipate witnessing the splitting of an entity, e.g., an amoeba, or a cloud, or a plant, or a brain: the splitting, the emerging of two out of one, is anticipated from within my horizon as something that will figure from within my horizon, the same horizon from within which it is anticipated. Where there is now a oneness, I anticipate a twoness. But the anticipation of a twoness itself presupposes a oneness. Here we refer not to the oneness, the unity, out of which the twoness emerges, but the oneness of the horizon from within which the twoness is anticipated to emerge. For this must be the same horizon as that from within which the twoness is anticipated, viz., my horizon (my life, my consciousness).

What could it be, then, to anticipate the doubling of my horizon? As anticipated, the doubling would be anticipated as figuring within the same horizon as that from within which it is anticipated: my horizon. But if the anticipated doubling is the doubling of my horizon, this is incoherent. There is a conflict between what I anticipate and what is presupposed by what I anticipate. In anticipating the doubling of my horizon, the oneness or unity of my horizon, the oneness of the very subject matter that I anticipate doubling, is presupposed.

All right. The incoherence that we have uncovered here, i.e., the experiential incoherence implicit in the prospect of division, is not touched by introducing a novel way of counting persons, or by replacing questions about the identity of persons with questions about their survival, or by explaining why division does not seem like death. At the same time that it entails the doubling of my horizon, the prospect of division presupposes the oneness or unity of my horizon. The doubling of my horizon does not make sense experientially. It does not make sense as a way things might be, or develop, from within my horizon.

23.8 The Unity of Consciousness

It might be of interest to compare the impossibility of imagining my horizon doubling with the impossibility of imagining there being nothing present from within my horizon (4.5). This too, we said, is an experiential impossibility. In the case of the empty horizon, there is NOTHING—hence nothing to imagine (hence no horizon). In the case of the doubled horizon, what is to be imagined is at odds with the unity presupposed in the imagining of it. In both cases, the attempt to imagine the relevant state of affairs *exhibits* (12.4) the relevant impossibility.

The unity or oneness of my horizon is presupposed in imagining anything about my future, since to imagine something about my future is at least to imagine something figuring one way or another from within my horizon. Thus the unity of my horizon cannot be compared with that of a substance or entity in the world; or again with the unity of something happening in the world, a phenomenon. In these cases, there is no impossibility of imagining a division or splitting. There is no problem imagining, say, a rock or a tree or an animal or the brain of an animal being divided. Similarly, however we individuate a particular phenomenon—an event, an ongoing bit of activity, etc.—we can always imagine the event or activity being interrupted in a way that temporally splits it into two and thus destroys its unity. In contrast, the unity of the horizon from within which such a split is imagined, this will always be presupposed. Here we have a unity whose destruction cannot be imagined.

The unity that is presupposed in imagination (as well as memory and anticipation) and therefore cannot be assimilated to that of an entity or phenomenon in the world is, I believe, what philosophers are getting at when (taking their cue from Kant) they speak of "the necessary unity of consciousness." When in philosophy we assert the (necessary) unity of consciousness we give expression to our grasp of an experiential impossibility, of something that does not make sense as a way things might be or develop within my horizon, our grasp of an impossibility that (like the impossibility of an empty horizon) is exhibited in the attempt to imagine it (12.4), viz., the impossibility of my horizon becoming two. The necessity of the unity of consciousness is an experiential necessity.

The unity of consciousness is not the unity of a material thing. Kant in the Second Paralogism draws attention to the mistake of inferring from this that it must be the unity of an immaterial thing. A bit of matter, like my brain, can always be divided, whereas in the case of a soul there is nothing to divide. (Souls are "simple.") But whether or not the world contains souls, the unity of consciousness is not the unity of a soul. It is a different kind of unity. The unity of consciousness is presupposed in looking to the future and past, and again in imagining possible futures and pasts. You cannot say this of the soul. When, say, I imagine (or anticipate) X appearing around the corner, is X imagined as appearing from within my soul—from within an *immaterial part of world*? Souls, spirits, have nothing to with this. That from within which X is imagined as appearing, my horizon, is not part of the world, material or immaterial, but that from within which the world appears, the horizon of the world.

The necessary unity of consciousness may strike us as an empty idea. Consciousness, we say, cannot be divided like a material thing. What exactly are we excluding? The doubling, the twoness, of my horizon. Yes, but what is that? The problem might be presented as follows. If someone were to ask us to show him a picture of which we can say "Here is what is being excluded," a picture of the horizon doubled, we would have nothing to show him. The only pictures we have are pictures in which things are thus-and-so from within the horizon—pictures in which the unity of the horizon is presupposed. Either we show a picture that presupposes horizonal unity or we have nothing to show. We have, then, no way of showing what is excluded. Might we not then wonder whether there is anything to be excluded, whether the assertion of the necessary unity of consciousness is an empty assertion?

Of course, this talk about "showing a picture" of the horizon doubled is a metaphor for imagining the doubling. Thus if we try to imagine what is excluded, we imagine, perhaps, something like a split visual field or body-space, or perhaps cooperating subjects of will, all of which presuppose the unity of my horizon. The excluded state of affairs, this we cannot imagine. Either what we imagine presupposes horizonal unity, or we have nothing—no "picture" to show of the excluded state of affairs.

Nor will it do here first to imagine how things are for R, say, and then how things are for L. There is no difficulty with this, but what we thereby imagine, one by one, is simply how things are within two separate horizons. We might have chosen *any* two horizons, like yours and mine. Surely this, that there might be two separate horizons, is not what we mean to exclude when we speak of the necessary unity of consciousness.

To repeat, either what we imagine presupposes the unity of the horizon, or we come up with nothing. Does this mean that nothing is excluded, that the philosophical assertion of the necessary unity of consciousness is in that sense empty? Look at it like this: If you understand why in this case we have nothing to show, that is, nothing to imagine, why therefore we might be tempted to dismiss the philosophical assertion of as empty, then you understand the point of the assertion:—you understand what we are getting at in philosophy when we assert the necessary unity of consciousness.

23.9 The Puzzle of Division

The necessary unity of consciousness is an experiential impossibility whose source lies in the way the unity of the horizonal subject matter is always presupposed. Given the presupposed unity, the prospect of division, of my horizon (my life) doubling does not make sense. It is an experiential impossibility. Yet given the causal-HP fact about my horizon and my brain, i.e., the fact that my brain maintains my horizon and how things are from within it, if the conditions of the division thought experiment were realized, my horizon, my life, would double. There is, in terms of the division of my brain, a (perhaps causally impossible) way of accounting for how the doubling of my horizon might come to pass. It is, in other words, metaphysically possible that something that does not make sense experientially should nevertheless be realized: it is metaphysically possible that the world should be tampered with in a way that forces (causally) into being an experientially impossible state of affairs.

Of course, were I faced by the immediate prospect of division, its metaphysical possibility would make it no easier to grasp or make sense of experientially. The prospect would remain impossible as a way that things might be or develop from within my experience. By the same token, the experiential impossibility of the prospect would make it no less something that might be realized. Thus I might find myself in a situation in which I *know* that my life (horizon) will double, that there will be two lives each of which is "my" life, yet without being able to make sense (experientially) of what I know. Events in the world would be about to override the necessary unity of the horizon of the world, the necessary unity of consciousness. I would be faced by the fact that something impossible is about to happen; faced, you could say, by an impossible fact.

We observed earlier (23.5) that, in the division case, the question "Who will I be?" can be given an answer that avoids any embarrassment about the identity or counting of the entities involved. We can say, on a certain understanding, that I will be both R and L—not (obviously) that the human being that I am, JV, will be identical with both R and L (that would violate the logic of identity), but that both R and L will be "me," the one that "I am," in the positional sense. Just as it is JV who now occupies the subject position within my horizon, in the future R and L will each be at the center of a horizon that is my horizon. However, we also pointed out that, while this may provide an answer to the "Who will I be?" question, it raises the puzzle in a new form. The answer assumes that there will be two horizons where there is now one, and that both horizons are my horizon. But my horizon cannot double—this does not make sense experientially. My horizon cannot double, yet, given the conditions of the division thought experiment, it would double. Here we have the real puzzle of division.

Does it have a solution? Or a dissolution? My view is that the puzzle is simply contained in the implications of a metaphysically possible situation. It has no solution. The main elements of the puzzle—the necessary unity of the horizon (consciousness) and the causal-HP fact about the horizon and the brain—are there for philosophy to reflect upon. The unity of consciousness is not in any sense a product of philosophical reflection but is rather uncovered in philosophical reflection. And the causal-HP fact is part of our picture of the world. Insofar as the puzzle, i.e., the metaphysical possibility of finding myself faced by an experientially impossible fact, is implicit in the combination of the necessary unity of consciousness and the causal-HP fact, it is already there for us. It is there for us whether we discover it philosophically or not.

24. Conclusion: The Extraphilosophical Puzzles

24.1 The Extra- versus Purely Philosophical Puzzles

The puzzle of division is another example of what we have we called an extraphilosophical puzzle (Int.9–10).[1] The extraphilosophical puzzles contrast with the purely philosophical puzzles. In one way, of course, the extraphilosophical puzzles are philosophical: their analysis or articulation requires philosophical reflection—categories, ways of thinking, that are philosophical. However, whereas in the purely philosophical case philosophy, by exploiting some antecedent confusion or unclarity on our part, generates the puzzlement and is thereby responsible for it, in the extraphilosophical case the elements of the puzzle are facts or truths known by us independently of philosophy. In this case, we are not guilty of unclarity or confusion: the puzzle is simply there for us; and it will remain there, whether or not we uncover it philosophically.

We have in the course of the book discussed six extraphilosophical puzzles. In addition to the puzzle of division (chapter 23), there are the two puzzles of death (chapter 11), the puzzle of the causation of consciousness (chapter 11), and the puzzles of memory and experience (chapter 21). We shall—this will involve some repetition of ideas already presented—conclude by briefly considering how these puzzles are connected to one another and their place in the book as a whole.

The purely philosophical puzzles—like the paradoxes of confirmation, or the paradox of the heap, or Zeno's paradoxes about motion—are in a real sense *due* to philosophical reflection. Of course there is a contribution from outside philosophy: the antecedent unclarity or confusion on our part. Philosophy devises an argument that exploits this unclarity, etc., an argument that seems correct but whose conclusion is patently unacceptable. So, confronted by the arguments, we are puzzled. Apart from the arguments, however, there would be no puzzlement. Moreover, insofar as the arguments exploit a confusion or unclarity on our part, they contain a mistake. Since philosophy has devised the arguments, it must take upon itself the task of exposing the confusion, etc., and thereby the mistake in the arguments. It is the task of philosophy, in other words, to solve the puzzles.

---

[1] See also *The Puzzle Of Experience*, chap. 9.

Positive instances of a universal generalization tend to confirm it; objects can move from one place to another; starting with one grain of sand and adding other grains one at a time eventually yields a heap. Are such things in and of themselves puzzling? They seem evidently true. Yet if someone takes you through Zeno's arguments, say, you may be puzzled by motion. Similarly, creating a heap does not, in and of itself, seem puzzling; nor does confirming a generalization. Given the sorites argument, however, or the argument that just by checking the objects in your room you could confirm the hypothesis that all ravens are black, creating a heap, or confirming a generalization, can seem puzzling. Philosophy is responsible for inciting our puzzlement in these cases; so it is responsible too for clearing up our puzzlement. The whole business, you could say, is internal to philosophy.

The extraphilosophical puzzles, in contrast, depend not on some unclarity or confusion exploited by philosophy but on our grasp of certain facts or truths grasped by us independently of philosophy. The puzzles, since they are implicit in these extraphilosophically grasped truths, have the capacity to break into our lives and make themselves known to us without any help from philosophy. They have the capacity to puzzle us extraphilosophically.

Recall, for example, how Wittgenstein represents our puzzlement about the causation of consciousness (11.4). "I, for example, turn my attention in a peculiar way on to my own consciousness, and, astonished, say to my self: THIS is supposed to be produced by a process in the brain." I am puzzled, and my puzzlement is (Wittgenstein says) accompanied by some odd behavior (staring vacantly, etc.). Why am I puzzled? It is not because I have worked through an argument or analysis that seems to establish that THIS, my consciousness, could not be produced by what is happening in my brain, that that is impossible (in the way that, say, the sorites reasoning seems to establish that by adding grains of sand, one by one, it is impossible that I should ever produce a heap). Yet that is how the causation of THIS by the activity of my brain seems: *impossible*. It seems impossible despite being—here I part company with Wittgenstein— a *fact*. What is grasped as a fact presents itself as impossible, hence as puzzling. It presents itself this way directly, without the benefit of philosophical reflection. I have not reasoned, or argued, or analyzed, my way into this puzzlement.

Or take the example of Ivan Ilyich (7.4). Ivan is unable to understand the fact that he will die. He is now open to that fact, to what it means, in a way that he has never been open to it before, but he cannot understand it. "It can't—it can't be, and yet it is! How has it happened? How am I to understand it?" He cannot understand it; he is puzzled. He is puzzled because it, the fact of his death, seems impossible ("it can't be"); impossible, but nevertheless a fact ("and yet it is"). Has Ivan been pursuing an argument or analysis here? Is the seeming impossibility of what faces him a *conclusion* that he has drawn? Nothing of the sort. In being struck by the fact that he will die, Ivan is struck by its impossibility. So he is puzzled.

We might speak of two levels here. If at the surface (outside philosophy) we are puzzled, this is because we sense or grasp in an unarticulated way a puzzle that is there for us at a deeper level. We sense the puzzle, but without having explicitly analyzed it. The task of analyzing the puzzle—of bringing to light the elements that are there for us at the deeper level and making clear how they give rise to the puzzle—this belongs to philosophical reflection. Our extraphilosophical grasp of the puzzles is compatible with our never making explicit the elements of which they consist, the facts from which they derive: compatible with our never reflecting on the puzzles philosophically. Indeed, it is compatible with the puzzles never breaking into everyday consciousness, with our never being extraphilosophically puzzled by the puzzles that are always there for us. I may go through life never finding the prospect of death incomprehensible, or being puzzled by the fact that my consciousness is caused by what is happening now in my brain.

Our puzzlement in such cases is the symptom of an underlying puzzle. We are puzzled extraphilosophically because we sense, we in some way grasp, the underlying puzzle. In the case remarked on by Wittgenstein, the underlying puzzle is the puzzle of the causation of consciousness (11.4); in the death case, as we explained, there are two underlying puzzles: the temporal and solipsistic puzzles of death (11.3, 11.4). The puzzles that underlie our surface puzzlement in these cases do not have solutions. The philosophical task is not to solve the puzzles but to understand them: to make clear in what they consist and, thereby, to understand our extraphilosophical puzzlement.

If this is right, if there are these puzzles that we grasp and that have a way of disturbing us outside philosophy, can it be out of place that philosophy should attempt to understand them? Since the puzzles are there *for us*, seeking to understand them is a way of seeking to understand ourselves. Is this not what has always been asked of us in philosophy, that we should to seek to understand ourselves?

Let us, now, with the aim of relating and organizing them in different ways, think back over the six extraphilosophical puzzles.

24.2 The Puzzle of Division as an Extraphilosophical Puzzle

The puzzle of division stands, in a way, by itself. Although the elements of the puzzle are there for us extraphilosophically, the puzzle does not manifest itself outside of philosophical reflection. In this respect, the puzzle of division differs from the other extraphilosophical puzzles. (We might say that it is an imperfect example of an extraphilosophical puzzle.)

To have an object of comparison, let us remind ourselves how the puzzles of death manifest themselves outside philosophical reflection. Ivan, when he stops kidding himself about what is going on and admits to himself that he is dying, finds the fact of his death impossible and therefore, since it is a fact, incomprehensible (7.4). He cannot understand it. Death, when it strikes us in the right way (when it really hits home) strikes us as incomprehensible.

We all know: I will die. About the *fact* of death, there is not much for philosophy to say. It is the impossibility of death that calls for philosophical reflection—to make clear, first, what death means, and second, in light of what it means, in what way it is impossible. Death is the prospect of absolute (unrelativized) once-and-for-all NOTHINGNESS, the once-and-for-all ceasing to be of the horizon. Of course, in order to grasp this explicitly, philosophically, we must explicitly grasp the horizon, the subject matter to which the world and infinity of space and time are internal. We must (as we tried to do in our reflections on the dream hypothesis) let the horizon, THIS, come into the open for us.

The meaning of death—absolute and final NOTHINGNESS—entails solipsism, that my horizon includes all others (chapter 10). Yet I am committed to (O): I am with Others, that is, with subjects whose horizons are coordinate with mine, metaphysical equals (6.4–5, 6.9). The underlying conflict here, which we implicitly grasp, is the solipsistic impossibility of death. Of course we know death is a fact. An impossible fact. Thus if its meaning gets through to us, the fact seems incomprehensible. In the case of the temporal puzzle of death, the impossibility derives from the status of my horizon as outside time (whatever is in time is internal to my horizon). What is outside time cannot cease to be. Death, however, is precisely the ceasing to be of my horizon (11.3). We are confronted, then, by something incomprehensible: by the ceasing of what cannot cease to be, by an impossible fact.

Consider now the puzzle of division. Death, we said, confronts us with an impossible fact. Division does not confront us with an impossible fact. It does not, in the first place, confront us with a fact.

Death is a causal necessity (it will be because it must be); division may well be causally impossible. Metaphysically, however, it is not impossible. My brain, as a physical object, might be divided, the two halves enhanced and separately transplanted. This is metaphysically, if not causally, possible. Given our causal entrapment in the world—that is, given the causal HP-fact: that my brain is causally responsible for the inseparable duality of both the continued existence and phenomenology (how things are from within) of my horizon—if such a division were to occur, my horizon would exist twice over: there would be two horizons, both of which were "mine." This prospect makes sense metaphysically. We can tell a coherent story in which everything is accounted for. But it does not make sense experientially. It is at odds with the necessary unity of experience, and thus is experientially impossible. Yet if I found myself in the metaphysically possible situation of being faced by division, I would know, just as we all in fact always do know about death, that something impossible (in this case, experientially) will be (chapter 23).

Note: *if* I found myself . . . In fact, I do not. Division is not something I actually face, or ever will face. It is only a possibility conjured up in a philosophical thought experiment, a metaphysical possibility. In contrast to puzzlement about death, without philosophical reflection there is no puzzlement about division. Hence there is no extraphilosophical manifestation of the underlying puzzle, no extraphilosophical incomprehension at the fact that I will become two. There is no such incomprehension because there is no such fact.

Suppose there were creatures that multiplied in the manner of our thought experiment about division. These creatures would have to deal with the fact of division in the way we must deal with the fact of death. Just as we may without any contribution from philosophy find the fact of death impossible and hence incomprehensible, they would be subject to extraphilosophical puzzlement about division. (Instead of "The Death of Ivan Ilyich," Tolstoy's counterpart in this world might have written "The Division of Ivan Ilyich.")

24.3 The Puzzle of Division and the Puzzle of the Causation of Consciousness

The two puzzles of death that we have distinguished concern different impossibilities. One impossibility derives from solipsism, the fact that my horizon is the all-inclusive horizon; the other from the fact that my horizon, the subject matter whose ceasing to be is my death, is outside time. With the latter puzzle, the temporal puzzle of death, we are in the neighborhood of the puzzle of the causation of consciousness (11.7). If my horizon, my consciousness (in the horizonal sense), is outside time, it must be outside the range of causation. Yet we know that it is not outside the range of causation. I know—we all know; this is something we picked up in picking up our picture of the world—that my consciousness and how things are from within it are maintained by the activity of my brain (the causal HP-fact). We are causally entrapped in the world. Thus if my brain were destroyed, or radically interfered with, there would be NOTHING (as in death): there would cease to be such a thing as my consciousness. (Do we not know this?) It is impossible that my consciousness should stand in a causal relation to anything; but the fact is that it stands in a causal relation to what is happening in my brain. This is the puzzle of the causation of consciousness.

The task of making clear in what exactly the puzzle consists—the explicit working out of things, including the explicit bringing into view of the horizonal subject matter, that is, of consciousness in the horizonal sense—belongs to philosophical reflection. This, however, does not prevent a sense of the impossibility from breaking into our thoughts outside of philosophical reflection. It is part of our picture of the world, something we all know, that consciousness is the product of what happens in my brain. Yet this fact can present itself to us as impossible. "How could THIS, my consciousness, be the product of what is going on now in my brain?" It can strike this way apart from any kind of philosophical reasoning or analysis, quite apart from philosophical reflection.

Wittgenstein, as we saw (11.7), seems to regard puzzlement about the causation of consciousness as the result of a perverse philosophical confusion. "I turn my attention in a particular way on to my own consciousness, and, astonished, say to myself: THIS is supposed to be produced by a process in the brain!" This "turning my attention on to my own consciousness" is, he says, "surely the queerest thing there could be!" My view of what is going on here is that the puzzlement is neither essentially philosophical, nor due to confusion. The causation of consciousness strikes us as an impossible fact. It strikes us this way, we are puzzled, because we sense an underlying puzzle—a puzzle that philosophy may articulate for us but that is there for us independently of philosophy.

It should be clear now that, given the necessary unity of consciousness, the puzzle of division is only a few steps removed from the puzzle of the causation of consciousness. In fact, we might think of the puzzle of division as a special case of the latter puzzle. My brain, as a bit of matter, is divisible. If the fact about material division is taken in conjunction with the fact that my brain causally maintains my horizon, we have, in essence, the metaphysical possibility of horizonal doubling: the possibility of causally forcing into existence two horizons, both of which are my horizon.

I say we have this possibility "in essence" because, given what we know about the brain, dividing it up in just any old way would not achieve horizonal division. Moreover, assuming the brain is divided hemispherically, horizonal doubling would not result unless we further assume that each hemisphere has been properly enhanced. Still, the kernel of the metaphysical possibility of horizonal doubling is implicit in the fact of the brain's divisibility plus the causal HP-fact, both of which are known to us independently of philosophy. Implicit then in facts known to us independently of philosophy is the metaphysical possibility of a state of affairs that does not make sense experientially, a state of affairs that if realized would clash the necessary unity of consciousness.

But as we said, we are not actually faced by division. Division, unlike death, is only a metaphysical possibility. Thus with respect to division there is no fact whose impossibility might puzzle us extraphilosophically. Without the thought experiments and reasoning—that is, without philosophy doing its bit—there would be no puzzlement about division. In this respect, the puzzle of division resembles the purely philosophical puzzles. Yet in contrast to the purely philosophical puzzles, philosophy does not create the puzzle of division. Puzzlement about division depends not on philosophy exploiting a pre-philosophical confusion or unclarity on our part but rather on philosophy bringing to light a metaphysical possibility implicit in facts that are there, and known by us, whether we or not we engage in philosophical reflection.

24.4 Our Causal Entrapment in the World

The fact of our causal entrapment in the world—the causal-HP fact—suggests another way of organizing the extraphilosophical puzzles. This fact, as we have just seen, has a role in the puzzles of division and the causation of consciousness. It has a role also in the puzzles of experience and memory (Int.10, 21.7). But we must note differences here: differences, that is, among the puzzles of causal entrapment (as we might call them).

There are two sides or aspects of our causal entrapment (22.2): the causation by my brain of how things are from within the horizon (the phenomenological side) and the fact that my brain causally maintains in existence the horizon itself (the horizonal side). Since there is no horizon in the absence of presence from within it, and no possibility of presence except from within the horizon, these two sides of our causal entrapment are inseparable. The puzzles of the causation of consciousness and division involve the horizonal side of our causal entrapment, the puzzles of experience and memory, the phenomenological side. Let us consider the latter two puzzles.

When we reflect on the fact that my brain is causally responsible for what now figures as now present/appearing, we get the puzzle of experience; when we reflect on the fact that my brain is causally responsible for what now figures as then present/appearing, we get the puzzle of memory. In each case there is an argument that forces on us the conclusion that what is directly available cannot be what we know it to be, that it cannot be the world/the past that is directly available (21.7); thus, since something is directly available, we seem driven to the conclusion that it must be an object that exists only from within the horizon (an internal object): a representation of an object in the world, or an event in the past.

We know the world and its past are directly available, that is to say, we know it, but we are not open to—we have not philosophically discovered—what we know (which is more or less how we go through life). Here we come to something else that distinguishes the puzzles of experience and memory from the other extraphilosophical puzzles. (See Int.10 and 21.7.) Philosophical discovery, we have said, presupposes resistance (Int.4, Int.7). In the case of the availability of the world and its past, the resistance presupposed by philosophical discovery is provided by philosophy itself: by the very arguments that yield the conclusions that conflict with what we know and thereby generate the puzzles. Thus in working through the arguments that by generating resistance put us in a position to discover philosophically the facts of direct availability (facts that we already know), we at the same time philosophically discover the puzzles. But once again, the puzzles that we thereby discover are already there for us, implicit in the fact of our causal entrapment and the facts of direct availability.

Our grasp of the fact that the causation of the world extends to our consciousness, the fact that we are in this sense causally entrapped in the world, does not depend on philosophy but is part of our world-picture. Thus the direct availability of the world/past may strike us as impossible without the benefit of philosophy, that is, without arguments or analysis, or any kind of philosophical lead-up whatever. Notice, though, it strikes us this way, if it does, not by itself but only in light of the extraphilosophically grasped fact of our causal entrapment in the world.

By itself, the fact of our causal entrapment does not strike us as impossible. It is just part of our world-picture. Nor, by itself, does the direct availability of the world/past from within our horizon strike us as impossible. This is where we start from, a fact that is built into the situation in which we find ourselves. It is thus a fact that we already know when, in philosophy, we engage in the reasoning that establishes that it is *not* a fact, and thereby put ourselves philosophically in a position to become open to the fact, to discover what we already know. What strikes us (if it does) as impossible outside philosophy are the two facts taken together: the two facts in light of each other. It is as if we thought, "How, given that my brain is causally responsible for the way things now are within my experience, could *this* object be part of the world?"[2] Or, "How, given that my brain is causally responsible for the way things now are in memory, could *that* (the event I am now fixing on in memory) be a past event?"

---

[2] See *The Puzzle of Experience*, 9.4–11.

This kind of puzzlement—though obviously not our presentation of it—is philosophically innocent. Given our world-picture, we are (if we are) struck by the impossibility of the fact that the world/past is directly available from within consciousness. What we know to be a *fact* seems *impossible*. "How could this be?" Outside philosophy, we have only a sense of the impossibility. We lack an analysis of it. The analysis of the impossibility and thereby of the underlying puzzles, the puzzles of experience and memory, belongs to philosophy. Philosophy thus uncovers and takes apart for us puzzles that in an unarticulated form are already there for us, and have the potential to disturb us, outside philosophy.

Such, then, are the four puzzles of causal entrapment. One of these, the puzzle of the causation of consciousness, is, as we have remarked, closely related to the temporal puzzle of death. The temporal impossibility of death is the impossibility of my horizon, the subject matter to which time is internal and which therefore is itself outside time, ceasing to be. Of course, it *will* cease to be. Now, insofar as this same subject matter, the subject matter of my death, my horizon—that is, my consciousness in the horizonal sense—is outside time, it is outside the scope of causation. Yet we know that it is maintained in existence by the activity of the brain. You will recognize that we have arrived at the puzzle of the causation of consciousness.

In one respect, then, the solipsistic puzzle of death stands alone among the extraphilosophical puzzles. The other puzzles depend either on an aspect of our causal entrapment, or on something that is presupposed by our causal entrapment, viz., on our place in time. The impossibility that generates the solipsistic puzzle of death depends on neither time nor causation, but (in a certain sense) on absoluteness. It is the impossibility not of something that is outside time ceasing to be, or being caused to be, but the impossibility of a ceasing to be that is both absolute, that, in other words, entails absolute (unrelativized) NOTHINGNESS, and yet leaves other horizons untouched, the impossibility entailed in the thought that aims to generalize the ungeneralizable absoluteness that faces us in facing death, the thought that "it is the same for all of us" (11.5).

24.5 The Extraphilosophical Puzzles and the Horizonal Subject Matter

We are, each of us—it seems—at the center of a horizon that not only contains the world and the infinity of space and time but, impossibly, both includes and is coordinate with all other horizons, a horizon, that is, whose ceasing to be entails a NOTHINGNESS that is both absolute and, impossibly, separately faced by all of us (the solipsistic puzzle of death); a horizon that, despite being outside time, will, impossibly, cease to be (the temporal puzzle of death); a horizon that, despite being, since it is outside time, outside the range of causation, is, impossibly, causally maintained in existence by the activity of my brain (the puzzle of the causation of consciousness); a horizon that, despite being necessarily unified, could, given its causal dependence on the bit of matter that is my brain, be caused, impossibly, to double (the puzzle of division); a horizon from within which, despite the direct availability of the world and the past, things are as they are because, impossibly, of what is going on right now in my brain (the puzzles of experience and memory).

So, one way or another, the extraphilosophical puzzles all concern the same problematic subject matter: the horizonal self, the subject matter to which the world and the infinity of space and time are internal and which is nothing in itself; the subject matter that is "mine" in a way that nothing else is and by being at the center of which a certain human being is "me"; the subject matter of the DH and death: my horizon (life, experience, consciousness). They concern the subject matter that initially emerged in our reflections on the DH and with which we have been occupied throughout the book. It should be clear, then, that the puzzles are not a sideshow curiosity here but are, in different ways, puzzles about the central subject matter of the book.

We said at the outset (1.1) that our real purpose in raising the DH was not to raise the issue of dream skepticism (although that was inevitable), but to ask about the meaning and hence the subject matter of the DH, and in this way to allow the subject matter of the DH philosophically to come into view: to let ourselves become open to it. In raising the DH we were preparing the ground for our reflections on death and the self as well as for an analysis of the extraphilosophical puzzles. Unless the horizon is first transformed from something known-but-hidden into an explicit topic of philosophical reflection, we lack what we need for insight not just into the meaning of death and the self, and therefore into the familiar philosophical problems in this area (for example, the problems concerning first-personal reference and our first-personal identity in time), but into the uncanny confrontation with impossible facts and the consequent failure of comprehension to which we are vulnerable outside philosophy.

These remarks will serve, I hope, to provide a retrospective sense of the book as a whole and the place within it of the extraphilosophical puzzles. Notice, the horizonal subject matter must be philosophically discovered in advance of appealing to it in the analysis of the puzzles. Yet if we focus on the manifestation of the puzzles outside philosophy, on the brute failure of comprehension in the face of certain facts (such as the fact that I will die, or that THIS is maintained in existence by the activity of my

brain), gaining insight into our incomprehension or puzzlement may, insofar as it depends on reference to the horizon, reinforce our initial philosophical discovery of the horizon, the very subject matter without discovering which we would have lacked what is necessary to gain the insight
into our puzzlement. That is to say, if by reference to the horizon we are
able to uncover the source of our puzzlement, this may indirectly have
the effect of bringing us back to that same problematic subject matter and
thus of reinforcing our openness to it, of reinforcing our initial philosophical discovery.

The horizonal subject matter has figured not just in our analysis of the
extraphilosophical puzzles; it has played an essential role in all of the
topics we have discussed in the book, for example in our discussion of
what makes a particular human being the one that "I am" (the phenomenology of the subject position), and in our discussion of the first person,
and of death and solipsism, and so on. Here, too, insofar as we are able
to gain insight into these matters via reference to the horizonal subject
matter, our initial discovery of the subject matter is reinforced.

Such reinforcement, let us note, is nothing like the confirmation of a
hypothesis in science, where the fact that the hypothesis enables us to
explain such-and-such data is taken as a reason for accepting it. That
there is such a subject matter as THIS, as the horizon to which the world
and the infinity of space and time is internal, is not a hypothesis but a fact
to which, the idea is, we can become open (in becoming open to the subject matter itself). Thus it is not something we "posit" in the way scientists
posit the existence of theoretical entities. The existence of the horizon,
that to which we become open, is, if I am right, something of whose existence we *already know.* Can we say this about the existence of theoretical
entities? (Did we already know of the existence of neutrinos and quarks?)
The horizon emerges in our reflections on the DH, and then turns out to
play a role in the analysis of the death and the self, etc., as well as in
the analysis of our extraphilosophical puzzlement. But we knew of it
all along.

Maybe—going back on something we said above—there is another possibility. Suppose that, although nothing happens when we follow the reflections on the DH, we accept the existence of the horizon on faith, or
just play along with the idea; and then, once we see how it can be philosophically put to use, *then* we make the discovery. Our reflections on the
DH kick in, as it were, retrospectively. It might happen even now, at this
late stage (or is that too much to hope for?). On the other hand, it might
not happen at all, before or after. It might never happen.

Either way, this is what the book has been aiming at. It may be regarded
as a single protracted attempt to uncover the horizon, to bring this subject
matter philosophically into view. However, nothing in the book—in our

initial reflections on the DH, or our reflections on death and the self, or our reflections on the extraphilosophical puzzles, or anything else—purports to be an *argument* that there is such a subject matter. Even where we have offered arguments, like the argument from internality (1.3), the point, as we said, was not rationally to force acceptance of the fact that there is a subject matter that contains the totality of the world and the infinity of space and time but to get ourselves to become open to something of which we already know, philosophically to discover this subject matter. Thus it will always remain open to someone who has followed our discussions to maintain that he has not discovered anything, that there is nothing to discover.

There is a limit to what we can do here. Recall the case of self-deception (Int.3, Int.4). The self-deceived person is not open to something about himself that he already knows. If we accuse him of self-deception and he denies it, we will naturally take the denial as just another expression of the basic self-deception. Is there a way to move things forward? Perhaps we remind the person of things he has said and done, draw attention to various aspects of his behavior, ask him to imagine how he would react in this or that situation. The aim is simply to get him to become open to the truth about himself, open to what he already knows. We may use arguments here; but they are just another means to the same end. We can use whatever we please. If something works, it works.

Similarly, there are no arguments that establish the existence of the horizonal subject matter; no rational way, then, to force someone to accept that there is such a subject matter. Suppose someone listens to us and says that he has failed to make the "discovery." As in the case of self-deception, we have no recourse but more of the same. We keep talking. The person to whom we are talking will in the end become open to what we want him to see, to what he already knows, or he will not become open to it.

Two things are true here. One is that talking (pointing things out, and so on) is all we can do, and the other is that talking is not enough. We talk and talk in philosophy, as in our self-preoccupations, but at some point we must become open to what we are talking about. This may not happen. What then? Sooner or later we will grow tired of talking—and then, well, that will be that.

You may object: we are assuming that it is *we* who are philosophically open, and that someone who listens but does not see what we are talking about is closed off from what he knows. Of course we are assuming that. How else should it be? If we think we see something, we think it is there to be seen.[3] So we attempt to direct the Other's attention to what is there,

[3] Cf. the earlier discussion of philosophical modesty and presumptuousness in Int.5.

or rather, to what we think is there. For just as it goes without saying that if we think we see something we think it is there to be seen, it goes without saying that we can think we see something when nothing is there. We know this, we are aware of our fallibility, and yet we remain certain. It is a minor mystery that the reflective mind, while nervously looking back over its shoulder, manages to move ahead with complete certainty.

Bibliography

Allison, H. *Kant's Transcendental Idealism*. Yale University Press, 1983.

Anscombe, G.E.M. "Causality and Determination." In *The Collected Papers of G.E.M. Anscombe*. Blackwell, 1981.

Augustine. *Confessions*. Trans. E. B. Pusey. Henry Regnery, 1948.

Austin, J. L. *Sense and Sensibilia*. Oxford University Press, 1962.

Ayer, A. J. "Fatalism." In *The Concept of a Person*. Macmillan, 1964.

———. *The Foundations of Empirical Knowledge*. Macmillan, 1964.

Block, N. "Mental Pictures and Cognitive Science." *Philosophical Review*. 1983.

Brentano, F. *Psychology from an Empirical Standpoint*. Ed. O. Kraus, trans. A. C. Rancurello, D. B. Terrell, and L. McAlister. Routledge and Kegan Paul, 1973.

Brod, M. *Franz Kafka: A Biography*. Schocken Books, 1963.

Campbell, J. *Past, Space, and Self*. MIT Press, 1994.

Cassam, Q. *Self and World*. Oxford University Press, 1997.

Chisolm, R. *The First Person*. The Harvester Press, 1981.

Dante. *Inferno*. Trans. C. S. Singleton. Princeton University Press, 1977.

Danto, A. "Basic Actions." *American Philosophical Quarterly* 2 (1965).

———. "What We Can Do." *The Journal of Philosophy* 60 (1963).

Davidson, D., "Actions, Reasons and Causes." *Essays on Actions and Events*. Oxford University Press, 1980.

———. "On Saying That." *Inquiries into Truth and Interpretation*. Oxford University Press, 1984.

Descartes, R. *Philosophical Works of Descartes*. Trans. Elizabeth Haldane and G.R.T. Ross. Dover, 1955.

Eliot, G. *Middlemarch*. Oxford University Press, 1996.

Evans, G. *The Varieties of Reference*. Oxford University Press, 1982.

Frankfurt, H. *Demons, Dreamers, and Madmen*. Bobbs-Merrill, 1970.

Frege, G. "The Thought." Reprinted in *Philosophical Logic*. Ed. P. F. Strawson Oxford University Press, 1967.

Geach, P. *Mental Acts*. Routledge and Kegan Paul, 1957.

Hart, W. D. *The Engines of the Soul*. Cambridge University Press, 1988.

Heidegger, M. *Being and Time*. Trans. J. Macquarrie and E. Robinson. Basil Blackwell, 1973.

Heidegger, "The End of Philosophy and the Task of Thinking." In *Basic Writings, Martin Heidegger*. Ed. D. F. Krell Routledge, 1994.

Hume, D. *An Inquiry Concerning Human Understanding*. Library of Liberal Arts Press, 1955.

———. *A Treatise of Human Nature*. Ed. L. A. Selby-Bigge. Oxford University Press, 1960.

Husserl, E. *Cartesian Meditations*. Trans. D. Cairns, Kluwer, 1995.

Husserl, E. *Ideas*. Trans. W. R. Boyce Gibson. George Allen and Unwin, 1958.

Johnston, M. "Human Beings." *The Journal of Philosophy*, 1987.

Kant, I. *The Critique of Pure Reason*. Trans. N. Kemp Smith. Macmillan, 1990.

Kripke, S. *Naming and Necessity*. Basil Blackwell, 1980.

———. *Wittgenstein on Rules and Private Language*. Basil Blackwell, 1982.

Lewis, D. *Philosophical Papers*. Oxford University Press, 1983.

Locke, J. *An Essay Concerning Human Understanding*.

Luria, A. R. *The Man with a Shattered World*. Penguin Books, 1975.

Mach, E. *The Analysis of Sensations*. Trans. C. M. Williams. Dover Publications, 1959.

Malcolm, Norman. *Dreaming*. Routledge and Kegan Paul, 1959.

Martin, M. "Sight and Touch." In *The Contents of Experience*. Ed. Tim Crane. Cambridge University Press, 1992.

McDowell, J. "Criteria, Defeasibility and Knowledge." *Proceedings of the British Academy*, 68 (1982).

———. *Mind and World*. Harvard Unversity Press, 1994.

Mellor, D. H. *Real Time II*. Routledge, 1998.

Merleau-Ponty, M. *The Phenomenology of Perception*. Trans. C. Smith. Routledge and Kegan Paul, 1962.

Moore, A. *Points of View*. Oxford University Press, 1997.

Moore, G. E. "Proof of the External World." In *Philosophical Papers*. Collier Books, 1962.

Nagel, T. "Brain Bisection and the Unity of Consciousness." *Synthese* 22 (1971).

———. *The View from Nowhere*. Oxford University Press, 1986.

Noonan, H. *Personal Identity*. Routledge, 1989.

Nozick, R. *Philosophical Explanations*. Oxford University Press, 1981.

O'Shaughnessy, B. *The Will*. Cambridge University Press, 1980.

Parfit, D. "Personal Identity." *Philosophical Review*, January 1971.

———. *Reasons and Persons*. Oxford University Press, 1986.

Pears, D. *The False Prison*. Oxford University Press, 1988.

Perry, J. "Can the Self Divide?" *Journal of Philosophy* 63 (1972).

———. "Frege on Demonstratives." *Philosophical Review* 86 (1977).

Plato. *Meno*. Trans. W.K.C. Guthrie. Ed. E. Hamilton and H. Cairns. Pantheon, 1961.

Putnam, H. Reason, *Truth and History*. Cambridge University Press, 1981.

Roth, P. *The Dying Animal*. Vintage, 2002.

Russell, B. *The Analysis of Mind*. George Allen and Unwin, 1921.

———. *Human Knowledge*. Simon and Schuster, 1948.

———. *An Inquiry into Meaning and Truth*. George Allen and Unwin, 1940.

Ryle, G. "It Was to Be," In *Dilemmas*. Cambridge University Press, 1953.

Sartre, J. P. *Being and Nothingness*. Trans. H Barnes. Methuen, 1969.

Schopenhauer, A. *The World as Will and Representation*. Trans. E.F.J. Payne. Dover, 1969.

Shoemaker, S. "Persons and Their Pasts." *American Philosophical Quarterly*, October 1970.

———. "Reference and Self-Awareness." *The Journal of Philosophy* 65, 19 (October 1968).

Snowdon, P. "Perception, Vision and Causation." *Proceedings of the Aristotelian Society* 81 (1980/1).

———. "Personal Identity and Brain Transplants." in *Human Beings*, ed. D. Cockburn. Cambridge University Press, 1991.

———. "Persons and Personal Identity." In *Essays For David Wiggins*. Ed. S. Lovibond and S. G. Williams. Blackwell, 1999.

———. "Persons, Animals and Ourselves," In *The Person and the Human Mind*. Ed. C. Gill. Oxford University Press, 1990.

Strawson, P. F. *The Bounds of Sense*. Methuen, 1966.

———. *Individuals*. Methuen, 1961.

Stroud, B. *The Significance of Philosophical Scepticism*. Oxford University Press, 1984.

Tolstoy, L. *The Death of Ivan Ilyich*. Trans. R. Edmonds. Penguin Classics, 1960.

Tye, M. "A Representational Theory of Pains and Their Phenomenal Character," In *Philosophical Perspectives*, vol. 9. Ed. J. Tomberlin, Ridgeview, 1990.

Valberg, J. J. *The Puzzle of Experience*. Oxford University Press, 1992.

Velleman, D., "Self to Self," *Philosophical Review*, January 1996.

Wiggins, D. "Essentialism, Continuity, and Identity," *Synthese*, 1974.

———. *Identity and Spatio-Temporal Continuity*. Basil Blackwell, 1967.

———. *Sameness and Substance*. Oxford University Press, 1984.

Wilkes, K. *Real People*. Oxford University Press, 1988.

Williams, B. *Descartes*. Penguin Books, 1978.

———. *Problems of the Self*. Cambridge University Press, 1973.

———. "Wittgenstein and Idealism." In *Understanding Wittgenstein*. Ed. G. Vesey. Royal Institute of Philosophy Lectures, vol. 7. Macmillan, 1974.

Wittgenstein, L. *The Blue and Brown Books*. Harper Torchbooks, 1958.

———. *On Certainty*. Trans. D. Paul & G.E.M. Anscombe. Basil Blackwell, 1969.

———. *Notebooks 1914–1916*. Ed. G. H. von Wright and G.E.M. Anscombe, trans. G.E.M. Anscombe. 2nd ed. Basil Blackwell, 1979.

———. "Notes For Lectures On 'Private Experience' and 'Sense Data.' " *Philosophical Review* 77 (July 1968). Reprinted in *Philosophical Occasions*. Ed. James C. Klagge and Alfred Nordman. Hackett Publishing Co, 1993.

———. *Philosophical Investigations*. Trans. G.E.M. Anscombe. Basil Blackwell & Mott, 1958.

———. *Philosophical Remarks*. Blackwell, 1975.

———. *Tractatus Logico-Philosophicus*. Trans. D. F. Pears and B. F. McGuinness. Humanities Press, 1961.

Wollheim, R. *The Thread of Life*. Harvard University Press, 1984.

Index

action. *See* will
afterimages, 48, 52, 94, 300. *See also*
   internal objects
aloneness: of the dying subject, 228–232;
   as essence of solipsism, 187–188; and
   negativism, 198–200; Wittgenstein's solipsism and, 188–198
anaesthesia, 37; super, 274–275
analysis, conceptual. *See* conceptual
   analysis
Anscombe, G.E.M., 8n, 322–324, 327n,
   329, 330n, 335, 345, 347–350, 353,
   356–357. *See* "I"
appearing, of myself. *See* centrality (and
   the positional conception of the self),
   perceptual
Aristotle, 194n8
attitudes *de se*, 351–354. *See also* first person
Augustine, 412n
Austin, J. L., 108n4, 421n
Ayer, A. J., 109, 409n

becoming open (being open). *See* openness
belief: as a form of seeming, 213; and principle of supervenience, 256n
biological processes, and death. *See* death,
   biological
Block, Ned, 304n12
bodily continuity, 447
bodily sensation. *See* body-space, and
   sensation
body-space: ontological dependence of my
   body-space on my body, 304–307; and
   the phenomenology of the subject position, 297–307; and sensation, 287,
   297–307, 350n8
brain, the: and biological death, 168–170;
   bisection of, 452–453n2; and causal entrapment, 480–482; and causal-phenom-
   enological/horizonal fact, 434–435, 479;
   causal role of, and the extraphilosophical puzzles, 21–24, 232–234, 475–484;
   and death, 165, 168–170, 173–179,

222–226, 232–234; and dreaming, 64–
66, 89–90, 94, 98–100, 106, 114–118;
and the horizon, 222–227, 257–259 (*see
also* causal-phenomenological/horizonal
fact); and memory, 422–431, and personal identity, 277–279, 374, 386, 389,
434–473 (*see also* division, the puzzle
of); and phenomenology of the subject
position, 279–281, 320; and the stream
of my mental states, 173–177, 222–223;
in a vat, 118n. *See also* consciousness,
causation of
Brentano, 194n8
Brod, Max, 230n15
Butler, 440

Campbell, John, 232–233n18, 345n3
Cartesian souls: Cartesian argument for,
237–254; and circle of first person, 338;
and emptiness at the center of my horizon, 356; and the horizonal-versus-phe-
nomenal conception of mind, 94, 98;
and Kant's paralogisms, 401–405; and
naturalising the self, 261–263; and the
paralogism of imagination, 237–263; as
part of the "world," 48; and personal
identity, 375–380, 441–443; and spatial
properties, 238–239; and the subject-ver-
sus-dreamer contrast, 62; and the subject
matter of death, 172–178
Cassam, Quassim, 278n
causal argument (regarding objects of experience), 424–426; memory version of,
420–422
causal entrapment in the world, 22,
480–482
causal-horizonal fact, 434, 436, 439
causal-phenomenological fact, 429–430,
434, 436. *See also* experience, puzzle of,
and puzzle of memory
causal-phenomenological/horizonal fact,
435, 450–453, 468–469, 472–473; and
brain, 434–436; and causal entrapment
in the world, 480–482; and NOTHING-
NESS, 436–439